HAVE FORK WILL TRAVEL:

A Practical Handbook for

Food & Drink Tourism Professionals

Published by World Food Travel Association

Erik Wolf, Executive Director

Editor, Jenn Bussell

Editor, Caralyn Campbell

Editor, Wendy Lange-Faria

Editor, Kathy McAree

Co-authored by an amazingly talented group of over 70 professionals from two dozen countries.

Published by World Food Travel Association, Portland, Oregon, USA.

The information presented in this book is presented as-is, without representation of warranty, and for informational purposes only and is sold with the understanding that the Publisher is not rendering professional advice. The intent of the authors is to present information to help in your personal and/or professional development. In the event you or your organization use any of the information in this book, the authors, contributors, editors and publisher assume no responsibility for your actions.

This book is a unique collaborative effort by dozens of contributors from around the world. Since often many contributors worked on a single chapter, it is impossible to identify who contributed which portions. Chapters may include examples, perspectives and opinions that represent one or many contributors, and do not necessarily represent the views of the Publisher.

Some material included in this standard print version may not be included in e-books or print-on demand.

For general information about the Association and its products and services or for customer support, please visit www.worldfoodtravel.org. The World Food Travel Association is registered as a 501 (c) 3 non-profit educational institution in the United States of America.

Library of Congress Control Number: 2013957969

Library of Congress Cataloging-in-Publication Date:
Wolf, Erik
      Have Fork Will Travel: A Practical Handbook for Food & Drink Tourism Professionals
      p. cm.
ISBN-13: 978-1490533995
ISBN-10: 1490533990
        1. Tourism industry – marketing. 2. Tourism industry – development. 3.
        Market segmentation. I. Wolf, Erik II .World Food Travel Association III. Title

Table of Contents

Section Four: Issues & Ideas in Food Tourism

Section Five: Wrapping It Up

Supporters

The authors and editorial team of *Have Fork Will Travel*, as well as the Association, would like to thank the following organizations that supported this project (listed alphabetically). Coordinating a book with so many authors in so many countries was just part of this enormous task. We sincerely thank the parties below. We could not have done it without you. Thank you all.

California Culinary & Wellness Adventures
Sonoma, California, USA
(+1) 707-484-2151
www.CaliforniaCulinaryAdventures.com
www.CaliforniaCulinaryWellnessAdventures.com

California Culinary & Wellness Adventures combines culinary activities, wellness opportunities, and exciting adventures to create uniquely tailored travel experiences. Packages include events and activities that will rejuvenate and replenish the sophisticated traveler. Our emphasis is on experiencing the relaxing environment and breathtaking views of the Sonoma and Napa Valley wine country in Northern California, while partaking in the culinary delights of the region. This can include a farm-to-fork experience, wine making and tasting events, tours and demos of local gourmet foods, and dining at renowned restaurants and cafes. We also provide SOUL Food experiences through fun nutrition and cooking activities. SOUL Food is: Seasonal, Organic, Unprocessed and Local food. We aim to tantalize the taste buds of the connoisseur food traveler. Our region is famous for its relaxing health spas in a Mediterranean climate with natural springs and mineral water. For the more active, the hills, trails, valleys and waterways welcome those looking for invigorating outdoor exercise and activities.

Ecuador Ministry of Tourism
Quito, Pichincha, Ecuador
www.ecuador.travel
www.turismo.gob.ec

The Ministry of Tourism of Ecuador is the directorate that leads all touristic activities in Ecuador and develops the touristic sector in a conscious, sustainable and competitive way. Its roles are to regulate, plan, manage, promote and control tourism. The Ministry of Tourism guarantees that the touristic activities deliver economic income, placing Ecuador in the list of the most valued destinations in Latin America, improving Ecuadorian quality of life through social, economic and environmental development. Our main goal is to strengthen Conscious Tourism as an activity that generates social, economic and sustainable development, contributing to the achievement of the Plan Nacional del Buen Vivir 2013-2017 (National Plan of Good Living) and placing Ecuador as a touristic destination due to its exceptional cultural and natural diversity. The Subsecretaria de Gestión Turística (Tourism Management Office) develops touristic activities through regulation, control and project development. It also develops touristic products by considering the existing potential in each territory.

Tourisme Montréal
Greater Montréal Convention & Tourism Bureau
Montréal, Québec, Canada
(+1) 514-844 5400
www.tourisme-montreal.org   www.facebook.com/Montreal

Tourisme Montréal is responsible for providing leadership in the concerted efforts of hospitality and promotion in order to position the city as a culinary destination in the leisure and business travel markets. It is also responsible for developing Montréal's tourism product in accordance with the ever-changing conditions of the market. Culinary tourism is one of the organization's priority niches, and in 2011 the Organization launched an integrated marketing strategy to attract food lovers. It is also responsible for the city's new restaurant week, TASTE MTL (held annually in early November). Follow us @Montreal on Twitter.

Wellness Tourism Worldwide
Los Angeles, California, USA
www.wellnesstourismworldwide.com
www.facebook.com/wellnesstourismworldwide   www.twitter.com/wtwtweets

Wellness Tourism Worldwide (WTW)'s mission is to improve well-being and economic growth through travel providing market intelligence, education, and promotion of wellness travel to destinations, suppliers, sellers and consumers. Our team is responsible for tourism education, development, branding and promotion, healthy destination accreditation, spa operations, hotel management, leisure travel sales, hospital administration & health promotion. WTW publishes the Wellness Travel Journal (WTJ), a monthly e-publication inspiring, educating and motivating readers to invest in themselves through wellness vacations and retreats. Our B2C approach offers advertisers a direct line to consumers worldwide while also linking buyers to suppliers, making WTJ a valuable resource for industry and consumers alike.

West Sweden Tourist Board
Gothenburg, Sweden
www.vastsverige.com/en   www.explorewestsweden.com
www.facebook.com/GothenburgWestSweden

Founded in 1999, the West Sweden Tourist Board (WSTB) is fully owned and funded by Region Västra Götaland. The aim is to be "*Scandinavia's most visited, appreciated and profitable tourism region.*" The WSTB is responsible for the region's development and international marketing – an easy task, since West Sweden is unique in the heart of Scandinavia - a breathtaking mix of coastline, islands, lakes and thick forests, offering visitors everything from lobster safaris and sea kayaking across the Marine National Park to historic manor houses and art museums. Vibrant Gothenburg, the region's gateway, is a coastal city with a lively cultural scene, stylish shopping and a fast-growing reputation as a foodie hotbed. Strategic development areas include transport infrastructure, targeted marketing combining traditional PR with new media, research and analysis and training and education for SMEs to ensure quality with the view that the entire tourism industry should be socially, environmentally and economically sustainable. The tourism industry is one of the most important regional sectors. Last year it had a turnover of SEK 35 billion and employs 24,000 people annually. Follow us @ WestSwedenTB on Twitter.

Acknowledgements

Erik Wolf

This book has been called a magnum opus and that it is. I know of no other travel industry niche that has brought together so many writers from so many countries to create such an important and evocative work than what our team created with *Have Fork Will Travel.*

Our first thanks goes out to nearly six dozen writers in two dozen countries. Without their vast expertise, limitless knowledge and patience for the process, this book never would have come together. Secondly I would like to thank my very talented team of editors who really proved their worth in solidifying this book into what you hold before you today. I have been blessed to work with some truly talented individuals on this project. Lastly I would like to thank my team at the World Food Travel Association as well as my Board of Directors for their support, insight and patience during this long process. I offer my sincere thanks to everyone who contributed to this book.

There are just a few special people who I would like to give special thanks to:

- To Bill Baker, who showed me that it could be done.

- To Linda Bell, who taught me that you can still learn something new every day.

- To Melody Johnson, who has been a loyal partner and inspiration, from the very beginning.

- To Don Monsour, for teaching me a thing or two about leadership.

- To Harold Partain, whose patience and wisdom I admire.

- To Lisa Schroeder, who was never too busy to listen to my ideas.

- To Barbara Steinfeld, whose energy and passion are contagious, and who supported our work from the very beginning.

- To Garry Taylor who helps me work out complex ideas.

And to all our passionate Association members who I love hearing from day after day. We would not have an industry without your support.

The Association and our writers and editors would also like to acknowledge a few industry experts who graciously shared their time and ideas for *Have Fork, Will Travel:*

Temi Adamoledun, Steve Butcher, Craig Culhane, John Dandeneau, Steve Kaufer, Jamie MacBain, Barb Morgen, Patrick Nelson, and Chris Perkins

And lastly, we would like to graciously acknowledge the following industry peers who each gave their time to review a chapter in their area of expertise (listed alphabetically by first name):

Alberto Amore, Canterbury, New Zealand
Annie Stewart, Sydney, New South Wales, Australia
Antonella Marcucci - Lucca, Tuscany, Italy
Benedicto Bernardo, Manila, Philippines

Bertha Bedolla, Queretaro, Mexico
Bill J. Gregorash, Thunder Bay, Ontario, Canada
Charles Wolinsky, Bra, Italy
Chef Carlos Gallardo, Ecuador
Dimitris Karagiannis, Athens, Greece
Dimitris Koutoulas, Patras, Greece
Dolores Wiarco Dweck, San Diego, California, USA
Edwina Golombek, Marrakech, Morocco
Emily Faraone, Burlington, Vermont, USA
Giorgia Baillieu, Bergamot, Italy
Harold D. Partain, CTC, CCTP, Dallas, Texas, USA
Hilda Morales-Nieves, Mayagüez, Puerto Rico
Hiran Roy, Christchurch, New Zealand
Jonathan Rogan, Long Beach, California, USA
José María Puyuelo Arilla, Zaragoza, Aragón, Spain
Judith Klinger, New York City, New York, USA
Karma Brophy, Victoria, British Columbia, Canada
Kim Shambrook, Chicago, Illinois, USA
Laura Morgan, Portland, Oregon, USA
Lisa Kehler RD, Winnipeg MB, Canada
Liz Mazzei, Brooklyn, New York, USA
Maria del Rosario Vásquez Argüello. Puerto Ordaz, Venezuela
Matthew Mejia, Indianapolis, Indiana, USA
Mimi Stockmann, Kirkland, Washington, USA
Pamela Faith Balagué, Paris, France
Raean Lane, Stockton, California, USA
Rebecca Leheup, Toronto, Ontario, Canada
Rodney Wedge, Atlanta, Georgia, USA
Sabrina del Ben, Calgary, Alberta, Canada
Serena Guidobaldi, Firenze, Italy
Shang Guan Fang Ping (Diana), Shanghai, China
Tara Nurin, Philadelphia, Pennsylvania, USA
Teresa B. Day, Baton Rouge, Louisiana, USA
Ulpiano J. Vázquez-Martínez, Madrid, Spain
Valerie Dean, Orange County, California, USA
Yury Ustrov, Gratallops, Tarragona, Catalonia, Spain

There are so many more people who we could not include by name here, and of course there are bound to be a few people whose names we inadvertently missed. If this is the case with you, please accept our sincerest apologies and contact us so we can correct the oversight immediately.

SECTION ONE

INDUSTRY BACKGROUND
& STRATEGY

Introduction to This Book

Erik Wolf

Even before the International Culinary Tourism Association was first conceived, I published a white paper called *Culinary Tourism: The Hidden Harvest*, which eventually became a book of the same name. It set out the basic tenets of what makes food and drink such important parts of the tourism industry. Rather than repeat the basics of culinary tourism, which were outlined in the white paper and book, *Have Fork Will Travel,* is designed to be a completely new discussion of the issues in and around the world's fastest-growing travel industry niche: food tourism.

Since we published *Culinary Tourism: The Hidden Harvest* in 2006, a lot has changed in our industry. We have experienced the world's worst financial crisis since the Great Depression. We have seen the launch of the largest commercial airplane in history, the Airbus A380. We have witnessed three of our planet's most severe natural disasters ever, the 2004 Indian Ocean tsunami, Hurricane Katrina and Hurricane Sandy, and we regularly hear about the increasing effects of climate change. We have watched mobile phones evolve from simple communication tools, into truly portable computers, and as a result, they drive profound improvement in our overall travel experience. We have seen Internet speed increase by an order of magnitude in most countries around the world, giving consumers more information and power than ever before.

Beyond technology, we have seen consumer interest in food pedigree rise exponentially, largely due to influential television programming and partly due to other reasons such as health, fair trade, the buy local movement and others. We take these interests, concerns and desires about food and drink with us when we travel. It is a fact that food touches every aspect of our daily lives, a position explored by *FoodWorx: The Future of Food*, an annual conference produced by our Association. By all accounts, food and drink are essential, fundamental components of who we are and what we do. It only makes sense that travel marketers take this into account when they develop and promote their products.

While the past few years have been difficult for many of us, this has been a time to reflect and grow as individuals and professionals, and our industry has matured as well. Less successful businesses shut down, and new ideas took off. We are witnessing a great flux and it is both exciting and unnerving.

Given all of the changes in our industry, as well as the world in the past few years, one thing remains consistent: food and drink continue to be the basic foundation that all visitors enjoy no matter their country of origin, religion, gender, age, or any other differentiating criteria. Eating and drinking are fundamental and ubiquitous parts of the tourism experience for all people. In the 10 years since our Association was founded, we showed that culture is not just found in a museum; it can also be found on a dinner plate. Marketers tell us that the more human senses we involve in marketing, the greater and longer lasting the impression will be on the consumer. Food and drink have more potential than any other tourism experience or special interest to create a long lasting impression. This is because food and drink involve all five of the human senses: sight, smell, taste, touch, and sound.

In the past 10 years we have also come to learn that the behavior of foodies largely transcends borders. Initial research in the food tourism industry was performed by national tourist organizations such as the Australian Tourism Commission in the late 1990s. A few years later the Canadian Tourism Commission continued food traveler research with its TAMS (Travel Attitudinal Motivation Survey) study, the first version of which was published in 2004. Our own

Association published research in 2007 about American culinary travelers. We conducted new PsychoCulinary profiling research in 2009 about the psychographic behaviors of food travelers, and in 2013 we announced brand new research on American culinary travelers, with lessons applicable to industry practitioners in other countries as well. We found that while some differences exist among food travelers, such differences are largely based on culture; there is a shared basic foundation of similar core preferences and expectations around food and drink experiences everywhere. Meeting the needs that visitors have for a positive food and drink experience is what this book is all about.

There have been many books published about both food and tourism. Few books, however, address the issues and ideas at the intersection of both industries. This book is a compendium of thoughts, ideas, issues, solutions, and struggles in our food, drink, travel and hospitality industries. Many will find herein a valuable toolbox of tactics and strategies that you can implement yourself. We will look at every possible angle of our industry, from providers of products and services, to the unique needs of destination marketing organizations, to the special needs of trade associations and other groups. We also explore the needs of journalists and academics. This will be regarded as a reference book to some, and an indispensable handbook to others. The book does not need to be read in any certain order. We invite you to read first the chapters that appeal most to you. Come back later to read other chapters as your interest or needs may change.

We made a conscious effort in the planning of this book to write in a tone that was friendly and approachable and not overly formal or academic. While we certainly respect the work that academia does to drive our understanding in the food, drink, travel and hospitality industries, it is not our intent to present reams of research. Research goes quickly out of date, and new research is always just around the corner. Our intent is to present practical information of relevance to practitioners in our industry. We respect your valuable time as a reader, and have attempted to present points as succinctly as possible to help save you time and get your work done more efficiently. If you find terms with which you are unfamiliar, the glossary at the end of the book may help. Non-American readers will appreciate our efforts to present information in a non-USA-centric manner. While worthwhile examples are included from the USA (as well as elsewhere), we have taken every effort to avoid insensitive references to miles, gallons and dollars wherever possible. For those whose native language is not English, we have attempted to eliminate as much slang as possible. We want this book to be understood by, and useful to, as many people as possible around the world. Lastly, any references to "the Association" naturally refer to the World Food Travel Association.

Certainly we hope that *Have Fork Will Travel* will find its way to classrooms, although it is intentionally not written with the rigor that an advanced academic textbook requires. While academic references are incorporated throughout, we remind academics that the purpose of *Have Fork Will Travel* is not to serve as a compilation of food and drink tourism research, rather the book is written with the practitioner in mind. Still, for undergraduate hospitality or foodservice students, discussion questions have been added following most chapters to make the instructor's work easier, and to incite thoughtful discussion among students. Higher level academic students may notice that the book's content does not go into enough depth for their needs, and rightly so; that is not the intent of this book.

Just a quick note about transparency: no business paid to be mentioned as a case study in this book. If a case study was written by the business owner, we took careful steps to de-emphasize the influence of the business owner by writing the chapter in the third person whenever possible. We have also made every attempt to cite every relevant source or quote. With such a large project and so many authors, it is possible something may have slipped through. If this is the case, please accept our sincerest apologies and do let us know so that we can credit the source appropriately.

All visitors eat and drink and therefore food tourism planning should be the cornerstone of all tourism product development and marketing initiatives. Readers should expect to glean tactical tools and tips for direct application to your own situation or business. There are plenty of case studies and examples strewn throughout the book. Call-outs draw attention to special concepts or content that lends itself better to table or diagram layout.

It is also our intent for the following pages to provoke thought and help guide the further development of our industry. We wholeheartedly believe that you will find this book a wealth of practical information. Best of luck in your food tourism development and promotion!

Erik Wolf
Executive Director
World Food Travel Association
Portland, Oregon, USA
January 2014
fork@worldfoodtravel.org

Introduction to the Food Tourism Industry

Erik Wolf

This chapter looks at when and how the food tourism industry came to be. It discusses the terms culinary tourism and food tourism and how they evolved. Lastly, this chapter looks at the growth of our industry in the past 10 years. We will also look at specific subsets of our industry, such as gourmet tourism and wine tourism, and how they fit into the overall food tourism industry.

INTRODUCTION

How old is the food tourism industry? That is a hard question to answer. By one account you could say that the industry started in 1999 when academician Lucy long coined the term "food tourism."[1] By another account, one could say that the industry started in 2003 when the International Culinary Tourism Association was founded. By still another measure, one could say that food tourism has been around for millennia, if you consider the spice routes of Central Asia, or traders on the Seven Seas of yore.

In 1999, when Lucy long first used the term "culinary tourism," the term was not well known or understood outside of academia. Food tourism industry founder Erik Wolf wrote a white paper about food tourism that was published in 2001. This white paper was the first public, industry discussion that presented the notion of food and drink as attractions to visitors. The white paper generated a strong buzz, which was ultimately the impetus to create the International Culinary Tourism Association, which was founded in 2003 in Portland, Oregon, USA.

The International Culinary Tourism Association rebranded as the World Food Travel Association in 2012. The Association's reason for rebranding is a good place to start the discussion of the variance of terms in our industry. The Association rebranded because of confusion about its mission and goals. In the English language, the word "culinary" connotes higher-end experiences. While the Association supports all segments of the food tourism industry, research the Association published in 2010 showed that only 8.1% of foodies self-identify with a "gourmet" (PsychoCulinary) profile.[2] In other words, the overwhelming majority of people – and travelers – just like great food and drink, and not necessarily the expensive kind. Therefore the Association adopted the terms "food travel" and "food tourism" to represent more accurately our overall industry.

When people hear the phrase "culinary tourism" or "food tourism" for the first time, they often do not know what to think. These terms are still relatively new. Translation of these terms into languages other than English and re-translation back to English can lead to a broad variation in meaning. For example, "food tourism" can become the equivalent of "gastronomic tourism" in Spanish or French, but remains "food tourism" in Swedish. Wine tourism can become the equivalent of eno-tourism in Italian. For simplicity's sake, we will use the one term "food tourism" to denote the entire food and drink tourism industry, as defined in this chapter.

While the food and drink tourism industry is now more than 10 years old as a defined segment of the tourism industry, an understanding of the industry is still new among many professionals in our industry worldwide. Consequently the very professionals who work in our industry do not always understand the benefits of being involved in food and drink tourism.

The notion of being involved in the food and drink tourism industry can take any of a number of different forms. It can be as simple as a restaurant that serves visitors but does nothing else, or can be as complex as a destination marketing organization that researches and creates a formal food and drink tourism strategy.

Therefore, we present the following overarching terms and definitions to help our industry come to a common understanding:

Wine tourism	pursuit and enjoyment of wine and wine-related experiences while traveling
Beer tourism	pursuit and enjoyment of beer and beer-related experiences while traveling
Gourmet tourism	pursuit and enjoyment of premium and expensive food and drink experiences while traveling
Commodity tourism	pursuit and enjoyment of specific agricultural commodities – either raw or value-added while traveling (examples include chocolate, coffee, tea and seafood)

With so much potential for confusion, we present a standard and now, widely accepted, definition of "food tourism":

> *"The pursuit and enjoyment of unique and memorable food and drink experiences, both far and near."*

We say "food tourism", but drinking beverages is an implied and associated activity. It is also cumbersome to say "food and drink tourism" which is why we shortened the term to "food tourism." In this book, we use "food tourism" to imply "food and drink tourism" in most cases.

We need to clarify "far and near". In addition to traveling across country or the world to eat or drink, we can also be food travelers in the regions, cities and neighborhoods where we live. If you rarely leave your neighborhood and travel across town to a new neighborhood to go to a special grocery store or to eat out, you are a "food traveler" in your own backyard. The act of traveling is implied because most people travel at least across their own town, if not the region, the country and even the planet.

Often destination marketers are primarily concerned with attracting overnight visitors. This may be due to an organizational mandate, spending restrictions or another reason. A commonly accepted practice in the travel industry is to recognize one as a visitor (tourist) if he or she travels 50+ miles (80+ km), a status quo definition that we challenge. In many destinations, the highest portion of non-lodging sales come from local residents. The exception would be areas with high concentrations of tourists like Mexican coastal areas, ski resorts, Caribbean resorts, and similar destinations.

In mega-cities like Los Angeles, Mexico City and London, one can travel for 2 hours or even longer just to get to the other side of the city (perhaps a distance of 25 miles/40 km). Traveling to the other side of the city to visit a restaurant or food truck would therefore not be considered as "travel", according to the common industry view, even if the person decided to spend the night in that new area. For people to travel to a new area with absolutely no connection to that new area (no friends, do not work in the area, do not normally drive through the area, probably would not return for a long time), would that person not be a visitor? According to current tourism industry measures, the answer would be "no." We argue yes and when defining culinary travelers, propose to discount distance and measure time traveled instead. The distance covered is not as important as the fact that we are always on the move. We are all "travelers" of a sort and we are all "eaters." Therefore, we can also all be regarded as "food travelers."

Trade participants in the food tourism industry are currently classified into 19 sub-sectors, which are grouped under "Food and Drink", "Travel and Hospitality" and "Related Businesses" (see chart below). Consumers are obviously part of the food tourism system, although they are not the focus of this book. Definitions for each sector are found following this diagram.

WORLD'S FOOD TOURISM INDUSTRY

FOOD & BEVERAGE

- RESTAURANTS, BARS, ALL FOOD & DRINK SERVICE
- FOOD PRODUCERS & MANUFACTURERS
- DRINK PRODUCERS & MANUFACTURERS
- FOOD & DRINK DISTRIBUTORS
- COOKING SCHOOLS & CLASSES
- CULINARY EVENTS
- CULINARY RETAIL & GROCERY
- FARMS & FARMERS' MARKETS

TRAVEL & HOSPITALITY

- DESTINATION MARKETING ORGANIZATIONS
- CULINARY TOUR OPERATORS, PACKAGES, GUIDES & TRAVEL AGENTS
- CULINARY LODGING
- CULINARY ATTRACTIONS
- MEETINGS & CONVENTIONS

RELATED GROUPS

- TRADE GROUPS & ASSOCIATIONS
- STUDENTS & RESEARCHERS
- MEDIA
- PROFESSIONAL SERVICES
- TECHNOLOGY PLATFORMS
- GOVERNMENT

CONSUMERS

- CONSUMERS

© World Food Travel Association

Restaurants, Bars, Tasting Rooms, Catering & Other Food & Drink Service
This category includes locations that offer unique, quality experiences with a focus on area food products. Uniqueness may be found in the food, the service, the interior design, the setting or, all of these. Generally, chain restaurants will be excluded unless they meet the above criteria. This is generally a very broad category and includes restaurants, cafes, delis, takeaways, street vendors, hawker stands, exceptional hotel restaurants, specialty dine-in/take-out stores (like bakery, candy shop, ice cream stores), caterers, bars, pubs, lounges, clubs, (possibly) nightclubs, breweries, wineries, and distilleries. Businesses in this category may also overlap to some extent with Culinary Retail & Grocery.

Food & Drink Producers & Manufacturers
Oriented towards factory production and includes processors, factories and packers. This would include for example, a place where coffee beans are packaged for distribution; an ice cream factory; a potato chip (crisp) processing facility; a soda (soft drink) bottling plant, etc.

Food & Drink Distributors
A company that collects food and drink products from producers and distributes them to its customers.

Cooking Schools & Classes
This sector includes any kind of stand-alone cooking or culinary school, either for vocational or part-time instruction. This can also include cooking lessons in people's homes. Class length can vary quite widely, from two hours to two days to two weeks to two years. It includes both hobby cooks as well as professional tradesmen.

Culinary Events
This sector includes events with a focus on local food products or experience and which are open to the public. It includes all food, wine, beer and other types of culinary-oriented events where food or drink is the primary focus. The events may have a charity component, but if the charity component is the focus, then it is not defined as a food or drink event. For example, a fundraiser for a heart association that has great food and drink does not qualify as a food or drink event. However, a food/drink event whose beneficiary is the heart association would qualify.

Culinary Retail & Grocery
These are retail stores that offer gourmet food and drink products, many of which are locally produced. This category includes culinary gift shops, gourmet stores, better quality liquor stores, wine stores, kitchen gadget stores, cookbook stores, etc. This sector does not typically include regular book stores or gift shops that have a cookbook or gadget section. Department stores are typically not included in this sector unless the experience is exceptional and unique, such as the cooking demos and gourmet grocery at Macy's Union Square in San Francisco, California, USA or Fortnum & Mason in London, United Kingdom.

Farms & Farmers' Markets
We include this agricultural sector because the seeds of cuisine are in agriculture. Agriculture is what makes cuisine possible, yet it is very different in its approach and concerns from the overall food and drink industry. This sector includes farms, orchards and self-picking facilities, as well as actual farmers' markets. It can even include local markets such as the Queen Victoria market in Melbourne, Victoria, Australia. This category does not typically include animal slaughterhouses or children's agritainment[3] type farm experiences. Many times we see destination marketing organizations embracing agritourism and calling it food tourism, or believing that agritourism is sufficient to market instead of food tourism. While food and drink

have their roots in agriculture and there is some overlap between food tourism and agritourism, the appeal of food and drink tourism goes well beyond the farm experience.[4]

Destination Marketing Organizations
Some destinations are more regarded for their culinary offerings than others. That said, nearly every place has a culinary story to tell. Destinations are also like a glue that binds together all of the other food tourism components. Destinations are a key uniting force in food tourism because they are usually the organizations that drive food tourism product development and promotion.[5]

Culinary Tour Operators, Packages, Guides & Travel Agents
This sector includes any kind of culinary tour, culinary tour guide, wine guide, or culinary tour package. It also includes travel agents and consultants who specialize in culinary travel.

Culinary Lodging
Culinary lodging includes a hotel, resort, bed and breakfast or other accommodation that has a focus on local food products. This typically includes bed & breakfasts and inns, and can sometimes include small boutique hotels. It should be noted that culinary lodging does NOT include a larger hotel that happens to have a great restaurant (if it qualifies, the restaurant alone would be included). This category usually also includes resorts and spas.

Culinary Attractions
This is a special category dedicated to unique sights such as a famous chef's home, a culinary museum, a place where a recipe was created, a bar where a drink was first invented and served, a movie star's favorite romantic restaurant, etc. This category can also include culinary museums, monuments, and places.

Meetings & Conventions
This sector includes both meeting centers and meeting planners. Meeting centers are not just convention centers and hotels, but smaller unique venues as well. Meeting planners can also serve as DMCs – who do more than just plan a meeting for an inbound group.

Trade Groups & Associations
This includes food, drink, travel and hospitality-oriented trade groups as well as food, drink, travel, and hospitality industry associations.

Students & Researchers
Students and researchers (academia) provide new knowledge and help to grow our industry. They provide research in the form of statistics, studies and methodologies that can be utilized by various components of our industry.

Media
This sector includes any kind of culinary media outlet. This sector has the potential to be quite crowded as it can include a wide variety of resources. In print, a dedicated foodie magazine dedicated to a town or region qualifies. A junky ad-filled or menus-only restaurant guide does not qualify as culinary media (we would call it advertising). This category includes editorial-oriented media only and typically includes audio/video publishers (includes CD/DVD/MP3); books; magazines & newspapers; websites, blogs and content providers.

Professional Services
This sector can include a variety of professional services such as marketing, advertising, branding, legal, accounting, human resources and others.

Technology Platforms

Technology platforms can include a wide variety of technology software. Today the most common technology platforms are the software as a service application, which refers to services delivered online. A number of these platforms serve the food, drink, travel and hospitality industries.

Government

A government body interested in food tourism can be one of several types of agencies, including a department or ministry of economic development, export, agriculture or even tourism. It is not unusual to find some destination marketing organizations, especially national tourist offices, which are structured as governmental entities.

State of Our Industry Today

Last year, 2013, marked the 10 year anniversary for both the World Food Travel Association (formerly International Culinary Tourism Association) and our formal industry as a whole. A lot has happened in the past 10 years for our industry, and a lot will happen in the next 10 years.

Our Association itself has grown from nothing to being the world's largest community of food and drink tourism professionals, currently with more than 18,000 people in 135 countries. We provided a framework for our industry's development, with a lexicon of common terms, educational tools, and media support. We initiated the move away from the phrase "culinary tourism" as the descriptor of our industry when our research showed that the use of "culinary" connotes high-end experiences, and people misunderstood the purpose of both our industry and our Association. Transitioning to the phrase "food tourism" has been successful and well-received. As an example of how the rest of the industry has begun to follow our lead, a survey of Google news alerts now shows prevalence using the term "food tourism", whereas 5 years ago, we found more Google news alerts using the term "culinary tourism."

In the decade since our industry was founded, food tourism has grown to become one of the most popular niches in the tourism industry. Everyone eats and drinks so food and drink are products relevant to 100% of visitors or customers. Not every traveler chooses to go shopping or play golf, but every traveler eats and drinks. We can work hard to help our visitors have unique and memorable food and drink experiences, or we can let visitors frequent the chains they know from home.

In the past 10 years, we have seen a number of notable industry accomplishments, such as Scotland's Gourmet Trail and fantastic, former EatScotland.com website. We have seen chef baseball cards as magazine inserts placed by the Las Vegas Convention & Visitors Authority. We have seen Singapore, Spain and Montreal place food imagery in tourism advertisements. We have seen the advent of regional culinary guidebooks like Oregon Culinary Escapes and Norway's National Tourist Routes. We have seen countries like Peru, Ecuador and Sweden undertake national food branding campaigns, which are tied into their national tourism strategies. We have seen regions within countries like the West Sweden Tourist Board take a leadership role in setting standards and training. And our industry is just getting started.

The Association continues to spread the food tourism message around the world. Our staff has delivered seminars and speeches to approximately 30,000 individuals so far world-wide, certified almost 400 students as food tourism professionals, and performed food tourism development work in nearly two dozen countries. More countries seem to be catching on, notably in Latin America, and just a few murmurs are being heard from the Middle East and Africa, which bodes well for further development in our industry. The Association appreciates the support of our industry, without which we would not exist.

We witness that many destination marketing organizations continue to pursue food tourism development and promotions, but many of them still do not understand our industry fully. For example, we still see menu guides and restaurant guides (featuring chains) commonly used to attract foodie travelers. We also still see destination marketers seeking to promote their best (i.e. most expensive) culinary experiences, assuming this is what foodie travelers want. With only 8.1% of foodies self-identifying as "gourmet," destination marketers could be missing nearly 92% of their potential universe of customers. Perhaps most importantly, we see a lot of tourism offices undertaking food tourism tactics, without any strategy in place. This is akin to driving to your destination without a roadmap or GPS. You might get to your goal in the end, but it will probably take you a lot longer, cost you more, and you will make a lot of wrong turns along the way.

CONCLUSION

We know cash is tight – the fallout from the 2008 global financial crisis, which we referred to as the "Dark Ages of Food Tourism" is nearly over. While things have not necessarily improved, many of us have come to accept a new norm. The shock of the crisis is now over for many of us. This is a great time to gather research and strategize your food tourism products for this decade and beyond.

DISCUSSION QUESTIONS

1. Consider the various food tourism industry sectors. Are there any new ones you would add or any that you would remove or condense with another sector? If so, why?
2. The English word "foodie" means different things to different people. In some cases, it can mean just a food lover. In other cases, people perceive a "foodie" as someone with a more gourmet profile. Discuss the term "foodie" and what it means to you and your geographic area. If English is not your area's language, what slang terms do you use to describe food enthusiasts and what connotations do these terms have?
3. Discuss the industry's shift from using the term "culinary tourism" to "food tourism". Which do prefer, and why?

ENDNOTES

[1] Long, Lucy M. 1999. Foodways: Using Food to Teach Folklore Theories and Methods. *Digest: An Interdisciplinary Study of Food and Foodways* 19:32–6.
[2] PsychoCulinary Profile of Culinary Travelers, International Culinary Tourism Association, 2010 [report not published externally].
[3] For unfamiliar words or industry-specific terms, we refer the reader to the *Glossary*.
[4] For further discussion of the role of agriculture in food tourism, refer to the *Special Role of Agriculture* chapter in this book.
[5] Please refer to the *Food Tourism Industry Stakeholders* chapter in this book for a discussion of specific sector business goals, benefits and challenges.

What's Your Situation?

Erik Wolf

This chapter focuses on self-assessment. Where are you in the food tourism process? What goals have you set and what are examples of specific and realistic goals? Are you learning about food tourism for the first time? Are you assessing your potential for product development or an existing product? Are you ready for a food tourism strategy, or to refine an existing strategy? Or are you already implementing your strategy or product launch? Perhaps you are reviewing (re-educating) yourself and your programs - the cycle begins again. We will also look at the EASI framework developed by the WFTA and other industry tools for self-assessment.

INTRODUCTION

Every food, drink, travel, or hospitality professional is eventually faced with one important dilemma, "Food tourism sounds interesting. What is it and how can I get involved?" When people hear the phrase "food tourism" or "culinary tourism" for the first time, they often do not know what to think. We defined these terms in the Introduction to Food Tourism chapter.

Understandably the term "food tourism" is a bit enigmatic to the uninitiated. Even without an explanation, some small business owners might deny any interest in food tourism, perhaps a reaction to the ubiquity of food and drink and non-belief in the need to target a separate market of consumers. Most destination marketers and consumers in the more developed world eat at least three times per day. Because of the ubiquity of eating, they may not feel that food and drink are special enough to warrant a special effort to promote to travelers. Yet there is a growing market of food lovers whose destination selection is partially or completely influenced by their interest in food. It is therefore in every destination's interest to become acquainted with this new tourism niche.

Determining Your Situation

No matter whether food tourism is new to you, your business, organization or destination, every business owner and organization can benefit from understanding your own situation. Are you completely new to the industry and the terms? Have you been practicing "something like food tourism" for a while but never knew what to call it? Or perhaps your organization has been engaged in both the food and travel industries for some time and fully understands what food tourism is and how it can benefit both the organization and community. Regardless of your stage or process, we offer several tools to help you assess yourself, your business, your organization or your destination.

SWOT Analysis

A classic tool in strategy and marketing circles is the SWOT analysis, which we will only touch on briefly due to its pervasiveness. In SWOT, S stands for Strengths, W stands for Weaknesses, O stands for Opportunities and T stands for Threats. Strengths and weaknesses are internal and present, while opportunities and threats are external and often future-oriented. The assessment is typically arranged in a grid as in Diagram 1. Then the various items as they pertain to you, your business, your group or your destination are written into the appropriate quadrant. There are plenty of resources available to help you complete a SWOT analysis.[1]

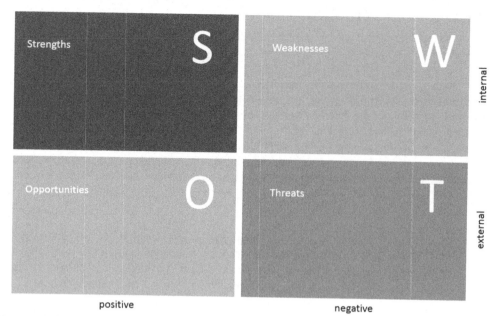

Diagram 1: SWOT Matrix. *Credit: World Food Travel Association*

VRIO Analysis

Another assessment tool that is usually applied to individual businesses and products is VRIO, or Value-Rarity-Imitability-Organization.[2] The tools relate to how valuable your product is, how rare it is, how imitable it is and whether and how well your organization harnesses these tools. Assessments are usually laid out in a table as in Diagram 2. The far right column in the table assesses the competitive implication for each item.

Valuable?	Rare?	Difficult to Imitate?	Supported by Organization?	Competitive Implications	Performance
no				competitive disadvantage	below normal
yes	no			competitive parity	normal
yes	yes	no		temporary competitive disadvantage	temporary above normal
yes	yes	yes	no	sustainable competitive disadvantage	sustainable above normal
yes	yes	yes	yes	sustainable competitive offer	sustainable above normal for you

Diagram 2: VRIO Matrix. *Credit: World Food Travel Association*

The EASI Process, or "Food Tourism is E.A.S.I."

A third framework designed specifically for the food tourism industry is EASI, where "EASI" is an acronym made from the first letters of the words Education, Assessment, Strategy and Implementation (see Diagram 3 below). These are the four major phases or steps, of the food and drink tourism industry. EASI was developed by the World Food Travel Association to help practitioners understand the basic workflow process in food and drink tourism development and promotion. Because EASI is the process of greatest relevance to the food tourism industry, we will discuss it in greater detail.

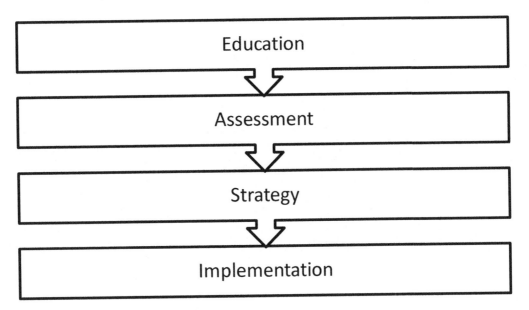

Diagram 3: The EASI process. *Credit: World Food Travel Association*

E for Education

Education is typically the first of four phases that applies to food tourism businesses. A professional first must be educated in food tourism, like the small business owner above who perhaps rejected any interest in participating in food tourism. Education includes learning the correct industry terminology, reading and understanding demographic and psychographic research about foodie travelers, attending food tourism conferences or learning online, becoming certified as a culinary travel professional, or reading this and other books that orient the business owner towards the food and drink tourism industry. Some professionals spend a great deal of time in this phase learning all they can, or even remain permanently in this phase, in the case of research professionals or consultants who specialize in this area. Other professionals, with sufficient food tourism knowledge for their specific needs may skip the Education phase and initiate the EASI process with the Assessment step. The fast pace at which food tourism is developing calls for frequent reading and educational coursework for any professional wishing to succeed in this field.

A for Assessment

The Assessment phase refers to taking an assessment of the tools, business processes and other assets a business has, or needs to have, in its inventory. It is not appropriate to go into assessment in great detail here, but suffice it to say that the Assessment phase can be split into two main tools: Experience Assessment and Asset Inventory Analysis.

An Experience Assessment helps both businesses and destinations improve both their products and service to their customers in the food and drink tourism industry. The Assessment can be as simple as a service journey analysis, or a more complex 360-degree analysis that includes on-site visits, interviews, and primary research. A service journey analysis describes a potential visitor or customer's service experience, from start to finish. For a visitor, it would start with the destination research and flight (train, etc.) booking process, airport arrival, customs/immigration if appropriate, airport transportation, hotel check-in, etc. For a customer in a restaurant for example, it would start with how the customer heard about the restaurant, whether they booked a table and the reservation process, parking or other transportation considerations and so on. These measures are then valued and ranked. It is literally qualitative analysis meets quantitative feedback. An Experience Assessment works for a wide variety of business types, including destination marketing organizations, food/drink/travel trade groups, hotel/restaurant management companies, and individual businesses (restaurant, winery, brewery, hotel, resort, spa, retail store, etc.). A Food & Drink Experience Assessment can serve as the cornerstone of a food tourism strategy.

The Asset Inventory Analysis is a tool derived from a common asset inventory platform. To be of true value, the destination or business needs to augment a classic asset inventory with food tourism-specific data points. Geolocation can also be performed on the data to identify clusters of critical mass. For example, one might expect a high concentration of restaurants in a city center. One might not be able to predict where a high concentration of cooking schools or bed and breakfast inns might be located. By creating a geolocation mash up, a destination marketer can see where businesses are, in relation to each other. This then provides a tool that can be harnessed in the creation of itineraries or lodging packages which can be promoted to food tourists.

Other Assessments

Of course other assessments can be performed, such as economic impact or environmental impact. In fact, an economic impact assessment should be performed before food tourism-specific assessments to determine whether developing a food tourism strategy is even advisable for a region. An environmental impact assessment is not a prerequisite for food tourism assessments, but it may be advisable if issues of sustainability and food waste are of interest to the destination.

The experience assessment and asset inventory analysis typically have the greatest impact on a food tourism strategy, which is the next phase. If no Assessment is performed, it is like building a house without an architect's plans. You might end up with a finished house, but it might not be on a solid foundation. Rickety walls and unstable stairs could cause the entire house to collapse, which would be a tremendous waste of time, energy and money.

S for Strategy

Once you have completed the assessment phase, you will know whether it makes sense to create a food tourism strategy. If so, then you can set realistic objectives and goals as part of the strategy. Within the strategy itself, you will define objectives and draft a plan.

Strategy is the third phase. It is like a road map for food tourism development. A strategy can be created by a business like a restaurant, by a group of businesses like a hotel management company, by a trade group that might focus on a specific sector like lodging or retail, or a destination marketing organization. Strategies can help all business types. It is not the place of this book to explain the minutiae of a food tourism strategy, however the interested reader should read the *Business Model Generation* chapter for a place to start.

I for Implementation

The last phase is Implementation by the business or group of businesses, or it can be a project implemented by the food tourism industry (such as a project sponsored by the WFTA). For businesses and destinations, implementation usually refers to the execution of the strategic plan. All too often we see one of two things. A business or destination will skip all three phases and begin with Implementation. This might look like a marketing campaign with few or no tracking mechanisms in place, and no way to tie the results from the campaign back into the plan for the next fiscal year. Or we see a business get to the strategy phase and stop, without any implementation. Such a scenario is usually an author who is paid handsomely for a beautiful food tourism strategy document, never to be seen or used again. Just as a strategy needs to be implemented, a proper implementation plan needs to take into account a way to measure progress, timing, and resolution of objectives.

If either a business or destination wishes to pursue food tourism seriously, it needs to:

1) Learn what food tourism is, and how it is different from gourmet tourism, wine tourism, and simply eating out at restaurants. (Education phase)
2) Figure out where it is in the process. Does it have a food/drink product or service that visitors would travel to experience? (Assessment phase)
3) Plan a roadmap for success. What are the target markets? What will your budget allow you to accomplish this year? What are competitors doing? (Strategy phase)
4) Do the work, and measure it. Feed the results back into the plan for next year. (Implementation phase)

We are all busy professionals. While we are preoccupied with our day-to-day lives, the world changes. Over a period of several years, trends and industries change. Whether you are new to it or it has been a while since you stepped through the EASI process, you may wish to evaluate your situation and see how the tools presented herein can benefit you, your business, your group or your destination. If you are going through a process like EASI again, going through the process a second time is always easier and faster. You learn how things have changed. You learn about new products and tools in the market that can help you do your job better, faster and for less money. We call this CPI, or continuous process of improvement.

CONCLUSION

Your first step is to figure out where you are in the EASI process. Do not skip a phase, but move as quickly as you are comfortable with. The faster you graduate through each of the phases, the faster you will be able to succeed in your food or drink tourism business.

DISCUSSION QUESTIONS

1. Where is your business, destination or organization in the EASI process?
2. Is it possible to be in two of the four processes at the same time? If so, explain.
3. What other assessment tools are you aware of? Which could apply to food tourism?

ENDNOTES

[1] Lavinsky, David. *Start at the End: How Companies Can Grow Bigger and Faster by Reversing Their Business Plan* (Wiley, 2012) 18-21.
[2] Peng, Mike W. *Global Business* (Cengage Learning, 2010) 102.

Food Tourism Industry Stakeholders

Lisa Chase, Santosh Kumar Mishra, & Erik Wolf

This chapter looks at the goals, benefits, challenges, and opportunities for getting involved in today's food and drink tourism industry. We will explain how the food and drink sector intersects with the travel and hospitality sector, and answer the question, "Why is there even a food tourism industry?"

INTRODUCTION

Why should business owners care about food and drink in the context of tourism? In fact, why does a food tourism industry even exist? According to the World Food Travel Association, it is a vital part of the tourism experience for visitors to experience the unique and memorable food and drink of a particular geographic area. Food tourism activities are broad and include much more than just dining out. For example, food events, cooking schools, cookbook stores, wineries and more are all part of the food and drink tourism experience. Unique and memorable experiences provided by culinary assets like these motivate people to choose to travel to one destination over another, according to data from the World Food Travel Association's 2007 research on culinary travelers.[1]

"Food tourism" as an industry is sometimes hard to understand because it represents the intersection of both food/drink and travel/hospitality, a phenomenon illustrated in Frans Johansson's book The Medici Effect.[2] The premise of the book is putting two formerly distinct products or industries together, and creating a new product or industry. That is exactly what food tourism is.

An everyday restaurant owner may see no immediate link between her business and travel/hospitality. Similarly, a lodging owner may see no immediate link between his business and food/drink. Business owners in these kinds of situations need help to understand how they fit into, and can benefit from, alignment with the food tourism industry. This means evaluating the goals, benefits, challenges and opportunities of the various types of businesses that comprise our food and drink tourism industry. Definitions and examples of the categories below are included in the Introduction to the Food Tourism Industry chapter in this book. Therefore, we will not repeat definitions of these business types here.

The interconnections between and among the various business types in our industry are complex and the resulting diagram would look like a map of communication traffic on the Internet. Yet it does make sense to divide the discussion of our industry's zeitgeist to better understand how the goals, benefits, challenges and opportunities of each of these business types can affect and benefit your own business:

- Small to medium sized businesses[3] (in general)
- Large businesses (in general)
- Trade groups & associations
- Students & researchers
- Media
- Professional services
- Destination marketing organizations
- Technology platforms
- Consumers

Note that not all goals, benefits, challenges and opportunities outlined below will apply to all business types.

Small Businesses in General

This category comprises a wide variety of business types, the only difference being the size of the business. Independent restaurants, hotels, wine stores and culinary tour operators, among other business types could be categorized in this group. There are a variety of ways to classify a business as "small" or "large", but the most common ways are looking at the annual revenue, number of paid staff or number of members or customers. How one classifies a business - as small or large - is subjective. Most of us would agree that a business with only one or two employees must be classified as small, but other people may find a business with 10 to 20 employees also small, yet it is large compared with the smaller two-employee company.

Industry Canada defines a small or medium business based on the number of employees. Firms producing goods are considered "small" if they have fewer than 100 employees. Firms producing services are considered "small" if they have 50 employees or fewer. Service firms with between 51 and 499 employees, or goods-producing firms with 101-499 employees, are considered "medium." The smallest of small businesses are called micro-enterprises, most often defined as having fewer than five employees. Firms with 501+ employees are considered "large" businesses. However you define them, sizes are relative.

Goals

Businesses may have other goals specific to their own unique business type, but as far as food and drink tourism is concerned, the following goals are a common denominator among most small businesses.

Making Money

One of the motivations of small food and drink tourism businesses is to make money. That means, for example, generating sufficient sales to meet or exceed goals, through more hotel rooms booked, more meeting delegates confirmed or more bottles of wine sold. Corollary goals are to increase the customer base, and the amount of per-trip spending by each customer. The more money made, the more the business owner may have to invest back into the business, and the more tax revenue that can be collected. New cash that comes into the community from visitors has a significantly higher economic multiplier (impact) than does cash spent by locals, because it grows the local economy. Without fresh cash from outside the area, a local economy can stagnate.

One way to make more money is to add value to the product and charge more. Agricultural producers add value by creating a prepared product (think turning milk and cream into ice cream), then higher prices can be charged for those agricultural commodities, especially if such products are sold direct to consumers at a farmers' market or farmstand. Direct-to-consumer sales gives an additional benefit that new visitors/consumers have a unique opportunity to learn about the agricultural products. This action, in turn, can expand the customer base and create new marketing opportunities; help to preserve heirloom species and traditional methods of food preparation and consumption (i.e. by creating greater awareness); and teach everyday consumers to appreciate where their food comes from.

Culinary Heritage & Preservation

Smaller business owners may also be interested in goals of preservation and promotion of local culinary culture and heritage. For example, preserving a time-honored method of making cheese or chocolate is a worthy reason to become a cheesemaker or chocolatier.

Small Business Benefits

Below are just a few small business benefits of being involved in food and drink tourism.

Pursue a Dream

One of the reasons we hear most often is that small business owners pursue a passion. For example, you may love cheese and decide to become an artisanal cheese producer, or you may have always had a lifelong goal to manage a bed-and-breakfast. Being in business for yourself gives you the freedom and flexibility to do whatever you want to do. This approach is not without challenges of course.

Creating New Markets

One benefit can be to create or target a new market segment. For example, Dry Soda out of Seattle, Washington, USA created a new beverage niche with low sugar sodas and is doing very well. It is also a brand that Seattleites are proud to call their own, helping to pique interest in Seattle as a culinary destination.

Education

Some food and drink businesses like cooking schools and classes have the opportunity to educate consumers and professionals alike by providing quality cooking instruction, either in a classroom or as a demonstration at an event.

Memory Creation

Marketers know that memories last longer when all five human senses are involved. Memories are created by experiences that we do not expect, perhaps out of our "comfort zone" like trying a new food, strange surroundings or personal service, which are often achieved through authenticity. What better way to leave an indelible impression than to involve food and drink as part of the visitor experience? Whether the tasting is at breakfast at a B&B, a cooking school in Italy, or a food event in Singapore, memories are still made by involving the tongue, nose, hands, eyes and ears.

Positive Word of Mouth and Repeat Business[4]

Consider your own behavior. If you have a great experience in a restaurant or really enjoy a particular beer or wine, you will tell your friends. Consider the meetings industry. Good food sells meeting space. Meeting planners want to keep the client and delegates happy and even turn them into "raving fans" so they will spread the word. A conventioneer who was impressed by the food and drink in a city may return with the family later to share the experience with them.

Critical Mass

A critical mass of a wide variety of food and drink business types gives a potential visitor a more compelling reason to visit a destination than if there are just a handful of food and drink resources. Economic development and tourism promotion officials should consider performing an asset inventory and assessment to determine the scope and quality of such resources. Plotting resources on a Google-style map is helpful to visualize where these resources are in relation to each other. This helps in the creation of itineraries and trails.

Small Business Challenges

Lack of Time, Money and Staff

Most small food tourism businesses face issues with insufficient time, money and staffing to do all the work that needs to be done. Many small business owners are sole proprietors or husband and wife teams. Frequently people like this are stretched financially and also stretched for time, through no fault of their own. It is simply the nature of running a small business.

More often than not, small business owners lack sufficient extra capital to be able to invest back into their business, which translates into difficulty in growing the business. This is a dangerous position because it means that a business can exhaust its operating capital quickly, or it could struggle without real growth for many years. It depends on the business owner's goals whether or not this is acceptable. Some people may be content without a lot of extra capital to invest, while others may not be happy at all. If outside investment is available, then this is a moot point.

Missed Personal Development Opportunities

Another challenge that small food tourism business owners face is the inability to take sufficient advantage of available educational and training opportunities, primarily due to lack of time. A local tourism office or a relevant trade association might make specific training available, such as in marketing, media relations, sales tactics or website design. However, if the small business owner does not have or will not make the time to take advantage of these sessions, or cannot afford the time away from the business, then they are unable to grow and benefit from them.

Cost to Quality of Life

It can be argued that working 60+ hours per week for a large corporation has a real cost in terms of quality of life. What many small business owners do not realize before starting a business is that they will work this much and usually more every week. Many small business owners operate their businesses out of their homes. A small cash flow or situation of understaffing means the proprietor has to do the work him- or herself. If the work does not get done, then the business fails. The solution is funding the business sufficiently (through product sales or investment) so that the small business owner can maintain his or her quality of life.

Propensity towards Weak Product Development and Marketing

Another challenge is how to make products attractive to foodies or how to provide new products/services geared towards food travelers. For example, you might make the best cooking marinades, but if you do not have the time to research and design an attractive label, they might not sell. A low cash flow can also mean an inability to perform regular marketing tasks, or the inability to schedule consistent marketing updates for new or current customers.

Product Appropriateness

Challenges to food and drink producers and manufacturers include the fact that often their products and services are not fully adapted to the needs of tourists. For example a sauce manufacturer may not see a clear fit with marketing its locally produced gourmet sauces to inbound visitors, preferring to keep its products for distribution and sale to local residents. They would miss the fact that foodies tend to spend huge sums of money on souvenir food and drink items and cooking gadgets, provided they know about the stores that sell these items in the first place.

Stunted Growth

A small business may not have a budget to translate marketing materials into multiple languages, or they may not be able to distribute a product outside of a certain geographic radius, or they might not be able to market and sell the product, especially in online marketplaces, which requires special skills. In some instances, these may not be realistic goals for small food and drink producers.

Bad Customer Experience

Many small providers are still unable or unwilling to accept credit or debit cards, which are universal forms of payment. If a business owner is unwilling to pay the credit card fee, then it should be built into the cost of the product or service. Thankfully with services like Square and PayPal, more small business owners are able to easily accept card payments in an affordable manner. When transacting with international customers, business owners are cautioned to be upfront about the fees charged to your customers for foreign exchange conversions. What might start out as a convenience for your customers could turn into a disaster when they realize they have to pay 3% more just for the privilege of paying in their own currency at the point of sale. Unfortunately, not much can be done regarding the fees banks charge, but we can do our part to make our customers aware of these charges.

Is it appropriate to offer signage (or menus) in multiple languages? Do you know the shipping policies for both airmail and common airlines serving the area, making it easy for visitors to ship your products home? Do customers have long waits to get into your establishment? If so, rethink your processes. Word-of-mouth is the most effective kind of promotion, and that includes bad word-of-mouth as well.

Customer Type: Local or Tourist

Sometimes it is not clear whether the customer is a visitor, a local resident or both. Such is the case with some cooking schools, and making this determination depends on the length of instruction. A culinary school with a two-year degree program is going after a different customer than is a cooking class that seeks to sell seats for a two-hour or two-day session. Consumers may be confused by what options are available in any given area. Another possible challenge is the language of instruction. Many smaller cooking class experiences, especially those of shorter duration, are located in rural areas where the instructors may speak only their native language. This would mean that an interpreter may be necessary, or more likely, it may be difficult for visitors to experience the training fully. Another challenge to cooking schools is online culinary instruction. Larger culinary schools will, of course, have a website and a published class curriculum, while smaller culinary classes may not even have a website. Factor in the volume of video recipes available online, and it becomes very difficult for consumers to make a decision. Consumers are overwhelmed by choice and for some of them, their only choice is to make no choice. The astute business owner will remove as many obstacles as possible from the purchase process.

Food events have a similar issue. Trying to reach out broadly to visitors to an area and entice them to be in your location for your particular food or drink event can be hard, if not also unrealistic. Unless the event is the main purpose of travel, many times a foodie will be disappointed to learn that he or she just missed (or will just miss) a great food event. Publicity and help from the tourism office can help reduce the instance of missed opportunities. Equally important is to plant the seed with traveling foodies that your areas hosts regular food events. It may not even occur to someone traveling for business to stay another day for a food event, unless they know about it in advance.

Lower Costs of Inputs & Higher Overall Cost

In recent years there has been downward pressure on pricing in agricultural commodities which has been making it increasingly difficult to make a profit in farming. Combine that with the fact that a large amount of prime agricultural land is being taken over by development or being purchased by larger corporations, and you can begin to see that farming is a difficult industry to be in. The consumer forgets that the costs of labor and energy (among other things) are increasing, making the overall product more expensive. Consumers see this as higher prices in their grocery stores.

For agriculture in particular, a solution to decreasing market prices is to find new distribution outlets. For example, direct sales to consumers. There has been an increase in supply of local and value-added products, which was spurred by consumer demand. In the more developed world, consumers are increasingly getting back to basics, including learning more about where our food comes from and the environmental impact of our actions just to put food on our table. Many consumers are interested in visiting farms and vineyards or volunteering on a farm for a day or longer. Learning how to grow, harvest, and prepare food is now an important part of "unique and memorable eating and drinking experiences."

Moving Target

Food travelers always look for new and different experiences. There are always new food tours, new wine routes, a new gourmet map or other type of lure. It is the job of the destination marketers, tour operators and travel agents to discover and package these new resources and market them accordingly.

It Doesn't Concern Us

Many small business owners (such as culinary retail shops) are unaware how they have an important role to play with food travelers. New customers are a new source of revenue. Even if only one sale is made one time, you can turn that into repeat business by leveraging your one-time customer's positive word-of-mouth among colleagues he knows in the area where the business operates.

The Great Unknown

Certain small businesses like culinary attractions, small culinary retail stores or out-of-the-way cafes may not be well-known or may be very hard to find. They may have a hard time attracting visitors and/or supporting their annual operating budget, as in the case of a culinary-themed museum.

Small Business Opportunities

The opportunities for businesses in this sector are also many.

Unparalleled Creativity

It may be easy for a small, locally owned ice cream shop, for example, to create truly unusual, complicated or risky flavors, which a large ice cream manufacturer would never think of doing. Examples are the Arbequina Olive Oil or Dandelion Sorbet with Spring Flowers flavors at Salt & Straw scoop shop in Portland, Oregon, USA. Small business owners are reminded that sometimes great ideas started by small businesses end up being adopted by larger corporations. Just look at what Starbucks did with the concept of the neighborhood coffeehouse. It was the "local" neighborhood feel and camaraderie of "being a regular" that Starbucks capitalized on by packaging for global use. Now it is fashionable and trendy to visit a Starbucks. Might the same extend to the purchase of unusual ice cream flavors?

Distribution

Distributors located in areas with high tourist concentrations, or high concentrations of meeting and convention hotels, will stand to do quite well financially as long as they provide good quality for a good price. A business in this sector could stand to do even better by diversifying its product portfolio to include a diverse range of locally sourced and artisanal products, whenever feasible. It is as much the job of the distributor's sales representative to ensure that the meeting and convention facilities know that the distributor carries a range of locally sourced products, as it is the meeting planner to ask if any locally made food and drink products are available. This would then help the meeting and convention planners to be able to offer something new and different to their delegates, a notion discussed in detail in the meeting and convention chapter.

Collaboration

Sometimes small food tourism businesses can group together for mutual benefit, such as the former Dine Originals independent restaurant association.[5] While the organization was in existence, its members had their own national website, a purchasing (discount) program and an annual conference. Working together, these businesses could effectively compete with big chains. These outlets can have an advantage over chains because of their authenticity, unique offerings, local personalities and local stories.

We say in English that a rising tide floats all boats. In other words, if we all work together, we will all benefit by making more sales. For example, food and drink events should ensure that their events are known to, and visibly promoted by, the local tourism office. The presumption is that people coming to the area will research activities to do while they are there. Another opportunity is for food and drink events to package their event tickets with tour operators or hotels, which in effect, become sales distribution channels for these events. Therefore it is in the hotel's best interest to actively seek out such partnerships, just as one example.

Large Businesses in General

This category also comprises a wide variety of business types. Larger corporations are typically focused on generating revenue and earning profits for shareholders. That said, many larger corporations are not indifferent to the benefits of highlighting the cuisine unique to the area in which they operate. This is especially true for airlines and hotels, and less relevant for other large businesses like rental car companies. For example Korean Airlines offers *bibimbap* as a main course choice in its coach class of service. *Bibimbap* is one of Korea's favorite national dishes. For those unfamiliar with this dish, Korean Airlines makes it very simple by providing a instructions how to assemble and enjoy the *bibimbap* meal. Air New Zealand is another airline that focuses on New Zealand made cheeses and other dairy products, wines, and meats as part of its meal service. It gives travelers a taste of things to come, or a pleasant memory of things enjoyed. Still, an airline is in the business of selling seats and at the highest possible price. A car rental company wants to rent more cars, and a hotel wants to ensure the highest possible occupancy rate at the highest possible room rate. Like small businesses, larger businesses want more sales too.

Goals

A large corporation may also be a good corporate citizen by engaging in community programs and charitable donations. An example of this is Whole Foods' commitment to supporting community programs, local fundraisers, and local non-profit organizations.[6]

Benefits

Large businesses stand to benefit from additional sales by foodie travelers. A secondary benefit is the extension of brand awareness into new markets.

Challenges

Perhaps the most significant challenge to food and drink tourism for large businesses is possible fierce competition from local providers.

Opportunities

Large businesses have an opportunity to establish a leadership position with regard to their business practices. Specifically with regards to things like commitments to sustainability, fair treatment of employees, worker rights, and so on. Large businesses also have the power to be able to foster consumer opinion and drive change by their sheer size and buying power. The US chain Chipotle is just one such example of a large corporation that is helping to change consumer awareness about the benefits of healthy eating by educating its customers about how its menu choices can be healthy.[7]

A Word about Chains

Chains often serve a need, but when we can make the effort, we *should* make the effort – to support the small, independent establishments if for no other reason than to help promote economic and community diversity and sustainability. You can get a McDonald's Big Mac or a Starbucks coffee in any major city in the world – and they will taste pretty much the same everywhere you go. Do you not want to try something you are unable to get at home when you travel? Many of us do, and many more of us need to learn to do so. That said, there is a certain group of consumers who are simply not interested in fine-tuning the particulars of their food or drink experience. These customers might be forever happy with the chain experience, or may even plan to visit a chain if they come from a community without the business they seek. Regardless of whether the customer seeks a chain or a locally owned business, first and foremost, the customer seeks what is comfortable and avoids what causes fear or doubt. This is strong evidence to know your customer (or visitor).

Some of us are scared to try local, independent establishments (for fear of wasted time, wasted money or embarrassment) so we rely on the *predictable* quality and the *consistency* of the big chain experience. As travelers, we should at least ask a local colleague or friend where the locals like to go – so we can then feel comfortable knowing that we will get a culinary experience of high quality and consistency – while supporting the local, independent establishment. Save the chains for airport dining on the way home. An argument can be made for differing health and safety standards, which might actually be harmful in some ways to visitors (i.e. in an instance where locals are used to different bacteria than are visitors). Travelers are always urged to use good judgment and if they find themselves in an environment where the quality or safety are suspect, try only small portions or forego altogether.

Chains serve a purpose. They are brands we can identify with, and frequently, they offer a quick meal at a predictable price. The can also serve as a reminder of home when we are far away from ours. Yet, chains do not need any help with marketing – many of them have their own marketing departments and dedicated budgets. It is the smaller, independent establishments that provide the charm that lures foodies to a destination in the first place. They are the unique and memorable establishments that create the memories that get visitors talking long after they return home. Travelers will spend some of their money in chains, but we have to make sure to spend our money in local, independent establishments as well. If we do not, then eating out while traveling will be no different from eating out when at home.

Trade Groups & Associations

Goals

The goal of trade groups and association is to pursue objectives of mutual benefit for the association or group and its members or constituents. Many of these groups engage in advocacy – taking a stand on an industry position.

Benefits

For groups or associations like these, being involved in the food and drink tourism industry may not match exactly the benefits for the group's members of being involved with the food tourism industry. For example, a winery may be concerned about exports or how its tasting room sales are doing, and less concerned about industry lobbying which the larger association or group might be primarily involved in. Still, that winery owner might want to hear relevant news from the larger association or group. A major benefit for smaller businesses to be affiliated with such organizations, is that larger organizations can serve as a single point of contact between the group's members and the larger food tourism industry.

Challenges

It can be very hard for these organizations to figure out the best way to work with the food tourism industry. Sometimes such larger associations are preoccupied with advocacy work and do little, if anything, else. Some of the larger restaurant associations are challenged because they receive the majority of their funding from large chains, but the majority of their members are small, local, and independent restaurants. This creates a challenge for the leadership of the restaurant association. For smaller industry associations, the challenge is trying to get a large number of small, independent producers or businesses to see the value of joining a membership-based organization. Many small business owners will not join unless they see a solid return on investment. In some countries, there is not a tradition of trade associations, so this particular type of infrastructure may not even exist, or it may not be strong. Small business owners are more reluctant than ever to pay membership dues. The return on investment needs to be proven first before such business owners will part with their hard earned cash.

The primary opportunity for trade associations and groups that participate in food tourism is the benefit their group's members can realize from being involved, such as group insurance, group purchasing contracts or group bank processing fee discounts. Groups and associations can typically negotiate better deals for their members, which can be positioned as a member benefit that helps justify the cost of member dues to those organizations.

Students and Researchers

Goals

Students and researchers of food and drink tourism seek to obtain funding for their research; publish said research; and for some, finding a job is also a goal.

Benefits

Students and researchers can make relevant contributions that help to advance the industry and benefit small businesses.

Challenges

One of the challenges to this group is that there are only a limited number of institutions where this kind of training is given, although the number seems to be growing every year. While there is only a limited amount of research in our field, available research seems to be growing as well. Another challenge to this sector is the ongoing lack of funding that researchers endure and the constant competition among grants and other funding applications that facilitate this area of research.

Opportunities

Research in our industry is growing, and more research is needed, for example, on new strategies based on future demands and how current technology is changing the way foodies make decisions, a recent example of which is using content analysis.

Media

Goals

Goals among media professionals today largely revolve around survival, by attracting new readers or viewers (a following) and advertisers.

Benefits

The benefits of culinary media being involved in the food tourism industry are to attract visitors and locals alike as subscribers to the publication, or viewers of the program, and by attracting new advertisers, which serves to increase revenue.

Challenges

One of the primary challenges in this sector is that advertising revenue has been reduced by a large order of magnitude so publications and programs of all kinds are having a hard time staying financially viable. A number of creative revenue models such as pay to play or paid content have been tried, with varying degrees of success. Another challenge is the constant need for new, high quality content. Consumers constantly seek the new, different and exciting. Successful journalists need to bring that to their followers on a regular basis.

Opportunities

The opportunities in this sector lie mostly in the online publishing industry, which has a very low production cost and virtually no cost of distribution. These facts make online publishing vastly more sustainable than more traditional forms of publishing. That said, opportunities still exist when the print media is highly targeted.

Professional Services

Goals

The goals of businesses in this sector (like media relations, advertising and legal professionals) are to provide quality services and develop a relationship with the food or drink business, with the corollary goal of selling additional services to the business over time.

Benefits

The food tourism benefit for these businesses is that as the food and drink tourism industry grows, there will be additional demand for a wide variety of professional services. More visitors mean that more services will be required, hence more demand for professional services.

Challenges

There are several challenges of serving the food and drink tourism industry. Many of these are very small businesses and may not have a budget earmarked for such professionals. A second challenge may be convincing the small business owner that such a service is actually needed. Small food and drink business owners may view marketing and branding work as an elective (nice to have and not required) component of their business. For such professional service providers, it can be very hard to find a sufficient amount of work from small business owners to keep a service provider gainfully employed. Additionally, the traditional financial model of a high monthly retainer is increasingly coming under fire, as business owners of all sizes question the return on investment of such arrangements.

Opportunities

The opportunities available to this sector are not huge, yet the need for services like these continue to grow at a nominal annual rate. With the additional growth of sub-sectors like artisanal foods, organics, and gluten-free, the need for services for advertising, media relations, and branding will increase as well.

Technology Platforms

Goals

The goal of technology platforms and their providers is to facilitate information exchange or to perform a function, such as to facilitate sales for participating businesses.

Benefits

The right technology solution can solve very real problems for a variety of businesses. For example, the online restaurant reservations system OpenTable.com revolutionized restaurant reservations and front-of-house management. A lot of restaurants suddenly had a very real problem solved.

Challenges

One of the starkest challenges for this sector is that technology is always changing. Software, hardware, systems, processes, are in a constant state of flux. By the time one solution is fully worked out, there may be a better – and cheaper - solution already in place. Therefore any technology platform will need astute leadership that can predict likely market changes and ready the company to take advantage of such changes as they occur.

Opportunities

The right technology platform can ascend quickly into stardom. Look at how quickly social deal platforms like LivingSocial and Groupon became popular. There were serious unforeseen disadvantages of platforms like these that made these kinds of companies become industry pariahs just as quickly. Any technology company seeking to solve a pain in the market would be well served by extensive advance market research. Additionally, cloud solutions where the customer runs an application directly from an external server on the internet, should grow as the cost for an individual business to install and maintain computer hardware and software is becoming prohibitive.

Destination Marketing Organizations

Goals

Destination goals include attracting visitors of all types (leisure, meetings, convention). Some destinations may provide information services to their community. Other destinations need to raise revenue to fund services. If the tourism office is a government body, then their goal would also be to provide a safe environment and adequate infrastructure and services to support tourism. If the tourism office is also an economic development entity, then it would also seek to create jobs.

Benefits

There are many benefits to a destination involved in food tourism. First there is the increased tax base from increased sales made by visitors. Next, additional jobs are created, many in suburban/rural areas. New infrastructure is typically not required until the destination experiences significant growth. Neighboring communities may benefit from overflow or transient business to and from a more popular destination. In many food destinations, traffic woes are temporary and/or seasonal. Another potentially significant benefit for tourism offices is new memberships from "hidden" businesses, i.e. those not normally involved with the local tourism office. In such instances, because the tourism office has made a strategic decision to be involved in food tourism, the restaurants in particular would be interested in the activities of that tourism office. Lastly, a food tourism initiative by a destination can lead to greater participation in and unity around, local product development/marketing initiatives.

Challenges

One of the most significant challenges to tourism offices is funding. Destinations need income to support current and new services for the community and for visitors. Another potential challenge is the lack of food and drink experiences (a.k.a. "assets") in sufficient quality or quantity to be of interest to visitors. Still another challenge is the actual structure of tourism offices themselves. Some are driven by memberships, while others have constituents. Still others are government entities with no members whatsoever. Trying to address the needs of each kind of tourism office is hard, as their needs and requirements are so different.

Opportunities

Destinations play a special strategic role. They are like the tip of an iceberg in their areas. They have the potential to influence a large base of members or constituents. Consequently some of the greatest opportunities in our industry involve the destination marketing organizations.

Consumers

Consumers are the end beneficiaries of great food and drink experiences, but employees and owners of every business mentioned herein have the potential of being foodie consumers (when they are not working) as well. In many ways, consumers are the most important group to understand.

Goals

Consumers want to travel and enjoy new and different culinary experiences. They want to discover new food products and for some, they may want to acquire bragging rights for stories to tell back home.

Visitors, especially from North America and Europe, now seek food experiences that are fresh, local organic, sustainable and seasonal (FLOSS), as well as authentic. Visitors are better educated than ever and have more information at their fingertips than at any time in history. If a food/drink experience is subpar, it is easy for the consumer to move on and find a suitable replacement. Food travelers have high expectations for their food experiences, no matter whether they originate in the developed or lesser developed world. The onus is on the business owner to ensure that the consumer's expectations are not just met, but exceeded.[8] When businesses satisfy a consumer's "unexpected" needs, they create "memories" that go well beyond basic satisfaction.

Benefits

Experiencing great food and drink can convey a wide range of benefits to consumers, namely: access to unique products; exclusive product sampling, purchase offers and club memberships; enjoyment of a higher quality experience; allure of being a trendsetter; bragging rights; satisfaction of helping to preserve natural resources and cultural heritage; creation of local ambassadors (i.e. enthusiastic residents); raising the bar (quality level) for uninvolved local businesses; unifying disjointed groups & communities; increased cultural appreciation; greater awareness of the need to protect food resources; support of sustainable food production practices; and preservation of choice in food and drink.

Food tourism provides consumers with direct avenues for supporting local farms and other businesses related to tourism, not just the restaurants. Protecting the environment (land, water, and air) is necessary to ensure a fresh, healthy supply of food from fruits and vegetables to fish and shellfish to meats and dairy.

Challenges

While every consumer has the potential to be a foodie, or at the very least, to be able to make conscientious and informed food purchase decisions, for many consumers, supporting, or even being aware of, local and independent food and drink experiences is simply not important. Many consumers are perfectly happy with their two-liter soft drink or high sodium/high fat hamburger that they receive through a fast food drive-through window. While this may be a stereotypical view of quickservice food outlets in the USA, this phenomenon is rapidly taking root in other countries as well. Reasons for this consumer view include apathy, programming by marketing messages, and a simple lack of education as to the importance of supporting the "long tail" of the food and drink industry, i.e. the ongoing threat to small, local and independent food and drink businesses. There can also simply be a lack of knowledge of local food experiences. All of these are significant hurdles to overcome to get the message out about the importance of unique and memorable food and drink experiences.

Opportunities

There are many opportunities for consumers. When consumers have access to better quality food, over time, in many cases, we can prevent or reverse obesity, diabetes, and high blood pressure, among other health benefits. By buying local food and drink, more profits are kept local and can be invested back into the community. This can help create new jobs, and taxes, and preserve the local culture. There is another opportunity for consumers to get involved because we want choice. If we do not support local and independent restaurants, then we run the risk of one day waking up to only one official coffee provider on Planet Earth. Or if you want a hamburger, you might have as many as two choices. Perhaps the very march towards globalization of the food, drink, travel and hospitality industries has helped to draw attention to consumers and even helped to shape the segment that we now know as food and drink tourism.

Local residents are also an opportunity themselves for the businesses owners. When we say food tourism, we tend to think of people arriving by airplane, or having taken a car or train a half-day or longer to get there. We often forget that we can travel several hours across some cities and therefore can be like tourists in our own cities. This applies to larger metropolitan areas like Los Angeles, Mexico City, London, Paris, Hong Kong, Seoul, and so on. Local residents might also be members of local food and drink clubs (such as a convivium (chapter) of Slow Food) and might be very interested in learning more about the unique and memorable food and drink experiences in the area. And while visitors will eventually return home, local residents will presumably stay all year-round.

CONCLUSION

Why is there even a food tourism industry? The answer is simple. All visitors must eat and drink, and food is one of the most personal experiences we can have. We all have to eat, whether at home or on holiday. The concept of food tourism is becoming the focal point of travel decision-making and one of the hallmark attractions of destinations around the world. All travelers have to purchase food or otherwise eat – whether in restaurants, cafes, bars or in grocery stores to cook themselves in self-catering lodging. More and more travelers seem to be placing more importance on their eating and drinking experiences.

In many locations, tourists provide a significant proportion of the market for restaurants and cafés around the world,[9] with dining out often being cited as one of the top three visitor activities.[10] Dining out is just one of the many facets of our industry. Our industry is an ecosystem that balances food and drink producers and providers with travel and hospitality providers, destination marketing organizations, trade groups and more.

Every one of the sectors mentioned has the potential to reap extensive benefits from food and drink tourism. While challenges exist, the opportunities are enormous as the food and drink tourism industry continues to grow in importance throughout the world.

DISCUSSION QUESTIONS

1. Many small business owners do not consider themselves part of the food tourism industry. What argument could you use to persuade them otherwise?
2. It can be confusing for some to think of local residents as food travelers, but in many ways they are. Discuss reasons why we can consider local residents to be food "travelers."
3. It is a large task to educate consumers about the need to support local and unique food and drink businesses. What suggestions would you make to help consumers understand the importance of supporting these businesses?

ENDNOTES

[1] International Culinary Tourism Association (2007), Profile of US Culinary Travelers.
[2] Johansson, Frans. Harvard Business Review Press, First Trade Paper Edition, 2006
[3] A commonly used term by economists and entrepreneurs is SME's (small to medium enterprises), although we have chosen not to use that term in this chapter.
[4] Readers interested in learning more about this subject should read the *Word of Mouth in Food Tourism Promotions* chapter in this book.
[5] Dine Originals was a USA-wide association of independent restaurants. It went defunct in the mid-2000s although the name is still being used by the Columbus, Ohio, USA chapter of the original association. The collective opinion is that the Association was a great idea but suffered from internal issues that were insurmountable. We still think there is an opportunity for an organization like this to thrive in many areas.
[6] Visit www.wholefoods.com to learn more about the company's community programs.
[7] Learn more about the company at www.chipotle.com.
[8] For an excellent discussion of this issue, see Raving Fans: A Revolutionary Approach to Customer Service by Ken Blanchard. William Morrow Publishers, First Edition, 1993.
[9] International Culinary Tourism Development (2010), State of the Culinary Tourism Industry Report & Readiness Index.
[10] According to the (US) National Restaurant Association, www.restaurant.org. While this may not be the case for non-American travelers, dining nevertheless remains a highly popular visitor activity, if for no other reason than all visitors eat.

Business Model Generation

Stormy Sweitzer

The food tourism industry is evolving and expanding at a record pace. On any given day, in even the most remote corners of the world, you can find a new business launching to meet the growing demand of travelers in search of authentic food and drink experiences. In a hyper-competitive business environment it is not enough to be a visionary with a great idea. Nor is there always time to spend months – or years – going through a labor-intensive discovery and planning process to bring your concept to market. Success will be achieved by the ability to quickly define and execute your idea. Helping you to ground it in reality is a turnkey assessment of market opportunity, customer need, and financial viability for your product or service. Business model generation is an innovative business planning methodology and digital toolbox that can enable you to design a custom business model ... your springboard to success.

INTRODUCTION

Clearly articulating the *who, what, when, where, why,* and *how* of your business is essential, but gone are the days of hypothetical business plans. Today's business climate calls for flexible, tested, and realistic approaches to starting your business before even committing your plan to paper.

Over the last few years, business model generation has emerged as an appealing complement, and sometimes alternative, to formal business planning. It allows you to formulate and test the core assumptions upon which your business idea is based, refine and clarify how you will operate and make money, and understand the relationships between different aspects of your business – the relationship between how you operate and your company's bottom line. Once you understand the mechanics of how the business functions and are confident that your approach will be successful, you are better able to articulate how your business will make money, as well as create financial estimates and analyze competition, risk and market conditions based on tested data, rather than mere assumption – things which make the formal business planning process more effective and complete.

In this chapter you will learn the art and science of business model generation, become familiar with a one-page tool to help you design and refine your business model, and explore ways to use content throughout *Have Fork, Will Travel* to aid in formulating and testing the various components of your model to ensure you start (or continue) your business in a sustainable manner.

Defining the Business Model

A business model describes how a company creates, delivers, and captures value. In other words, it is the logic behind how you will best serve your customers and earn a living from doing so. At its core, a business model is about serving the right customer with the right product or service in the right way and at the right time. This requires that you clearly identify the customers you wish to serve, understand their needs and wants, and develop products or services to address them. Real value – and your customers' willingness to pay you for it – is created when you are able to provide products or services in a way that solves a major problem, satisfies a real need, or fulfills a strong desire. And this overlap is what turns a good idea into a great business.

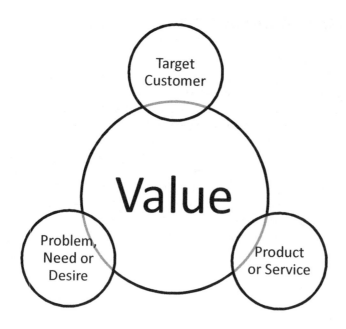

Diagram 1: Value Creation, *Credit: Stormy Sweitzer*

A business model also helps you describe what you need to do to deliver that value to your customers. This includes decisions around activities like marketing and product development, as well as partnerships and operations, even if you only articulate them at a high level.

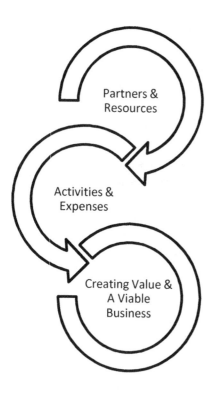

Diagram 2: How Business Models Work, *Credit: Stormy Sweitzer*

How you operate will affect the financial costs and benefits you receive from running your business in a particular way. Fortunately, the process of business model generation gives you the ability to think quickly and test assumptions about different ways to serve your customers so that you are best able to meet their needs and create a viable business when and where opportunity exists.

Business Model Generation

Business model generation is a term made popular by a variety of recent business books, though the term "business model" has been around for many years. What has not been as common is how to apply business model generation tools as way to launch a food or drink tourism business, or evolve the business you already have.

At a big picture level, business model generation is about asking questions and testing theories that help you define your new business or service idea, the benefit it produces, and how you get it out into the world. At a more granular level, it is about:

1. Who the idea serves and how you reach them.
2. What form the idea takes – a product or service, for example - and what problem it solves.
3. How you will do what you do – from operations to delivery.
4. And the part that always grounds us in reality, the costs and benefits – both financial and non-monetary – of pursuing this idea.

Some of the best examples of food tourism entrepreneur success stories are of those with a simple idea and approach and that have followed business model generation, perhaps not necessarily intending to, but discovering it afterward. The following two hypothetical examples, based loosely on currently operating businesses, show how a kernel of an idea can grow into a full-blown business by using business model generation.

Whether you work through the process on your own – or enlist the support of colleagues, friends, family, or mentors – the goals of business model generation are to produce:

●   Clarity of the logic behind your business idea – how does it all work?

●   Possible alternatives worth considering – such as how different marketing tactics might affect cost or reach.

●   Shared understanding among the people involved or a way to communicate important aspects of your business to others, so that everyone is in agreement.

●   An inventory of resources and partners you can draw on when needed.

●   Assumptions about how your business should work that you can test, assess for feasibility, and refine.

●   A foundation upon which to develop action plans or even a formal business plan.

Generating Your Business Model via the Canvas

The authors of *Business Model Generation: A Handbook for Visionaries, Game Changers, and Challengers* created a one-page canvas – or template – to help you focus on the most critical elements of a business or new service or product idea.[1] Since that time, there has been some discussion about the lean canvas, which is an evolution of the original business model canvas.[2] Both may work and depend on your individual needs. The World Food Travel Association favors the lean canvas and has updated this canvas for your use in the food tourism industry:

PROBLEM	SOLUTION	UNIQUE VALUE PROPOSITION	UNFAIR ADVANTAGE	CUSTOMER SEGMENTS
one short sentence that includes not more than 3 problems	one short sentence that includes not more than 3 features	one sentence, from your customer's perspective, not yours, how your company or product is different and why it is worth attention	what you offer than cannot be easily copied	customer groups who is your target?
ALTERNATIVES also called competitors	**KEY METRICS** tangible ways to measure your activities			**EARLY ADOPTERS** first customers
			CHANNELS what paths do you take to reach your customers?	

COST STRUCTURE	REVENUE STREAMS
what are your costs: acquisition, distribution, fixed, variable, staff how much money will you need now? in five years?	how will you sell your product/service customer lifetime value revenue vs gross margin

Diagram 3: Lean Business Model Canvas
Credit: World Food Travel Association

Think of the lean business model canvas as a balance sheet. The left side is about the product, including the benefits that the customers receive. The right side is about the market, including your customers, how you will reach them, and how you will derive revenue from them. Start by keeping the contents of your canvas simple. The canvas is a snapshot of what you are trying to accomplish. In other words, someone should be able to look at your canvas and understand, at a high level, what you are trying to accomplish.

The remainder of this chapter continues to address each part of the canvas and showcases how a fictional food tourism business, Food Walk, has implemented specific steps in the canvas to grow their company. While it is a fictional example used for illustrative purposes, Food Walk is based on a real collaboration of cottage-industry food and spirits artisans in a mid-sized agricultural community.

Customers

When using the canvas, most people like to start with the customer, i.e. the person or group of people to whom you hope to sell your food tourism products and services. Customers are possibly the most important element on your canvas. Knowing who your customer is informs how you interact with and serve them, and drives the rest of your business model. Are the people in your target market intrepid eaters or more-cautious travelers dipping their toes into unchartered culinary waters? Are they high turnover budget sleepers who want to spend their remaining cash on a one-of-a-kind food experience, or are their accommodations the cornerstone of a 360° luxury travel experience? Is your market comprised of health-minded, spa-cuisine seekers, adventure junkies and fearless followers of exotic fare, or indulgent diners looking forward to feast their way across the land, one celebrity chef at a time?

Perhaps your customer is a business partner or strategic alliance such as a travel agent, tourism board, or other professional group that you work with to market your product or service to your target customers? In this case, you actually have two unique customer bases to consider. You need to design services for the end customer (referred to as B2C ("business to consumer") marketing), but understand the dynamics of working with and providing value to your partner as well (referred to as B2B ("business to business") marketing).

Knowing your customer can help you communicate with them effectively, not just by knowing how to reach them, but by being able to speak their language, and to develop a way to serve them that works for both of you.

Case Study: Identifying Food Walk Customers

Food artisans in a thriving agricultural community heard from partnering retail outlets that customers liked their products, but that they wished they knew more about the producers. Some of the artisans were in the practice of giving impromptu tours of their small facilities and often got rave reviews and sold a lot of product in the process. The artisans banded together to create Food Walk, a structured way to provide customers what they wanted.

Value

Every successful and memorable food tourism product or service satisfies some need, solves some problem, or fulfills some desire for the customer who buys it. In other words, it helps the customer achieve something. The question to ask yourself in this phase of the business model canvas is, "What benefit does my specific product or service provide to my specific target customer?" Not theoretically, but in very real terms. It may be helpful to state it this way: "My business helps my customer _____," where you would fill in the thing your customer most wants or needs. For example the 'blank' could be "enjoy time with friends in a pleasurable way," or "explore the amazing food of an exotic locale," or "have a family-friendly excursion that educates and is enjoyable for all," or "experience the wine country of Oregon with an expert." Value is the reason that people will want to work with you time and again. These benefits are the value you provide them.

Defining and understanding your target customer can help you develop products that are specifically and uniquely designed to address their needs, interests, wants, and even fears – some of the factors you will discover in learning about the psychographics of your customers.

Case Study: Determining How Food Walk Creates Value

The Food Walk artisans determined that each of their customer groups - locals and tourists - had different needs and interests. Local customers wanted to know more about the artisans and how they created their products, to feel like they had a personal connection to the artisans and the animals, fruits, and vegetables they relied on for their goods, and to purchase directly from the producers when they could. Foodie visitors to the area liked being able to learn more about foods of the region more broadly. The artisans decided that the best way to accommodate these desires was to make themselves more available to local customers and tourists in a structured way. The artisans of Food Walk felt they could offer real value to both customer groups by offering regular tours of their small production facilities and tastings in their shops, as well as their interest in social pairing events.

Channels

The channel section of the business model canvas discusses marketing, advertising, and promotion of your product or service, and addresses how your customers will find you and buy food tourism services or products from you. Knowing your customer will help you figure out how to get your offerings in front of them in the right place and in the right way. It is important to do your homework and know the media preferences of your customers in order to successfully reach them, engage with them, and entice them to act. More specifically, keep the following in mind:

Channels can be promotional activities and resources that help you reach out to customers and create awareness, such as through your company website or a mass media ad campaign. Channels can also include any other form of outreach or marketing activity that gives potential customers the opportunity to learn about you and your offerings. These might include a webinar to potential customers, an introductory tasting event highlighting foods from a multi-week tour, or a brochure that you place in public areas around town. If you know your customers well, you will know which of these channels is likely to reach them and appeal to them most.

Channels help customers evaluate your service or product offer against alternatives so they know if what you offer is better than what somebody else can provide and how. Reviews on Travelocity (for example), testimonials on your own website, and transparency around what your offering includes – from meals and activities to engaging images and descriptions - can help customers do this effectively.

Channels are also how customers buy from you, or access your services or products. The most common ways these days are:

- Online, where people can browse for information, look for reviews, find pricing, and either make initial inquiries or purchase their travel directly.
- In person, such as at a brick-and-mortar agency or on-site ticket stand.
- By phone, often in follow up to a virtual or in-person visit.

Case Study: Channel Strategies for Getting the Word out About Food Walk

Through their conversations with tourists, Food Walk artisans learned that they needed a website with directions, a route map, and information about each artisan that they could advertise through the community tourism office website that visitors reviewed when making travel plans. They also realized that printed flyers and postcards would be helpful ways to get the word out when places with retail partners and at local inns. Finally, in hearing that Facebook was where the majority of both customers segments spent time online, they decided to create a page where they could share updates.

Customer Relationships

A customer relationship is how you stay in touch and interact with your customers. This can be anything from social media interactions on Facebook, Pinterest, or Twitter; sending out a monthly eNewsletter with upcoming offerings, tips, information from past trips, etc.; or in-person or phone communication. If your customers are older, they may not be keen on social media and a phone call might be best. If they are younger, text messages might be preferred. Knowing your customer will also help you figure out how your customers make decisions about their food tourism experiences so you can send the right message at the right time. For example, you might send out a "last-minute offer" post on Facebook for a two-hour market exploration tour in town, though you will likely need more persuasive and ongoing personal or email outreach to potential customers for a luxury, culinary tour of Southern Europe. This information allows you to focus your time and resources on the most influential communication channels.

Relationships are also about the entire experience a customer has in working with you. What experience do you want to create for customers that will help you build trust and maintain a relationship with them over the long term? Each of these choices will affect the resources you need and the costs of running your business.

Case Study: Maintaining Food Walk Customer Relationships

Keeping things simple, Food Walk decided to use their Facebook page as a place where artisans could post photos from their facilities, discuss new foods, have a link to their website, and share upcoming Food Walk events. They felt this was the most effective way to both create awareness and build interest among one-time visitors, and cultivate a relationship with loyal, local fans of their goods. It also allowed the participating artisans to create a united front, share resources, and build awareness of the region's food production.

Revenue

Revenue is the lifeblood of your business – it enables you to operate, to deliver your products and services, and to support your business goals. For that reason, you need to know what product or service your customers are actually willing to pay you for and how much they are willing to pay. Again, knowing your customers and designing an offer (a product or service) that appeals to their specific needs and preferences will increase the likelihood that your business will make money. For this portion of your business model, ask yourself:

- What are customers willing to pay for this new product or service?
- What alternatives do they have (e.g. can they get a similar experience for less money elsewhere)?
- How would customers like to pay for what you offer (e.g. credit card, check, PayPal; or payment distribution: lump sum or deposit with milestone payments)?
- If you have multiple product or service offerings, how do the ones you are describing here contribute to total income?

In some cases, adding a new service or product may not directly translate to increased revenue. Instead, you and your company might benefit in other ways – like improved customer relationships, increased productivity (which reduces cost), a more interesting customer experience, community support, greater willingness of customers to buy your core offerings, etc. Use the Revenue portion of your business plan to define these benefits as well.

In this section, it is beneficial to be as specific as possible. Run the numbers. Figure out what you can charge based on customer input. Estimate the number of people you think you can sell this offering to at that price. Write total estimated sales on your business model canvas. State the specific benefits you hope to gain by offering this new product or service. Knowing this information can help you determine if your business, product or service is worth the time and energy it may take to move it forward.

Case Study: Developing Food Walk Revenue Streams

Food Walk knew that most of the revenue from tours and events would come from on-site purchases and increased purchases through retail partners that were closer to where their customers did their regular shopping. They also believed they could generate income from ticket sales to monthly food fairs where participating artisans paired and showcased their food and beverage products. They decided to test this particular idea to make sure that the time and expenses needed to make it happen were outweighed by goodwill, revenue, and/or increased sales at retail outlets. Goals were set and numbers – ticket revenue, sales following the events, expenses were tracked. Finally, the group knew from past experience that they visitors to the area often inquired about gift baskets and whether they could order products online. A more coordinated effort would allow them to do this more effectively and bring in income from this additional sales channel.

Key Resources

When you think about starting up a food tourism business – or any business, for that matter, you really need to consider the time, money, technology, human resources, etc. needed to make all of the elements in your business model work. What do you need to develop your idea, what do you need to keep it running, what do you need in order to reach out to and stay in touch with your customers? Breaking this down, key resources are the essential physical, financial, intellectual and human resources that you will need in place to make your business model work. You will need to answer the following questions:

- What money you need to start things up – whether an entire business or the development of a new product or service.
- The nature of your products or services – are they virtual or in-person?
- What people you need and what training will be needed to bring them up to speed
- Whether you need supplies, materials, a physical space, or other tangible assets to run your business.

Different approaches require different resources. Consider ways that you can start small and lean and only acquire resources as you grow and can afford them. Alternatively, think about ways you can team up with others (partners) to access the resources you need.

In some canvas models, Key Resources is a separate section on the canvas. However, the updated version of the lean business model canvas included herein has omitted Key Resources, as we feel the components of that section can be placed elsewhere on the canvas.

Case Study: Putting Food Walk Resources to Work

Food Walk's activities did require some resources. The artisans had to be available during tastings and special events that either added time to their day or took away from production activities. By scheduling events at certain times of day, they were better able to manage this than they were when ad-hoc tours were requested. They pooled their resources to manage website and marketing activities.

Key Activities

Key Activities are the major activities you need to put in place to make your business, product, or service operate over time. The activities you conduct will depend on the nature of your specific business model, including the service or product offering, how it is delivered to your customers, and the type of relationship you establish with your customers. Be specific and realistic about what needs to happen, because how you operate will impact your resource needs and long-term costs. At a high strategic level, key activities might include sales and marketing; bookings and tour coordination; outreach to service vendors or partners; operation of your tour, class or tasting/dining experiences; customer service activities; technology maintenance; staff training; and financial management.

In some canvas models, Key Activities is a separate section on the canvas. However, the updated version of the lean business model canvas included herein has omitted Key Activites, as we feel the components of that section can be placed elsewhere on the canvas.

Case Study: Food Walk in Action

In the case of Food Walk, key activities included scheduled tour and tasting experiences, social media updates, flyer design and printing, outreach and delivery of flyers to area hotels and retailers (they tried to combine these with product delivery runs), special event planning and operation, and, finally, fulfillment of special and online orders.

Key Partners

Key Partners are those individuals and organizations that help you in making your business model work. They can give you greater access to resources you may not otherwise have and help you manage the risks that new business and offerings face when introduced to the marketplace. Partnerships can potentially help you:

- Operate more efficiently or on a bigger scale.
- Carry out activities that you are not able to do on your own.
- Reduce the risk of trying something new, because they have already learned what it takes.
- Learn or move quickly by being able to access others' knowledge/relationships.
- Acquire the resources you need.
- Build trust with customers that may not yet know who you are but which trust your partner's recommendations.

It can be helpful to think of partners in two ways:

1. Mentors, colleagues, and beta customers (trial while in development) that support you and help you develop your business and offerings.
2. Industry partners who you work with to market or provide value to customers. These may be suppliers, strategic partners, and even those beta customers that are now willing to help you get the word out.

Case Study: Partnering to Increase Food Walk's Reach

The Food Walk artisans saw each other as primary partners, but realized that they had partners in the organizations that would both benefit from Food Walk's existence and which could support it by making their customers aware of other businesses and things to do. Conversations took place, and all groups agreed on what needed to happen.

In some canvas models, Key Partners is a separate section on the canvas. However, the updated version of the lean business model canvas included herein has omitted Key Partners, as we feel the components of that section can be placed elsewhere on the canvas. For example, Early Adopters can include Key Partners who can drive early adoption of your product.

Costs

Once you have outlined all of the other aspects of your business model, you can determine how much it will cost you to operate it over time. This includes all of the costs involved in operating your business model, from developing your idea and inventory of goods to working with customers after they buy what you have to sell them. When it comes to revenue planning and projections it is helpful to do your homework. Research competitors' pricing; estimate your start-up costs and ongoing operational requirements; calculate how much each operating activity, marketing tactics, technology, and behind-the-scenes initiatives will cost you after your core resources are in place.

This calculation will help you put your revenue model into perspective. If offering a luxury tour with high-touch marketing costs you US$10,000 per customer, in addition to your monthly operating expenses, does the US$15,000 price tag you think people will pay cover what you need it to? If you provide two-hour market tours three times a week, can you justify the cost of an office space or does it make more sense to work from home? If possible, break your costs down into:

- **Fixed costs** – those that remain the same each month no matter how many customers you have, such as office space, website hosting fees, subscription advertising.

- **Variable costs** – the ones that fluctuate depending on the number of customers you have, such as the number of tours you conduct each month, the number of gift packages you go through at a retail shop, or the cost of hotel rooms if you reach a certain quantity of tour participants.

Consider where you can save on expenses without sacrificing too much of the customer experience or value that helps you remain unique. And know which things are not worth compromising so that you make sure to price your products and services appropriately.

Case Study: Assessing Food Walk Expenses

Food Walk saw their website and its maintenance, printing expenses, and the online shopping cart as fixed costs. They looked at staff time as a variable expense, because they realized that if the tours were popular, they might need additional staff to manage visitors, the cash register, and tasting preparation. They also expected to increase the frequency of tours, if they proved to be popular.

Formulating and Testing Assumptions

Sometimes when we have an idea, it is easy to go too far with it. One thing that business model generation allows us to do well is state assumptions, i.e. our beliefs about what customers value or what they might be willing to pay or how much we think it will cost to develop a new product or service. Testing those assumptions helps us move from 'what if' to 'what is.' This is a powerful step for ensuring that you have the right model in place. Once you have laid those assumptions out in your canvas you can put them to the test. In other words you can take actions to prove your assumptions, find your blind spots, and figure out how you need to change your business model to be successful. Think of testing as a learning experience that allows you to refine your business.

There are a number of ways you can test assumptions; how you test will be specific to your product or service. Here are some examples:

- Ask questions of potential customers; interview them about their needs, wants, and actions.
- Verify costs with potential vendors and test your own pricing on potential customers.
- Pilot a bare-bones version of an idea and see what kind of interest or feedback you get.
- Track and measure customer response after marketing in another language – does any behavior change?
- Pre-sell an experience or product based on the value you expect to provide – if enough people are on board (actually willing to put a deposit down, buy in advance), then move forward with developing it.

The canvas is a starting place intended to let you test, experiment, and make improvements in a low-cost way that helps you reduce the risk of starting something new, but do not let perfection get in your way. A business model is a guide for trying out ideas and working out any issues as you learn what works and what does not.

A proven business model also results in concrete data that can be presented in a formal business plan, if you ever want to write one. This not only provides confidence to you as a business owner, but also to potential investors, financiers, and partners, that your plan will work.

CONCLUSION

In this chapter, you learned the importance of having a business model and testing assumptions about how you will carry out your business to best serve your customers. By making use of the resources at your disposal and assessing the feasibility of how you will run your business, you will ensure that it is financially viable and realistic for you and the people who work for you. Use the canvas as a guide, a resource, and a map for charting your business success.

DISCUSSION QUESTIONS

1. How will evaluating your competitors help clarify your own business concept?
2. What steps or activities can you take to uncover what your target customers want, need, and expect from your business?
3. What role will social media play in establishing and growing customer relationships?

ENDNOTES

---

[1] Business Model Generation: A Handbook for Visionaries, Game Changers, and Challengers. Alexander Osterwalder and Yves Pigneur. Wiley, New York (2010).
[2] http://practicetrumpstheory.com/2012/02/why-lean-canvas

Economic Impact of Food & Drink Tourism

Lisa Chase and Lynn Ogryzlo

What are economic impacts and why do they matter? We know that food and drink travelers are valuable to our economies, but exactly how valuable? This chapter will explore economic estimation and impact of food tourism, examples of economic impact assessments in food tourism, recommendations for future economic impact studies and guidance for conducting such studies.

INTRODUCTION

The economic impacts of food tourism is the benefit that results from food tourism to a specific geographic area. Such economic benefits include additional sales, more income, higher tax revenue[1] and new jobs brought into a region. Economic impact analysis can occur at many different levels, ranging from a localized initiative impacting one, small community to a national or even global level.

Economic impacts are widely cited and often misunderstood. Rigorous economic impact studies of food tourism are hard to find. Some models that analyze economic impacts are the Capacity Utilization Model (CUM), Regional Economic Models Inc. (REMI) and the Impact Analysis for Planning (IMPLAN), each of which evaluates economic impacts in different ways, such as labor and fiscal impact of tourism in the local community; change in disposable personal income; and value added.[2] One of the major challenges of measuring economic impacts of food tourism is defining who is a food tourist and who is a local resident who happens to be buying food and drink products or eating out. While all tourists eat, what behavior qualifies as food tourism? Local residents eat as well, sometimes just because they are hungry, but other times to partake in "the pursuit and enjoyment of unique and memorable food and drink experiences, both far and near," which is the official definition of food tourism espoused by the World Food Travel Association.[3]

Just as food tourism may be difficult to define and measure, so is tourism in general. The World Travel & Tourism Council has been working on measuring the economic impacts of tourism for many years, so consistent estimates exist that are familiar to most people working in every segment of the tourism industry. According to the World Travel & Tourism Council, travel and tourism had the following economic impacts in 2012:[4]

- Direct contribution to world gross domestic product (GDP) and employment of US$2.1 trillion and 101 million jobs.
- Taking account of its combined direct, indirect and induced impacts, total economic contribution in 2012 was US$6.6 trillion in GDP; 260 million in jobs; US$760 billion in investment (2012 prices); and US$1.2 trillion in exports (2012 prices).
- This total contribution represents 9% of total economy GDP in 2012, 1 in 11 jobs, 5% of total economy investment and 5% of world exports.
- Direct contribution to the gross domestic product was expected to grow 3.1 % in 2013.

These are big numbers. Clearly, the global tourism industry has an impressive impact, whether positive like destination development for locals or negative like increased prices.[5] Each one of those tourists will generally eat a few times a day. While it is not known how many "unique and memorable food and drink experiences" are occurring during the visits, anecdotal evidence suggests that two of the most common questions asked by tourists is, "Where should I eat today?" and "What should I do today?" Often those questions are combined, leading to well-known food tourism experiences, like visiting champagne cellars in France, whisky distilleries in Scotland and olive groves in Italy. Specific segments of food tourism, such as wine tourism in Australia, are easier to study than food tourism in general because they are easier to define and identify.

Types of Economic Impacts

Different models are used to evaluate the economic impact in tourism. For the purposes of discussion, we will use the World Travel and Tourism Council model, which categorizes economic impacts into three distinct types: direct economic impacts, indirect economic impacts, and induced economic impacts. These models will then be applied to assess specific economic impacts of food tourism.

Direct Economic Impacts measure what is sometimes called the 'first round' of spending. This type of impact refers to direct transactions between tourists and the places they visit; such as that between the owner of a local restaurant and a tourist dining at that same restaurant.

Indirect Economic Impacts measure the re-spending of money within the local economy. The indirect impacts are the business-to-business transactions that are needed to allow for the direct impacts, and they benefit a broader set of economic sectors that serve food tourism businesses. For example, restaurants need to buy food from food service providers or distributors. Food service providers may buy products from local farms. These are indirect economic impacts as long as they stay within the local economy being measured.

Induced Economic Impacts go one step farther and include the impacts of household expenditures from the income earned in a directly or indirectly affected industry. The induced impacts include local spending on goods and services by people working to satisfy the direct and indirect effects. For example, restaurant workers and food service providers need a place to live. That money spent on rent or a home purchase is induced impact.

Total Economic Impacts are the sum of direct, indirect and induced impacts. Total impacts may be several times higher than direct impacts. This is known as the multiplier effect.

The *Multiplier Effect* or "chain of spending" measures how many times the spending on food and drink is re-spent within the given boundaries of the economic impact study (Figure 1). Multipliers vary greatly depending on the circumstances.

For example, a visitor might eat a meal in a chain restaurant owned by a distant corporate headquarters. The money spent to pay for the restaurant meal is the direct impact, or 'first round' spending. If the restaurant purchases food locally, that is considered indirect spending and contributes to the multiplier. If the restaurant's food is shipped in from a non-local supplier, that is considered leakage and does not contribute to the economic impact through indirect spending or the multiplier effect. Salaries and wages paid to restaurant employees living and spending money in the community would result in induced impacts. Those do contribute to the multiplier effect and total economic impact. Multipliers vary greatly depending on the size of the community, the goods and services available there, the types of food tourism establishments, and the spending decisions by residents. For local regions, tourism spending multipliers often fall somewhere between 1.0 and 1.5. They may be 2.0 or higher for larger regions with more goods and services.[6]

Enhancing the multiplier effect is a goal for many communities focused on local food tourism. If a restaurant buys meat from a local farmer and that farmer spends that revenue on local apples at a local store, and then that storekeeper goes out to dinner at a locally-owned restaurant in town, the cash keeps circulating within the community, leading to a higher multiplier, less leakage, and a greater economic impact on that community.

Figure 1: Economic Multiplier Effect of Tourism
Credit: World Food Travel Association

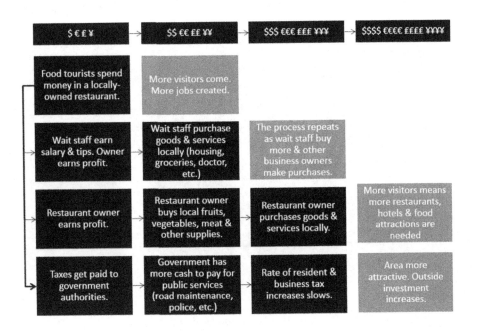

Practical Application of the Multiplier Effect

To increase the multiplier effect and keep money circulating in the community, some food tourism establishments purchase as much locally as possible. Liberty Hill Farm, a farm stay and working dairy farm in the state of Vermont, USA, makes a point of using locally grown and purchased ingredients in its delicious home-cooked breakfasts and dinners. Meals at the Kennetts have always been family-style, with guests and family members sitting around the large dining room table eating hearty, made-from-scratch meals together. Their dairy cows supply milk to Cabot Creamery Cooperative, where the Kennetts buy local Cabot butter and cheese. Beth Kennett, a ninth generation farmer, grew up helping her grandmother can and freeze everything from the garden and has always used local food in cooking without thinking much about it. Eating local and using the freshest ingredients was just what they did. When *Gourmet Magazine* did a story on Beth's cooking,[7] she realized that meals made with fresh, local food had become a large part of the attraction of her farm stay. It was not anything new for her, but it was exceptional for her guests.

The interest in local foods has grown exponentially during the past decade. Beth explains, "Agritourism and farm stays used to be something for kindergarteners. Families with young children were my niche. It's no longer just about school tours. Now, with the local food movement, college kids think farmers are cool. It's the college kids who are so excited about coming to the farm, and the 20-somethings and 30-somethings want to learn about growing and storing food. Everyone is becoming more aware of where their food comes. We are now part of the innovative local food movement."

Why Economic Impact Matters

Economic impacts are the underpinning of decisions made at all levels. Individual businesses need to understand their bottom line. Investments made at the community, regional, and national levels are based on potential economic impacts and return on investment. Without an understanding of economic impact, it is virtually impossible to make well-informed decisions concerning investments into food tourism.

Photo: Breakfast at Liberty Hill Farm, *Credit: Liberty Hill Farm*

Consumers' grocery budgets are often described in terms of food dollars (or euros or pounds, etc.) and each dollar (or euro or pound, etc.) spent has an impact on the economy. In the U.S., almost half of every food dollar (43 cents) goes directly to retailers and foodservice establishments according to the U.S. Department of Agriculture Economic Research Service (Figure 2).[8] Retail trade includes national supermarket chains, local food stores, and farmers' markets which account for 12 cents of every food dollar. Foodservice establishments include full-service restaurants, fast food outlets, caterers, cafeterias, and other places that prepare, serve, and sell food to the general public for a profit.[9] Foodservices account for almost one-third of the food dollar in the U.S. (31 cents), the largest portion of the food dollar, followed by food processing and retail trade, each at 22 cents.[10] The breakdown of the food dollar emphasizes the importance of how consumers spend their money.

Figure 2. Dividing Up the U.S. Food Dollar[11]
2001 Food Dollar [nominal]. *Credit: USDA*

Estimating Economic Impacts

Now that it has been established that it is important to measure economic impact, how does one derive the figures? There are several methods for estimating economic impact, ranging from simple and inexpensive to complex and costly. Regardless of the methods used, there are five essential stages of an economic impact study:

1. Define the scope of the study
2. Agree on logical assumptions
3. Determine current facts
4. Collect additional data as needed
5. Estimate a measureable impact based on facts and knowledge

To illustrate how one might measure the economic impact a business may have in a community, we will use a hypothetical example of a maple festival in Vermont. It is late winter and the sap is flowing from the sugar maple trees. An enterprising community decides to open its sugarhouses to the public so people can see how maple syrup is made, taste the varying flavors of maple, and sample different maple products. Restaurants in the area feature maple as an ingredient in many dishes, and roadside stands are set up with maple candies and creams (several communities in Vermont actually do this). The community comes together to promote the maple festival to food travelers far and wide.

1. Define the scope of the study

Following the stages above, it is essential to first decide on exactly what needs to be measured. In this case, the direct and secondary economic impacts of the weekend-long maple festival will be measured. Part of identifying the problem is defining the time and place. In this case, there is a distinct timeframe (a specific weekend) and a fixed geographic boundary around the community.

2. Agree on logical assumptions

This study is to be as straightforward and simple as possible so the following basic formula for estimating direct economic impacts of food travel will be used:

***Number of Food Travelers * Average Spending per Food Traveler =
Direct Economic Impact of Food Travel***

This looks simple enough, but coming up with the estimates of the numbers of food travelers and average spending may be difficult. Primary data collection through surveys and interviews of participating businesses, along with visitor counts, can provide the necessary information. An alternative method would be to charge an admission fee and track total ticket sales. Stage 2 (agree on logical assumptions), stage 3 (determine what facts are already known), and stage 4 (collect additional data as needed) are often used reiteratively. As facts are uncovered and data are collected, additional assumptions will be needed. For this hypothetical case, we will use a visitor count of people entering the event. To simplify calculations, this example will not differentiate between the types of visitors and will assume that average spending is the same across all visitors to the maple festival.

3. Determine current facts

As this is the first year of the festival, not much is known specific to the festival, but general data about tourism in Vermont and average spending per visitor does exist. The best way to calculate the average a visitor spends is to find out directly from the visitors who are the target of the study. Often surveys are used to ask visitors to calculate their spending on several items including transportation, lodging, souvenirs, and food and beverage of course. This has been done for Vermont visitors in general. Ideally the researcher would conduct a separate survey at the maple festival where they would interview a sample of visitors to get an estimate of how much the average visitor spends during that trip.

However, conducting a survey is not feasible for this particular hypothetical example. For this case, the average amount for visitor spending from another published study is used. Research conducted on Vermont's tourism industry indicates that the average amount a visitor spends in winter (December to March) is US$149 per person per trip.[12] This number will be used instead of conducting a survey at the maple festival, although it may over- or under-state the actual amount, depending on how different maple festival visitors are from other winter visitors. By using this number, it is assumed that visitors to the maple festival spend about the same amount as visitors from the general study. This is an assumption that may or may not be true. The more precise the number, the more reliable the economic impact estimate.

4. Collect additional data as needed

In addition to calculating the average spending of visitors, it is necessary to estimate the number of visitors based on reports from the entrance gates. Counting visitors may or may not be straightforward and estimates based on assumptions may be used. If the festival has monitored points of entry where visitors are counted, a precise estimate of the number of visitors will be available. If not, the size of the crowd may be estimated. Again, the more precise the number, the more reliable the economic impact estimate.

5. Estimate a measureable impact based on facts and knowledge

For this hypothetical example, 10,000 visitors attended the weekend-long maple festival the first year. Using the data from the study on Vermont's tourism industry, it is assumed that visitors spent US$60 on average. The formula would then look like:

10,000 visitors at the maple festival * US$60 spent per visitor on average
= US$600,000 in direct economic impact

The direct economic impact of the maple festival would be US$600,000. Not bad for a small town holding a festival for the first time.

To estimate total economic impact, including secondary impacts of indirect and induced effects, the formula includes a multiplier:[13]

Number of Food Travelers * Average Spending per Food Traveler * Multiplier
= Total Economic Impact of Food Travel

As discussed earlier, estimating the number of food travelers and their average expenditures can be challenging. The difficulty is compounded when including a multiplier. Sophisticated economic programs have been developed to estimate multipliers, such as IMPLAN and the Money-Generation Model.[14] These models require extensive data inputs, which can be costly to collect. Multipliers vary greatly depending on the size of the community, the goods and services available there, the types of food travel establishments, and spending decisions by residents. Remember that for small regions, tourism spending multipliers often fall somewhere between 1.0 and 2.0. They may be higher than 2.0 for larger regions with more goods and services.[15] These are rough estimates and should be specifically calculated for each situation.

Now to return to the hypothetical example of the maple festival. Assuming the data has been collected, the numbers have been run through the program, and a multiplier of 2.0 was generated the formula would be:

10,000 visitors to the maple festival * US$60 spent per visitor on average
* 2.0 multiplier = US$1,200,000 in direct economic impact

In this hypothetical example, the multiplier effectively doubles the value of the direct impact, from US$ 600,000 to US$1.2 million total impact. While multipliers are important for estimating indirect and induced effects, they are difficult to measure accurately. Keep in mind that the economic impact estimates that come out of a model are only as reliable as the data and assumptions that go into the model.

Examples of food travel economic impact studies

For the calculation above, a simple hypothetical example was used because real-world studies tend to be more complicated. Comprehensive studies of the economic impacts of food travel are in demand, but not many studies are available.[16] More studies are needed to better understand the current and future potential of food travel locally, regionally, and globally.

Measuring Food Tourism in Ontario, Canada

Ontario's Four-Year Food tourism Strategy and Action Plan uses data from multiple sources to estimate the economic impacts of different types of culinary tourists in Ontario. Using definitions from the World Food Travel Association's research, three segments of food travelers are defined:[17]

1. *Deliberate culinary tourists* engage in culinary experiences as a primary motivation for taking a trip
2. *Opportunistic culinary tourists* take the opportunity to seek and enjoy a culinary experience during a trip that was made for other purposes
3. *Accidental culinary tourists* enjoy an unexpected culinary experience if it is brought to their attention during a trip

Tourism research in Ontario suggests that deliberate culinary tourists accounted for 15% of all Ontario-destination trips, generating C$816 million of travel-related expenditures. Opportunistic and accidental culinary tourists generated an additional 18% of Ontario destination trips, with a total expenditure of C$955 million.[18] Note that these expenditures represent all spending on the trips, not just food tourism-related activities. These findings are significant for the development of Ontario's Food Tourism Strategy, such that the vision is to ensure that, "By 2015, food tourism in Ontario is valued as a leading contributor to a vibrant and sustainable tourism economy in the province."[19]

American Appetites for Food Travel

Two studies of the economic impact of food travel in the U.S. have been done, both spearheaded by the World Food Travel Association (formerly the International Culinary Tourism Association). The Association's 2007 study found that 27 million travelers, or 17% of American leisure travelers, engaged in food tourism during the three years preceding the study.[20] Food tourists spent US$1,194 per trip on average, of which US$425 was spent on food.[21] Based on these numbers, a rough estimate for direct economic impact of food tourism is US$32 billion during the 3 year period. Over US$11 billion was spent just on food and drink.[22] Further analysis showed that American foodies spend on average nearly US$100,000 per minute, every minute of the day, on food and drink while traveling, a staggering figure. Later research by the World Food Travel Association found that only 8.1% of foodies self-identify as being gourmet-oriented.[23] In other words, the overwhelming majority (almost 92%) of foodies just like great food and drink. This comes as a surprise to many small business owners and destination marketers, who often expect foodies to be wealthier, older and seeking only high-end experiences. Data from the 2007 research show that American foodies skewed middle-aged to younger; are definitely better educated; and are not necessarily rich (an average income of US$50,000 prevailed).[24]

Complementing that research, a 2011 LivingSocial "Dining Out" online survey found that the average American eats 4.8 meals per week in restaurants or 249 total restaurant meals per year (both dining in and take out).[25] There is more good news for food tourism: more than one-third of the survey respondents described themselves as "experimental eaters," one-quarter called themselves "foodies," and over ten percent considered themselves "locavores."[26]

More research needs to be conducted to measure national impacts or, better yet, a global study needs to be conducted using consistent methods to measure economic impact the same way in all countries, and compare the results by country. In the meantime, smaller communities have taken the initiative to measure their own impacts as needed.

Wine Industry in Napa Valley, California, USA

One of the most comprehensive studies available examines the economic impacts of the wine industry in Napa Valley, California, USA. Data were collected from all sectors of the industry involved in wine production and consumption, grape cultivation, and allied industries such as tourism, distribution, equipment, and suppliers.

Results indicate that the total annual economic impact of the Napa Valley wine industry is US$11 billion, including direct and secondary impacts, i.e. the actual measurement of the wine economy of the Napa Valley. As the geographic boundaries are enlarged, the multiplier effect is amplified so that the impact of the Napa Valley wine industry on the State of California as a whole is estimated to be US$15 billion, and the total impact of the Napa Valley wine industry on the United States economy is estimated to be US$42 billion.[27]

In addition to direct and secondary impacts, economic impact studies often include statistics on job creation and employment. In Napa Valley, the wine and vineyard sector is the county's largest employer, providing nearly 40,000 jobs including direct, indirect and induced effects.

Tax revenues are often included in economic impact studies as well. In Napa Valley, the wine and vineyard sector and its related activities are estimated to generate US$4 billion in taxes across state, local, and federal levels. You can imagine that the Napa Valley wine industry wants to emphasize those contributions to tax dollars when looking for government support and investment in its initiatives.

Focusing specifically on tourism, the study estimates that the wine and vineyard industry in Napa Valley attracts 3.5 million visitors, who spend an additional US$714 million in wine related tourism expenditures. This information can be used to encourage public and private investment in California's growing wine tourism industry.

Olive Oil Tourism in Italy

Because economic impact analyses can be helpful for encouraging investment, food travel niches around the world are working with researchers to conduct studies. According to the Italian olive oil producers' consortium, Unaprol, olive oil tourism generates more than €1.8 billion annually. The growing interest in quality olive oil has resulted in a boom in farm tourism with more than two million people a year visiting oil groves and mills to buy their oil straight from the source. Unaprol attributes the popularity of this form of tourism to "the increasing interest in quality and authenticity of olive oil, which today can only be guaranteed by buying the oil at its source or with the PDO (protected designation of origin) label."

In 2006, Italy recognized 17 olive oil "roads" or itineraries that tourists can use to find olive oil mills, olive-producing farms, restaurants, and holiday farms, all places where guests can purchase high quality olive oil and other local cuisine specialties.[28] Today in Tuscany alone there are 21 oil roads to visit.[29] As demand for food travel increases in Italy, the U.S., and around the world, there is an increased need for better information about the economic benefits of food travel.

CONCLUSION

More economic impact studies are needed at the global, national, and local levels to help inform decisions about investments in the developing food travel industry. Common terms and definitions need to be understood more broadly so that what is assessed or analyzed in one country, will be as close as possible to the comparative data from another country. While these studies may be time-consuming and costly to conduct, the benefits of having this research outweigh the costs because results can be used to inform decisions about policy and investments that strengthen the local economy. As economic impact studies become available, sharing results will elevate understanding of the importance of the industry and ultimately help everyone working in the food travel industry.

DISCUSSION QUESTIONS

1. Research and create an economic impact multiplier for food tourism in your area. Search for data and amend the multipliers in this chapter as necessary.
2. There are some industry players who would argue that food tourism is really a subset of tourism in general while others would argue that food tourism can be an economic driver all on its own. What do you think? Can food tourism be an economic driver on its own? Justify your position.
3. Locals and visitors alike must eat. How would you differentiate economic expenditure by food tourists and non-tourists?

ENDNOTES

[1] "Global Report on Food Tourism", World Tourism Organization, last accessed July 8, 2013, http://dtxtq4w60xqpw.cloudfront.net/sites/all/files/pdf/food_tourism_ok.pdf

[2] Bonn, M.A. (2008) A comparison of three economic impact models for applied hospitality and tourism research. In Tourism Economics. Vol. 14, n°4 p.769-789

[3] "What is Food Tourism", World Food Travel Association, last accessed July 9, 2013, www.worldfoodtravel.org/what-is-food-tourism/

[4] "Economic Impact Research, World Travel and Tourism Council, last accessed July 9, 2013, http://www.wttc.org/research/economic-impact-research/

[5] "Exploring the Full Economic impact of tourism for Policy making", World Tourism Organization, last accessed July 8, 2013, http://www2.unwto.org/es/node/35511

[6] "Multipliers", MGM2 Handbook, last accessed July 9, 2013, http://35.8.125.11/mgm2_new/econ/multipliers.htm

[7] Schulz, Warren. "Heart of the Country", *Gourmet Magazine*, June 2001, last accessed July 8, 2013, www.gourmet.com/magazine/2000s/2001/06/heartofthecountry?currentPage=1

[8] Canning, Patrick. "Food Dollar Series". United States Department of Agriculture Economic Research Service, last modified March 05, 2013, last accessed July 9 2013 www.ers.usda.gov/data-products/food-dollar-series.aspx#.UW_6Q7WkqbU

[9] Hayden, Stewart. "Food Service Industry". United States Department of Agriculture Economic Research Service, last modified May 26, 2012, last accessed July 9 2013, www.ers.usda.gov/topics/food-markets-prices/food-service-industry.aspx#.UW_xibWkqbU

[10] "Food Dollar Series", Economic Research Service, last accessed July 8, 2013, www.ers.usda.gov/data-products/food-dollar-series/documentation.aspx#.UgRj7jtFV1s

[11] Canning, Patrick 2011. Food Dollar Application. United States Department of Agriculture Economic Research Service. last accessed July 8,2013, www.ers.usda.gov/data-products/food-dollar-series/food-dollar-application.aspx#.UW_7oLWkqbV

[12] Chmura Economics & Analytics. 2012. Benchmark Study of the Economic Impact of Visitor Spending on the Vermont Economy – 2011: The Travel and Tourism Economy in Vermont, last accessed July 9, 2013, www.uvm.edu/tourismresearch/publications/Vermont_Tourism_2011.pdf

[13] Stynes, Daniel J. 1997. "Economic impacts of tourism". Illinois Bureau of Tourism, Department of Commerce and Community Affairs, last access July 9, 2013, https://www.msu.edu/course/prr/840/econimpact/pdf/ecimpvol1.pdf

[14] "Money Generation Model", MGM2impact, last accessed July 9, 2013, http://mgm2impact.com/

[15] MGM2 Handbook. http://35.8.125.11/mgm2_new/econ/multipliers.htm

[16] "Global Report on Food Tourism", World Tourism Organization, last modified 2012, last accessed July 9, 2013, http://dtxtq4w60xqpw.cloudfront.net/sites/all/files/pdf/food_tourism_ok.pdf

[17] "Culinary Tourism, a recipe for economic development success, Profile of US Culinary Travelers", International Culinary Tourism Association, last modified 2006, last accessed July 9, 2013, http://ontarioculinary.com/wp2011/wp-content/uploads/2012/06/OCTA-INFO.REBRAND.pdf

[18] "Ontario's Four-Year Food tourism Strategy and Action Plan 2011-2015", MTC, last accessed July 9, 2013,www.mtc.gov.on.ca/en/publications/Culinary_web.pdf

[19] Ibid.

[20] International Culinary Tourism Association and Travel Industry Association of America, Profile of US Culinary Travelers, Washington, D.C., 2007.

[21] Ibid.

[22] "Culinary Tourism, a recipe for economic development success, Profile of US Culinary Travelers, International Culinary Tourism Association, last modified 2006, last accessed July 9, 2013, http://ontarioculinary.com/wp2011/wp-content/uploads/2012/06/OCTA-INFO.REBRAND.pdf

[23] "State of the Culinary Tourism Industry Report and Readiness Index", International Culinary Tourism Development (2010), last accessed July 9, 2013, http://www.great-taste.net/tidbits-kudos/tidbits/new-2010-state-of-the-culinary-tourism-industry-report-readiness-index-now-available-to-trade-2/

[24] [24] International Culinary Tourism Association and Travel Industry Association of America, Profile of US Culinary Travelers, Washington, D.C., 2007.

[25] "Reservation Nation? Despite Recession, Americans Eat Whopping 250 Restaurant Meals Per Year", Living Social, last modified September 15 2011, last accessed July 9, 2013, https://corporate.livingsocial.com/inthenews/articles/43

[26] LivingSocial Dining Out Survey, Key Findings, Mandala Research, September 2011.

[27] Stonebridge Research. Economic Impact of the Napa Valley Wine Industry. 2008, Napa vintners, last accessed July 9, 2013, www.napavintners.com/downloads/2008_economic_impact_report.pdf

[28] Olive Oil Tourism on Rise in Italy. 2006. www.olives101.com/2006/11/21/olive-oil-tourism-on-rise-in-italy/

[29] "Roads list", Strade del Vino dell´Olio dei Sapori e dei Colori di Toscana, last accessed July 9, www.stradevinoditoscana.it/elenco_delle_strade/

Demographic History of Food Travelers

Donald Getz, Richard Robinson, & Sanja Vujicic

This chapter is about the history of demographic analysis of food tourists and draws on recent research offering comparisons of food tourist profiles from various countries.

INTRODUCTION

For many, food and drink consumption while traveling is perfunctory — a matter of refueling — so that visitors can get on with whatever it is they have traveled for; leisure in some cases or business in others. Some however, specifically seek out places, products, events and experiences that further gratify their urge to consume food and beverages. In this chapter we call these people 'foodies,' a broad term that also implies appreciation for noteworthy beverages. In this chapter we consider, evaluate and synthesize a range of research to address a fundamental question asked by students, educators, researchers, tourism industry operators, destination marketing organizations and policy and planners, "Who is the food tourist?"

This is an important question for two reasons. Firstly, all tourists must eat and drink. Various tourism stakeholders could be forgiven for their ambivalence vis-à-vis destinations servicing these basic needs. This is because a range of food and drink products, services and experiences exist invariably in their destination already. One would assume that surely such resources are sufficient to satiate the appetite and quench the thirst of all, but the most fastidious of travelers? Secondly, finding out who food tourists are is the first step in identifying whether indeed the range of food and beverage services and experiences typical of a tourism destination, are actually those for which people expressly interested in food and drink will travel. To lay the foundation to answer these questions we present a range of research that has begun to demographically profile food (and drink) tourists. We then comparatively evaluate this research before synthesizing the findings to present a cogent description of the demographic profile of the contemporary food tourist and present future research challenges.

Before continuing it is important to set the scope and delimitations of this chapter. Although the focus of this book is on food tourism per se, we face a similar challenge to that of many of the other contributors – that being that the food tourism field of study is still in its infancy. Indeed, although some research began to appear in the academic literature from as early as the mid-eighties it was not until the endeavors of the likes of Richards and Hjalager[1] (*Tourism and Gastronomy*, 2002); Hall, Sharples, Mitchell, Macionis and Cambourne (*Food Tourism Around the World: Development, Management, and Markets*, 2003); and Long (*Culinary Tourism*, 2004) that a consolidated and critical mass of research in the area began to develop, Long first described culinary tourism/tourists in her 1998 article,[2] which was later updated in her 2004 book, *Culinary Tourism*. Since 2005, academic literature in the area has begun to proliferate. Indeed, a recent study has found that 214 academic articles have been published relating to food tourism across the tourism, geography, environmental and cultural literatures, with just over 10% of these predating 2003[3] (Robinson & Tran, under review). At the same time a number of commissioned studies in English speaking countries were conducted, although the findings are not always available in the public domain. Nonetheless, significant studies were conducted in Canada (Travel Industry Association, 2001, Cuisine and Wine Interest Index), the USA (International Culinary Tourism Association and Travel Industry Association of America, 2007, Profile of Culinary Travelers) and Australia[4] (Sparks, Roberts, Deery, Davies & Brown, 2005, The Good Living Tourism: Lifestyle Aspects of Food and Wine Tourism) during these periods. Most recently in 2013, the World Food Travel Association (formerly International Culinary Tourism Association) published new research about American food travelers.

The differing focus of academic and broader and newer reports is important to note. Typically, academic research seeks to investigate a theoretical question. In the area of food and drink tourism, some topics typical of the literature, from the supply side, describe the formation of stakeholder networks and how these function (e.g. Forga & Valiente, 2012)[5] – or for the supply side, the motivation of tourists[6] (see Nicholson & Pearce, 2001 and Bonifice, 2003) – or our particular interest, levels of involvement (see Robinson and Getz, forthcoming). In other words academic researchers are not often interested in the demographics of their population beyond establishing some parameters for generalization, and hence rarely offer any detailed descriptors of their sample. On the other hand, the often larger scale commissioned reports are generally broader and more descriptive in objective and nature, and thus of considerable assistance for our task at hand. In this chapter we will analyze a selection of both these key sources.

It is also important to note that a critical mass of research in the area of wine tourism has also been published although less so for other beverages. Nonetheless, some work on beer, whisky, tea and coffee has been recently published. Hence, the delimitation of this chapter is bounded by the books and studies just mentioned, and the research efforts they subsequently spurred. Given the intrinsic relationship between food and drink the scope of this chapter also includes, where relevant, studies into drink tourism of the variants just described. There is one important qualifying caveat, namely that overwhelmingly studies regarding food (and drink) have examined the supply-side – that is descriptions and less frequently evaluations of different products, services, events and experiences that might satiate the appetite of food and drink tourists. The upshot of this is that not many studies have actually looked at who the potential food and drink tourist is and even more less so what they might want from a food and drink tourism experience. Working with these limitations, we set out to determine, from the existing body of work, the demographic profile of the food (and drink) tourist.

Key Literature and Sources

An examination of some of the key, typically large-scale, commissioned reports in terms of how they describe the food tourist will help us paint a more complete picture of food travelers. In 2007 the International Culinary Tourism Association (ICTA), together with the Travel Industry Association of America (TIA), published a Profile of Culinary Travelers.[7] Based on 2,364 responses from leisure travelers, the study concluded that a segment measured at 17% of the total sample could be described as 'culinary travelers.' This segment was identifiable because when traveling they reported participating in one or more of a selection of food- and drink-related activities such as dining out, mostly in destination or upmarket restaurants, for inimitable and/or memorable experiences; attending farmers' markets; participating in cooking classes; shopping for gourmet foodstuffs; attending food festivals, or even partaking in some wine tourist experiences. In terms of their demographic profiles the findings showed that these segmented food tourists were generally younger, not necessarily affluent, and definitely better educated. Indeed, 73% of the food tourist segment was aged between 18 and 54 with most of these in the middle aged bracket. More mature travelers were found to be less likely to be food tourists. Strikingly, in terms of the highest level of education measured in the study (i.e. university graduate level), the food tourists were nearly three times as likely as the general traveler to have attained this standard. The final key demographic indicator was income. While the raw figures do not necessarily categorically conclude that the food tourist has a significantly higher income, their expenditure in destination suggests they have higher than average discretionary income. For example, on average, the food tourist spent over one-third (36%) of their travel budgets on food-related activities. Among those interested in future culinary activities, going to restaurants for unique and memorable experiences, and local/regional cuisine, top the list. The generally expensive activity of dining out was also the most highly reported foodie pursuit. It does not matter if one dines out only for the experience or for necessity. In both situations one has the opportunity to try local and/or regional food.

Commissioned by the Canadian Tourism Commission, another survey of a comparable scale, though a little less focused than the ICTA/TIA research, was the Cuisine and Wine Interest Index, first conducted in 2001[8] and repeated again in 2007. The 2001 iteration (conducted by Lang Research), developed the cuisine and wine index from an analysis of the Travel Activities and Motivation Survey (TAMS), which was conducted in the USA and Canada. Consisting of responses to questions regarding motivations for, and activities undertaken during vacations taken over the previous two years, the most interesting finding was a predictive correlation between an interest in traveling for food and wine experiences and educational and income profiles with more highly educated folk and those with higher incomes more likely to seek out food and wine experiences than those on lower incomes or holding lower educational qualifications. In particular couples without children were identified as a key market segment.

Funded by the Cooperative Research Centre, a major project in Australia produced The Good Living Tourism: Lifestyle aspects of food and wine tourism publication. This project's research objectives focused on the lifestyle aspects of food and wine tourism and contained both supply side regional case studies and demand side consumer research. The consumer-based research attracted over 800 responses and interestingly the sample was biased towards female respondents (87%). In terms of the other demographics, mindful of the skew to females in the sample, over 78% of the sample were between 35 and 64 years of age and correspondingly, although only about a third of the sample (36%) were employed fulltime, nearly 60% reported household incomes over A$70,000.[9] Concurrently, over 60% of the sample had either graduate or post-graduate qualifications. Moreover, 82% of the sample reported being either married or in a stable relationship (Sparks et al., 2005). This respondent profile marks out the Australian food tourist, largely consistent with their American and Canadian counterparts, to be predominantly female, middle-aged of above average income, well-educated and with a partner.

Now consider some of the demographics available from academic studies. To continue the Australian focus, a recent study by Robinson and Getz (in press) also attracted a high percentage of female respondents (80%). Similar to the findings of Sparks et al. (2005) in this study, 74% of the sample reported being 'partnered' when asked about their relationship status. Moreover, 30% of the sample reported having dependents. In terms of education, the vast majority (80%) had attained at least some level of college. Income was measured on an individual rather than household basis and it was found that 50% of the sample reported earning more than A$60,000 in annual *individual* income.

One of the largest academic studies undertaken in the food tourism field was conducted by Kivela and Crotts (2006).[10] Their research into gastronomic tourists in Hong Kong, revealed some interesting findings that over a fifth of the respondents declared their primary reason for visiting Hong Kong was for the food. Yielding 1,067 useable questionnaires Kivela and Crotts' (2006) sample contained fewer females (49%) than males. However, 58% had a university/college degree at a minimum and 36% reported household incomes of over US$50,000. Still, over half the sample (56%) was between 36 and 65 years of age, as consistent with most other research.

Extrapolating from the data of Smith and Costello's 2009 study[11] of culinary tourists in Tennessee in southern United States, like Kivela and Crotts, they achieved a reasonably gender balanced sample (53% men and 47% women). However, 60% of their sample was between 32 and 60 years of age and 60% of the sample also reported household incomes of over US$50,000 with approximately 47% of the sample having a minimum of a bachelor's (university) degree. About 59% of the sample reported being married with about 13% of the sample being married with children. Another study in the United States,[12] by Kim et al. (2011), also reported a reasonably equitable gender ratio in their sample of tourists attending a food festival. According to age however, 64% of the sample was over 37 years of age and 62% were married. Nearly 56% of the sample reported holding at least a college degree and correspondingly 65% reported household incomes over US$60,000.

We choose to also profile a couple of studies outside of the United States, Canadian and Australian markets. A study conducted by Correia and colleagues (2008),[13] interviewed 377 gastronomic visitors to Portugal. Consistent with most studies we have showcased so far women (55%) outnumbered men, and 87% of the sample had an undergraduate degree or higher. The mean age was 37.5 years, with a standard deviation of 11.37 years thus marking the sample as early middle-aged and again consistent with previous studies. Another study from the Iberian peninsula,[14] by Sanchez-Canizares and Lopez-Guzman (2011), while finding an almost even gender balance, found 67% of their respondents to be between 30 and 60 years of age. Again, 65% had at least a certain level of degree a degree of some description from a university although income was not reported.

On the other hand a Korean food festival study by Kim[15] et al (2009) highlights some of the inherent difficulties in obtaining a true demographic picture of the food tourist. Their study focused on a food lover's festival that was qualitative in nature. Despite providing detailed demographics across a number of indicators that this paper deems worthy, the sample size was only 20 and all respondents were 35 years or older. Nonetheless, 65% of the sample was female and 80% held undergraduate degrees at a minimum. In contrast with other studies, and only 30% reported being employed full time.

Similarly, presenting other challenges to understanding the socio-demographic profile of the food tourist,[16] the study by Tse and Crotts (2005), as expert as it is in contributing to our understanding of visitor's propensity to experience exotic culinary traditions when travelling, only reports demographics in a correlation matrix to identify significance. This, like many other demand-side studies, does not contribute to our knowledge of the demographic profile of the food tourist, as useful as it is, as we will point out in our conclusions.

To conclude our analysis, given that we flagged the relationship between beverage interests, mostly wine, and food tourism pursuits, we profile a study of New Zealand winery visitors. In Hall and Mitchell's (2005)[17] analysis of 1,090 respondents they found a slight skew to female respondents (53.5%). In terms of age nearly 70% of the sample was between 30 and 60 years of age. Consistent with food tourists, a high proportion of the sample was well educated with 45% reporting a minimum of an undergraduate qualification. Only 20% of the sample reported a low income (< NZ$30,000) with only 30% recording upper or high incomes (> NZ$60,000). The majority of the income levels were average. Although this chapter focuses on food tourists, we see in this profile from wine tourists in New Zealand some correlations with other research, according to age, education and income.

Key Demographics

This section aims to synthesize the key demographics from extant studies and contributes some additional insights. Our chapter is not a formal meta-analysis, but a qualitative interpretation. It must be cautioned that the available studies are not really comparable in their definitions and methods. For example income is not always reported and when it is, sometimes it is individual income and other times household income. It is also probable that food tourists vary widely in their nature and habits, from region to region. Nevertheless, the generalizations made below constitute a useful starting point for those seeking market intelligence or planning a research exercise.

Age: Anyone can be a food lover. Age is hardly a restricting factor, although in this chapter the studies cited a prevalent age range between 30 and 60 years. But to be a food tourist requires independence, money, time and a strong desire to travel, all of which increase with age - up to a point. Seniors who travel for food experiences probably have a different set of needs and preferences than young couples without children, yet romance, learning, and novelty-seeking might appeal equally. It is important to avoid stereotyping and do the necessary research among target audiences before launching communications or developing products. Regardless, our synthesis of selected studies suggests the typical food tourist is most likely to be middle-aged, somewhere between 30-60 years.

Distance: Assessing how far someone will travel for a meal is difficult at best, and not necessarily entirely relevant, when all factors are considered. A commonly used definition of a "tourist" in the USA is anyone who travels 50+ miles (80+ km) from home. In other jurisdictions, a tourist is defined as anyone who makes an overnight stay. The search for unique food and drink experiences is behavior exhibited by locals and travelers alike. Traveling for a meal across a large metropolitan area like Los Angeles or London may turn a local resident into a food tourist in their own city. Similarly, people travel from rural locations to cities to eat, sometimes at chains.[18] A better question to ask is of the business, "who are your target markets?" Foodies are interested in interesting food and drink experiences both at home and while traveling. While relevant for the marketer and business owner, such is not really an issue of demographics, rather one of personal preference, individual needs and possibly a degree of psychographics.

Gender and Marital Status: Overall, definitely more females than males answered the surveys and indicated a high level of involvement with food, but to say that most food tourists are female would be flawed. Firstly, marketers recognize that women have a higher tendency to participate in research than men.[19] This should be a caution to researchers and those that interpret and use the research results. Indeed, most travel as couples, then as families, then as a group similar to wine tourists (Getz, 2000).[20] Men and women also tend to eat different types of food. Men seem to eat more meat, and women seem to eat healthier food. Men and women appear to share strong interests in wine and food, but when traveling they seek different benefits. The social dimensions seem to appeal more to women, while men seek out technical knowledge. Together, they must work out priorities and realistic itineraries. If children accompany the foodie couple, a whole new set of requirements enters the picture. Asking respondents whether they have children living at home will definitely help in segmentation.

Nationality: most of the available research on food travelers comes from has been done in Oceania, South Africa, North America and Europe, although the tourist's nationality may differ from the country in which the research takes place. Consequently, the majority of the world's population has been ignored and their food tourism preferences and propensities remain a great unknown. It can be said however that food tourism preferences mostly differ between nationalities, which makes it more important to conduct target market research between countries. Ideally, this would involve comparative behavioral studies in order to discover similarities and differences.

Education and Income: These variables are always highly correlated and therefore constitute a strong leading indicator regarding propensity to travel for any purpose. While lower and middle-income people might very well seek out good food experiences, especially when on holiday, destinations trying to attract dedicated food tourists will out of necessity concentrate on better-educated, higher-income travelers. That said, people of any income level like good food, and richer people do not necessarily seek expensive culinary experiences. Destinations should strive for a balance of affordable and mid-priced food experiences, with a smaller number of premium culinary experiences targeted at a smaller, higher income group.

Previous Travel Experience: A very good market differentiator is travel experience. The more one has traveled, especially if they traveled for a food experience, the more likely they can become interested in a specific destination and the easier it should be to communicate with them, such as through frequent flyer programs, tour companies, hotel chains and online.

Clustering: The level of sophistication in statistical analysis of available data sets on food tourists is not that high, but a couple of clustering efforts have been reported. This segmentation technique identifies a small number of groups, or clusters, described by important variables (see Ignatov and Smith, 2006; Smith and Costello, 2009).[21] Whether the socio-demographic profile of foodies stands up to further segmenting scrutiny is yet to be discovered.

Future Research

Large-scale, comparative studies are needed, particularly to include vast Asian and other populations that might become food tourists (Chang et al., 2010).[22] Advanced statistical techniques including discriminant analysis, clustering and meta-analysis will be necessary for both theory development and more refined market intelligence.

Market research, focused on potential tourists and at foodies at home, has to be matched by field research. Most wine tourism research in the early years was done at wineries, while most food tourism research has been done through large-scale surveys in particular populations. Of critical importance will be to test the products/experiences and the communication messages and methods by contacting real tourists during their visits. It is also useful to determine the information sources utilized by culinary tourists in order to know how to best communicate with this consumer group.

In terms of socio-demographics, the focus of this chapter, it is suggested that much more attention be given to the dynamics of couples as food tourists, including those who take children with them on trips. How do they work out their priorities and satisfy different needs? What travel and accommodation choices do they make and which types of food tourism experiences do they mutually negotiate? It is these types of future research that will inform destination marketers on how develop, package and promote their food assets in unison with their other destination offerings.

CONCLUSION

This study of selected leading research suggests some definite patterns in the demographic profile of food tourists and these should be of value to food tourism professionals, at least as a starting point when considering who their food products and experiences are likely to cater to and attract. Caution however, needs to be exercised on a number of counts. First, the demographic profile of the food tourist we have found to be consistent across many studies is likely not necessarily substantially different from the typical tourist, whether traveling for a broader, even mass, tourist experience or many other special interest niches. Income and maturity, which is associated with stability, are lubricants if not prerequisites, of travel and education, piques a certain inquisitiveness to discover the world around us. Secondly, some have questioned whether niche markets, indeed food tourists[23] (see McKercher et al., 2008) actually seek out experiences that are that vastly different to the ordinary tourist. Hence they question whether the time and effort dedicated by destination marketers in targeting food tourists specifically is warranted. While our current chapter does not answer this question, the work of our co-contributors surely does. To be sure, most of the world's population are not foodies, or potential food tourists, and not target markets for any given destination. Even if the target markets are not foodies per se, showcasing the local food experience does help to preserve the local culinary culture. Yet it will pay handsomely to focus research on foodies, test their level of involvement, match that with previous experience on food-related activities from previous travel experience, and then concentrate on the small niche segments that represent the best prospects. This means a heavy investment in original research but a rich vein of work is providing evidence that involvement in serious leisure pursuits matures into serious leisure careers, whereby individuals are prepared to travel to indulge their involvement, whether it be sport (Getz & Anderson, 2010)[24] or food.

As mentioned in the introduction, food is a ubiquitous destination product, service and experience. There is no doubt whatsoever that there are globally passionate foodies who seek to satiate their appetite for new food adventures by traveling to new and exotic destinations or for a different food experience. Only concentrated research efforts will unravel who they are, (beyond demographic profiling as useful as this is as a starting point), what they want and how to reach them.

Beyond this, there will likely be a trickle-down effect for destination marketers. The messages about products and experiences aimed at highly involved and experienced food tourists are also likely to help develop a positive destination image and thus spread, or filter downward, to attract lesser involved yet potential food tourists who can support sustainability of food tourism in a destination. By focusing on the most refined segment, effort and cost will be minimized. This however, in no way detracts from the importance of ensuring that every visitor has a good food experience.

DISCUSSION QUESTIONS

1. Do you think it is worth studying the demographics of food travelers or is the consumer base so broad, so diverse, that it is too hard to quantify from the perspective of food tourism?
2. Is the notion of niche markets becoming moot since travelers find interest in so many diverse niches?
3. Could all travelers potentially be food tourists? Discuss why or why not.

ENDNOTES

[1] Hjalager, A-M., & Richards, G. (2002). Gastronomy: an essential ingredient in tourism production and consumption Tourism and Gastronomy): Routledge, London.
[2] Long, L. M. (1998). Culinary tourism: A folkloristic perspective on eating and otherness. Southern Folklore, 55(3), 181-204.
[3] Robinson, R. N. S., & Getz, D. (in press). Profiling Potential Food Tourists: An Australian Study. British Food Journal.

68

[4] Sparks, B., Roberts, L., Deery, M., Davies, J., and Brown, L. (2005). Good Living Tourism: Lifestyle Aspects of Food and Wine Tourism. Gold Coast, Australia: Cooperative Research Centre for Sustainable Tourism.

[5] Forga, J. M. P., & Valiente, G. C. (2012). Costa Brava Culinary Tourism Routes and Relational Dynamics International Journal of Tourism Sciences, 12(3), 47-68.

[6] Nicholson, R., & Pearce, D. (2001). Why Do People Attend Events: A Comparative Analysis of Visitor Motivations at Four South Island Events. Journal of Travel Research, 39(4), 449-460.

[7] "TIAA (Travel Industry Association of America and International Culinary Tourism Association)" (2007). Profile of Culinary Travelers, 2007 Edition.

[8] "TAMS (Travel Activities and Motivation Survey)" (2001). Wine and Culinary. Lang Research Inc., Toronto. www.tourism.gov.on.ca/english/tourdiv/tams

[9] For reasons of space, it is beyond the scope of this chapter to provide additional details that might be applicable to segmentation from this research.

[10] Kivela, J., & Crotts, J. C. (2006). Tourism and Gastronomy: Gastronomy's Influence on How Tourists Experience a Destination. Journal of Hospitality & Tourism Research, 30(3), 354-377.

[11] Smith, S., & Costello, C. (2009). Segmenting Visitors to a Culinary Event: Motivations, Travel Behavior, and Expenditures. Journal of Hospitality Marketing and Management, 18(1), 44-67.

[12] Kim, M., Kim, Y. H., & Goh, B. K. (2011). An examination of food tourist's behavior: Using the modified theory of reasoned action. Tourism Management, 32(5), 1159-1165.

[13] Correia, A., Moital, M., Ferreira Da Costa, C., & Peres, R. (2008). The determinants of gastronomic tourists' satisfaction: A second-order factor analysis. Journal of Foodservice, 19(3), 164-176.

[14] Sánchez-Cañizares, S. M., &López-Guzmán, T. (2011). Gastronomy as a tourism resource: profile of the culinary tourist. Current Issues in Tourism, 15(3), 1-17.

[15] Kim, Y., Eves, A., & Scarles, C. (2009). Building a model of local food consumption on trips and holidays: A grounded theory approach. International Journal of Hospitality Management, 28(3), 423-431.

[16] Tse, P., & Crotts, J.C. (2005). Antecedents of novelty seeking: international visitor's propensity to experiment across Hong Kong's culinary traditions. Tourism Management, 26(6), 965-968.

[17]Hall, C. M., & Mitchell, R. (2005). Gastronomic tourism. Comparing food and wine tourism experiences. In M. Novelli (Ed.), Niche tourism. Contemporary issues, trends and cases (pp. 73-88). Oxford: Elsevier, Butterworth-Heinemann.

[18] For an interesting discussion of this topic, see "'When You're Here, You're Family': Culinary Tourism and the Olive Garden Restaurant" by Michael Mario Albrecht, Sage Publications, Tourist Studies 11(2) 99 –113.

[19] For an example see www.clickz.com/clickz/column/1721875/analytics-basics-understanding-survey-data

[20] Getz, D. (2000). Explore Wine Tourism: Management, Development and Destinations. Cognizant Communication Corporation.

[21] Ignatov, E., & Smith, S. (2006). Segmenting Canadian culinary tourists. Current Issues in Tourism, 9(3), 235-255.

[22] Chang, R. C., Kivela, J., &Mak, A. (2010). Food preferences of Chinese tourists. Annals of Tourism Research, 37(4), 989-1011.

[23] McKercher, B., Okumus, F., & Okumus, B. (2008). Food tourism as a viable market segment. It's all how you cook the numbers! Journal of Travel and Tourism Marketing, 25(2), 137-148.

[24] Getz, D. & Andersson, T.D. (2010). The event-tourist career trajectory: A study of high-involvement amateur distance runners. Scandinavian Journal of Hospitality and Tourism, 10(4), 468-491.

How Foodies Make Decisions

Sarika Chawla, Statia Elliot, Brian Wansink & Erik Wolf

For years marketers looked at demographic profiles to help us understand our customers. Eventually things like income, gender and level of education were not detailed enough and we turned to psychographics to allow us to construct a consumer profile to better understand consumer behavior and purchasing decisions. The problem – or opportunity – with food tourism is that everyone eats and drinks. Its appeal is universal. Still, interesting and memorable food experiences rank higher in importance for some people than others. This chapter looks at psychographic motivators to help us better understand decision making by foodies.

INTRODUCTION

"Research often treats culinary tourists as a relatively small, separate and homogeneous market,[1] when by common sense and biology we know that, with certainty, one hundred percent of travellers eat, making food and beverage perhaps the most connected activity to travel possible."[2]

If a chef or tour operator really wants to understand what type of culinary tourist may be most relevant for a potentially new food experience, they can focus development efforts with this person in mind. In this way, they will not be guessing and hoping to hit upon a new product that people might like. Focusing on specific, representative profiles of consumers can help guide the science of new product development, and it can suggest parameters of what is scientifically feasible and market relevant. At the same time this chapter provides necessary information and useful tools for those involved in marketing a destination.

The "traditional" method of obtaining consumer information is to use demographics to describe a product's potential consumers. Using demographic information to accomplish this is like using colors to describe night. While demographics describes the 'typical' generic consumer profiling of the 'ideal consumer' or 'brand champion' in very specific terms. This provides product developers a greater understanding of the people for whom they develop products and what are their hopes, perceptions, and aspirations.[3]

Exhibit 1 illustrates the differences between using demographic data and profiling to describe two hypothetical consumer segments for a dairy-based sports drink. The first segment might be generally characterized as "weight conscious young drinkers" and the second as "health conscious older drinkers." While the demographic data describes "people," it does not describe "a person" whom this development team would be able to visualize as they were working with their new product ideas. The consumer profiles in the right-hand column provide much more vivid qualities and characteristics than the demographic segments. This key distinction is the difference between understanding numbers and understanding motivations. Motivations explain why people buy, which we need to know for new product development.

The Power of Psychographics

Psychographic and "lifestyle" research are sometimes referred to as Attitude, Interests, and Opinion (AIO) research because the questions often focus on these types of questions. This research resembles both motivation research and conventional research. It resembles motivation research because a major aim is to draw recognizably human portraits of consumers, but it also resembles more conventional research in that these portraits can be analyzed using standard statistical tools.

	Demographic Segments	Consumer Psychographic Profiles
Segment 1 **"Weight Conscious Tourists"**	• ages 27-35 • typically middle school to high school level • low personal income • involved in school related activities including several types of sports	• Sees sports as a way to create an identity in a large school, and a good way to meet friends and potential dates. Many people admire athletes. • Impressing others is important • Being young is all about staying in shape and having fun. "I'll never get fat like my parents." • Not set in ways. Likes to try new things and seeks adventure whenever possible. • Immediate gratification is a must.
Segment 2 **"Health Conscious Tourists"**	• age 38-50 • college education • well-established in career • income US$30,000-$70,000 • 2 children • works out at gym 2x/week	• Career has been the main driving force in life • Keeping up a good social image in front of others is crucial • Appreciates value, but has enough money to feel secure • Every acquaintance is another opportunity to better social standing • Has elderly parent with failing health, beginning to realize what may lie ahead if health is ignored • Wants to devote more time to family in later period of career

Exhibit 1. Comparing Consumer Psychographic Profiles and Demographic Segments for a Dairy-Based Sports Drink

Using Psychographics to Understand Your Customers

Our understanding of travelers has evolved from viewing them as an undifferentiated, homogenous population ("people have opinions"), to viewing them on a more demographic basis ("So, what do women think of hotels that include breakfast as part of a package?"). While this evolution represented some improvement, there is still much that cannot be explained simply by grouping by demographic characteristics. For instance, why is it that two neighbors can have nearly the same background, income, and education, but have totally different political beliefs, own different types of cars, and have different preferences for food and travel?

Psychographic and individual difference measures enable us to further segment populations to explain why different people behave in different ways. When the term psychographics was introduced by Emanuel Demby in the 1960s, it was generally defined as "the use of psychological, sociological, and anthropological factors, self-concept, and lifestyle to determine how the market is segmented by the propensity of groups within the market—and their reasons—to make a particular decision about a product, person, or ideology."[4]

There are a number of different ways to generate consumer profiles, and some involve more experience and expertise than others.[5] One method to gather consumer behavior profiles is from directed interviews that ask potential consumers more about themselves than about the product.

These involve a basic interviewing method that asks people representative of potential markets a series of questions focusing on the type of person they are and on their specific goals, motivations, and aspirations in life and on a daily basis. The fundamental questions proposed by the researchers in this chapter (additional ones can be added) include:

• How would you describe yourself to others?
• How would you characterize your general view toward life?
• How would you describe your social life and the way you are around others?

- How would you ideally like to be seen by others?
- What are your hobbies?
- How would you spend the perfect weekend?
- Where and who would you ideally like to be in five years?
- What are your lifetime goals?

Being able to profile the personality, goals, and perceptions of representatives of the target market will help a team think in a more coordinated and creative way.

The power of understanding psychographics is that it is not only tells us what different individuals prefer, but also how they will behave. When considering culinary tourists, this more refined understanding can help craft a culinary experience that is unforgettable.

Pairing Food and Travel Experiences Using Psychographics

Food tourism has grown in popularity, new destinations around the world have emerged to satisfy the hunger, and our knowledge of culinary tourists as a sustainable segment of travelers has expanded. Sophisticated psychographic approaches to segmentation are helping destinations to match culinary product with consumer tastes and preferences. Like the pairing of food and wine, psychographic profiling reveals how travel and dining experiences can be effectively paired together to appeal to a range of traveler segments.

In 2010, the International Culinary Tourism Association published results from a survey to over 11,000 international respondents resulting in 13 *PsychoCulinary* profiles that reflect how people are motivated to make food experience decisions.[6] The top profiles of all respondents globally were: Localist, Novice, Eclectic, Organic and Authentic – five very different segments that range from the dedicated foodies who love local, organic and authentic fare at one extreme, to the novice foodie who is new to the experience at the other extreme, and with an eclectic segment in between who seems to like a bit of everything. The research went a long way to explaining how two friends can have vastly different opinions about one restaurant or one winery. The reason for their different opinions was rooted in their different expectations about the food experience. The study also dispelled the mistaken assumption that food travelers prefer premium and expensive experiences. The research showed exactly the opposite, with only 8.1% of respondents self-identifying with a Gourmet (or premium, high-end) PsychoCulinary profile. The overwhelming majority – nearly 92% - just wanted good food and drink without fuss.

Type	Primary %	Secondary %	Tertiary %
Gourmet	8.1	7.4	11.3
Authentic	8.8	9.8	10.7
Localist	11.0	11.7	10.4
Adventurer	8.1	8.9	10.1
Eclectic	9.2	10.7	9.2
Ambiance	7.1	7.8	8.6
Organic	8.9	9.9	8.0
Budget	7.3	6.3	6.7
Innovative	5.4	5.8	6.6
Social	6.8	6.2	6.3
Trendy	5.2	4.5	4.9
Novice	10.7	8.5	4.9
Vegetarian	3.3	2.4	2.3

Top 5 of Each Category

Primary	Localist
	Novice
	Eclectic
	Organic
	Authentic
Secondary	Localist
	Eclectic
	Organic
	Authentic
	Adventurer
Tertiary	Gourmet
	Authentic
	Localist
	Adventurer
	Eclectic

Exhibit 2: Top PsychoCulinary Rankings. *Credit: World Food Travel Association.*[7]

The 2007 culinary traveler study by the International Culinary Tourism Association (now the World Food Travel Association) and the Travel Industry Association of America noted that foodies on the road are much more active than general leisure travelers, taking part in cultural activities, spa services, and visits to parks and historic sites. They are also more likely to read travel and culinary publications, both offline and online, and motivationally, they seek a unique culinary experience that they cannot get at home.[8]

Similarly, the 2011 State of the American Traveler report from Destination Analysis, Inc. International (DAII) found that foodies and/or wine tourists are more likely to take leisure trips, are experiential, adventurous, willing to travel for a specific restaurant, interested in cultural or historical experiences, and are technologically savvy.

Perhaps most importantly for marketers, the study also found that foodies and wine tourist are also willing to spend on the experience.

- Non-foodies spent an average of US$780 on their most recent leisure trip;
- Foodie travelers spent an average of US$833;
- Wine tourists spent an average of US$1174[9]

The sum of the research to date confirms that the culinary travel market has great potential, and importantly, the types of culinary experiences available can drive destination choice. One way for destinations to take advantage of this market opportunity is to develop targeted communications and cross promotions. Profiling psychographic consumer characteristics can produce well-defined communities of interest that are not only reachable by marketers, but also are likely to already exist within the realm of social media. Some of the most well-known community sites are Facebook, Yelp, Pinterest and Flickr. A search of "culinary" related groups in Flickr produces a listing of over 500, ranging from a group named "I Ate This", with some 27,400 members and more than 515,000 posted photos, to culinary destination groups – Greece, Italy, France and so on – with only a few members each. "Food" in general has over 29,000 Flickr groups, while "travel" has close to 60,000. This collaborative categorization based on the freely chosen keywords allows users to join conversations with like-minded "friends" and form online communities of interest. The challenge for market researchers is to refine segmentation analysis in a way that mirrors these communities of interest.

New Insights to Culinary Travel

To capture psychographic characteristics of a broad cross-section of consumers, a web survey was conducted among Canadian adults aged 18+, who had taken at least one vacation during the last 12 months involving a minimum of one night away from home, excluding visits to a second home and business travel.[10] The final data set of 4,029 responses was almost evenly split between summer and winter season, and between short getaways and longer vacation trips, to reflect a good mix of travelers.

Consumers were profiled according to their primary motivation for travel, and behavioral preferences for a range of trip attributes categorized as urban vibe, nature, convenience, culture, pampering, and familiarity, with each attribute comprising a number of activities, including dining.

Factor clustering produced the following eight unique segments: Urban Gourmet, Intellectual Explorer, Indulgent Family, Indulgent Couples or Friends, Outdoor Family, Hedonistic Adventurer, Nautical Nature and Urban Hyperactive, presented in Exhibit 3 with corresponding visuals. This method of segmentation reflects a holistic approach that examines dining preferences within the context of travel preferences, to more accurately assess food consumption patterns during travel as a ubiquitous activity versus a special interest, more typically measured in isolation.

In Exhibit 3 we see that the restaurant experience is not only important to the urban gourmet (9% market share) – perhaps the most obvious foodie-type traveler – but also to the hedonistic adventurer (15%) and the urban hyperactive (11%) segments. It is actually the hedonistic adventurer who is most likely to incur the highest food expenditures. The consideration of these sub-segments of tourists with culinary interests beyond the urban gourmet niche increases the

74

target market from a small share of 9% of travelers, to a combined and profound total share of 35%. For many destination marketing organizations, it is much more feasible to develop and implement a campaign intended to reach over a third of the market, versus only 9%.

Browsing destination marketing organizations websites, it is clear that several already present their product offerings by category or segment – urban, adventure, culture – with dropdown tabs, for example, listing appropriate travel experiences. Surprisingly few, however, incorporate dining experiences within these product categories. More often restaurant listings appear as a distinct list, and the opportunity to pair experiences is lost. Exhibit 4 presents a sample of potential pairings of food and travel experiences that could be effectively expanded and adapted by many destinations. Characteristics associated with food tourism are used to profile sub-segments of travelers with culinary interests. Categories of dining preferences are also identified in Exhibit 4. The resulting psychographic segments are described below, listed in order of dining importance.

Exhibit 3: Psychographic Segments[11], *Credit: Ipsos Marketing*

Rank	Type	Description
1	Hedonistic Adventurer	Ready to spend and have fun. Want to be spoiled and have exotic and gourmet culinary experiences and haute cuisine. Baby boomers tourist with income, education, and desire to travel. Not afraid to try new destinations to find their paradise. More about experiences than location. Approx. 15% of the travel market and an attractive segment for culinary destinations with refined dining experiences.
2	Urban Hyperactive	The dining experience is important. Spends primarily on restaurants and shopping while on vacation. Prefers urban vibe, trendy places, exotic restaurants, bistros and cafes. This educated Generation X-type will visit museums and festivals, and enjoy nightlife to enrich a trip experience. Approx. 11% of the market and an important segment for culinary destinations that offer hip dining and travel experiences.
3	Urban Gourmet	Places great importance on dining while traveling, selecting city destinations offering not only a wide selection of exotic and haute cuisine restaurants, but other urban activities such as shopping and sightseeing. Seeks pleasure and will spend less on accommodation and transport so that they can indulge in fine dining. Likes the familiar and can be strong repeat visitors. Typically baby boomers with average income, they tend to travel and dine as a couple, and comprise approx. 9% of the travel market.
4	Indulgent Culinary Travelers	Couples and friends, notably the biggest travel segment at 20%, place high importance on dining, but above all, travel is about pampering for these Generation Y-type tourists. They seek fun dining options, from the exotic to steakhouses and rotisseries. Their vacation getaway is about relaxing together without worry. Whether in a well-known destination or one that is less accessible, this is a mobile, active cohort, who wants it all -- from swimming, to fine dining, to an evening show.
5	Intellectual Explorer	Looking for a cultural experience. Mature travelers attracted to destinations featuring museums, historic sites and natural beauty. Dining is important too, particularly neighborhood-type local restaurants and farm-to-fork outdoor dining experiences. These educated tourists choose affordable accommodation and dining to be able to spend more on their preferred cultural activities, and to travel away from the big cities. Approx. 10%

of the market.

6	Indulgent Family	Attracted to practical and organized travel, making dining more important for function than fun. Typically families with young children, this segment understandably looks for family-type dining, including quick serve restaurants and all-inclusive buffets. Then off to the pool or park, or another family-oriented activity. They represent approximately an 11% market share.
7	Nautical Nature	Drawn to nature destinations, preferably for swimming and other nautical sports. A range of demographics, common features of this segment are preferences for pampering, convenience and safety when traveling. Dining is a secondary consideration, with selections including basic family restaurants, fast food, and pizzerias – low cost, fast and simple fare. They make up about 13% of the travel market.
8	Outdoor Adventurer	Families who want to get out of the city and enjoy a getaway in a natural setting. Not looking for cultural enrichment, nor contact with locals, nor fine dining. Restaurant preferences – primarily for need versus want – lean toward basic family dining and fast food. Though 12% of the market, they are a lower income segment without much interest in culinary destinations.

Exhibit 4: Sample Pairings of Food and Travel Experiences[12], *Credit: Ipsos Marketing*

Experience	Urban	Adventure	Nightlife	Culture
Travel	shopping sightseeing	parks zoos	festivals theater	museums historic sites
Culinary	trendy restaurants, food festivals, meet artisan food makers	farm stays, vineyard hikes, mountaintop dining	bistros, gastropub tour, progressive dinner	cooking class, market tour, ethnic neighborhood tour

This depth of tourism analysis allows destinations to match their food offerings with particular communities of interest to maximize marketing impact. For example, haute cuisine restaurant experiences are sought after by the urban gourmet (9%) and the hedonistic adventurer (15%) segments. However, exotic restaurant experiences are sought after by these two segments as well as the urban hyperactive (11%) and the indulgent couples or friends customers (20%). Now the potential reach expands to 55% of the market, thereby substantiating the development of a food tourism marketing campaign. In this manner, culinary tourists are not treated as a small niche segment, but as a diversified community, linked by a shared passion for food, yet touched in different ways depending on their traveler segment profile.

These study results may also explain the range of market share statistics often reported in food tourism research, from relatively low figures (e.g. 9% if only the urban gourmet segment is counted) to relatively high figures (e.g. 76% if all segments that rated the restaurant experience as important are counted). As a methodology, psychographic profiling presents an approach to help marketers identify actionable segments with the growth of social networks as a marketing media, it can support and inform tourism destination communications on how to effectively pair food and travel experiences.

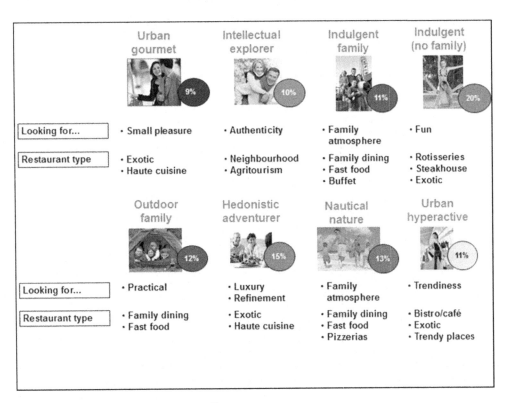

Photo Credit: Ipsos Marketing (2011).[13]

Discovery, Adventure and Culture

Targeting the food traveler is not as simple as promoting restaurants and hoping guests will come. Food travelers do not all think in the same way and may seek entirely different types of experiences on the road. The Indulgent Culinary Traveler, Urban Hyperactive and Intellectual Explorer travelers are heavily motivated by culinary offerings in a destination, and may choose where they travel based on the types of culinary experiences available.

For the vast majority of travelers, however, food can still rank high in importance without being the deciding factor. Whether it is making sure to eat a lobster roll in Maine or dim sum in San Francisco, finding food or drinks that are unique or indigenous to the destination is a crucial part of the travel experience.

Overall, what unifies food travelers of all types are the elements of discovery, adventure and culture. Instead of marketing food as a standalone activity, one approach is to "pair" it with other experiences. Remember 100% of travelers to a destination will eat, so food and drink should form a prominent foundation for every tourism development program.

Indulgent Culinary Travel

One of the earliest marketers of food tourism is the Santa Rosa, California-based Food & Wine Trails, which markets high-end, custom programs in Europe and California, and epicurean-themed cruises. "These are people with time and money," explains President Larry Martin. "These are people who are interested in the joy and the pleasure of the table; people who want to press farther into the nuances of the culture."[14]

While the typical audience for a high-end, Food & Wine Trails product tends to be affluent baby boomers, Martin notes that millennials in their 30s are now joining the culinary scene in droves. Similarly, while wine tourism was traditionally a more male audience, women have been participating more often in the last five years. Martin explains that the foodie who follows TV personality chefs, like *Top Chef and Hell's Kitchen* or The Food Network programs, is not his target audience. "Without question, those shows have increased the public's interest in food and wine, but it's not my market. The person I'm selling to isn't watching TV, they're cooking five nights a week." The niche audience for an intensive culinary tour craves access: a back-of-the-house tour of a winery, learning to cook regional cuisine, visiting the markets with a chef, meeting artisans and winemakers, and even something as simple as having lunch at a local's home.

Because Food & Wine Trails offers a higher-end product, its audience tends to be boomers who have the means to spend on personalized experiences that offer lifelong bragging rights. While the vineyards of Bordeaux may be well-trod, a customized trip can include a driver and wine expert guide, private estate tours and meals at Michelin-starred restaurants. Those kinds of activities cannot simply be bundled as a mass-market experience that anyone can do.

Hedonistic Adventurous Culinary Travel

Launched in 2001, California-based Access Trips provides exclusive learning adventures. Its products mostly involved outdoor adventure, whether it was surfing in Costa Rica or snowboarding in New Zealand. In 2010, CEO Tamar Lowell launched the company's first non-sport programs, which was a series of culinary tours to Morocco, Thailand and Japan. "We were blown away," reports Lowell. From 2011 to 2012, Access Trips saw a 94% increase in participation in its culinary products, mostly due to the Morocco tour.

Lowell explains that the audience for these tours, whether sports or culinary, are explorers who want to go "somewhere amazing in the world and develop a new skill." When they added culinary tours, the age demographics began to skew older. "We now see just as many people in their 50s and 60s as their 20s and 30s. I'm not surprised. People in their 60s and 70s tend to be interested in culinary travel more than mountain biking. The general profile of our culinary tour participant is female, some gay men, and a few honeymooners." These tours, she explains, appeal to people who want to see a country from a culinary angle, but not exclusively so. "They're really into eating and they look at our itinerary and think it sounds like crazy fun. "Morocco is our most popular tour, by far. People are fascinated by Morocco, and it's stable, but it's not an easy place to travel by yourself."

Intellectual Explorer: Culture

In Oaxaca, Mexico, Chef Susana Trilling owns and operates "Seasons of My Heart", a cooking school/ B&B/ tour operator. An American-born chef, Trilling is considered one of the pioneers of Oaxacan cooking schools, and is credited with bringing the local cuisine into the mainstream consciousness through her school and subsequent cookbook and PBS network series. Because of Trilling's reputation and her presence in Mexico, her program tends to attract more professional chefs and restaurant groups than does a typical cooking school. Her core audience for both one-day courses and fully immersive week-long tours is the traveling foodie who wants to learn about the culture through the lens of food.

In addition to cooking lessons and meeting local artisans, Trilling also offers specialized courses in mushroom foraging and tours to other regions of Mexico. One of her most popular courses is the "Día de los Muertos" program, a 7-day course that includes cooking traditional holiday food along with meeting and working with artists, visiting graveyards and participating in the festivities in Oaxaca. "We've always had foodies coming, people who have been to cooking schools all over the world," says Trilling. She has noticed that her audience is not just women traveling in pairs or solo. The cultural aspect of her courses also attracts those looking for a bonding experience, such as honeymooning couples and destination weddings; families with young kids who like the hands-on aspect; professional couples; and second marriages.

While Trilling's program offers a complete immersion into local cooking, an organized group tour can attract a similar audience without being as cooking oriented. The Los Angeles-based Brendan Vacations, which offers a number of escorted tours, recently launched with Slow Food Italia and Slow Food Travel to create a cultural-culinary program. Four programs in Italy and two in France involve the traditional tour bus and sightseeing tours, but also include a culinary expert guide, tastings and meeting local producers. A tour may involve experiences such as visiting a farm that breeds rare rabbits for meat, sampling cheese in a 15th century farmhouse, and visiting a Sicilian pastry shop that still uses medieval recipes. Every vendor on the itinerary has to be approved by Slow Food: restaurants, hotels, food shops and wineries. These packages, part of Brendan's Boutique Journeys, are limited to 24 people (a typical tour is closer to 30-40) and departure is guaranteed even with two people on the trip; accommodations are in boutique properties, using the "hub and spoke" model of staying one city for two or three nights and venturing on day trips.

According to Nico Zenner, president of Brendan Vacations, this style of packaged travel is a direct response to customers' desire to immerse themselves in the local culture, using food as the catalyst. These culinary tours tend to attract people who have already been on the traditional sightseeing trip and now want a slower-paced, more thorough travel experience. This format blends the old model of "escorted tour" and the more modern "flexible independent travel" to give travelers the comfort of having a framework in place (flights, hotels, daily activities) but also having choices within those activities, leisure time, and access to the local culture that is not readily available on other itineraries.

Intellectual Explorer: History

Not all destinations are known for their culinary offerings so it may require attracting one traveler profile and introducing the food through that perspective.

Virginia's wine scene has exploded in recent years, with locavore dining growing alongside the wineries. Most visitors to Virginia are history seekers who tour Colonial Williamsburg, explore nearby Washington, D.C., and visit the homes of the country's founding fathers.

The Virginia Tourism Corporation (VTC) collected data on 3,422 household-trips taken to Virginia from July 2010 to July 2011. According to the 2011 Leisure Travel Profile of Virginia, 14% of leisure travelers visited historic sites or churches and 6% visited old homes and mansions. Only 2% listed wine tasting and winery tours. VTC has already identified the need to make prospective visitors aware of the state's "fantastic lodging and culinary offerings."

Only in recent years has Virginia begun capitalizing on its history to reach foodies. It coined the term "First in Wine," referring to the state's 400-year-old winemaking history. Virginia has several AVAs and wine trails, several of which have been paired with historic tourism. There is the Colonial Virginia Wine Trail in the Hampton Roads area, which includes Williamsburg; the Jefferson Heritage Trail connects Thomas Jefferson's Monticello to his retreat in Lynchburg. Meanwhile, historic venues are incorporating culinary experiences, like Mount Vernon, which features a carefully restored distillery from George Washington's days, and Colonial Williamsburg, which showcases age-old food preparation techniques, fine dining and an 18th century-style tavern.

Nature Lovers & Outdoor Adventurers

Sonoma County, California, USA is a mecca for food and wine lovers of all types, whether high-end wine enthusiasts, restaurant fanatics or serious cooks. "For food and wine tourism, boomers are the number one audience," says Tim Zahner, director of Sonoma County Tourism. "They tend to be higher income, spend more money, and drink wine at least twice a week." But others include millenials — younger travelers who cannot splurge as much, but who can be converted to choose Sonoma if given the right information. This is the audience that might be interested in the newer culinary trends like trying food trucks or attending an artisan cheese festival. This group is often intrigued by the concept of agritourism, something that Sonoma does well. The people who are interested in food are also interested in where it comes from," explains Zahner.

According to the 2012 Sonoma County Annual Tourism Report, which surveyed local business owners and tourism executives, in addition to wine, Sonoma's most attractive assets to visitors are scenery (average rating of 4.32/5) and cuisine (3.9/5). The most reported niche markets in the county are cycling (47.6%) followed by ecotourism/agritourism (12.5%). Sonoma is made for agritourism, where visitors can get an inside look of a working farm, and which could include hiking a vineyard, spending the night at a winery, picking produce with a chef, making cheese, or a number of other hands-on, immersive experiences that connect to the source of the food.

Hyperactive Culinary Travel

Not to be overlooked is the foodie who idolizes chefs and who loves to be on the cutting edge of food trends. Houston, Texas, USA is home to "Where the Chefs Eat", a chef-led tour of ethnic and local establishments that the city's top chefs like to attend. Overall, the tours tend to resonate more with locals than out-of-towners. The most popular tours are led by Brian Caswell and Monica Pope, both of whom have appeared on high-profile cooking competition shows.

"The Houston foodie likes going to restaurants and having relationships with the chefs," says Lindsey Brown, director of marketing and public relations for the Greater Houston Convention and Visitors Bureau. "They want to say they're friends with the chef, they're adventurous, and they're savvy about social media." The program has successfully paired tasting with other immersive experiences: the oyster tour, led by Caswell, involves learning how to shuck and visiting local seafood counters to learn the difference in varieties, before dining at several oyster bars. A pig-themed tour follows the trend of nose-to-tail dining by taking visitors to a local butcher before tasting different ethnic preparations. These kinds of creative endeavors are a triple benefit in tourism terms: 1) it shows off a side of Houston that most people never see; 2) it highlights the city's undiscovered foodie scene; and 3) it taps into the trendy culinary traveler profile's sense of adventure and discovery.

CONCLUSION

The identification of sub-segments of culinary tourists provides opportunity for destinations to expand food and wine product offerings to larger communities of interest. The identification of specific communities in terms of their primary motivator, needs and preferences, provides a foundation that is particularly well suited for social media-based campaigns, to reach individuals that have joined a community according to their passion, not because of a particular company or destination. Instead, a destination can build awareness by infiltrating or even creating social media communities of interest. For example, a community of travelers interested in exotic restaurants may include the urban gourmet, the hedonistic adventurer, the indulgent traveler, and the hyperactive urbanite. Specific restaurant matches can be shared with communities of interest to best meet their culinary desires.

Psychographics can provide useful information to help owners of different types of food and travel businesses to correctly fine-tune their target markets and messaging. In this way, the business owner will create marketing strategies that are more sustainable in the long term.

DISCUSSION QUESTIONS

1. Using the various psychographic models, what might a future and more globally suitable psychographic model of food travelers look like?
2. Why is income not necessarily a good measure of someone's propensity to engage in food tourism?
3. If gourmet-oriented foodies only represent 8.1% of foodies, according to the World Travel Association, what could food tourism professionals do differently to market to more of a mainstream audience?

ENDNOTES

[1] Ignatov, E., Smith, S., 2006. Segmenting Canadian culinary tourists. Current Issues in Tourism 9 (3), 235–255.

[2] Elliot, Statia and Durand, Luc (2011). Mapping Culinary Tourist Communities of Interest across Traveler Segments. Travel and Tourism Research Association, European Chapter Conference Proceedings.

[3] Zaltman, G. & R. Coulter (1995). Seeing the voice of the customer: metaphor-based advertising research.Journal of Advertising Research, 35:4, 35-51.

[4] Emanuel H. Demby, "Psychographics Revisited: The Birth of a Technique," Marketing News, 2 January 1989, 21

[5] Wansink, B.(1994). The customer profiling technique: Its validation and application. Journal of Targeting, Measurement and Analysis for Marketing, July, 1994, pgs. 18-23.

[6]International Culinary Tourism Association (2010). State of the Food tourism Industry Report. Chapter 4: New PsychoCulinary Research.

[7] Ibid.

[8] International Culinary Tourism Association, Profile of U.S. Culinary Travelers, 2007.

[9] Destination Analysts Inc International. Food, Wine & Travel: The Perfect Pairing. State of the American Traveler. 2011.
Ipsos Marketing (2011). Naked Foods: Canadians on the Road, by L. Durand, President, Ipsos Marketing, Ipsos ASI and Ipsos Public Affairs, Montreal QC Canada.

[10] Ibid.

[11] Personal interview with Luc Durand, President, Ipsos Marketing (2011), Montreal, QC Canada.

[12] Ibid.

[13] The authors acknowledge and thank Luc Durand, President, Ipsos, Quebec, for the traveler segmentation data and analysis.

[14] Author interview with Food and Wine Trails President Larry Martin, January 2013.

SECTION TWO

BAKING THE CAKE:

PRODUCT DEVELOPMENT
IN FOOD TOURISM

Developing a Food & Drink Tourism Framework

Gloria Rodríguez with Marco Fuso

This chapter presents the framework of a food tourism development program. This initial step involves creating the conditions needed in order to develop food tourism in a given destination. The chapter covers the complete framework creation process, from the identification of the stakeholders involved to the final outcome of producing a food tourism development plan. Participation, collaboration, public-private cooperation and local community representation are all important issues that are covered in the chapter and that are essential to the development of this tourism niche. Details of some existing food tourism development frameworks are provided as examples, as are references to existing methodology that can be consulted when requiring additional support.

INTRODUCTION

Other chapters of this book present the benefits that developing food and drink tourism may bring to an ample array of stakeholders. In this chapter we will look at the conditions that need to be created in order to make this development possible.

The characteristics of the food tourism niche, where a large number of different stakeholders and interests converge, present specific challenges that need to be addressed in order to unleash its full potential. The tools and recommendations presented in this chapter are based on tourism planning methodology, project management theory and the analysis of food tourism development scenarios around the world. Previous research by a number of authors has also been consulted to provide additional support to the concepts and guidelines presented.

Information portrayed in this chapter will provide the reader a comprehensive view of the complete framework creation process, from the identification of the stakeholders to the final outcome of producing a food tourism development plan. Although the main beneficiaries of this information are typically the authorities or associations in charge of tourism/economic development, the chapter provides valuable information for any food tourism stakeholder — whether they are a small food producer, a public administration, a research institution, etc.

By highlighting the different but highly relevant roles that each of these stakeholders has in the development of food tourism, the chapter can help these stakeholders understand the importance of their participation for the success of their region as a food tourism destination.

Recognizing the Stakeholders

One of the first steps needed for the successful implementation of food tourism is the identification of the stakeholders that can play a relevant part. These players — or stakeholders in project management terminology — are "the persons or organizations ... who are actively involved in the project or whose interests may be positively or negatively affected by the performance of completion of the project".[1]

Food tourism stakeholders include:

- Public administrations at different levels (local, regional, national, multinational and international) and in different areas (tourism, culture, agriculture, commerce, foreign relations, etc.) who are responsible for defining food tourism development policies and who may provide support for private initiatives in this area.

- Businesses and NGOs in the areas of tourism, culture, food and health, commerce, research, media, etc., who provide services directly to the food tourism industry and benefit from any development in this area. The most relevant of these stakeholders are described in the *Introduction to the Food Tourism Industry* chapter.
- The local community, who receives the direct impact of any development strategies, constitutes the workforce for most food tourism services, and acts as host for the food traveler.
- The visitors, or food travelers, who provide income for the region with their consumption of basic tourism and food tourism services, and who are the main source of information on motivation to travel, service quality perception and even new product development possibilities, if appropriately questioned.

Identifying and involving all stakeholders at an early stage in food tourism development is key for three fundamental reasons:

- To consider the objectives of all stakeholders affected by this development, which is fundamental in order to define a development strategy that truly benefits them all (or, at least, the vast majority).
- To enable active involvement of all stakeholders, which will ensure that all actions needed for this development are carried out.
- To foresee potential negative reactions of some stakeholders, and plan to mitigate or counteract them, to ensure success of the initiative.

The Price of Ignoring

Failure to recognize some of the varying perspectives in food tourism may result in action plans that are derailed or delayed due to active opposition of ignored stakeholders. This is the most likely result of failing to consider, for example, the local community as a stakeholder when it is by far the group of people who will be affected the most by any local development actions.[2] Considering the local community an important player in food tourism development will ensure that their needs are heard and will gather their support to the initiative, which will be essential in avoiding opposition. Since the local community is, in effect, the host to any incoming visitors, it is of outmost importance that they are committed to the development of this niche as they are often the most visible face of the destination.

Mistakes in identifying all stakeholders can also prevent some necessary actions to be carried out when the stakeholders that can best perform those actions are not considered from the start. This has proven to be an issue, for example, in destinations where food tourism was initially considered as only involving the hospitality and restaurant business. When you leave food growers, distributors or manufacturers, cooking schools and other related businesses out of your stakeholder list, you may find that you have no support to create essential food tourism products such as classes, tastings, demos, tours that include production fields, markets, etc.

A less fatal but also common mistake when setting the stage for food tourism development is considering some of the stakeholder's mentioned above solely as 'providers' to a food tourism industry that is led by other stakeholders. The problem with this approach is that 'providers' without a true voice will hardly be willing to make the additional effort needed to create the new products or services that may be needed for a specific destination to fully and effectively develop food tourism. Your food manufacturers, distributors or producers, for example, whose main activity is not tourism-related, may not be willing to create tourism activities around their assets unless you convince them of the benefits and involve them in the food tourism development decisions. Other potential service providers to the food tourism industry, such as research centers, they may not have established teams with sufficient food tourism knowledge, may not be able or willing to invest in creating these teams if they are not involved from the start in the development strategy, given voice and/or support. Even professional services, such as tourism consultants, may find it hard to provide services in this area if they lack the expertise and cannot foresee a true benefit. A similar scenario can occur with the media. In general, if your development of food tourism requires investment from a certain set of stakeholders, they will need to be considered stakeholders, and involved from the start, to ensure their active participation and their commitment to this development.

Aside from hindering development, failing to identify and involve all relevant stakeholders can have a more profound negative impact, i.e. limited development. Food tourism, as discussed in previous chapters, can generate benefits that go well beyond an increase in visitor numbers. These benefits can include, among others, improvements in local food production and distribution,[3] strengthening of local identity and creativity,[4] promotion of intercultural dialogue[5] and even maintenance of biodiversity.[6] For food tourism to truly generate these wide-scope benefits, then its development must be holistic.

Understanding the Challenges

Effective and far-reaching development of food tourism requires participation of a large number of stakeholders. These stakeholders include public administrations at different levels and in different areas; small, medium and large businesses and NGOs of various sectors; and less structured groups of people such as the local community and the visitors. The fragmented nature of this industry into such a large and diverse group of stakeholders is possibly the most widely recognized challenge to the development of food and drink tourism.[7]

The enormous differences in stakeholder objectives are one of the first hurdles faced by the development of this niche.[8] While some stakeholders will be aiming at increasing the number of visitors, others are only interested in selling their products and may not even consider themselves as part of the tourism industry. The wineries or olive oil producers are a good example, most of whom are interested in visitors not for tourism, but for on-premise sales and to improve the awareness of their products. Cooking schools are somewhat similar, and so are restaurants. Both of these types of businesses see their market as being primarily local and regional residents.[9]

Another important obstacle associated to the fragmentation of the industry is that most stakeholders have limited resources to assign to developing food tourism. Many of the stakeholders involved in this industry are small local companies such as restaurants, cooking schools or artisanal food producers who cannot afford to invest in marketing to tourists, translation services, or the infrastructure needed to support the needs of visitors. Even without budget restraints, many stakeholders may not be committed to development of this niche because they cannot envision its potential, cannot see what their role in it could be, or perceive that they do not have the support they need to pursue it.

Knowledge of the industry needs is also scarce and fragmented among the stakeholders. The food and drink industry, for example, presents a general lack of experience in regards to tourism.[10] While tourism stakeholders may be familiar with general tourists' expectations, they are typically less knowledgeable of the cultural aspects of food tourism. Both the tourism and the cultural stakeholders will be fully ignorant of the needs of the food industry and neither of the above may have the slightest idea of who their food tourist is and may have to rely on research institutions to provide this information.

The fact that businesses involved in this development fall in different areas (food & agriculture, tourism, culture, commerce, etc.) often causes difficulties in determining which public administration should promote this development.[11] Food tourism, however, is an interdisciplinary field that requires support from various administrative areas. While the tourism administration may want to promote it for obvious reasons, the food administration may also want to ensure that this development entails increased food production and/or local consumption. The cultural administration will be involved in issues such as culinary culture conservation and proper communication, which is also essential to ensure the authenticity and territorial identity that food tourists demand. The commerce administration will also have a say in development, as it watches over the needs of the food retail industry. Employment administrations will also be interested, and the list goes on. In many countries, the splitting of responsibilities among different public administrations is strict, and interaction among them can be difficult and cumbersome.

The need to involve both public and private stakeholders in development of food tourism can also pose a challenge to timely development of food tourism, as the interaction between public administrations and private stakeholders is often regulated by a strict and official communication protocol that is ineffective for pursuing a shared goal.

The Power of Collaboration

We discussed that some of the biggest challenges of developing food tourism are related to the enormous fragmentation of the industry, which is comprised of a large number of very different stakeholders. Successful and effective development, as we have also discussed, can only be accomplished if all stakeholders participate in this development, voicing their needs and contributing their expertise and resources.

Coordination of such a large and heterogeneous set of stakeholders can be done in a number of ways, but typically involves creating a collaborative structure/network, where all stakeholders are represented and where they can all contribute their knowledge, resources and views. Building collaborative networks has been widely suggested in recent research as essential for sustainable development of food tourism.[12]

To ensure effectiveness of this collaborative network, unified management is needed to coordinate and lead the development efforts. Unified management of the network should be exercised via a management body that is highly representative of the various types of stakeholders in order to maintain commitment from all of them to the alliance.

A common management structure can support the communication flows that are necessary to produce a unified strategy which is in line with all stakeholders' objectives; it can also make the most of the resources that are scattered across the different stakeholders – be in it the form of funding or skills. Unified management will also be more effective in raising external funding and better positioned to procure external services at competitive prices. An example of some of the points mentioned here is the procurement of e-commerce platforms, which may be out of reach for individual businesses but can be easily undertaken by a partnership where each contributes its share of the cost.

The benefits of collaborative networks in food tourism development can be summarized as follows:

Unified management ➜ Effective
Unified strategy ➜ Focused
Unified efforts ➜ Stronger
All feel involved ➜ Motivated
All contribute expertise ➜ Knowledgeable

Benefits of Collaborative Networks in Food Tourism

A number of countries have already implemented this type of collaboration structures, with various degrees of stakeholder participation. From the less inclusive scope of Saborea España, which is comprised, at management level, of the restaurant association, professional chefs associations and the association of DMOs,[13] to the wider scope of Prove Portugal, which recognizes that "Tourism of Portugal, Regional Tourism Organizations and Island Territories, Business and Professional Associations, Central (Economy, Agriculture and Fishing, Culture) and Local Administration Organizations, professional Public and Private Organizations – all have an important role to play."[14] Future research can provide interesting data in regards to the efficiency and scope of the results attained by these different management structures.

Creating an Effective Food Tourism Development Partnership

Taking the Lead

As seen earlier, a unified approach towards development of food tourism is the most effective way to ensure sustainable development of this niche. A unified approach, however, will not happen spontaneously; it will need a driving force that can involve all necessary stakeholders and provide the initial support needed to create a common working structure.

The initiative to bring all stakeholders together can originate with any of them, but is best undertaken by a widely recognized institution that can legitimately pursue development of food tourism. In most European countries, where public administrations are large, the initiative to established national food tourism frameworks has been undertaken by the national tourism administrations. This is the case of the frameworks mentioned for Spain and Portugal, and also the case of Ireland.[15] Some other initiatives, such as Genuss Region Östereich,[16] in Austria, were promoted by public administrations responsible for agriculture. In geographies with smaller public administrations, the initiative can be promoted by professional associations, privately managed destination tourism bureaus or visitors associations.

Taking the lead for the establishment of a food tourism framework should ideally be part of a wider scope strategy at the leading institution, and not an isolated idea that may respond to an exceptional opportunity or situation. Framing the development of food tourism inside a solid and stable development policy of wider scope ensures sustained support from the leading institution and a better chance at gathering support from other stakeholders.[17]

Securing Initial Funding

Until the partnership is effectively created and an internal funding strategy has been defined and implemented, the leading organization should be prepared to cover the costs that will be generated during the partnership setup. These costs are mainly comprised of labor, basic office infrastructure and resources, meeting costs and travel. Some initial planning will be necessary in order to accurately forecast these costs and secure funding, either from the lead organization, a group of initial partners, or any other source.

Identifying the Stakeholders to Involve

For the food tourism development framework to be effective, as we have widely discussed in previous sections, it must include the views and resources of all stakeholders who can play a part in it. It is therefore important that a first inventory is done to determine who is who in the region where the partnership will be established: what food manufacturers exist, what tour operators, culinary schools, etc., and who best represents them in order to reach out to them.[18] Relevant public administrations in the areas of tourism, culture, food and health, etc. should also be considered, as well as professional associations and NGOs that may be active in these areas. Representation options for the local community and the visitors should also be planned for. A stakeholder register, as described by the Project Management Institute, can be a useful tool at this point to gather information about all potential partners or participants.[19] This document will also be of great help, once the partnership is established, to ensure appropriate communication with all stakeholders.

Securing Stakeholder Participation

Once the region's stakeholders have been identified, a comprehensive communication strategy should be devised by the leading organization to raise awareness and engage/enlist support from as many food tourism stakeholders as possible. Awareness building efforts typically consists of:

- Communicating the benefits of food tourism development;
- Explaining the need for collaboration among stakeholders; and
- Presenting the benefits of becoming actively involved.

It is important to bear in mind that not all stakeholders may be willing or able to participate in the food tourism development framework at this early stage. Setting up a truly representative and effective partnership may take some time, especially in regions with no food tourism background. Regions where similar stakeholders are not organized in associations or other representative bodies may also pose a challenge at this step. To avoid excessive delays in the partnership setup, a limited group of stakeholders can be enlisted to promote the creation of an initial working structure that can be later enlarged, as other stakeholders become interested.

Participation in the partnership can be structured in different ways. Some stakeholders may want to play a very active 'promoter' role; others may want to take an external role and collaborate only in a particular area via collaboration agreements; others may choose to participate in a consultant role; and others may ask to be simply kept informed of the actions. The level of implication in the partnership should ideally depend on the stakeholder's degree of potential impact and interest in food tourism development. In practice, however, the level of involvement may be affected by the degree of knowledge of the niche and its potential, and by the resources that each stakeholder can assign to this task. When the partnership creation is promoted by a public administration, every effort should be made to ensure that these, or other impediments, do not get in the way, and that relevant stakeholders can participate in a role that is in accordance to their potential impact on the common mission of developing food tourism.

Agreeing on Mission Scope

Once the initial set of participants has been identified, it is advisable to promote discussion about, and agreement among participating stakeholders on, the scope of the partnership's mission. This step will ensure that all stakeholders can contribute their vision of what the partnership should pursue, which will result in a stronger and on a clear understanding of the partnership's global mission by all involved.[20]

90

Some disagreements are bound to happen at this stage, but this should not deter the leading organization from promoting this discussion. Disagreements or differences in understanding of the partnership's mission are best tackled now, when they can be discussed without jeopardizing the continuity of action plans that will have already consumed a certain amount of resources.

Regardless of who the leading organization might be, this institution will normally have a partial interest in food tourism development, which will be shaped by the institution's ultimate mission. When the DMO is the leading organization, for example, the partnership creation is promoted by a stakeholder who is specifically focused on increasing visitor numbers and spending. This stakeholder, however, may be unfamiliar with other equally important food tourism benefits, such as local employment, reinforcement of local culture, increase of local food sales, etc., and may have not included them in the initial scope of the partnership. When the leading organization takes a step back and this point, it creates the conditions needed for the construction of a common mission that covers a wider range of development areas.

Defining the Organization and Work Methodology

The leading organization's last role as promoter of the partnership is to facilitate the establishment of a set of procedures to regulate its functions. Clearly documented procedures are essential to transform a heterogeneous group of food tourism stakeholders into an effective team capable of pursuing common goals.

Working procedures for a food tourism partnership can follow a pre-established pattern that the leading organization promotes. This is the case, for example, in Mexico, where the National Tourism Administration promotes the creation of 'Tourism Product Clubs,' a collaboration system aimed at developing specific tourism niches that was initially created by the Canadian Tourism Commission.[21]

Collaboration models can also be created specifically for a food tourism development partnership, either by the leading organization or by the initial stakeholders. In either case, the resulting set of working procedures must have ample support from the participating stakeholders in order to maintain their interest and commitment to the initiative.

Working procedures for a food tourism development partnership may differ in content and level of detail but should always cover, at least, the following areas:

Roles: A clear organizational structure for the partnership should be defined, with precise splitting of responsibilities for the management and the non-management roles. This organizational structure should be able to lead and coordinate stakeholders once the partnership has been fully set up. Although the leading organization will always be an important stakeholder, and may therefore maintain a relevant role in the partnership, its function - once the partnership is fully set up - will normally be substantially different from the initial leading role, and will need to be clearly defined to avoid excessive interference.

Directives to determine how the management and non-management positions will be filled and how they will be updated should also be defined at this stage. This set of procedures should be designed bearing in mind that new stakeholders may be incorporated at later stages. Those future stakeholders should be given the opportunity to participate in the partnership in a role according to their potential impact in food tourism development, and not dependent on the time that they joined. Procedures that are designed to incorporate new stakeholders and give them the appropriate level of responsibility make the partnership attractive and open for stakeholders who may not have been initially interested or able to participate, those who may not have been initially recognized as relevant for food tourism, or those who may appear later in the form of new businesses or organizations that did not previously exist.

Communication: To ensure effective communication among physically and functionally distant stakeholders, clear internal communication processes must be defined. The partnership's internal communication procedures must be designed taking into consideration the communication limitations of each stakeholder and effectively enable them to 1) voice their views; 2) participate in project work; and 3) receive timely communications. These procedures can include face to face meetings, technology platforms and anything in between, as long as they are adapted to the real communication needs of the partnership.

Communication needs may be different if the partnership's scope is local, regional or national. Geographically limited partnerships, for example, may rely on face to face meetings which may be impracticable for larger-scope networks. The partnership's maturity can also be accompanied by more complex communication demands, as advanced common projects will require intense data sharing. The implementation of a shared commercialization platform, for example, is a good example of a scenario where very detailed communication procedures are needed to define the product data input and other data processing with the help of a technological tool.

Membership: Basic rules describing the requirements and steps to become a member should be clearly defined and published to facilitate the incorporation of new stakeholders while maintaining the partnership's focus and effectiveness. Membership requirements should be designed taking into account a wide range of potential future partners, who may not have been recognized, able or existing at the setup stage, and who can contribute valid knowledge and resources for the development of food tourism. In this respect it is particularly important that membership rules do not to restrict access exclusively to businesses or institutions similar to the initial participating stakeholders.

Funding: For the partnership to be able to function, beyond the initial support of the leading organization, a detailed funding strategy must be defined and implemented. Although the leading organization may provide sustained financial support for the initiative, this support will rarely cover all the partnership's costs, as it will be expected that other partners contribute funds in accordance with the benefits that the partnership will provide them. Internal funding procedures will therefore need to be defined to complement the leading organization's financial contribution and to cover the most basic partnership's costs, when that contribution ceases to exist.

All of the above mentioned working procedures can, and should, evolve with time, as the partnership grows and new needs arise. The initial regulations should therefore be flexible enough to allow for reconfiguration without risking the partnership's existence. Transparency and clearness of the procedures are also fundamental to avoid differences in interpretations and to keep the partnership truly open and attractive for new members.

Creating a Food Tourism Development Plan

With a solid working structure, a funding plan and a clear mission, a food tourism development partnership is ready to tackle the task of developing this niche in a given region. Developing food tourism in a collaborative way will follow the same general steps applicable to a generic tourism development plan[22] and can be summarized as follows:

Analyzing the Current Food Tourism Development Situation

A sustainable and successful food tourism development plan must be based in thorough analysis of the current state of food tourism development. This analysis will help the partnership understand the issues that food tourism development faces in the region and design a strategy to overcome them. Basic analysis of the region's degree of development of food tourism can be performed via the World Food Travel Association's E.A.S.I. methodology, for example.[23] Additional quantitative and qualitative analysis will also be needed in order to provide a good basis in which to base an effective development strategy.

Food tourism development analysis for a specific region will normally be split into analysis of the resources, offer, demand, and positioning of the destination. It can also include benchmarking of the destination against destinations that may be especially successful in certain aspects.

Defining a Unified Development Strategy

The food tourism development partnership can now design a development strategy aimed at overcoming the current weaknesses of the industry and the threats it faces, taking advantage of its strengths and opportunities. Defining a development strategy normally entails two main steps: 1) definition of strategic goals; and 2) agreement on tactics to reach these goals. Ireland's National Food Tourism Implementation Framework provides a good example that illustrates these actions.[24] Its development framework cites the following strategic goals:

- Quality and value – Ensuring that the quality of food and service offered to visitors (...) is of consistently high standard and competitively priced. (...)

- Availability – Expanding the number and variety of food-related experiences (...).

- Authenticity – Ensuring that all food experiences promoted to visitors offer a unique and distinctive Irish flavour (...).

And, as strategies to attain these goals:

- Research and benchmarking – Supporting fact-based planning and decision-making.

- Business and sector support – Helping industry operators to build their capabilities and improve business performance.

- Marketing and promotion – Strengthening the positioning of Ireland as a food tourism destination.

Creating Implementation/Operational Plans

To realize the partnership's strategic goals, the above strategies need to be further refined into tangible and measurable objectives and accompanied by specific action plans to reach them. This process, known as operational planning, translates the more generic goals and strategies into very tangible project plans, with very specific objectives, resources and timelines.

To reach the Irish strategic goals of *Quality*, *Availability* and *Authenticity*, via the strategy of creating *Business and Sector Support*, for example, the Irish Food Tourism partnership decided to put in place a specific project to "Develop education and training programs that seek to build individual and collective capabilities to deliver high quality Irish food experiences".[25] Under this generic title, a very specific project plan must be defined that specifies the expected outcomes, the budget and resources to be used, and the deadline for completion. The definition of a set of operational plans, consisting on specific implementation projects, will drive the partnership, project by project, closer to its established goals.

Managing Operational Plans/Projects to Completion

Although it is not the objective of this chapter to explain project management methodology, it is important to remind the reader that operational planning, which will result in a set of specific implementation projects, must be followed by strong project management in order to ensure project success.[26] Solid and standardized project management methodology will prove invaluable at this stage, as it can help manage the complex projects that will result from a food tourism development strategy; projects that will typically involve a large number of stakeholders across a number of very different organizations. A standardized project management methodology will also ensure correct closure of implementation projects, which should ideally assess project success and detail lessons learned.[27]

Reviewing Accomplishments and Redefining Strategy

Aside from the individual project success assessment, it benefits the partnership to evaluate and report on the success of the complete strategy. Assessing the success of the food tourism development strategy entails measuring the degree to which the completion of the implementation projects have effectively helped reach the previously defined strategic goals. In Ireland's example above, this step involves measuring how much the development of "education and training programs" has impacted the "quality and value, availability and authenticity" of the food experiences.

A second level of assessment would be to measure the degree to which reaching those strategic goals has truly impacted development in the region, in the terms that were intended by the food tourism development strategy. Reviewing these accomplishments and reporting on them is an integral part of any development plan, but also a frequently overlooked step. Skipping this important step is often caused by the difficulty of evaluating results which are often intangible and, others, by the fear that reporting will highlight the shortcomings of a poor development plan. Ignoring this fundamental step, however, will prevent the partnership from fully understanding the mistakes made and from learning from them, which is essential in order to refocus the partnership's strategy into a truly effective plan. Failing to report on results will also turn the partnership into an opaque structure that may create mistrust from stakeholders, in particular those who may not be directly involved in the planning. A regular and comprehensive review of the actions undertaken by the partnership is therefore highly recommended, both as a tool to correct potential deviations and as a communication tool to demonstrate transparency.

CONCLUSION

Effective development of food tourism that generates wide-ranging benefits requires the participation of a large and varied set of stakeholders. These stakeholders include public administrations at different levels and in different areas; small, medium and large businesses and NGO's of various sectors; and less structured groups of people such as the local community and the visitors. Active involvement of all these stakeholders in food tourism development efforts contributes resources to the cause, as well as diversity of perspectives, both important to ensure efficient implementation of a development strategy and effective accomplishment of development goals.

A collaborative approach to food tourism development requires a unified management structure and a clear set of working procedures that can support the coordination of all stakeholders. These procedures should be detailed enough to avoid confusion, overlapping of tasks, or divergence in focus, but flexible enough to accommodate changes in the partnership, in particular those related to the incorporation of new stakeholders.

A well-structured food tourism development partnership is best positioned to design and implement an effective food tourism development plan. Food tourism development plans should be based on ample research and follow a solid planning and project management methodology in order to ensure coherence with agreed mission and effective completion of planned actions.

A stable food tourism partnership that is widely representative of the industry stakeholders and that follows solid working methods can effectively pursue the development of this niche to the benefit of all involved.

DISCUSSION QUESTIONS

1. Does your area have a food tourism strategic plan? If so, how does its structure match the recommendations in this chapter?
2. What might be some challenges of involving both local and regional or national governments? How could such challenges be overcome?
3. What are some ways to involve stakeholders that may not otherwise participate, especially small businesses with only one or two employees?

ENDNOTES

[1] PMI, 2008, p. 23.
[2] Van der Stoep, 2000.
[3] Tresserras, Medina & Matamala, 2007.
[4] Richards, 2012.
[5] Wolf, 2006.
[6] Hall, Mitchell & Sharples, 2003.
[7] e.g. Hall & Sharples, 2003; Medina & Tresserras, 2007; Richards, 2012.
[8] Espeitx, 2007.
[9] Hall, 2008.
[10] Hall & Sharples, 2003.
[11] Ruiz de Lera, 2012
[12] e.g. Richards, 2009; Hall, 2008; Ruiz de Lera, 2012
[13] www.tastingspain.es/que_es.php
[14] www.taste-portugal.com/sobre-o-programa/about-program
[15] www.failteireland.ie/In-Your-Sector/Food-Tourism-in-Ireland.aspx
[16] www.genuss-region.at
[17] Hall, 2012.
[18] A praiseworthy example of efforts in this area is the LEADER-funded Project "Pon Aragón en tu mesa", which has produced extensive data on this subject. (see ponaragonentumesa.com).
[19] PMI, 2008, p. 248-251.
[20] Boyne & Hall, 2003.
[21] SECTUR, 2001.
[22] Literature in the area of tourism planning is extensive. Examples for further reference on this matter are: UNWTO, 2007, chapter II; Goeldner & Brent Ritchie, 2009 (first edition 1972), chapter 16; Tribe (2005 & 2010) and Schulte, 2003, chapter IV.
[23] Educate, Assess, Implement and Strategize. See www.worldfoodtravel.org for more information.
[24] Failte Ireland, National Food Tourism Implementation Framework, 2010, p. 10.
[25] Failte Ireland, p. 18.

[26] Two project and task management tools used effectively by the World Food Travel Association are TeamWorkPM.net and todoist.com.

[27] Further information on project closure can be consulted in PMI, 2008, chapters 3.7 and 4.6.

Creating a Food & Drink Tourism Product Inventory

Gloria Rodríguez

This chapter is mainly written to benefit destination management organizations and trade associations wishing to promote the development of food tourism in their region. The information and tools provided here will help these organizations identify and assess the food tourism products that exist in their region. Understanding product potential and product deficit is critical for destinations to fully exploit the potential of food tourism. Creating concise product inventories is a powerful tool that will help a destination better understand the composition and characteristics of its existing food tourism offering.

INTRODUCTION

Identifying and understanding a destination's current food tourism offer is essential in order to determine the effectiveness of a food tourism strategy and to make any necessary adjustments.

Correct assessment of a destination's food tourism offer begins with the compilation of a food tourism product inventory. This step is particularly relevant in food tourism, as many potential tourism products may be "hidden" in the form of food related services that were not initially created for tourists. Identifying all products that can be marketed to the food tourist will help a destination assess its food tourism potential and define an effective strategy to pursue it. Product inventories can also help determine if a critical mass of products exists and may uncover otherwise hidden opportunities.

Although the creation of this type of inventory may seem like a simple task, it is often obstructed by a widespread misconception of the terms "asset", "product", "offer", etc. To facilitate the task of creating a precise food tourism product inventory, this chapter begins by clarifying the above mentioned terms. Once the term food tourism product is clear, we address, step by step, the tasks of building a product inventory for a specific destination or region.

Semantics

Even though tourism development is a widely studied discipline, the relatively new food tourism niche is still a scarcely explored subject.[1] As a result, many of the basic concepts that are needed for a correct definition of its components are still unclear, undefined, or simply understood differently by some of the players involved. For the specific task of inventorying a destination's food tourism offer, there are a number of concepts that must be first clarified to avoid confusion that can lead to incorrect or incomplete inventory results.

The Food Tourist

Understanding food tourism as a form of cultural tourism, we will consider the food tourist to be the person whose motivation to travel outside of his/her normal place of residence is the desire to experience food and drink culture in any of its possible manifestations. This definition, based on the conceptual definition of cultural tourism proposed by ATLAS[2] should be understood in its broadest sense, to encompass all possible activities that allow a visitor to experience a destination's food and drink culture. Food tourism activities may include, among others, visits to primary or secondary food producers, food festivals, restaurants, cooking schools or specialist tours.[3] The list of possible activities is not, however, restricted to these; any food or drink related activity in which a visitor can participate and that enables him/her to experience food could be considered a food tourism activity. Maintaining this broad concept of food tourism is important in order to fully exploit the possibilities that food tourism presents.

Food Assets

In the framework of food and drink tourism, we will use the term food asset to refer to any food or drink related element present at a given destination and associated to the local food and drink culture. These assets may be:

- tangible (a specific vegetable variety, a food or drink production infrastructure or even a food or drink production landscape),
- intangible (a food/drink processing technique, a food/drink consumption tradition, etc.)
- mixed (a food- or drink-related local business, a food or drink museum, etc.)

Food Tourism Attraction

The more restrictive term of food tourism attraction will be used to name a food asset that is capable of attracting visitors to a given destination. In order for this asset to be considered an attraction it will therefore need to be known by potential visitors, interesting to them, and accessible.

Food Tourism Product

A food tourism product, on the other hand, is a product (or service) that visitors can procure in order to experience one or several food or drink assets. To be considered a food tourism product, the food-related service must be therefore priced, distributed and promoted.[4] A food tourism product can be a guided tour, a local cuisine class, meal service at a restaurant, or any other food-related service available for tourists.

Food Tourism Offer

Finally, we will define a destination's food tourism offer as the complete set of food tourism products that can be consumed/experienced/enjoyed in a given destination.

From Asset to Attraction to Product

Asset to Attraction

Although all of your food assets will be valuable elements of your food culture, not all of them may constitute effective food tourism attractions. For a food asset to be considered a food attraction, it will need to be known, interesting and accessible to visitors. Most likely, however, not all of you food assets will arouse interest in your target market. Among the potentially interesting assets, not all of them will be sufficiently known outside of your region. Even attractive and well known assets do not constitute food tourism attractions unless they are accessible to visitors.

Making your assets accessible to visitors entails:

- Communicating where, when and how these assets can be experienced/enjoyed
- Creating/ensuring physical access to assets (e.g. constructing access paths to production fields, building exhibition premises or museums for tangible food-related elements, etc.)

- Creating/ensuring intellectual access to assets (translating information, providing guided services, providing written descriptions, etc.)

A common mistake in this area is forgetting that accessibility is vital and investing in promoting food and drink assets that cannot be easily experienced by visitors. Take a country's or region's traditional cuisine, for example. This is an intangible food-related asset that is commonly used to promote as a significant tourist attraction. Ask yourself, however, what are the chances that a given food tourist will be able to experience this asset as advertised or as expected? Will they have a way to easily locate it or, in other words, to differentiate traditional from non-traditional cuisine? Is there a certification/information system at restaurants/food shops/etc. that visitors can rely on to ensure they experience "the real thing"? Are you providing sufficient background information about this asset to visitors? Is it in their language? Is your traditional cuisine even available at restaurants, or are your traditional dishes only really prepared in private homes? If so, do visitors have a way to procure a home-made food experience?

These are some examples of accessibility issues that can render a valuable food asset impossible or difficult to experience for visitors. Promotion of food assets under these conditions will generate expectations in your food tourists that are impossible to fulfill. Luring visitors to your destination with promises of joys you can hardly guarantee will harm your brand image quickly, as visitors are now keen to share their opinions and take other travelers' opinions quite seriously.

Attractions to Products

Your food attractions, properly communicated and promoted, can encourage a potential food tourist travel. These tourism flows can generate regional income in the form of:

- Visitor expenditure on basic tourism services (accommodation, transport, etc.)
- Visitor expenditure on services procured to experience the food attractions (food sales, food tours, food classes, etc.)

While you can certainly take advantage of your 'open-access' food and drink attractions by capitalizing of the expenditure that visitors will make on basic services at your destination, a more profitable approach would be to build additional services that feed on this attraction and offer the tourist additional ways to enjoy it. This process is what we call food tourism product creation. Creating innovative and interesting ways to experience your food and drink attractions (i.e. building new food and drink tourism products) will give your destination a myriad of possibilities to generate additional income from visitors.

Food tourism products/services provide not only an additional means of generating income for our destination, but also an additional means for visitors to enjoy your food assets. These products/services can even become an attraction on their own right, drawing additional visitors that may have otherwise not chosen your destination. Famous food events around the world are a good example. Based on the local food assets, food events typically provide an interesting way for visitors to experience these assets and attract many visitors that may have not chosen the destination if this product were not available.

The most common food tourism products, and an essential part of any food tourism offer, are your local cuisine restaurants (or, strictly speaking, the dining services offered at these restaurants). Although consumption is an essential activity for the food tourist, it is important to remember that is it not the only way to experience food. The food tourist, being essentially a cultural tourist, is not just interested in tasting, but also in learning, in observing, in participating of food or drink activities of all sorts. In general, the more interesting and varied your food tourism offer is, the more chances at success your destination will have in food and drink tourism.

Identifying Your Food Tourism Products

Once clarified what a food tourism product is, the task of inventorying is a matter of careful observation. As we saw before, your food tourism offer will be composed of the food tourism products available in the market for tourist consumption/enjoyment in your destination. Your food tourism product inventory will not include, therefore, your food assets or food attractions, unless they are effective commercial products. Your local cuisine, for example, will not be included in this inventory; your wineries will not necessarily be part of it either, unless they offer cellar door sales, tastings, or any other paid service accessible to visitors.

To facilitate the task of pointing out the products available at your destination, the table below can be used as guide of potential food and drink tourism products. By examining each category carefully you should be able to uncover all existing products in your area.

Resource Type	Service Type	Product Type	Example
Basic (themed) services	Lodging	food and drink themed accommodation	chocolate hotel www.hotelchocolate.com.mx
		accommodation in food and drink premises or surroundings other	hotel at winery www.hotel-marquesderiscal.com
	Transport	transport routes serving one or various food and drink assets food and drink themed transport	wine bus stopping at various wineries and/or vineyards apfelwein tram www.ebbelwei-express.com
		other	
Food and drink services	Consumption	a la carte dining, snaking or drinking	restaurant menu
		set-price dining, snaking, or drinking	tasting menu at restaurant
		tastings	paid product tasting event
		catering services	hire a cook
		other	
	Purchase	permanent markets	food hall
		temporary markets	open air farmer's market
		specialty shops	spice shop
		other	
	Education	cooking classes	regional cuisine class
		food and drink production classes	herb growing class, beer-making class
		other classes (food history, culture, preservation, etc.)	wine pairing class

		congresses	e.g. Yale Food Symposium www.yalefoodsymposium.org
		other	
	Visit	admittance to food and drink exhibits, museums, etc.	rice museum (http://www.irri.org/)
		guided visits to any food-related asset	guided visit to fruit plantation
		other	
	Participation	practice activities	pick-your-own fruit
		creative activities	recipe development event
		games	food contests
		other	
	Rental	food preparation infrastructure, equipment or space (do your own)	open kitchens (www.kitchenclub.es)
		food consumption infrastructure, equipment or space (bring your own)	table rental at near-water locations
		food production infrastructure, equipment or space (grow/breed your own)	self-gardening allotments
		other	
	Mixed	products including several of the above food and drink services (priced as a whole).	food tours including several visits, multi-activity food events, cooking class + dinner products, etc.
	Enhanced	products including one or various food and drink services + additional (non-basic) services (such as cultural activities), priced as a whole.	medieval staged dinner, movie + recreation of dinner seen, etc.
Packaged services	Lodging + food and drink	hotel + meal packages	romantic weekend package including room and dinner.
		hotel + other food and drink services	food experience package including overnight, fruit picking and fruit-themed cooking class.
	Transport + food and drink	ride + meal packages	bus ride from neighboring cities and pre-set menu at special restaurant in your destination.
		ride + other food and drink services	mushroom picking excursion including transport to area and supervised picking.

| Lodging + transportation + food and drink | hotel + transport to destination + food and drink services | wine-themed weekend including flight, overnight at hotel, visit to winery, wine tasting and wine purchase. |
| Flexible | personalized products | culinary on-demand tours |

When working with the list above, remember that only paid and established services available for visitors can be considered effective food and drink tourism products. Free activities or services that are not regularly offered do not constitute commercial products.

When inventorying your food tourism products, it is also wise to differentiate between the business that offers the service and the service itself. A cooking school, for example, will be a food and drink related business, but the food and drink tourism product will be the class (or set of classes) that are offered and open to external visitors.

Completing Your Inventory

For your food tourism product inventory to be useful, it will need to reflect not only the complete list of products available in your destination, but also a minimum set of characteristics that can help you assess the performance, potential, and limitations of each product, and of your offer as a whole.

The product characteristics that will need to be recorded to facilitate assessment of your offer will largely depend on the objectives that you have defined for your food tourism development strategy. If your destination's objectives fall exclusively in the realm of economic growth, you will be looking at recording, in your inventory, attributes like: sales figures, profitability numbers, tax collected, employment generated, etc. If your objectives include improvements in the environmental area, you will want to record other attributes such as: ratio of local vs. imported resources used, pollution generated, etc. Sociocultural objectives may be assessed in your inventory if you include: degree to which product respects/reflects local traditions, number of local users of the products (or ratio of local vs. external users of the product) or capacity building potential of product on local community.[5]

Other more specific attributes will be needed in order to help you assess, in greater depth, the potential for improvement of your food tourism products. The most relevant of these attributes will normally be those that help you assess potential sales growth. The product attributes that will help you best assess this potential will be those that reflect how well your products are adapted to your demand. This will entail including in your inventory the attributes that reflect how well your product is adapted to the expectations of the food tourist[6] and, among these, to those that are particularly important for your destination's target market.

Although the attributes that can best reflect your offer's adequacy for demand may vary from region to region, there are some product characteristics that will always be relevant for today's food tourism and should always be considered in your inventory. Among these, consider:

- Opening times (to ensure tourist-appropriate)
- Exact location (to determine critical mass)
- Languages supported
- Cultural value of food asset(s) involved

- Level of interpretation provided
- Level of visitor participation permitted
- Distribution methods (where are the products available for purchase, is e-commerce an option, etc.)
- Communication methods (where are the products advertised, when, how, etc.)

To make inventory building practical, you should only aim to reflect the product attributes that have the largest impact in attracting and satisfying your target market. This will obviously require in-depth knowledge of your demand characteristics, in the form of statistical studies that should have been performed before you attempt to build your inventory.

For your inventory to be truly effective, it is important that it is dimensioned correctly, i.e. steering away from over-detailed charts but also away from simple products lists that will offer insufficient data for your analysis.

Challenges to Inventory Assessment

While we present straightforward advice to collect data about and build a food and drink tourism product inventory, a few challenges may arise in creating such an inventory.

Urban destinations, for example, with large numbers of food tourism products, may find it difficult to detail each product individually. In those cases, an effective strategy is to group products with similar characteristics. In your inventory you would reflect the product type (e.g. local cuisine restaurants) and the number of similar products that exist, together with the characteristics that they share and that you have determined as relevant. Further breakdown of this initial list may be needed at a later stage, if your strategy calls for further analysis or action upon one or several product types. At that point, more exhaustive inventories can be produced with the help of automated processes.

Rural destinations, on the other hand, may encounter issues with incomplete, inexact or altogether missing addresses. Businesses in scarcely populated areas or areas with little urban planning may offer "descriptive" addresses of which visitors may, or may not, make sense of.[7] Inexact or missing addresses make geo-mapping impossible and complicate the task of creating visitor maps. Great geographic distance between businesses is another issue that often arises in rural destinations. In areas with a small density of food or drink related businesses, it may be difficult to define the geographical area that the inventory should cover, striking a balance between covering a sufficient number of businesses and limiting the inventory to an area that can be easily shown on a visitor map.

Another potential challenge may be difficulties obtaining recent, quality tourism data and visitor spending. Data about spending on food and drink may not exist, in which case we recommend using the 23-28% of total visitor spending rule presented elsewhere in this book. It is also possible that the number and type of visitor arrivals is unknown. Some destinations do a better job of measuring inbound visitor data than others. It is highly likely that the businesses in question may not have a clear picture of what percent of their total income is attributable to visitors from outside their area. In that case, credit card companies can be of help. If the business accepts credit cards, it may contact its credit card processor for customer origin data, which all payment processors have access to. This data, provided in aggregate to avoid privacy issues, can provide insightful information regarding customer origin, both in terms of percentage of sales attributable to tourism and in the form of demographics of these external visitors.

In general, the most challenging part of building a regional inventory will be to populate it with reliable data that must be collected from a diverse range of businesses. Creating a simple questionnaire, providing businesses support to complete it and gaining their collaboration by communicating the ample benefits of the analysis can go a long way in facilitating this task.

CONCLUSION

Food tourism product inventories can be a powerful tool for an effective assessment of a destination's food and drink tourism offer. Building these inventories entails correct identification of existing food tourism products and careful selection of their most relevant characteristics.

The task of identifying food and drink tourism products is often obstructed by a generalized misunderstanding of the term food and drink tourism product. This confusion can result in inaccurate or incomplete inventories, which will lead to incorrect offer assessment and, ultimately, to ineffective food tourism development strategies.

Correct identification of the most relevant product characteristics is also key to effective inventorying. This task will require previous statistical analysis of your demand's expectations as well as throughout understanding of the destination's ultimate goals for developing food and drink tourism.

With a complete and accurate food tourism product inventory in hand, you will be best armed to assess your current food and drink tourism offer and to make the adjustments needed in order to convert it into a set of products that can truly help you reach your development goals.

DISCUSSION QUESTIONS

1. What unique challenges would a very large metropolitan area have to create a complete and reliable food tourism asset inventory?
2. An inventory could go out of date very quickly. What could a tourism office do to prevent this from happening?
3. What is a suitable geographic area around which to do a food tourism asset inventory? In other words, how far out from a town or city should an inventory reach?

ENDNOTES

[1] e.g. Hall & Sharples, 2003; Medina & Tresserras, 2007; Richards, 2012
[2] Association for Tourism and Leisure Education (www.atlas-euro.org), Definitions found at Richards, 1996, 23.
[3] Hall & Mitchell, 2001.
[4] See UNWTO's *tourism resource to tourism product* process definition (UNWTO, 1998, 187).
[5] A complete list of sustainable tourism indicators can be consulted in UNWTO (2005).
[6] Further study of these characteristics is provided in this book in the *How Foodies Make Decisions* chapter.
[7] For example, Fleur's Place in Moreaki, Otago, New Zealand, a fish restaurant popular with locals and visitors alike, is located off a dirt road on a small headland on the ocean, a considerable distance from the main highway and a solid hour's drive north of Dunedin, the nearest town. By nearly everyone's opinion, the restaurant is worth the trip. When asking directions, visitors are told simply to turn right or left (depending on the original direction) and "drive to the end of the road and you'll see it." Technically the restaurant does have a physical address but no one seems to use it.

Special Role of Agriculture

Tracy Berno, Urban Laurin, & Giorgos Maltezakis

This chapter discusses the role of agriculture in food tourism and the relationship between tourism and agriculture. Included are case studies showcasing best practices from the South Pacific, Greece and Sweden.

INTRODUCTION

With an abundance of print and online articles, the instructional nature of television programming and more travel experience overall, travelers today increasingly demand more authentic experiences. The preparation and types of food provide a powerful, multi-sensory means of expressing one's local culture and heritage. As such, a distinctive local cuisine provides an unparalleled marketing opportunity for any destination. Local foods, supported by local agriculture, therefore, can be key for tourism development. As Boyne, Williams and Hall (2001, 5)[1] point out, "...where destination areas' [high quality] food and beverage [and other] production are [used] to strengthen the tourism product, and tourists are encouraged to purchase and consume locally produced agricultural products thereby stimulating local primary production sectors, we see a bi-directional development process – food production for tourism and tourism for food production."

Agriculture is a prerequisite for food tourism as the seeds of cuisine are in agriculture. It is agriculture that produces most of the raw materials that tourists eat. Many farmers refine raw materials into finished products. Direct sales and visits with producers create experiences for tourists, and sales and customer contact for the farmers. More and more farmers are developing their business to include tourism and culinary experiences because they see the need to diversify and the financial benefit that follows. Such tourism contributes to the economic and social development in the rural sector. As a result of these linkages, the benefits of linking tourism and agriculture go beyond the actual product "on the plate." Some of the direct and indirect benefits of linking agriculture and tourism are:

- Increased economic development
- Pride of place, generating attractive, vital and viable rural areas
- A vibrant and locally distinctive tourism product

This chapter examines some of the benefits to the food tourist and food producers, while addressing some of the possible corresponding challenges.

Special Role of Agriculture

Agriculture provides a basis for which a visitor may be introduced to a new culture. When looking at agriculture, the experience for the visitor has a certain totality in the ways culinary cultures are presented. Understanding the systems within which agricultural practices engage into the shaping of a local culture and how both culture and environment interact within a certain social and geographical space, introduces to the tourist a fuller picture of the culture at hand. In other words it is the way culture is communicated through food as a total process that includes production (agritourism, farm visits, visits to vegetable gardens etc.), preparation (cooking classes, fermentation processes), and consumption (end products, wine tastings, fine dining) that make sense as a culinary journey.

Setting agriculture as the starting point of any culinary trip is the perfect introduction to an authentic and original lifestyle the visitor is about to experience. Agricultural practices become the start of a unique and memorable experience that will introduce the visitor to a brand new world full of flavors and aromas. It combines the ingenuity of the human mind together with what the environment has to offer, as well as, the cultural, social, and economic interconnections that come with it. According to Cai, Gartner and Manner (2009) tourists that engage in these types of activities are looking for elements that create a much simpler way of life than the ones they follow back home in both psychological and physical terms, which in turn is reflected in their culture through hospitality.

The authentic experience for the tourist is also within the romantic, often exotic, character of an agricultural area. The originality of practices used for the production of the essential materials and produce incorporated in a cuisine creates a feeling which is often outside the everyday visitor experience. Distinct from the urban spaces most of us are used to, we often lose touch with the love and attention to detail shown by farmers and people of rural areas when it comes to the actual production of food. Hall (2003) in the example of French wine and food tourism marketing practices and the ways within which the French countryside is depicted in local brochures, contends that the use of images depicting the cultural dimension food in French society is rarely depicted. Instead, there is the general demonstration of food products as simple materials used for cooking. However it is the ways people use these ingredients and the importance they hold for the local people that make the region attractive as a culinary destination. A grandmother painting eggs for Greek Orthodox Easter is much more appealing visual to the traveler than the painted egg by itself.

Agriculture and Food: Fast to Slow Food Movement

This movement towards 'authentic' regional or local cuisine is not exclusive to the domain of tourism. In response to the growth of "fast food", the concept of "slow food" or sustainable cuisine has emerged. Believing that in the name of productivity, contemporary society ("Fast Life") has changed humans' ways of being, threatening the environment and landscapes, the sustainable cuisine movement considers that the defense against these unsustainable practices should begin with the rediscovery of regional foods and cooking. The movement has progressed from a sole focus on pure gastronomy towards ecology and a dedication to sustaining the land and farmers who produce artisan foods. "The "eco" [organic] part of [this] eco-gastronomic movement necessitate[s] a new focus on education of the entire food continuum, from soil to table."[2] Thus the "slow food" movement makes the critical linkage between agriculture and cuisine.

The increasing appeal of gastronomy and locally sourced cuisine in tourism results in part from these processes in society at large. People's interests in food quality, ecological concerns about the needs for increased sustainable agricultural practices, health and nutrition concerns, a more sophisticated knowledge of food and beverages and acquired information about different cuisines are impacting upon tourists' expectations and behaviors.[3]

Agriculture and the Tourist Experience

Food tourism is a beneficial activity for travelers that choose it consciously as part of their "tourist experience" or unconsciously in a search to satisfy their hunger. The benefits of such choice differ in nature and purpose due to the multifaceted character of food tourism itself. Taking as a starting point its undoubtedly entertaining nature, food tourism becomes a playful and tasty medium for a culture to be introduced to the visitor through the authentic and original personality of a cuisine and its products, as well as, an interactive learning experience for all kinds of visitors whether they are interested in history, culture, cooking techniques and practices or even sheer interest for the flavors of the place of interest.

All tourists must eat, and tourists experience a place through a meal. But tourists also "consume" the area's landscape, by either eating out or eating to enrich the earth, providing a negative or positive contribution to sustainability. With mainly cows, but also other ruminants, grazing the local landscape supports not only meat and dairy products, but the grazing animals also contribute to increased protective layers of humus. More mull gives higher carbon sinks which reduces the threat of climate change. Sustainable meals are thus an essential part of a sustainable location.

Many farmers take the ethos of sustainability even further with the stance that soil is one of the most complex and important ecosystems in the world and that soil biodiversity and health are the key to human health and well-being (Andersen, 2000). Drawing on the best of traditional agricultural practices, they aim to improve the quality of the soils to improve the vitamin and mineral content of food they produce, believing that the first fundamental of biological farming is to consider people, namely their health and well-being as a function of the food and environment as it is produced on the farm. The second fundamental is valuing and understanding the soil and its biology as the basis for all fertility — the ultimate in farm-to-fork health and nutrition. By integrating the best of science, sustainable agriculture and traditional knowledge, many farmers are directly and indirectly making a contribution to local cuisine as a unique tourism attribute, strengthening the relationship between farm-to-fork along the entire value chain (Oliver, Berno & Ram, forthcoming).

Extending this notion of a systems approach to agriculture, one can view the cow as a common denominator for sustainable development in practice. Increasingly acclaimed Allan Savory clarifies how cows and other grazing animals are the only ones that can help humanity to face the challenges of global supply of food and water, while quickly reducing the amount of carbon dioxide in the atmosphere to prehistoric levels. Savory's model is called "Holistic Management."[4]

Allan Savory with the Savory Institute conveys knowledge on how we can plan grazing in such a way that the fertility of the soil constantly increases. Grazing animals eat or trample down vegetation that is rich in carbon. In their stomachs, microorganisms break down cellulose and lignin. This nutritious mixture becomes feces returned to the soil and recharges the humus supply. A significant positive effect is that the carbon sink created by the grass roots also means that the soil has a greater capacity to retain water, so that there is still water in the soil during dry periods. Pastures can bind four times more carbon than rainforests.

The tourism industry can take advantage of the growing interest in sustainable food systems, sustainable cuisine and food tourism by promoting and using more local products throughout the industry, while at the same time, meeting travelers' needs for an authentic, quality experience. By forging stronger linkages between agriculture and tourism through the development and promotion of sustainable cuisine, a symbiotic relationship between these sectors can be established.

Case Study: South Pacific

One way of operationalizing the articulation between agriculture, sustainable cuisine and the tourism industry is the development and promotion of the "farm to table" concept that promotes a high quality tourism product through the value chain, supporting the use of local agricultural products within the tourism industry.[5] The farm to table concept does not have to stop at just the dining experience, it can also lead to a range of related direct and indirect agritourism activities and products including agricultural commodity festivals, farm visits, factory tours and value added products such as souvenir food purchases, further enhancing the local community's benefits.

The farm to table concept does not just involve farmers and restaurateurs. To operationalize the farm to table concept successfully, a broad range of stakeholders must be involved. These include interests such as relevant government ministries (e.g., tourism, agriculture, fisheries, environment), national food production, pastoral and agricultural associations, providers of tourism and hospitality education, chefs and/or hotel management, national and local tourism organizations, communities of interest (i.e., rural producers, individuals with relevant expertise etc.) and others with interests in rural development, agricultural and/or tourism sectors. Implemented well, the farm to table concept links agriculture, sustainable cuisine and the tourism industry, resulting in positive outcomes for a broad range of beneficiaries.

Issues in the South Pacific

Despite an abundance of locally produced foods and food products, in most South Pacific island nations, much of the food served in the tourism sector is imported. There are many reasons for the reliance on imported agricultural products in South Pacific island countries including colonial heritage, product availability and price, and consistency and quality of local products.[6] Other reasons may include that tourists demand foods that are often not grown in the host region, or tourists are reticent to try local foods or local cuisines. Also posing threats to local foods are "international" menus (which often include versions of local dishes rather than authentic local food) favored by many large hotel and resort chains and the proliferation of multinational fast food and restaurant chains at the expense of small locally owned enterprises.

Tourism and agriculture are both critical to the economies of most South Pacific island countries and many countries have identified the need to improve food choice and quality (i.e. the tourism product) and reduce food imports (improve economic retention) as part of their overall tourism strategies. Concurrently, the agricultural sector has identified the need to diversify markets for products as the local market is too small. This identification has resulted in an emphasis on export-led strategies, often excluding small-scale producers, which have achieved varying degrees of success and sustainability. There is opportunity however, to bring the market to the product by using tourism as the conduit.

Addressing the Problem: The Farm-To-Table Concept - A Value Chain Approach

The benefits of tourism to a destination can be enhanced by expanding the backward economic linkages by increasing the amount of local foods used by the tourism industry. Creating and strengthening these backward linkages between tourism and the food production sectors can provide a local market for locally produced products, while at the same time, enhancing tourist experiences by providing them with the opportunity to consume high quality local produce. Potentially, food in the South Pacific can be positioned as one of the components of the tourism paradigm: agriculture provides the product; culture provides the authenticity; and, tourism provides the infrastructure and services.

Best Practice: Food Tourism as a Tool for Development

Recent research undertaken in the South Pacific on the relationship between tourism, food and agricultural production[7] identified a range of facilitators and barriers to increasing the use of local products in the tourism industry. Two of the issues identified in the research were the need to highlight the food of the Pacific in a way that would appeal to the tourist palate (create a food tourism product), and the need for a resource, such as a cookbook, to communicate this.

108

In response to this, a cookbook based on the culture, cooking and festivals of six South Pacific nations was developed.[8] The book is underpinned by a philosophy of sustainable tourism, sustainable agriculture and sustainable cuisine. It was developed to highlight South Pacific cuisine as a tourism asset, and as a tool to create linkages between the farmers and the tourism sector through the farm-to-table concept. The farm-to-table concept promotes a high quality tourism product through a value chain approach, supporting the use of local agricultural products within the tourism industry. The book was designed to improve the quality of the food offered to the South Pacific region's tourism market, so that the demand for the food is increased and local prosperity grows as a result. More than just a cookbook, it sought to promote a new facet of South Pacific culture; enhance the tourism product; contribute to sustainability (cultural, environmental and economic); and, create new opportunities for sustainable livelihoods.

Lessons Learned

The book, particularly its unique approach to food tourism and agricultural development, has received international recognition and acclaim.[9] The book is now being used for cookery training and has been the basis for recent promotion of tourism and trade between New Zealand and the Pacific islands. It is commonly used by hospitality providers in the South Pacific region. The international community's positive response to the book has demonstrated that there is genuine interest in the cuisine of the South Pacific. This creates an opportunity to continue to build on this interest by using the book as a foundation for farm-to-table projects in the Pacific region, and as a means to further facilitate food tourism.

The production and use of a regional cookbook as a tool for food tourism development is a model that can be applied to other destinations. For example, based on the success of the South Pacific cookbook, the authors are now working with the Samoan Tourism Authority and the non-governmental organization Women in Business Development to develop a cookbook based on the "Organic Samoa" concept. The book will be used as a means of marketing Samoan food as a component of the tourism product of the country, which helps differentiate Samoa from other Pacific countries, and establishes it as a food tourism destination. As part of this, an evaluation of the impact of the book as a tool for development will be undertaken.

Case Study: Greece

Greece is a country with long tradition in tourism and hospitality, as well as a country with a long and very interesting culinary tradition. Historically Greece has been the crossroads of many civilizations whose various cuisines have influenced and evolved Greek cuisine into how we regard it today. The great Classical Greece era had its own distinct flavors of sweet and sour with the use of wheat, barley, fish, honey and citrus, and of course wine and olive oil that influenced Europe as a whole. The later presence of Romans, Byzantines, and Venetians brought a different twist to the recipes where more acidity was added to food with the use of tomatoes, for example. Finally the Ottomans with their 400 year rule brought in the use of spices in the everyday cuisine. The interaction of all these cultures resulted in what is known today as Greek cuisine.

Issues in Greece

Greece has been an attractive summer tourism destination for several decades. Great clean waters, with fabulous beaches, and clean blue skies were the iconic representations of the country. Big hotels, luxury accommodations, small rooms for rent, tourist shops and even small villages targeting tourists proliferated uncontrollably. Previously, the food had nothing to do with culture. The food experience was limited to hotels where international cuisines were available, and the most famous Greek dishes were limited to moussaka, tzatziki and souvlaki. However, along with demand came high prices which did not match the service offered to visitors. Additionally the emergence of markets with similar tourism products such as Turkey, Egypt, and Spain, shifted popularity from Greece, which resulted in the downfall of the touristic product which offered nothing more than sea and sun. Thus the urgent need for the creation of new tourist products was born.

Addressing the Problem: Greece's Strategic Approach

Due to the global economic crisis of 2008-2011, as well as the urgent need for development of new products within the tourism sector, authorities shifted their attention to alternative modes of tourism which included food tourism. The general consent was that the tourist "Sea-Sun" model had long passed. Thus it was time to highlight the assets of the country. The Greek diet was quickly identified as such an asset. On one hand, the global shift of attention to gastronomy, and on the other hand the already successful models of food tourism in countries such as Italy and France created the perfect conditions for the emergence of a new product that would attract global travelers and make their journey a memorable experience. At the same time there was a global interest in the health benefits of Mediterranean cuisine, with particular attention to the dietary habits of the Greek islanders.

Although the public sector lacked the financial resources for a strong reinforcement of efforts that underline food tourism, there was a considerable effort from the Ministries of Tourism and Agriculture, to define a culinary terroir through advertising campaigns in international media. Most credit, though, should be given to individual efforts that joined forces to introduce the culinary culture of Greece to visitors. Municipalities and local authorities endorse such efforts to their best extent. Financial aid in the form of European Union funds for tourism is prioritized and individuals or businesses that want to focus on food tourism are typically funded. The most important factor is that those who deal with food tourism in Greece are people who make an honest effort due to their love and passion not only for their country, but also for their food. Some tourism-related governmental associations organize conferences and seminars in order to inform businesses about food tourism in general and the benefits of incorporating culinary dimensions in their tourist offerings in order to make their products more attractive.

Best Practices: Involving Tourists

The best practices that underline Greece as a food tourism destination are myriad and continue to increase. Numerous and thematic hotels, where visitors are introduced to a wide range of culinary practices, and where local, regional, and seasonal food is served. In these hotels visitors have the opportunity to get involved in agricultural activities, take cooking classes, and participate in wine tastings. Everyday more and more food tourism oriented businesses arise, either new or adapted to this brand new tourism model for Greece.

Another practice is that of wine tourism. The wine producers of different areas famous for their wines, or grape varieties, such as Crete, create networks or trails where visitors have the opportunity to follow wine roads that lead them to a variety of wineries with wine productions specific to an area. Although the effort is both collective and very serious, a lot of work needs to be done in order to compete with pioneers of the wine tourism market such as Italy or France.

Tourist offices with attention to culinary tours are slowly starting to build products that relate immediately to the promotion of food in their area of interest. These tourist offices offer specialized tours to people who are interested in exploring the places they visit with food having the protagonist role.

At the micro level, small villages in rural areas, often secluded from major tourist destinations organize events and set up their entire summer production as a means to attract visitors from tourist areas with the sole purpose to try their food. Specialized cuisine and expertise on a specific endemic ingredient is celebrated and becomes the focus of visitor attention. In Crete, for example, in Lasithi, there is a three day festival celebrating potatoes, which are cooked in every way imaginable and offered to visitors to try free or charge. Other practices such as the incorporation of local cuisine in hotels, the organization of seminars and lectures that aim in the further development of food tourism as a tourist product are also in the food tourism development agenda.

Lessons Learned

Despite the financial crisis that devastated Greece, there are serious efforts to put the country on the food travel map, and introduce Greek dietary habits to the world. The general belief is that by doing so, other industry sectors will simultaneously benefit such as the international trade of Greek prepared food products as well as its agricultural industry.

With the exception of hotels and perhaps some other specifically focused businesses, the majority of the efforts mentioned above also provide an insight to the agricultural practices involved in the Greek food concept. Islands, such as Crete or Lesvos, offer tourists the opportunity to visit farms, get their hands dirty by planting produce or picking straight from the plants, and harvesting grapes and olives. By providing such a holistic experience to the tourist, visitors may carry the memory home and even begin to apply what they learn and experience into their own home gardens.

Case Study: Sweden

Sweden is experiencing an interesting dichotomy in food tourism. While the country is enjoying some success with the Sweden: The New Culinary Nation campaign, by most accounts, the program is still neither well-known or a raving success. There are areas in Sweden, notably the region of West Sweden, where Gothenburg is located, that are doing a commendable job in promoting their area's culinary assets.[10] Still, much more work remains to be done.

As far as Swedish agriculture, local and traditional foods have basically disappeared from the tourist landscape and have been "forgotten" by the typical visitor. In fact, the Swedish food industry is largely characterized by commercialized thinking.

Issues for Sweden

Alcohol was a product that was affected by Sweden's state monopoly in the 1900s. The effect was such that this entire industry suffered as the production of fruit and berry wines and spirits disappeared.

Driving forces for this development for the rest of the food industry were both government and farmers' organizations. In 1933, a historic agreement was reached between the parties in power to reduce unemployment and develop a welfare state. The settlement was called "cow trade." The Social Democrats passed policies to reduce unemployment and the Farmers Party succeeded with its call for regulated agricultural policies that led to better prices and conditions of the farmers. Support was given to the growth of the dairy cooperative movement, which took over the handling of milk from the many small private dairies. A strict requirement for pasteurization was introduced in 1937, with the strong support of farmer's cooperatives. The remaining small private dairies quickly disappeared. This trend continued with the industrialization of meat, grain and other agricultural products.

The local food artisan tradition has all but died out. The old craft and recipes are long forgotten. In recent decades, however, interest in artisanal foods has increased. But the many years with the dominance of the industry have created several problems.

Addressing the Problem: Rejuvenating Local Traditions

One solution is to retrieve the traditions and recipes that are forgotten, but which are important for food tourism. Today there are food artisans around the country and many of them are farmers; however, many of them are copying each other and make similar products. A publicly funded Institute for food artisans has for many years used a cheese expert from France and a meat master from Germany. Today Swedish producers often make German sausage and French cheese. Instead of getting an exciting variation and new discovered traditional products, Sweden has a lot of copies, a fact which does not attract food tourists.

Quality is another issue being addressed in Sweden. In the countries which have kept their traditions, standards of quality are quickly defined. Sooner or later, poor food quality reflects back on the artisans. Another challenge is to create definitions of what is local food. The EU has rules on appellations, but there are few products in Sweden that meet the requirements. One example thus far is bleak roe from Kalix – there are few other genuine Swedish products. The debate is intense concerning the definition of gastronomic region or "local" foods. Is a region the division made by the country for its administrative needs? Is a gastronomic region a traditional landscape, a river, a part of a coast? What does terroir mean in a country without the tradition of terroir? Currently, Sweden is working to define exactly what their food tourism product should look like - and to create an authentic food tourism product, that is precisely what needs to be done.

Best Practice: Creating New Traditions

Despite some of the challenges, there is an exciting development of innovative food artisans. Even old traditions have always had a beginning, and therefore new traditions can develop. This notion of developing a new tradition is particularly true in beer production, where a revolution has taken place. A decade ago, there were about a dozen breweries in Sweden. Currently there are over 70, most of which are very small and are often run by farmers. They produce not only traditional Swedish beer, but are also creating new traditions (or in some cases awakening dormant traditions).

Even the Vikings' popular honey-based beverage Mjöd (mead) has come back, after being forgotten for centuries. The production of fruit and berry wines are on the way back as well. The greatest success has been for the sparkling SAV, made of birch sap using the champagne method, and has quickly become an export success, mainly to Asia. The recipe for SAV comes from 1785.

Sweden is rapidly developing into an exciting wine country. Today there are 250 vine growers in Sweden. Most of these vintners grow wine as a hobby, but more than 70 of them are working professionally in the area of producing wine and developing wine tourism.

While some argue that one should compare Swedish wines with those from Germany or France's Loire Valley, others believe that the Swedish wines should be launched with their own identity. There are wineries from Skåne in the south to just outside Stockholm in the middle of the country. The many hours of sunshine in this northerly climate actually facilitate the growth of grapes. Growers discuss intensively whether to regard Swedish wine as something uniform, or whether to highlight different districts by developing appellations.

Lessons Learned

In a country that has forgotten its traditions, or in a country where brand new products evolve and traditions change, it is obviously important to have an open dialogue about how to combine innovative ideas, with the preservation of the old traditions. The dialogue is also relevant for the classic culinary countries. There is a risk that old traditions, and established regulations can be an obstacle to exciting agriculture experiences that modern food tourists seek. Specific lessons learned include:

- Agriculture is at the heart of food tourism - agriculture provides the product; culture provides the authenticity; and tourism provides the infrastructure and services
- Agriculture/tourism linkages can create unique and authentic opportunities for both producers and food tourists
- Agriculture/food tourism linkages can be a powerful tool for economic development and sustainable rural livelihoods
- Food tourism can be used as a means to rejuvenate traditional agricultural and artisan practices, or as a vehicle to create new ones
- Every destination is slightly different, so agriculture and food tourism must be considered in context.

CONCLUSION

Agriculture is an essential component of sustainable food tourism and there are numerous benefits to a broad range of stakeholders that can be derived from enhancing and sustaining agriculture-tourism linkages in this context. The potential to contribute to rural development and sustainable livelihoods, support for the agricultural and artisan food sectors and reduced economic leakage in the tourism sector are just a few of the potential positive outcomes. Tourists also benefit through the opportunity to experience authentic local culture and heritage, and engage in a meaningful way with local producers and suppliers. However, the way forward for agriculture and food tourism linkages requires careful consideration. There are lessons to be learned from successful linkages already achieved that can serve as examples as to how these linkages can be implemented and sustained.

DISCUSSION QUESTIONS

1. How can a rural, predominantly agricultural community participate in food tourism?
2. How are circumstances in the case study examples different from a predominantly agricultural country such as one in Africa or Asia?
3. What steps are being taken in developing agricultural communities to create a sustainable food tourism industry?

ENDNOTES

---

[1] Stephen Boyne, Fiona Williams & Derek Hall, "Rural Tourism and Food Production: Opportunities for Sustainable Tourism". Paper presented at the RICS Foundation Roots Conference, London, England, 12 – 13 November, 2001.
[2] Patrick Martins. "Introduction." In *Slow Food*, edited by Carlo Petrini., xiv. White River Junction: Chelsea Green Publishing Company, 2001.
[3] Jan Vidar Haukeland and Jens Kr Steen Jacobsen, "Gastronomy in the Periphery: Food and Cuisine as Tourism Attractions at the Top of Europe". Paper presented at the 10th Nordic Tourism Research Conference, Vasa, Finland, 18-20 October, 2001.
[4] www.savoryinstitute.com

[5] Tracy Berno. "Sustainability on a Plate: Linking Agriculture and Food in the Fiji Islands Tourism Industry". In *Tourism and Agriculture: New geographies of consumption, production and rural restructuring,* edited by Rebecca Torres & Janet Momsen, 87-103. London: Routledge, 2011.

[6] Tracy Berno, Fiji Grown: From Farm to Restaurant (keynote presentation to the FAO/Ministry of Agriculture Fiji Grown Workshop, Korolevu, Fiji 26 – 28 February, 2003).

[7] Tracy Berno. "Bridging Sustainable Agriculture and Sustainable Tourism to Enhance Sustainability." In *Sustainable Development Policy and Administration*, edited by Gedeon Mudacumura, Desta Mebratu & M. Shamsul Haque, 208-223. New York: Taylor & Francis, 2006.

[8] Robert Oliver, Tracy Berno & Shiri Ram. *Me'a Kai: The Food and Flavours of the South Pacific.* Auckland: Random House, 2010.

[9] "New Zealand Chef Wins Cookbook of the Year in Surprise Upset." *The Independent,* 7 March 2011. Accessed January 3, 2013. www.independent.co.uk/life-style/food-and-drink/new-zealand-chef-wins-cookbook-of-the-year-in-surprise-upset-2235249.html

[10] For more discussion of West Sweden's progress in food tourism development and promotion, readers are referred to the *Best Practices in Destination Food Tourism Branding* chapter later in this book.

The Food & Drink Tourism Service Journey

Katrin Rippel, Michael Schafer, & Erik Wolf

The notion of a service journey for a business or destination is relatively new, but understanding it can give you and your business renewed success. A service journey (also called a customer journey map) looks at every possible customer touchpoint — how a customer begins thinking about your business or destination, their discovery process, interrelated aspects and other businesses, their actual experience and follow-up/post-experience. Taking what you learn from a service journey assessment and applying it to the continuous process of improvement that every business must go through to continue to develop, can improve your overall customer experience and generate positive word of mouth. This chapter offers some practical tips of things that can improve your customer (or visitor) service journey.

INTRODUCTION

Good service is crucial to success in the hospitality business and tourism industry. Tourists frequently look forward to experiencing the local food and beverages as much or more than any other aspect of their travels. Our job as hospitality professionals is to provide the best service journey possible to our guests. In other words, we must exceed their expectations. A customer service journey analysis should be part of the overall food and drink tourism experience assessment.

The Service Journey

A tourist's service journey is comprised of three progressive stages. The first stage is expectation of the experience. Expectation is followed by the actual experience itself. Lastly and perhaps most importantly, is the memory that the experience creates. This chapter will guide you in exceeding guest expectations, giving them a wonderful experience and creating positive lasting memories they cannot wait to share with others. For you, that means new business. Think and reflect on your own travels. Did you enjoy planning your trip? Was it a pleasure or a pain? When you arrived at your destination, was it disappointing or better than you expected? Did you vow never to return or did you tweet about your great experience and post photo albums of evidence on Facebook?

Credit: World Food Travel Association

Expectations (Pre-Arrival)

Before we make a food purchase or travel decision, customers and travelers go through a discovery process. The process may include asking friends, family and colleagues their opinion; searching the Internet; researching newspapers, magazines and books; consulting reviews; and similar practices. The process also includes the actual booking experience (transportation, lodging, restaurant, etc. These acts form a perception of the destination before the guest visits it. Think about your own behavior. Before you spend money on food or travel, you want to make sure that you are making a good decision. The same holds true with your customers or visitors to your destination.

When it comes to new food and drink experiences, we often experience initial fear and doubt. Many decide not to pursue or try such experiences because it is easier to do what is familiar (such as choose to eat at a well-known chain restaurant). Fear and doubt need to be removed before the customer makes a purchase. There is a tremendous amount of work that a business owner or destination marketer must do to convince the foodie to try their food, drink or destination. The initial research and discovery process includes every customer touchpoint up to the actual experience itself. Following are some ways to enhance your customers' or visitors' pre-arrival expectations.

> **Fear and doubt need to be minimized before the customer makes a purchase.**

From the moment our guests (and we mean guests, not customers) start searching the Internet for your website, it is our job to make their service journey as easy as possible. If you treat your customers as guests, they become more than just customers; they may eventually become brand ambassadors for your business. Your mission statement, business plan, and values must reflect that the guest is your reason for being. You only have one chance to make a first impression. Design your website to be as user-friendly as possible. You might want to consider hiring a usability (UX) expert to help. Be sure to use compelling photography on your home page. Do not be modest or understated. You have about 3 seconds to make a positive impression, or the website visitor will move on. Consult web designer friends or YouTube videos to get ideas. If you have the resources to offer the visitor their choice of language, you will be ahead of your competition.

Many business owners are incredibly busy today, and sometimes too busy to worry about the details. Yet getting details right is absolutely critical, not just to the success of your business or destination, it is also critical to positioning your business or destination above your competitors. An example is the Ritz Carlton hotel chain, which maintains a customer database that is updated regularly across all of the chain's properties. This means that a guest who first checks into a Ritz Carlton in Beijing and requests a special kind of pillow, will have that pillow request automatically fulfilled when he or she checks into the Ritz Carlton in Bahrain in the following month.[1] The simple act of remembering your customer preferences is an example of getting the details right.

From where do your visitors or customers originate? If you are not sure, analyze your website's traffic for country domains (i.e., .fr for France, .ru for Russia, etc.). Who visits your site most frequently? If you add foreign languages to your existing website, it makes destination planning much more comfortable for visitors from your target markets. Studies show that over 50%, in some countries up to 60%, of tourists buy only from websites presented in their own language.[2] More on translations later.

Ask your local Chamber of Commerce or tourist office for facts and figures about international tourism to your region. Mine your own data (i.e. guest registrations and email lists). Once your guests have arrived, ask your employees to give you feedback about what your guests talk about and what languages they speak.

Keep content simple. From descriptions of your establishment or destination to training your team, keeping it simple whenever possible ensures a premium experience for your guests, especially in their pre-trip phase. For example, simplify your website content. Clarify your target market(s). Are you advertising on "foodie" websites, blogs devoted to beer drinkers or web pages for wine enthusiasts? Are you focused on a specific market due to your unique location or facilities? Avoid slang, jargon and other colloquialisms that may confuse people whose native language is not yours. Use correct grammar so if someone is using Google translate or a similar translation service, your grammar will not confuse the machine translation. While you may think speaking colloquially is friendly or part of your character, save that for once your visitors arrive. You want people from other countries or cultures to understand what your business offers. If you make it too difficult for them before they arrive, they may never come.

Current trends indicate that your guests probably interact more via mobile devices than computers, especially in emerging countries. If you do not create (or need) a mobile app, keep your website simple so it is easily viewed on mobile devices. Savvy web designers can now design one website template (based on "responsive" design for the techies) so that it will render correctly on both regular computers and mobile devices. Gone are the days when you had to design two different websites. A solid mobile strategy can give your business a boost, especially in countries with high penetration of mobile devices, such as China, India, the USA, the UK, Russia, Brazil and Indonesia.

Complete website localization, i.e. faithfully reproducing an exact copy of all content in one or more additional languages, is expensive and is not always necessary. As an alternative solution, use a shorter amount of content and provide a synopsis of your points in the other language, or define key pages that should be translated professionally. Keep in mind that regular news updates will need regular translation. Consider asking a friend or colleague whose language and culture are the same as that of your target market to point out anything that might be confusing or potentially offensive, like sometimes is unexpectedly the case with pictures. Remember to translate keywords, metatags and your website description as well, so foreign language search engines can find your website. Of course if you have the budget and want to demonstrate your commitment to your target markets by translating everything professionally, the decision is yours to make.

Machine Translation vs. Human Translation

With all the new developments and widely accessible translation tools such as Google Translate, it is very possible that one day human translators will be replaced by machine translation. Machine translation has come a long way, and it still has a long way to go. However, languages are full of synonyms, ambiguity and rules that a machine cannot easily distinguish and resolve. Translation is not simply replacing the source word with the foreign language word, but rather involves cultural, grammatical, syntactic and semantic knowledge to completely convey the meaning and intent of a text.

An excellent test of machine translation is to paste content from your brochure or website into Google Translate or Babelfish. Translate it into another language of your choice, and then translate it back into your own language. You will be amused by the results. You will quickly recognize the limitation of machine translation in websites and for marketing materials. That said, most international customers are used to using machine translation to get the general gist of what is meant. In most cases, such translation is good enough for things like a simple website. Machine translation should never be used for your printed marketing collateral, however. Spend the money for proper human translation so that your intended message lives on with the correct meaning.

Remember, if you provide content in a foreign language, you may also receive customer inquiries in that language. Are you prepared to respond to those foreign language inquiries? If you use human translation, keep your word count low. Translation is typically charged on a per-word basis, with a certain minimum. Avoid embedded text on images, which cannot be translated by machines. Also, keep in mind that most text translations expand the space required by 10-30% depending on the language. A page with graphics that looks perfect in English will often be off-balance in the translated version. Avoid translating news like the latest updates, which are costly to maintain across localized sites. Frequent news means frequent translation and higher cost.

Be Global, Talk Social

In a recent survey, TripAdvisor claimed over half of the respondents (53%) would not book a hotel if they did not find a suitable review of that property. It also states also that responsive hotels attract more business.[3] Do not be overly concerned about getting an occasional negative review. If you respond promptly, it shows that you care, and no one is perfect. The survey says that 78% write a review because they want to share their good experiences with other travelers. User reviews can be an important facet of your marketing plan. Go beyond Facebook and Twitter. Determine the essential social networking sites for your target markets. For example, YouTube videos about your business or product are quite valuable but rarely used. Remember, if "a picture is worth a thousand words" then "a video is surely worth a hundred thousand words."

Create and nurture relationships with other businesses in your village, city, state, province, region and country. Collaborate with complimentary service providers. Jointly promote holidays and events that are part of the cultural fabric of your locale. Find ways to engage your team, your vendors, affiliates, and even your competitors. If a tradition does not exist, create one. Each and every tradition from grape harvests to Oktoberfest had a beginning, sometime, somewhere. These types of things visitors want to learn during their pre-trip discovery phase.

Be consistent. Spend the money to design a distinctive, memorable logo for your business. Use it throughout your website, marketing materials, signage, menus, and each and every touchpoint with your guests. Ensure that every use of your logo is with consistent colors, size and placement. A professional looking logo helps convey confidence to a potential new customer or visitors.

On Site Experiences

After the customer or visitor has spent considerable time anticipating the experience, now the time has come for their actual experience. This can include their arrival and initial impressions; and subsequent experiences during the duration of their stay (if a destination or lodging property).The experience is not a single event. It is the sum of the visitor's or customer's entire interaction with your product or service.

Things your guests will look for are the memorability of your product or service. Is the experience memorable in a positive way? Was it a good value? Were quality souvenirs available at a fair price? If the food and drink are not so memorable, the overall experience can still be memorable if combined with a nice view, a heritage site or other remarkable and memorable feature. Below are tips how to improve the on-site customer or visitor experience.

Consider how training your service providers ("team") to educate and enlighten tourists is vitally important. If you want to find out the mindset of your team ask them a simple question: "What business are we in?" Their responses may surprise you. Often you will hear "the food business", "the service industry" or "the food and beverage business". Unfortunately, these are not the correct answers. We are all in the same business, whether we own a 60 seat diner, run a Michelin starred kitchen or have a wine bar. What business is it? In a word, hospitality. In the everyday operations of a service business, this raison d'être frequently takes a back seat to all of the other demands on our time and resources.

Hire team members who genuinely like to serve others. It is much easier to train someone in a specific job function than it is to teach them to like people. If you are not sure if staff members are service oriented, use your intuition and observe them in action. There are plenty of people seeking jobs. You do not need to hire an underperformer. If service is not inherent in the employee's character, find someone else for whom service is second nature.

The word "hospitality" means "the friendly reception and treatment of guests or strangers".[4] This phrase says so much. The ancient Greeks defined status by how hospitable someone was. The better the host you were, the higher your status. In ancient Celtic society, you were responsible for not only providing food and drink to your guests; you also had to protect them from harm. In the Sahara desert, nomadic Bedouins follow a custom that requires them to feed and shelter even their enemies, knowing that their foes are bound to reciprocate.[5]

From our perspective, hospitality is providing the best possible products and service to our guests. As you know, our goal is to exceed our guest's expectations. Creating and building relationships with our guests is our number one priority. Before social media, the formula was "if a guest loved their experience, they told one person, if they didn't, they told ten people." That is no longer the case thanks to social media. Today if just one guest has a less than pleasurable experience, they can wreak havoc on your reputation.

What can you do to ensure your guests sing your praise in social media? Here are three actions to instill in each of your team members. First, follow the Ritz-Carlton motto of "We are Ladies and Gentlemen serving Ladies and Gentlemen." Instill in your employees (or team) that they are ladies and gentlemen serving ladies and gentlemen. Some of your team members may be far from being either a lady or a gentleman. Your guests may not fit that profile either. The point is to change not only their perception of your guests, but to alter their self-perception.

Next, train your team to think first about their guests, then about themselves. This is not quite the golden rule of "treat others as you wish to be treated", but a variation on that rule. When the guest accepts your offer of a glass of water, ask them if they prefer tap or bottled water, no ice or lots of ice, etc. Most Americans like ice in their beverages, while Europeans prefer little, if any. Demonstrate the anticipation of your guest's needs and desires.

Last, and certainly not least, demand that your staff smile, at each other, at you, and most importantly, at your guests. It may sound obvious, but look around, observe your team in action, and see how often they smile. A genuine smile is the universal symbol of greeting. Greet and treat your guests the best you can, they are your raison d'être.

Here are some additional ways to enhance a guest's overall experience during their trip. There are a few phrases that many servers use regularly and phrases that better illustrate your commitment to service. While these are colloquial to the English language, the equivalent behavior and words probably exist in your own local area and language so you can adapt accordingly to your own situation.

1. How are YOU GUYS tonight?
    Just omit the word GUYS. How are you tonight?

2. Are WE ready to order cocktails?
    The use of WE can sound condescending or infantilizing. Better to say "Are YOU ready to order cocktails?"

3. Are you still WORKING ON that?

WORKING ON a dish sounds like a chore. Better to ask: May I CLEAR your plate?

4. JUST ONE tonight?
    If a guest is dining alone, make that person feel good about spending the evening in your establishment, not that they do not have any friends. Better to ask, "One in your party this evening?" or "What is the name on the reservation?"

5. NO PROBLEM
    NO PROBLEM introduces negativity and implies that the speaker's act of service might, in fact, be a problem, at least some of the time. Better to say ABSOLUTELY, RIGHT AWAY, or OF COURSE. We prefer the very gracious "MY PLEASURE" – what one often hears in South Africa.

In the service industry, servers should avoid touching patrons regardless of the perceived level of familiarity. While tapping you on the shoulder while taking your order may not bother you personally, it may infuriate someone else. Team member should keep their hands to themselves..

Getting service right is of critical importance. An example of in-depth training is the German concept of an apprenticeship. Usually for approximately three years, an employee studies as an apprentice. Such programs are found in hotels/restaurants and also in schools and universities (in the programs of general education, culinary arts, service, or administration). The apprentice is paid a small salary. The apprenticeship may be in a nice hotel or restaurant, or in a family run operation.

Create a consistent program of training, perhaps in partnership with vendors and affiliates. Use the resources of other, perhaps more well-established companies. In the USA, beer wholesalers have resources that they will share with their customers. Promotions, translations, contests, and other marketing tools may be available to you. If you are not sure, be sure to ask. What resources are available in your sector, and in your country?

Beverage service can be difficult when serving both regular guests and visitors from around the globe. Sensitivity, observation, a genuine sense of warmth, a sense of humor and an open mind are all keys to superior beverage service. As with food, serving hot beverages hot, and cold beverages cold, is crucial to ensuring an experience that your guest will not only remember, but will tell their friends and family about. And of course, fingers should never be placed around the rim of the glass or cup when serving.

When beverages are part of meal service in a business that serves a large number of tourists, consider not using ice at all or using only bottled water or triple-filtered water for ice cubes. This may not seem to be worth the effort or cost, but many visitors do not tolerate well the differences in water. This is most often noticed by visitors who travel between the more developed world and the lesser developed world. Avoidance of ice and tap water is something that your customers might forget, but you should anticipate the needs of your guests.

In-depth knowledge of your product is crucial to your success. If your focus is primarily on local, regional or national products your team must know these offerings thoroughly. Spelling, pronunciation, history, local relationships are all features your guests are curious about. Tell a story. People love stories, which are how we communicated and learned for thousands of years. Historical anecdotes and humor are both good to weave into stories. Everyone loves to laugh. Sometimes an owner, chef or winemaker are the story themselves.

Many tourists seek beverages that are indigenous to their destination. Feature products made locally. Consider offering "specials" that feature beverages produced from your locale. If your region makes beer, feature those beers. Remember, the guest can get the big multinational beer brands back home. If your area produces wine, offer your guests the local favorites. Explain to them why imported brands are not available (or not recommended) and offer them a suitable alternative. Do not just serve California or French wines just because your visitors ask for it (they may not know to order anything else). Many spirits are specialties of the country or city where they are produced, frequently with little or no distribution elsewhere. Promote those beverages and your guests will thank you by spreading the word about them. If alcohol is not customary in your area, simply substitute "sparkling water," "fruit juice." "soft drink," or "tea/coffee".

What is your business you known for? What are the specialties of your area? Is it a particular type of meat/fruit/vegetable? Is the preparation unique? Are your local cheeses famous? Do you offer specialty produce with a short growing season? Are the locally-made spirits unique? How are they unlike any other beverages? Answering these questions, and similar inquiries, is very important in your analysis of how to create the most memorable experience possible for your guests.

Another way to enhance your visitors' experience during their trip is to offer user-friendly menus, wine lists, beer lists and cocktail lists, which are vital to the success of foodservice establishments. A menu that is too long can have an opposite effect from what is intended and leave your guest feeling frustrated and unable to decide. Accuracy is paramount, as is simplicity. Keep it simple. Describe your food or drink simply yet enticingly. Mention locally sourced ingredients when relevant. Avoid cliché phrases about the food's preparation. If your business is destination marketing, evaluate your signage. How easy do you make it for visitors to experience your destination's culinary delights? Do you mark a wine route or cheese trail, for example?

Translating a menu is highly recommended in areas with high concentrations of tourists. After taking an honest assessment of your assets and resources, make key decisions on how to approach your service for international guests. Translating your restaurant menu into two or three (or more) languages is a relatively small investment with a large potential return. Handing guests your restaurant menu in their native language can make a huge difference to a guest who barely speaks, much less reads your language. Languages are full of synonyms, ambiguity and complicated rules. To save time, cost and effort, consider creating a multilingual menu. Consider the use of photos if you think your target market might appreciate it, as is often done in Asian countries. If you are able to say, guests will appreciate knowing where a dish originated or where the ingredients came from. If your guests want their meat well done, then do not argue with them. Give them what they want.

Food allergies are, unfortunately, becoming more frequent. Perhaps the best way to address this topic is to simply ask your guests if they suffer from any food allergies, although they should advise you in advance. If they do, a well-trained server will ensure that information is communicated to the chef in your kitchen. If not, you might open yourself up to legal action if your patron gets sick or even dies. It is not a pleasant subject to discuss, but an important one nevertheless.

Always give your guests a positively memorable experience because afterwards they will share it with their friends or family and may even be a repeat customer. If your guests do not have a positive experience, they will also share that with everyone they know.

Creating a Seamless Customer Experience

After you have determined the unique products, services and experiences you want to offer your guests, partner with the providers of these products. If you sell a lot of wine, cross-market your business with the winery that makes that award-winning wine which you feature on your wine list. If beer is your specialty, after your guests enjoy a local brewery tour, ask the guide direct them to you for a fabulous food and pairing with that brewery's beers. The possibilities are endless.

Does it make sense to create a tiered level of service? In other words, is a VIP offering advantageous? If you offer a delicious prix fixe menu paired with local wines, consider offering a VIP pairing with exclusive, limited availability wines. The suitability varies with the food or drink experience offered and expectations of your target market.

The very nature of travel often crosses language and cultural boundaries. It involves complex planning, a substantial amount of money, long flights or drives, new environments, new cultures and foreign languages. In essence, it means moving out of one's own comfort zone. Being welcomed in a guest's native language helps newly arrived tourists to feel comfortable in the "exotic" environment.

Knowing about cultural differences of your guests can go a long way to winning their hearts and wallets. Patrons in most European restaurants are used to requesting the bill only when they are ready to pay the bill. Presenting the bill without the guest asking is perceived as "kicking them out" before they are ready to leave. This obviously does not help create pleasant memories.

Memories (Post Trip)

After the experience is over, the customer or visitor will reflect upon his or her experience, sometimes for several weeks. Each reflection builds more layers of memory. As time goes on, the customer or visitor will speak to friends, family and colleagues and either endorse or defame your product or destination. Which would you prefer? Word-of-mouth is the least expensive and most effective kind of promotion, and it can either be positive or negative. Ultimately, you want your customers to provide an endorsement of their experience. The memories that your guests have and share with others are your greatest marketing tool. If your customers or visitors request a follow up, be sure to do so. Stay connected with past guests and consider inviting them to connect with you on social media. Developing and maintaining loyalty is one of the keys to long-term success.

Customers sense integrity and enthusiasm. When you and your team love what you do it shows. Your magnetism draws guests back again and again when you create experiences that leave positive memories. You create the brand ambassadors mentioned earlier. Quality will be remembered long after price has been forgotten. If this kind of magnetism is not in your character, then run things behind the scenes and hire someone to be the smiling face of your business. You will be amazed at how a genuine, smiling face can increase sales.

CONCLUSION

"Yesterday is but today's memory, and tomorrow is today's dream," said poet and philosopher Kahlil Gibran. Use your skills to help your guests create wonderful, vivid memories of their visit to your business. Exceeding expectations is the start for marvelous experiences that leave lasting memories. You must guide your guests every step of the way on their service journey. "Rome wasn't built in a day". It takes time to establish a business or change business processes and habits. Success happens in small steps. As Lao Tzu said centuries ago, "The journey of a thousand miles begins with a single step".

DISCUSSION QUESTIONS

1. Map out a service journey of your own customers or visitors. If components are missing, research them. What problem areas can you identify?
2. How would you handle a problem customer – the type that is always right and is quite happy to argue with you in a loud voice until they get what they want?
3. Do you follow up with your guests or visitors right after the trip while they are presumably spreading positive word of mouth about their experience? If not, consider doing so to either give an extra boost to your guests' communications about their experience or to remind them to do so. What would such post-trip communications look like?

ENDNOTES

[1] "Take it from Ritz – Carlton: Data is nothing without the personal touches", Joseph Michelli, Customer think, last modified August 18 2008, last accessed July 14 2013, www.customerthink.com/article/data_nothing_personal_ritz_carlton

[2] "Can't Read, Won't Buy: Why Language Matters on Global Websites". Donald DePalma, Benjamin Sargent, Renato Beninatto. Common Sense Advisory, last modified September 2006, last accessed July 15 2013, www.commonsenseadvisory.com/Portals/_default/Knowledgebase/ArticleImages/060926_R_global_consumer_Preview.pdf

[3] "Survey finds half of TripAdvisor Users will not book a hotel that has no reviews". TripAdvisor, last modified November 14 2012, last accessed July 15 2013, www.tripadvisor.com/PressCenter-i5569-c1-Press_Releases.html

[4] The Free Dictionary. TheFreeDictionary.com

[5] "Honor codes of the Bedouin". Wikipedia, last modified February 11 2012, last accessed July 15 2013, http://en.wikipedia.org/wiki/Diyafa

Food Tourism Where Little Agriculture Exists

Wendy Lange-Faria and Erik Wolf

Contrary to conventional thinking, not every food tourism destination has an abundant local or sustainable food system to supply it. In this chapter we will explore how destinations with little to no nearby agriculture have successfully created a unique culinary brand, and targeted prospective domestic and international visitors in search of unique and memorable food and drink experiences in such regions where little agriculture exists.

INTRODUCTION

Food tourism affords a visitor the opportunity to enjoy a wide variety of offerings and immersive education about local culinary products and the artisans behind them. At its core, food tourism allows visitors to experience a new culture and its food customs, heritage, and history. Many of the world's preeminent food tourism destinations are enshrouded by robust agricultural communities. To wit, consider Sonoma, California; Tuscany, Italy; and Loire Valley, France. These destinations have no shortage of high-quality agricultural products and are instantly recognized by most foodies. That said, there is another kind of foodie destination – one without much agriculture at all. In this chapter we will look at Las Vegas, Iceland, Sweden and Jordan for inspiring ideas for similar destinations.

"Sin City" as Culinary Mecca

Las Vegas is affectionately referred to as sin city. There seems to be something for everyone within the city's borders, and that includes foodies. The 40 million people who visit the city each year employ 35,000 people in restaurants on the Strip alone. County-wide, the 2012 economic impact of these 40 million visitors was US$8 billion.[1] How does a city with a metropolitan population of around 2 million, feed 42 million people per year? Las Vegas, in spite of its desert location and with a remarkably small farm-to-market system for its current dense population of around two million,[2] has established itself as one of the world's preeminent culinary destinations. Obviously the food has to be imported - and a lot of it. For example, foodservice businesses in the city use 60,000 pounds (27,216 kg) of shrimp per day, more than the rest of the daily United States shrimp consumption combined.[3] Much of that is imported from Asia, although efforts are being made to farm the required shrimp locally.[4] Still, the desert climate around Las Vegas does support crops that do well in high heat and low moisture conditions, like dates, pomegranates and onions, although that alone would be a very boring diet for 42 million people.

A few decades ago, the food scene in Las Vegas consisted of not much more than 99-cent buffets. In the 1990s, a hotel building boom began a profound transformation of the city in every way, from lodging to entertainment to shopping and dining. It is no surprise that along with the glitz and glamor of fancy shows like Siegfried & Roy, consumers began to see glitz and glamor in celebrity chef-owned restaurants like Todd English's Olives or venues with dramatic architecture like Aureole. While the hotel boom continued, smart hoteliers wanted to capture more of the visitors' share of wallet. To prevent guests from dining off-property, hotels like the Bellagio, Paris and Wynn created their own high-quality dining experiences. The massive and beautiful Aria/Vdara hotel complex managed by MGM Properties, supports almost 20 quality restaurants. City-wide, there is no shortage of eateries owned by celebrity chefs like Charlie Palmer, Wolfgang Puck, Michael Mina, Emeril Lagasse, Guy Savoy, Tom Colicchio and Joël Robuchon, just to name a few.

Las Vegas is a metropolitan area with a well-developed urban infrastructure. It is also not far from California, where many agricultural products are grown. Las Vegas does not need a robust agricultural community around it because of extensive agriculture nearby. What makes Las Vegas stand out is chef talent and the drama that surrounds the city's culinary offerings. For destinations in a similar situation, leveraging chef talent and creativity may be an option worth exploring.

More than Ice in Iceland

Contrary to what many might expect, Iceland does have some agriculture. Besides robust fishing, the country's farms produce lamb, potatoes, carrots, cabbage, berries, mushrooms, leeks and other cold weather fruits and vegetables. While Iceland does not produce many raw ingredients, its longer summer daylight hours mean larger vegetables. And of course, farmers use greenhouses to grow other fruits and vegetables, but strangely, no one hears of tomatoes or bananas imported from Iceland. So how did Iceland establish itself as a food-worthy destination? It did so largely thanks to talented chefs like Siggi Hall, Eythor Runarsson and Gunnar Karl Gislason, not to mention a commitment to celebrating traditions and its readily available Icelandic ingredients. Among all that is available in Iceland, the country is well-known for its lamb, fish, dairy products and wild berries.

As the Icelandic education system began to take formal shape in the early 20th century, proud Icelanders took steps to document their culinary heritage and recipes, which were later published in cookbooks. At the same time, Reykjavik was growing as the country's capital and largest city. New residents in Reykjavik kept the traditions such as popular midwinter festivals where they served "Icelandic food", traditional country foods served Þorramatur (buffet-style). Therefore historic traditions were nicely preserved. At the same time, Iceland's fishermen found a market for their high-quality fish, which boosted the country's economy. Increased affluence meant the ability to afford more fruits and vegetables and other imported foodstuffs. New and different foodstuffs gave rise to experimentation.

The country's affluence continued but it was really the launch of the New Nordic Food movement in the early 2000s that gave Iceland, and Sweden (below), the impetus to aggressively develop and promote their cuisines to the world. In 2005 the Nordic Council of Ministers created the New Nordic Food manifesto as a means of increasing the production and consumption of traditional, local food.[5] One of the observations made (curiously, one might argue this same theme is prevalent in the modern world) was that the industrialization of food products and massive exports system has stifled the development of much local, small-scale (and in some cases subsistence agriculture) food production. The Nordic countries noticed the lack of diversity in food inspired by mass food industrialization – and are paying attention. And from there the "ball started rolling" on the New Nordic food wave.

Iceland is participating full force in this New Nordic food wave. The produce, as indicated above is key to food tourism activities playing an integral role in the selection of fresh, local ingredients used in the kitchens and restaurants across the country.[6] Many of the Icelandic chef trainees participate in the Nordic Congress (Nordisk Kongress) to promote the culinary industry, particularly among its younger generation.[7] The NKF Congress also holds a "Cook Scandinavia" contest. Icelandic and other Nordic chefs also participate in Bocuse d'Or, which helps spread awareness of their talents.

A Unique Selling Proposition

Iceland brands its food with adjectives such as fresh, sustainably produced and pure, drawing on the nuances of the country's distinctive characteristics, such as the Icelandic coastal waters and clean pastoral landscapes, which emphasize the elements of purity and simplicity.[8] A number of Icelandic chefs are noteworthy for bringing Icelandic cuisine to the shores of North America. Iceland Naturally, a group comprised of iconic Icelandic brands, including food and drink that are marketed to the Americas.[9] Icelandic chefs have promoted the country in North America via a series of "Taste of Iceland" celebrations featuring Icelandic culture and food.[10] This four-day festival represents a classic example of bringing the culture and food experience to a destination – a unique twist bringing the destination to the tourist instead of bringing the tourist to the destination:[11] "Experience the vibrant culture of Iceland without even leaving your city! A Taste of Iceland is a free four-day event that celebrates Iceland's food, music, and culture. Get a taste of what life is like in Iceland and enjoy the best of the country's culture and lifestyle through a series of events...A Taste of Iceland is presented by Iceland Naturally, in cooperation with Icelandair, Reyka Vodka, 66 [degrees] North, Blue Lagoon, Icelandic Glacial Water, and Visit Iceland...".[12]

For the purposes of this discussion we will now look first to the food product of Iceland and then turn to the chefs of Iceland, both of which have really helped shape the direction of food tourism for the nation.

Icelandic Food

It is well-known that Iceland is a fishing nation. Wild fish caught in this country account for a good portion of the Icelandic diet. The country promotes its wild caught fish which is caught in sustainably managed clean waters through an intense marketing program called Iceland Responsible Fisheries.[13] A primary export product, the seafood program is carefully branded by a consortium of fisheries that came together to establish this program. This program not only protects the pedigree of the seafood but also the fishery stocks at the same time. There is a certification program based out of the FAO (Food and Agriculture Organization of the United Nations) and a logo that clearly identifies the nation's fish product – and at the same time clearly differentiates the product as coming from Iceland and *only* Iceland. There is also a clear message of the brand here that will resonate with many a visitor will respond to: "sustainable use of marine resources for the benefit of future generations."[14]

Lamb is another traditional ingredient found in Iceland – sheep farming practiced in many a remote area throughout the country. Sheep are sent to graze free-range in the mountain pastures for the summer.[15]

Iceland is completely self-sufficient when it comes to dairy products. A number of milk products are produced including the unique Icelandic *skyr* native to the country since around 1000 A.D.[16] *Skyr* is a curd made from skimmed milk and often served whipped with milk and cream. There is also *mysa*, which is made from *skyr* and use instead of wine for cooking fish. Other typical dairy products include *súrmjólk*, a sour milk eaten at breakfast with muesli and brown sugar; *mysingur*, a sweet spread made form whey and popular with children; and *mysostur*, a brown cheese made from whey.

Interestingly enough, despite the more rugged climate, vegetables are grown in Iceland with the assistance of geothermal energy and electric lights. Tomatoes, cucumbers, green peppers and different varieties of lettuce may be grown year round in greenhouses. Traditional outdoor crops include carrots, rhubarb, rutabaga, cabbage, leeks, cauliflower and kale. There have even has been some successful cases of growing canola and barley.[17]

The Icelandic Chef

There are two training programs in Iceland for aspiring chefs; one is the Hospitality and Culinary School of Iceland[18] and the other is the Kopavogur Institute of Education which works in partnership with the University Cesar Ritz in Switzerland to deliver a culinary program in Iceland.[19] The chef education program is based on a partnership between workplaces and the school. The apprentice signs up a four year contract with a restaurant/hotel of a professional level qualified to educate young chefs. The apprentice spends 36 full months in the workplace and the remaining 12 months in school.[20]

Klúbbur Matreiðslumeistara (KM) (Icelandic Chefs Association) is the national entity that promotes a variety of initiatives designed to promote the culinary heritage of food in and food culture in Iceland. Founded in 1972, the KM was established to promote the culinary arts and dialogue about food and culture in Iceland. This organization coordinates the efforts of the Iceland Culinary Team, mentoring young chefs to compete in Nordic and international competitions. Among the noteworthy activities of the association are the Icelandic Chefs competition, Food Days festival, and Nordic Chef of the Year.[21]

Team Iceland. Pictured are: Hákon Már Örvarsson, Þráinn Frey Vigfússon, Viktor Örn Andrésson, Fannar Vernharðsson, Garðar Kári Garðarsson, Bjarni Siguróli Jakobsson, Hafsteinn Ólafsson, Ylfa Helgadóttir, Axel Clausen, Daníel Cochran, Þorkell Sigríðarson and María Shramko. *Photo Credit: Rafn Rafnsson*

One of the main forms of recognition for KM is the Icelandic Chef of the Year award that is coordinated by the same Association. The Association selects a chef of the year that is based on a series of criteria, including the use of local ingredients. In addition to this initiative, the Association promotes a variety of initiatives in order to further Icelandic food and culture. Some key activities used to drive culinary innovation in the country include:

- Coordination and funding of the Icelandic Culinary Team that represents Iceland in major culinary competitions worldwide. This team promotes the pride and spirit of the food products and food experience of Iceland.
- Operation Ungkokka Iceland is a group of young chefs who train and compete in the various Nordic organizations for Iceland and internationally, with the World Association of Chef Societies (WACS)
- Coordinates and hosts a Food Day festival contest to showcase Icelandic specific food manufacturing. There are also cooking competitions among local chefs from around Iceland, urging people to use specialties from each corner of the country in order to promote restaurants and to encourage the tourism industry to think locally about their food and menus.
- Participate with the other Nordic countries in the annual "Nordic Chef of the Year".
- Coordinates competitions in Iceland for aspiring young chefs under 23 years of age. The first and second place winners compete with their Nordic colleagues.
- Hosts an annual Gala Dinner bringing together the country's most celebrated chefs to prepare a meal for a special contingent of guests including the President of Iceland – all to celebrate the best of Iceland's food and drink.[22]

Iceland as Part of the Nordic Food Movement

Iceland is closely connected to the overall Nordic Food movement. As such it is also part of the Nordic Chefs Association, a non-politically oriented entity involving the countries of Iceland, Denmark, Finland, Norway and Sweden. The organization's purpose is to promote and unite the culinary profession within the Nordic countries. One of the interesting awards that the countries participate in is that of the Cordon Rouge – a medal with the flags of the Nordic countries along with a diploma along with the Nordic Chefs Association insignia.[23]

A Look at Sweden

Like Iceland, Sweden has similar issues of a colder climate with shorter growing seasons. However, Sweden has made efforts to promote its food tourism resources and is a particularly interesting example for a number of reasons. If you think Swedish cuisine is just meatballs covered in gravy, you will be pleasantly surprised.

Swedes are nature-loving, environmentally minded and outdoorsy people who love great food, especially on special occasions and holidays like Cinnamon Bun day, Midsommar, Semla season, crayfish parties, Easter and Julbord. The country is quite large, running 1,500 km (932 miles) from top to bottom. In Sweden's southern area (Skåne, known as Sweden's Tuscany), fertile plains abound, while forests, rivers and seas throughout the country provide a wealth of agricultural bounty, which most people do not expect for a country so far north. Fish, game, berries, mushrooms, potatoes and a variety of liquors are local ingredients commonly encountered on Swedish menus. Like Iceland, Swedish farms use greenhouses to grow fruits and vegetables that would otherwise not grow in any of its climatic zones. Native Sápmi people in Lapland have also contributed their culinary heritage to Swedish cuisine, with reindeer and other indigenous ingredients.

While foodies around the world may not necessarily look forward to the next offer of pickled herring, as in Iceland, it is the chefs who are making a name for Sweden. Current noted restaurants include Mathias Dahlgren and Frantzén/ Lindeberg, each of which have two Michelin stars. And Magnus Nilsson of Fäviken in Järpen (rural western Sweden) made it into the 2013 list of world's top 50 restaurants.[24] Foodies also will recognize the name of Marcus Samuelsson, who heads up restaurants in both Gothenburg and New York City. Swedish chefs welcome imported ingredients and ideas, fuse them with Swedish produce and proteins, and let the creations stand on their own merit. Even the finest dining establishments in Sweden are relaxed and less of a "scene" like in major world capitals. This puts non-gourmet foodies at ease, while still satisfying those with higher-end expectations.

Sweden produces a variety of quality agricultural products, many of which are organic, which plays to the Swedish notion of healthy eating. While many regions around the world are known for their high quality agricultural ingredients, Sweden, like Iceland, has had to try a little harder to compete with the reputations of France and Italy. And Sweden, like Iceland, has done quite well making a name for itself, largely thanks to its talented chef pool and strategic push by the government.

Jordan's Unexpected Delights

The Kingdom of Jordan's first delight is *karam*, a custom where guests are treated like kings. It may sound like mere lip service, but all visitors receive the warmest possible reception, complete with food and drink appropriate for whatever the occasion. Genuine hospitality that never seems to end is noticed by visitors from the moment they arrive, and continues for the duration of their trip. Jordanians are not putting on airs; this is how they treat all guests. One could easily say that Jordanians inherently understand the word "hospitable."

A quiet country surrounded by noisy neighbors is how Jordanians jokingly refer to themselves. There is some truth to that. A country known for the arid yet stunning UNESCO World Heritage Site at Petra, sandy Roman ruins, and striking desert vistas does not necessarily portend amazing culinary adventures, yet Jordan is a foodie's unexpected dream come true.

Local food production includes olives, lamb and the fish which comes from the country's southern port in Aqaba. Few people are aware that in the country's northwestern Jordan Valley, a dizzying array of fruits and vegetables are grown, although irrigation is an issue that seriously threatens this bounty. Jordanian grocery stores are full of herbs, grains and every possible fruit and vegetable one could want, including some of the largest cabbages seen on the planet. Most of the agricultural produce is surprisingly grown in Jordan, with a few exceptions being imported from Syria, Egypt, South Africa and even the USA. The imports are the exception to the rule however, which surprises visitors who expect Jordan to be nothing more than a land of desert sand.

Jordan has benefitted from a stable political and economic climate, however recent immigration waves are taking a toll on the infrastructure and testing the limits of *karam*. Jordanians also benefit from a cohesive family unit and family traditions where recipes and culinary stories are handed down from generation to generation, helping to preserve culinary culture and know-how. While hummus, kebabs, lavash style bread and tabouleh are common throughout the Levant region, the freshness and quality of the ingredients is another unexpected delight for visitors, who often proclaim their discovery of the best hummus, falafel or best lemonade they have ever had. Jordan does have a few national dishes that visitors can enjoy as well. Perhaps most importantly, Jordanian food is made fresh, with lots of fresh fruits, vegetables, meats and fish. While organic ingredients are not widely promoted, the consensus is that most agricultural produce is at least biodynamic. Food tastes better to Western visitors because it is fresher than what they are typically used to. And it was made with *karam* in mind. One does not expect to find so much produce in the middle of one of the most arid regions on Earth, yet there it is. Jordan's ingredients combined with Jordanian hospitality are a win-win for foodie visitors.

CONCLUSION

A foodie destination does not need to be an agricultural powerhouse like California or rural France. Ingredients may differ, but there are an almost endless variety of lesser known ingredients and dishes from furthest corners of the planet, waiting for foodies to discover. Westerners may need to look beyond the ubiquitous hamburgers and sandwiches, and Asians may need to be more adventurous with cuisines other than their own. Even when traveling in harsh climates and remote areas, great food can be enjoyed. In fact, it is unexpected destinations like these that offer foodies new and different experiences, which is exactly what they seek as bragging rights. Not everyone wants to visit San Francisco, Tuscany and Paris, and in fact, many foodies already have and are seeking "the next big thing."

DISCUSSION QUESTIONS

1. Traveling to the nether regions of the planet may give foodies access to some unexpected food and drink experiences – some wonderful and others less so. How would you position food or drink that may be considered "uncustomary" for your area's regular visitors? How would you get them to try it?
2. If a very hot, very cold or very remote destination is known for striking natural scenery, famous archeological ruins, or some of the world's best entertainment, how would a destination marketer begin to diversify the destination's product offerings and add more food and drink activities into the product portfolio? In other words, if a destination is known so strongly for one major type of experience, how can marketers get visitors to start celebrating its food and drink, provided of course that they merit celebration?
3. Areas that are very hot, very cold or very remote must import a lot of their food in order to serve visitors. Consider the sustainability around importing so much food. Should such destinations or foodservice businesses be doing this or should they promote more of what they grow locally. For example, coconuts in The Philippines. Discuss the pros and cons of importing whatever the visitors desire vs. what is more realistic and sustainable.

ENDNOTES

[1] www.nytimes.com/2012/06/27/dining/examining-the-las-vegas-food-scene.html
[2] www.lvcva.com/includes/content/images/media/docs/Population-2011.pdf
[3] www.venere.com/blog/las-vegas-fun-facts
[4] www.fastcoexist.com/1678733/growing-local-shrimp-in-vegas-with-the-ocean-hundreds-of-miles-away
[5] The New Nordic Cuisine. (2013). Retrieved August 6, 2013 from http://denmark.dk/en/green-living/nordic-cuisine/the-new-nordic-cuisine/
[6] www.chef.is/v.asp?page=44&Article_ID=64   Retrieved July 22, 2013.
[7] http://bit.ly/1bXGeuR Retrieved July 22, 2013.
[8] www.icelandnaturally.com/culture/food/nr/9   Retrieved June 24, 2013.
[9] www.icelandnaturally.com/about/ Retrieved June 24, 2013.
[10] http://crosscut.com/2012/10/12/food/110958/iceland-comes-calling-staple-fancy/ Retrieved June 24, 2013 and http://rickshawmag.com/2013/taste-of-iceland/
[11] www.youtube.com/icelandnaturally   Retrieved July 26, 2013
[12] http://tasteoficeland.tumblr.com/ Retrieved July 24, 2013.
[13] Email correspondence by Wendy Lange-Faria with Gudný Káradóttir, Director, Products and Services and Marketing Manager, Iceland Responsible Fisheries. [August 6, 2013]
[14] Iceland Responsible Fisheries. (2013). Retrieved August 7, 2013 from http://responsiblefisheries.is/news-and-media/videos/

[15] Email correspondence between author and Gudný Káradóttir, Director, Products and Services and Marketing Manager, Iceland Responsible Fisheries. [August 6, 2013]

[16] Skyr. (2013). Retrieved August 6, 2013 from www.skyr.is/goals/

[17] Email correspondence between author and Gudný Káradóttir, Director, Products and Services and Marketing Manager, Iceland Responsible Fisheries. [August 6, 2013]

[18] European Association of Hotel and Tourism Schools. (2008). Retrieved August 6, 2013 from www.aeht.eu/en/useful-links/hospitality-education/192-iceland

[19] www.aeht.eu/en/useful-links/hospitality-education/192-iceland- Retrieved July 22, 2013

[20] Email conversation between author and Hafliði Halldórsson, President, Icelandic Chefs Association and National Culinary Team Iceland; Board Member, Nordic Chefs Association, 7 August 2013.

[21] www.facebook.com/KlubburMatreidslumeistara/info   Retrieved August 6, 2013

[22] Ibid

[23] www.facebook.com/groups/131046610294054/permalink/492301750835203/

[24] www.theworlds50best.com/list/1-50-winners/

SECTION THREE

SECTOR CASE STUDIES

Tourism Offices & Trade Groups

Margaret Jeffares and Erik Wolf

Tourism office and trade groups are the tip of the iceberg with regard to representing the interests and activities of an entire area. To smaller businesses, the workings of such groups may be a bit mysterious. This chapter will explain how Visit Sweden, Taste of Nova Scotia and Good Food Ireland are organized, including salient points about their operations and promotions.

INTRODUCTION

Many foodservice producers spend their entire careers without giving a thought to working with a local tourism office or trade group. They may think they are in the business of producing, growing or otherwise furnishing food and drink, and nothing more. Yet issues of seasonality, crises like bird flu, and increasing competition from chains mean that for the first time, many food and drink producers and providers now must look for new ways to distribute their products and make sales. Attracting visitors is a great way to boost sales, but can be hard for an individual business owner to do it alone. This is why it makes sense to reach out to a tourism office or trade group for help.

VisitSweden

Mention Sweden to a potential traveler and thoughts of cold weather, attractive blonds, Vikings and even vodka come to mind. Stereotypes aside, Sweden has garnered a worthy reputation in the food world, and is now achieving that same reputation specifically in the food and drink tourism world. Sweden is the result of a "perfect storm" of all the variables needed to create a sustainable and successful food tourism destination.

Swedish Chefs Unseat the French

The seeds of Sweden's rise to fame in culinary circles were planted back in the 1970s when Swedish chefs were represented in European culinary competitions. Swedish chefs began winning these competitions, much to the surprise of the French, whose country hosted some of the more prominent events, including the renowned "Bocuse d'Or". Building on that confidence, for two or so decades, Sweden's chefs began experimenting with many of their country's high quality ingredients, and fusing them with influences from other cultures. European history has brought a number of influences into Swedish cuisine, notably from the French. So the idea of experimenting and evolving recipes is endemic in the mindset of today's Swedish chefs.

Commitment to Fresh and Organic Ingredients

One noteworthy Swedish Chef is Magnus Nilsson, of the restaurant Fäviken, located near Sweden's western border with Norway. He has always understood the importance of quality, fresh food. As a child and into his teens, he would hunt, fish, forage and cook with his family. His grandparents lived on a small farm and survived more or less almost entirely from what their own land produced. These principles would later influence the philosophy of his restaurant. After finishing school, he moved to the south of Sweden, where he learned to master many of the essential cooking techniques in a restaurant called Kattegat in Skåne, and later on at Pontus at the Green House in Stockholm. These establishments gave him a glimpse of the determination and skill necessary to run an ambitious and successful restaurant. Following these experiences, Magnus worked for Pascal Barbot at L'Astrance in Paris. He began as a trainee before returning as a chef de partie in the pastry and cold starters section after a short stint at L'Arpège. Eventually he returned to Sweden and took the helm at the kitchen of a successful restaurant in Stockholm while perusing his passion for wine. Magnus decided to study at a sommelier school, setting his sights on becoming a master of wine. At this time, Magnus was introduced to Fäviken Magasinet, the restaurant he now runs, located on a remote farm in Western Sweden. In 2008, he joined as a sommelier, helping the Brummer family to establish their wine cellar as well as working in the kitchen. After three months, the owner called for a change in direction and Magnus was enlisted to transform the restaurant into how it operates today. Amongst the proposals, Magnus suggested that local produce should be used, and he began by tending to a small vegetable patch at the side of the estate. This first step was important, because it made Magnus realize that the kitchen could source restaurant produce in the immediate vicinity of the restaurant. Magnus took over the restaurant as his own. He continued to get good reviews in Swedish national publications. Fäviken was the first restaurant outside of Stockholm to get a review of 25/25 in *Dagens Industri*, a Swedish daily business newspaper, and has been ranked number one in Sweden numerous times. It is also number 34 in the 2013 list of World's 50 Best Restaurants.[1] In October 2012, Magnus released his first cookbook entitled Fäviken, offering an insight into his fascinating restaurant, which only seats 16 guests per night. Chef Nilsson's commitment to using fresh, local ingredients is key to making his restaurant a culinary experience or attraction, for locals and tourists alike.

Public Government Commitment

Concurrently with Chef Nilsson's rise to fame was the edict from Swedish Minister for Rural Affairs, Eskil Erlandsson. The minister announced in 2008 his vision to make Sweden the "New Culinary Nation." Citing long days of summertime daylight; a unique climate and landscape that begets unique produce; a diversity of produce and manufacturing methods; a booming food industry; and a commitment to animal health, welfare and organic cultivation, Minister Erlandsson knew that growing tourism could position Sweden as an exemplary model of food tourism. With this edict, the wheels of a new movement began to turn.

Sweden: The New Culinary Nation

As part of its commitment to develop Sweden as the New Culinary Nation,[2] the Swedish government invests a large sum each year to help drive the program forward. The investment also pays for a general manager to develop the project. Anne-Marie Hovstadius, who was hired to fill that role. During her tenure, VisitSweden (the national tourist organization funded in part by the Swedish government) began to develop the foundation of a culinary brand strategy. Tenets of the strategy included hosting an annual Matlandet (Country of Food) Conference and participation in Ny Nordsik Mat (New Nordic Food), a dialogue of ministers and other culinarians from the Nordic countries who have committed to working together to develop an image for the region's cuisine, which shares many similarities. VisitSweden also regularly hosts qualified food journalists and bloggers to experience what the new culinary nation is all about. And it works with Sweden's regions such as Gothenburg and West Sweden; to help build regional food identities that support the country's national food identity. VisitSweden knows the value of partnerships and together with Gothenburg & Company[3] (the city's tourism office) and the West Sweden Tourist Board, hosted the World Food Travel Summit in Gothenburg in 2013.

In many ways, Sweden is in the best possible position as a food tourism destination. The country has a legion of creative chefs who want to use Swedish produce; high quality agricultural products from the sea and land; national government commitment; a dedicated program manager; funding; and an action plan with specific projects that deliver results as part of the destination marketing organization's key performance indicators. Not every destination can emulate this model, but it is a model worthy of study for specific lessons of relevance.

Good Food Ireland

Margaret Jeffares, Executive Director of Good Food Ireland (GFI),[4] grew up on a farm on the west coast of Ireland in County Clare, with plenty of agriculture and animals. Those with agricultural roots will understand that farming is a way of life. It was not unexpected when she ended up moving to the southeast corner of Ireland, to County Wexford to marry her farming husband Des and to make a life on a Ballykelly Farm. While working on the farm, Margaret gained an even greater respect and admiration for the people who grow, rear and make the food we eat. Ireland's traditions and cultural core are at the very heart of the small and medium sized farms that spread all over the island and which have been hugely influential in forming Ireland as a nation. Now Ireland is part of the European Union and its markets are global. Margaret saw change on the horizon and knew that many Irish farming families would need to diversify and create new commercial opportunities and value added products in order to compete successfully.

How it All Began

Margaret's career was not in farming, but in tourism marketing and development, from airline to tour operations, to hotels and visitor attractions. In the early 2000s, there were a number of food scares, both global and local, that had a significant effect on Ireland's tourism industry. Food security became a common discussion and consumers all around the world were beginning to give greater attention to sources of their food. During this time, Margaret's organization operated a central bookings service for international visitors coming to Ireland. The shift in consumer behavior was clearly evident. For the first time, she witnessed strong visitor demand for information around restaurants in Ireland and where to eat.

A Time for Innovation

At this time, the challenges surrounding the tourism industry were not just from a downturn of international visitors but affected domestic tourism also. The industry began to change and evolve. Alcohol licensing laws in pubs forced them to develop a greater food offering. Incentivized hotels were built, increasing bed inventory. Restaurants and traditional accommodation providers were now operating in a far more competitive environment and in clear need of recognition. From knowing and working with these operators, it was obvious that there was one thing that so many of them had in common, but no one was really identifying or celebrating it. That was their commitment to using local food produce. Margaret saw the opportunity. If she could create a resource that would highlight those tourism providers committed to using local food and produce, it would drive international visitors to their businesses, bringing greater opportunity and increased incomes for farmers, fishermen and food producers. She would need to create a brand that would tangibly link for the first time Ireland's two biggest industries, the agriculture/ food sector and the tourism/ hospitality sector. The end goal would be to guarantee the best that Ireland offered from producers, retailers and food service, for both tourists and domestic consumers who demanded and expected only the best.

Good Food Ireland as a Brand

The brand would become the consumer facing endorsement, the core products and services for the consumer offering and uniting force for members subscribing to the brand. However, to be true to the customer and industry alike, then the new business would have to deliver on its promise. Therefore a brand strategy was created with strict entry criteria based on this commitment to Irish ingredients. Then in late 2006, the Good Food Ireland (GFI) brand was launched. GFI's proposition is straightforward: quality assurance for everyone who simply loves good food. The brand governs everything the organization produces and is present in all consumer touchpoints.

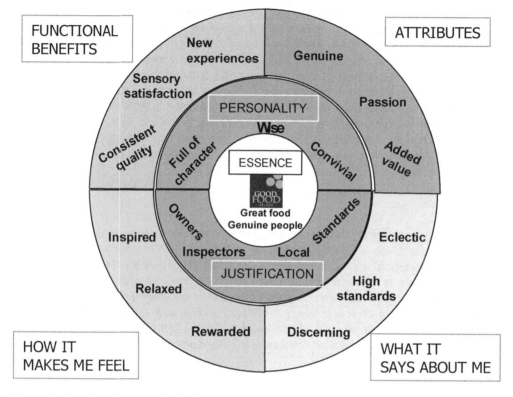

Figure 1: Growing Support; Credit: Good Food Ireland

Most of 2007 was spent building consensus. The leadership traveled around Ireland to present the vision to industry, seek feedback and opinions, and to build support. GFI did receive huge support from people who were eager to support this vision in every way. In November 2007, Good Food Ireland, along with 70 founding member businesses, officially launched its brand at Dublin's Shelbourne Hotel, with the then Minister for Arts, Sport and Tourism.

Growing the Business

With the brand to the fore, Good Food Ireland operates as a services company, promoting a network of selected members who produce, prepare and serve the highest quality local food experience. The ambition is to be the number one food tourism resource "for everyone who simply loves good food." During the years that followed, three main objectives were determined:

1) to market the brand domestically and internationally to drive business; 2) to grow the membership base to meet customers' needs and 3) to communicate the philosophy of GFI to government, food and tourist boards and relevant associations both north and south of the island. A number of key industry and business leaders, with varying areas of expertise, came together on a voluntary basis in support of the vision. A Steering Group was formed and Chairman appointed.

Good Food Ireland is a big vision and with a small office team of just three in the beginning and very limited financial resources. It was extremely challenging. However, its leaders never stopped believing in the philosophy of GFI and that it was right and good for consumers, the industry and for Ireland as a whole. As time moved on, some matched marketing funding was secured from Tourism Ireland and strong corporate partnerships were developed.

Business Model

Brand Standards

An independent team of quality assurance representatives were appointed on a contract basis to inspect industry businesses prior to joining to ensure that their philosophy met the Good Food Ireland consumer promise. The GFI team was very conscious of being critical of people who ran a business and ensured that the inspectors who were appointed had a proven track record in the food and hospitality sector in industry. Membership approval is subject to satisfying the Good Food Ireland criteria based on:

- The quality of the food, ingredients and taste, prioritizing Irish foods
- The use of local and seasonal produce
- The championing of local artisan producers
- The personality of the cuisine and hospitality of the service
- The quality of accommodation and authenticity of product
- Value for money and consistency of the offer

Customers

Good Food Ireland customers fall into two clearly defined categories — members and consumers. Members are at the heart of GFI, but consumers are the lifeblood. Both need to be healthy and in steady supply. The Membership pool is drawn from a diverse base, identified by the needs of our consumer and includes the following:

- restaurants & cafes – fine dining, bistros, visitor attractions, restaurants etc.
- culinary accommodation – hotels, country houses, guesthouses, B&BS, farmhouses
- food shops – delis and gourmet shops, butchers, bakeries etc.
- food producers & microbreweries open to public – including farmers and fishermen

Good Food Ireland Approved Providers

The prime benefits that Good Food Ireland offers its approved members are:

- Endorsement as a premium local food experience, through a recognized and unique national brand.
- Access to, and recognition by, a wider audience i.e. driving business to their doors through established and successful marketing activities at local, national and international levels.[5]
- The significant collective marketing effort that GFI musters on behalf of its individual members, the scale and scope of this would be unattainable for the majority of the members whose businesses are small and have little or no marketing budget
- immediate cost effective route to market through existing and new business platforms
- Access to business platforms and marketing distribution that as individual companies they could not reach.

- Support through an already established network of like-minded people. The marketing effect drives consumer business to their doors and there begins the cross-fertilization in the network.[6]
- Opportunity for formal and casual contacts. These liaisons enable like-minded people to share ideas and source the best foods and services.
- Access to education and mentor program based on existing industry needs analysis, information on best practice and consumer trends with proven operating protocol and toolkit. New support programs are developed in line with industry requirements. Members also receive a variety of templates that will them develop all aspects of their business. Often we coordinate with other organizations and government agencies to tailor "how to?" guides on e.g. networking, developing supply/local sourcing channels, marketing your business, how to manage cross-referrals etc.

Figure 2: Good Food Ireland Business Model; *Credit: Good Food Ireland*

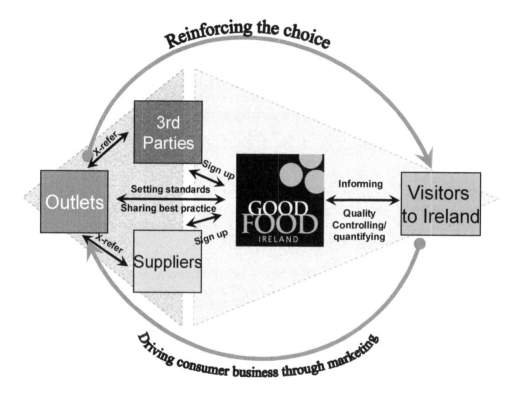

For Everyone Who Simply Loves Good Food

According to GFI, consumer audiences are characterized by having:

- Demanding and developing palates: they increasingly want sensory rewards and satisfaction, without the attendant risks of cost or dissatisfaction
- An expectation of good, attentive and well informed service: they like to be looked after and to know things
- Occasionally compromise on food in today's lifestyle, but they will not compromise on taste or on quality and health

- A keen eye on the food learning process, using the acquired information to justify purchases: require provenance and nutritional detail, and to justify where they eat: seek recommendation, inspect premises
- They are generally not food snobs but genuine aficionados/epicures: use all senses to evaluate the food and eating experience
- Appreciate being pointed in the right direction but not being told what to do or think

Good Food Ireland's marketing efforts have taken the organization all over the world in collaboration with Tourism Ireland to promote the brand and industry providers behind the island's destination message. The proposition has been tailored to meet the two key drivers for visitors to Ireland – scenery and people. Good Food Ireland therefore promotes the people behind the food, telling their story and communicating their message.

Vision Becomes Reality

In early 2013, GFI commissioned a survey to discover the effectiveness of its programs. Ninety-four percent of Approved Providers increased their purchases of Irish food under the influence of Good Food Ireland, directly contributing around €50 million to the Irish economy. Ninety seven percent expected their turnover to increase or remain the same in 2013. Again, 94% believed that there was a need for increased marketing of food tourism and that Good Food Ireland's integrated food tourism strategy and website uniquely fill this gap.

Having got the statistical reassurance, GFI further invested in driving the next phase of the vision. Now commencing its sixth year in business this is an exciting time with a critical mass of almost 600 members behind the brand and a strong food tourism consumer presence. A new consumer focused website has just been launched with a call to action around "My Food Trip" and online shop selling artisan Irish food products world-wide.

Good Food Ireland will continue to evolve. The market has created the opportunity and GFI will embrace it strategically to meet its ambition. The company is still in its infancy but new business ventures that are mutually reinforcing the core business are being created to meet consumer needs. GFI will continue to provide an even greater cultural and authentic food experience for the consumer that is unique to Ireland, so visitors can immerse themselves in the very heart and essence of Ireland, its food and its people. GFI extends its deepest gratitude to all those who believed in its vision.

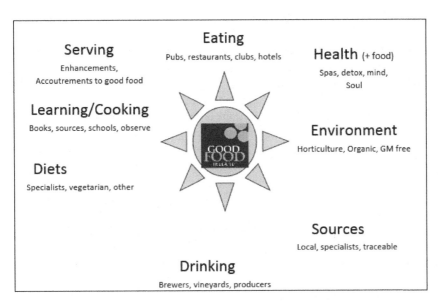

Figure 3: Good Food Ireland Network; *Credit: Good Food Ireland*

Taste of Nova Scotia: Leave No Stone Unturned

Taste of Nova Scotia is a not-for-profit, member-driven association that is dedicated to providing authentic culinary experiences through a unique, province-wide marketing program. Its members are committed to offering the very best culinary experiences and products that the province has to offer. At the helm of Taste of Nova Scotia (TNS) is Janice Ruddock, who has effectively led the organization through several successes since 2007. She has an unwritten philosophy to "leave no stone unturned". In other words, she believes partnerships and success can come from every corner of the province, and from places where one might least expect.

History

Originally, TNS was created by the Nova Scotia Department of Agriculture to encourage Nova Scotians to buy fresh local peas, instead of canned peas. On a larger scale it set the stage for the province's buy local campaign, although buying local is something many Nova Scotians have been doing for a long time. The organization's purpose fit well with the approach that many of its citizens had already embraced. In 1991, the Taste of Nova Scotia Society was established to support the province's restaurants. Later in 1995, the Taste of Nova Scotia Quality Food Council was established to support producers. It was not until 2007, under the leadership of executive director Janice Ruddock that the two organizations merged to form the current Taste of Nova Scotia, which represents both restaurants and producers. Having one unified, rebranded Taste of Nova Scotia association for all of the quality restaurants, producers and processors in the province, provides a greater opportunity to promote local culinary experiences, represent industry and grow members' businesses.

Stringent Membership Process

To become a TNS member, producers and processors must submit an application and samples of their products. The business undergoes a site inspection and the products are assessed to ensure adherence to Taste of Nova Scotia standards and criteria. Restaurants submit an application and their menu, and also undergo a site inspection and commit to serving seasonal, local ingredients. All TNS businesses must be Nova Scotia owned and operated.

Successes

Since its inception in 2007, the organization has achieved the following notable successes:

- A stable, internationally recognized brand: From our Land. From our Sea. From our Hands
- Taste of Nova Scotia beverage education seminars: Working with restaurants and chefs to embrace Nova Scotia wines
- Nova Scotia Culinary Guide: Both print and app versions. The iPhone app is a best-in-class example of an organization of food and drink producers working to promote tourism.
- Prestige Awards: Annual celebration of excellence to honor producers and restaurants that provide exceptional culinary products and experiences. Winners chosen from consumer nominations and committee scrutiny are announced during the annual Tourism Industry Association of Nova Scotia's (TIANS) Tourism Summit.
- Media: TNS is fortunate to be in a position where it is approached regularly by media for content. For example, Jamie Oliver is in love with Nova Scotia's lobsters, which is not a bad position for TNS to be in. With success comes a caveat that organizations in this position tend to be more reactive than proactive with media requests. At some point when new competition fights for consumer attention, the balance will need to be more proactive, which TNS has acknowledged.

- Overview: Some of our accomplishments, significant media exposure (developing local relationships, being the "go to" for culinary info, Jamie Oliver spread). Media familiarization tours with the tourism office.
- Export Initiatives: TNS works with Atlantic Canada Opportunities Agency (ACOA); the Department of Foreign Affairs and International Trade (DFAIT); and local experts to facilitate opportunities for its members to grow their businesses outside Canadian borders. TNS members now sell products around the world. Examples include Acadian Maple syrup, Terra Beata cranberries, Nova Scotia wine, Gidney Fisheries, Victoria Co-op, Clearwater Seafoods and Louisbourg Seafoods.
- World Food Travel Summit: Hosted the world's largest gathering of food tourism professionals, effectively putting the province on the map of the industry world-wide, and adding to its exposure with media.
- Roving Receptions: local, national and international business receptions and also at the 2012 Olympics. TNS partners see the value in having a Taste of Nova Scotia branded reception. This may include wine tasting, bringing a Nova Scotia chef to cook at the host destination, and TNS member product sampling
- Effective partnerships: TNS partners with a range of provincial organizations such as Select Nova Scotia, the Winery Association of Nova Scotia (WANS), Destination Halifax, the Tourism Industry Association of Nova Scotia (TIANS), Nova Scotia Association of Chefs & Cooks and the Restaurant Association of Nova Scotia (RANS), which all work with TNS to promote Nova Scotia's quality culinary experiences and products. Within the community Nova Scotia Business Inc. (NSBI), Waterfront Development and Blue Nose Marathon all support the organizations work. Even the government supports the organization's work, with endorsement coming from the Nova Scotia Department of Agriculture, Fisheries and Aquaculture; ACOA as well as the Nova Scotia Department of Economic and Rural Development.

Challenges

While all appears rosy, there are always a few areas in need of attention. Like with many other organizations and destinations, funding is a perpetual challenge. Current funding for TNS is secured through membership fees, government funding for specific projects and third-party event management. A long-term goal of the organization is to become completely self-sufficient. The organization has lots of ideas of additional projects it can take on, but funding is always an issue, with funding for current programs a priority.

TNS also faces challenges encouraging locals to buy local and support the province's agriculture industry, a problem frequently faced by similar organizations around the world. While there is no easy solution, visibility at events and show throughout the province, strong partnerships and great media coverage give the organization visibility and respect by trade and consumers alike.

Lessons Learned

While in many regions and countries, there are producer organizations like TNS, it is rare to find the components that have come together as completely as with TNS. Effective and passionate leadership; an engaged board of directors; a small team with complementary skill sets; high quality food and drink products; a naturally beautiful area; and great partners have helped to make Taste of Nova Scotia the success it is today. Similar regions and groups should be inspired from the TNS case study and remember to leave no stone unturned.

Nova Scotia has a plethora of local products, talented chefs and authentic culinary experiences. The province's biggest asset is the passion of its people and the access to fresh, local, quality ingredients. Working with this foundation, Taste of Nova Scotia is taking the culinary scene in Nova Scotia to new heights. Each year new local, national and international opportunities present themselves. To grow its members' businesses will continue to be its number one goal.

CONCLUSION

In many ways, destination marketing organizations like VisitSweden and trade groups like Good Food Ireland and Taste of Nova Scotia, are some of the most important pieces in the food and drink tourism puzzle. These organizations provide strategic direction, leadership, marketing ideas and programs including some distribution outlets, and even funding on limited levels. These organizations are like glue which holds together the food and drink tourism industry for the areas they oversee. While two of these organizations are national and one is provincial, the concept of a tourism office or trade group can apply to regional and even local levels. If none exist in your area, then perhaps this chapter will provide inspirational ideas as to what can be done in your area.

Food and drink tourism industry professionals are encouraged to study these organizations for inspiration and ideas. There is an opportunity in areas without trade groups like TNS or GFI to create such groups to shepherd development and promotion of unique food and drink resources, which are key components of a successful food and drink tourism program.

DISCUSSION QUESTIONS

1. In what ways do trade organizations like GFI and TNS serve as DMOs? In what ways are they different from DMOs?
2. Both organizations represent small areas and have members who believe in the organizations' missions. What problems might exist with larger geographic areas or producers who are concerned solely about their own profit and well-being?
3. What solutions can you present to overcome the issues of a managing a larger geographic area or of convincing single-focused producers of the value of participating in an organization like these?

ENDNOTES

[1] "Number 31 – 40" The world`s 50 best restaurants, last accessed July 17, 2013, www.theworlds50best.com/list/1-50-winners/#t31-40
[2] "Sweden, the new culinary nation", Visit Sweden, last accessed July 17, 2013, www.visitsweden.com/sweden/Featured/Sweden-the-new-culinary-nation/
[3] www.Goteborg.com
[4] www.goodfoodireland.ie
[5] The significant collective marketing effort that GFI musters on behalf of its individual members, the scale and scope of this would be unattainable for the majority of the members whose businesses are small and have little or no marketing budget.
[6] Additionally the network provides the opportunity for formal and casual contacts. These liaisons enable like-minded people to share ideas and source the best foods and services.

Culinary Tours, Guides, Packages & Agents

Nicole Biscardi, Carlotta Casciola, Martin Hrabec, Harold Partain, & Erik Wolf

This chapter delves into different aspects of culinary tour operations, including common terminology, product development, marketing and customer satisfaction.

INTRODUCTION

The notion of eating and drinking one's way around the world is appealing on many levels. Many people who enter the food tourism industry decide to become a culinary tour operator or guide because of such appeal. However, it takes a lot of work and effort to succeed as a culinary tour operator, travel agent, or guide. This chapter is a comprehensive guide for anyone who wants to create and develop food tourism products or packages and send or receive food-loving guests.

Current Food Tourism Market

The growing popularity of food tourism in recent years has presented a new set of opportunities within the travel and tourism industry, resulting in the emergence of several new roles specific to the food tourism sector. In response to this growing need for professionals specifically focused on food tourism, there have been long-time industry participants who have simply shifted their professional focus towards culinary travel in an effort to capitalize on some of these new opportunities. There also exists an entirely new set of entrants into the travel and tourism industry, who are entering the business and taking on roles specifically addressing the needs of the food tourism sector.

Entering into the food tourism market, regardless of your impetus, requires a high level of commitment. Successful participants build their food tourism businesses upon a strong foundation of understanding the basic principles and best practices in the greater travel and tourism industry. Local knowledge and expertise are necessary components, as well as an existing network of potential clients and partners in your prospective market. As with any new business, having a solid business plan detailing your concept and its financial feasibility is essential. Calling on local professionals for assistance with in-depth financial planning, legal advice, and insurance, are crucial to your success when planning any new venture in the food tourism industry.

The specialization and expertise of food tourism professionals is an essential component to their success, and as a result we find that many industry participants choose to focus on a specific sub-sector in which to operate. For example, a food tourism professional may choose to focus their business around a specific destination or geographic region. Some professionals may choose to market exclusively to a specific demographic, for example, women or senior citizens. Others may choose to focus on a particular product or service offering, such as wine tourism, hands-on instructional culinary programs, or agritourism.

Defining New Roles

This sector is not a large sector of our food tourism industry, but it is a very important one. At its most basic, the sector includes culinary tour operators (both outbound and inbound), tour guides, tour packages, and travel agents and counselors. This chapter will review these terms to ensure a common understanding for our industry.

Culinary Tour Operator

A culinary tour operator is the individual who, or organization that, plans, organizes, and executes the logistics of a group of culinary tourists. It is generally responsible for arranging the complete itinerary, including the transportation, lodging, activities, tours, excursions and of course meals. An example of a culinary tour operator is Gourmet on Tour, based in London.[1] A tour operator can be outbound (for example UK to India), or inbound (such as a company located in Peru that receives culinary travelers to Peru from all over the world). In such an example, the company in Peru is referred to as a receptive operator, because it receives visitors.

Culinary tour operators can sell their products and services through a variety of channels, including wholesale (B2B, or business to business), retail (B2C, or business to consumer), or some combination of both.

Tour operators must be proactive in educating their agency base, informing them in detail of the unique selling points of their products and services. This enables the agents to be well versed in the value proposition that the operator is offering, and assists them in effectively communicating this to their clients.

Culinary operators often offer prepackaged itineraries for groups of travelers, and provide these itineraries in a ready-made fashion for the selling agents to market to individuals or groups of clients. In addition to providing prepackaged itineraries, culinary operators should provide agents with comprehensive marketing materials detailing their products and services, so that the agent can in turn, use these materials to advertise and promote the culinary tours to their client base. Although much of this information can be shared electronically, regular sales calls and live presentations to agents are extremely effective methods by which operators can increase awareness of their offerings, and in turn, increase sales. Due to the geographic separation of many operators from their sales agents, alternative technology-driven educational methods such as webinars, conference calls, newsletters and regular email communications, are now used to keep agents abreast of the latest information available to help support and facilitate the sales process.

Another important reason for operators to stay in close contact with their agents is to receive valuable feedback from the customers of food tourism products and services. Agents are in direct and often frequent contact with their clients, and can provide operators with a tremendous amount of relevant information regarding the demographics, preferences, interests and trends amongst the customer base. Culinary operators can also actively solicit post-trip feedback from customers via their sales network, which can be a valuable source of information for operators. This information can be used to improve and enhance the quality of service and enhance the value proposition of the operator's product and service offerings.

Wholesale Culinary Tour Operator

Culinary tour operators who conduct their business in a wholesale capacity sell their products and services by relying explicitly on third-party agents to sell their experiences to the consumer. The operator's client is essentially the travel/culinary agents or group travel organizers who actively market the experiences to their client base. In order for a culinary operator to be a successful wholesaler, they must play an active role in supporting the selling process of travel agents in a number of ways.

There are few truly wholesale tour operators offering only culinary tours and working through the travel agent/affiliate network. Typically one finds a more traditional tour operator offering a division or special group of tours that are principally sold through their traditional agent network. An example of this is the California-based Classic Journeys.[2]

There are several inbound companies now who offer their products through travel agencies/affiliates and will gladly work with consultants to help organize a specific itinerary. However, these companies also work directly with the consumer and offer a series of specific travel dates and itineraries that both an individual or travel agent can book. A Taste of Spain is one company that works with this business model.[3] Another interesting example is the New York City-based Tour de Forks. The company works with a travel agency consortium and actively solicits travel agencies to work with them. [4]

Culinary operators who sell their products and services wholesale do not need a direct network of consumers. This allows the operator to focus more of their talent and resources on operational aspects of the business, such as improving the quality of products and services. The costs to the operator associated with selling through an agency are generally low, because operators who employ the wholesale channel for selling their products and services generally compensate their selling agents by way of a commission. Rates for culinary tour operators' products and services are typically offered to selling agents at a net pricing level. The net price, determined by the operator, is the amount of money that the operator must be paid for services rendered. The agent's commission is an amount charged to the consumer in excess of the operator's net price, and is generally in the 10-12% range.

Retail Culinary Tour Operators

Culinary tour operators may also operate in a retail capacity, selling their products and services directly to the consumer, without any involvement of a third-party agent. In this case, the operator generally employs a sales staff responsible for sales. The direct sales function of a culinary operator is quite similar to that of third party selling agents. These individuals are responsible for actively advertising and promoting the operator's products and services to potential consumers.

Many culinary operators who sell directly to consumers utilize web-based methods for conducting their sales activities. Comprehensive websites and web-based marketing activities are commonly relied upon to generate direct sales. An operator must develop and maintain an extensive network and database of potential clients, and actively market to these individuals and groups on an ongoing basis. Lead generation is a crucial aspect of building and maintaining a viable database and network of consumers for the operator's sales staff to target for direct sales.

Potential benefits of culinary operators directly employing their own sales staff are that the operator will possess a greater level of quality control over the sales process. In addition, employing a retail sales channel presents the opportunity for an operator to keep a greater portion of the revenue from each sale "in house," as internal sales staff are also generally compensated by a commission structure, which would pay the salesperson a percentage of each sale they make. This commission will generally represent a large portion of the sales staff compensation, keeping the operator's fixed costs for maintaining an internal sales staff relatively low.

There is often crossover between culinary tour guide, culinary travel agent and culinary tour wholesaler. Examples of companies that could fit in many different categories include Gourmet on Tour,[5] Momma Margaret's Italy Cooking Schools,[6] and The International Kitchen.[7]

Culinary Travel Agent

A culinary travel agent is a sales agent who specializes in the sale of food tourism experiences. Such an agent may work for a typical generalist travel agency, and be the individual that specifically sells food tourism itineraries as part of the agency's overall service offering. The culinary agent is typically the designated person within an agency who exclusively works with clients seeking a food tourism experience. Alternatively, a culinary agent may be employed by an agency that specializes solely in food tourism. Irrespective of the type of agency in which the culinary agent operates. Such an agent is essentially an industry specialist with a strong network of connections and a high level of expertise in the food tourism world. Culinary agents possess the ability to utilize the products and enlist the services of numerous incoming culinary tour operators in order to provide culinary experiences for their clients.

Culinary agents are sometimes remote or home-based employees of a greater travel agency network. A culinary agent is typically compensated by receiving a commission equal to a percentage of their sales. Often these agents are not paid a base salary, and are granted access to utilize the parent agency's network affiliates, often in exchange for a franchise fee.

In order for a culinary agent to succeed, they must work hard to source, develop and maintain a well-targeted client base. Many successful culinary agents are active members within their communities and have close ties to organizations and groups of individuals who actively engage in food tourism. For example, a culinary agent may source leads from relative activity-specific groups such as cooking schools and wine clubs, as well as from demographic-specific groups like womens' or senior citizens' travel clubs or associations.

Culinary Tour Guide or Culinary Tour Host?

There is an important difference between a Culinary Tour Guide and a Culinary Tour Host. A culinary tour host is an individual who accompanies culinary travelers throughout their food tourism experience. The host's primary role is to act as the coordinator and leader of the tourism activities throughout the duration of the culinary travel experience. In the case of small culinary group travel, the guide usually accompanies the group for the duration of their itinerary at no additional cost, as the revenues from the paying passengers usually cover the expense of a Tour Guide. Sometimes the culinary agent who sold the group tour actively participates in the travel experience acting as a guide.

In most countries it is not permitted for a non-native, non-registered or otherwise not legally qualified person to serve as a tour guide. A tour guide must be licensed in order to lecture or discuss on-site in most public places. A tour guide must be a truly specialized individual for the specific region or issue and have passed all the required examinations and licensing.

Sometimes a Tour Host can also be a Tour Guide. These situations would be in private homes, gardens, other non-public places, and in the van or on the motorcoach. A chef, for instance, would be more than qualified to discuss, demonstrate, lecture, and instruct hands-on cooking classes, but not necessarily lecture in public places. Local laws and protocol must be respected. If you have a strong Tour Host, it may not always be necessary to hire a Tour Guide for the duration of the journey. Locals can be hired to cover specific needs. A guide who steps on to a motorcoach to provide a brief lecture or introduction to an area or an attraction is called a "step on guide."

Tour Hosts fill in the gaps not covered by the Tour Guides. Depending on the journey, there may be several local guides, but there is only one Tour Host, whose main responsibility is to bring cohesion to the itinerary.

Culinary tours comprise various individual products that may be sold separately or bundled with additional travel products and services. Often culinary travel products are arranged and sold as complete itinerary packages with transportation, lodging and activities combined together. In addition to the daily scheduled culinary activities, a package may also include transportation (air, land, or both), lodging, and other group events. Common food tourism products include cooking classes, guided market visits, ingredient shopping, wine tasting, vineyard tours, market or farm visits, meet the winemaker/brewer/distiller, expert lectures, special dinners, and demonstrations. A meal itself is not considered a "product" unless it contains special features or experiences that make it positively memorable. Otherwise it is simply a meal, or sustenance. To accompany typical food tour activities, many operators and agencies arrange special souvenirs. Aprons, cookbooks or recipes, journals, utensils, or non-perishable specialty food items like olive oil are commonly offered as complimentary gifts for travelers to bring home. If the package is created by a culinary tour operator, they will distribute it to their travel agency network to advertise and promote to their own network of clients.

Develop Your Tour Product

No matter if your primary business is as a tour operator or in destination marketing, ideas for a successful food tour can be gleaned from a variety of sources, such as colleagues, employees, clients, your competition, your own research on product gaps and market needs, and successful examples seen in other destinations. Be careful not to simply copy a package or trail offered in other regions or destinations. While such ideas may be good or successful in their home markets, what works elsewhere, may not work in your area. Not to mention it would be unethical to copy someone else's work. If an idea inspires you, the smart tour operator or destination marketer will find a way to add value to it to make it their own. Insert unique content specific to your destination, place or company. Think about what is the best, most interesting, most tempting in the place where you want to take or invite your clients. Think about stories that can be told and woven in with the history or the people. It does not matter whether the food is famous, but an interesting story is a must.

Other sources of inspiration for itineraries and activities include the internet, magazines, and brochures from the local tourism office. Develop a unique selling proposition (USP) to design a unique food tourism experience. What can you offer that no one else will be able to offer? It could be access to a winery that is normally closed to the public, or a taste of an early release of a special beer or cheese. Analyze your idea in terms of your ability to realize it, organize it, and fund it, and in terms of its suitability for your customers.

The next step is to define your food tourism product. The purpose of your product may be to promote; 1) a destination or specific region; 2) a specific product or appellation; 3) a specific manufacturing process; or 4) a story of the food and place, which may be told by an animated local resident. When developing your product, ask yourself the following questions:

- Who is the target market?
- What content and experience comprise our product?
- What client needs or expectations are satisfied?
- Does our product leverage regional or national tourism products and strategies?
- How is our product different from our competition?
- What are the costs of the various components of our product, and how will we price it?
- How do we measure our success?

Write a SWOT Analysis

A number of internal and external factors can affect the quality of the product and its potential for success, for example:

- Do we have enough financial resources to cover the costs?
- Do we have sufficient options, capacity and skilled staff to make the product happen?
- Do we have enough reliable, quality suppliers to get all necessary goods and ingredients?
- Is the destination's positioning strong enough to support our product?
- How will our tour product impact the destination?
- How will the market, competitors, and clients react?
- Does customer research prove an interest in our product?

At this stage of planning, writing a SWOT (strengths, weaknesses, opportunities, threats) analysis should either confirm your product or encourage you to make adjustments. Also consider creating a Lean Business Model Canvas discussed in the beginning of this book. We encourage you to write out the analysis, rather than using computer software. The actual act of physically writing out the information tends to draw out important concepts that are lodged deep in your suconscious.

Scheduling Your Tour

Often food and drink experiences are available at specific times of the year, such as around harvest time, which may feature festivals or similar events. Many countries produce a harvest calendar for their agricultural commodities. Other times a food tour needs to be synchronized with agricultural production. For example, the harvest of grapes and making of wine; the harvest of olives, saffron, truffles or anything else, and the making of their value-added products.

In the case of customized tours, not all of the food and drink experiences requested are available when the clients want to travel. In such cases, get to know your client's priorities to help them make the best second choice. In Mediterranean countries, grape harvesting season varies from the end of August to the beginning of November; olives are picked from the end of October to December; January and February are the months for black truffle hunting. Saffron harvesting is even more delicate because the exact dates are only known a few days in advance and saffron harvest lasts no more than 10 days. If saffron is the priority, the client may be not able to experience the grape harvest or have to skip black truffle picking. In the southern hemisphere, add approximately 6 months to each of the dates above, although climatic zones can easily affect that time estimate. You also need to check for national holidays and national vacation periods. For example, much of Europe goes on holiday in August. While it may be prime time for visitors from North America to visit Europe, and it may suit your schedule as well, will enough attractions be open and will there be enough people available to work to execute your tour?

Weather may also contribute to the success or failure of a tour. It is important to explain to the client the probable weather conditions for the experience you offer. For example, Brazilians who are used to a warm climate most of the time may not enjoy truffle hunting in mid-winter in Italy. Most of the time, producers can propose other suitable experiences outside harvest. At non-harvest times, wineries may be able to offer a series of other wine experiences such as artwork, performances, or wine tasting activities (wine tasting sessions, blind tastings, create your own wine, etc.). In the case of specific or popular local events, it is important to make a reservation in advance. Always get confirmations in writing.

Specific food tour products might be challenging to integrate into your program. The plan for a gourmet dinner with Mangalitsa pork products will look different from a plan for a two-day culinary trip to harvest fruit in the highlands. If you want to create a good food tourism product, you need to find, create and communicate what is special and unique about your product. When finalizing your tour itinerary, you should have:

- A clear and detailed schedule of tasks, roles and responsibilities of your team members
- List of contracted or agreed suppliers for all necessary ingredients or components
- Logistics of supplies – how will you get them to the venues?
- Visitor logistics in case you plan to move the clients, i.e. from restaurant to farm and back
- Adequate team training about the program, the products, etc.
- Activities and amenities that complete the guest experience - decorations, inventory, music, gifts, story ...
- Budget and financial plan for upcoming event (if included), pricing of services
- A solid idea of your target customer

Marketing Food Tours

Food tour customers come from a number of sources including: current customers; customer referrals; conference and incentive customers; and even from specific countries of origin or specific groups. If you run regular, scheduled tours (such as a food walking tour of a city), then you should count on walk-up business as well.

It is beyond the scope of this chapter to give a specific prescription how to market culinary tours, primarily because there are so many possible variables it is impossible to prescribe a "one size fits all" solution. Still, many of the marketing techniques for food tours are similar to other tourism products and services with one main difference: the publication of an itinerary or program. Do not include too many specifics which would make it easy for your competitors to copy. For example, instead of saying "You will visit the DeCameron Winery and meet winemaker Mike and his wife Sue who will explain the history of the winery," you should say something like "Visit a local winery to meet the winemaker who will explain how he got started in the wine business." Below are some helpful reminders for both new and veteran food tour professionals.

- On the first page of your leaflet, newsletter, e-mail, or website, you must feature your unique selling proposition (USP). Use two to three sentences, not just a list of what you offer.
- Promote equally all of the five human senses
- Answer the usual, but unspoken question, "Why should client choose just your product?"
- Tell the truth (say to your clients: buy X and you will get Y)
- Remember that a tourism product is an *experience*, not a checklist
- Be different than your competitors
- Innovate (even only in small things) in your product development

Selling the Tours

You may have a great food tour and your website and brochure may look very professional, but if you make it hard for the customer to buy, they will move on and buy a similar, but still satisfactory product from someone else. The following suggestions can help prevent this:

- Include a regular toll phone number on your website. Use the (+xx) x-xxx-xxxx standard international phone format where the (+xx) is where you would put your country code. This seems obvious but the overwhelming majority of food tour operators either have no phone number on their website or do not include a country code.

- Avoid using words that spell numbers as part of a phone number. Telephone dial pads are not the same in every country, and some phones do not put the alphabet on the phone pads. Use your regular phone number and avoid the temptation to be cute.
- Toll-free numbers no longer have the appeal they once had. They are an additional and not inconsequential cost to your business and most people use mobile phones or office phones today. The cost to call you to make a booking is easily absorbed by your customer.
- How will your customer actually book with you? Do you have to take the information manually? Not only do you probably not have the time to do that, but your customers do not have the time for a manual sale process either. Consider using an online tool like checkfront.com to manage the booking process for you.
- What forms of payment do you accept? If you accept credit or debit cards, say which ones. Be aware that some countries call the same type of card by two different names. For example, EuroCard is simply a MasterCard in Europe, however it is often referred to as a EuroCard in businesses. In this example, by stating that you only accept MasterCard, you might be confusing a potential customer. The same rule applies for country-specific names for debit cards (like Solo or Electron in the U.K.) or country-specific credit cards (like Carte Aurore in France).
- If you want to pass along the cost of the bank processing fees to your customer, check to see if it is even allowed. In some jurisdictions, it is illegal to add a percentage on top of the product cost to cover bank fees. If this is the case, and even if it is not, consider increasing the base price of your tour by enough percent to cover the bank fees. Telling your customer that there will be an additional 5% added to the tour cost when they are ready to pay you is a disincentive that could actually cost you the entire sale. Think like your customers.

Custom Tours

While good client knowledge is important when designing a culinary tour or any other food experience, it is absolutely essential in the case of customized tour. Communication between the clients and the provider is very important in order to counsel and support the client's choice. Most important is the understanding of your client's motivation for the food tour. Practical information is basic to start designing a custom itinerary: length of the stay, budget available, kind of accommodation, services to be included (tour leader, transportation, guides, logistics) and any other specific requirements must be known in advance.

Pricing Food Tours

A great number of factors can affect the price of your tours. Suffice it to say, there is no simple formula. Obviously it is important to factor in the cost of the site visits, product samplings, meals and local transportation. Other components you might not expect are bank fees, foreign currency fluctuations, advance deposits and legal licensing requirements. The Association offers a webinar on how to start a culinary tour company.[8] It goes into the broad range of pricing issues that will help you to understand the best way to calculate a sustainable tour price.

Understanding Your Customers

Before you design an itinerary, you need to understand truly who your customers are. This means their demographics (origin, age, culture/religion, language, gender, income, social status); travel preferences for group or individual travel, and purchasing behavior (psychographics). There are many ways how to describe and classify food tourism clients. For simplification we classify them below in three broad yet fundamental categories. Depending on this profile and level of food and drink experience, changes may need to be made. Also refer to the World Food Travel Association's PsychoCulinary profiles of foodies which may help you more precisely define your customers.[9]

Food & Drink Professionals

This group includes chefs, winemakers, sommeliers, and wine and food importers/retailers. Wine professionals, for example, are looking for a technical visit of wineries and meeting with the winemaker or winery owner to exchange their experiences. They may ask to visit several cellars per day and have a professional wine tasting including a large number of regional wines, and/or specific appellations or grape varietals. In many ways, this *professional kind of food traveler* is the most demanding.

Food & Drink Enthusiasts

In the case of wine lovers, they tend to look for a *combination of classic and technical visits* to a famous winemaker combined with a few smaller producers. They appreciate insider tips and seek authentic experiences. They look for wine tasting with the purpose of buying wine at a good price, or at least cheaper than they can buy it in their country of origin. This is not always possible if the winery has a contract of exclusivity with the wine importer. Included in this category are wine club visitors who often travel with their spouses or with a group of friends. Even if food and drink experiences are the main motivation of the trip, they appreciate a casual itinerary including time for relaxation, shopping, art, and culture.

Food & Drink Epicureans

The greater majority of food and drink travelers seek food and drink experiences with the purpose of *knowing a different culture* through the pleasure of food and drink. They are neither professionals nor enthusiasts, but enjoy all around food and drink. They seek a more relaxed itinerary where food and drink experiences are combined with other travel attractions such as culture, art, nature, business, and so on.

Customers as a Market of One

A concept the Association has pioneered is that of "nanodemography", which adds the dimensions of individuality and time to psychographics. The basic premise is that we are all individuals who change our behaviors multiple times per day. Marketers need to plan accordingly. For example, someone may start the day as a Caucasian male businessman in his mid-30s seeking a professional food experience, such as a business lunch. As the day progresses, he may seek a more casual or authentic experience, such as a local café. By the time the evening comes, he may seek a social or trendy experience. All are valid behaviors and segmentation profiles. The lesson to be learned is not to restrict your clients to one particular type of experience because their preferences can actually change, and frequently. Someone with a Gourmet PyschoCulinary profile may still appreciate a humble falafel stand on the street. Ask your clients lots of questions before they arrive.

Customer Expectations

The success of any culinary tour or event is always a key factor in how we can meet the expectation of customers, especially in case of open tours and events. It is quite a hard job since we often do not know the structure of the group, background of clients, age, gender, social status or even their expectations. During the booking process, ask clients as many questions as possible to know them better. Another important source of information is feedback and data from previous customers and visitors. Such information in aggregate might be available from the local or regional tourism authority, or it could be gleaned by post-trip surveys which you send to your own customers. There are many methods and ways how we can gain customer feedback – statistics, questionnaires, online forum on a website, thank-you e-mails with a request for an opinion, but the best and most objective feedback is from personal and ongoing communication with your customers. Personal communication makes clients feel they are important, welcomed and well cared for, and helps to make them feel fully satisfied.

Customer Satisfaction

Ensuring your customer's satisfaction is of utmost importance. After all, if our customers are not happy, they will most certainly talk about the experience and not in a flattering way. Therefore, ask yourself if you meet the following requirements:

- Do you provide flawless and professional service?
- Are you and your team friendly and willing?
- Are your business practices fair and honest?
- Experience, experience, experience – do you offer one?
- Do you make your customers feel welcomed?
- Do you show your customers respect?

This seems like common sense, but many companies fail in these areas. Also consider:

- Do you know your customer's service journey?[10] If not, map it out. Pay attention to the customer's first impression – in person, by phone, online or by email.
- Create a vision of service quality, which will lead your operations and decision making. Share it with your customers.
- Check, evaluate, and promote team excellence.
- Streamline your operational processes. Avoid confusion and ambiguity.
- Educate your customers and provide them with regular information about new products, events, enhancements and service innovations.
- Receive, analyze and evaluate your customer feedback. Encourage your team to solicit customer feedback.
- Orient your products to the needs of specific customer groups - elderly, foreigners, families, children, business clients, etc.
- Be realistic in your offering. It´s better to under-promise and over-deliver than vice versa.
- Do not try to satisfy everyone. It is better to satisfy fewer clients 100% of the time than a larger number of clients only 50% of the time.
- Even the most friendly and guest-orientated approach does not solve all problems. Clients also need high quality information and quality service.
- Superior technical infrastructure is nothing without friendly and helpful staff.
- Talk to customers, ask them, show your interest and offer help – especially if they look uncomfortable. It is the only chance to solve and prevent potential problems.
- Handle guest complaints in proper way – as a useful feedback and not as a stressor.
- If you make a mistake, claim responsibility and do whatever it takes to make it right.
- Maintaining an existing customer is many times cheaper than acquiring a new one - keep that in mind constantly.
- Remind customers that you have not forgotten them, even if they have not visited you for a long time - e-mailing of special offers, birthday cards, newsletters, etc.
- Every customer is different. Do not look at that as a problem, but as something to make your daily work more interesting.
- Returning, satisfied guests are the best measure of your ROI.

CONCLUSION

It is difficult to forecast what it is like to work with food tour products in various markets. In well-developed food tourism countries like Italy, France, or Spain, culinary services are typically delivered in an established and predictable way where expectations and deliverables can be clearly defined. In emerging food tourism markets, such as those in Eastern Europe, Southeast Asia and Africa, food tourism products are still being defined. Suppliers and buyers are searching, testing, experimenting and exploring old, forgotten traditions and indigenous culinary heritage, and restoring traditional artisan food production. This can lead to problems like service failures and misunderstandings in what food tourism really means. These countries still have huge potential for further development, countless interesting stories waiting to be told, and the traditional food products waiting to be tasted.

DISCUSSION QUESTIONS

1. How might planning a culinary tour in Sweden differ from planning one in Thailand? What would be some of the differences in planning, and how would you overcome them?
2. How would you manage foreign exchange fluctuations in your product pricing?
3. What kinds of legal terms and conditions should you have in place in order to offer a professional culinary tour?

ENDNOTES

[1] www.gourmetontour.com
[2] www.classicjourneys.com/culinary
[3] www.atasteofspain.com
[4] www.tourdeforks.com
[5] www.gourmetontour.com
[6] www.italycookingschools.com
[7] www.theinternationalkitchen.com
[8] Visit www.worldfoodtravel.org and search for "webinar".
[9] This is explained in the *How Foodies Make Decisions* chapter in this book.
[10] For more about the customer service journey, read the chapter in this book entitled *The Food & Drink Tourism Service Journey.*

Food Tourism in Emerging Destinations:
The Case of Ecuador

Ayako Ezaki, Carlos Gallardo, & Carolina Perez

Food is of universal interest, no matter our gender, religion, income, level of education or any other difference. While many of the world's more glamorous cities and wine regions have garnered reputations as food tourism leaders, emerging destinations hold great promise to attract adventurous or bored food travelers. Many foodies have already toured Europe or the wine country in the western USA, and they now seek the new and different. Emerging destinations can give them just that. This is often where foodies can access true flavors, unadulterated by the influence of multinational chains; original recipes as they were intended to be served; and foods with ingredients that were picked or raised near where they are served. This chapter will look at a case study of Ecuador, an emerging culinary destination, explore how it orchestrated its rise, and draw conclusions about what other emerging food destinations can do to capitalize on food tourism.

INTRODUCTION

Mountains, highlands, tropical coastal regions, islands, Amazon jungle, and multiple ethnic and cultural groups are just some of the ingredients that make Ecuador a unique culinary destination. Visitors can find local foods and culinary traditions on every corner, and these offer an exciting combination of ancestral knowledge, community involvement, local recipes, and products from Ecuador's four distinct regions: the Amazon rainforest, Andes highlands, Pacific Coast and the Galapagos Archipelago. Ecuador is an interesting example for emerging food travel destinations around the world, as it demonstrates the possibility for a new and different approach to a destination's culinary identity, shaped by biodiversity, preservation of indigenous recipes, and different varieties of agricultural products coming from the land where they originated. It is an exciting model, which shows that culinary experiences are not only shaped by recipes, flavors, and ingredients, but enriched by traditional beliefs, local customs, and biological and cultural diversity.

Ecuador: Biological, Geographic & Culinary Diversity

What is Ecuadorian food? Unlike Mexican or Argentinian food, the culinary identity of this small South American country is not well known. Part of the reason for this may be Ecuador's approach to defining its own culinary identity differently; not by focusing on and marketing iconic dishes and typical styles, but by finding uniqueness in its diverse culinary traditions.

Ecuador is one of the 13 countries in the world whose territories are on the path of the Equator, and one of the only two countries in the world that are on the Equator and have mountains of significant elevation: Ecuador with the Andes (5,790 m /18,996 ft above sea level at summit), and Kenya with Mount Kenya (5,199 m /17,057 ft at summit). Ecuador's location in the tropics, the earth's biodiversity hotbed, and its unique geological features make the country an incredible living museum of ecological and biological diversity. In fact, Ecuador is one of the 17 mega-diverse countries that "Have within their borders more than two thirds of our planet's biological wealth, its biodiversity."[1]

Ecuador consists of four distinct geographical regions – Amazonia (the Amazon rainforest) on the east; La Sierra (Andes highlands) in the central part of the country all the way from the northern border with Colombia to the southern border with Peru; Costa (Pacific Coast) on the west; and the Galapagos Archipelago.[2] These regions have distinct geological and climatic characteristics, which have played an important role in forming Ecuador's regional cuisines and culinary traditions. One of the benefits of having four different regions in one country is the resulting culinary diversity. Ecuador's culinary identity is an exciting and diverse mix of local flavors that reflect regional climate, geography and cultural traditions.

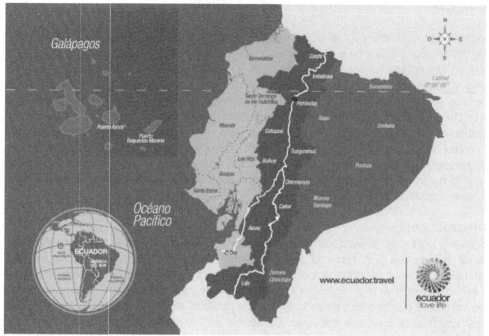

Credit: Ecuador Ministry of Tourism

Ecuador has 24 provinces, each of which has its own unique recipes, exceptional agricultural products, particular ways of seasoning, and cooking methods that express the communities' cultural and historical backgrounds. Below are some delicious examples of typical Ecuadorian dishes with unique regional variations.

Soups

Some call Ecuador "country of the soups"[3] and they might be right. There are numerous local soup recipes in Ecuador that showcase the country's agricultural and cultural diversity. Andean lands are blessed with nutrient-rich ancestral grains, cereals and roots, all main ingredients for soups commonly associated with this region: potato soup, or locro, quinoa soup, and many others. In the coastal region, the Pacific Ocean brings quality seafood to the table, allowing locals to prepare soups with green plantain in most cases; or sometimes with coconut milk or peanuts. In an effort to rediscover and bring back traditional recipes, gastronomic experts have identified more than 50 soup recipes.

Fanesca, the traditional soup usually served during Holy week, is part of the celebration of Lent across Ecuador, but each region – some may even say each household – has its own recipe for this traditional dish. There are also numerous accounts as to how exactly this tradition started. "Some suggest it is an Inca dish introduced to Ecuador when these people invaded form the south; others claim it was brought to the country by the first Christians; while another version will have you believe that a certain Juana invented it in a mountain hacienda during Colonial times ('Juanesca,' in the style of Juana, became 'Fanesca'). The less pious believe that the harvesting of grains and legumes in the Andean highlands simply combined fortuitously with the time of Lent."[4]

Fanesca is not only a combination of Andean grains and local ingredients, it also represents an interaction of religious beliefs, cultural influences and Ecuadorian family values. Indigenous communities will all agree that Fanesca was originally made by boiling a variety of nutritious grains from Ecuadorian highlands to honor harvesting seasons. When the Spaniards arrived to the "land of cinnamon" – as they called it – some new ingredients such as milk were added and it served as a fulfilling dish to help Catholic followers who were not permitted to eat meat during the Holy week. In the Catholic version, twelve grains were said to represent the twelve apostles. Five hundred years later, this soup is certainly a blessing for most Catholic families and an excuse to gather family members to share valuable moments while working together on its laborious preparation process. Fanesca is usually accompanied by various family dishes and offers a great culinary experience that highlights local tradition and lifestyle.

Image of Ecuadorian fanseca soup, a national staple.
Credit: Ecuadorian Association of Chefs

Envueltos

Wrapping food in Ecuador is not merely a trendy or easy way to serve food, it is an ancestral tradition. This tradition survived the Spanish conquest and is today still very much alive, in every home as part of family gatherings, celebrations, and even as treats to offer guests. Envueltos, which simply means "wrapped", is a culinary technique that has been used by indigenous communities for centuries, and typically refers to wrapped food made with local and native ingredients such as corn, hominy and even green plantain. There are countless possibilities of different types of dishes that can be wrapped, and ingredients that can be used. For example, one of the favorite breakfast or afternoon snacks of most Ecuadorians is corn dough (salty or sweet) wrapped in corn or achira leaves. In the coastal region, Envueltos of fish wrapped in banana leaves are common, whereas the fish Envueltos in the Amazon are usually wrapped in bijao leaves. In the Andean highlands, visitors will find a local cafe, restaurant or welcoming family offering a Tamal or Humita with a cup of coffee to warm up a cold afternoon.

Ceviche

In the coastal region, seafood is naturally the most important part of the local flavor. Ceviche is considered a delicacy in Ecuador, and while ceviche is popular in many parts of Central and South America's coastal regions, recipes in Ecuador are not the same as those from Peru or Chile. Ecuadorian ceviches feature quality local seafood such as large prawns or lobster, and each ceviche recipe is different. Depending on the region, ceviche recipes may vary, experimenting with a combination of different ingredients such as lemon juice, orange, tomato, onions, and green pepper. Each community will also eat ceviche differently; some with fried plantain, others with toasted corn or rice.

This emblematic dish is so attached to the national culinary identity that the recipe's fame has migrated to the highlands and to the Amazon region. Provinces that have no seafood have learned ways to use the products of their lands to create their own ceviches, such as Lupini Ceviche and Volquetero Ceviche (volquetero is a popular snack made with lupini beans, plantain chips and tuna). Ceviches in different parts of Ecuador may be prepared differently, but one thing that all Ecuadorians share when it comes to ceviche is that it is eaten at any time of the day, for breakfast, brunch or lunch, and it is commonly believed that it will help anyone to overcome a hangover. Ecuadorian ceviche definitely offers a complete and diverse culinary experience for travelers.

Hot Peppers

Ecuadorian Amazon is well known for being home to many types of hot peppers in a plethora of colors and sizes: red, green, orange, large, round and small. Ecuadorians have eaten sauces made from hot peppers since ancestral times, which helps to explain why different hot sauces coming from the Amazon will always find acceptance all around the country, especially if they are mixed with native fruits. These products are also enjoyed by food lovers and market-goers in the big cities today.

A Good Way of Life – for People, for Communities, and for Nature

The Constitution of Ecuador declares that the Republic of Ecuador strives to build "a new form of public coexistence, in diversity and in harmony with nature, to achieve "sumakkawsay," or good quality of life, and it grants rights to all living things, as specified in the following passage from the country's constitution, "Persons, communities, peoples, nations and communities are bearers of rights and shall enjoy the rights guaranteed to them in the Constitution and in international instruments. Nature shall be the subject of those rights that the Constitution recognizes for it."[5] (Title II, Chapter One, Article 10).

With an emphasis on the importance of coexistence, Ecuador as a tourism destination embraces the idea of "love life" (ama la vida),[6] and the approach to sharing experiences that invites everyone to be able to love life. That is why the concept of "conscious tourism," which promotes the values of peace, friendship, respect and love for life, is at the core of Ecuador's efforts to create and market a uniquely diverse destination filled with different stories, cultural backgrounds, and ways of expressing cultural identities, understanding the world and interacting with the natural world.

Food, as an important means of cultural expression, is an essential part of embracing harmonious coexistence among people, communities and nature. In addition, food travel (the slow, local, and authentic kind) is an excellent example of conscious tourism in action, offering visitors an insight into one of the most important aspects of local life, one intricately connected to the reasons why Ecuadorians love and celebrate life.

Conscious tourism also promotes ecological and sustainable practices that many rural, agro-ecological farms and markets around the country represent. In order to preserve nutritional integrity and agricultural diversity, various private and public initiatives – such as agro-ecological movements, networks that safeguard seeds, campaigns for responsible consumption and food sovereignty – have been implemented across the country. Travelers also benefit from these efforts, as authentic culinary traditions highlighting ecological, ancestral and healthy products enrich visitor experiences. Another essential ingredient of conscious tourism is the ability to transform lives by achieving spiritual growth both for visitors and for local communities. What allows this mutually beneficial process is the desire to share authentic lifestyles and to create opportunities to spend quality time.

With its indigenous foods and non-industrial processes and organic farming, Ecuador takes a conscious approach to food tourism, which plays a critical role in shaping the country's tourism brand. Slowness is key to food tourism in Ecuador.[7] Local, traditional and authentic foods should not be served in compulsory stops in order to satisfy feeding needs within busy itineraries, but should be enjoyed by savoring each bite, getting to know each ingredient personally, being involved in harvesting processes, learning about communities' beliefs through storytelling, and sharing meals at family and community tables.

To accomplish these goals, Ecuador's Ministry of Tourism has developed different types of tourism programs that provide the opportunities for local communities[8] to use culinary and agricultural resources as tools to achieve sustainable economic development. By empowering communities to use their culinary skills and ancestral knowledge to generate jobs and create tourism businesses, these programs aim to become self-sustaining in the long term.

This type of inclusive tourism development model reflects the key goals of the Culinary Tourism, Community Tourism and Agritourism division, as part of the Ministry's Department of Tourist Products Direction ("Dirección De Productos"), which creates opportunities for Ecuadorians and travelers to "love life" through love of food.[9]

Ecuador's Food Tourism Experiences

Ecuador's rich culinary culture and heritage allows visitors to experience indigenous and local communities' traditional knowledge in food production and preparation, creative family recipes utilizing local produce, local festivals and other celebrations that include seasonal ingredients, all of which are things other emerging destinations can emulate. Below are some examples of slow, local, and authentic food tourism experiences visitors can expect to find in Ecuador.

Local Markets

One of the best ways to get to know a local way of life is to visit a market where locals eat, shop and socialize. This is true almost anywhere in the world – as markets bring together things that are truly meaningful and necessary in life: food for the family, interactions with friends and neighbors, connections with one's community, and ways to participate in and support the local economy – and this is certainly true in Ecuador as well. These markets bring local and organic fruits and vegetables, homemade jams, cereals, cookies, breads, cheeses, honeys, quality Ecuadorian chocolates and coffee – and more – directly to consumers.

Visitors can also enjoy unique local specialties such as quinoa and amaranth breads, hot pepper sauces with tropical fruits and edible rose petals.

161

The national government has also developed programs to create "Healthy Markets" that offer agricultural products and traditional foods along with health standards and educational materials to inform consumers, tourists and community members about local food heritage.

Tropical Fruits

For travelers who are vegetarian or vegan, Ecuador's fruits are probably the most exciting and convenient (and nutritiously important) aspect of eating locally while in Ecuador – although they are certainly not the only meat- or dairy-free options that are delicious and authentic. In large cities like Quito, Cuenca and Guayaquil, and in small towns and villages across Ecuador, visitors can find an impressive variety of tropical (and subtropical) fruits in local markets. Fruit juices, fruit salads, desserts made with fresh fruits, and other dishes featuring fresh fruits are also very common in many restaurants, cafes, and markets.

While a large selection of Ecuadorian fresh fruits can be available almost everywhere in the country, the best way to find and enjoy some of the more 'unusual' fruits is to look for those that are regionally unique.

Guanabana (soursop) fruit at a produce market in downtown Quito.
Credit: World Food Travel Association

In the coastal region, tropical fruits are part of everyday meals. There are many types of banana, which are used for soups, snacks, and desserts. Other tropical fruits commonly eaten in the coastal region include melons, pineapples, oranges, coconut, and mangos, just to name a few. In addition to these common tropical fruits, visitors will also spot many unusual (sometimes strange-looking) ones, such as:

162

- *Borojo*: The large, round, brown fruit from the tropical rainforest tree borojo, which grows in some parts of Colombia, Ecuador, and Panama.[10]
- *Guanabana* (Soursop): The fruit from Annonamuricata, native to some Central American and northern South American countries.
- *Grosellas* (star gooseberry): The edible small yellow berries from the Phyllanthusacidus plant grown commonly in Southeast Asia and Latin America.

Avocados are found in the coastal region, in the highlands and in the Amazon. Each region gives them a special characteristic: the ones from the coast are sweeter than the ones from the highlands and in the Amazon grow wild and are rough-skinned.

One of the most popular local fruit varieties in the highlands is the "tree tomato" (tamarillo), a citric fruit native to the Andean region. Tree tomatoes are used as part of many different dishes, from desserts and juices, to hot pepper sauces. With a wide variety of fruits available – such as apples, pears, grapes, peaches, nectarine, mortiño (wild blueberry or hucklberry), blackberries, and plums – the Andean region offers a great selection of local juices and special drinks, such as Rosero, which is made with fruit juice, hominy (dried maize kernels) and spices. The diversity of native fruits is so important to the communities in the highlands that farms within protected areas in the region exist to protect around 600 native and exotic fruit species.

Chonta, a round red fruit with a high nutritional value, eaten both raw and cooked, is a native fruit found in the Amazon region of Ecuador. It is used to make chicha, a fermented drink that is prepared by the elders and consumed in celebrations to honor spirits and nature. Even the Chonta worm that grows in these fruits is eaten by native communities. Naranjilla is also a unique fruit native to the Amazon, also cultivated in the highlands, and commonly eaten around the country. Its particular acid flavor is used to prepare drinks, desserts and traditional meat dishes.

Slow Travel & Regional Food Experiences

Cotopaxi

In the Andean highlands, there are many community tourism projects that serve as windows to local gastronomic traditions. In the province of Cotopaxi (named after one of the highest active volcanoes in the world), travelers can enjoy a unique slow food travel experience: a train ride through impressive landscapes and rural communities, a walk to the community restaurant in the cold air beneath the volcano, to enjoy the taste of native produce from the mountains and local markets. The community restaurant is established inside a protected ecological area and the community that manages it is well trained. Traditional dishes such as bean soup, potato soup and potato patties are cooked and served by the local community.

Cañar

In the Andean province of Cañar, where visitors find one of the most important archeological vestiges of the country, there are community associations specialized in the harvest of quinoa and the making of products such as cookies and ice creams. Community centers offer visitors the opportunity to learn about traditional agriculture, fishing activities and to taste recipes from local products such as Andean cereals and grains. Community centers are ideal places to find authentic and pure products straight from the local land. The indigenous people have a traditional way of sharing and eating the "gifts of the land" called Pamba Mesa, an ancestral tradition that originated as a way to honor the Earth, or Pacha Mama, who provides communities with food. People sit on the ground and share native products such as corn,

163

hominy, potatoes, beans, hot peppers, sambo seeds (Andean squash), carrots, and the different kinds of Andean tubers such as mashua and oca; all of these simply boiled to enjoy their natural taste.

Bolivar

The province Bolivar, also in the Andean highlands, is called "The Barn of Ecuador" as it is known as the producer of a wide variety of Andean and tropical foods. The entrepreneurial spirit of the community has brought much attention from food enthusiasts, as the locals here have successfully created a cooperative model to support their local economy. To provide an income source for more than 150 local families, they have created their own production chain, from milking cows, to artisanal production and the commercialization of their high quality products around the country. With this cooperative approach, established over 40 years ago, the local community started writing their own history, and they are now well known for their variety of Andean cheeses. Visitors can also find a variety of products such as chocolates made with Ecuadorian "Fino de Aroma" cacao, sausages, yoghurt, wild mushrooms, and oils. Inside lodging projects and the tourist office (managed by local youth), visitors can have their own tasting menus and learn about how food converted a poor town into a productive, self-sustaining community as a result of the people's struggle and creativity.

Agritourism

Another way that Ecuador displays its diverse culinary and gastronomic offerings is through agritourism models. All around the country visitors can learn about the cooking process of traditional recipes from harvesting to tasting experiences. Local farms, haciendas, countryside projects and markets offer great food travel experiences for visitors in all four regions of the country.

In the cloud forest region (northern Ecuador), many community projects have been developed to conserve the forest and to encourage sustainable agritourism development. These initiatives include such activities as staying with local families, participating in the making of artisanal, organic and additive-free jams and fresh cheeses, working in organic gardens, helping feed animals, and of course, dining in local restaurants. An important fact that makes these experiences even more special is that these recipes have been created by local women, adding a special aspect to the experience: women are empowered through local culinary heritage.

In the coastal region, especially in the province of Manabí, sustainable farms offer visitors the opportunity to find food forests, vegetable gardens, animal farms, and activities focused on health and well-being, such as mediation, yoga and educational workshops. The local products that can be found in these tropical areas include manioc, coffee, cacao, tropical fruits, banana, rice and of course, traditional dishes prepared with green plantain, peanut and seafood or typical foods wrapped in plantain leaves. Visitors at these farms can harvest the local ingredients that will be prepared with ancestral recipes to make for a very special lunch experience.

Culinary Routes

The Ministry of Tourism supports food tourism and local culinary heritage by creating "culinary routes"[11] that promote agricultural products or traditional recipes. International travelers can discover that the concept "terroir" (special characteristics of a certain place expressed in agricultural products) can travel from European lands to a small Latin country where different regions, cultural traditions, biodiversity, geographical and climate conditions give each local recipe a specific flavor.

Along the "Ruta del Spondylus" (Spondylus Route), visitors can follow the coastline from north to south, enjoying a variety of local recipes that combine seafood with tropical flavors and particular culinary techniques.

"Cacao Routes" are emerging in different parts of Ecuador. Scientific studies have shown that "Fino de Aroma" cacao originated in the Amazon. Since this type of cacao is only found in Ecuador, it is a source of national pride. Another interesting fact is that every territory that grows cacao pods has its own unique, territorial organoleptic characteristics. In fact, organoleptic maps have been created by government research for each territory with their own chocolate flavor and aroma wheel by working with community associations that produce cacao and make their own chocolates. Agritourism and the traditional dishes that can be found in every region, is a key factor in creating gastronomic tourist routes. In Ecuador, "chocolate tasting" could become a new trend in the way that wine tasting has become popular around the world. Wine routes have become famous because of wine's ability to arouse passions for the diversity of aromas and flavors from each territory. Ecuador might not be known – yet – for grape and wine production, but it is certain that cacao and chocolate can awake new passion in food lovers.

Ecuador also has potential to create "Coffee Routes," because many regions of the country produce high quality, mostly organic, coffee. Many Ecuadorian coffee brands are certified not only as organic but also as fair trade, although there is a national effort underway to take this one step further with "Equal Trade" certification. Each year, local producers create associations supported by strong private coffee institutions offering training and technical support.

Every year private and public institutions aim to promote gastronomic culture and incentivize tourism by organizing theme fairs for cacao, chocolate and coffee in different cities. Fairs include producer displays, conferences, tasting sessions and contests. Currently the Ministry of Tourism is working not only on the creation of tourist products but also on strategies to professionalize local gastronomic experiences. Along with a specialized governmental training institution, government will work together in creating educational programs in order to train and certify chocolatiers and baristas.

Huecas: Locals' Best Kept Secrets

Another face of Ecuador's slow food tourism experiences can be found in "Huecas," small, local food establishments originating in colonial times, where most traditional food preparation methods can be found. Huecas offer home-style dishes cooked by locals who are keeping alive the culinary secrets of the country. These places are managed by families, who have mastered unique traditional culinary techniques and transmitted these traditions orally from generation to generation. Every Ecuadorian knows a hidden gem, a hidden corner in their community, where they can find their favorite Hueca. Ecuadorian chefs research these places to identify traditional recipes and the national government is working to train Huecas in heritage and tourism management in order to maintain the Hueca traditions that help to make Ecuador's culinary identity so unique.

Indigenous Cultures, Traditional Knowledge & Culinary Heritage

Ecuador is not only home to biodiversity hotspots, but also magnificent ethnic diversity; incredibly rich ancient cultural traditions and indigenous beliefs, customs, languages, artistic expressions, and ways of life. The traditional cultures of Ecuador's many native communities have unique characteristics that are closely tied to the natural environment of the Coast, the Highlands, and the Rainforest. Visiting and learning about these communities' rich living cultures and traditions is one of the most attractive and enriching experiences for travelers, and those who are in search of authentic culinary travel experiences in Ecuador will find the traditional knowledge of the Indigenous peoples particularly intriguing.

As seen in the example of Fanesca, many traditional recipes are closely linked to local celebrations, ancestral beliefs, and religious rituals, and they have become unique symbols of Ecuador's culture that embraces diversity. "Colada morada" is another such example. Prepared during "Day of the Dead" or "All Hallows Eve" celebrations, this purple-colored beverage is made with black corn flour – one of the many varieties of corn found in the country – fruits, herbs and several spices such as cloves, cinnamon, and sweet peppers. According to the indigenous ancestral beliefs, this unique drink was made as an offering to their deceased family members that maintained a living spirit in another world. The offer was complemented with guaguas de pan ("childrens' breads"), so named because they are shaped to resemble a child's figure. Today, every Ecuadorian family prepares this combination to honor their loved ones who have departed. They maintain the local tradition of linking food with ancestral traditions, using culinary practices keeps history alive.

Among the most important spiritual celebrations by Indigenous communities are IntiRaymi, or the Sun Festivals. Closely linked to culinary heritage and agricultural traditions, these celebrations honor the summer solstice and harvesting times to thank the Earth for the bounty that it provides for families and communities. Later in the year similar celebrations honor the harvest of seven varieties of corn, and serving a fermented drink called Chicha de Yamor. According to ancestral beliefs, corn represents fertility and this is why it is an important part of many Indigenous food traditions and celebrations.

For the Amazon's indigenous tribes, the Chonta fruit is an important symbol of their lives, exhibiting a close connection to nature. When they harvest this fruit, an important ritual directed by the elder of the community takes place. Children participate in the harvesting process and women prepare Chicha de Chonta, a fermented Chonta drink. While the drink is fermenting, the community dances to the beat of the drum, expressing their gratitude to the spirits for seasons of plenty.

Indigenous communities maintain nutritionally rich natural diets, as they believe that chacras (small spaces containing natural and varied crops) are spaces where nature, gods and humans coexist in a continuous spiritual exchange. This is why agriculture is considered a sacred ritual to honor nature's gifts, which nurture not only their physical bodies but also their souls.

The "Rescate de los Sabores Tradicionales del Ecuador" ("Rescuing Ecuador's Traditional Flavors")[12] project is one of several examples of a local chef's work to discover, learn and share Ecuadorian ancestral recipes. The project, managed by the Ecuadorian Chefs Association with the support of local governments and a private university, contributes to efforts to keep these culinary traditions alive by engaging younger generations. For more than six years, a specialized team has been traveling around the country searching for local kitchens, traditional cooking tools, farms, and recipes, and investigating products that are emblematic to each province of the country. This culinary journey has resulted in books, events, scientific studies, and local awareness-raising efforts to encourage Ecuadorians to proudly acknowledge their traditional foods.

Cacao, shrimp, quinoa, and banana, for example, are all local and traditional products that have given life to unique recipes. The country has 24 provinces, each with particular soil and climate characteristics, which also means that there are numerous traditional recipes that derive from the many quality local and traditional products. Even more, the journey to identify and highlight traditional ingredients and recipes engages young local cooks. This is important

166

because they are literally the future of Ecuador's national identity, including, of course, its culinary culture.

Lessons for Emerging Food Tourism Destinations

(1) Find and craft food tourism strategies that complement the country's tourism goals.

The bilingual guidebook Ecuador Culinario - Saberes y Sabores ("Ecuadorian Culinary Art – Knowledge and Flavors")[13] produced by the Ministry of Tourism of Ecuador in 2012 is an excellent example of destination-wide efforts in Ecuador to educate people (both travelers and locals) about the country's rich culinary heritage and diversity, and to strengthen the country's culinary identity in a way that is consistent with key national tourism strategies and priorities. The task to select the recipes was the responsibility of a committee formed by the public and private sector. The book was validated by local universities and written both in English and Spanish. Additionally, each province of the country has regional tourism offices that have also invested in creating regional culinary guides to accomplish the same goal. These guides are more than just a list of recipes and cooking instructions, they showcase the country's culinary richness through an emblematic dish, drink and festivity from each province, and include historic and heritage information; some even have nutritional components.

Every year, Ecuador participates in international tourist fairs in different countries of the world. The country has a commitment to bring as part of its tourist products, a display of local gastronomy. For this purpose, it's an important task to establish emblematic menus, agricultural products and communicational concepts to show the world. This task is being developed by a team work between universities, private and public areas specialized in gastronomy, culinary heritage and tourism.

(2) Embrace authenticity and strive to be different.

Not every destination needs to (or can successfully manage to) find and market a particular dish – or even a type of food – that can be an emblem of their culinary identity. As Ecuador's example shows, establishing a country's reputation as a food travel destination does not have to rely on having one distinct type of cuisine, but can instead highlight different colors, flavors, stories, and identities that are represented within the destination. It is clear that in Ecuador, diversity is the spice of life that enriches its culinary heritage, and a key aspect of its tourism potential. Rather than finding one way to define and describe its cuisine, Ecuador has invested in efforts to harness the country's passion for food, to discover and learn from ancestral beliefs, and to preserve traditional recipes and culinary practices that are the foundation of Ecuadorian cuisine today and in the future.

(3) Engage and empower local communities.

Local farmers, chefs, business owners, street food vendors, tour guides, and others who are on the frontline of customer interactions in food travel destinations have the important challenge and opportunity to directly impact the experience and memory of the food traveler. It is therefore crucial to invest in opportunities within the destination that help local people – who are the faces of the destination's food travel identity – to embrace their culinary heritage and to be proud of their culinary traditions and expressions. Culinary routes in Ecuador, with an inclusive and social model, are being designed to allow travelers to discover the uniqueness of each region while helping local communities to become self-sustaining. In addition to promoting culinary experiences featuring agritourism and community-based tourism products, the Ministry of Tourism has created "Saber con Sabor" (Knowledge with Flavor), large gastronomic fairs offering public spaces for small producers, communities, professionals, students, historians and researchers from all around the country to come together to celebrate local culinary heritage and traditions. The first fair took place in 2011 in Guayaquil and brought together almost 16,000 visitors. The "Saber con Sabor" fair is intended to be repeated as an ongoing event.

(4) Promote collaboration among private, public and academic sectors.

Ecuador's efforts to develop and promote local gastronomy by preserving ancestral traditions and original recipes have been supported by talented local chefs that have strived to prioritize national gastronomy by developing research projects, writing books detailing regional recipes, training Ecuadorian chefs abroad, and investigating in local ingredients and their culinary uses. In addition, in recent years universities and culinary schools have also joined in these efforts, by adjusting their academic programs to place more emphasis on Ecuadorian cuisine. A variety of food-related conferences, fairs, and events have also helped to motivate students and youths in embracing the unique national food identify of Ecuador.

The national government is also working to support these initiatives. In 2012, the Ministry of Tourism and the Heritage Ministry, the National Association of Chefs and the Culinary Academy came together through an agreement, to unite efforts and to collaborate in developing strategies for agriculture, food research, culinary tourism, and promoting local gastronomy. This collaborative approach has made it possible to find a middle ground between preserving heritage and traditions and creating modern and appealing ways to promote local food for travelers.

CONCLUSION

The secret to creating a successful food travel destination in emerging areas like Ecuador is to create a dialogue among governmental teams, professionals and academic institutions to formally organize efforts to preserve biodiversity, heritage, and local flavors. Then the stakeholders must write a food tourism strategy that unites these concepts. While other developing areas may also have extraordinary and unique cuisines, without a solid food tourism strategy and buy-in from the government, their success is limited.

All of this has made Ecuador a promising food travel destination that is increasingly recognized around the world. This is one reason why "Ecuador is snapping at Peru's heels as a foodie destination, with a more varied natural larder, and young chefs happy to mix things up at a new wave of restaurants."[14] Another example of how these strategies have worked is the recognition that Ecuador´s geography has contributed unique assets to its food, "Altitude and geography play a prominent role in Ecuadorian cooking, with cooks in the Andean highlands preparing quite different dishes from their counterparts along the coast."[15]

DISCUSSION QUESTIONS

1. Choose an emerging destination with food tourism potential. Which of the tactics in Ecuador's portfolio might work for the destination in question?
2. How might the tactics used by Ecuador need to be modified by countries physically larger in size, and also by countries smaller in size?
3. Local empowerment is a recurring theme in food tourism development. Are locals sufficiently empowered in your destination chosen in question 1? If not, what steps can be taken to adequately empower them?

ENDNOTES

[1]"Megadiversity: The 17 biodiversity superstars", Conservation International, last modified 1998, last accessed July 11, 2013, www.conservation.org/documentaries/Pages/megadiversity.aspx

[2]*This is Ecuador;* Thisisecuador.com

[3]"Culinary Tourism: Discover Ecuador through great soups", Lance Andrew Brashear, last modified October 22, 2012, last accessed July 7 2013, www.lan.com/onlyinsouthamerica/2012/10/culinary-tourism-discover-ecuador-through-great-soups

[4]"The Fanesca Soup – A mortal sin during Holy Week?", Dominic Hamilton, This is Ecuador, last accessed July 11, 2013, www.thisisecuador.com/component/content/article/13-this-months-recommended/187-typical-dish-of-the-month-fanesca-soup.html

[5]"Republic of Ecuador – Constitution of 2008", Georgetown University Political Database of the Americas, last modified January 31, 2011, last accessed July 11 2013, http://pdba.georgetown.edu/Constitutions/Ecuador/english08.html

[6]*Ecuador ama la vida.* Turismo.gob.ec

[7]"Slow Tourism: el placer de ir despacio", Ecuador.travel, last modified February 4, 2013, last accessed July 11 2013, http://ecuador.travel/micrositios/blog_tur/

[8]"Consolida Turismo comunitario", Ecuador´s Ministry of Tourism, last accessed July 12, 2013, http://servicios.turismo.gob.ec/index.php/?option=com_content&view=article&id=37

[9]"Author's personal interview with Ecuador Ministry of Tourism, June 6, 2013.

[10]"What is Borojo", Borojo.net, last accessed July 12, 2013, www.borojo.net

[11]*Train Routes.* Ecuadorbytrain.com

[12]"El libro sabor de mi Ecuador, sera elaborado por jóvenes ecuatorianos", Ecuador´s Ministry of Tourism, last modified April 5 2013, last accessed July 12, 2013, www.turismo.gob.ec/el-libro-saber-de-mi-pais-sera-elaborado-por-jovenes-ecuatorianos/

[13]"Ecuador Culinario – Saberes y Sabores", Ecuador.travel, last modified April 8, 2013, last accessed, July 12 2013, www.ecuador.travel/descargas/file/3-ecuador-culinario-saberes-y-sabores

[14]"Food in Ecuador: a lesson in diversity", Ben Quinn, The Guardian, Last modified February 1 2013, last accessed July 12, 2013, www.guardian.co.uk/travel/2013/feb/01/ecuador-quito-food-restaurants-cuisine.

[15]"Sampling the regional dishes and delicacies of Ecuador", Regis St Louis, BBC Travel, last modified February 3 2011, last accessed July 12, 2013, www.bbc.com/travel/feature/20110127-regional-dishes-and-delicacies-of-ecuador

Cooking Schools & Classes

Lynne M. Bennett and Jeremy Freemantle

This chapter provides historical context and an overview of how cooking schools and classes have evolved, including specific information on how to start a cooking school or classes and how to transition into and involve the local community. This chapter also includes a case study about African Relish, a rural, recreational, destination cooking school in South Africa.

INTRODUCTION

Culinary schools and classes have always been driven by media. Television and cooking shows drive people to seek out cooking experiences away from home. Corporations like Sur La Table[1] and Williams-Sonoma[2] have also capitalized on the growing culinary interests of consumers and now both of these culinary retail stores offer cooking classes, demonstrations, cookbook author events, and culinary vacations. For instance, after the release of the movie *Julie and Julia*, Sur La Table capitalized on the popularity of the book that was the basis for the movie; it held a monthly cooking class based on a chapter of the book. The class included entertainment, gathering, and learning recipes.

Cooking schools and classes greatly benefit the food tourism industry. They can also have a positive economic impact on an entire town and community, and all the businesses that operate in that locale.

Creating a new food tourism destination includes knowing your market, being clear on the real target market, understanding break-even calculations and strategies, and building a business plan that will deliver profits. Other considerations include funding (self-funding versus venture capital); networking and collaboration with industry partners, suppliers, and local government to build the brand; community marketing and development, which will support the entire community and help drive business to the cooking school; and learning how to improvise during low season with innovative offerings, special rates, and packages. When operating under this model, it allows the creation of individualized classes based on needs and desires that is market-driven.

Ramekins Culinary School, Events & Inn

Located just blocks from the beautiful downtown square in Sonoma, California, USA, Ramekins is owned by Darius and Sarah Anderson. This elegant, Tuscan-style culinary school and inn offers private hands-on demonstrations and cooking classes, catering, culinary retreats, kids' classes, as well as a wide variety of special themed events throughout the year.

The success of this cooking school lies in the owners' ability to stay booked both in high and low seasons by utilizing the region's multitude of culinary experts, artisans, farms, and wineries. Any part of the beautiful facility can be utilized — the kitchen, courtyard, meeting rooms, or inn — so weddings, family reunions, and organizational and corporate events keep the booking calendar full. Also, Ramekins does a fantastic job of promoting local products in their cooking classes while including tours to regional locations.

Classes and products go hand in hand at this culinary school. As experts in marketing, some of their products include winemaker dinners, themed classes such as "Winter in Paris" or "French Quarter Cuisine" with their French chef Pierre Lagourgue, citrus marmalade jam class with Blue Chair Fruit Company, and contemporary Indian dishes with chef Neela Paniz. One promotion invited students to kick off spring with a culinary fling by taking a "Springtime in France" class with chef Pierre Lagourgue. After a day of cooking and shopping, students can relax at the inn just upstairs.[3] By marketing the Sonoma region around seasonal calendar themes and incorporating regional products, artisans, and experts, Ramekins provides endless possibilities.

Bauman College Natural Chef Training Program

Culinary trends in today's food world include a range of organic, nutritional, holistic, locally-grown, seasonal and therapeutic food preparations that demand a new mastery in culinary arts. Out of this growing demand emerged the concept of Natural Chefs and the Natural Chefs Training Program developed by Sonoma, California-based Bauman College, which specializes in holistic nutrition and culinary arts. This program educates culinary arts students and certifies them as Natural Chefs.

"Natural Chefs are in great demand as the need for good nutrition and healthy lifestyle choices becomes more apparent in our fast-paced world. Natural Chefs are trained to provide delicious, nourishing, and beautifully presented meals to those who wish to avoid or recover from illness and those who want to reach their optimal health."

Graduates of this program have gone on to establish great culinary careers by becoming cookbook authors, accomplished restaurant chefs, personal and private chefs, corporate chefs, caterers, and business owners. Others have developed successful careers in product development, recipe testing, counseling, and consulting.[4]

Ecco La Cucina[5]

Eat like a Tuscan, drink like a Tuscan, and tour with a Tuscan. "The Italians revel in the joy and community that good food fosters. Gina loves living and working in Tuscany because the people and culture are so closely connected to the foods they eat and the wines they drink. Ecco la Cucina uses the freshest of ingredients to prepare classic Tuscan dishes that are easy to master and delicious to eat. The pairing of our daily menus with local wines makes for an unforgettable dining experience!"

Chef Gina Stipo is an Italian-American author and passionate regional wine and food enthusiast based in Siena, Italy. Dedicated to Tuscan cuisine, history, and culture, Gina's unique teaching methods give her students the opportunity to cook and learn in a relaxing environment in Tuscany, a world-renowned culinary region.

If someone only has one day, the school recommends they take a hands-on cooking class located in a restored 900-year-old flour mill in Siena. For those with more time, an immersion-style culinary tour is available, where guests experience the surrounding countryside, local artisans, culinary products, farms, and taste some of the finest Chianti wine the region has to offer, all while getting an insider's perspective on the region.

Ecco La Cucina offers individualized hands-on cooking sessions, wine education and tastings, local restaurant event meals, regional highlights, and visits to goat cheese farms, farm-to-table tastings, and olive oil specialists. It is a successful model that is replicable in other geographies.

A Formal Cooking School: Culinary Institute of America[6]

In 1946, two exceptional women, Frances Roth and Katharine Angell, began an amazing journey on the path to what we now know as the Culinary Institute of America (CIA). They opened the New Haven Restaurant Institute in New Haven, Connecticut providing hands-on instruction in the culinary arts that was so successful it inspired the community to start the first campus in New York. Later that year, the CIA began to set a new standard for culinary excellence, professional education, and training. This rich tradition has carried on for more than six decades and today still stands at the forefront of innovation in the culinary arts world. "Almost every profession has an outstanding training ground. The military has West Point, music has Julliard, and the culinary arts has The Institute *(CIA)*," shared Craig Claiborne, Celebrated Author and Food Critic at *The New York Times*.[7]

As a not-for-profit college, the CIA offers associates and bachelor's degrees with a cross section of culinary arts majors such as baking and pastry arts, culinary science, as well as several certificate programs. As a world leader in culinary education, it provides professional excellence in health, wellness, sustainability, world cuisines, cultural resources and research, and professional conferences. The CIA has three culinary campuses located in the United States: Hyde Park, New York; St. Helena, California; and San Antonio, Texas. The Institute's only location outside the USA is in Singapore. The CIA's claim to culinary excellence lies in its ability to establish student-run restaurants. By dining at one of the numerous CIA's restaurants, you can eat a great meal today with one of the world's famous chefs of tomorrow.[8]

A student in this program will learn how to understand food, as well as incorporating this professional approach into their management studies. Students who earn a diploma in Culinary & Catering Management, Hospitality & Tourism Management, or Leisure & Resort Management are uniquely trained to meet the industry's challenging and competitive demands.

Recreational Cooking Versus Formal Culinary Schools

The reference to a culinary journey to a far-off place to attend cooking classes has become like a badge of honor, if not the pinnacle of amateur culinary prestige. Most of these vacations are enjoyed at one of a growing number of cooking schools around the globe. The term *cooking school* is used generically and has caused a fair amount of confusion as to what it actually means.

The term *school* suggests that students attend an institution in order to come away with a qualification at the end of a prescribed period of time. This is true of the professional chef school environments that have strict curricula, assessment processes, etc. Recreational cooking schools, on the other hand, are loosely structured with an emphasis on conviviality, social interaction, and enjoying good food and wine in a great location. Perhaps the confusion lies in the use of the word *school*, which has an immediate connotation and evokes a certain expectation. We can say then that a cooking school focuses on culinary arts and sciences; it assesses students' qualifications and awards diplomas to those who pass

Build It and They Might Come: Culinary Training in Rural South Africa

Food tourism and culture are inextricably linked insofar as food or a nation's cuisine defines the personality of that culture. The climate, ingredients, cooking methods passed down over millennia, religious rites and interventions, invasions by other cultures, colonialism, and many other influences have shaped the cuisines and cultures of the world.

The global ascent in popularity of food and cooking has spawned a myriad of new trends, such as television chefs, dedicated cooking channels, recreational cooking schools, and home cooking lessons. Cookbook publishing has expanded exponentially despite the trend toward e-books. Food blogging has become a launchpad for many new food celebrities and authors. Thus, the establishment of a plethora of cooking schools, both recreational and formal, and other food tourism-related products are obvious consequences of these developments.

The concept of recreational cooking schools is not a new one, and long-established schools are scattered worldwide, inviting tourists to experience their country's culinary culture and food heritage. Progressively, more people are participating in cooking as a recreational pastime. Cooking schools are a perfect forum for sharing food cultures, embedding a sense of conviviality around food, and encouraging people to slow down and savor more of the sensual aspects of food, discarding the "bite-and-run" mentality.

In South Africa, which only recently emerged from the darkness of apartheid isolation, the concept of food tourism is quite new. A great appetite for food knowledge, and most importantly, food integrity, is now developing. Locals and tourists alike increasingly want to know about the provenance of food, fair trade status, and production methods.

Although launching a new recreational cooking school in a remote, rural South African location came with huge challenges, the African Relish example can be used by other aspiring cooking school entrepreneurs to further develop their products in similar remote locations.

The first challenge was to define the cooking school's mission statement. This proved more difficult than originally anticipated, as the concept of recreational cooking schools is unfamiliar in this region of the world and required careful branding and marketing to convey the essence of the business to prospective customers. The location that was chosen provided further challenges as it is situated in a remote and wild part of the country known as The Great Karoo, an arid, semi-desert vastness covering almost two-thirds of the area of South Africa. The area has great historical, paleontological, and archaeological significance and was home to two groups of Africa's original indigenous peoples, the Khoi-Khoin and San. The climate is harsh, the environment pristine, the air pure, and the night skies legendary for their clarity and brilliance. Yet, despite all these positive elements and natural attractions, the destination's remoteness was still an obstacle.

The distance to market proved to be a significant challenge. Cape Town is a renowned, major tourist hub for inbound visitors. Most visitors have itineraries planned from that epicenter radiating out to day-trip attractions, such as Robben Island, Table Mountain, Cape Point, West Coast National Park, the Stellenbosch Winelands, and others. The visitor who is prepared to travel further afield is typically an adventurous, self-driven road tripper who enjoys planning a linear itinerary that includes a greater number of destinations on a major route. However, there are also adventurous souls looking for unique experiences and destinations that are on the road less travelled.

The next challenge was choosing a village that was not a high profile tourism destination, was not on a major tourist route, and was generally used by travelers as an overnight stop. Prince Albert was the one location that stood out, a mere 250 miles (400 km) from Cape Town.

It was obvious that this town, nestled at the foot of the world-famous Swartberg Pass, had an enormous appeal with its quaint, well-preserved, historical architecture and abundant water flowing out of the Swartberg Mountain range. This entire mountain wilderness area has been declared a World Heritage Site, with its innumerable attractions. The African Relish owners saw this unique geographical situation with its added cultural and culinary appeal as an opportunity to create a brand. They focused on the business itself: its identity, unique selling propositions, and all the peripheral marketing collateral to take to market. It soon became evident that the more the school scratched the surface, the more it discovered benefits and attractions that would appeal directly to the food traveler. However, they realized that in order to attract visitors, they would have to devise a much broader marketing and branding strategy to build the profile of the village and the area as a whole. This responsibility would normally fall to the local tourism authority, but it was soon evident that the local authority had little to no capacity to undertake an effective marketing and promotional campaign. They also did not have a budget that could extend to building a major branding campaign for the town. So they came up with an alternate plan: to reach out to the food and lifestyle media with a story about a few passionate individuals who were launching a destination-based cooking school called African Relish,[9] which would showcase South Africa's rich culinary heritage and culture.

The media was provided with a press release to that effect, and the response from the media was overwhelmingly positive. They latched onto the uniqueness of this concept and the fact that food tourism was a relatively new pastime in the area. And since the food revolution is still in relative infancy, anything new and different immediately sparked interest. With the positive press reaction, suddenly the village of Prince Albert was "on the map." The number of visitors to the area began to increase and has continued to do so.

Nurturing local acceptance was also a challenge, as the village is historically a conservative community and sometimes wary of new ideas and change. The school needed to convince the villagers of the numerous opportunities so that they, in turn, would help promote it. It was as important to convince them that African Relish and the broader marketing effort would be good for the town in the long term and to ease their concerns regarding any gold-rush-style influx of development and congestion that could threaten the serenity and lifestyle they hold so dear.

The Market for Cooking Schools and Classes

Starting a new business of any kind carries with it the inherent dangers of making incorrect assumptions of all kinds, not least of which is identifying the primary target market. This is a simple and fundamental tenet of any marketing strategy or business plan that can profoundly affect the success of a business in the short to medium term.

Common experience is one where valuable lessons are learned and timely corrections made in order to realign marketing focus. Research was carried out involving a great number of cooking schools around the world. African Relish's leaders interviewed numerous smaller businesses to see what worked and what did not. Luckily, the world's culinary community is willing to share information. There is a great generosity when it comes to collaboration and networking, and in particular, in sharing personal stories of success and failure. Therefore, when assumptions are made, they are based on solid information.

In the case of African Relish, the owners decided that the primary target market would be inbound, international culinary travelers looking for an alternative to traditional destinations, seeking instead a "South African *Tuscany*" style experience. The school discounted local travelers, assuming that South Africans were still starry-eyed with the prospect of travelling to Europe rather than exploring their own country. The owners assumed there would be a flood of international visitors desiring to experience South Africa in general, and this new cooking school in particular.

External factors play a significant role in the roll out of any strategic plan; this includes factors over which there is no control, such as political upheaval and economic shifts. These can either work in favor of the broad business plan, or conversely, can have a negative impact on initial projections. It is advisable to build contingencies and alternative strategies into one's plan and create "what if" scenarios to anticipate as much as possible what might go wrong.

Identifying the target market requires focus, research, and a great deal relying on one's gut feelings. It is not an exact science. It is important, however, to decide first the unique differentiator of your business, know your competition, and ascertain what markets they are targeting. Decide what your product is, and do not try to be all things to all people. Be prepared to adjust the strategy as you fine-tune your market focus.

Funding Your Dream

One of the most challenging and difficult decisions to make regarding a start-up cooking school is the source of funding. Readers interested in learning more about this subject are referred to the chapter *Bringing In the Dough: Creative Funding Models*.

Community Development

It is the responsibility of every business to contribute to ensuring the stability of the community in which it operates. It is self-evident that stable and sustainable communities can only exist under certain socioeconomic conditions and circumstances. The community must have a viable business environment. There must be sufficient employment, a stable local government, and essential services must be in place for communities to operate with any stability.

There is a great difference between community development and economic development, and these two concepts should not be confused. Community development involves the social aspect of community well-being; it addresses health, education, nutrition, and the social and recreational issues of a community. Economic development is direct investment in, and the establishment of, businesses that will drive job creation, skills development, and have a positive spin-off on the greater community.

In the real world, many businesses do not regard community development as their direct responsibility but rather assume that government is solely responsible for it. In fact, businesses are often critical of the government for its apparent lack of delivery in this area. Furthermore, many businesses do not consciously approach their strategies with the broader issue of economic development and community development in mind. This dichotomy is much more visible in a small community, and conversely, the positive impact of a more enlightened approach is even more visible.

The Importance of Supporting Local Producers

During the research phase, when deciding where to locate a new cooking school or other food tourism-focused business, it is vital to know the local culture, the local politics, and to do an audit of the local agriculture, artisanal producers, and livestock farmers. Share your vision with them and ask them what they can provide. Ensure they understand what you are trying to achieve and secure their support and commitment. One of the most attractive aspects of a rural cooking experience for visitors is the opportunity to meet suppliers and producers firsthand, to follow the process from farm-to-fork, and to observe good methods. It is a process that adds enormous experiential value to the entire scenario and ensures that visitors leave with a great sense of fulfillment.

The suppliers and producers, in turn, have the opportunity to engage with end users and to find out what is important to them regarding food and its production. With contemporary society's fast pace of living, having the opportunity to go to the source and meet the farmer is a great attraction and helps people to slow down and reconnect with their food.

Supporting local industry and producers in rural areas has a significant positive impact on a small economy. It is important to contain local and visitors' spending to ensure that it does not leak to larger centers. In many smaller towns and villages there is limited retail opportunity for essentials, and therefore residents and visitors are forced to go further afield for essential purchases, whereas if there is local support for local business, then the spending is contained. It is rather a chicken-and-egg situation, where the retail outlet must first exist before the spending can take place. However, if a culture of cross-business support can be encouraged and support for local producers becomes second nature, then the environment will be created for a ground swell of enterprise development opportunities to be explored.

There is also an opportunity to use bartering in smaller areas. It was historically the logical solution for smaller communities to support one another and encourage the production of all essential requirements that could be swapped out on an equitable basis. There is no reason that this system cannot work in a modern context, given the high cost of fuel and transport. It makes perfect sense to encourage the barter system.

Get Creative in the Low Season

For many tourism areas, such as coastal resorts, a low season poses a challenge for businesses to maintain incoming revenue. Some businesses follow a strategy of "making hay while the sun shines," or, inflating prices during the high season to compensate for the quiet times ahead. This is a very short-sighted strategy and one that assumes that tourists are uninformed. Tourists may feel "trapped" for the period they are on holiday at the resort/village, thereby decreasing the chances they will return or refer the destination to friends. The strategy is not sustainable, and businesses that follow it create the perception amongst visitors that all businesses located at this particular destination follow suit. Even if there are businesses in a locality that do price fairly, they may be perceived as following the same business practices. So their businesses are ultimately affected by the unscrupulous actions of others.

The more sustainable choice is to apply a fair-pricing strategy whereby normal market-related pricing models are employed during the peak season, which will create customer loyalty and a good chance of repeat business. Then, during the low season, a series of special packages and special deals can be offered to help increase business.

Think of alternative revenue streams to generate extra low season income. Cooking schools and other food tourism businesses have the perfect opportunity to offer other services like wine tours, catering to the local community, event management, food product development and packaging, and farmers' markets.

Diversifying the Cooking School Experience

Visitors to a recreational cooking school will invariably be happy to spend most of their time cooking and eating. However, it is as important for them to experience a broader profile of the town or community they are visiting as it is to learn about the culinary treasures. A good mix of added cultural, natural history, and historical and sporting activities extends the brand experience by including other pastimes, such as adventure cycling, bird watching, hiking, botanical, and archaeological and paleontological pursuits with the culinary/cooking experience.

Meeting the Producers

Meeting the producers may sound like something that would happen in Hollywood, except that these producers have their fingers firmly in the soil. Food travelers, by their very nature, are keen to meet producers and artisan farmers who have returned to ethical and natural methods. So much of what we eat today is mass-produced and masked with all kinds of additives, colorings, stabilizers, flavor enhancers and more. Lists of scientific hieroglyphics on packaging boggle the mind. There is a groundswell back to the natural way of farming and producing. This movement has transcended the trendy phase and is now founded in a real conscious and fundamental need to get back to basics. So many environmental, socioeconomic, and purely economic factors now dictate that we need to explore alternatives to the way we have come to live. Ironically, these so-called alternatives are merely the way our ancestors lived for centuries; we have simply forgotten about them.

An immense sense of satisfaction can be derived from meeting these producers. The visitor experience will be enhanced dramatically. Visitors to cooking schools who have the opportunity to pick fresh fruit and vegetables from the land and select livestock or poultry at the source and return to the kitchen to create their own culinary masterpieces experience something truly special indeed—something not many people have the privilege of doing.

Value-Added Experiences

The experiential tourism environment creates wonderful opportunities for visitors to meet and engage with locals. For visitors to a cooking school, what would be better than to have the opportunity to meet traditional herbalists and wild food foragers? Indigenous people are often very knowledgeable about wild plants, both edible and medicinal. South Africa has a particularly rich and diverse mix of cultures, each with its own unique culinary heritage and knowledge to share, giving visitors a great value-added experience and a real glimpse inside a different culture.

Staying Competitive & Flexible

To drive local economic development, African Relish is launching SUSTAIN 360, a non-profit entity. The new company will be extending its core business and knowledge of food tourism to other segments of the local economy, principally to promote growth and opportunities for young people and to promote the products and services of the district. Relevant sectors will include agriculture, eco-conservancy, small businesses, and tourism development in general.

By developing sustainable programs and projects in several areas, including food tourism; agritourism; nutrition; health; and environment, Sustain360 will support the municipal mandate for local economic development. In particular, it will ensure skills transfer and economic opportunity for young people.

The future success of African Relish depends on its working partnerships with municipalities, tourism offices, local farmers, Western Cape restaurants/hotels/chef schools, international food tourism initiatives, and high-profile celebrity chefs and others attached to the food industry. Such partnerships will help to forge a new curriculum that can be one that is unique to the local area.

Looking Back Four Years Later

While African Relish set out in the beginning to create a destination-based food tourism product, Ralph Waldo Emerson's words rang loud and clear, "Life is a journey, not a destination." Its owners believe that the journey actually never ends. If we decide that we have arrived at the destination, then that journey of discovery and wonderment would be deemed to be over. There would be nothing new to explore.

It all started with a dream of creating a business built around the broader food experience, something the owners have always been passionate about. The cliché notwithstanding, the school's leadership has always felt connected to food, excited by discovering new ingredients, meeting eccentric and genius producers, reveling in culinary conviviality, and sharing in the generosity of spirit of like-minded people. The world of food has opened up the school and its instructors to world cultures and cross-cultural understanding. Four years later, the owners see clearly what worked well and what did not. And they can identify where the opportunities are for future growth, and so the journey continues.

CONCLUSION

The global ascent in the popularity of food and cooking has naturally spawned an increased enrollment in cooking schools throughout the world. Progressively, more people are participating in cooking as a recreational pastime. The reference to a culinary journey in a far-off place to attend cooking classes has become like a badge of honor for food travelers. Visitors to a recreational cooking school will invariably be happy to spend most of their time cooking and eating. However, it is important for visitors to experience a broader profile of the place they are visiting, and business owners to enable their endeavor to benefit the entire community. The experiential tourism environment creates wonderful opportunities for visitors to meet and engage with locals, giving them a value-added vacation and a real glimpse inside a different culture.

DISCUSSION QUESTIONS

1. What are some of the ways to ensure year round success for cooking schools?
2. Does it make sense for cooking schools to market to both locals and visitors, or one or the other? Discuss the pros and cons of each approach.
3. In what ways can cooking schools benefit the local communities where they operate?

ENDNOTES

---

[1] www.surlatable.com
[2] www.williams-sonoma.com
[3] www.ramekins.com
[4] www.baumancollege.org
[5] www.eccolacucina.com
[6] www.ciachef.edu
[7] www.ciachef.edu/about-the-cia
[8] www.ciarestaurants.com
[9] www.africanrelish.com

Culinary Attractions

Lynne M. Bennett, Catherine Morellon, & Katerine-Lune Rollet

This chapter defines the enigmatic "culinary attractions" category and presents three case studies of successful culinary attraction businesses.

INTRODUCTION

There exists a group of food tourism experiences that are hard to classify. Some might be considered dining, others as museums and still others simply a retail store. Yet something truly unique about these experiences captures the attention and passion of foodies. A wine museum like Vinopolis near London's Borough Market, gives foodies two major food and drink attractions within walking distance of each other. The Scottish Whisky Heritage Centre in Edinburgh, Scotland, UK is another must-experience attraction for foodies. Scotland is famous for whisky so what better place to learn all about it than an interpretive tasting museum? This chapter will define our understanding of culinary attractions and provide several solid examples that can serve as models for similar types of businesses that could inspire similar businesses elsewhere.

Defining Culinary Attractions

According to the World Food Tourism Association, a *culinary attraction* "is any kind of food or drink business that is recognized in a special manner for an exceptional, one-of-a-kind experience."[1] This special category can include a famous chef's home, a culinary museum, a restaurant where a recipe was first created, a bar where a drink was first invented and served, or even a movie star's favorite restaurant.[2]

The Market for Culinary Attractions

Globally, there is an emerging green, sustainable marketing effort that aims to replace the fast-food sector that has done "little to connect local cultures and images with the act of eating."[3] Traditionally culinary attractions were used either like publicity stunts to garner press attention (think of the world's largest hamburger), or to educate the public (think of a chef demonstration). The following list of examples shows how some businesses have historically used creative marketing strategies to draw people to their venues.

- **Buena Vista Café,** in San Francisco, has *served Irish Coffee since 1952*. This is an example of an attraction promoted by locals (the travel writer of the *San Francisco Chronicle* and the mayor) that succeeded beyond its wildest dreams — to date, serving over 30 million Irish Coffees.

- **Coney Island**, *where the American hot dog was first sold* at a stand that is now internationally known as *Nathan's Famous*. Their annual hot dog eating contest has been held for over 40 years on the fourth of July and has gained worldwide recognition. In 2011 over 40,000 spectators attended the event, and an additional 1,949 million viewers watched the live broadcast.

- **Museums Featuring Culinary History:** *Julia Child's Kitchen*, used as the set of three television shows and the testing ground for many of her recipes featured in her cookbook, is now an exhibit in the *Smithsonian Museum* in Washington D.C., USA. The *Southern Food and Beverage Museum*, located in New Orleans, Louisiana, USA, aims to celebrate the cultural treasures of the region, where food is the art on display. Johnson and Wales

University, located in the US State of Rhode Island, has a *Culinary Arts Museum* that is devoted to educating, preserving, and interpreting the culinary and hospitality service industry.

- **James Beard House** is located in the heart of New York City and was once the *home of James Beard*, the celebrated television personality and cookbook author. A foundation was established in his honor to showcase culinary events by food artisans and writers from all over the world.

Developing and Selling a Culinary Attraction

To be successful when promoting a culinary attraction, today culinary entrepreneurs and businesses need to develop innovative and strategic marketing strategies to remain competitive in the marketplace.[4] With an emerging value-oriented, community-based, sustainable-centered view of global tourism, new opportunities are arising for entrepreneurs and businesses to develop and promote their unique culinary attractions. A secondary role of culinary attractions in the tourism industry is to help develop and sustain regional identities for communities, while at the same time creating a successful "repeat business" model.[5]

Faith Popcorn, futurist, founder and CEO of Brain Reserve, spoke at the International Spa Association 2011 conference. She described a new worldwide trend emerging that is moving away from the traumas of recession "into a culture that is focused on reinvention, renewal, inspiration, elevation, connection, nurturance, transparency and honesty."[6] She also explained the movement towards substance over superficiality, where the individual "is inextricably woven into the context of community" that includes a sense of personal wellbeing, that is interconnected with friends, family community, and the planet.[7] Culinary attraction businesses have an opportunity to tap into this emerging trend by weaving these elements into their services, events, activities, and products that they are developing to attract foodies.

In the book *Visions for a Global Tourism Industry: Creating and Sustaining Competitive Strategies*,[8] Kivla and Crofts suggest that, in order for culinary destinations to become successful gastronomy providers, they need to educate tourists about why the local cuisine and its associated culture are unique to their destination.[9] By experiencing a local culture through their food, tourists can establish a relationship with that destination and feel good about their experiences. The local industries can then benefit from this type of business model in order to increase their revenues. The following three case studies serve to illustrate this concept.

Marché des Saveurs, Montreal, Canada[10]

Antonio Drouin and Suzanne Bergeron did not expect in 1998 that a "small project to keep them busy during their retirement" would become a major destination for food tourism in Montreal.[11] Fifteen years later, the Marché des Saveurs is a pioneering retail concept that is a leading light for Quebec gastronomy. It provides a showcase for 4000 Quebec producers and 7000 Quebec food products. Marché des Saveurs is now a full-fledged family business (their daughter Isabelle Drouin and her partner Simon have now joined) located inside the busiest public market in North America, Marché Jean-Talon (Jean-Talon Market). The store is now so well respected that it was visited by Carlo Petrini (Slow Food founder) and Ferran Adria (chef/owner of Spain's former El Bulli) and has been mentioned in articles in *The New York Times*, *Los Angeles Times*, *Le Monde*, and Japan's *Asahi Shimbun*.

In the beginning, tourists represented only 15% of the store's customers and those tourists were probably already at the market before they found out about Marché des Saveurs. Now tourists represent 35% of its customers and 45% of its revenue. The road to this point was long, and was built upon a foundation of quality, customer service, education, and authenticity. "Customers are searching for authenticity. The best proof? I am even selling them ketchup and relish ... as long as it is authentic!" reported Isabelle Drouin, with a smile on her face.

From One Market to Another

The adventure of Marché des Saveurs began in a small 400 square foot (37 sq m) store called the Maison des Vins et Boissons artisanales du Québec (The House of Artisanal Quebec Wine and Beverages) in Marché Maisonneuve, a smaller public market located in Montreal's east end. This shop came about as a confluence of three events. First, Drouin and Bergeron were no strangers to retail, they had run a chain of magazine shops in the past and already had entrepreneurial experience. Second, the rules for the sale of craft alcohol in Quebec had just changed (all alcohol sales in Quebec are regulated by a government monopoly). Third, a friend, who was a meat producer, asked them to represent his products. One thing led to another, and over time other producers asked the couple to represent them as well. The result was a portfolio of products that was large enough to open a shop. The opening was a success and they received wide media coverage. They built on this success by expanding with stalls at two other Montreal markets: Marché Atwater and Marché Jean-Talon.

In the late 1990s, celebrity chefs and the public conversation about eating locally was not as prevalent as today. Nevertheless, shortly after opening, tour guides began dropping by the stalls with their groups. An offering developed where tourists tasted several products such as ice cider and alcohol made from maple syrup, "but we did not want to work with just anyone and simply become a bus stop. We wanted to develop a loyal customer base," said Bergeron.

With their successful promotion of local wines at their first shop, food producers across the province began to ask them for representation as well. They were now faced with the decision of whether they would also sell food. If they did so, they would need a larger location. An exciting opportunity existed at Marché Jean-Talon. The Jean-Talon market opened back in 1933 and is part of Montreal's "DNA". It has about 300 vendors during the height of the summer season and remains busy throughout the year. The challenge was the size of the proposed premises at the market, a huge 4,000 square foot (370 sq m) space.

Antonio Drouin assessed the feasibility of the new business (to be renamed Marché des Saveurs) in this way: "There were two indicators that made us believe in our project: the parking lot was always full and we offered an original concept: Marché des Saveurs would sell only 100% Quebec products." The parking lot was always full because Montrealers have always been foodies who love their local produce, and the opportunity to enjoy other kinds of local products while already shopping at the market was sure to be a hit. The concept was so original that there really were no competitors. Inside the Marché des Saveurs was the first cheese counter to offer only 100% Quebec cheeses and shelves full of Quebec canned and non-perishable products, side by side with Quebec alcohol products.

Obtaining products for the store was made easier by the structure of the artisanal food retail business. It was very difficult for producers who lived up to an eight hour drive from Montreal to rent a stall in the market and be present every day during the summer. Marché des Saveurs became the retailer for these producers, showcasing the products and becoming the link between Montreal and the producers. In this regard, Drouin and Bergeron were truly visionary; they accomplished this at a time when eating local was not a trend or even really present in people's minds.

Marché des Saveurs was supposed to open on June 24, 2000 for Saint-Jean Baptiste day, Quebec's national holiday. Instead it opened on July 4th and perhaps not surprisingly, its first customers were Americans (July 4 is the USA's national Independence Day). The years passed and sales steadily increased to the point that five years later they invested C$500,000 to enlarge the shop.

Things have not always been easy. An unexpected blow happened in 2006. Following a complaint from eight supermarket owners, the Marché des Saveurs' right to sell alcohol was challenged. The couple fought hard to maintain their rights and collected 20,000 signatures on a petition that they presented to the Quebec National Assembly. After several months of struggle, an agreement was reached. They could continue to sell alcohol but only as a legal entity separate from the food store, and inside the store they needed to install walls between the food and alcohol sections, so that it would be a completely separate shop. This was a tough blow and it had a significant financial impact on the business. The shortfall in revenue as a result of these changes is still C$60,000 per year.

The Mission of the Marché des Saveurs

Over the years, fresh products, such as meat and cheese, have taken more and more space on the shelves of Marche des Saveurs; however, the biggest sellers are still maple syrup products (15% of total sales). Isabelle Drouin summed up this state of affairs in the following way: "Because of the language barrier, it is difficult to make groups of tourists who speak another language taste something different than what they want (and expect), which is usually maple syrup products and ice wine. For the tourists that we can communicate with (in English or French), the educational style of the shop allows them to discover other products. For example, products made from native plants or alcohol made from cloudberries."

Marché des Saveurs hosts groups of culinary tourists brought by tour operators. For the price of C$7-$10 per person, participants are offered an in-store taste experience. When groups arrive at the store, Isabelle Drouin paints for them a portrait of the family business, and explains that, while common in Europe, the promotion of regional products is a relatively recent phenomenon in Quebec. The tourists then sample products from the store including cheeses, sausages from Kamouraska, blueberry juice, marinated fiddleheads and much more.

The store is also beneficial for producers. Those that produce non-perishable goods rent a space on the shelves and put their products on consignment. They then receive a monthly check with the percentage of their goods sold. For some producers, the sales at Marché des Saveurs represent 50% of their total sales.

In order to meet Marché des Saveurs' mission to allow customers to discover the flavors of Quebec, producers whose products are sold in the store must commit to come to the store three times a year to provide an educational tasting of their products. This tasting includes a description of the product origin, its preparation, and a small sample. This type of educational tasting transforms the Marché des Saveurs from a simple food tourism destination into an agritourism experience as well. Building on the gastronomic tourist's need to be an explorer, Marché des Saveurs creates an environment full of new experiences that makes customers feel like they are kids in a candy shop. Foodie visitors are given the opportunity to feel that they have lived a unique experience and that they themselves discovered these new products that they tasted for the first time.

Reasons for Success

Several reasons explain the success of the Marché des Saveurs as a food tourism destination:

- **Competition:** There is simply not a lot of competition for the store. Supermarkets, which have large infrastructures, find it difficult to sell regional products, which are often prepared in small quantities and have unstable supply. For example, Bergeron said: "Every week I go to the bus station to pick up packages from producers from across the province. A manager of a supermarket does not have the time to offer this kind of personalized service." Marché des Saveurs is one of the few places where you can find local food products because they make this kind of effort.

- **Culinary Ambassadors:** The Canadian trade delegations abroad have also provided a great showcase for Marché des Saveurs. In Chicago, New York, and Japan, Canadian diplomats gave gifts from Marche des Saveurs that garnered media visibility and attracted tourists.

- **Media:** The owners stated plainly: "We have always been very spoiled by the press. They always gave us great visibility regionally and internationally." It is interesting to note that Marché des Saveurs did not create a media relations plan. Their very business model was inherently newsworthy. The media were already interested in what they were doing.

- **Gifts:** Many of the products sold in the store make nice gifts. They are small enough to fit into luggage and are packaged in a way that allows them to travel well. For example, in December, their biggest buyers are Europeans now living Montreal. When returning to their home country for Christmas, they want to give Quebec products to their family to discover.

- **Partnerships:** In developing their market, the owners met with hotel concierges who in turn prompted tourists to visit the shop. Similarly, through contacts with organizations such as Tourism Montreal, Marché des Saveurs also became a proposed activity for large groups or conferences taking place in the city.

- **Emerging Interest in Food Tourism:** The increase in tourism in Montreal combined with the increasing interest in culinary tours, the trendiness of being a "foodie," and a more educated population with regards to food, has created a gastronomic explosion in recent years and has certainly brought a lot of new visitors to the shop.

- **Quality Customer Service:** The employees at the shop love food — and it shows. This family run business has a very low turnover rate (some employees have been working there since the shop opened 12 years ago). Marché des Saveurs makes sure that its customers have a sampling and a great time: "For 12 years, there is not a child who leaves this store without a chocolate candy or a slice of cheese," says Bergeron.

In the 15 years since the opening of the original shop, the whole family has experienced a real learning curve in growing and managing their business. In 2011, their efforts were rewarded when they received an Edna Award, which honors Canadian individuals who promote regional cuisine. It was the first time that anyone from Quebec had received the award.

Siam Winery, Bangkok, Thailand

Thailand is a popular destination for tourists from around the globe. All who come will find sun, sea, culture and fun, but few visitors would expect to find a winery in Thailand. Yet that is exactly what the uninitiated will find at Siam Winery, located in Samutsakorn province, a 45-minute drive from central Bangkok. It is a perfect surprise for foodies who are explorers by nature and love discovering new and different food and drink experiences.

Siam Winery uses 100% Thai-grown grapes, another unexpected fact. Its success had led to the emergence of the term "New Latitude Wines," used to refer to wine produced in latitudes previously unexpected, notably between the 14th and 18th northern parallels. Thanks to modern winemaking technology, now wine grapes can grow in tropical countries. In addition to Thailand, other countries crossing these parallels, namely Brazil, China, India, Indonesia, and Vietnam have begun developing their wine industries in earnest. Besides the obvious potential revenue from domestic and export sales, many of these regions already enjoy a robust tourism industry. With increasing wine grape production, these destinations are maneuvering themselves to be the next wine tourism destinations.

Siam Winery was founded in 1986 by inventor of the Red Bull energy drink, Khun Chalerm Yoovidya. The winery has already won several international medals for its Monsoon Valley label, and produces 20 varieties in its state-of-the-art facility with an annual capacity of 30 million liters from its 300 acres (121 ha) of vineyards. It is Southeast Asia's leading wine producer with approximately 1000 employees. Grapes are harvested twice annually due to the warm climate. Wine is transported in air conditioned trucks for maximum quality assurance. Siam Winery's wines are available at better resorts throughout Thailand and in retail shops throughout the region.

The winery welcomes more than 150,000 visitors annually at its Hua Hin vineyard location, built on a former elephant corral. Appropriately, vineyard tours take place on the backs of elephants. After the tour, visitors taste the wines and watch a short video about the winery. Meals can be purchased in The Sala, a multi-use Thai-style wooden facility featuring a restaurant, retail shop and meeting center overlooking the vineyards and nearby mountains. Naturally the restaurant's food focuses on locally sourced ingredients that complement the wines. The Sala was designed by Sylvia Soh, an award-winning architect who also designed the Hua Hin visitor center.

Is Hua Hin the next Napa? Who can say, but it is well on its way. Siam Winery's founders have successfully positioned the company as a force to be reckoned with, regarding both retail sales and tourism. Who would ever forget touring a winery in the tropics on the back of an elephant? Some might call it a gimmick, but it is an appropriate feature for the area. And in Siam Winery's case, it works, evidenced by its 150,000 visitors per year.

Indigenous Food-Based Culinary Attractions

With the successful international transportations systems of the second half of the twentieth century, eating food from other countries has been as simple as driving to the local grocery store or ethnic restaurant. It is easy to forget that many of the foods we consume have their origins someplace else. The macadamia nut, is one such food. Most people in the northern hemisphere believe macadamia's origin is Hawaii. Its actual origin is Australia.

For thousands of years the aborigines of Australia ate this native nut, which was found in the rainforests of eastern Australia. Natives called the nut *gyndl, jindilli or boombera*.[12] Of the variety of species, two have edible nuts that can be eaten raw.[13] In the 1850s, while visiting Brisbane in Queensland, Australia, British botanist Walter Hill and German botanist Ferdinand Von Meuller noticed these magnificent trees. Von Meuller was so impressed with the tree that he named the nut *Macadamia integrifolia,* after Dr. John McAdam, a prominent scientist of the time.[14] In 1882 the first commercial macadamia orchard was planted at Rous Mill, near the town of Lismore in New South Wales, Australia, about 200 km (≈124 miles) from Brisbane,[15] where it was discovered by the two botanists. In the 1930s the macadamia was successfully harvested and marketed in Australia by Steve Angus and his brothers who formed Macadamia Nuts Pty. Ltd. However, it was not until 1964, when the business was moved to Brisbane at Slacks Creek, that the first macadamia processing plant was built.[16]

The macadamia nut is the only native Australian crop plant that has been cultivated and produced as a commercial product.[17] As for the Hawaiian connection, the macadamia was brought to Hawaii in the early 1880s, but it was 1925 before it was cultivated as an edible nut in Honolulu.[18]

The Macadamia as a Culinary Attraction: Summerland House Farm[19]

Less than 20 km (≈12 miles) from the town of Lismore, New South Wales, Australia, where the first commercial macadamia orchard was planted, culinary enthusiasts and visitors will find the Summerland House Farm, located in the town of Alstonville. This is a 172-acre (70 ha) working macadamia and avocado farm that is located on the Alstonville plateau and has sweeping views of the eastern coastline. It has over 7,000 trees that produce about 1,500 tons (1361 metric tons) of macadamias each year.[20] It is also a very popular large-scale agritourism destination with 150,000+ annual visitors.[21] Culinary attractions at this farm include:

- **Farm Tractor Tours:** Visitors can take a tractor-train ride through the macadamia and avocado orchards and see the trees while learning about the history and cultivation of the macadamia. Bus tours and community groups can also arrange for private tours.
- **The Grocer:** Their onsite store showcases a wide range of macadamia products from their farm, including fresh, local fruit and vegetables selected from farms throughout the region, and award winning, local gourmet foods, wines, and body products.
- **Nursery:** Visitors can purchase a variety of native plants, exotic trees and shrubs, citrus trees, grasses and indoor plants.
- **Hydroponic Tomatoes:** Visitors can tour the state-of-the-art hydroponic tomato facility where 4,000 tomato plants are grown and harvested for national markets.
- **Summerland House Farm Café:** The café provides a variety of foods from simple to gourmet, showcasing locally grown and produced foods.
- **Monthly and Year-round Events:** include the "Make it, Bake it, Grow it Market" held the first Sunday of every month, showcasing locally produced and made goods; an Annual Country Fair (September), and Australia Day on the Farm (January).
- **Special Events:** from weddings to conferences. With three outdoor courtyards and several conference rooms, the farm can accommodate up to 230 people or cater up to 200 people for a private event.
- **Kid Friendly Activities:** include a water park, playground, and mini golf course.
- **Museum:** dedicated to the inspirational life of the founder of the farm, Lionel Watts.

In addition to being a unique culinary attraction in the heart of macadamia land, Summerland House Farm is also renowned for its successful and unique business enterprise. It is run by the nonprofit, *House With No Steps* (established in 1972), which provides employment programs for over 90 employees with disabilities.[22] Founder Lionel Watts developed this business as a result of his personal struggle to find rehabilitation programs and employment after a long recovery from poliomyelitis, an illness that left him a quadriplegic in 1956.[23]

The diverse business model for this farm also includes a large agricultural hub that houses a large-scale packing and distribution system for avocadoes, tomatoes, and tropical fruits from regional farmers, which are sent off to major wholesale markets and supermarkets in Australia.[24]

The Summerland House Farm is a successful culinary attraction because it features the discovery and cultivation history of an ancient food now marketed for a worldwide modern society and also has a unique and diverse marketing strategy that has enabled it to be successful. Its diversity of produce, services, attractions, activities, and community building philosophy, as well as its successful marketing strategy, is a model for any entrepreneur who is looking to develop a culinary attraction based on the origins of a food.

In addition, this thriving indigenous food production business has added value to the community through its nonprofit business model that employs and supports those with disabilities. By bringing awareness to the larger community about the employment challenges faced by the disabled, Summerland House Farm has been able to demonstrate that everyone can make a positive contribution to society despite any perceived limitations they may have. Summerland House Farm is a brilliant example of a culinary attraction being synonymous with amusement, entertainment, and fun, while at the same time being philanthropic and community-based. It is also one of the best examples of how one food item can enhance the region's economic sustainability while at the same time exposing tourists to Australian culinary culture and history.

There are other examples of culinary attractions in Australia that feature the macadamia and make a contribution to the area by increasing food tourism. Their success is dependent on their marking strategies, diversification and local community support. In addition, the influential and fast moving world of digital technology, requires culinary attractions to have a strategic online presence in order to draw international tourists to their website. The Summerland House Farm website is very thorough in providing visitors with detailed information about their farm, services and products, which are complemented by enticing images. Of the other examples listed below, some have very informative and detailed websites, while others were sparse with insufficient information for the online food traveler.

Other Examples of Macadamia Culinary Attraction in Australia

Business/Location	Type	Culinary Attraction	Other
The Macadamia Castle 1699 Pacific Highway Knockrow NSW 2479 Australia www.macadamiacastl e.com.au	**6 acre (2.4 ha) Animal Park:** Featuring native and farmyard animals, birds and reptiles.	**Nut Bar:** Featuring macadamia products. **Retail Shop:** Includes a *fine food* section that contains the largest range of local produce in the region, with over 200 locally made products. **Café:** Serves freshly prepared local produce and food.	**Family friendly:** Mini golf course, keeper talks, interactive animal experiences.

Lorne Valley Macadamia Farm and Café
1181 Lorne Road
Lorne NSW 2439
Australia
www.lornevalleymacadamiafarm.com

Macadamia Plantation: growing, harvesting and processing macadamia nuts. Features 20 tree varieties ranging from 6 to 22 years old, producing between 600-650 tons annually.

Farm Tours: of plantation includes information talks on the tree cycle, harvesting, machinery, and processing.
Café: Described as "beach meets bush": decorated with vintage surfboards positioned throughout the exposed hardwood rafters, old street signs and farming tools. Visitors can enjoy a selection of freshly made macadamia products.
Shop: macadamia and local food products, cosmetics and face and body creams.

This family farm is one of the region's most popular attractions. The farm owners are shareholders of Nambucca Macnuts, a co-op structured as a private company.

Nutworks and The Chocolate Factory:
37 Pioneer Road
Yandina, QLD 4561
Australia
www.nutworks.com.au

Macadamia & Chocolate Factory: located in the heart of a natural macadamia growing region of the Sunshine Coast in Hinterland.

Factory Tours: Tours of Macadamia processing can be viewed during harvesting season (April to November). Year around tours of chocolate coating and flavoring/roasting process.
Retail Shop: featuring factory products.
Café: Includes macadamia treats.
Chocolate Making Workshops: Offered during holidays.

Started as a small factory farm in 1990s with six employees. Now a major employer of the region. Nuts sourced from most growing areas in Queensland. Products from the company's factory are exported worldwide.

| Yarramalong Macadamia Nut Farm: 34 Macadamia Lane Wyong Creek NSW 2259 Australia www.yarramalongmacadamiafarm.com.au | Macadamia Farm: Established around 1972, when named the Barkala Plantation. Contains rare older macadamia cultivars. | Farm Tour: of 600 mature macadamia trees. Firefly Bistro: Features fresh lunches, snacks and coffee. Dishes incorporate macadamias. Most items are made from produce grown on the farm. Retail Shop: Macadamia nut products. | A biodynamic farm where only natural products are used. 100% on-site rainwater harvesting and composting systems. Farm goal is towards 100% self-sufficiency. |
| Medowie Macadamias 672 Medowie Road Medowie NSW 2318 Australia www.medowiemacadamias.com.au | A Family-run Macadamia Farm: This 12-acre (4.8 ha) farm was established in 1980 and grows five varieties of macadamia trees. | Farm Tours: For groups and bus tours to demonstrate the growing, harvesting and processing of macadamias. Café & Store: serves a large variety of sweets, cakes and macadamia products. Online Gift Shop: includes items like chili flavored macadamia nuts and brittle, raw nuts and cracking tools, and a large range of beauty supplies, oils, and gifts. | The family is involved in every stage of the business, from harvesting of the nuts to experimenting with new, tasty products that can be purchased at the cafe or online. |

Success Factors: Tying it All Together

A number of factors can contribute to the successful marketing, development, management and operation of culinary attractions:

- **Food Origins:** Can include history, culture, tradition, agriculture, location, local foods, food-ways and food traditions.
- **Food Heritage:** Regional culinary dishes featured as part of the experience.
- **Culinary Education:** Centered on the region's unique food, site and/or attraction provide a more meaningful experience to the tourist.
- **Unique Cultural Experience:** Tied into the cultural and food heritage of the region.
- **Culinary Networking:** Developing culinary tour packages with local and regional travel experts to enhance the regions cultural and food specialties.

- **Cultivating Economic Growth and Sustainability:** To promote culinary attractions and provide economic growth opportunities for the region.
- **Marketing:** Both local and international, using the digital technology resources of the Internet, to include web content and internet marketing media connections to generate positive reviews and drive business to the culinary site.

CONCLUSION

For culinary attractions to be successful, one must understand what drives food tourism. Indigenous food, local ingredients, cultural presentations, healthiness, freshness and the relationship of the food, people and place of culture, can all be tied into creating a fun, desirable experience that contributes to successfully establishing a sustainable culinary attraction.[25] The three case studies presented above demonstrate the importance of the experience that the culinary attraction produces for that specific region. A culinary attraction also needs to have the ability to tell a story, because it conveys some aspect of the culture of the region being visited and lends itself more readily to repeat business.[26]

DISCUSSION QUESTIONS

1. Besides a farmers' market, unique retail store or unique dining experience, what other examples of culinary attractions can you think of?
2. Can a culinary attraction be built, or is it something that must evolve naturally over time?
3. Consider the story and business model of Napa Valley's COPIA, which is now closed. What circumstances would need to be different, or what could this culinary attraction have done differently, for COPIA to have remained open?

ENDNOTES

[1] "Asset Inventory & Lucky 13 Business Types.pdf". International Culinary Tourism Association. 2010. Retrieved on May 10, 2012, www.worldfoodtravel.org
[2] Ibid.
[3] Kasimoglu, M., editor. Visions for Global Tourism Industry: Creating and Sustaining Competitive Strategies. (2012), p. 101. InTech. (ISBN: 978-953-51-0520-6). Quoted Source page 101: Ching-Shu Su and Jeou-Shyan Horng. Recent Developments in Research and Future Directions of Culinary Tourism: A Review. Graduate Institute of Tourism and Hospitality Management, Jinwen University of Science & Technology and Department of Hospitality Management, De Lin Institute of Technology.
[4] Ibid.
[5] Ibid.
[6] Wuttke, M. Be A Leader, Change the World. Organic Spa Magazine, April 20, 2012. p. 33.
[7] Ibid.
[8] Kasimoglu, M., editor. Visions for Global Tourism Industry: Creating and Sustaining Competitive Strategies. (2012). InTech. ISBN: 978-953-51-0520-6.
[9] Kasimoglu, M., editor. Visions for Global Tourism Industry: Creating and Sustaining Competitive Strategies. (2012), p. 101. InTech. (ISBN: 978-953-51-0520-6). Quoted From page 104: Ching-Shu Su and Jeou-Shyan Horng. Recent Developments in Research and Future Directions of Culinary Tourism: A Review. Graduate Institute of Tourism and Hospitality Management, Jinwen University of Science & Technology and Department of Hospitality Management, De Lin Institute of Technology. Reference Source: Kivela, J., & Crotts, J. C. (2006). Tourism and gastronomy: gastronomy's influence on how tourists experience a destination. Journal of Hospitality & Tourism Research, 30 (3), 354-377.
[10] www.lemarchedessaveurs.com
[11] Telephone interview by Katerine-Lune Rollet with Antonio Drouin and Isabelle Drouin, owners of Marché des Saveurs, December 2012.
[12] Macadamia Castle, retrieved on May 30, 2013, www.macadamiacastle.com.au/about-macadamias/history

[13] Australian Macadamia Society, retrieved on May 30, 2013, http://macadamias.org
[14] Ibid.
[15] McConachie, I. "The Macadamia Story", Retrieved on May 31, 2013, www.mnmsnuthouse.com/yahoo_site_admin/assets/docs/themacadamiastory.287114127.html
[16] The Macadamia Castle, retrieved May 30, 2013 www.macadamiacastle.com.au/about-macadamias/history
[17] Australian Macadamia Society, retrieved on May 30, 2013, http://macadamias.org
[18] The Macadamia Castle, retrieved May 30, 2013 www.macadamiacastle.com.au/about-macadamias/history
[19] Guide at a glance: Alstonville, December 2, 2012. Rouse Hill – Stanhope Gardens News, Retrieved on May 31, 2013, www.rhsgnews.com.au/story/1158402/guide-at-a-glance-alstonville
[20] Summerland House Farm, retrieved on May 31, 2013 www.summerlandhousefarm.com.au
[21] Ibid.
[22] Ibid.
[23] Ibid.
[24] Ibid.
[25] Kasimoglu, M., editor. Visions for Global Tourism Industry: Creating and Sustaining Competitive Strategies. (2012), p. 107. InTech. (ISBN: 978-953-51-0520-6). Quoted Source page 101: Ching-Shu Su and Jeou-Shyan Horng. Recent Developments in Research and Future Directions of Culinary Tourism: A Review. Graduate Institute of Tourism and Hospitality Management, Jinwen University of Science & Technology and Department of Hospitality Management, De Lin Institute of Technology.
[26] Ibid.

Culinary Lodging

Lynne M. Bennett and Lee Jolliffe

For some travelers, a hotel is just a hotel — a place to spend the night. For foodies, hotels can serve as an opportunity to extend their culinary adventure. This chapter highlights the relevance of themed lodging in food tourism. It defines and discusses the development of culinary lodging, providing case studies illustrating best practices in the marketing, development and management of this niche type of accommodation property.

INTRODUCTION

Culinary lodging, defined as "lodging or accommodation with a culinary or cuisine focus or theme," can take a number of forms, such as 1) lodging provided at or near the site of food cultivation or production, where related to the offerings of the facility and 2) lodging that includes a dedicated culinary or cuisine focused experience component forming a major theme for the facility.[1] At these types of properties, both food and more refined cuisine can provide a major motivation for guests to choose these over alternate accommodations. Culinary lodging thus contributes to the culinary product of the destinations where they are located.

With the popularity of food tourism, destination organizations have developed food tourism policies and some have defined "culinary lodging." For example, the food tourism policy of the government of Alberta, Canada defines food tourism lodging as "including hotels, resorts, bed and breakfasts, and other accommodation that focuses on providing Alberta Food and Drink."[2] Within the category of culinary lodging, numerous types of accommodation properties, ranging from urban and rural bed and breakfast inns, to city hotels to destination resorts and inns with cooking schools, are illustrated in Table 1.

Table 1. Culinary Lodging Types

Type	Criteria	Examples
Culinary Hotels and Resorts	Cuisine is a central focus in on-site restaurants, reflecting local food-ways and culinary expertise.	Switzerland[3] categorizes culinary hotels, i.e. Gasthof Gyrenbad Auberge de Soleil,[4] Napa Valley, California, USA
Culinary Themed Accommodations	Adopted a culinary theme, providing a focus for cuisine related activities.	The Chocolate Boutique Hotel,[5] Bournemouth, U.K. Safari West,[6] Santa Rosa, California
Culinary Production Related Accommodations	Local food and/or drink production reflected by the design, menu and activities provided.	Heritance Tea Factory Hotel,[7] Sri Lanka
Culinary Experience	Participation in cuisine is encouraged, i.e. incorporating cooking schools.	Time for Lime,[8] Koh Lanta Island, Thailand Ramekins Culinary School, Events and Inn,[9] Sonoma, California, USA

A variety of types of culinary lodging thus form part of the food tourism supply chain.[10] These accommodation types reflect and are often linked to other local culinary resources, such as local markets, and food-related attractions and activities. Various types of accommodations can have "special food and drink" features, such as its kind and caliber, or an attraction such as a cooking school.[11] However, while many types of culinary attractions may only attract day visitors, dedicated culinary lodgings provide a range of activities that can contribute to lengthening the stay of tourists in a particular area.

The Market for Culinary Lodging

Food travelers need lodging. It follows that culinary lodging developed to meet the needs and interests of food travelers. Marketing for culinary lodging lends itself to the arena of individualized culinary adventures and wellness travel experiences, thus meeting the demands of the culinary travel 'foodie' enthusiasts. Choosing culinary lodging allows individuals to either stay for a weekend or longer, to experience a complete culinary adventure. They can get into the soil, feel the dirt, taste the results, and can even bring these adventures home to their own kitchen table and friends. The benefit to the culinary lodging industry of promoting culinary experiences is the repeat business, allowing the culinary marketing expert to focus on seasonal venues.

To know your market is to know your region, as well as its history and environs, this is the key to marketing culinary lodging. For example, the Napa and Sonoma Valleys focus on their legendary vineyards and local winemaking, attracting this kind of visitor to the area. The food tourism industry grew naturally in this rich agricultural environment, and further development of this region led to it becoming a well-known destination, and contributed to the restaurant industry's growth and success. Here the culinary expertise became a new trend involving growing, preparing, and serving fresh, local, organic, gourmet food in farm-to-table settings.

Culinary travelers have a unique profile in that they are well-traveled, use all five senses to experience all that a region has to offer, and are a highly loyal group that returns to the destination to further their culinary experiences. Marketing to those travelers must include awakening those senses as well as showing the culinary traveler how to bring their experiences home with them. Savvy travelers want those experiences to continue beyond their vacation.

Culinary lodging has brought repeat business for weddings, catering, cooking classes, seasonal classes, the new "kids can cook" movement, hands-on classes, and private cooking classes. Currently, the trend is moving toward wellness, which opens up the need for longer stays in culinary lodging. Now the marketing niche can extend into more than culinary packages by including wellness travel packages.

Wellness tourism has become more than just a spa experience; it now has incorporated culinary aspects in terms of healthy diets and cuisines. A wellness tourist is a consumer that travels to pursue holistic, preventive, or lifestyle-based services. Wellness tourism is "the sum of all the relationships and phenomena resulting from a journey and residence by people whose main motive is to preserve or promote their health."[12] According to Wellness Tourism Worldwide, the spa industry has realized that there is an emerging market in wellness travel that includes foods and healthy diets. With this new trend, spas are seeking to appeal to this changing demographic and are actively seeking to reposition themselves in this industry.[13]

The following case studies demonstrate how varying types of lodging contribute to food tourism by adopting distinct culinary themes, while also catering to different niches in the food tourism market. In particular these cases also show how local food and drink production and farm-to-table approaches can be complemented by global culinary traditions and standards. This

194

approach adds value to a number of specialty resort operations while appealing to the growing market of food tourism.

Calistoga Ranch of Auberge du Soleil, Napa Valley California, USA

Calistoga Ranch is located in the beautiful and secluded Upper Napa Valley, in Northern California (USA). It is situated in a canyon on 157 acres (64 ha) amidst the oak and redwood forest and hills. This estate-type setting offers deluxe one or two bedroom lodges. This pristine ranch can accommodate visitors with a choice of 48 private free-standing lodges surrounded in a natural and secluded setting. The Ranch is also available for weddings, business conferences, and events. Calistoga Ranch provides several possible escapes or packages that include: Wellness Spa, Indulge Your Senses, and Taste of the Good Life, just to name a few.[14]

This property contributes to a unique type of food tourism. Legendary Napa Valley, known for world-class wines, ingredients, and local produce, provides the inspiration for dining at this ranch. Travelers can experience Michelin-rated farm-to-table dining that is created as a local twist on Mediterranean cuisine.

Calistoga Ranch, owned by Auberge du Soleil, is one of 500 Relais & Chateaux properties, a collection of the finest hotels and gourmet restaurants in the world.[15] Established in France in 1954, the mission of Relais & Chateaux is to spread its art de vivre across the globe by selecting properties with a truly unique character. Their responsible luxury commitment incorporates local and worldwide affiliations and programs within the Green Spa Network and the Napa Valley Wine Trail Association. Each Relais & Chateaux property is privately owned and uniquely operated. Taking advantage of their local lodging expertise, Calistoga Ranch can provide an in-depth group or private culinary lodging experience.

Calistoga Ranch is a good example of extending culinary lodging locally and globally by using their private resort setting. This ranch-style lodging offers visitors cultural events and locally influenced cuisine. This finely stated ranch lodging further contributes to the legendary luxuries of the region for food tourism, by enriching each guest's stay and wellness experience.

Ramekins Culinary School, Events & Inn

Ramekins is both a culinary school and an inn located in the historic town of Sonoma, California, near the rolling Mayacamas Mountain range.[16] Guests can visit the Mission San Francisco Solano de Sonoma in town or take a scenic drive through the vineyards to visit the Jack London Historical State Park and learn about emerging sustainable farming practices of the early twentieth century. Ramekins is an elegant, Tuscan-style culinary school and lodge that offers a culinary experience that can include private or hands-on demonstration and cooking classes in the fully equipped professional demonstration kitchen for up to 36 guests, culinary retreats, and kids classes. Class themes vary from season to season and feature local ingredients.

Participants can learn how to bake a perfect loaf of sourdough bread, brew their own batch of micro-brewed beer, preserve summer fruits, or prepare authentic international meals in classes such as Cuisine Dans Les Rues De Paris, Exploring Burmese Cuisine, Favorites from Bacar, Memories of Italy, and Introduction to Vietnamese Cooking. Classes are taught by visiting chefs and culinary instructors. Their wide range of classes vary in skill level and interests. Ramekins has a farm-to-table philosophy that teaches guests the importance of working with local farmers and food artisans. Ramekins is unique in that it provides luxury accommodations to its culinary guests. Guests can relax in their rustic French antique furnished rooms constructed of rammed earth walls that create a naturally controlled tempered environment, or they can also choose to enjoy a relaxing spa treatment or lounge in their private courtyard surrounded by native plant landscaping.

Safari West, Santa Rosa, California, USA

Safari West is a 400-acre (162 ha) award winning wildlife preserve nestled in the wine country of Sonoma County, California (USA). Safari West is a true Wildlife Preserve and Five Star Rated African Tent Camp.[17] In this Sonoma Serengeti one can relax in an authentic African tent while wild animals graze nearby. Different from the normal hotel, guests will experience the fun and adventuresome pace of Africa—while in California—and relish their natural world surroundings, in a relaxing atmosphere, while leaving their emails, deadlines, and worries behind. One of only six in North America, Safari West has earned a prestigious membership in the American Zoo and Aquarium Association. Established in 1989 by Peter Lang, Safari West brings conservation programs for endangered and extinct-in-the wild animals to its visitors. Their ongoing mission of wildlife preservation is through breeding, education, research, and public interaction.

Lodging on this wildlife preserve includes 30 luxury tent cabins where one wakes up to the serenade of the African savannah. Guests experience an authentic safari tour in a refurbished jeep where they can get up close to giraffes, gazelles, zebras, and other animals inhabiting the preserve. This is Africa, but in the glorious wine country of Sonoma, California. Guests can also wander through their gift shop to view and purchase from a collection of African artisan masks, books, cookbooks, and other mementos.

Safari West is also an example of a unique lodging niche that provides its guests with African culinary opportunities along with their safari experience. Local chefs put a twist on African cuisine by using a special blend of spices and flavors on their ranch style barbecue. Guests can also participate in wine tasting by sampling and comparing locally grown wines with their specially selected imported African wines. Guests can dine indoors surrounded by African décor, or they can enjoy the views of the Sonoma Serengeti from the terrace.

This culinary lodging, located on a game preserve, has been repurposed as a luxury and vacation destination. Although tourists can come just for the day, by extending their stay they can take advantage of a genuine culinary lodging experience, which includes sleeping in a safari tent on the Sonoma Serengeti and dining on gourmet African-styled meals. Safari West also provides a complete massage service to rejuvenate their guests after a long day of trekking. Safari West provides this one-of-a-kind-exotic setting for weddings, reunions, business conferences, and private retreats.

Developing & Managing Culinary Lodging

The following case studies further demonstrate both the different types of culinary lodging and also the diversity of their development and management. Providing best practice examples they also serve to highlight the potential for existing lodging facilities to be converted to culinary lodging, with an increased focus, in particular, on local cuisines and experiences sought out by culinary tourists.

Heritance Tea Factory Hotel, Nuwara Eliya, Sri Lanka

This luxury hotel with 54 guest rooms is located in a converted historic tea factory building, set amid the tea gardens of the Hethersett Estate in the central hill country tea growing area of Sri Lanka. The building, constructed in the mid-1930s, was converted to a hotel by Aitken Spence and Company and opened in 1996. Guests are greeted on arrival by a cup of hot-spiced tea.

196

The hotel is surrounded by tea gardens. It is possible to see women picking tea year-round and to participate in nature tours of the gardens and surrounding area. Within the hotel, guests can view collections related to the history of the estate, and some of the equipment of the former tea factory incorporated in the renovation. Souvenir packages of tea picked and processed on site are available in the hotel shop. Guests are able to pluck their own tea and follow it through the production process in the hotel's Mini Tea Factory, taking home a unique souvenir.

There are a number of dining experiences with menus using fresh organic vegetables, herbs and tea produced on the estate. The main restaurant features a buffet and a special menu with tea accompanying every course, while a converted rail car has a menu created by the chef for each party. The historic rail car dining experience provided is uniquely linked to the heritage of tea production here, as the railway was established for the tea industry.

The property contributes to a niche type of food and drink tourism, namely tea tourism,[18] in this tea-producing region.[19] There are complementary forms of culinary lodging in the area such as Ceylon Tea Trails,[20] a network of four colonial era tea planter bungalows, repurposed as luxury holiday accommodations, complete with butler service and gourmet meals. This range of tea heritage properties contributes to the attractiveness of the region for food tourism, offering accommodations that reflect the area's rich tea heritage and culture.

Time for Lime, Koh Lanta Island, Thailand

Time for Lime is a cooking school, Bungalow and Beach Bar operation located on Klong Dao Beach, near Krabi, Koh Lanta Island in Thailand. The school offers lessons focusing on Thai cuisine and participants can stay on site in one of the nine basic bungalows located in a tropical garden behind the school. The school's founder Junie Kovacs and local Thai chefs provide instruction. Daily classes emphasize ingredients and substitutes as well as preparation methods and lessons include an apron and recipes. Non-cooking partners are welcomed as "Lazy Chefs" to relax at the beach bar while their partners cook. A dining experience is incorporated into the lessons as participants and partners sample the products of the instruction.

Cooking schools, both residential and non-residential, are an important attraction for food-related tourism.[21] Time for Lime offers an educational experience in an authentic residential beachfront setting that is appealing to culinary tourists. Participants in the Cooking School are able to gain knowledge of local ingredients, as well where to find possible substitutes once they are home in Europe or North America. A weekly menu of lessons allows participants to gain progressive culinary expertise as they learn how to prepare different Thai dishes and supplementary daily lessons are also available. Profits go to the Lanta Animal Shelter.

By linking accommodation with a cooking experience, Time for Lime offers an intensive culinary experience in a residential setting. By offering daily lessons, this site is able to appeal to other culinary motivated visitors who are not looking for a residential setting. In addition the Beach Bar is able to offer a beachfront experience for casual culinary tourists wishing to sample traditional and fusion Thai cuisine.

Success Factors: Tying it All Together

A number of factors identified below contribute to the successful marketing, development, management and operation of culinary lodging:

- Culinary Resources – history, culture, tradition, agriculture, location, local foods, food-ways and food traditions.

- Culinary Expertise – local culinary professionals who can implement the desired concepts, ability to deliver a quality culinary product and experience, marketing and management of culinary aspects in synergy with the lodging.

- Culinary Networking – synergy with local, regional and national food tourism plans and policies, partnership with local suppliers.

- Culinary Lodging – the uniqueness of the location, cuisine and accommodations, tied into the history, geography and culture, which provide for high quality service, ambiance, authenticity and specialized venues.

CONCLUSION

Culinary lodging can provide a direct benefit to food tourism by providing an enriched, educational and more intensive culinary and gastronomic experience to tourists, at the same time lengthening the stay of visitors to the area. Destinations wishing to focus on food tourism can strengthen their product offering by encouraging the development of culinary focused accommodations. Best practice missions, whereby accommodation operators have the opportunity for study visits to successful culinary lodging operations, can also contribute to the establishment of new culinary-focused accommodations. The culinary lodging case studies should benefit culinary and tourism professionals who wish to expand or diversify into the culinary lodging industry.

DISCUSSION QUESTIONS

1. What kinds of culinary lodging exist in your community?
2. Explain the difference between a culinary lodging property and a regular lodging property.
3. Could there be a market for moderately priced culinary accommodations? If so, what would the business model look like and how would it compare to higher-end culinary accommodations?

ENDNOTES

---

[1] International Culinary Tourism Association, Culinary Tourism: The Hidden Harvest, Kendall Hunt, Iowa, 2006.
[2] "Alberta Culinary Tourism Alliance". http://albertaculinary.com (accessed January 5, 2013)
[3] "MySwitzerland.com". www.myswitzerland.com/en/culinary-hotels.html (accessed January 2, 2013)
[4] "Auberge du Soleil". www.aubergedusoleil.com (accessed May 16, 2013)
[5] "The Chocolate Boutique Hotel". www.thechocolateboutiquehotel.co.uk (accessed January 26, 2013)
[6] "Heritance Tea Factory". www.heritancehotels.com/teafactory (accessed January 27, 2013)
[7] "Safari West". www.safariwest.com/home (accessed May 16, 2013)
[8] "Time for Lime". www.timeforlime.net (accessed January 27, 2013)
[9] "Ramekins Culinary School, Events & Inn" www.ramekins.com (accessed May 22, 2013,)
[10] S. L. J. Smith and H. Xiao. "Food tourism Supply Chains: A Preliminary Examination," Journal of Travel Research 46 (3) (2008): 289–299.
[11] P. Boniface. *Tasting Tourism: Travelling for Food and Drink* (Ashgate Publishing Limited, 2003).
[12] H. Mueller, and E. Lanz Kaufmann. "Wellness tourism: Market analysis of a special health tourism segment and implications for the hotel industry". Journal of Vacation Marketing, 17(3), (2011): 5-17.

[13] Wellness Tourism Worldwide. www.wellnesstourismworldwide.com/articles.html#sthash.O4CnhN6d.rmFnZf2C.dpbs (accessed May 24, 2013)

[14] "Calistoga Ranch". www.calistogaranch.com/accommodations.html (accessed May 17, 2013)

[15] "Auberge du Soleil". www.aubergedusoleil.com/about/the-auberge-story (accessed May 17, 2013)

[16] "Ramekins Culinary School, Events & Inn" www.ramekins.com (accessed May 22, 2013)

[17] "Safari West". www.safariwest.com/home (accessed May 16, 2013)

[18] Those interested in learning more about tea tourism are encouraged to read *The Role of Drinks: Promoting Tourism through Beverage Trails* chapter in this book.

[19] L. Jolliffe and M. S. M. Aslam. "Tea Heritage Tourism: Evidence from Sri Lanka, Journal of Heritage Tourism". 4(4) (2009): 331–344.

[20] "Ceylon Tea Trails". www.teatrails.com (accessed January 25, 2013)

[21] P. Boniface. *Tasting Tourism: Travelling for Food and Drink* (Ashgate Publishing Limited, 2003).

Culinary Media

Sarika Chawla, Prajakta Remulkar, & Janet Welch

The culinary media industry has gone through dramatic transformations in recent years. Two decades ago, food writing was largely about restaurant reviews written by opinionated critics and recipes developed by a magazine's test kitchen. Today, advertising revenue has all but dried up and consumers are wielding a tremendous influence on both consumer behavior and culinary journalism. This chapter looks at the current state of culinary media and offers a variety of ways to leverage culinary media successfully in today's marketplace.

INTRODUCTION

Food has become increasingly important in the travel industry. More and more travelers admit to choosing vacation destinations based on food and drink alone. That voracious appetite for all kinds of good food is increasingly highlighted in media, in paid advertising and feature stories, and in traditional and social channels, both professionally and customer-written. Consequently the way stories are published and trends are made has changed. For example:

- A newspaper restaurant critic today stands at an equal position with thousands of reviewing customers, through blogs, user-generated reviews and social media.

- A culinary trend can now be invented by a local chef and gain international recognition, such as the Kogi fusion food truck in Los Angeles[1] that inspired a modern culinary phenomenon, explored later in this chapter.

- Potential traveling customers gain their destination information by accessing an ever-increasing list of media resources, so a multi-pronged approach is generally the most effective tool in reaching customers. One article in a leading magazine may be a coveted hit, but a consumer may be just as influenced by a chef who they have seen on television and who is also active on Twitter, or a dining experience that has appeared on food blogs and recommended on a social review website such as Yelp.

This chapter is an overview of food tourism media channels, providing a discussion on traditional and new media as well as digital self-publishing. It illustrates the success of such channels through the presentation of real-life media strategy case studies. It is important to note that the media climate is constantly changing. Today's media will be enhanced, revised and replaced. The astute media planner in food and drink tourism will continue a quest for the appropriate media mix every time.

How Journalists Cultivate Stories

In most cases, the press industry is not as "organic" as it is made out to be. It does not happen often that a writer, driven by wanderlust, stumbles into a regional culinary delight that has yet to be discovered by outsiders. Many times, these stories are packaged by a public relations (PR) or marketing team and pitched to media. The hope is that enough press coverage will resonate with travelers and convert them to choose that destination over others. That is not to say it is not deserving of attention. If a culinary story has merit and, if the experience is that good, then people will come.

Major food destinations such as France, Italy, Thailand, and California get covered frequently as writers return to these places again and again trying to uncover the next new story: the best macaroons in Paris; how the truffles of Marche compare to those in Umbria and Piedmont; how modern restaurants measure up to street food in Bangkok; and the newest artisan producer in California wine country. However there is only so much marketing budget to go around. Even so, these prominent food destinations have marketing and public relations experts hard at work generating story ideas, coordinating with journalists, and coming up with the next "big" story.

How can a smaller destination or individual operator compete? The good news is that modern media outlets are now on a 24/7 cycle and always in need of content. Provide a good story, and chances are someone will pick up on it. Nevertheless, it is very easy to get lost in the clutter with so many media outlets available to potential audience. There is no standard media plan for a travel provider or destination. The best plan is to think of media placement as a multi-pronged, ongoing strategy.

Television, print magazines, newspapers, radio, online, social media, and mobile applications are the cornerstones of any media plan. In theory, the plan for any product — food tourism or otherwise — should be simple:

- Define your product
- Identify your audience
- Target and contact key journalists
- Measure success in attendance, clicks, purchases, or other ways

Of course, it is not that simple and one needs to identify which type of media is most likely to bring new business. In addition one needs to know how best to measure awareness and how to convince a journalist or editor to cover one's story. The following section outlines the main types of media that can be used for features on food and drink.

Types of Media

Newspapers

Achieving a story in old-school print media generates a sense of credibility and legitimacy. Online versions of articles mean inbound links to your website and a longer impact as the content is available longer. However, circulation is decreasing and content is limited. A print publication has an extremely short shelf life. Getting the attention of an editor or writer at a top-tier publication may require the expertise of a PR professional with those contacts.

Magazines

Emerging technology with tablets and online content allows people to access the material in a dynamic, interactive form. Coverage in a major print publication still garners respect and credibility. Nevertheless circulation is decreasing and editorial content is sometimes traded for paid advertisements. Lead times can be extremely long, often 6-12 months.

Websites and Blogs

People of all ages consume Internet content at an astonishing pace. Online content is available and searchable for a long period of time. It is possible to track incoming traffic from online media sources. Online outlets have a quick turnaround time, providing instant gratification. High-profile blogs and websites can have incredible reach, with thousands or even millions of readers. The trouble is that the Internet is a vast place, with thousands of culinary travel stories competing for attention. Content gets stale very quickly as new information is updated constantly and many bloggers do not have significant audience reach.

Social Media

Facebook, Twitter, Pinterest, Instagram, and Google+ are engaging and visual, with potentially enormous audiences. Information can be disseminated with the click of a button, whether it is to announce a new product, promotion or news. However misinformation runs rampant. It is difficult to stand out in a sea of social-media outlets. Gaining an audience and credibility requires ongoing engagement and updates, not simply promotional posts. Furthermore, posts to these outlets only reach people who happen to be on your particular page at one point in time. A lot of potential viewers/readers – and customers – can fall through the cracks.

Direct Online Mail

You can send special offers and announcements to a highly targeted audience, tailor them to seasons or events, and directly measure the response through clicks. Newsletters have space for advertisements and traceable links. This requires building a significant database of e-newsletter subscribers, which is a time-consuming process and only a fraction of recipients (currently, usually less than 20%) actually open the message.[2]

User-Generated Sites

Everyone can be a critic and share their personal experiences. Consumers tend to trust their peers when it comes to respected sites such as TripAdvisor, Yelp and Chowhound. Providers have a direct link to their audience and can adjust their product based on specific feedback. On the other hand there has been controversy over the validity of some posts, whether it is owners posting positive reviews of their own product or disgruntled ex-employees posting negative reviews.

Radio

Online technology allows a bigger audience to access radio shows around the globe, including in cars and on smartphones, not to mention live streaming or recorded Internet radio shows. An on-air interview can be engaging and lively, which may resonate with audiences more than text. Yet, radio content is fleeting. Websites of smaller stations are not very robust or well-staffed.

Television

Television reaches a wide audience and has a high media value. It is easy to showcase a venue, destination or experience in its best light. Chefs and destinations who get repeated exposure on television benefit from top of mind recall. Nonetheless, getting your product on television often requires a PR professional with an extensive list of contacts. The information is fleeting and can be buried among today's 24-hour news cycle of content.

Mobile Apps

This is a growing outlet in which people have access to information and promotions at their fingertips. A 2012 study from the Pew Internet Project showed that: 88% of American adults have a cell phone, 57% have a laptop, 19% own an e-book reader, 19% have a tablet computer and 63% go online wirelessly with one of those devices. Apps can be used to convert directly into bookings and traffic through smartphones and tablets.[3] However like all new technologies apps may not yet reach a wide audience, particularly the coveted market of affluent Baby Boomers. Ideally an app should fulfill some kind of purpose (like booking something) or conveying useful information, otherwise it is nothing more than a website that has been optimized for mobile technology. Having analyzed the main media channels, the next section focuses on identifying the most appropriate media for food and drink products.

Which Media Is Right For You? How to Build a Media Plan

"Every dollar spent in one place is a dollar not spent somewhere else," explains Tim Zahner, Chief Marketing Officer of Sonoma County (California, USA) Tourism. "So you have to evaluate the impact your marketing dollar will have and what the likely return is." There is the magic number of advertising revenue. One article in Food & Wine magazine is worth a certain amount of cash in advertising, whether it is a glossy feature with photos or an accompanying sidebar. However measuring that in terms of conversion (how many people are actually booking trips based on that article) is nearly impossible. The beauty of online press is that you can literally track where your clicks come from, and the younger generation of food-obsessed people gets information from a variety of online sources. A hit on Grubstreet, SmittenKitchen or Eater can be just as effective as a traditional magazine, if not as sexy. "We have to look at the ad equivalent, that's what we're targeted on," says Emma de Vadder Regional Director North America at VisitEngland. "There are the big hits, like the Today Show and far-reaching print, which have high ad value. "But these days we also want to work with bloggers and online outlets because the story stays up there."

A visit to ChicagoFoodPlanet.com reveals an ongoing dedication to cultivating media attention. Links to media mentions in outlets such as CNN, ABC, The Travel Channel, USA Today and many more resonate that this company's media strategy is robust and proactive. Beyond traditional media, ChicagoFoodPlanet engages visitors to join their conversation on social media channels, including Facebook, Twitter, Yelp, YouTube and TripAdvisor. The company offers three food-tour options in vibrant Chicago neighborhoods. Shane Kost, owner of Chicago Food Planet Food Tours, says "In today's competitive market for culinary tourism, it's important to have feet in both the traditional and social media /online marketing." Kost's media strategy has evolved since the company's inception. "When we started Chicago Food Planet Food Tours in 2006, this was the social media landscape: Facebook was a private company targeting mostly college students; TripAdvisor was important, now it's hugely important; Twitter didn't exist and Yelp was just starting to operate outside of California. Now all of these media channels are important to master and pursue, and there will undoubtedly be new ones in the years to come," says Kost. While return on investment (ROI) is not always easy to track, Kost recommends staying on task. "Sometimes with social media, for example, the ROI is less tangible and quantifiable. But it has its role and cannot be put aside," argues Kost.

Building Credibility through Media Coverage

The California-based Access Trips launched its culinary program in 2010 and was overwhelmed by the response — a 94% increase from 2011 to 2012. As it is a small operation with a limited budget, CEO Tamar Lowell puts a lot of emphasis on online PR rather than advertising. "We're still figuring out what works," she explains. "But how do you define [what] "works?" Is it creating credibility? Driving traffic to our site? You cannot measure awareness."

While it is difficult to track which media leads to what bookings, scoring a major publication does have a great benefit as it establishes credibility and becomes part of the press kit to generate more media, as the following example shows. Susana Trilling, a successful chef, restaurateur and owner of Seasons of my Heart culinary school and Bed and Breakfast in Oaxaca, Mexico, has been teaching in this region for almost 20 years. Initially, her clients were local Oaxacan women wanting to learn American dishes. In 1997 she wrote an article about Oaxaca's moles for Chile Pepper Magazine which garnered her international attention. "That's when more people started calling me right away" she recalls. The cover story appealed to the niche audience of "chili heads" and, because she wrote the story herself, it gave her even more credence as an expert in the cuisine. Later on she met a bureau chief for *BusinessWeek* magazine in Mexico and hosted her for a few days, which turned into a feature story. While she cannot track whether that article brought in customers, it did give a sense of credibility when promoting to prospective clients. Since then, Trilling has published a book called Seasons of My Heart, A Culinary Journey through Oaxaca, Mexico and hosted a 13-part television series for PBS (Public Broadcasting System television channel) by the same name—resulting in more legitimacy through various forms of media.

Proven Methods for Generating Media Attention

Tell a Story: Branding and Consistent Messages as the Structure of Effective Media Messages

Passionate about their mission to help farms and dairies deliver their fresh products to Bay Area restaurants, two restaurant heavy hitters joined forces in a small town north of San Francisco. First, Sue Conley founded Tomales Bay Foods in Point Reyes Station as a marketing vehicle for farmers and local artisan cheesemakers. Then Peggy Smith joined in and Cowgirl Creamery opened in 1997 producing cheese from local milk. Their first location was a renovated hay barn that housed a cheese making room. What makes the Cowgirl Creamery story remarkable to the media and customers is the dedication to their marketing brand and a consistent message. It is a simple story that is conveyed in every product, every culinary tour and every bit of media coverage. "We are just telling our story. We are passionate about what we do," says Vivien Straus of Cowgirl Creamery. "The owners are passionate about saving small farms and connecting consumers to where their food is grown. We're simply letting people know what we feel is important to us, the agricultural community and the community at large." This message is transmitted in every clip of media coverage. Content that is compelling and consistent with the company brand tells a story of media coverage success.

Identify a Trend: Does Your Product Align With A Current Media Hot Topic?

Everyone loves a trend. It gives marketers a pitchable concept. It gives journalists a framework for a number of stories and it gives consumers a sense of discovery and the "cutting-edge" factor. The Los Angeles food truck scene is a prime example of all the pieces fitting together. In 2007, a group of friends asked the classic "what if X meets Y" question and fused traditional Korean food staples with California-Mexican street food, launching the Kogi BBQ truck. Contrary to what the subsequent media frenzy might suggest, the Kogi truck was not an instant success. Nor were food trucks a new concept in Los Angeles. But throw in a classically trained Korean chef, the inventive use of social media as a marketing tool, and a serious economic crisis, and it was the perfect storm. Since its inception, Kogi has been featured in *Food & Wine*, *Bon Appétit*, and *TIME*, among others. The idea grew into a trend and then a phenomenon, with dozens of food trucks getting media attention. Other forms of non-traditional dining, such as stationary food carts, roving supper clubs and pop-up restaurants, became part of the story. Food truck festivals sprang up all over the country, and food trucks were showcased on numerous television shows. Most travelers, at any price point, are looking for bragging rights, whether it is a roadside stand on their drive home or dinner at the Michelin-starred restaurant they booked months in advance. An early trend such as the Kogi BBQ food truck is something that gave travelers and locals alike something to talk about, and it sparked future food truck entrepreneurs around the country.

While VisitEngland credits the 2012 Olympics as a successful vehicle for food, drink and lifestyle coverage, Emma de Vadder, explains, "The number one reason why people go to England is the history and heritage, to see the castles and palaces. But globally, everyone is interested in food, some more than others, and it can help to enhance your vacation." One of Britain's newer trends is that those historic castles and palaces are incorporating restaurants, cafes and tea rooms, bringing in top-tier chefs and sourcing their products locally.

Another way Britain has succeeded recently is by capitalizing on the "trail" concept, an attractive pitch for journalists. By marketing local providers in a loosely connected route, usually self-guided, it is a natural piece filled with content, unique stories and opportunities to compare and contrast. Again it echoes a sense of discovery as the traveler literally wanders down the road from point to point.

From the Devon "Cream Tea Trail" to the "Rail Ale Trail" to the enduring pub crawl, the entire landscape is rich with food travel journeys. In 2012, Birmingham was named a top foodie destination by The New York Times and "foodiest town" by BBC Olive Magazine—but the real story driver is the city's "Balti Triangle," a collection of more than 50 Indian-style Balti restaurants, which has been profiled on the BBC, The Guardian and The Telegraph, to name a few.

Substance Over Style: If There's a Food Trend in the Media, Tasty Food Must Follow

Journalists are constantly under pressure to be on the cutting edge. They are expected to anticipate the next big trend, and every year there are roundups of the next up-and-coming culinary hotspot, like Peru, the Caribbean and...Louisville, Kentucky[4]? That's right, in the course of one year, the Southern city we most associate with bourbon was named among the "Foodiest" Cities by Bon Appétit magazine, one of the top 10 "Tastiest Towns" by Southern Living magazine, and one of the "Best Foodie Getaways around the World" by Zagat. Media begets media. If one major publication "discovers" a story, others are sure to follow. However if there is limited substance, the same story simply gets repeated, but not developed, and that does not resonate with audiences. Zach Everson, editor of Eater Louisville, launched in November 2012, notes, "The joke around town is that if a travel article about Louisville focuses on the English Grill, where the hot brown was invented, the just-shuttered Lynn's Paradise Cafe and the Urban Bourbon Trail, it's clear the writer never visited the city. Sadly, I've noticed plenty of articles of that variety." On the contrary, when there is substance, new discoveries and simply delicious food or fun experiences, the story can really succeed. Everson points to the explosion of "modern restaurants" in Louisville as the driving force behind the onslaught of media attention: from authentic Mayan cuisine to the trendy Proof on Main at the 21c Museum Hotel, to farm-to-table restaurants. It is those newer, cutting-edge experiences that generate the kind of media that sticks, and ultimately reaches the top-tier publications that resonate with audiences.

"Pair" a Culinary Story: Develop Stories for Specific Targeted Audiences

Destination marketers have the burden that even if their region is particularly known for food and wine — like Sonoma County, California — they still have to give weight to other types of tourism other than the coveted food-and-wine-loving market, even if it is the number-one market. Food enthusiasts, meeting planners, gay/lesbian travelers, and brides are all markets that Sonoma also targets through advertising and editorial media. The creative solution is to tie the food experience with other potential stories. Sonoma is not just a great destination for wine and food, it is an agricultural breadbasket where visitors can literally see where their food comes from: vineyards, dairy farms, ranches, cheese makers. Luxury hotels and inns do not just have great restaurants; they also have spas and bucolic vistas that make for great romantic getaways. All that agricultural land means plenty of outdoor space for golf, hiking trails and off-roading. The climate that makes grape wine growing so ideal is partly due to the nearby coast, which opens up a whole new dynamic.

It is even possible to pair a major cultural event with a food angle. In England, it seemed almost a calculated decision when Prince William and his bride chose an English-made sparkling wine, Chapel Down, for a private reception at Buckingham Palace. The idea was to celebrate English wines and the media picked up on it. Soon after, the Kent-produced wine took home first prize from the prestigious International Wine Challenge, sparking another round of media. "We have seen an increase in visitors to our vineyard in the past two years," says Brand Manager Sally Streeter. "It is hard to judge whether this is due to one particular piece of media coverage [but] the royal wedding and the international awards that we have won have definitely contributed to the increased awareness of Chapel Down wines."

Invent a Product: Develop a Unique "Hook" for Journalists and Their Readers

Sometimes, a good story can appear when you get the right people in a room. Few Americans think of Houston as a foodie city, but members of the Houston Convention and Visitors Bureau took note when several local chefs began garnering national attention. So they brought those four chefs into a room to figure out what they could do that is different and interesting. The first idea was a behind-the-scenes tour of the chefs' kitchens. As the meeting progressed, the chefs began comparing notes about where they liked to eat in their free time. From that gathering came the hugely successful "Where the Chefs Eat" food tours, with Houston's top chefs leading the tours into the city's eateries.

For a writer, it is a perfect story: celebrity chefs (two of the most popular tours are led by Bryan Caswell, who appeared on 'The Next Iron Chef', and Monica Pope, a contestant on 'Top Chef Masters'); ethnic, "mom 'n' pop" establishments (tours range from Chinese to Indian to barbecue to crawfish); and that sense of discovery, where participants are experiencing a side of the city they would never learn about otherwise. Since then, Houston has also associated its culinary offerings with other stories. For example, *Smithsonian Magazine* is writing a story on Houston being one of the most diverse cities in America, profiling locals from a variety of industries, including a Hispanic chef.

Publicist Maureen Poschman, who represents the Aspen (Colorado, USA) Chamber of Commerce, explains that while Aspen's famous food and wine festival is its cornerstone summer event, generating other culinary media can require some creativity. Launched in 2011, the Aspen Mac and Cheese Festival is a block-party-style event that takes place in autumn, traditionally low season for ski resorts. It is free and attended mostly by locals. Media coverage was mostly in the *Denver Post* and *Aspen Times*, but in 2012, *Yahoo! Shine* covered the event on video and brought in more than 1 million views. For a platform that focuses on a mostly female audience, coverage of a macaroni and cheese festival may not make the most sense, but Yahoo! reported that it was their third most-watched video to date. Local officials are also considering the idea of inviting other chefs from around the country to compete in the local event, which would also raise awareness with a larger audience. However, it is not always a case of "if you host a food festival, the media will follow." Also in 2011, a luxury hotel in Aspen hosted a summer barbecue festival which drew criticism and protests from local businesses. The event, held downtown on the last weekend in August, blocked access to local restaurants and business, and billowing smoke from the cookers forced at least one shop to close down for a day. The event, which local officials had hoped to grow into a major attraction in the coming years, did not return the following year.

Capitalizing on the Celebrity Factor: How Can You Align Your Product with Star Power?

Today we are experiencing a new phenomenon where almost any chef who appears on television enough times becomes a celebrity. The old model of cooking show where a chef stood in a kitchen demonstrating with pre-chopped ingredients gave way to a rise of competition shows. Suddenly programs like 'Top Chef' brought high-caliber, albeit less famous, chefs into the spotlight, and revealed not just their culinary prowess, but their personalities. This ushered in the new wave of chef celebrities as the new rock stars. Programs such as 'Life After Top Chef' usually mean ample air time, local media around the premiere, interviews after being ousted, and then—if the personality has any sort of following— lots of public appearances. Appearing on 'Top Chef' has allowed even non-winners to attract business from audiences hoping to see the chefs in person and to get the funding to launch their own restaurants. Food and wine festivals around the country use recognizable television personalities in their marketing materials. It is famous faces from television that journalists notice, whether it is for calendar listings or feature stories. Recognition from television can be helpful in generating attention, however it cannot be the only driving force to sell a product.

Signature Travel Network, which markets its member travel agents such as Food and Wine Trails, briefly partnered with the Food Network Kitchen to sell an 11-night Mediterranean cruise, mostly highlighting the appearance of Chef Anne Burrell - a familiar face on a number of food shows. The package included cooking demos and VIP events on board. But the product did not sell and the partnership ended. The reason being that serious culinary travelers — the ones willing to spend money on a food-themed cruise, were not tempted by glitz of rubbing shoulders with a "celebrity chef" that they recognized from television.

Yet, there are culinary cruises that have succeeded for several years. Experts explain that this is due to the richness of the culinary experiences and reaching out to a targeted audience. Buck Banks of Newman PR in Miami consults major cruise lines that recognize dining and travel cannot be separated. "The industry-wide trend started years ago when Todd English consulted on the Queen Mary 2. He was the first to put his name on a dining experience at sea," says Banks. "Today, celebrity and other well-known chefs go onboard, help develop recipes, collaborate with chefs and extend their expertise for serving. These experiences are wildly popular with cruising customers." This strategy can be seen on almost all of the cruise lines today.

For example, Holland America partnered with *Food & Wine* magazine to create a Culinary Arts Theater. *Bon Appétit* has a longstanding partnership with Oceania Cruises, which includes classes in a state-of-the-art kitchen and tours of local markets and shops led by chefs, and more specialized cruises that are a 10-day food festival in themselves. Silversea has a series of Relais & Chateaux L'Ecole des Chefs trips that include market tours and cooking classes, wine pairings inspired by the region, and dining at Michelin-starred restaurants. The participating chefs receive mentions in the press materials, but they are not the focus.

Reaching out to a targeted geographical area can be just as crucial as blanketing the general foodie market. They know that if a well-known Chicago chef is appearing on a cruise, they can target media placements in Chicago and fill the ship. Media can be targeted regionally and that kind of niche marketing works."

The US State of Virginia has a reputable travel PR firm promoting its various attractions to the media, and one region of Virginia has its own champion. Patrick Evans-Hylton is a Norfolk-based chef, writer and cookbook author whose personal interests have spurred him to promote the Chesapeake Bay region as its unofficial ambassador. Evans-Hylton travels the country to educate industry people about the original settlers of Jamestown and writes about different preparations such as roasted oysters or the origins of smoked ham. He also maintains an active Facebook page, with over 5,000 followers, linking to articles on local chefs, events, and photos of his own restaurant experiences. When he promotes his own products — cooking classes, cookbooks or food products — they are related to or inspired by the Chesapeake Bay. Hiring a talented public relations firm or dedicated "public relations" done by a local personality can both be effective means to an end.

That kind of organic promotion from an ambassador speaks volumes to followers, making a region seem that much more accessible and intriguing. The challenge is that it requires pure passion for the subject, not a targeted marketing strategy, and it is difficult to measure how that translates into visitors.

Blogs Build Loyal Followers

Tamar Lowell from the aforementioned Access Trips writes a regular column for the *Huffington Post*, where she posts about topics such as Adventure Travel Trends and The Flavors of Thailand. When Access Trips launched a culinary program in Sonoma, she posted a story on the Hidden Charms of California Wine Country. Not only does the story link back to the company's website, but it explains her own experiences exploring Sonoma and how it led to the creation of a tour package. Those kinds of topics resonate with the audience she hopes to reach, inspire them to learn more, and then drive traffic back to the company's site.

Another small operation is Divina Cucina, located in the heart of Tuscany in Colle di Val D'Elsa. Judy Witts Francini has been teaching since 1988, offering both one-day and week-long culinary experiences. In 1997, she began offering market-to-table programs, taking visitors to shop for products and ingredients, followed by a cooking class. Over the years, she's garnered an impressive array of press, including being listed in *National Geographic's* Food Journeys of a Lifetime, a mention in *Food & Wine* magazine, and various radio and television appearances. But it is the Internet that has been her most consistent source of attention. Francini notes that one-day programs have grown, partly because 1997 was also the year Italians got connected to the Internet. She explains that pre-Internet, a one-time ad in *Wine Spectator* cost US$2,500 in a special edition (which could pay for itself in a week-long course). As she runs her business by herself, her attention is mostly on online and social media. Since 2003, she has regularly updated a blog which includes a guide to her own favorite trattorias and wine bars throughout Tuscany and a photo-heavy guide to what she is personally cooking or eating, along with the ingredients and recipes that inspire her. Her social media pages are quite active, where fans can see what she has made for lunch, what is growing in her garden, or which local food artisan she is having a meal with that day. Her online media outlets are a source of inspiration as much as information, and lend a sense of credibility that she is a culinary expert in this region. So when a traveler is making that all-important decision of where to go and how to accomplish travel goals, this one-person operation becomes a viable option.

Like other media discussed earlier, blogging also has both pros and cons.

Pros of Blogging

Blogs have a number of advantages. For example, an audience of engaged blog readers can serve as ambassadors to pass along the blog's content to their friends and colleagues. "Engaging" readers means providing high quality content that is updated on a regular basis, usually at least weekly. Engaging can include allowing readers to post comments and make their own recommendations. Engagement can also include the use of badges and buttons linking the blog with social media such as Facebook, Twitter and Yelp, thus helping to increase brand recognition, social engagement, and audience reach. Blogging is a convenient platform for the promotion of new things such as a new vendor at a farmers' market, a food festival or a new culinary hot spot.

Furthermore, blogs can be aligned with tracking tools such as Facebook Insights, Google Analytics, and LinkedIn Analytics in order to measure marketing promotions. These tracking tools help to optimize the traffic, generate detailed statistics and help guide efficient marketing. Blogs can be efficiently used to push the current links and updates to giant content aggregators (which gather and then re-distribute content) such as Delicious, Sphinn, and Reddit among others.

Cons of Blogging

Writing a blog requires some care. A primary concern is ensuring the quality of the readers visiting the blog, since misuse of the content by some audiences could damage the brand. Secondly, continuity has to be maintained. Blogs are becoming the face of a business and can attract viewership and thus future and loyal customers. Unless content about products, customer testimonials and events is updated on a regular basis, such as weekly or monthly at the very least, blogging could lead to reduced interest and eventually create difficulty in managing your customer base. Thirdly, if external material is used to build content, credit has to be given to the original writer. Plagiarism is illegal, and by simply asking permission you can save yourself from getting into trouble. Finally, bloggers need to ensure that they practice blogging in an ethical and legal manner. The respective country laws on the subject matter need to be consulted.

Journalist Relationships & Press Releases

Fostering relationships with media representatives is essential for future success. This can be achieved by delivering compelling stories, honoring commitments and being upfront. Also showing personal interest in your media contacts as people and not as your personal servants will go a long way towards getting the results you want. In most instances, you will be promoting your business, people, events or contests in positive ways. But things can go wrong in business that may attract media attention so you need journalists to be understanding if you need their help to manage a future crisis. Beneficial media relationships can be built through the following initiatives:

- Identify the topic of your press release.[5] An opening, the hiring of a new chef, a special event are all worth alerting an audience. From the journalist's perspective, think about seasonality, how your story fits into a larger trend, and whether your announcement is useful to readers.

- Build a database of writers in your key target zone. It may not always be the obvious food or travel publication. Think about gay lifestyle outlets, women's magazines, hyper-local blogs, meetings and convention trade publications, and other audiences that might be part of your audience.

- Obtain the editor's contact information. If it's not readily available or you can only find a general inbox, do your due diligence by performing online searches, or simply pick up the phone and call the publication.

- Send a press release or announcement to the editor via email. Use attachments wisely. Editors often get flooded by information, so include the key points in the body of your email.

- Mail programs such as MailChimp, ConstantContact or iContact work well, but be aware that some browsers may prevent images from appearing, and an editor working at a fast pace may skip over any blocked images

- Avoid careless errors like failed mail mergers ("Dear Firstname Lastname") or addressing the editor by the wrong name or by mentioning the wrong publication.

- Keep the subject of the email simple and to the point. Avoid all capitalization, or false familiarity like "Hey, I thought you should see this."

- Focus on just the "who, what, where, why, when", and one or two images. Remember, editors are scanning for information and keywords that resonate with them. Too much information and they may gloss over it.

- If possible, provide a link to high-resolution images and/or video.

- It is recommended to call an editor only once to follow up, but be prepared to answer questions immediately or provide new information. Simply saying, "Did you get my press release?" is not enough, and no one wants to hear a rehearsed script recapping the release. Engage in conversation, ask about their editorial calendar and anything they may be working on, and how they prefer you follow up and when.

- If a journalist requests more information, images or to arrange an interview, get back to them quickly. Writers are often on tight deadlines and simply missing their call asking for a photo could mean being cut out of a story completely.

Managing your relationships with the media takes a personal touch. The above suggestions are just suggestions, but are sourced from years of experience. Failing to follow many of the above guidelines could mean less than successful results with your journalist contacts.

The Importance of User-Generated Media: Customers Are Journalists Too

Before the advent of social media, marketing and media plans referenced the value of "word-of-mouth referrals." It was touted that a customer review, good or bad, would be magnified exponentially to friends and colleagues. Social media channels are word-of-mouth referrals on steroids. Blogs, Instagram photos, Twitter messages, Facebook likes, etc… give the customer the power to write, critique and publish in an instant. The following example is a clear illustration of the power of social media.

Hawaii Food Tours has been in business since 2004. Matthew Gray, a former food critic and television personality in his own right, founded the company located in Honolulu. "My first four years in business were very difficult. Not only was the culinary tour industry an unknown product, so was my business. So I was educating potential customers on what we were, all the while trying to sell them a tour." Matthew remembers running hotel in-room television spots and using other traditional media channels. He also sent thousands of press releases and email blasts, and then followed up every one of them on the phone. He gained some notable coverage on *MSNBC* and *Food Network*. "My perseverance paid off," he says.

Today Hawaii Food Tours has a Facebook page, YouTube channel and still distributes an email newsletter. Yet TripAdvisor's strength in the Hawaiian tourism industry was a game-changer. The online resource for tourists to find location activities and also review experiences, good or bad, is a clear leader in customer referrals. "We track sourcing for each and every tour customer. TripAdvisor is credited with a whopping 95% of Hawaii Food Tours customers. The tours are almost always sold out. Now all we need to do is deliver a quality product and exemplary service. Our customers do the rest on TripAdvisor reviews," says Matthew.

Are Press Trips Worth It?

Flying in a small group of journalists to experience your product or destination can be effective only to a point. Some popular publications, such as *The New York Times*, do not allow their contributors to accept press trips or any other free products or services in exchange for editorial coverage. Others are more lax or do not ask questions. Transparency to your audience is increasingly important. Consumers are increasingly unforgiving, therefore integrity is more important now than ever. The trick with press trips is to avoid the perception of bribery. You cannot "require" a certain amount of coverage, or within a specific period of time, or that it all be positive, nor is it appropriate to pester writers. Unless your press trip is timed to a new launch (hotel restaurant, culinary tour, food trail, etc...), it is better to host writers on a case-by-case basis. Then you can work closely with journalists to tailor the experience to their interests and follow up more effectively to ensure that a story comes from the trip.

CONCLUSION

Below are lessons to help food tourism providers develop a successful media plan:

- Media channels constantly change. Use the appropriate media outlet.
- Measure effectiveness and adjust accordingly.
- Each and every media mention builds company awareness and credibility.
- Establish your brand, develop stories that resonate with your target audience and remain consistent with company values and messaging.
- Leverage trends to your advantage if appropriate. If your story fits with a current hot topic in the media, jump in with your quality content.
- Deliver excellent products promised in your media coverage. If delivery fails, good media coverage may morph into bad.
- Branding and consistent messages are the structure of effective media plans. Tell your story in a unique way, from a different angle.
- Blogs build loyal followers for your brand, website and products.
- On-going communications with media representatives foster beneficial relationships in good times and bad.
- Heed the power of customer-generated content. Social media is "word-of-mouth" marketing referrals in exponential terms.

- The media mix that meets company goals for budget and time invested and delivers return on investment for sales goals is a delicate balance. A strategy to be an early adopter, to discard the useless and adopt what is effective, promises to be an on-going challenge as the food tourism industry and media channels continue to evolve.

DISCUSSION QUESTIONS

1. Create a media plan for your business, group or destination. Which channels are most important to achieve your goals?
2. How could a crisis affect your media plan? How would you handle a crisis?
3. Will all print media eventually die? When is print media still useful?

ENDNOTES

[1] Kogi BBQ is a fusion of Korean and Mexican cuisines. More information at http://kogibbq.com
[2] Email open statistics vary by business type, industry and quality of the relationship between the business and the email recipients. Currently the World Food Travel Association's email open rate is in the 20% range. Other business types might only see about 9%. Open rates above 25% are extremely rare.
[3] Duggan, M and Rainie, L. "Cell Phone Activities 2012" (2012). Accessed at www.pewinternet.org/Reports/2012/cell-activities.aspx
[4] Louisville, Kentucky, USA is the gateway to the American bourbon industry.
[5] It is beyond the scope of this chapter to discuss proper press release formatting. Interested readers are encouraged to explore this topic further using other resources.

Culinary Retail & Grocery

Georgia Baillieu, Måns Falck, & Erik Wolf

Few people other than foodies appreciate culinary retail and grocery stores as a visitor attraction. Yet, ask any foodie and they usually cannot wait to take a stroll through gourmet shops, wine stores and other culinary troves. This chapter will look at the role of culinary retail shops and markets in the global food travel and tourism industry, featuring a case study from Sweden.

INTRODUCTION

There is something moving about walking through the aisles of a grocery store in another country. New smells and sights can affect the visitor in profound ways. New products, new brands, new beverages, new fruits and vegetables, new spices and of course often a new language help to turn a trip to an everyday grocery store into something more like a Disneyland of food for the food traveler.

More Than Big Boxes

Food travelers seek out a variety of food and drink stores, including chain grocery stores like Tesco in the UK, referred to as "Big Boxes" because some chain stores resemble an enormous box. Foodies also enjoy local and independent grocery stores such as Zabar's in New York City and we seek out wine, beer and liquor stores such as Lavinia in Paris, France.

Foodies enjoy roaming fruit and vegetable markets and other public markets like Seattle's Pike Place Market, even if we cannot purchase the fresh foods for use during our stay. Another great example are the many street corner outdoor markets found all over Seoul, Korea. Some stretch for quite a way and sell everything from fresh chiles and other spices to vegetables to meat and fish. Such an experience is unexpected by the visitor but a delight to discover.

Additionally, a smaller and independent grocery store offers more charm than you might find at a "Big Box" store. Consider Antica Macellaria Folorni (pictured left) in Greve in Chianti, Italy, which is designed like a hands-on art museum, with beautiful walls of packaged meat and antique kitchen devices on display, along with other unique wares for purchase.

It is not unknown for foodies to allow extra space in their luggage, or to even bring an extra suitcase, in order to bring home their food finds. With restrictions on carrying liquids on board an aircraft, foodies are now forced to set aside even more room in their luggage for exotic cordials or premium spirits. Most tourism offices can produce data that show that shopping is one of the top three visitor activities in their area. Foodies may or may not be looking for a new purse, pair of shoes or overcoat, but they will definitely be looking for unusual and high quality food and drink items to bring home.

Stockholm's Cajsa Warg[1]

Cajsa Warg in Stockholm originated as a reaction to the three major grocery chains that dominated the Swedish market for a century. The founders behind Cajsa Warg wanted to create a food store for food enthusiasts. The first store opened in 1996 on Södermalm, a fashionable yet somewhat alternative part of Stockholm with a strong concentration of artists, musicians and actors. Since then the area has gradually become the home of a number of different culinary institutions. Following a customer suggestion, the owners also opened up the basement kitchen to groups wanting to cook together under the direction of an instructor. A catering business was added, again based on requests from enthusiastic customers who wanted to enjoy the personal service and excellent food at special events and parties.

The business concept of Cajsa Warg was unique when the first store opened and is still unchanged today: food should be fun to shop for, easy to cook and good to eat. The owners are passionate about taste and customer service and their ambition is to expand the business through new shops in suitable locations around the city. In 2010 the second store opened in fashionable Vasastan offering a larger store area and adjoining kitchens for group cooking sessions. The location is rather unique, an old cinema with high ceiling, round windows and lots of charm.

Photo Credit: Cajsa Warg

Fun to Shop

To ensure a positive shopping experience, the atmosphere is radically different from the chain stores that dominate Swedish retail. The store is built in oak wood and as many as possible of the refrigerators and other appliances are covered with oak panel. At any time, staff offer customers tastes of a variety of products. Often suppliers are invited to present their products in which case the focus is clearly on the story around the products offered. To ensure a positive ambience, classical music is played and the store is filled with the aroma of cooking food.

Cajsa Warg is a complete grocery store with a clear focus on quality food. At the exit where one would normally find chewing gum, instead you find ready-made food attractively displayed. Also the choice of bulk products has been reduced — in each category one product has been selected, as an example you will find only one brand of soap but you can be sure that this one is the best possible choice in its category.

The staff is key to the overall experience. All are passionate food lovers that are regularly trained on new products and encouraged to experiment in common cooking sessions. Once a month, all 50 employees gather and cook together with a given theme. This way they all get to taste numerous variants of each product and the inspiration provided by the creative forum is useful during customer encounters. Staff is normally hired from aspirants walking through the door with a specific culinary interest. The key test is ability to handle customers and to provide good service.

Easy to Cook

At Cajsa Warg the customer is given a full range of options when it comes to level of cooking experience. There are always raw products available to cook from scratch but there are also meals available where the basics have already been prepared. A typical example could be fresh salmon filled with a feta cheese mousse that can be combined with a lemon zest potato mash and basil cream. This way a properly cooked meal can be prepared in matter of minutes from fresh ingredients. There is also a refrigerated unit filled with ready-made food, produced in-store for the customer that wants to just heat up a fully cooked meal. The staff are all keen cooks at various levels, which allows them to advise customers on their choices. While such dishes are obviously convenient for local residents, visitors can also purchase many of them to eat in their hotel rooms or in the local park, weather permiting.

Another key element at Cajsa Warg is the layout of the cold cases where the intention is to create culinary inspiration. In the case presenting the meat shoppers will also find suitable combinations such as risotto, salads and different kind of sauces. This not only makes it easy to put together a good meal but also creates a much more attractive presentation of the food.

Good to Eat

The last, but most important pillar of the Cajsa Warg concept, is taste. Throughout the years a unique product offering has been developed. With the unique position in the Swedish grocery market, the Cajsa Warg team is contacted by thousands of producers and suppliers every year. All of these are carefully tasted and reviewed before being offered to customers.

Long before the current trend of locally cultivated products, Cajsa Warg worked actively on finding local producers, not compromising when it comes to taste. The same goes for the organic philosophy. Organic products are always preferred but taste is always the base for selection. Many of the producers have through the years become personal friends with the Cajsa Warg team and they thoroughly enjoy presenting their beloved articles in the store. The team regularly visits producers to learn more about the background of the products, and also to further develop the ultimate taste experience of the store's products.

In total there are 250 suppliers, with an annual turnover of €2 million. While larger chains may only allow individual stores to decide on 10% of their product offering, Cajsa Warg has the opportunity to fully adjust the offering to its particular customer base.

The unwillingness to compromise on taste also limits what Cajsa Warg can offer. While the ambition is to provide a full range of groceries, Cajsa Warg is more strictly limited by seasons than most other stores in Sweden. Instead customers are encouraged to find alternatives to products that are currently out of season and unavailable. At any time on large boards customers can see which seasonal products are especially good. This approach helps reduce the carbon footprint and lowers food transportation costs.

To further emphasize the internal and external knowledge of taste, Cajsa Warg regularly arranges blind tasting activities inviting renowned chefs as well as press, and most importantly, regular customers. Most often it is clear that quality and passion of producers beat the large-scale budget alternatives but there are also cases where surprises appear, sometimes people are just so used to artificial tastes that they do not recognize and enjoy the real thing.

Cajsa Warg as a Culinary Institution

Ever since the birth of the idea, Cajsa Warg has provided food enthusiasts with a one-stop shop for all occasions. While it should be a joy to come in and stock up for a weekend cooking event with long lists of specialty ingredients and fancy products, it should be equally enjoyable to rush in and shop for a late, easy dinner on a weekday or a tourist's take-away lunch. In fact, regular customers provide the base of Cajsa Warg's overall financial equation. Due to the geographical boundary to every day shopping, yet another group of customers come to Cajsa Warg regularly for special occasions. For example, the Christmas holiday attracts customers that would not normally travel the distance from their home to Cajsa Warg for every day shopping.

Lastly, there are a relatively high number of food tourists that travel from other regions in Sweden or from abroad. They are attracted by the unique collection of quality products and by the unique atmosphere that is an experience for any food enthusiast. In total, approximately 30% of customers visiting Cajsa Warg are visitors who neither live nor work in the neighborhood.

Based on the customer profile, the Cajsa Warg marketing strategy has always been focused on the target customer – food-loving neighbors that do most of their food shopping at Cajsa Warg. Hence, most of the marketing activities are focused on in-store communication. Another marketing activity has been mini tasting delegations where Cajsa Warg staff walk around in the neighborhood offering potential customers a selection of in-store-produced items to attract customers to come and shop.

Cajsa Warg became an early favorite of food journalists, simply because of its position as an alternative to the large food chains that dominate the Swedish market. This special relationship has been carefully nourished through the years and Cajsa Warg is often mentioned as the place to find special ingredients or referred to for its taste sessions. It is most likely media relations that explain the relatively high share of food tourists that find their way to the stores that are really off the typical tourist track.

It is clear, however, that the most important marketing channel for Cajsa Warg is its existing customers. Cajsa Warg fans can be found all over Stockholm and suggestions for new locations are regularly made by customers who want to have easier access to their favorite food store. These existing customers interact regularly with Cajsa Warg through the weekly newsletters informing them of new arrivals, seasonal highlights and dinner suggestions. These enthusiasts are an important word-of-mouth resource for foodies traveling to Stockholm.

Issues

Some countries strictly forbid the import of certain foodstuffs. For example, anyone caught trying to sneak honey into New Zealand is met with a stiff fine on the spot. The USA is notorious for confiscating imported meats and cheeses from air travelers, sometimes with good reason and other times on pure whim. And of course, there are restrictions varying from one country to the next on how much liquor and wine visitors can transport. Often food store owners are unaware of such international regulations, especially if they serve a largely local population and only receive the occasional tourist. Most foodies are at least somewhat aware of what they can and cannot import to their home countries. Still, in stores with a high concentration of tourist business, the shop owner would do well to caution the well-intentioned customer that perhaps the pate and raw goat's cheese best be eaten before heading to the airport.

Lastly, grocery stores have a responsibility to reduce material waste. Many recycle cardboard boxes, which is a great start, but then they give consumers their purchases in plastic bags. An exemplary retailer is New Seasons Market in Portland, Oregon, USA, which has achieve "zero waste".[2] Culinary retail stores have an opportunity to educate consumers on ways to reduce, reuse and recycle, such as bringing their own carry bags, or purchasing a reusable bag. Such stores also have a responsibility to reduce food waste. In some jurisdictions, food that is past its sell-by date, but which has not yet spoiled, can be donated to shelters for people in need. In other jurisdictions, laws forbid the donation of food, citing reasons of health and hygiene. While the reasons for such laws sometimes make sense, surely there is a middle ground where more potentially wasted food could be donated before it spoils. Reducing food waste can also help to curb greenhouse gas emissions by depositing less organic waste into landfills.

Western Australia's Providore[3]

Providore in Margaret River, Western Australia, recently voted one of Australia's Top 100 Gourmet Experiences by *Australian Traveller Magazine*, is a contemporary model based on the grand country houses of Europe, each of which had a vegetable garden, orchard, olive grove and vineyard. This concept has been used to create a culinary retail outlet and a small restaurant, where everything consumed is grown before your eyes. Customers and visitors can meander through the half-acre (0.2 ha) vegetable garden that provides the restaurant with the freshest ingredients, with the chef preparing dishes only reflecting what is in season. The onsite vineyards and olive grove allow customers to see directly where their products are coming from. The on-site store showcases an award winning selection of wines and liquors and a huge range of homemade jams, preserves, olive oils, sauces, dressings, spice mixes and desserts.

Providore is not easy to get to, in that it is outside Margaret River itself and requires a drive through the local wine region to get there. All products, marmalades, chutneys, dukkah, salad dressings and marinades to name a few, are produced in small batches in ever-changing combinations. All products are beautifully displayed, also allowing visitors to sample before purchase. Providore has continued to attract visitors not only from Australia but from all over the globe and has become a popular stop for many food and wine tours of the region.

CONCLUSION

Culinary retail and grocery stores of all kinds and price points have an opportunity to expand their customer base to inbound visitors. While they may argue that a one-time purchase is not worth their effort to woo new customers, would they have the same reaction to 20 new visitors spending an equivalent of US$100 each in their store each month? What store owner would say no to an extra US$2000 or equivalent monthly? To reach larger numbers of visitors, such store owners should speak with their local tourism office and local food tour operators about increasing visibility with tourists. The potential for word-of-mouth promotion is high, as visitors share their new foodstuffs with friends and family back home, not to mention with their colleagues or friends who live local where the store is located. Those friends and family then might like to visit the destination too, and hunt for their own stash of food souvenirs. Either way, there is certainly an economic impact to the local community by visitors importing fresh cash into the local economy through local food and drink store purchases.

DISCUSSION QUESTIONS

1. Often culinary retail stores are marketed only to locals. What are the benefits and drawbacks of marketing this type of business only to local residents?
2. Could an ordinary grocery store be interesting to food travelers? Why or why not?
3. What issues might food travelers face when buying food and drink products with the intent to bring them home? List possible issues and offer solutions for each.

ENDNOTES

[1] www.cajsawarg.se
[2] For more information about the store's Zero Waste program, read www.opb.org/news/blog/ecotrope/how-new-seasons-market-recycled-its-way-to-zero-waste and also http://initforgood.newseasonsmarket.com/zero-home
[3] www.providore.com.au

Developing a Food Tourism Destination

Carlotta Casciola, Urban Laurin, & Erik Wolf

This chapter begins by discussing the role of food in the development of a destination. It continues by reflecting on the ways to develop a food tourism destination through positioning, branding and innovation. Next, a way of organizing food tourism destinations is proposed along with best practices for each of these categories. The chapter concludes with a story of how Scandinavia is developing its food tourism offering through positioning, branding and innovative practices.

INTRODUCTION

The destination is like the tip of the iceberg in any kind of tourism. Everything a visitor experiences is wrapped into the destination experience. The planning that takes place at the destination level is spearheaded by a destination marketing organization (DMO), whether it is a non-profit membership-based organization, local government, economic development office, or national tourism organization. No matter the DMO format, it will still oversee the planning and promotion of all tourism products, including food tourism, where food tourism is of interest.

Food in Destination Development

Everyone has to eat. Though often overlooked by tourism stakeholders, food is unquestionably a real part of the visitor's experience and therein lies great opportunity for the aspiring food tourism destination.[1] In fact, the meal is the activity most often mentioned by tourists as most important when visiting a destination. Data suggest that the majority of visitors spend anywhere from 23-28% of their total travel budget on food and drink while traveling.[2] Furthermore, many tourists share their food travel experiences and will attach that feeling to the destination itself. Those who are dissatisfied with the meals, often avoid returning to a destination based on this bad experience.[3] Research also suggests that tourists search for engaging experiences, especially when it comes to food.[4] Authentic experiences are becoming increasingly important which includes elements of local and cultural food experiences.[5]

Food is not just about appeasing the tourist's hunger.[6] The aesthetic design of the meal can be important, such as how the restaurant or farmers' market is designed, how the table is laid or how the tasting room at the winery is set up. The quality of the meal can be compared with the quality of a symphony orchestra or a theater where the artistic design and presentation are just as important as the food itself.[7] The meal is also a social and cultural process, when the tourists have a chance to share their views, collect impressions, reflect on and discuss their experiences.[8]

A long list of countries and regions now recognize this link between food and tourism and are developing strategies to meet the growing demand from visitors. We offer three key reasons why a destination should consider food and drink as visitor attractions:

- Tourists spend a large portion (23-28%) of their travel budget on food.
- Eating is an activity that stimulates all of the senses, particularly taste and smell.[9] As such, these senses become associated with a destination and the memory of that destination becomes that much stronger.
- Visitors are increasingly interested in local and sustainably produced food. Those destinations that overlook this will miss additional opportunities.

Having established that food tourism does play a central role in the development of a destination, the next section outlines issues DMOs should consider when developing their food tourism offerings.

Positioning a Food Tourism Destination

Typically a tourism destination can be defined geographically. It can be a loosely defined area such as the Mediterranean or Scandinavia. For food tourism there are a number of traditionally established regions that evoke images such as Tuscany in Italy, Provence in France or California's Napa Valley. These type of "food landscapes" are established by tradition. Over time they have become widely associated with particular types of food and drink. While a food tourism destination may be a loose geographic area, it can also be a city, such as Copenhagen, the restaurant capital of Europe.[10] It could also be a neighborhood in a city, such as Chinatown in London or New York, filled with Chinese restaurants or a village in the countryside famous for its wines or local food.

To develop a food destination, the concept of a foodscape or "winescape" becomes a useful term on which to build a solid foundation. A foodscape concept relates to the actual *place* where food is prepared or delivered. This sense of place becomes associated with the food/drink experience and forms the essence of a foodscape. An example is the interaction between the chef of a restaurant and the tourist; where the food is prepared by the chef, enjoyed by the tourist, but where the actual experience may be associated with a strong sense of place — for example, in a restaurant that was a former monastery. The food, the personal interaction, the service and the venue combine to form the foodscape.[11]

Positioning a destination around the concept of a foodscape requires the creation of a special experience unique to the destination, and successful destinations in the food tourism domain do this well. Given that food is the key ingredient, tourism development needs to take into account all five human senses to create clearly differentiated experiences. The idea is to create conditions that provide the visitor with an outstanding, memorable and hopefully non-replicable experience. For the individual businesses within a given destination, it is important to position their products and experiences, to create a foodscape. The restaurant or the farmer's own shop must consider the facility's exterior as well as the surrounding environment, signage and parking lot, the interior such as furniture, crockery, decor, design, aromas, flavors and service quality.

In order to create an attractive food tourism destination, the whole experience becomes important to success and how the visitor perceives the destination. To accomplish this, businesses and DMOs must work together to create a particular foodscape. Collaboration is absolutely crucial to accomplish this goal, and critical given the competition between various food tourism destinations from which the visitor may choose.

Branding a Food Tourism Destination

Since place is such an important part of food tourism, associating food with the sense of place is useful to help brand a destination. A sense of place with regard to food tourism concerns the subjective, personal and emotional attachments and relationships that people have with a place. This sense of place is often applied to people who permanently live in a place, and reflects how they feel about their community.[12]

The sense of place is important as tourists search for authentic food experiences when they explore different destinations. In food tourism development, it is the local citizens' own sense of place that is the basis for storytelling about products and food experiences. Many potential tourists already have a sense of the place or destination, as they have read tourist brochures or information online.[13] When they visit the food destination, their sense of the place is developed and enhanced.

Collaboration between businesses and tourist offices is important. Equally important is the relationship between locals and tourists. Both locals and tourists can smell and taste a destination. This experience of a place can evoke strong memories of sense of place for the visitor. Additionally, this experience also provides local food tourism operators with clues as to how best to develop the meal experiences so that they reflect the culture of a particular destination. This concept is a key brand differentiator for a food tourism destination.

Innovation in Food Tourism

Many destinations do not have a long history with food, wine or other beverages that attract tourists. As interest in food tourism grows, it is important to develop food tourism in a destination where food traditions are missing or have been forgotten. Credibility and authenticity are key to success. The challenge for new food destinations is to create a story; to use local ingredients and culinary traditions to formulate a new story or retell an old one.

While some destinations have positioned and branded themselves over a long period of time, others are creating their own niche and brand of food tourism. One such example is that of the Nordic countries which are not traditionally known as food tourism destinations. That said, recently a number of chefs emerging from these countries have won major international competitions. As a result of these competitions, many of these countries have suddenly become famous for their restaurants. For example, Noma in Copenhagen is currently regarded as one of the best restaurants in the world.[14] Noma and other restaurants have encouraged local food producers to develop higher quality sausages, cheeses, beer, and other products. An overnight success, the notion of New Nordic Food is becoming known worldwide.[15]

A destination's stakeholders are naturally diverse. To work effectively as a food tourism destination, the businesses, the DMOs, and everyone involved in tourism must cooperate in a transparent system.[16] Effective food tourism destinations are about collaboration - stakeholders must feel a strong sense of belonging within their community and culture and a sense of togetherness. In such a collaborative model, the visitor experiences a common feeling for a destination, which is ultimately the positioning that a food tourism destination will acquire. One example of how such a model may work practically is where the destination's best chefs work directly with local farmers, back and forth, to produce the finest local meat, vegetables, cheese and other products.

The idea of mobilizing key players is also important. Many successful destinations, especially emerging ones, often have a visionary who takes the lead and inspires others, creating newsworthiness. Robert Mondavi and the development of Napa Valley as a wine destination is one such example. The dramatic effect of Noma for food tourism in Copenhagen is another stellar example where one person or group created a media buzz around food tourism for a particular destination.

Another possible determinant of success is that of resource sharing. Stakeholders in a destination who promote and share with each other both in terms of knowledge and resources are positioned better for success than those who do not take such an approach. This is particularly true in our contemporary network society, where technology and internet communication represent the strongholds towards a reciprocal cultural enrichment.[17] This form of innovation is currently known as crowdsourcing and open innovation. New entrepreneurs should be welcomed to fill the holes in the value chain. If a food destination lacks, for example, a restaurant, farmers with quality products or a local brewery, the tourism office or local government needs to work with the local businesses to create an environment in which entrepreneurs would want to fill those gaps.

Cooperation and competition, can the two really work together? To reiterate, cooperation and collaboration are key to success. There will always be competition for resources and for customers. This will occur equally within a destination and between destinations. Perhaps it is necessary to establish a balance between the two. Accept that the competition exists but also acknowledge that in order to strengthen a destination brand, to develop joint products and packaging and to help each other market a destination overall, cooperation is the best way to succeed. The term "co-opetition" (i.e. cooperative competition) is often used to define how a successful destination might work.

So far this chapter has covered positioning, branding and innovating. Effective destination development needs to involve everyone at all levels of the food tourism system. Destination marketing organizations and tourism organizations play a key role in positioning, branding and innovation in food tourism development. However, the decisive players are the actual businesses and entrepreneurs themselves.

Individual Food Tourism Providers

A food destination is characterized by a variety of different businesses and people who depend on each other, at least in the context of a food tourism destination. Strong networks increase the destination's competitiveness.[18] Many entrepreneurs in food tourism are small business owners, such as farmers or food artisans. While they may be skilled in producing raw materials or food of the highest quality, they may or may not have a good understanding of the customer or market. In fact, many times these producers would not consider themselves part of the food tourism system. They just produce the food. However, many tourists love to visit these producers and buy their products. It is also important for restaurants in food destinations to feature locally-sourced food and drink. Food "artisans" can be seen as the artists of food and tourism, and as an artist they perhaps need a manager in their network. This manager can be another entrepreneur, as a restaurant or a tourist company, or the DMO.

Funding Food Tourism Development[19]

Destination development requires access to capital for entrepreneurs as well as for the DMOs. One of the challenges concerns the rural location of many food tourism activities. Many rural areas tend to be low in capital and banks can be reluctant to finance food and tourism efforts in areas that are not well developed. An exception to this rule and a beacon of encouragement in the agricultural world is the Bank of North Dakota (BND), in the US state of North Dakota. The BND is known as an anomaly in the U.S. banking system because it is the only state-owned bank in the country that serves as a funding resource in partnership with other financial institutions, economic development groups and guaranty agencies.[20] In an era where banks seem to be losing money, the BND has been profitable nine years in a row. The bank is known for its programs to invest in, and guarantee investments of, farm and ranch financing; livestock retention and improvement; farm income diversification; irrigation programs; and value-added equity financing. In essence, the state bank is kind of a combination bank, venture capital firm and government guarantee agency all in one. The BND is highly regarded in the American agricultural community and a model worthy of consideration for extending the idea into value-added food production, with an eye towards food tourism as a tool for economic development.

Many destinations have been known to organize themselves and manage to raise their own money through their own networks. This is known as crowdfunding. The primary aim of a crowdfunding mechanism is to provide the financial means to leverage entrepreneurship when implementing a new product. Crowdfunding can certainly be applied to food tourism projects and worthy of exploration. What is needed are local venture capital markets with tools that make it easy for ordinary people to share the risk with their local business community. Tools are needed to replenish the equity in the small business and union balance sheets. In Sweden, the Destination Åre tourism office provides one interesting example of innovative thinking concerning crowdfunding and crowd equity.[21]

Local stakeholders form the so-called local capital company where ordinary people can lend money earmarked for specific investments. With the help of this money the local capital company acts as a shareholder in companies that need capital. They can also provide assistance and advice to common interests for investors and the companies. The administration is very cost effective with the help of the Internet. Suddenly local residents can begin to take control of local development. But they can get additional funds if the "public" channels tax money through the local capital companies. Then public funds can act as equity in small businesses. When local capital companies are entrusted to manage public money in the local economy's interests, perspective changes from top-down to bottom-up and greater potential for a more economically sustainable society.

Best Practices for Promoting Food Tourism in Destinations

One way to view a destination is by using four specific categories that vary according to the level of motivation the traveler has to visit a destination for its food and drink. The main criteria in the matrix developed below (Diagram 1) is whether the primary motivation is food and drink or another motivation (e.g. culture, nature, business, etc.).

1. Destinations where food and drink are the primary reasons for travel, which are well known and already have a strong food and drink tourism brand.
2. Destinations where other motivations are the main reason for travel but food and drink tourism is not always relevant.
3. Destinations where food and drink as well as other motivations have similar importance as the main reasons for travel.
4. Emerging destinations with varying degrees of development with regard to food and drink, culture, nature and business tourism.

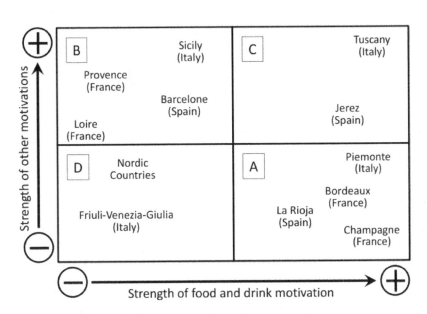

Diagram 1: Food as Primary vs Other Motivation; *Credit: Carla Casciola*

Examples of Regions and Best Practices

1. Destinations where food and drink are the primary reasons for travel, which are well known and already have a strong food and drink tourism brand

La Rioja

La Rioja is the most famous Spanish wine appellation and widely considered the most popular wine destination in Spain. Its wines have a reputation of aging well. However in the last decade, the market has demanded a few modern style wines favored by the likes of noted wine critic Robert Parker.

DMOs in the area use the fame of their wines for promotional activities. In the past 10 years, the official tourism board of la Rioja started an aggressive promotional campaign based on the fame of its wines with the following quote: "La Rioja, la Tierra con Nombre de Vino" (La Rioja, the land with the name of wine), their logo was depicted as a vine with a leaf. The fame of La Rioja DOC is certainly connected to its historical and well-known wine producer status.

During the last decade, some wineries invested in architecture, converting this area into a leading destination for winery architecture. Historical wineries with updates designed by world-famous architects, such as Marques de Riscal with Frank Gehry; Lopez de Heredia with Zaha Hadid; and Viña Real with Phillippe Mazieres) are popular, as well as new wineries investing in architecture from the start such as Ysios by Calatrava; Alcorta by Ignacio Quemada; Baigorri by Iñaki Aspiazu; and Darien by Jesus Marino Pascual.

However La Rioja wine appellation covers two different political regions: La Rioja proper and part of the Basque country called Rioja Alavesa. The two regions are not united politically or with regards to marketing, in fact, the two regions have different marketing plans and in some cases, compete with each other for visitors. This situation only generates confusion for foreign tourists, for example, each region has a wine map where wineries of the other region are not included even if they are only a few minutes away.

La Rioja is a clear example of a region where tourism is generated by the fame of its wineries. Rioja tourism boards are very active with plans directed to attract any category of visitors, not only wine lovers. In just 10 years, the tourism board was able to place La Rioja on the map of tourism destinations.

2. Destinations where other motivations are the main reason for travel but food and drink tourism is not always relevant.

Loire Valley, France

The Loire is a clear example of a region where visitors travel because of the attraction to art and culture. Many visitors are drawn especially to the famous castles of this region, which characterizes the Loire tourism image. The valley's wine, however, is known to be inexpensive and does not age well. Out of several small winery producers, few, if any, are well-known. What tourists do not know is that in the Loire valley, there are a great number of biodynamic and natural wine producers, a segment of the wine industry that is booming. In particular, Nicolas Joly, pioneer and leading personality of the biodynamic wine movement, is located within the Loire Valley. Also some of the most important natural/biodynamic wine fairs are held here and this could be an important selling point to promote wine tourism.

Along the Loire River there are a great number of wine appellations. However, there are no wineries well known enough to attract a large following of food and drink tourists. Most visitors mainly travel here to visit castles, but once there may decide to visit a winery, or other food and drink producer. As an emerging destination for food and drink tourism, wineries are not always prepared to receive visitors, DMOs and the wine appellation control authorities have the important task to train and support them.

This is another case where DMOs and food and drink resources can benefit from increased synergy. In this region food and drink resources need the support of the local tourism board. Wine producers and the food and drink board could use the fame of the castles to strengthen their brand and image and attract standard tourists to their wineries. From the other side even if tourism in the Loire Valley is mature, they could use wine to attract the niche market of those who seek out natural/biodynamic wines.

3. *Destinations where food and drink as well as other motivations have similar importance as the main reasons for travel.*

Jerez, Spain

Jerez is a famous destination both for its famous wines and brandies and for other travel resources such as Flamenco, Horses, Cultural Heritage, and nature. Jerez wines are famous worldwide, but suffer from a poor image. Abroad their image as sweet, low-quality wine. In Spain they are considered a cheap white wine drunk during Ferias. That being said, Jerez produces some exceptional wines too, although such wines are typically only known to wine professionals.

There are some challenges in changing this image. Jerez wines have a complex classification that is difficult to understand, including Fino, Manzanilla, Amontillado, Oloroso and Palo Cortado. They also have fortified wines. However due to the recognition of the Jerez name, Jerez wineries receive a large number of visitors, but those visits are mainly from tourists coming to the area for reasons other than food and drink. The Consejo Regulador (Regulating Council) of Wines & Brandy de Jerez is making an effort to change this situation through:

- Specific trainers named "Official Jerez Wines & Brandies Specialist and Trainer" to promote high quality Jerez & Brandy wines and improve the region's image;
- Support and training for wineries that would like to receive visitors; and
- Leading the Jerez wines & brandy route, to promote wine tourism to its members.

Jerez is a clear example of a destination where wine is a key product that could bring in additional higher quality visitors while improving the destination's image. The DMOs and Jerez Wines Council have the same goal. By improving the image of Jerez wines and brandies, Jerez will be able to improve its destination image.

4. *Emerging destinations with varying degrees of development with regard to food and drink, culture, nature and business tourism.*

Friuli Venezia Giulia (FVG), Italy

FVG is an example of an emerging tourism destination in general, but with a lot of potential for the development of a more specific food and drink tourism plan as well. Part of the reason FVG is as yet undiscovered is because of its history and geographical position. The region's borders with Austria and Slovenia have moved several times due to frequent war and conflict nearby and these circumstances have left a rich cultural heritage that is now an attractive selling point for the region. The area has also traditionally been disregarded because of the fame and draw of nearby Venice. However, here again is an opportunity to convert a disadvantage into an advantage for tourism purposes.

Regarding food and drink tourism specifically, local DMOs have found a selling point in the complex history thanks to the amazingly rich regional cuisine that reflects the area's middle-European heritage with Hungarian, Jewish, Slovenian, Austrian and Greek-influenced dishes. FVG has several products with controlled origin domains and several Slow Food Presidia. Its leading food and drink resources are Prosciutto di San Daniele, coffee (home to Illy) and 14 different wine appellations such as Collio, Piccolit and Ramandolo.

In the past few years the regional tourism board has started an aggressive and well-structured promotional plan using food and drink. Sea, culture and mountains are the main selling points. Food and drink producers are creating associations, wine routes and councils to promote their products and food and drink tourism. The official tourism board supports food and drink institutions and associations to create and promote food and drink tourism experiences, including food and drink routes. One of the best examples is the Collio producer association. They have a very creative brand with the image of quality, authenticity, and passion. They promote both quality of their products and also the image of a poetic place of ancient vineyards on rolling hills, a place to stay among friends.

FVG is a clear example of an emerging tourism region where food and drink resources work together with other tourism resources (art, culture and nature) to develop the image of the products and of the destination. The FVG tourism board considers food and drink resources a strategic asset and a vehicle of the culture and of the image of this land.

The Story of the Nordic Countries

The Nordic countries Denmark, Finland, Iceland, Norway and Sweden have a long tradition of cooperation through the Nordic Council of Ministers, and during the last decade, food and food tourism has been a top priority.

In 2004, a gathering took place in Copenhagen which included some of the region's best chefs. Together they developed "the manifesto for the new Nordic cuisine" that states "as Nordic chefs we find that the time has now come for us to create a New Nordic Kitchen, which in virtue of its good taste and special character compares favourably with the standard of the greatest kitchens of the world." [22] The aims of New Nordic Cuisine are:

1. "To express the purity, freshness, simplicity and ethics we wish to associate with our region.
2. To reflect the changing of the seasons in the meals we make.
3. To base our cooking on ingredients and produce whose characteristics are particularly excellent in our climates, landscapes and waterways.
4. To combine the demand for good taste with modern knowledge of health and well-being.
5. To promote Nordic products and the variety of Nordic producers – and to spread the word about their underlying cultures.
6. To promote animal welfare and a sound production process in our seas, on our farmland and in the wild.
7. To develop potentially new applications of traditional Nordic food products.
8. To combine the best in Nordic cookery and culinary traditions with impulses from abroad.
9. To combine local self-sufficiency with regional sharing of high-quality products.

10. To join forces with consumer representatives, other cooking craftsmen, agriculture, the fishing, food , retail and wholesale industries, researchers, teachers, politicians and authorities on this project for the benefit and advantage of everyone in the Nordic countries."

The Nordic Council of Ministers has since worked closely with the New Nordic Food project. Consequently, international interest in Nordic Food has grown considerably. Young and entrepreneurial chefs in the Nordic countries have been inspired by the forerunners who signed the manifesto in 2004.

The success story of Restaurant Noma in Copenhagen may be the prime example of the growing interest in food from the region. Restaurant Noma's concept, mixing Nordic culinary traditions and ingredients with modern and innovative cooking techniques has won the hearts of foodies around the globe. For three consecutive years (2010, 2011 and 2012), Noma was chosen as the world's best restaurant by the jury of the prestigious contest The World's 50 Best Restaurants. Nordic chefs have become increasingly prominent on the winners stand in the biannual world championships for chefs, the Bocuse d´Or.

The Economist, in its special report about the Nordic Countries states that "one of the world´s blandest regions has become one of its most creative. Twenty years ago the Nordic region was a cultural backwater... The restaurants offered meatballs or pale versions of Italian or French favourites. ..The Backwater has now turned into an entrepôt ... Copenhagen is the restaurant capital of Europe, largely thanks to Noma, which has been rated among the world´s best restaurants ... and to its founders, Claus Meyer and René Redzepi. Mr Redzepi, the head chef, eschews the standard fare of Mediterranean cooking such as olive oil and sun-dried tomatoes in favour of local products such as mushrooms, cloudberries, seaweed and flowers, which he collects from beaches and hedgerows." [23]

TIME Magazine goes even further and presents the concept of "Nomanomics: How one restaurant is changing Denmark's economy".[24] *TIME* states that "Noma's real success hasn't been to bring a really great, really expensive restaurant to Copenhagen's harbour, it's been to change the way people — from local businessmen with expense accounts to dishevelled backpackers with the last of their savings in their pockets — look at and experience Denmark the country." Matt Goulding, who penned the article and who coined the term "Nomanomics" spoke about this very issue at the 2013 World Food Travel Summit in Gothenburg, Sweden.

Noma's success story inspires others to develop business related to food tourism. Several former employees of Noma have opened their own restaurants around Copenhagen. Many cheesemongers, brewmasters, bloggers, oystermen, farmers and fishermen are benefitting from the impact of Noma. Denmark was once a culinary desert, now it leads in food tourism.

One of the activities from the Nordic Council of ministers is "Nordic Food Diplomacy - culinary experiences that highlight and strengthen the Nordic countries' unique values at home and abroad." One important goal is to strengthen the Nordic brand around the world, not just the food tourism brand.

Although Sweden participates in New Nordic Food, it has largely chosen to go its own way. The Swedish government initiated in 2008 a vision to make Sweden the "New Culinary Nation." Its manifesto states that "long, light spring and summer evenings, diversity of produce and manufacturing methods, unique nature and good chefs – are the reason why Sweden will become the new culinary nation in Europe."[25] Increased food tourism is one method that is supported to fulfill this vision. The Swedish state and regions invests a lot of money into different projects in order to support this development. While the development in Denmark has its base in the world-famous Noma Restaurant, the development in Sweden is initiated by the government. The purpose of the vision is to create jobs and growth in Sweden and a number of objectives must be met by 2020. The total amount so far spent on the vision is just over SEK 1.1 billion, which was funded by both government and EU funds.

An evaluation published in early 2013 asked whether "Sweden - the New Culinary Nation" has so far had any effect on the hospitality industry in general.[26] The only measurable effect on the tourism industry so far appears to be in marketing. VisitSweden's mission to raise awareness of Swedish food abroad has been successful and generated a great deal of publicity. The evaluation also states that another positive effect is on attitudes and knowledge. During the last four years, the vision has become well-known and well established in the Swedish food and drink industry. It has also given rise to increased collaboration between companies, organizations and government agencies. However, without a base of entrepreneurs that are inspired by competition, or "co-opetition", as is the case with Noma and Denmark, and with one of the world's most oppressive taxation systems, it is difficult to generate strong development and capital investment.

CONCLUSION

It is no easy task to promote food and drink tourism to a destination. Some regions with a long-standing tradition of food and drink excellence, like California's Napa Valley or Italy's Tuscany, almost sell themselves. Still other outstanding culinary destinations like Ecuador and Peru, Lebanon and Jordan, and Singapore and Thailand, are not as well known. Advancing the consumer's awareness of the food-worthiness of these destinations takes time, money and effort. Most importantly, a destination needs strong vision, strong leadership and a clear food tourism strategy, as is the case with Sweden.

DISCUSSION QUESTIONS

1. Some destinations have strong vision and strong leadership, but resistant locals. How would you develop a strategy to overcome the locals' resistance to change?
2. As more and more great food and drink destinations emerge, they will take more from the visitors' share of wallet, which will reduce food and drink tourism revenue in the traditional food tourism destinations. How could you prevent this from happening to traditional food tourism destinations?
3. Funding is key to development and promotion of food tourism. If a destination has absolutely no chance or receiving grant money or other government funds, how would you suggest it raise enough money to fund an annual operating budget?

ENDNOTES

[1] Wolf, Erik. (2006). *Culinary Tourism: The Hidden Harvest*. Iowa: Kendall Hunt Publishing, 2006. p. 51
[2] State of the Culinary Tourism Industry Report & Readiness Index, World Food Travel Association, 2010.
[3] McIntosh, R., C. Goeldner, & J. Richie. (1995) *Tourism: Principles, Practices, Philosophies* (7th ed). New York: Wiley.
[4] Cohen 1996 p. 94, Prentice 1996 p. 5, Pine II & Gilmore 1999 p. 163.
Gupta & Vajic 2000 p. 35
[5] Boniface, P. 2003, Cohen-Hattland & Kerber 2004, Getz & Cheyne 1997 p. 142, Jesiam, Mattson Sullivan 2004, Edensor 2000 p. 325, Gartner 1996 p. 360, Ryan 1997 p. 39, Taylor 200 p. 8
[6] Jacobsen & Haukeland. 2002

[7] Auty, S. 1992, George 2006, Hansen 2005, Jacobsen & Haukeland 2002, O'Neil & al 2002, Hansen 2005, Reeves & Bednar 1995, Steve & Simone 2005

[8] Chang 1977. Tse, Sinh & Yin 2002

[9] Wolf, p. 52-55.

[10] Economist Feb 2nd 2013

[11] Bitner, M.J. Servicescapes: the impact of physical surroundings on customers and employees. *Journal of Marketing* 56, pp 57-71.

[12] Cooper & Hall 2008, p. 116

[13] Bramwell, B. & Rawding, L. (1996) Tourism marketing images of industrial cities, Annals of Tourism Research, 23(1), pp. 201 – 221.

[14] www.theworlds50best.com

[15] http://newnordicfood.org

[16] Hjalager & al 2008

[17] http://henryjenkins.org/2009/02/if_it_doesnt_spread_its_dead_p_5.html

[18] Baggio & Cooper 2010; Novelli, Schmitz & Spencer 2006

[19] For a more detailed discussion of this subject, readers are directed to the Bringing in the Dough: Creative Funding Models chapter in this book.

[20] http://banknd.nd.gov

[21] www.youtube.com/watch?v=88ksYFsleto

[22] www.foodandwine.com/articles/manifesto-for-a-new-nordic-cuisine (last accessed 21 June 2013)

[23] The Economist, Feb 2-8, 2013

[24] Goulding, Matt, TIME Magazine, 14 February 2013.

[25] www.government.se/sb/d/11310/a/117765

[26] www.visitsweden.com/sweden/Featured/Sweden-the-new-culinary-nation

Restaurants, Catering & Other Foodservice in Tourism

Jenn Bussell, Jesse Eisenhuth, Corinne Rober, & Erik Wolf

This chapter explores the unique and important role that restaurants, caterers, street food and other foodservice providers play in the food tourism industry.

INTRODUCTION

Launching a foodservice business is challenging in today's tough economic climate. You need the right kind of business model for the right kind of customers in the right location. Launching a new foodservice business is hard enough, but keeping your business operating successfully is equally as hard. To that end, diversifying your business model may be an important part of your success. Before we look at how different components of the foodservice industry fit into tourism and hospitality, we need to understand the different types of foodservice and a little bit about the issues they may face as part of the food tourism industry.

Types of Foodservice

We need to start by defining the different food-related business types discussed in this chapter, namely restaurants, caterers, street food and miscellaneous other foodservice providers. They each play a unique role in the food tourism world which we will discuss.

Restaurants and Cafes

Let's begin with the most common business type, the restaurant. These are traditionally brick and mortar establishments and really can serve as the backbone for an area's food tourism scene. Everything to provide a unique and memorable food experience is housed under one roof, from kitchens to guest seating. Restaurants can be depended upon to be open consistently and provide the same experience in just about any type of weather condition. This is a comforting feeling to any tourist that may not be familiar with the area but is looking to have a pleasant experience no matter what the conditions may be outside. Restaurants also provide consistent orders of products from food and beverage vendor. The restaurant environment can be the most stable of all food tourism outlets and allow not only for the guests to plan their trips but also the operator to plan great experiences well in advance.

Caterers

The second type of business we will discuss is the caterer. These are the people that can provide food just about anywhere. It can be difficult to define this type of business operation due to the diversity that many of them have in menu, service styles and service locations. Some caterers have brick and mortar buildings most commonly referred to as banquet halls or other permanent facilities such as museums, gardens or other cultural institutions. With these types of caterers, the kitchens, storage areas and venue are typically located within one building or on one piece of property. Other caterers, known as offsite caterers, can have a kitchen and production facility in one location where they store and prepare for an event only to load everything into transportation vehicles and take to a location where the actual event will take place. With modern equipment, foodie events can be held almost anywhere.

Street Food

Not every traveler is interested in fine dining and expensive wine. In fact, only about 8% of food travelers identify as having a "gourmet' profile.[1] That means the overwhelming majority of foodies just like good food and drink, no matter where they find it. While cafes, diners and family restaurants can all offer great food, the street food experience is one of the most popular types of experiences in the food tourism industry. Street food can range from falafel stand on the side of the road, to the trendy new food cart/truck scene that is sweeping North America in particular, to the sometimes very well appointed hawker centers in places like Singapore. It even includes the meat kebabs and fresh pressed sugar cane juice in Zanzibar.

Health and hygiene are issues to be considered just like in brick and mortar restaurants, especially when foodies travel to countries with standards different from what they would find at home. For example, a foodie could make every possible attempt to avoid ingesting water in a new destination, only to have the worst happen because crushed ice was used in a lovely lemonade drink. The drink would not be tasty if it were not cold, and the ice is ground so fine, it is hardly noticeable. The astute drink purveyor selling his wares in a highly trafficked tourist area should have chilled the beverage in a refrigerator and avoided ice altogether.

Food Markets

Similar in experience to buying food and drink on the street outdoor markets are increasingly popular. Markets can be outdoors such as the lovely Portland, Oregon, USA downtown farmers' market, partly covered like the London Borough Market, or entirely enclosed like Saluhallen in Gothenburg, Sweden. Such markets are part grocery store, part farmers' market and even sometimes part café. Vendors can usually purchase booths at such markets for much less than a brick and mortar storefront. While a contract may be required for an entire season, paying rent at a market booth from May until October saves the vendor having to pay rent in the colder winter months. It is an interesting option for farmers, cheesemakers and artisanal food and drink manufacturers.

Miscellaneous Foodservice Providers

Finally, the most diverse business group are local food service providers. Street food vendors and food markets are considered food service providers, but have a more detailed definition of who they are. Anyone else that serves food can be placed in this last category. This is where some great food events can happen. Say you go on a brewery tour and during the tour they may provide you with samples of their beer along with small bites of food that pair well with each beer. That brewery tour is technically a foodservice provider. There are thousands of unique examples, but you can understand how large this business group can be.

Getting Started in Foodservice

We have all heard about how hard it is to start a restaurant and keep it financially viable. The current economic climate has not helped matters in the past few years, but hope is in sight. However, if you know what you are doing and do your research, the data concerning new restaurants is not all doom and gloom.

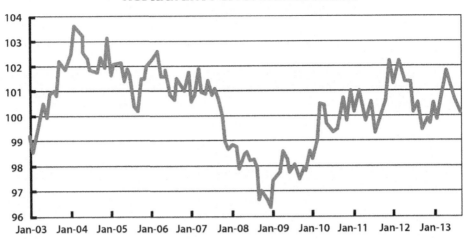

Restaurant Performance Index

Table 1: Showing US restaurant performance index, from January 2003 to January 2013. Note the horizontal middle line with a median of 100. *Credit: (U.S.) National Restaurant Association*[2]

In the last couple of years, there seems to have been a dramatic increase in locals supporting their local economies. This is no more evident than the recent explosion of farmers' markets, especially in North America, but also in New Zealand, Sweden and elsewhere. This may stem from the hard times many of us faced over the past few years. Now that economies throughout the world are slowly improving, people are not forgetting those tough times and desire to strengthen their own communities. Also, with the increasing number of outbreaks of food borne illnesses, many people are starting to care about the sources of their food. When they go to a local restaurant or family-owned place, they may feel more at ease that the food is from a reputable source. Whether true or not, a sense of community comforts guests.

The restaurant industry is hard to get started in, but not impossible. You may have heard that running a restaurant is long hours and hard work. Anyone looking to start a new restaurant, catering or local foodservice business should themselves review the many assessments that have been done on the industry. This will prepare you for some of the pitfalls you will inevitably face. Two of the most important things you can do before you look to open a business are first complete a concept brief and business plan. Next, conduct a competitive set analysis. You need to know the competition surrounding you and what they are doing.

Creating a Foodservice Vision

Creating a foodservice establishment means putting together a vision that meets the needs of your guests. Who are your target customers? Are you looking to attract domestic or international travelers, or do you prefer to cater to the local residents, or even a combination of both? As the business owner or operator, you must decide this before you can create a plan to attract customers. Situations vary all around the world so there is not one right or wrong answer. It means you must consider all aspects of the area, the guests you will attract and the vision you are inspired by. The creation of the vision is a combination of all these factors creatively packaged. The task is less daunting if you use an integrity-based statement to help direct your project.

One way to do this is using an approach like SOHL (Sustainable, Organic, Healthy/ Handcrafted, and Local/Living). The strength of SOHL is its ability to make connections and drive interdependence. It will expose both the strengths and weaknesses of your vision while revealing the relationship between the mission and the connections to others. The relationship between all these factors is the core that will pull the vision together. Its cohesive nature, will strengthen your focus, thus defining a strong model to develop & market. Staying true to the goals of an operation and connecting to as many resources as possible, will broaden its appeal.

Determine your mission statement then go through the list of questions below to define your direction or determine its viability. The questions listed are merely suggestions. You should add or adjust according to your vision. This is one way to create your foodservice brand.

Sustainable

- Is the mission sustainable, i.e. sustainable financially, physically, emotionally, environmentally?
- Does it support the area by working synergistically with the attributes of the community?
- Is your vision sustainable to the area and its inhabitants by offering opportunity for growth and providing quality jobs?
- Will you be promoting sustainable agriculture and environmental awareness in connection to food?
- Will all of your purchases support your vision? If so, how?
- What are the factors that might limit your level of commitment?
- Does the area have the workforce, products or resources needed to uphold your vision?
- Will you integrate a management style that is sustainable, effective, productive, motivating and progressive?
- Does the model give back to the community?
- Do you offer jobs that promote personal growth and job satisfaction?

Organic

- Are you true to who you are? Do your habits in management, purchasing and decision-making reflect your mission?
- Is the vision or model unique/organic to your area or simply unique/organic?
- Are 100% of products you buy certified organic, or are some biodynamic, or just "local"? If you say it is organic, you have to be able to prove it. Organic certification in some locales is so expensive, that farmers forego it, but everyone may know that the produce is all, or mostly organic.
- Do you have a statement on your menu about the pedigree of your products? By pedigree, we mean can you document the source of everything you sell? And if it is organic, do you say so on your menu?

Handcrafted/Healthful

- Does your work environment reflect your goals? Is it clean, healthy, and safe?
- Is the way you operate your business congruent with a healthful lifestyle?
- Do you contribute to the welfare of your patrons and community in all aspects of your operation?
- Do you nurture interdependence while promoting independent growth?
- Do you support the local culture by supporting handcrafted, locally sourced products that will enhance the attraction and connection?

Local/Living

- How do you support the local culture? Do you contribute to the welfare of your community both locally and visiting guests?
- Do you spend your profits in the local community as much as is feasible?
- Will the experience you offer resonate with the desire of guests visiting the area or will it stand alone and be a destination in itself?
- Will you offer local products? If so to what extent will it be part of your vision?
- How do you define healthy living and will you promote it? How? Will this model allow you to live a healthy lifestyle?

From your mission statement and answering the above questions, you will be able to determine your marketing direction. To thrive, first understand that we all are interdependent. This means that we are all valuable resources to each other and that these "resources," when combined or synergized become far more powerful than the sum of the parts. Creating relationships that will support your vision is the most critical part of marketing. Marketing is about creating a relationship to an idea and then relaying that effectively. For instance, if you have determined that the connection to agriculture will be a pivotal point in your mission, the obvious relationships to develop will be with local farmers. This relationship is a strong marketing opportunity. Cross-promotion on websites, collaboration on promotions such as farm-to-table dinners or even holding farmers' markets featuring your partners are a few ideas to explore.

Develop a visual association to the mission to use promotionally, for instance a logo or brochure. This will stand to represent your entire concept. Going through the exercise of developing a vision and validating the vision by using something such as the SOHL set of guidelines, will also reveal the relationships needed for marketing.

The connection to others should tie into your mission and brand. It will bring forward endless ideas to help develop your identity, as well as giving you opportunities for free promotion. Newspapers, tourism organizations or publications are all looking for events to post and stories that connect to their readers. Tell a story about what you do and why it is great for the area. How long has your establishment been in business? Why are you different or what makes you connected to the area? Once you start to connect to the media outlets available to you, these connections will strengthen your ability to reach others by word of mouth. Consider the impact an article has over a paid advertisement and seek opportunities to get your establishment written about. Send out press releases that tell the reader what you are doing that benefits them. Some businesses will send out a press release about everything they do, small or large. This has become a great marketing strategy with very little effort or cost. Many do not get any attention but the more you send out, the better your chance of some getting picked up by a local media outlet. Certifications that relate to your niche, may also unveil more marketing opportunities at little to no cost. Does the DMO for your area produce tour maps that connect wineries, breweries, farm-to-table restaurants, farms, cheese producers, artisan galleries and environmentally sustainable businesses? Are there any opportunities for you to connect to these publications? If not, is there a need for a type of organization that would make connections for collective marketing? All of this work in making connections is marketing. The sum of your marketing does not need to be expensive but it should be a lot of work. If it is not, you are not doing it right.

Your greatest asset will be your staff. The vision and mission of your operation are translated through the actions and opinions of your staff. Their knowledge and enthusiasm for your product is vital to your success. Managing this valuable tool will create word of mouth marketing on several levels. Local customers respond to what staff members relay about establishments, management, successes and failures. A staff that respects an establishment will in turn bring forward satisfied guests. Do not overlook this marketing opportunity. Strengthening your staff will strengthen your business. Operate from the principles set forth in your mission statement and directed by the brand you create.

Social media is another opportunity to reach out to others who are interested in your product. Once again being led by your mission, seek opportunities to connect to others that are like-minded. Your staff will also be your best promoters. If you treat them well, they will nurture repeat guests, build awareness, and attract new guests. Invest in them and they will invest in your business whether they realize it or not.

Restaurant Business Diversification: Flour + Water

Developing deeper customer relationships has always been a goal of San Francisco restaurant Flour + Water, a 2010 finalist for the James Beard "Best New Restaurant" award.

The restaurant's decision to expand into the culinary event market happened organically. Flour + Water's owner, executive chef and three-time finalist for the James Beard 'Rising Star Chef' award (2011-2013) Thomas McNaughton, was known for his unique creation of regional Italian pastas not normally found in American restaurants. Guests were delighted and intrigued, and the team at Flour + Water found themselves being asked quite often, "How was it made?"

Chef McNaughton learned how to make pasta from a group of old ladies in Bologna, Italy and he truly enjoyed the personal, hands-on experience. Based on their frequent questions about the pasta dishes he prepared, Chef McNaughton believed guests might also love to learn these same techniques and about the special ingredients that go into making some of the world's best pastas in an intimate setting.

"Pasta-making and cooking classes have helped us to educate and connect personally with our community and our best customers, and of course it is a nice benefit that the classes create a new revenue stream on the restaurant's slowest night," said Temi Adamolekun, director of marketing for Flour + Water. "The classes connect us on a deeper level with our community, and have inspired a new customer base from all over the West coast to fly in for just for this unique experience."

Flour + Water currently offers a two-part class focused on the building blocks of pasta making. During the first pasta class (Pasta Class I), Chef McNaughton talks about the variety of flat noodles and pasta dough found regionally throughout Italy, with an overview of their ingredients, textures and uses. Students then practice mixing dough, explore making flat noodles such as garganelli using a hand-cranked pasta machine, and hand cutting noodles such as orecchiette with a knife.

The second class (Pasta Class II) offers students an introduction to the world of stuffed pastas. Students make a variety of filled pastas in different shapes made with a ravioli based dough, including: cappelletti, francobolli, and agnolotti. Special attention is given to various fillings including meat, ricotta and vegetable purees.

Pasta classes are taught in the Flour + Water test kitchen in San Francisco, and each student is greeted with a glass of Prosecco upon arrival. Students taste everything made in the class and leave with fresh pasta to cook at home, with a recipe book to follow. At the end of each class, the group sits down to a dinner and wine pairing prepared just for them by the Flour + Water team.

After working with Chef McNaughton on the pasta class concept and high caliber classroom experience designed to mirror the Flour + Water dining experience, Adamolekun researched different low-cost methods to building awareness and getting people to sign up for their new pasta making classes. In addition to marketing the classes on the Flour + Water website in a newly created 'events' section, Adamolekun evaluated different options for both promoting the classes and selling tickets. Adamolekun chose to partner with Seattle-based Brown Paper Tickets because they provide, in her words, "excellent customer service, ease and control of setting up events." In addition, Adamolekun was impressed by Brown Paper Tickets' extensive database of registered users in search of local food events. "This enables us to appeal to [more] people who might not have found us otherwise," added Adamolekun.

The success of Flour + Water's pasta making classes has paved the way for additional diversification, and the restaurant will be launching a new class product called the "Weekend Pasta Project" for customers who want to replicate their Flour + Water dining experience at home. These classes will provide an opportunity for attendees to learn about and purchase an easily prepared memory of their Flour + Water experience. "We have created a new customer base, a new revenue stream, and a vehicle for new product sales, all at the same time," Adamolekun said.

When asked what advice she can offer to other restaurant owners interested in diversifying their business with a culinary class or event space, Adamolekun offered, "Focus on what people love about your restaurant … whether it's the techniques, the produce, the style of food … and recreate a more intimate and enjoyable experience for people."

Thriving in Spite of Seasonality

Most businesses experience a downtime. What do you do to minimize loss or differentiate yourself during this time? As you are considering how to keep your business thriving in the downtime think of these few questions. Are you in a part of the world that has changing seasons? How do the seasons change your business? How can you "minimize the loss" to your business when you are not busy? What can you do to keep people coming in during the off season? Think about your community. It is likely your business will not be the only one suffering during the off-season. Partner with those other businesses. Are you a business that is slow in the summer? Partner with a local farmer and offer a farm to table dinner. Many farmers will have their best products in the warmer months. Hold a culinary demonstration for young and old with the local farmer. This can benefit both your business and the farmer's business. Do you have a local brewery in your area? Partner with them to have a beer release party at your business. Is your business slow in the colder months? Have a fire and ice party creating a theme and menu items around fire and ice, bringing in ice carvers to make statues to decorate the event.

Use holidays to your advantage as well. Most people spend a little more around the holidays and are looking for things to do with their family, so give them something to spend their money on. Seasonal, holiday and activity-based events featuring the area should be explored.

Working with your local DMO to develop events that support the assets of an area is also a very viable option during slow times. Look up your local DMO and give them a call. They are probably already having meetings and working with other local companies. They can help focus on available resources and will help identify the collective strengths of an area. Another great thing to do during your slow season is hold fundraisers and benefits that could position your establishment as a good community member and draw new customers to your business.

Supporting local growers, producers, artisans, retail, and activity-based organizations creates great relationships in your community and the surrounding area. Coming together as a group allows the food tourism industry in your region to drive financial growth and community well-being during lean times of the year.

CONCLUSION

Many of us are inspired to open a foodservice business. It can be a fun and rewarding experience for many to cook for others. The reality is often very different from the idea. However, chefs are artists and are truly passionate about what they do. Yet many small business owners are at a disadvantage because they do not have sufficient business skills to steer their businesses through tough times. Chefs are known to work 18 hour days or more, often six days a week. There is no time for marketing or education with a schedule like that. To help overcome this burden, foodservice entrepreneurs are strongly encouraged to liaise with their local or regional tourism office for assistance. Tourism offices can help to generate sales and marketing opportunities and make it literally no harder than signing your name to an agreement. Independent restaurants, street food and similar experiences are perhaps at the very core of the food traveler's experience.

DISCUSSION QUESTIONS

1. Chef/owners are often in a situation where they have no time to do marketing or pursue additional training, but they really must do so in order to grow their business. What advice would you give the chef/owner?
2. Often restaurant and food cart owners do not see the benefit of working with a local tourism office. How would you persuade them to think otherwise?
3. Starting a restaurant can take a considerable amount of cash that many people simply cannot raise. What advice would you give a prospective restaurant entrepreneur in this situation?

ENDNOTES

---

[1] PsychoCulinary Profiling Research, International Culinary Tourism Association, 2010, published for internal use only.
[2] www.restaurant.org/News-Research/Research/Restaurants-The-Economy/RPI last accessed 1 December 2013.

The Role of Drinks:
Promoting Tourism through Beverage Trails

Wendy Lange-Faria and F. Xavier Medina

This chapter delves into three popular beverages — tea, wine and whisky — and presents models of how businesses in each of these industries are participating successfully in the food and drink tourism industry. Lessons learned may be applicable to drink businesses in other destinations.

INTRODUCTION

Tea, wine and whisky are three popular beverages, each with its own unique histories and stories that tourists find appealing. In this chapter we examine tea tourism in India and Sri Lanka; wine tourism in Hungary; and whisky tourism in Scotland. This chapter will look at the types of consumers each of these attract; sustainability, responsible tourism and authenticity; and offer a few opportunities and challenges they face in the context of the overall food and drink tourism industry. Naturally, there is tremendous interest in other beverages of all kinds from coffee to fruit juices to mineral waters to other alcoholic beverages. Space precludes us from discussing every beverage type uniquely.

Tea & Tea Tourism

Tea tourism may be defined as "a tourist experiencing history, culture and traditions related to the consumption of tea."[1] Tea has a long history, considered to be everything from an agricultural commodity to a beverage to a meal service to a past time. Whether it is intricate tea ceremonies in Japan, tea plantations and the cultivation of tea in India, visiting tea museums in England, the samovar tradition in Russia, or the chá of Brazil, tea spans the globe. Tea is a staple in the Middle East, Asia, parts of Africa and even parts of Europe. Given the rich traditions and history of tea, the growth in this sector is likely to increase. Entire books have been dedicated to the topic of tea and tourism.[2]

Tea tourism is steadily gaining in popularity. Tea tourists are generally those who are interested in different teas and tea cultures. Research shows that they tend to be young professionals between the ages of 31-40.[3] Tea culture and tea tourism seemingly go hand in hand. Visitors typically soak up the entire experience, visiting tea gardens, enjoying tea culture experiences and picking the tea leaves. From a marketing perspective, promoting tea knowledge is just as important as promoting the tea product.[4] The following quote outlines some of the intriguing history behind tea:

> Tea, coffee and cola are three major beverages widely consumed in the world (Yang, 2007). And tea is an integral part of food service (Jolliffe, 2007). As widely accepted, China is the homeland of tea, the Chinese started to use tea as medicine and food 4,000 years ago (Emperor Shennon's Herbal Classics cited in Li, 1993). [During the] Han Dynasty, tea became [a] special beverage among the royal families. Since [the] Tang Dynasty, tea drinking became a daily social vogue and enjoyed from the royal family and courtiers, down to ordinary people. Ancient Chinese intellectuals left behind a great volume of poems, chimed verses, songs, paintings and ballads about tea. Tea drinking was regarded as the high fashion, from which derived tea rituals and tea arts (Yang, 2007). Tea related tourism has parallels with food related tourism such as wine tourism, which has been investigated by many researchers (Dembardt, 2003; Williams and Dossa 2003; Brown et al 2007). As pointed out by Jolliffe (2007), tea tourism has

a lot in common with wine tourism in terms of its history and the connections with travel. In the industry, it has already become a niche tourism program in many regions in China, such as Hangzhou, Wuyi Mountain area, Wuyuan and Xinyang etc (Shen, 2005; Huang and Wang, 2005; Shen, 2007).[5]

Tea tourism today, particularly in the areas of Sri Lanka, India and China, is very closely linked to sustainable tourism initiatives. Tea has been seen as a means toward developing sustainable communities — generating income for the locals and thereby reducing poverty. One such example of tea being a conduit for sustainable tourism is a tea factory in Darjeeling that offers tours to visitors.

India, Sri Lanka & Beyond

Tea tourism is especially on the rise in India. Two of India's prime tea growing areas, Darjeeling and Assam, offer many the opportunity to observe the process of local women picking the tea leaves, tourists then get to sample the teas and enjoy the tea plantation lifestyle. More and more tea estates and gardens in India are opening their doors to tourists in an effort to generate new sources of revenue.[6] Many of these estates, not only educate the visitor on the art of tea cultivation and harvest, but also offer insights into a long and intense history — an authentic experience dating back to the origins of the plantations.

Tea trails have gained popularity in recent years in the northeast of India, parts of the south and certainly in Sri Lanka. Indians consume the highest percentage of the world's tea but there is increasing interest from North Americans as well, in the art and science of tea-making.[7] One of the draws to India is the romanticized version of the tea planter's idyllic lifestyle. The legacy and image of the British colonial rule still exists, with managers of the estates ruling the estate or garden with a large contingent of servants and very strict protocols. This type of system can, however, raise questions around ethics.

It is interesting to note, in a recent tourism article the prices quoted for accommodation on a recommended tea trail were as follows:

IF YOU GO ... TEA TRAIL ACCOMMODATIONS

The Heritage Bungalow, Balipara, India, double occupancy, US$460 including meals. Other bungalows are US$156, including meals, www.wildmahseer.com

Windamere, Darjeeling, India, Colonial Suite, double occupancy, US$210 including meals, www.windamerehotel.com

Maikabari, Kurseong, India, homestays US$11 per person including meals. Tea is free, www.makaibari.com

---

While a homestay may be cheaper than a hotel, one would be remiss not to question the value of staying in someone's private home. Certainly in the western world, where the equivalent of a homestay might be a bed and breakfast, the prices, while lower than a hotel, typically would not be quite as dramatic as seen in this example. What is the value we place on an authentic experience and how do we define fair pay versus exploitation?

Origin of Tea Tourism

According to USA Today, tea tourism came about as follows:

> "Smaller, private estates began welcoming guests in the 1990s as a marketing strategy to help pull them out of a worldwide tea glut. Another slump followed in the early 2000s when India opened up its markets to cheaper imports, forcing some growers to seek alternative sources of revenue. There's been no looking back. Around Darjeeling are nearly 90 tea estates, including Makaibari, the producer of India's first organic tea and a pioneer in tea tourism, offering 21 homestays with estate workers and an upmarket residence. Its factory has changed very little since it was erected in 1859, and barely relies on modern technology to produce high-end tea for export to the United States and Europe."[8]

Though this quote fails to show how the lack of modern technology is actually a positive since Makaibari uses artisanal tea production methods which yield better results, it appears to be on the right path in terms of contributing directly back to the community. Makaibari is located in the region of Kurseong in Darjeeling. Operated by Rajah Banerjee, the factory uses the tea harvested by seven different nearby villages employing sustainable environmental and social practices. Not only following sustainable forest management practices whereby forest cover is protected and various species of animals may continue to coexist, the factory has employed a number of practices that build local communities.

> "In 1994 a joint body was instituted by the Makaibari tea estate to regulate the activity of the seven villages and also take up developmental work. Each family on the estate is provided with their own cows, which they use for milk and manure. The manure converts its methane into cooking fuel called "bio-gas" - a non-polluting renewable energy source on tap. This system benefits not only the environment and help save the forests. [sic] It also decreases the workload of the women who otherwise have to get up hours before they start plucking to bring firewood back to their houses. Surplus milk and manure can be sold outside the estate. It is indeed this culture at Makaibari that not only liberates the land, but its people - especially women. Makaibari has 450 children and currently maintains a negative birthrate. One woman supervisor has 20 men working under her--an extreme rarity on tea estates. Makaibari's Ladies' Joint Body is a group formed by elected members who are in charge of allocating funds to projects and programs on the farm. The premium earned through Fair Trade tea sales has enabled the working community at Makaibari to take an active role to participate holistically to improve their lifestyle...."[9]

Ethics of Tea Tourism

Ethics are an overarching issue that apply to tourism generally, and are important in food and beverage tourism as well. Given that much of the world's tea is grown in economically disadvantaged areas, there is a temptation to exploit the lives of people who are eking out a living picking tea leaves or providing accommodation to tourists. On one hand, this might be called sustainability (providing employment opportunities for locals), there is another side. Many of these tea factories were started by wealthier individuals or companies, lending to some forms of exploitation — not unlike the colonialism that occurred in North America and India and other parts of the world. Initial tea plantations in India and Ceylon, for example, established huge businesses but also used the local workforce, keeping the costs very low by paying very little to the workers.[10] Many tourists today desire new and authentic experiences. We see this in slum tourism that takes place in many of the world's great cities, for example.[11] The curious eyes of tourists can be a form of exploitation, where certain companies or individuals gain at the continued exploitation of others. On the other hand, when this form of tourism is used to foster economic development in a community, individual entrepreneurs can be lauded and people in those locales actually engage in capacity building activities for their communities, then this type of tourism can be truly successful.

Opportunities for Tea Tourism

Apart from sustainability in tea tourism, this industry faces a number of emerging trends. A number of experiences in the Far East provide a fleeting glance of the potential of tea tourism.[12] For example, on Mainland China there are six tea-exporting provinces. In Taiwan there is a growing fruit and flora trend around tea that many visitors find attractive. Different sorts of teas unique to their respective region are another draw for the tourist — everything from Malaysian milk tea to horse-milk tea in Tibet, to apple tea in Turkey. Darjeeling, as indicated in the example above, has developed factory visits, local host accommodations, and tea plantations. Other places offer tea festivals.[13] The possibilities are almost endless.

In China, "The Forgotten Road" was expounded on by National Geographic, "Chinese tea and Tibetan horses were long traded on a legendary trail. Today remnants of the passageway reveal grand vistas – and a surprising new commerce."[14] The Silk Road excerpt below provides another fascinating example of the lure of tea tourism to the adventuresome traveler.

> The Silk Road connecting the cultures of the East and West is probably one of the most well-known and significant trade routes in all of history. Tucked in the verdant landscape of southwestern China, however, is a lesser-known route that parallels the Silk Road in cultural and historical importance. This other ancient route spans an impressive 2,350 kilometers, traversing some of the most diverse and mutable terrains in the world. For thousands of years, travelers have been lured across its snow-capped mountains, precipitous canyons and lively streaming rivers to discover some of the most beautiful landscapes in all of China.
>
> As its name suggests, the *Chamadao*, literally translated as 'Tea Horse Road' or 'Tea Horse Path', was a central trade route for exchanging Tibetan horses and Chinese tea. The corridor came to play a crucial role in the communication and exchange between the cultures of present-day Yunnan, Sichuan and Tibet, with the route passing through, among a number of important posts, the volcanic ranges of Tengchong, the colourful culture and dwellings of the Khamba people in Changdu, the breathtaking gorges of Lijiang, through Tibet as far as Burma and India.[15]

Tea has been part of the history and economy of Sri Lanka, otherwise known as the *Isle of Tea*, since the 19th Century.[16] It is surmised that the continued development of tea tourism in this part of the world will add significant economic value to Sri Lanka.[17] The following table outlines the types of tea tourism activities available in Sri Lanka.

Table 1. Typology of tea tourism supply in Sri Lanka.[18]

TYPE	VARIATION	EXAMPLE
Retail	Stores and boutiques	Mlesna tea boutiques
Lodging	Tea hotels Tea character Tea boutique hotel Tea bungalows Tea ecolodges	Tea factory hotel Bandarawela hotel Ceylon tea trail Kelbourne–Haputale Fishing hut
Factories	Tea estate factories Tea mini factories	Pedro tea estate factory Tea factory hotel, mini factory
Attractions	Museums and interpretive centers Tea estates and landscapes Natural attractions	Ceylon tea museum Tea research institute Tea estates Waterfalls, springs, mountains
Food service	Cafe´s and restaurants	Pedro tea estate tea house St. Claire tea centre Art of tea cafe´, 'The tea cup'
Recreational activities	High tea Tea trail/trekking Tea processing Tea livelihood/culture	St. Claire tea centre Castlereagh tea trail Labukkeli tea factory Rosita–Dimbulle tea estate

This study also shows interesting trends among tea tourists, many of which fall under the category of "accidental visitors" who come across the tea and corresponding culture. They appear to enjoy visiting the tea gardens, and tend to stay on average anywhere from one to seven nights at an accommodation. Guests seem to enjoy the relaxed, home-style environment and friendly climate.[19]

Developing tea-related tourism activities has a great deal of potential, as the above examples suggest. The entire experience around tea that appeals to visitors appears to be the authenticity of the entire experience — the climate, the picking of tea leaves, the unique types of tea and uses for that tea, the history and the culture of the tea, the atmosphere and heritage of the location and the experience of the local lifestyle. Another side of tea tourism that has been briefly, albeit importantly, touched on is the issues around ethics and sustainability. All of these elements appear to be important when developing tea related tourism products.

Wine & Wine Tourism in Hungary's Tokaj-Hegyalja Wine Region

Since 1990 Hungary's Tokaj-Hegyalja grape growing region, the most important and internationally known region in Hungary, experienced a renaissance with regard to both the production of wine and its image abroad. Within this promising panorama, to which we should add the inscription of the Tokaj-Hegyalja region as a historic cultural landscape by UNESCO in 2002, the promotion of tourism, and wine tourism in particular, has been aggressive. Since the late 1980s and early 1990s, and together with high-profile institutional plans, a number of small private initiatives relating to rural tourism have been started in the different municipal areas that comprise the region and, especially in its capital Tokaj.

Tokaj History[20]

Tokaji[21] has always been an internationally appreciated wine and is considered one of the gems of the oenological world. It began life around 1630, the year, as legend goes, when evangelist preacher Laczkó Máté Szepsi, having delayed the harvest for days because of the struggle against the Ottomans, decided he could not lose his crop and harvested the grapes even though they had been infected with botrytis. The resulting wine was a complete surprise and he presented it as an Easter gift at the table of his lady, Szuszanna Lórántffy, daughter of the Prince of Transylvania, György Rákóczi I.[22] From then on, Tokaji *Aszú* wine began its glorious history.[23]

The Latin phrase "*Vinum regum, Rex vinorum*" (wine of kings, king of wines) is attributed to the French King Louis XIV, who, it is said, had a particular predilection for the sweet wines of Tokaj.[24] However, throughout history he is not the only noteworthy fan to praise its properties and to drink it. Peter the Great and Tsarina Elizabeth Petrovna, Napoleon III, Empress Eugenie, Gustav III of Sweden and many other well-known figures, including Beethoven, Rossini, Liszt, Schubert, Göethe and Paracelsus all enjoyed Tokaji. Schubert even wrote the song "Lob des Tokayers" (Tokaj eulogy, D. 248, Op. posth. 118, No.4) in its honor, extolling the wine of the region. Tokaji is even quoted in the Hungarian national anthem.

Following the fall of the Berlin Wall and the Iron Curtain in 1989, the new democratic Hungarian government began a series of improvements. Together with the new private sector, which restarted the production and sale of wine, the age known as the Tokaji "renaissance" began. As writer Hugh Johnson who knows the region well said, "I arrived in Tokaj in 1989. It was a cold, sad and depressed region and 18 years on, it now enjoys its spring, with everything it needs to offer the visitor."[25] [26]

The "renaissance" of Tokaj and its wine brought with it a speedy "revolution" in the region. Big international investors from the wine sectors in France, Spain, the United States, Germany and Japan, took over vineyard management, refined production and standardized exports. Hungarian producers were swept along by the dynamics of the situation and have largely embraced the changes and modernization of their structures.[27] Today there are plans for collaboration between the private and public sectors and the creation of a Tokaj wine route with the participation of some 60 vineyards scattered throughout the area. The recent embrace of wine tourism in the past 20 years has had a few unusual consequences, giving rise to an interesting (although not mass) influx of international visitors to the region. UNESCO's declaration of the Tokaj-Hegyalja as a World Heritage Site helped boost interest among prospective visitors.

Wine Tourism and Rural Accommodation

Over the last two decades, the socioeconomic changes in the region directly influenced the prospects of small producers and farmers. Given the ambitious and technologically innovative strategies of the large companies in the sector, small producers find themselves the "guardians of tradition" and the *local heritage* of the region.[28] Within this new situation, tourism takes on an important role in terms of local and family economies. The links to the land and traditions of the region put small producers in a privileged position with local knowledge and wisdom, while at the same time making them exceptional spokespeople when explaining their land and lifestyle. A number of initiatives linked to rural wine tourism began in the early 1990s and have developed into new seasonal income for small economies.

The role and initiative of women takes on special significance within these new circumstances. While men continue to occupy themselves with their small farms and production, it has been the women who have taken up the reins for converting their homes, or a part of them, into rural accommodation or B&Bs; and it is the women who are in charge of running them including their seasonal maintenance. However, this characteristic is not unique to the Tokaj-Hegyalja region, nor is it unusual in other areas. As Téchoueyres points out in relation to France's Aquitaine region, "For some women [this type of family business] becomes the means that helps them find their place in the operation, parallel or complementary to the role of their husband. What it brings is the possibility of seeing people, as well as their being recognized for what they do." [29]

Whisky & Whisky Tourism

Branded as the only malt whisky trail in the world, the Malt Whisky Trail of Scotland consists of iconic distilleries steeped in history and tradition. This unique trail affords the savvy drink traveler to learn about the creation of this drink while experiencing the nuances of fine whisky.

Whisky distilleries were founded in an environment rich in the highest quality ingredients: pure, clear spring water and abundant supplies of fragrant golden barley. On the whisky trail of Speyside, you'll find more than half of Scotland's malt whisky distilleries, each with its own warm welcome and an invitation to see, smell, taste, and absorb the magic of whisky. Each whisky distillery on the tour follows its own traditions, lore and recipes for everything from malting the barley to the height and size of its stills. All offer visitors a sample of the finished product and some include an informative nosing and tasting while others give insight into the complex art of blending whisky and malt.

> "Tourists can follow the world-famous Malt Whisky Trail through Speyside to seven working distilleries, including a fascinating cooperage and a historic distillery. From Benromach to Dallas Dhu, a perfect time capsule of whisky-making; from Glen Moray to Strathisla, home and heart of Chivas Regal; from the Glen Grant distillery to the Speyside Cooperage where real coopers work with incredible speed and skill; from Glenfiddich to The Glenlivet and the Cardhu distillery, Scotland's whisky trail signposts lead one through the picturesque lush countryside of Speyside, the world's favourite malt whisky region. Come for a weekend in May, or in September for the whisky festivals, when distilleries, whisky shops, bars, pubs and whole villages welcome visitors with drams, special nosings, ceilidhs and other parties. Come at any time to enjoy famous names and share well-kept secrets with knowledgeable locals in well-stocked bars and friendly pubs."[30]

Scotland has recognized the specialness of its whisky, which is one reason for the creation of the Whisky Ambassador training program.[31] The program trains and certifies bartenders in the subject of Scotch whisky. Students are taught how to discern differences in smell and taste, from peat to grass to cloves and other aromas and flavors. The whisky product is further differentiated in that it is the United Kingdom's only accredited whisky training for the licensed trade.[32]

There are a number of consistent trail characteristics that appeal to food and beverage tourists.[33] Such trails:

- Provide the visitor with a history and the unique context of the product [Scotland's Malt Whisky Trail provides a history of whisky.]
- Send a clear brand message [Whisky trail provides clear pictures and information on each distillery on the trail.]

- Identify the trail with a clear theme and memorable slogan [The only malt whisky trail in the world.]
- Include quality photography [Whisky trail website uses high resolution photographs.]
- Link the product with a calendar of events [the "What's On" tab on the Whisky Trail homepage.]
- Use an effective search engine to explore the site.
- Feature organized itineraries that suit the diverse needs of trail users. [The Malt Whisky Trail is at the top of Google rankings]
- Add appeal with unique or unusual products (Scotland's Malt Whisky Trail states "Whisky, Uisghe Beatha, The Water of Life, has evolved over more than 500 years to give the range of rich single malts, complex pure malts and distinctive Scotch blends we know today.")[34]

Certainly whisky trails and the whisky ambassador program make Scotland stand out in the whisky market, but that is only part of the equation. Scotch whisky is world renowned and the brand stands solid in markets all around the world. Indeed Scotch whisky consumption is expected to grow in the emerging economies of Asia, South America, and Africa.[35] How has it managed to become so successful? There is a long standing tradition of Scottish whisky that is well established – the strong taste trail network and the whisky ambassador program are two such examples that the tourist can experience while in Scotland. Back at home, the reputation of the whisky is well-established already. In effect, the lesson learned here is that the tourism aspect is building on an already well-established brand.

In recent years, whisky manufacturing has taken hold in India and China. Japan also produces whisky. While ingredients, terroir and flavor profiles may differ, the question must be asked, what happens to Scotch whisky when high quality substitutes are available at much lower price points? While Scotch whisky is protected by European Union and World Trade Organisation law,[36] there is no law against anyone else making a Scotch-like whisky and calling it something else.

CONCLUSION

As we have seen, the opportunities abound for tourism in the tea, wine and whisky markets. Tea tourism is a developing niche market with many opportunities given the rich culture and heritage that surrounds it. However, issues of sustainability also need to be considered when developing this form of tourism. Wine tourism is a very well-developed industry and this chapter outlined some of the challenges and opportunities found in the wine region of Eastern Europe. Finally, whisky tourism is the legacy of a strong brand with further potential for development, and an opportunity for further protection as well.

These three beverages enjoy a common thread of tradition. When bringing tourism into the mix, it is critical to convey to the visitor the unique traditions around the beverage, from how it is made, to how it is served and indeed, every possible viewpoint and story that surrounds the beverage. Food travelers largely seek authenticity. While the product itself is of interest, the story around it is what compels the tourist to visit.

DISCUSSION QUESTIONS

1. Considering other beverages that could be featured in drink tourism, give examples of destinations where fruit juice, soda pop and mineral water are attractions to visitors.
2. Consider the culture of sharing tea, coffee, beer, wine or any other beverage with a colleague, friend or family member. What is it about the experience of sharing a beloved beverage that brings people closer together?
3. Pretend you work for a destination marketing organization. Create a drink trail. What features would you put on the trail? How would you promote it?

ENDNOTES

[1] Jolliffe, L. *Tea and tourism: Tourists, traditions and transformations.* 2007. Accessed June 2, 2013. http://bit.ly/15uqDze

[2] Ibid.

[3] Cheng, S., Xu, F., and Zhang, Y. "Tourists' attitudes towards tea tourism: A case study in Xinyang, China." *Journal of Travel and Tourism* Marketing 27(2) (2010): 211-220. Accessed June 2, 2013. http://bit.ly/15uzfG0

[4] Ibid.

[5] Ibid.

[6] USA Today. "Tea tourism draws devotees to India". Accessed June 5, 2013. http://usat.ly/107FvyH

[7] Ibid.

[8] Gray, D. "India experiences growth in tea tourism". Accessed June 2, 2013. http://bit.ly/ZmQSGl

[9] "Makaibari Tea Estates". Accessed June 2, 2013. http://bit.ly/12oIDgP

[10] Jolliffe, L. *Tea and tourism: Tourists, traditions and transformations.* 2007. Accessed June 2, 2013. http://bit.ly/15uqDze

[11] BBC News. "Slum tourism: Patronising or social enlightenment?" Accessed June 5, 2013. http://bbc.in/TshCnz

[12] Jolliffe, L. *Tea and tourism: Tourists, traditions and transformations.* 2007. Accessed June 18, 2013.

[13] Ibid.

[14] GoChina. "Tourism along the Tea Horse Road". Accessed June 4, 2013. http://bit.ly/14erioN

[15] "Tea Horse Road". Accessed June 4, 2013. http://bit.ly/11fK0ao

[16] Jolliffe, L. and Aslam, M. "Tea heritage tourism: Evidence from Sri Lanka." *Journal of Heritage Tourism* 4(4) (2009): 331-344. [Electronic version]

[17] Ibid.

[18] Ibid.

[19] Ibid.

[20] For more information about the development of the wine industry in Hungary, especially since its years under Communist rule, see ALKONYI, Lázsló . *Tokaj: A szabadság bora / Tokaj: The Wine of Freedom.* Budapest, Spread Bt. (Borbarát), 2000.

[21] We will be talking about the Tokaj region and while talking about its wine, we will use the declined term, "Tokaji" (which in Hungarian literally means "of Tokaj".

[22] cf. Alkony, 2000: 84-87

[23] *Aszú* is the Hungarian term used to designate specifically the wine resulting from the fermentation of grapes that have been infected (and *dried* directly on the vine) by *botrytis cinérea.*

[24] Alkony, 2000: 84

[25] Johnson, Hugh. Foreword to *Tokaj. A Companion for the Bibulous Traveller,* by D. Copp. Budapest: PrintXBudavár, 2007.

[26] Copp, David. *Tokaj. A Companion for the Bibulous Traveller.* Budapest: PrintXBudavár, 2007.

[27] Atkin, Tim. "Tradition and Innovation in the Tokaj Region" (pdf). Accessed October, 2009). www.docstoc.com/docs/4031194/TRADITION-AND-INNOVATION-IN-THE-TOKAJ-REGION-Tim-Atkin-TRADITION

[28] Cros, Szusza and Luginbühl, Yves. "Enjeux territoriaux du patrimoine à Tokaj Hegyalya (Hongrie)". In *Campagnes de tous nos désirs. Patrimoines et nouveaux usages sociaux* edited

by M, Rautenberg., A, Micoud.,L,Bérard. and Ph, Marchenay, 36. Paris: Éditions de la Maison des Sciences de l'Homme, 2000.

[29] Téchoueyres, Isabelle. "Patrimoine alimentaire et dynamiques territoriales: Questionnements et tendances dans le Sud Ouest de la France", in *Patrimonio gastronómico y turismo cultural en el Mediterráneo* edited by J, Tresserras, and F. X. Medina, 257-258. Barcelona: Ibertur.

[30] "Scotland's Malt Whisky Trail". Accessed June 2, 2013. www.maltwhiskytrail.com/

[31] http://www.thewhiskyambassador.com

[32] "Whisky Ambassador". Accessed June 5, 2013. http://bit.ly/KuvLua

[33] Jacobs, H. *A selected internet guide to culinary trails*. Ted Rogers School of Hospitality and Tourism Management, 2010.

[34] Ibid.

[35] Fraser, D. "How Scotch whisky conquered the world". Accessed June 5, 2013. http://bbc.in/UztUGv

[36] http://bit.ly/11KDJ6h

Farms & Farmers' Markets

Lynne M. Bennett, Rasto Kirn, & Crystal Miller

While agricultural tourism and agriculture are not food tourism per se, the seeds of cuisine are found in agriculture. Therefore there is a solid business case to include agriculture in a discussion of food tourism. This chapter will look at agriculture and agritourism, and present some best practices examples of farmers' markets.

INTRODUCTION

An increasing number of consumers and travelers alike are interested in the origins of their food. This interest has set the stage for rural economic development in the form of agricultural tourism. A central and well-known component to local food systems includes farms and farmers' markets, which is a form of agricultural tourism, also referred to as "agritourism." Agritourism can be broadly defined as any agricultural operation serving consumers that may include retail sales and provision of services involving food, fiber, flowers, trees, shrubs, and any other farm products.[1] Two emerging components of agritourism are activities and events centered around farmers' markets and farms. Agritourism differs from food tourism in that agritourism is inherently rural, while food tourism is predominantly urban, but can be rural as well. Also, food tourism tends to focus on prepared food and drink, while agritourism focuses more on the raw ingredients and the farming experience.

The Market for Farmers' Markets and Farm Visits

Farmers' markets and farm visits connect travelers to local food culture while offering a wide variety of activities focused on local agriculture and cuisine. Agritourism can also be an opportunity to build partnerships and collaborations that promote more sustainable economic development for urban and rural areas, support farm preservation and increase farmers' livelihood, while helping create diverse and memorable food tourism experiences for travelers. To fully understand the current trend of food tourism's relationship with agricultural tourism, a brief review of farms and farmers' markets is needed.

Old World Farming and its European Influences

The historical story of Europe is not only about the many kingdoms and wars, but also of the lesser known lives of ordinary people. Europeans lived largely in the countryside until the last century, when more people began moving into the cities. The work of the local inhabitants was connected to nature and their products were eco-centric. Their inherited experience and expertise were passed down from generation to generation. Travel distances were far, so people were very connected on the local level. Local cuisines developed that still today distinguish countries and regions of the Old World. Most people know at least something about the historical influence of French, Italian, Greek, Spanish and Scandinavian food worldwide. This contribution aims to open the door from the local farms and farmers market into the simple kitchen that evolved in the New World. Today, there is a food movement to get back to the basics.[2] The Old World way of eating is now becoming the mainstay in the modern countries of central Europe and America and are influencing the food culture of today on a global scale.[3]

From Old World Farms to Farmers Markets

To survive during the Middle Ages, villagers often worked as traders and craftsmen, while at the same time needing to harvest their gardens for food production. With the development of trade in the Middle Ages, large urban clusters, also known as agglomerations, were formed. As the population grew, a growing number of villagers could no longer be fed by suburban gardens. Out of this problem grew a solution: "the fair day." Once a week, farmers and artisans from neighboring villages would come to sell their produce and artisan products. These "fair days" or "markets" always took place in larger towns. Even today, traditional food markets are not generally held at small farms, but in towns. In the same tradition, they are open or covered outdoor marketplaces where the sellers and buyers do business. One of the oldest continuing markets in Europe is the Borough Market in London, England. North America's oldest market is located in Halifax, Nova Scotia, Canada.

The Borough Market

The Borough Market is located in London, England, near the famous London Bridge, and is open six days a week. The market started in 1014, and over the centuries has been moved to different locations. It remains one of the oldest and largest food markets in London, if not the world. At one time, it was situated near the Globe Tavern public house, built in 1872, located along the path of the River Thames. This strategic historical location has contributed to the market's present day growth.[4]

Throughout history, the Borough Market has focused on selling fruits and vegetables. However, due to the recent food movement around London and the surrounding areas, the market has expanded to include gourmet foods and artisan bakers. It also specializes in wholesale and retail foods, both globally and locally sourced. The market houses over 100 individual stalls and "all of our traders share a love of food and many of them make, grow or rear the produce they sell so now, just as in 1755."[5]

The historical location of the market around the transportation center of London has been problematic throughout history. In 1755, British officials closed the market by an Act of Parliament in order to reduce the congestion it caused. In response, a group of Southwark residents raised £6,000 to purchase land to reopen the market. The market is the only fully independent market in London and is owned by a charitable trust.[6] The market has received two prestigious awards: the 2008 National Association of British Market Authorities' Award for "Best Specialty Market" and the 2010 London Lifestyle Award for "London Food Market of the Year."

Halifax Farmers' Market

The Halifax Farmers' Market, in Nova Scotia, Canada, was founded in 1750 and is the oldest continuously operating market in North America.[7] On any given day the market can have up to 250 vendors specializing in selling local produce, foods, crafts, and products from Nova Scotia. On its busiest days the market will attract over 12,000 visitors.[8] Although organic foods, artisan products, and handmade crafts are core to the market, the demand for access to and direct contact with local farmers and food producers drives this experience.[9]

From 1983 to 2010, the market was located in the Alexander Keith Nova Scotia Brewery Building. In November 2010 the market moved to its new home on the seaport in a renovated shipping warehouse owned by the Halifax Port Authority and is now referred to as "Halifax Seaport Farmers' Market."[10] The redeveloped Halifax Seaport waterfront, which extends from Piers 19 to 23, has become a popular destination for locals, as well as over 252,000 annual cruise ship travelers from around the world. The 56,000 square foot (5203 sq m) permanent indoor facility, with outdoor features and open public plaza, was specifically designed for the market by Lydon Lynch Architects, Halifax, Canada.[11] It is also a LEED Platinum-certified building sustainably designed to integrate four wind turbines, solar-thermal panels, geothermal wells, water harvesting, a green wall and green roof made of living plants, with other sustainable features as well.[12] The port also houses the Canadian Museum of Immigration, the Nova Scotia College of Art & Design, cruise terminals, and offices.[13]

Along with the establishment of farmers' markets, where food is sold directly from farmer to consumer, the role of farming has also evolved.

Twenty-First Century Farming

Although the primary goal of agriculture is food production, even with government subsidies, farmers often need other gainful activities on the farm to survive. One good way for farmers to do this is through "farm tourism," where visitors can rest or enjoy farm activities in a natural environment. A central farm activity is consuming homemade food and drink in an authentic environment, including homemade wine from the farm or from a local winery. Many farms also have their own farm store to supplement their income. In some places a tourist can spend more days on the farm and "help" in traditional tasks.

In Austria, there are over 10,000 farms solely engaged in tourism activities.[14] These activities include farm and vineyard tours, farm stays and educational workshops, farms stores and stands, wine tasting and tours of the vineyard, homegrown farm meals with the farmers, hosting and participating in local food fairs, festivals and events. In Slovenia there are thousands of farms that engage in these gainful agri-business activities, over 500 of which deal with daily trips and tourism.

Farms in the New Era

The structure of farms and farming has experienced many transformations during the past two centuries. Farming moved from family operated farms to the large corporate industrialization of mono-agriculture farming. Over time, the negative effects of commercial farming intensified, as did their negative influences on the environment and the health of farm workers and consumers.[15]

The current trend is moving away from the large commercial farms in favor of small and medium sized farms working to reestablish more sustainable farming methods, coming to be known as the alternative food system. It arises out of concern for issues such as biodiversity loss, global competition, environmental degradation, economic downturns, and consumer influence.[16] The concept is that an alternative food system is sustainable and offers an alternate model to conventional agriculture. The overarching concept of an alternative food system is to include practices such as organic farming, aquaculture, direct marketing such as community supported agriculture (CSA), farmers' markets, and community based farming. Engaging in these alternative practices typically requires farmers to build or strengthen new skills sets and it encourages diversification.

Farm diversification offers farms several benefits including reducing environmental impacts, entry into niche markets, creating new agriculture industries which can strengthen rural communities, decreasing economic risks, and creating a more sustainable food system.[17] Agritourism fits nicely into this model. It can consist of local farms providing attractions and activities on their farm while inviting local residents and tourists to participate. In the U.S. alone there are 23,350 farms that provide some kind of agritourism services.[18]

The Growing Food Movement and Agritourism

In 1986, Carlo Petrini founded the Slow Food Movement in Italy as a movement against the industrialization of food that became not only toxic to the land and the consumers, but also which created a monoculture of tasteless food.[19] He realized that in order to keep alternative food choices alive he had to show consumers that they had the power to choose the type and quality of food they eat. He understood that the industrialization of food was standardizing taste and leading to the annihilation of thousands of food varieties and flavors.[20]

In addition he saw that "it was imperative for an eco-gastronomic movement to exist – one that was ecologically minded and concerned with sustainability, and one that acknowledged the connection between the plate and the planet. With preservation of taste at the forefront, he sought to support and protect small growers and artisanal producers, support and protect the physical environment, and promote biodiversity."[21]

While Petrini galvanized the sustainable food advocates throughout Europe and thereby created a movement in Europe, Alice Waters was bringing the same awareness to the San Francisco Bay Area in northern California. Waters, a well-known and highly regarded chef, author, and owner of Chez Panisse Restaurant in Berkeley, "is an American pioneer of a culinary philosophy that maintains that cooking should be based on the finest and freshest seasonal ingredients that are produced sustainably and locally."[22] As a passionate advocate for a local food economy, for the past 40 years, Waters created an integrated community of local farmers, ranchers, and food artisans dedicated to sustainable agriculture practices to supply local restaurants with the finest and freshest variety of ingredients available. With farmers selling directly to restaurants, they have created a new form of "farmers' marketing" by providing organic, sustainable, local produce, meats, and artisanal foods directly to the restaurants.[23] There is also a growing movement for restaurants having their own "kitchen garden" where they grow seasonal produce and herbs to supplement their kitchens. Alice Waters' philosophy of cooking with only local, fresh, seasonal, organic, and unprocessed food complements the values of the Slow Food Movement.

As this movement evolved, it was only natural that Petrini and Waters would meet and form international alliances. Waters, now as the Vice President of Slow Food International, continues to bring food awareness and advocacy to the sustainable food movement which includes 100,000 Slow Food Movement members in over 130 countries.[24] This international food movement has brought a new food consciousness to the general population, so much so, that their culinary appetites now play an important role when making travel plans.[25] This marriage of food and travel opened up opportunities for agritourism worldwide: travelers can readily include farm-to-fork experiences as they travel abroad.

With the stage now set, local farmers, ranchers, food artisans and entrepreneurs, including farmers' market associations, have a chance to tap into the agritourism business in a creative manner. Some examples of creative marking and the development of new niches include mobile farmers markets, on-site farm stores open to the public, on-site education programs, tours and cooking demos, and commercial kitchens founded by farmers.

Farmers' Markets

Farmers' markets are often defined by their local and regional context and therefore remain diverse in their composition and purpose. The composition is dependent on region, weather, access to space, and community support. Farmers markets are found in shopping centers, in streets, banks, hospitals, art centers, indoor shopping centers, arenas, empty lots, and many other areas where permitted by local jurisdictions. The main purpose for farmers' markets is to provide fresh regional food to local residents and support local agriculture.[26] They can also serve as strong connectors along food tourism trails and create destinations that attract tourism in rural communities, such as the development of local and regional food festivals.

Farmers' markets create an alternative to non-local food systems and are becoming a social institution in many communities. Furthermore, many farmers' markets are quickly surpassing the role of direct-marketing channels for farmers.[27] Rather than going to the grocery stores to make their food purchases, consumers are migrating towards buying many of their food products directly from food producers. In the United States, between 1994 and 2011 there was a fourfold increase in new farmers markets, numbering to over 7000.[28] Roles that farmers' markets can fulfill include providing a venue for nutritional education, cooking demonstrations, food security and social justice education, community building, supporting the local food movement, and entrepreneurial incubators for food artisans.

Doing Business

Management and Marketing Issues

The food tourism industry has an opportunity to engage travelers ranging from the food conscious to the average hungry traveler by building partnerships with farmers, local food processors, and food service professionals. Forging these relationships will allow tourism associations and agritourism producers to coordinate travel packages that integrate agritourism opportunities, create culinary tourism trails that include agritourism attractions, and develop joint marketing efforts through television, print, web, and word-of-mouth.

Traditional marketing campaign methods such as brochures, signage, radio and television, need to be enhanced with new multimedia methods. This includes dynamic websites, social media (e.g. Facebook, LinkedIn, Twitter, Pinterest, blogging) and applications developed for smart-phones and tablets. Farmers and farmers' market managers need to stay on top of the constantly changing electronic media tools available to them to remain competitive and to be successful.

Some of the tools to develop a successful farmers' market agri-business include incorporating well-conceived branding, marketing, partnerships, and networking practices, both locally and globally. Collaborating and networking with local, national and international tourism associations can also greatly benefit the visibility of the emerging agritourism entrepreneur. Technology can enhance collaboration efforts among local and regional food system stakeholders to build sustainable food systems. Examples include developing food system infrastructure; pooling funds for joint marketing, promotion, research, and events; developing work groups and food policy councils; and establishing forums for stakeholders to share their challenges and successes. Collaborative initiatives help nurture the relationships that are necessary for local and regional food systems to succeed.

Branding and Positioning

Engaging in collaborative marketing provides agritourism operators the opportunity to reach a wider audience, while giving tourism associations and visitor bureaus more attractions to promote within the region. Additionally, aligning small agritourism attractions with larger, reputable travel and tourism associations provides immediate brand association for the smaller attractions. Branding can be seen as the development of a product or service beyond its tangible utility; it is the promise of an experience and/or quality of your product or service that you make to the customer (often referred to as a "brand promise"). Networking with trustworthy tourism associations and businesses in a particular region is a strategic way to strengthen or establish brands.

Farmers as Leisure Providers

Transitioning from a traditional commodity business that focuses on wholesale sales and exports, to one that sells a product, service, or an experience directly to the consumer is often a challenge for many farmers. Research reveals that farmers resist identifying themselves as anything other than a producer or farmer and viewing themselves as a leisure provider would mean a loss of identity.[29] Yet, as agritourism continues to grow, it is crucial to understand the farmers' role as a leisure provider.

Promoting a farmers' market as a leisure experience for consumers[30] is also an emerging topic in the recreation and leisure fields, but just like other forms of leisure provision, it requires thoughtful facilitation to be successful.[31] Including farmers in planning market events, programming, and services can serve as an introduction to this new provider role, as well as create educational opportunities for farmers to learn about delivering a leisure experience. Collaboration among parks and recreation departments, tourism associations, and farmers' market management can help build opportunities for farmers to explore this role, gain knowledge and skills, and develop their capacity to provide leisure experiences.

Food tourism presents an opportunity for communities to build upon their local agricultural assets by transforming their farms and farmers' markets into destinations. Farmers' market growth shows continued increases, up from 1,200 in 1980 to 4,385 in 2006[32] and while agritourism growth has actually declined by 17%, the income generated by these operations has dramatically increased by 236%.[33] This may reflect a decrease of new agritourism ventures, but with a 236% increase in income from existing operations, it also reflects a strong diversification option for farmers wanting or needing to increase revenue.

Below are examples of individuals and organizations that created successful farm-to-fork enterprises. These endeavors not only help sustain the local food system, but they also have created agritourism opportunities.

Interview with a Slovenian Farmer

Agriculture should be one of the more important domestic economic industries, but in Slovenia it brings less than 2% of GDP.[34] The main stakeholders of agriculture in Slovenia are mostly small, individual farms. In the 1980s, some Slovenian farmers saw that the current farming practices were producing low quality food. A few brave farmers began moving towards organic farming principles that focus on quality rather than quantity of crops. Mrs. Varja Stergar from Stergar farm on Pohorje is one such farmer. She shares her story:[35]

> From an early age my husband and I were "ecologically oriented." We did not know this expression at that time, but we both lived this way. Inheriting our farm, we tried to organize the whole process in a sustainable way. At the end of the 1990s, directives for organic farming were adopted by the government. We told ourselves, "This is it!" We began to educate ourselves on organic farming principles and we put our farm under state control. After two years of organic farming, we were registered by the government as organic farmers.
>
> We moved towards organic farming because we saw that chemical fertilizers were killing the life in the soil and permeating the ground and water with harmful chemicals. Instead of chemical fertilizers we feed our crops natural manure. By causing the plants to naturally search for nutrients in the soil, they become more resistant and protect

themselves with the production of natural vitamins. The added benefit of people eating organic vegetables and fruits is that they do not need food supplements.

Another important factor of organic food production is the importance to minimizing the length of the path from producer to final consumer. The produce is then able to retain vitamins and nutrients for consumers. Due to the small size of Slovenia, this is not a major problem: most of the food could be of local origin.

Organic farming has become possible because of the European Directive that requires states to subsidize farms. In France, a higher level of food awareness has produced a "partnership agriculture," where local people have chosen to purchase healthier food from local organic farmers. In this partnership, farmers are able to stay on their farm because the local people are financially supporting them by paying farmers in advance for the next season of crops, and even offering their own physical labor on the farm. The people of our region are not yet at this level of sustainable food consciousness.

We are now a well-established farm and are members of the Biodar group, the strongest organic association in Slovenia. With food packaged bearing the mark BIODAR, it is possible to trace the origin of food from farm-to-table. "BIODAR-made" confirms that the product is of organic origin and from the field or stable to the shelves controlled by the control organizations. We stand for our products with all my heart: we believe that organic food is not only healthier, but it is also much more delicious. Just compare our apples or onions with those from a supermarket. Even domestic flour is of better quality and more nutritious.

We are still improving the workflow on our farm. We have created our own "partnership agriculture" and are delivering crops for regular customers twice a week and selling our produce at our organic farmers market. We are constantly learning new ways to farm sustainably.

Marin Organic: Nonprofit Organic Producers' Cooperative

Marin Organic, located in northern California (USA), was founded in 2001 by a conglomerate of farmers, ranchers, agricultural advisors, and marketing experts in order to promote the producers and consumers of Marin County.

The mission of the organization is to support local organic producers "whose livelihood is based on a respect for nature and a sense of place."[36] Their focus is to create an ecological, social, and economic food system to support their local communities. They achieve these goals through their various programs that support the local farmers. These include education and outreach programs to provide farmers with information on how to improve their farming and management practices economically, environmentally and socially. The cooperative provides assistance on marketing and public education to help producers bring their products to market. They form alliances and coalitions to strengthen relationships with businesses, government, and other organizations to build a more sustainable and equitable local food system to serve as a regional, state, national, and international model. In addition to holding fundraising farm-to-fork, food author, and culinary food events, Marin Organic has also created an Eat Local Guide Map. Consumers use this guide when buying groceries or dining out and are encouraged to select businesses that support local farmers and producers. This benefits growers, producers, businesses and consumers alike, allowing everyone to thrive economically year round. By using this model, lasting regional relationships are created. Local farmers' markets are important partners of Marin Organic. Marin Organic members have "Marin Organic" signs posted at their food stalls to inform shoppers that, indeed, their produce is local and organic. By purchasing their products consumers are helping to sustain local businesses and the local food-shed.

Agricultural Institute of Marin, a Farmers' Markets Association

Agricultural Institute of Marin's (AIM) is a farmers' market management nonprofit association that is located in Northern California (USA). In 1983, AIM opened its first farmers market at the Marin Civic Center in the town of San Rafael. This was the first Certified Farmers' Market in Marin County. AIM's mission is to promote a viable food system, to educate the public about the benefits of buying fresh and locally grown food, and to bring farmers and communities together AIM now manages eight Certified Farmers' Markets in northern California (USA), representing over 500 family farms, artisans, and specialty food purveyors. The Sunday Marin Civic Center Farmers Market is now the third largest farmers market in California.

At all their farmers markets, AIM integrates public education around nutrition and the economic benefits of purchasing local, sustainable, and organic foods grown directly by the farmers. AIM's educational programs include Market Tours and Eat Local 101, workshops that inform and inspire eaters looking for a deeper connection to the food they eat. The programs include seasonal tastings, chef demonstrations, and interactive displays on healthy eating. AIM also has a farm-to-fork outreach and distribution program to encourage schools, institutions, food service programs and businesses to buy directly from local producers. AIM has created partnerships with over 40 schools, restaurants, cafes, bistros, corporate cafeterias, and catering services throughout the Bay area.

The Agricultural Institute of Marin also provides business marketing and outreach support for the food producers. AIM's marketing campaign puts faces on the food producers, farmers and the lands they work and live on. By creating biographical stories, complemented by photos of the food producers' farming habitat, AIM helps connect the consumers to the hands that feed them. Along with their website, AIM's monthly e-newsletters, which reach over 5,000 readers, and the full-page ads they place in over two dozen local publications featuring the farmers and their personal stories enable shoppers at the market to develop a personal connection with the food vendors.

Currently, AIM is working towards building a permanent year-round pavilion in San Rafael, California. It will be dedicated to local agriculture and will serve the community, the local farmers, ranchers, specialty food purveyors, artisans, agricultural organizations and the public. It will include a retail promenade with a bakery/cafe, butcher shop with locally sourced meats and fish, local cheese & dairy shop, specialty grocery and restaurant. AIM hopes to add a commercial kitchen, where eaters can learn and farmers and food purveyors can showcase. Business incubator and training programs are also planned to help local farmers diversify their production.[37]

Pike Place Market

Pike Place Market, located in Seattle, Washington (USA), was established in 1906 to connect the locals to the farmers, and today is "internationally recognized as America's premier farmers' market."[38] It is also fondly known as Seattle's "neighborhood market," sitting on a nine-acre (3.6 ha) historic district in the rolling hills of downtown Seattle near the Wharf. Although food is the focus of this market, it is also known as one of the largest year-round craft markets in the United States, featuring local, sustainable, and handcrafted goods.

The market's history includes tales of immigration and urban renewal and today, Pike Place Market is regarded as "The Soul of Seattle".[39] Unique to Pike Place Market are daily espresso and market tours where one can meet the local food producers, while taking in the ambiance and history of the area. This is really a bird's eye view of a local village where you can interact with the butchers who know where their meat came from, the farmers who grow their own food, and the fishermen who just hauled in the catch of the day.

Pike Place Market is an innovator in social-agricultural entrepreneurship. Its heritage programs and commitment to community services have been instrumental in the development of new programs, such as a free health clinic, senior center, low-income housing, childcare center and establishment of a Farmer Relief Fund.

CONCLUSION

Farmers and farmers' markets have a long history of providing locally grown food to their communities. The development of industrialized mass food production and processed foods of the twentieth century disengaged many urban people from the land and the local food production that once was a part of daily family and community life. With the resurgence and growth of food movements worldwide, along with education and outreach by food producers and supporting associations, local food products are once again being integrated into many people's daily lives.

Aligning this growth with a target population of food savvy, health-conscious, culture-seeking travelers, the integration of agritourism elements such as farm visits and farmers' markets is a necessary part of the food tourism offering, wherever feasible. As potential for food tourism grows, it is critical for tourism and agriculture industries to build networks, partnerships, and alliances within the communities where they operate and across regions and industries to ensure sustainability of these ventures.

DISCUSSION QUESTIONS

1. How can farmers and farmers' market organizers work to enhance opportunity to create agritourism operations?
2. What are the benefits of food tourism and agritourism for farmers, communities, local businesses? In what ways do these two forms of tourism help each other, or conflict with each other?
3. What stakeholders should be included in the conversation when developing an agritourism operation? Why?

ENDNOTES

[1] Che, D., Veeck, A., and Veeck, G. (2005). Sustaining Production and Strengthening the Agritourism Product: Linkages among Michigan Agritourism Destinations. Agriculture and Human Values, 22(2): 225-234.

[2] Pollan, Michael. "How Change Is Going to Come in the Food System," The Nation, October 3, 2011.

[3] Lappé, Frances Moore, "The Food Movement: Its Power and Possibilities." The Nation, October 3, 2011. Retrieved from: www.thenation.com/article/163403/food-movement-its-power-and-possibilities#

[4] www.boroughmarket.org.uk

[5] Ibid.

[6] Ibid.

[7] Malone, Alanna. "Halifax Seaport Farmers' Market." GreenSource: The Magazine of Sustainable Design. July 2012. Halifax, Canada. Retrieved from: http://greensource.construction.com/green_building_projects/2012/1207-halifax-seaport-farmers-market.asp

[8] Malone, 2012

[9] Forrestall, Monica, "In Halifax, an Old Market Gets a New Home" New York Times, August 14, 2011, p. TR5. . Retrieved from: http://travel.nytimes.com/2011/08/14/travel/in-halifax-an-old-market-gets-a-new-home.html?_r=0

[10] Malone, 2012.

[11] Malone, 2012

[12] Malone, 2012

[13] www.cruisehalifax.ca and www.portofhalifax.ca

[14] STATcube - Statistical Database of Statistics Austria. (2013). 20130502 http-__statcube.at_superwebguest_login.do_guest=guest&db=def1459.pdf. Retrieved from: www.statistik.at

[15] Altieri, M. (2009). The Ecological Impacts of Large-Scale Agrofuel Monoculture Production Systems in the Americas. Bulletin of Science, Technology & Society, 29(3): 236-244; and Eastwood, R., Lipton, M., and Newell, A. (2010). Farm Size. In Handbook of Agricultural Economics, Vol. 4 (pp. 3323-3397). Elsevier, BV: Academic Press; and Hanson, J.D., Hendrickson, J., and Archer, D. (2008). Challenges for Maintaining Sustainable Agricultural Systems in the United States. Renewable Agriculture and Food Systems: 23(4), 325-334.

[16] Altieri, M. (2009). Agroecology, Small Farms, and Food Sovereignty. Monthly Review, 61(3): 102-113, and Horrigan, L., Lawrence, R., and Walker, P. (2002). How Sustainable Agriculture Can Address the Environmental and Human Health Harms of Industrial Agriculture. Environmental Health Perspectives, 110(5): 445-456.

[17] Fritz, M. and Myers, R. (2004). Diversifying Cropping Systems. Sustainable Agriculture Network, USDA-SARE Outreach. Retrieved from: www.sare.org/Learning-Center/Bulletins/National-SARE-Bulletins/Diversifying-Cropping-Systems.

[18] U.S. Census Bureau. (2007). National Quickfacts. Retrieved from: http://quickstats.nass.usda.gov/results/203C6378-59FA-349A-99BA-C54471B7858C

[19] See Slow Food International www.slowfood.com and Slow Food USA www.slowfoodusa.org

[20] History of Slow Food. (2013). Retrieved from: www.slowfoodusa.org/index.php/about_us/details/manifesto

[21] www.slowfoodusa.org

[22] www.chezpanisse.com

[23] McNamee, Thomas. Alice Waters and Chez Panisse: The Romantic, Impractical, Often Eccentric, Ultimately Brilliant Making of a Food Revolution. The Penguin Press, New York, 2007

[24] Slow Food. (2013) retrieved from www.slowfood.com and Slow Food USA (2013) retrieved from www.slowfoodusa.org

[25] Long, Lucy. Culinary Tourism. University Press of Kentucky, 2004.

[26] Lappé.

[27] Stephenson, G. (2008). Farmers' Markets: Success, Failure, and Management Ecology. Amherst, New York: Cambria Press.

[28] Lappé.

[29] Sharpley, R. and Vass, A. (2006). Tourism, Farming and Diversification: An Attitudinal Study. Tourism Management, 27: 1040-1052.

[30] Farmer, J., Chancellor, C., Gooding, A., Shubowitz, D., and Bryant, A. (2011). Journal of Park and Recreation Administration, 29(3): 11-23.

[31] Lee, Y. (1999). Research Update: How Do Individuals Experience Leisure? Parks and Recreation, 34(2): 40-46.

[32] U.S. Department of Agriculture. (2006). Farmers Market Growth. Census of Agriculture, National Agriculture Marketing Service. 2007.

[33] U.S. Department of Agriculture. (2007). Agricultural Diversification. Census of Agriculture, National Agriculture Marketing Service. 2007.

[34] SURS-Statistical Office of the Republic of Slovenia (2013). 20130502 Gross domestic product and gross national income by TRANSACTIONS,_BR_ MEASURES and YEAR. Retrieved from: www.stat.si/eng/koledar.asp?pod=3&kon=19&DatumOd=1.1.2005&DatumDo=Date%28%29

[35] Author interview with Mrs. Varja Stergar, Stergar Farm, Pohorje, Slovenia, 13 February 2013.

[36] www.MarinOrganic.org

[37] www.agriculturalinstitute.org/our-story

[38] www.pikeplacemarket.org

[39] Ibid.

Food & Drink Events: Great Ideas or False Panaceas?

Karolina Buczkowska, Colm Folan, & Erik Wolf

Food and drink festivals and events can be worthwhile projects when done right and an unfortunate waste of money when poorly executed. One of the biggest misperceptions among destination marketers and would-be entrepreneurs is that an area *needs* a food festival, and that creating a big food festival will be a panacea, bringing in thousands of visitors and providing a much-needed infusion of cash into the local community, which is not necessarily the case. This chapter will look at food and drink events from a number of angles and offer advice for potential food and drink event producers.

INTRODUCTION

One measure of economic development is how much fresh cash comes into a community from outside of the community, allowing for investment and growth to occur. The premise is that new growth cannot occur from stagnant cash, or local cash that is recirculated. Creating a festival or event seems to be an obvious way to bring in a lot of cash all at once, but the reality is not so simple. Food events do not necessarily drive significant economic development. Many event producers will admit that it takes a minimum of three years for an event to prove its success. That said, a potential event producer needs to find the right formula and location for an event to work. Creating a successful food or drink event is not as successful as "build it and they will come."

Just Say No to Commodities & Ice Cream Socials

Often an event will be planned around an agricultural commodity like apples, corn, watermelon or another fruit or vegetable. While it is fun for kids to see a corn maze (popular in the USA) or to observe apple art (popular in Sweden), commodities like these, with few exceptions, do not tend to attract large numbers of non-local visitors. Local residents may be looking for activities for kids or may enjoy a watermelon eating contest, but these will not entice someone to fly hours to participate or to overnight. Even regional visitors who might attend such events on a day trip leave very little cash behind in the community. The net economic impact is small. Still such events serve a definite purpose for local residents. Similarly, an ice cream social is a popular event phenomenon in the United States and dates back almost 200 years. Who would love a bowl of rich ice cream on a hot summer day? Almost everyone. And who would fly hours to do it with strangers? Almost no one. Yet, we have witnessed several instances of communities that market an agricultural commodity or ice cream event through the local tourism office.

One notable exception to this position is the Gilroy Garlic Festival held in California, USA. This three-day summer celebration has entertained almost 4 million visitors and raised almost US$10 million for the benefit of local non-profit organizations since its inception in 1979. The festival now welcomes over 100,000 visitors annually, netting a yearly estimated economic impact to the town of up to US$10 million. The festival is one of the largest food festivals in the USA and provides a best-in-class example of using a commodity product (garlic) in the festival itself. Garlic-rich foods like garlic ice cream and garlic french fries are readily available, as they should be in this type of festival. Compare this experience to the Half Moon Bay (California) Pumpkin Festival, which features few if any pumpkin foods for sale. A pumpkin enthusiast would be severely disappointed.

Another Reason to Visit

Some geographically challenged destinations may seek to organize a food festival to drive visitation in the off season. This is the case with the Singapore Food Festival held every July, not the best time to visit a seaside city on the Equator. Still, the event, which is organized by the Singapore Tourism Board, has been held for two decades and is certainly worth a visit by regional visitors. Truly, walking around Singapore is like a food festival every day, with hawker centers everywhere. One hardly needs a food festival for a reason to visit Singapore or to try its food. Still, for those who have never visited, the food festival provides a tempting incentive.

Case Study: Saint Martin's Croissant Feast

There is probably no other city in the world that celebrates the name-day of one of its main streets, especially in late autumn. For almost 20 years now, in Poznan (Poland)[1], such an event takes place on November 11, commemorating St. Martin, the street patron. Poznań is associated with St. Martin's day thanks to the small catholic St. Martin's church, which originally stood in a settlement outside the walls of Poznan.

Photo: St. Martin's croissants *Photo Credit: Karolina Buczkowska*

Each year, from early October to late November, citizens of Poznan eat 500-600 tons (2.5 million pieces) of St. Martin's croissants (*rogale swietomarcinskie* in Polish). On November 11 alone (Poland's Independence Day), 120 tons (108,862 kg) are eaten. Thousands of Poznanians and tourists alike participate in the feast and Poland's Independence Day that takes place on the same day. Everybody in the region buys and eats considerable amounts of 'rogale' on that day. Locals are very proud that their sweet delicacy is protected by patent and since 2008 by the EU's protected geographical indication program (PGI).

Product History

The tradition of 'rogale' was born in Poznan in November 11, 1891, when the Rector of St. Martin's Parish asked the faithful during the mass to do something for the poor, as their patron used to do. Jozef Melzer, a baker from a local confectionery heard this at the mass and persuaded the bakery owner to bake the croissants, because, as the legend says, it commemorates his dream. His nighttime reveries had St. Martin entering the city on a white horse that lost its golden horseshoe. The very next morning, the baker whipped up horseshoe-shaped croissants filled with almonds, white poppy seeds and nuts, and gave them to the poor, while the wealthier dwellers of Poznan had to buy the delicacy. The custom was recognized in 1901 by the Association of Confectioners.

Today each patisserie has its own carefully guarded recipe for the perfect croissant. Locals know that although they all look the same, they certainly do not all taste the same. Moreover, the recipe has been continuously improved over time. In November 2003, a genuine St. Martin's croissant was made from puff Danish pastry and filled 35% with a filling made from white poppy seeds, vanilla, ground dates or figs, sugar, cream, raisins, butter and orange zest. The weight of one 'rogal' is strictly defined between 150 and 250 g. One piece can have as many as 1000 calories, but on November 11, no one is concerned with dieting.

If a confectionery wants to use the name 'St. Martin's Croissants', it must obtain a certificate by the Poznań Traditional St. Martin's Croissants Chapter, which was initiated by the Poznan Confectioners and Bakers Guild, the Chamber of Crafts and the Poznan City Hall. Certificates are valid for one year only, so patisseries have to apply for it each year before the Saint Martin's Name-Day. Currently in the Wielkopolska Region more than 100 confectioners have an appropriate certificate. The price of rogale may seem high at 30 PLN (€8)/kg or 9-10 PLN (€2.50) per piece. In some patisseries the price is even higher. For Poznanians, it does not matter because they could not imagine celebrating the November 11 without them.

Event Particulars

The first St. Martin Street Name-Day was organized in 1994 by the Zamek Cultural Centre, bringing the ancient tradition of public celebrations of patron saints alive again. Today 'Zamek' is the main organizer of the event but many other institutions from St. Martin Street cooperate with it: libraries, bookstores, cultural associations, cinemas, the Music Academy, etc. Every year the event starts with a high mass in St. Martin's Church. Afterwards, St. Martin, dressed in a Roman legionnaire's costume and riding a white horse, heads a colorful parade up St. Martin Street to the square in front of the 'Zamek' Cultural Centre (formerly the Prussian Emperor's castle). There, the mayor hands him the keys to the city, starting the celebrations.

The parade features several hundred artists, performers, children, clowns, members of historical reenactment groups, stilt walkers, men named Martin, and of course, bakers carrying croissants. Colorful and historic machines, artificial St. Martin's horses and patriotic elements (for Poland's Independence Day) make the parade more interesting and spectacular. St. Martin Street Name-Day event is associated with the charity action "Help your neighbors survive winter" conducted since 1994 by the 'Zamek' in collaboration with the 'Barka' Foundation for Mutual Help.

Year-Round Impact

Croissants are not only for feasts or to be eaten in November. People can buy them in Poznan cake shops all year round. Since 2011 people have been able to order Poznan's sweet croissants online and have them delivered. The reputation of the Poznan croissants goes even beyond the city and region. Since 2000, the Poznan City Office has been sending these delicacies to the President and Prime Minister of the Republic of Poland, ambassadors and mayors of all provincial cities treating them as a showcase of Poznan and an important element of the city's promotion. The festival has put Poznan on the map, giving rise to other events and more reasons to visit year-round.

Arthur's Day: A Festival or Marketing Master Class

The festival business is steadily growing worldwide. Food and drink festivals seem to be increasing in popularity, especially in the niche craft-beer market. Beer festivals are generally organized events during which a variety of beers are available for tasting and purchase. Beer festivals often coincide with beer exhibitions that tend to concentrate on the craft side and beer tastings, whereas the festival generally concentrates on the consumption of the product, along with accompanying food and entertainment. The Oktoberfest held every year in Munich, Germany, is perhaps the world's best known beer event, but a marketing campaign by an Irish brewer, has the Munich festival firmly in its target sights.

Ireland by its culture, nature and location lies on the periphery of Europe, and relies heavily on tourism as a valuable source of foreign exchange. Food festivals are an integral and valuable part of the tourism offer in Ireland. They range in style and scale from the recent emergence of pop-up style themed festivals, to long established food and cultural festivals which draw in thousands of tourists and are valuable income multipliers in the regions. Because tourism activity is often concentrated in areas that lack an intensive industry base, it is credited with having a significant regional distributive effect.[2]

The Tourism and Hospitality industry in Ireland[3] employs a core workforce of over 120,000 people across 16,500 businesses. Add to this part-time, volunteer and casual labor, the tourism and hospitality workforce may exceed 180,000.[4] The United Kingdom is Ireland's largest tourism market, accounting for 45% of international arrivals, followed by the rest of Europe at 35%. The USA accounts for 15% of international visitors annually.

Ireland, because of its peripheral location, has not been immune to the recent economic downturn and has had to face severe financial challenges in competing in an increasingly unsure marketplace. Rory McCarthy, Failte Ireland's Festivals and Events Officer, recognizes these mounting difficulties:

"Festivals and events play a key role in developing and promoting Ireland as a destination and we are working hard to ensure that the festivals and events sector can survive the current tough times. We will continue to assist the festivals and events industry in driving tourism, animating destinations and improving the visitor experience of Ireland."[5]

In terms of participation, over 400,000 international visitors attended festivals in Ireland in 2010.

- 40% of adults in Ireland attend festivals, and 72% of these spend money on lodging
- More than 2 million bed nights are generated by festivals from the domestic market alone
- €448 million was generated by festivals in Ireland in 2010, of which €300 million originated from domestic and overseas visitors who traveled specifically to attend a festival

Recently, scholars within and outside traditional disciplines have been examining festivals with regard to an increasing variety of issues: their roles in establishing place and group identity; the social and cultural impacts of festivals and festival tourism; creation of social and cultural capital through festival production; fostering the arts and preserving traditions; and a variety of personal outcomes from participation in festivals, including learning, acquired social and

266

cultural capital, and healthfulness. The value and worth of festivals to society and culture has been addressed, as well as the imputed need for festivity, but research on these important issues has been slim.[6]

Guinness Stout is an unofficial but an undeniable symbol of Ireland, and perhaps has been the drink of choice for many over the generations. Guinness is a long established Irish brand that is a leading beer brand in many countries. However, the brand is only recently emerging from a spate of falling growth, as it struggled to compete with other international brands. The company has concentrated on developing its successful "event advertising" format, whereby its innovative style of advertisements has been well received by consumers. In fact, the Guinness brand has won numerous national and international advertising awards over the years.

With a growing concern over falling Guinness stout sales in Ireland and overseas, Diageo (owners of the Guinness brand) decided that to increase sales and awareness of the Guinness brand, it was necessary to promote the brand to new and "lapsed" customers who may have been lulled away by lighter or cheaper alternatives.[7]

However to show the grasp that the Guinness brand has on Ireland and its influence as a worldwide brand, it is interesting to note that the Guinness Storehouse[8] (the Guinness Brewery exhibition and conference center) is officially Ireland's most visited visitor attraction, with over 1 million visitors in 2011. That said, perhaps the greatest coup that the brewery pulled off was the marketing master class called "Arthur's Day".

Not just satisfied with having the most popular visitor attraction in Ireland, to help "celebrate" the 250th anniversary of the signing of the lease for the Guinness brewery, Diageo, turned what was originally designed as a marketing campaign, into an annual "toast" to the founder of Guinness and inadvertently (or deliberately) created an annual "beer festival." The difference between this festival and others is the international aspect. Celebrated in many major cities across the world, Guinness drinkers are expected to raise a glass to the memory of Arthur Guinness at 17:59 in reference to 1759, the year the Guinness Brewery was established. The first events took place in the cities of Dublin, Kuala Lumpur, Lagos, and New York on 23 September 2009. The event was broadcast internationally on Sky TV, ITV2 and DirecTV. Six million euros were pledged by Diageo to the Arthur Guinness Fund.[9] The celebration was endorsed by several high-profile names, such as Rock star Bob Geldof, film director Guy Ritchie, footballers Michael Essien and Peter Crouch and supermodel Sophie Dahl.

As Andy Fennel,[10] Chief Marketing Officer for Diageo states, "It's a simple idea. Create a new consumption moment for a brand that everybody loves, but not everybody drinks every week - simple, strategic intent. Do that with boldness, do that with conviction and do that with flare based on an insight into how consumers relate to each other and to the brand currently. What you get is a [250 year anniversary programme] which was hugely successful, and we're really excited about repeating it this year and next year, and the year after. We're going to need to refresh it, but hopefully you understand the point, that it's just what Arthur was trying to do 250 years ago. We just need to apply those fundamentals to the current context".

Not everyone is enthused with the idea as Andy Fennel. Criticism has been rife, pointing particularly to the idea of celebrating an alcoholic beverage in a country which is seeing soaring health issues directly as a result of below cost and loss leader sales in supermarkets and in the off-licence (liquor store) trade. As Eimear O'Toole of the Guardian Newspaper[11] points out, "... This leads me to my biggest issue with the Arthur's Day phenomenon. Of course, I think it's irresponsible for a corporation to promote a national day of drinking in a country already straining under the social costs of alcohol abuse. Do they not sell enough fecking hats on Paddy's Day? But mostly I regret that at a time when "Irishness" needs a serious rebrand, we are allowing our national image to be exploited by multinationals, allowing stereotypes of a drunken Irish populace to be propagated for the benefit of shareholders."

In a statement hitting back at the criticism, Diageo said: "We promote responsible drinking and discourage alcohol misuse year-round through our support of Drinkware.ie and other resources for consumers. We are also in regular dialogue with publicans and venue managers. As a consequence of these efforts, the overwhelming majority of consumers in Dublin and nationwide behaved responsibly throughout Arthur's Day."

Whatever the rights and wrongs, Diageo has created a marketing and festival phenomenon. In comparison to other festivals in Ireland, none can match the sheer size and scale of the Guinness initiative. Not only do they have to compete with a globally recognized product, they also have to compete with the Guinness corporate sponsorship of other national festivals[12] and sporting events. Guinness is an ever-present brand which tends to consume the identity of any festival, be it a Jazz festival in Cork, or an Oyster festival in Redbank, New Jersey, USA.

Is Arthur's day a festival? Technically, no. It does not compare with the Oktoberfest or other beer festivals in terms of a core festival identity, or in the selection of beers. That said, the Guinness brand more than makes up for this in terms of the spread of associated festival activity, particularly food and entertainment. Rather than having a core and augmented product in a centralized location, Diageo has created a completely different type of festival- a satellite festival of almost global proportions concentrated in a moment- *"to Arthur!"*

Reasons for Success

Not every community has the history of St. Martin's or the clout of Guinness, and that is fine. Other successful types of food and drink events include the Aspen Food & Wine Classic (Colorado, USA); South Beach Wine & Food Festival (Miami, USA); Salone del Gusto (Italy); Garlic Festival (Isle of Wight, England, UK); La Tomatina (Valencia, Spain),[13] Galway Oyster Festival (Galway, Ireland); the Good Food & Wine Show (South Africa) and the Fancy Food Show (USA). These events represent a variety of general food and drink shows; commodity shows; and even a food industry trade show. This variety of shows demonstrates that there is no fast formula for the kind or location for a successful food and drink event. These and other food events are successful because they have the following common denominators: 1) paid staff and leadership; 2) a committed board of advisors; 3) an extensive team of committed volunteers; and 4) a quality product or experience worth promoting.

Issues

One important issue that seems to be overlooked by the majority of food and drink events is that of food waste. Any event attendee will tell you that events usually serve way too much food and when probed further, the event patron will admit that he or she left quite a bit of food on their plate. An immediate step that event producers can take, is to donate uneaten (and unserved) food to local charities. Some event producers do this, but laws vary by municipality. Some food (dairy products) may not be donated at all, while other food (meat) must be donated within 4 hours of cooking. While these kinds of laws are designed to protect people, they can often be over-protective. Hundreds of thousands of tons of food gets sent to landfills each year.

Another serious consideration for event producers is that of packaging waste, such as with paper or plastic plates, plastic utensils and cups and paper napkins. Using ceramic plates and glassware is an obvious solution to minimizing packaging waste, however for large scale events this is not often possible. Event producers need to be environmentally sensitive and proactively take steps to minimize waste that their events produce. Plastic plates and cups can be washed and recycled, but you will not find many people at events going through the trash bins afterwards. These days however, there are plates and cutlery already made from recycled plastic or paper as well as from other eco-friendly materials such as sugarcane and potato starch. Another option is packaging made from corn, bamboo or hemp, which are compostable and biodegradable. Paper napkins might also be able to be recycled.

An interesting, alternative approach to reducing waste is Way Out West, a music festival that takes place annually in Gothenburg, Sweden. While the event is not a food festival per se, the event organizers decided to serve only vegetarian food. By serving only vegetarian cuisine, the stress on the environment from the production of meat is kept at a minimum. Water is also conserved by serving vegetables rather than meat. This solution will not work for all events, but it is an interesting approach.

CONCLUSION

Event producers, destination marketers, lodging properties and other businesses with a vested interest in a successful event, need to work together and find the right formula to realize success. Sometimes the right formula takes a few years to work out the problems. Working together and forging strong partnerships is the best formula for a successful event. Working alone without the support of the local community or tourism office or local businesses or newspaper is a certain formula for failure. Whether you choose to produce a food event for fun, to promote low season arrivals, to support destination branding or any other reason, be sure you have a sustainable formula and buy-in from all parties affected. You will be glad you did.

DISCUSSION QUESTIONS

1. What could a destination with only one major agricultural commodity do to create a successful food tourism event?
2. Which event utensils, plates and cups are available in your area and are made of corn, bamboo, hemp or other natural fibers? How many event producers in your area use them?
3. Should a meeting planner produce a food event (instead of a consumer/volunteer)? What would be the benefits and drawbacks of this scenario?

ENDNOTES

[1] Poznan is the capital of the Voivodeship of Wielkopolska (Great Poland Region) and is the fifth largest city in Poland, with over 550,000 inhabitants. It is one of the oldest cities in Poland where the Polish State was born 1000 years ago. Today, Poznań is an important center for trade, services, industry, culture, sport, higher education, and science.

[2] Failte Ireland is the Irish government body with responsibility for tourism planning and policy (Tourism Facts 2011) www.failteireland.ie

[3] Tourism Ireland is responsible for marketing the island of Ireland overseas. Information on Tourism Ireland's marketing activities and the performance of overseas tourism to the island of Ireland is available at www.tourismireland.com/corporate/

[4] Irish Central Statistics Office www.cso.ie/en/statistics/labourmarket/

[5] www.failteireland.ie/News-Features/News-Library/Teaching-Festivals-to-Survive-and-Thrive-in-Diffic.aspx

[6] Gertz. D "The Nature and Scope of Festival Studies" *International Journal of Event Management Research* Volume 5,, no. 1 (2010)

[7] "Guinness Case Study: Utilizing a Major Anniversary to Reinvigorate a Brand" *Harvard Business Review* (2009) http://web.ebscohost.com/ehost/pdfviewer/pdfviewer?sid=df7b831d-2cb8-46fb-b0ad-10915b1d9357%40sessionmgr112&vid=6&hid=118

[8] www.guinness-storehouse.com/en/Index.aspx?gclid=CJvUg7Pkz7YCFcFAMgod4HwAfw

[9] www.guinness.com/en-ie/arthursday/AGF.html

[10] www.diageo.com/Lists/Resources/Attachments/603/Marketing%20-%20Web.pdf

[11] www.guardian.co.uk/commentisfree/2012/oct/02/guinness-arthurs-day-diageo-ireland

[12] http://guinnessjazzfestival.com/

[13] While La Tomatina is not a food festival per se, it does involve an agricultural commodity.

Food & Drink Manufacturing

Livio Colapinto, Kathrin Fehervary, & David Wilson

How can food and drink manufacturers support food and drink tourism? Today's food tourists are more inquisitive than ever and demand to know the specifics of how and where food is produced. This chapter describes a number of food and drink manufacturers — from the U.S., the U.K., Italy and Austria — and how they have successfully approached food manufacturing from the perspective of responsibility, safety and quality, with an eye towards food tourism. It concludes with a final example from the Zotter factory in Austria where sustainability, quality and transparency are packaged together in a fabulous example of touristic innovation.

INTRODUCTION

While there is an interest in factory and food production facilities in the way of tours and sampling experiences, there remain legitimate concerns surrounding responsibility (in how the food is produced, how employees are treated, how the community is served and how to thrive as a business); safety (keeping food safe for human consumption and uncontaminated); and quality (maintaining an authentic product that is distinct to a region be it through history, production processes or based on tradition and history). Responsibility, safety and quality form the pillars of this chapter.

Responsibility

Ben & Jerry's Ice Cream: Three Pillars of Sustainability

Ben & Jerry's began in the US state of Vermont with two friends taking a US$5 correspondence course on how to make ice cream. As the story unfolds, Ben & Jerry's ice cream was used to build the "world's largest ice cream sundae" weighing 27,102 pounds (12,293 kg). The ice cream gained quickly in popularity and the company went public in 1984. It has maintained its popularity ever since.

Some of the more noteworthy events that may have contributed to the rise in popularity for Ben & Jerry's included some key positioning. The proactive owners considered not only economic profitability, but also social responsibility and environmental well-being. The pillars of sustainability, which also echoes the triple bottom line philosophy that has gained a strong foothold in today's biggest companies.

Indeed, Ben and Jerry's does have an ice cream factory tour, where a person can view the ice cream making process (behind glass windows for safety reasons) and sample the flavors. However, it appears that the success of this brand today has very little to do with the factory tours and much more to do with the commitment to getting involved with the community and interacting with people — as well as constant innovation. This company provides an excellent example of what corporate social responsibility can and should look like in this century. To this end, there are a few key areas in which Ben & Jerry's has excelled and that have paradoxically helped the company to do very well:

- Recognition that their customers are real people with real names, faces, personalities and values. Everything the company does from the factory tour, to naming ice cream, to operating a circus bus takes the brand out to real people in real time.

- Creation of solutions to issues that extend beyond the company. Note that Ben & Jerry's, while selling ice cream, at the same time managed to help farmers, support the environment and even support street performers.
- Understanding the needs of the various stakeholders. Ben and Jerry's contributes to the community of which they are part while at the same time benefitting the company. In industry jargon, this is joint-value creation.

An additional responsibility that food and drink manufacturers have is to avoid the triumph of overpackaging that besets many of today's food and drink products. Complicated lids with multiple types of plastic and shrink wrap plastic that are not recyclable, or extra boxing that may be recyclable but nevertheless adds cost to production, weight to shipping and which contributes to the decimation of our valuable forest lands. As consumers think more and more about sustainability, those manufacturers that do not think ahead about what packaging is truly essential vs. what is a nice-to-have, may suffer the wrath of consumers.

Safety

Cadbury World: Risk Management

Public health and safety is a common concern in the food and drink manufacturing world. Strategically managing the risk is key and knowing what to do when a problem occurs. And problems do arise when it comes to food; no individual and no business can ever be completely immune.

In mid-2006, Cadbury (a name synonymous with chocolate, ranking fourth in the world supply of confections) suddenly recalled seven of its products in the U.K. and Ireland due to contamination concerns with Salmonella montevideo.[1] Cadbury, aside from being synonymous with chocolate was also famous for its Bournville project that housed employees in communities in close proximity to the factory and became known for its corporate social responsibility focus as early as the 19th Century — an early pioneer in the area of sustainability. With the creation of Cadbury World, it has also gained major recognition as a tourist attraction, providing memorable chocolate factory tours.[2]

When it comes to food manufacturing, issues of safety become particularly relevant for businesses and consumers alike. Aside from making certain that guidelines and governmental standard protocols are followed, the case of Cadbury also underscores some very key risk management principles that the company implemented effectively, thereby restoring public faith and maintaining a credible, positive image in the face of a potentially disastrous situation. The way Cadbury handled the situation is noteworthy and applicable to any large scale food manufacturing organization:

"Cadbury...highlighted the importance of differing stakeholder needs, the ongoing tussle between consumer needs and other key stakeholders, the timing of response in issuing a recall, effective strategic planning, conducting a risk assessment and scenario planning for a company. During a crisis event, organizations have to endure intensive stakeholder scrutiny, thus highlighting the need for effective crisis communication responses in order to maintain and protect a firm's reputation. If companies fail to conduct the appropriate stakeholder research then they may well risk losing their hard won reputations that have taken decades to create."[3]

Quality

Parma: Model of Success & International Acclaim

Parmigiano Reggiano. Barilla Pasta. Prosciutto di Parma. These products and many more have become synonymous with the Emilia Romagna (Po Valley) region of north central Italy. Not only are these products well branded internationally, but they are also leading brands due to their superior quality. Tourists who visit the region may observe the process of making prosciutto, and visit a number of different ham producers along the "road of ham and wine" or other itineraries, including the "Road of Culatello" in Zibello or the "Road of Porcini Mushrooms" in Borgotaro.[4] Below is the story of Parmigiano Reggiano, highlighting where the product is made, how it is made and the consortium that monitors the production. Indeed, the story is one of enormous success.

> Parmigiano Reggiano: is a PDO (Protected Designation of Origin) product. This means that its distinctive features and its link with the area of origin are guaranteed by a system of EU rules designed to protect both consumers and producers. Production is carried out according to the product specification of the PDO, and it's certified by the independent body "Dipartimento Controllo Qualità". The trademark "Parmigiano Reggiano" can only be put on a cheese 1) produced and processed in the place of origin or 2) produced according to strict rules, which require precise production methods (Production Standard), controlled feeding of the cows (Feeding Regulation) and qualitative selection and marking (Marking Regulation). Milk and cheese production takes place in the provinces [sic] of Parma, Reggio Emilia, Modena, Bologna to the west of the Reno River and Mantua to the east of the Po River. The quality is dependent on the place of origin, the natural feed and the high quality milk free of additives. During the long aging process, natural fermenting agents in the milk give the cheese its particular flavor and texture, in other words, its typicality.[5]

Of equal importance to the story is the unique way in which Parmigiano Reggiano is made — a long history and tradition unchanged since the 11th Century:

> Parmigiano Reggiano is part of the history, tradition and hard work of the people who create it. Essentially it depends on the knowledge of everyone involved in making it. Produced since the year 1200, Parmigiano Reggiano was first made at the Benedictine monasteries in the area between the Po River and the Apennine mountains. What makes Parmigiano Reggiano special is the human factor. This cheese owes its unique qualities to the cooperation between the milk producer and the cheese maker, who transforms the milk into the cheese and looks after the maturing process.[6]

Also important is the care with which the product and Parma name are protected:

> Finally, to define and maintain the upstanding quality assurance that really has brought about the international acclaim for this product, there exists the Consorzio del Formaggio Parmigiano Reggiano, a consortium that includes all the cheese houses that produce Parmigiano Reggiano. The responsibilities of the Consortium include regulating use of the certification marks and protecting Parmigiano Reggiano from imitations; distributing information about Parmigiano Reggiano and promoting its purchase and use; and improving and perfecting Parmigiano Reggiano's qualities to safeguard its uniqueness and special characteristics. The Consortium is also officially charged with the important duty of applying the certification and identifying marks of Parmigiano Reggiano cheese – the distinctive signs of conformity to the Regulations

of the Protected Designation of Origin (PDO), granted by the regulatory body of the EU. The Consortium is entrusted by law to regulate the production and trade of Parmigiano Reggiano and employs monitoring agents with the same qualifications as public safety officers. The Consortium is a non-profit organization.[7]

Best Practices: How Parma Achieved Success

- Cooperation: Both Parmigiano and Parma ham producers have a long history of a strong cooperative society that led to the creation of a consortium of regulatory bodies representing all the producers and aimed at the protection and supervision of all manufacturing protocols.

- Product awareness campaign to the international community: To date, this consortium works to support national and international marketing campaigns and product awareness programs. Over 150 producers of Prosciutto di Parma and 400 of Parmigiano Reggiano benefit from joint promotional programs all year-round.

- Attention to food safety: They also work collectively to improve their lobbying power such as working with EU food safety regulators in food production area tours. Thanks to this Consortium the prosciutto and the Parmigiano Reggiano now provide hours ("open-days") and incoming guided tours to the factory. This offering attracts both scholars and independent travelers.

- Encouraging entrepreneurship: The combination of cooperation between food producers and entrepreneurship within the food manufacturing industry has firmly established Parma's food production culture and reputation. By way of example, various private and public entities have started investing in the district and branding Parma as the Italian food capital icon.

Barilla: A World Leader in Pasta Manufacturing[8]

Barilla, one of the world's leading pasta manufacturers with a history of over 125 years, has witnessed the momentum of Parma and perhaps that is what influenced the opening of the Academia Barilla, a place "dedicated to the arts, culture, and the diffusion of knowledge"[9] of Italian gastronomy. Since 2004, a 2500 square meter (26,910 sq ft) venue with 18 kitchens set the stage for professional cooking classes, custom designed courses, product tastings and pairings all founded on the active participation of its guests. An auditorium, baking and sensory analysis labs, training rooms and food library complete the offering with the aim of drawing closer to future bearers of regional cuisine and culture. Building on its success, since 2010 Barilla has introduced a series of culinary tours of their region and northern Italy.

All of Barilla's well-devised culinary resources may be for naught in light of their Chairman Guido Barilla's anti-gay comments that appeared in global media in September 2013, when Mr. Barilla said Barilla Pasta would never feature same-sex couples in its advertising and he then prompted gay people to eat another brand of pasta.[10] While Barilla may know how to make pasta and sauce, it seems that at least one of the company's owners has a thing to learn about grace and hospitality towards potential customers. Such a scandal will almost certainly have an adverse economic and visitor impact on Barilla's home town of Parma, Italy.[11]

New Product Development and Innovation

What is the reason why a food producer, no matter how difficult to reach, becomes a must-visit for food travelers? To answer these questions, we look no further than the *Zotter Schokoladen Manufactur*, located in Styria in the southeastern corner of Austria.

Zotter Factory

With a product range of some 300 different chocolate creations, Zotter is "by far the most innovative company in the chocolate industry"[12] and ranks eighth among the best chocolate manufacturers worldwide according to research conducted on over 271 companies from 38 countries. If consistent innovation and high quality are the two true values of this success story in the food industry the third — diversification — is what allowed Zotter's factory to become the most exceptional chocolate destination open to the public, second only to Willy Wonka.

Creating opportunity

As a former confectioner with premises in the center of Styria's state capital Graz, Josef Zotter was known from the beginning of his career for his extraordinary creativity. In the late 1990s, after some idle time — both personal and professional — and under the threat of bankruptcy, Josef decided to relocate his production in the former stable of his parents' farm in Riegersburg, where he founded the Zotter Chocolate Company. The decision to move away from the big city and step back in the countryside proves to be the most crucial decision of his business life.

Innovative packaging and a focus on sustainability

With designer A. Gratze, he transformed the packaging into artwork, designing product lines with different themes. He traveled to the cocoa growing countries of Venezuela, Peru, and Bolivia, and sought direct contact with the farmers. In Europe, Zotter is the only manufacturer producing organic and fair trade bean-to-bar chocolate with recyclable packaging. Every new product introduced by Master Zotter builds upon the foundation of his previous successes. By the year 2000, with increasing demand, Zotter expanded the manufacturing division and decided to open his factory operations to visitors, creating a virtual tourism revolution in the region.

Chocolate Theatre

First, in 2007, came the Chocolate Theatre, a brand-new edu-tainment concept that provides insights and tangible experiences in the context of a factory showroom to provide transparency, openness and closeness to the customer. Tourists are guided with audio devices in nine languages. They can take a direct look into the production, see how the work is carried out, visit creative tasting stations like the Drinking Chocolate, where the colored bars travel along a wire and can be picked and melted in warm milk to perfection. The walking theater involves all senses, with music playing from the tropical forests, aromas and textures of dozens of organic ingredients, all the while overlooking the production lines and tasting up to 100 different chocolate creations.

Just as important as the taste and quality of the chocolate, are the company's commitments to sustainability and fair trade, as the company's website proves:

> Zotter produces individual chocolate for individual people to savour each moment. The diversified Zotter assortment is a reference to the biological variety of chocolate. "The

assortment is nothing but a small extract of what the cocoa bean with its countless aromatic components renders possible in terms of biological diversity." ... The inventor Josef Zotter has constantly invested in his products. He has been involved in fair trade since 2004, in 2005 his company converted to organic and in 2006 he opened his own Chocolate Factory. For this reason he is the only manufacturer in Europe who produces chocolates bean-to-bar organically and through fair trade! Using hand-scooped chocolates, the creative chocolate maker from Riegersburg has managed to upset our familiar view of the world of chocolate. Bacon Bits in chocolate, Pumpkin Seeds with Marzipan and Apples and Carrots with Ginger surrounded by chocolate are just a few of the company's offerings. Since the opening of the Chocolate Factory Josef Zotter has ranked among the few quality chocolate makers around the world whose chocolate production processes are all located under the same roof. From the roasting of the cocoa beans, to the rolling up, to the finishing touches in the conching plant, everything is carried out with a high degree of sensitivity. In this way Zotter clearly positions himself against standardized mass production and the concentration of the chocolate market. In his Chocolate Factory there is no run-of-the-mill processing and the entire manufacturing process is transparent and tangible for visitors in the Chocolate Theatre.[13]

Edible Zoo

In 2011 Josef Zotter came up with his largest-scale idea yet, to offer visitors the Edible Zoo, a 27 hectare (67 acre) farm. The Edible Zoo invites adults and children alike to explore the organic farm, pet livestock animals while learning about animal breeds and fruit and vegetable varieties. The on-site restaurant Essbar also serves food directly from the farm.

In 2011 alone, 200,000 tickets were sold for the theater and zoo. Projections for 2012 were near 250,000 with over 15 full-time employees (out of 130 total) dedicated to welcome and reception services alone. According to the local area tourism office, in the last 10 years other artisan food producers (vinegar, pumpkin seed oil, bread, preserves) have opened their doors to the public in Riegersburg and surrounding areas. Old farms have been restored in order to offer tourists hospitality year-round. New tourism packages including the sensational medieval Riegersburg Castle have been welcome additions to the regional tourism offerings as well. Nearby businesses can also benefit from the overflow and success of one key business.

In less than five years from its public opening, Zotter's represents the second most popular destination in Styria, second only to the Graz historic center, a UNESCO heritage site since 1999. In just two decades of chocolate making, Zotter has achieved an exemplary business model where suppliers, employees, clients, and tourists all have their voice heard. The case of Josef Zotter is one great example of the evolution of food tourism entrepreneurship worldwide and how a focus on quality and sustainability are contributing factors to great success.

CONCLUSION

Food and drink manufacturers must face a number of issues to work successfully with tourists. Some manufacturers already work with tourists, and quite well, like the Ben & Jerry's factory in the US State of Vermont. Other manufacturers like Zotter have taken an older tradition like chocolate making and made it a public attraction. Still other manufacturers like Parma's cheesemakers count on the history and tradition of their product as the main visitor draw. Successful food manufacturers consider the overall visitor experience, from a positive welcome at a dedicated visitor's center (Zotter and Cadbury), to an informative tour of the facilities, to a final product tasting. Product sampling is a must. Whether an ice cream lover is pursuing her dream to visit the birthplace of Ben and Jerry's or an animal lover seeks out the Edible Zoo at

Zotter's Chocolate Factory, food and drink manufacturer factory tours are an important part of the visitor experience. Such visits increase brand awareness, increase customer loyalty & sales, and potentially increase exports when the visitors go home and ask for new product lines (or for the product itself if it is not carried by their local store). When food and drink factory tours are not offered, the local residents and tourism office alike should initiate a dialogue with the factory to see why tours are not offered and explore ways to offer tours to increase visitation to the area. Consumers fiercely support their favorite brands. Why deny them the opportunity to spend more money in your business or community?

DISCUSSION QUESTIONS

1. What could a food manufacturer do to meet the demands of its fans if laws prevent the manufacturing facility from hosting tours?
2. How can a small food or drink manufacturer create a compelling visitor experience, without large amounts of cash or staff, or a dramatic visitor center?
3. Do you agree that corporate responsibility, safety and quality are suitable pillars that all food and drink manufacturing companies must address in order to be successful tourist attractions? If not, why not?

ENDNOTES

[1] Carroll, C. "Defying a reputational crisis – Cadbury's Salmonella Scare: Why are Customers willing to Forgive and Forget?" *Corporate Reputation Review* 12 (2009) 64-82.

[2] Ibid.

[3] Ibid.

[4] "Visits at the Ham factories along the Roads of taste." Accessed May 22, 2013. http://turismo.comune.parma.it/tportalparma/application/tportal/engine/pubblica.jsp?db=tportalparma&id=VisualizzalAT_en&transformJava=true&NREC=PR00COM-AAAAAJZJ

[5] Accessed May 22, 2013. www.parmigiano-reggiano.it/american/made_1/default.aspx

[6] Ibid.

[7] Accessed May 22, 2013. www.parmigiano-reggiano.it/american/consortium_2/default.aspx

[8] www.academiabarilla.com

[9] www.academiabarilla.com/italian-food-academy/principles/default.aspx

[10] www.dailymail.co.uk/news/article-2433573/Barilla-pasta-faces-boycott-chairmans-homophobic-comments.html

[11] www.nydailynews.com/life-style/eats/barilla-fix-anti-gay-scandal-article-1.1506397

[12] Der Schokoladentester. Die besten Schokoladen und Pralinen der Welt. Was dahinter steckt und worauf wir gerne verzichten. Georg Bernardini

[13] www.zotter.at/en/about-zotter.html

Technology in Food & Drink Tourism

Jenn Bussell, Paulina Salach, & Erik Wolf

This chapter discusses the types of technologies used in, or available to, today's food tourism industry. The chapter addresses website design, applications for smartphones and tablets, online reservations systems, online deal tools, loyalty programs and social communities.

INTRODUCTION

Technology can be an enabler if used properly, allowing your business to grow rapidly, reduce operating costs, and manage a number of functions that were previously done manually. If misused, technology can be a black hole for time and distract a business owner from the task at hand, namely generating profit and customer satisfaction. Often a business owner believes they need a solution such as accounting. They will search for an online solution, make a decision and things should continue seamlessly. That is not always the case, however. A strategy is needed for which technology tools will be used and how they will interact with each other, if at all. Technology can also be used to engage customers and prospects, distribute special offers and measure customer satisfaction. Again, a plan is needed to illuminate how information from these services feeds back into the overall business plan.

In the online accounting software scenario, the solution is not as simple as choosing a platform such as FreshBooks.com or Xero.com. The astute business owner needs to probe deeper. Do these accounting platforms synchronize with credit card payments and online banking? If so, is the synchronization real-time or is it manual? Do you have to export data and then reimport it into the accounting system, or can this all be done automatically? Will the solution need to tie into sales from your website? How will it handle offline sales by check or cash? What kinds of reports will it provide you? Can you share access to the accounting solution with your accountant or do you need to purchase an additional license? A sound technology strategy is crucial to your peace of mind as a business owner, and to saving you time, money and effort.

Websites

Today a company's website is like a doorway to the world, much like a brochure used to be used many decades ago. Brochures are still used today, but have nowhere near the breadth of information or flexibility that a website can offer. Before a company embarks upon the sometimes arduous task of building its own website, it needs to decide what kind of website it needs. The type of website could be informational, advertorial, transactional, purely mobile, or a combination of all these. Many quality resources are available online that can teach a business owner how to create mobile, e-commerce, or advertising related websites. This article will cover the most popular type of website, namely the informational one.

The use, capabilities, and content of websites today is vastly superior to, and expanded from, what was seen just 10 years ago. This change was largely driven by tremendous advances in technology. Now small business owners can do a lot more than they ever could, and at a fraction of the development cost of just a few years ago.

One of the most flexible website platforms available today is WordPress. WordPress started as a blogging platform and quickly grew to accommodate ever increasing needs from small business owners and individual writers. Over time, WordPress made it quite easy to use something called a plug-in to perform tasks like member registration, anti-spam filtering, social media sharing, and even e-commerce. WordPress grew so fast in popularity for two main reasons: cost and ease of use.

As for cost, the website owner simply needed to purchase a theme, usually less than US $50, apply the theme to the basic WordPress software, and the design work was done. Of course the small business owner can do a lot more with WordPress and plugins, but that was the only financial expenditure required, apart from hosting the website itself.

As for ease of use, to get the most out of WordPress, it helps to have some minor HTML skills, but even those are not required to maintain a WordPress website. All a user needs to do is click "edit page," change the text they want and then click save. It is literally that simple. Inserting photos and other graphics in the website is a little more complicated but it is years ahead in ease and simplicity than any other platform on the market today. All-in-one website platform companies such as Wix, Weebly, and Basekit have a long way to go before they begin to approach the flexibility, simplicity and ease of use that WordPress currently offers.

WordPress offers small business owners a way to have a professional online presence without any of the headaches and very little of the cost of other solutions. Small business owners with more budget can still higher a web designer, but we recommend staying with the WordPress platform for most small business needs. WordPress allows for e-commerce functionality so merchandise can be sold. Other third-party plug-ins can easily integrate into and extend the WordPress platform. For example one can use ZenDesk for customer service and use a widget on the website that plugs right into WordPress itself.

Before launching a website, a business owner needs to plan out what elements will go where on the website. Search for "wireframe" online to find a tool that will help you do just this. One popular tool from Balsamiq.com allows the designer, or business owner, to literally put together how the website will look before it even goes live. One does not enter content into a wireframe. Instead, you layout placeholders for text, videos, pictures, logos, navigation buttons and so on. Show your mockups to friends and colleagues to get their input. Once you are happy with the final design, you can implement it using one of the templates you choose. Depending on the template you choose, you may need a web designer to assist with the template layout.

Smartphones, Tablets & Application

The smartphones of today are truly small computers that we can take with us everywhere. As technologies improve, smartphones get even smarter. As of this writing, a new technology called near field communication or NFC, promises to revolutionize the sharing of information and the payment of small point-of-purchase transactions. Still, one of the most basic functions that mobile phones provide, namely SMS or short messaging service, is still one of the most widely used tools worldwide, with 6 billion messages being sent per day in the US and 8.6 trillion text messages sent annually world-wide.[1]

One of the most useful features that smartphones offer is the ability to use applications (apps). For food travelers, apps can perform a variety of tasks like currency conversion, metric to imperial measurement conversion, weather forecasting, language translation, off-line PDF reading and more. Apps are also being used by the food and travel industries to bring a wealth of new information to current and potential customers. For example, in the food industry, Yelp and UrbanSpoon provide apps for users to check popular opinions from other diners about restaurants. In the travel industry, apps are commonly used either for reservations such as Kayak.com or TripIt.com, or with destination information. Apps can also combine food with travel, as is the case with the Taste of Nova Scotia app. The beauty of this quickly evolving technology, is that not only can the user access useful information about the food, drink, and culinary culture of a destination, now a user can get maps and directions in real time to add real value to the act of travel itself. Travelers are able to get more done in less time, and at a lower cost, than ever before. As time goes on, mobile bandwidth will increase, this speed and flexibilities of mobile phones will increase, and the sophistication of apps will also increase. In the near future we could have high definition live video, real-time reservation booking of complex travel itineraries, and real-time translation of sound and video files, from foreign language sources.

Native apps utilize all the functionalities and capacities of the smartphone device (iPhone-iPad-Android), and they offer customers a different brand experience. However they can be expensive to develop and must be developed for specific devices and launched via the Apple Store or Google Play store, two ecosystems where the willingness to pay is very low, especially on Google Play, where free apps are the norm.

The alternative to developing a native app is to build a mobile web app. Mobile Web Apps offer a low-cost app developed in HTML 5, readable by Android, iOS, and other smartphones and tablets. Using a "responsive" website design, which resizes content to fit the available screen (i.e. you no longer need to develop a mobile version of your website), is the first step towards developing a suitable mobile web app. As for strategy, consider using a mobile web app to acquire new customers and develop a native app to keep those customers. For most small business owners, a mobile web app is probably the easiest and most cost effective way to have an app presence.

Apps are certainly not required for small businesses, but they have found a place in the hearts of consumers and have become ubiquitous. In other words, apps are not going away any time soon. It may not make sense for a small business owner to have an app for their restaurant, or inn or cooking school, but small business owners should work with content aggregators, travel reservation websites, and other information publishers, to ensure that their businesses are adequately represented on these platforms and that their businesses stay top of mind with travelers. The price of remaining silent in the world of apps could mean the difference between business survival and closure.

Loyalty Programs

Another benefit that smartphones have brought to consumers, as well as small business owners, is the ability to manage a complete electronic customer loyalty program. Gone are the days of overly complex databases, an overzealous salesperson spying a huge potential commission, and a 6 to 7 figure price tag for software that required a team of people to design and manage, and which was likely outdated before it was even deployed, due to its complexity. Today's electronic loyalty programs are so simple, that one person alone could manage it. Good examples of loyalty programs that work well for food and drink businesses are Perka (getperka.com) and Perx (getperx.com). Perka tailors customer loyalty programs to encourage repeat visits by customers and improve sales. Merchants can reward customers for purchases of one or several products or services at once. Perka has an app for both the iPhone and Android phones, which means that it has the potential to penetrate the majority of the smart phone owner market. The beauty of these cards is that the customer no longer needs to keep a wallet full of cards that can get lost, misplaced, stolen or destroyed. The assumption is that customers carry their mobile phones with them everywhere and that they will have their mobile phone with them when they are in the business that accepts the electronic loyalty card.

Other Considerations

According to Rafat Ali, the founder of Skift, a travel intelligence startup, "food tourism has the potential to be the next big growth market as the hunger for more authentic and local experiences among tourists rise."[2] Over the past few years, an increased number of tourists have begun choosing their travel destination based on the gastronomic offerings of the region. This newfound love for gastronomy and its importance for tourists has put the food tourism industry at the forefront. Talib Rafali, the UNWTO (United Nations World Tourism Organization) Secretary General, states that "tourists are attracted to local produce and many destinations are centering their product development and marketing accordingly. This gives destinations a unique way to market themselves and appeal to those travelers that seek to explore the destination through its flavors."[3]

The leading role of gastronomy in the choice of destination by tourists has resulted in the growth of gastronomic offerings based on high-quality local products and the creation of a unique market for food tourism.[4] More and more food tours, cooking classes, food festivals and events, farmers' markets, foodie trips, and all sorts of boutique businesses are springing up worldwide, seeking to take advantage of this new foodie market.

It is essential, however, for businesses in the food tourism industry, to use new and innovative ways to promote themselves, differentiate their company from competitors and brand their images. To promote your business, it used to be simple. Hire a publicity firm, give them freedom to craft savvy and creative public relations campaigns and hope for positive feedback from pitches to journalists. To quantify campaign results, publicists use the AVE (advertising value equivalent) principle, which assumes that editorial coverage was at least 2.5 times more valuable than paid advertising. The seemingly higher value of the press hit makes the publicist look good, although there is not a straightforward measurement between public relations and advertisement. For years, credibility of this practice has been widely debated among industry professionals and the practice is generally viewed today as inaccurate and invalid.

Community Platforms

Even into the mid-2000s, advertising money was spent to attain media coverage primarily in print, television and radio. Today, promoting your brand and reaching an audience that can be converted into paying customers requires the use of several technology platforms that are within a reach of a button. Whether you decide to hire a social media manager or decide to do it yourself, you have to choose wisely from all the platforms available or you will fall far behind your competitors. Community websites including Facebook, Trip Advisor, Yelp, Foursquare, LinkedIn, Pinterest and Google+ are great tools that are important for brand promotion. Most of them are relatively easy to use once you understand them.

Facebook is undeniably the most popular and largest community platform with about 1 billion users. In 2012, Facebook launched Facebook pages for business, a powerful tool that when used correctly, can produce significant return on investment. The Facebook business page allows you to tell the audience exactly what your brand does and actively interact in the form of comments, photos and videos. Your page should be visually appealing, i.e. have great photography on the page and in your cover photo, include links to your website or booking page and convey a clear message of what your business does. For example, if you own a food tour company, you might want your landing page to have high quality images of items your guests will sample on the tour. You want people wishing they were eating that dish right now. Your cover photo is also very important. It is the first thing people see when they go to your page so it needs to be first class. Not only must it look good, it has to explain what you do.

Engagement with users on a regular basis is critical on all social media sites. Companies should be aware of their clients' perceptions, complaints and criticisms, and consistently monitor responses to their posts. The main rule, according to the Hotel Management Group Blog, is to keep content new, interesting, and engaging to encourage interactions and discussions with users. Post relevant content about your company but also about the destination. The tour company should post information about events happening in the city and tips for travelers. Become a go-to guide for travelers; this will increase your readership. You want people to trust you and make them feel like they need to book your tour while on vacation or they would be missing out.

Running offers and promotions on your page will also generate buzz. Who does not like free stuff or a good deal? It builds brand loyalty and trust among present and future clients. For example, Argentina Wine Tours urged fans to share their flyer and by doing so, customers participated in a chance to win a free wine tasting at a bodega. It shows a simple and quick call to action.

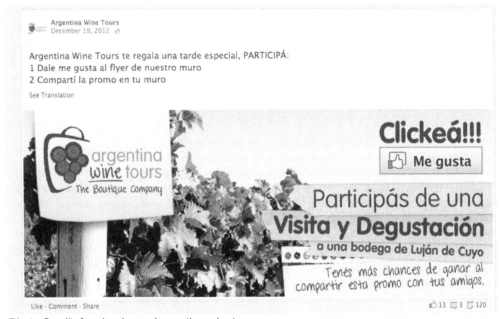

Photo Credit: facebook.com/argentina.winetours

If you want to promote your business more, you can take advantage of ads on Facebook. According to Tom Demers, co-founder and managing partner at Measured SEM, a search engine marketing firm, "one of the strongest uses for Facebook ads is to get people in a very specific demographic to like your Facebook page so that you can then message to them over time."[5] For example, if you offer cooking classes in a villa in Tuscany, you can target your ads to people that enjoy cooking, love Italy and like to travel. You can also target specific countries, cities and age groups.

Another great Facebook feature is the use of insights to measure how effectively you are engaging with your fans through posts and ads. After publishing a post, you can see how well it is doing. If you created a successful post, you can turn it into a sponsored story or an ad. Advertising on Facebook is relatively inexpensive compared to traditional means of advertising and gives you a great deal of control. Perhaps the best thing is that it can only cost as little as US$5 per day since you set your daily spending limit.

Another key platform for business promotion is TripAdvisor. According to its website, TripAdvisor is the world's largest travel website, offering trusted advice from real travelers. With over 60 million unique monthly visitors, as published in a study by Media Metrix in July 2012, TripAdvisor has tremendous global reach. Today many travelers rely on TripAdvisor as their sole resource to book their entire trip. On TripAdvisor, you can book a hotel, a restaurant and even a tour. In its forums, you can learn about events. With everyone so busy nowadays, TripAdvisor allows for a quick and easy booking process. It has become a trusted source among users, as people tend to believe their peers more than a traditional ad paid for by the advertiser.

Setting up a business on TripAdvisor is free and the management of your listing is easy. You must create a description of your business and as with Facebook, upload high quality, appealing images. Your guests will be able to upload images later on but you maintain control, especially over your primary photo.

Engagement with your users is essential and should be done right away. Do not wait too long to respond to a review. Set up an email alert to advise you once someone has written. Do not use a template response; tailor your response to each customer. People look at these things and want to see that you are involved with your customers on a regular basis. Daniel Edward Craig, social media and marketing blogger for the travel industry, says that responding to reviews shows that you care about your customers and it allows you to reinforce the positive aspects of your business and change opinions of the negative reviews. He also suggests using a friendly and conversational tone. Eventually your business will get a bad review. You cannot please everyone and it is the nature of the game. When responding to negative reviews, respond promptly, be professional, be courteous and lastly, do apologize.

According to a tutorial published in 2011, the Australian Tourism Data Warehouse summed up TripAdvisor when they wrote, "having a business listed on the travel site, which generates regular positive reviews, should be a cost effective, efficient and credible way to reach potential customers."

Another user-generated content site that has become popular for business promotion is Yelp, which is a much-improved, digital yellow pages. Yelp allows businesses to input their information such as hours of operation, telephone number, neighborhood, and details like the nearest public transit stations and whether or not credit cards are accepted.

Yelp, as Foursquare (discussed later), allows the business owner to create special check-in offers for their customers. When a customer checks into the restaurant through the application on their smart phone or tablet, they can redeem an offer that was created by the establishment. For example, restaurants can offer a happy hour special or a 15% discount to be redeemable on location after check-in. Every time the business creates a check-in offer or other deal, Yelp puts it into their announcements directory for that city. Users can also search the Yelp app by deals, thus increasing exposure for your business. The bottom line, offers and deals promote brand loyalty, convert into repeat checks-ins and increase your presence on the web and among customers.

Businesses that greatly benefit from Yelp are restaurants. Ippudo in New York City does a good job displaying all of its pertinent information (see below). It is important for your information to be complete, correct and that you keep it current. A neglected or incomplete profile will cause the customer to leave your page and go to the competition. Users write reviews and the management has the ability to respond, and as previously mentioned, this provides an essential way to connect with customers. With close to 5,000 Yelp reviews, total-check-ins, and bookmarks by users, Ippudo made Yelp's Top 10 Restaurants of 2011 list.

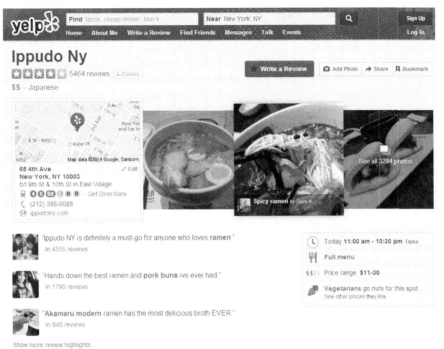

Photo Credit: Yelp.com

Foursquare, the check-in king, is the world's leading location-based social network. For a business, it can translate into a large customer base that is built and maintained through announcing deals, offering coupons and giving tips. The site offers free exposure through check-ins. When someone checks-in to your business, the check-in appears on that person's Foursquare account. It can also be shared on that person's Facebook and Twitter account, potentially reaching hundreds and thousands of their friends or followers. According to Felicia Baratz-Sabaneg of getbusymedia.com, "the check-in acts as a personal endorsement, and the very best type of business is that which is generated by word of mouth."[6]

Foursquare is free and has great potential so use it to your advantage. Like Yelp, Foursquare is also a helpful tool for restaurants. Incentivize people to check-in to your business by offering individual or group deals. For example, give away a free dessert to a table with 4 or more check-ins. Similar to Facebook, Foursquare also gives you access to back-end analytics. Find out who your recurring customers are and reward them. They will thank you via Foursquare, sharing that gratitude on the web.

Many people already have a profile on LinkedIn, the world's largest professional network. The site has proved to be instrumental in building valuable business connections. It allows its users to create interactive resumes and connect to business professionals within your industry. In addition to a personal profile, LinkedIn users can also create a business page to promote their company and network with employees and companies all over the world. Joining LinkedIn groups of interest can be beneficial to connecting with people in your industry, sharing insights and establishing credibility. You can learn a lot about what your peers are their doing and gain as well as offer valuable tips.

A relatively new entrant in the industry is Pinterest. This visual medium has taken the world by storm and become one of the most addictive platforms. On Pinterest, users create virtual boards by topic where they pin their own images or videos and media shared from other websites. With over 20,000 followers and 38 different boards, companies like Bon Appétit have taken advantage of this powerful platform to connect with new and existing customers displaying boards ranging from restaurant design, contests, travel and one dedicated to bloggers. Since pins are meant to be linked, when someone repins a pin from one of your boards, it carries with it the link to your website or the original destination. Another user that wants to learn more can simply click on the link and be brought to your site.

Another great benefit of Pinterest is that it transcends the language barrier. Jill Lloyd, senior PR & social media manager at Expedia says, "one of the advantages of Pinterest compared to other social platforms is that language is not essential, which offers a wider reach." Lloyd adds, "We know that in certain cultures images are more powerful than text. While Germans tend to make choices based on fact, the French are more likely to be swayed by a stunning image."[7]

Last but not least among the top community platforms is Google+. Google+ is important primarily because it is owned by Google, still one of the most popular search engines in the world. The main reason to be on Google+ is SEO (search engine optimization). Sites on Google+ tend to be indexed quicker and show up higher on rankings in search results. The core of Google+ is its effective and frequent use of keywords. If you want your site to come up on Google, use relevant keywords in your profile and in all your posts.

In addition to community websites, tactical tools like Twitter, email and Flickr should be used in promoting your business. Twitter allows you to share information about your business in real-time. John Markus, author of an article on how to use Twitter to promote a food truck business, suggests including photos and videos in addition to information into your tweets to keep your followers engaged and interested. He also suggests joining discussions on trending topics.

A great way to maximize exposure on Twitter is mastering the art of the hashtag (#), a number sign (pound sign in the UK) preceding a word or topic. Hashtags, according to Josh Catone of openforum.com are used to 'catalog and connect tweets about a specific topic.'[8] You can use hashtags that have already been created, or come up with a unique one. When creating new hashtag however, make it short and sweet. Since you only have 140 characters to create a tweet, save that space for crucial information you want to convey. For example, create a new hashtag related to a food event you will be hosting in your city. This helps you keep track of the discussions and gives you a great outlet to get the word out. Link your Twitter page to your website and Facebook page, and other social media you are using. This facilitates the customer in navigating through all your information in a timely fashion. The easier you make it for people, the more willing they will be to spend time learning about what you offer.

Do not ignore more traditional tools like email marketing. The main goal of email marketing is reminding customers about your business and connecting with them on a regular basis. Within seconds, you could reach your loyal customers and continue building a trust-worthy relationship with them. None of this will work however, if you do not have a solid database of clientele. You do not want to waste your time, sending emails to people who just do not care. Ven Tesh of blasho.com, advises against buying lists and advocates gathering natural and organic email lists which will be more effective in the long run. To attain these unique lists, ask people to sign up on your website and entice them by creating contests. Give away a free cheese tasting or offer a discount. A variety of email marketing services are available, although MailChimp.com is one of the most popular such services.[9]

Flickr, a photo-sharing site owned by Yahoo, allows you to tell a story through photos and join groups of interest to you. It can also be a great promotional tool. Even though Flickr prohibits advertising, it does not mean you cannot draw people to your product or service through indirect marketing. However, you do have to understand how it works or you will just be wasting your time. Digital marketing and social media consultant, Jeff Bullas, gives a great tip on how to draw people from third party sites to your Flickr account. He suggests embedding links on your blog and sharing it on Twitter, Facebook and Pinterest.

Another tip for effective Flickr use is proper labeling of photos, this will allow people to find you or stumble upon you in a search. When tagging a photo, be specific and use several descriptive words. Always tag your website URL and business name.

Blogging is the last technology platform for promotion in the food tourism industry. There are a lot of bloggers nowadays, but why? Blogging has become a part of daily life for online users, whether reading blogs or contributing to them. Blogs are free and can be highly personalized. Search engines index blogs and frequently used keywords can increase your exposure and result in higher ranking. If you want to start a blog, integrate it into your website if possible. You can also use a blogging platform like WordPress or Tumblr but remember to always include links to any other website you own on your blog. Share your blog posts on other social media website for additional exposure.

No matter which technology platform you decide to use, and you should use several, make sure you are an active member. Create fresh, intriguing content and update frequently. Engage your readers by creating contests and offering freebies or a modest discount. Link all your sites and make them work in synergy.

Online Booking Systems

"The trigger for food tourism expansion in other countries is technology and providing access to – and the ability to purchase tickets for – food and drink classes, events, and tours," Steve Butcher, CEO, Brown Paper Tickets. "Central America...South America...Africa...everywhere has something [special] to offer. With better communication through technology people can now shop and plan food excursions before they even leave on their trip. Making it simple to find a French champagne tour or a pizza making class in Naples will definitely grow the food industries that celebrate every country's local cuisine and culture."

Advances in technology are arguably the most potent driver of change within the global travel industry, and food travel is no exception. In today's food travel and tourism sector, success is determined not only by delivering unique and memorable experiences coupled with consistently high levels of service. It is driven by the ability to create and distribute compelling, accessible, and instantly bookable offers online.

For gastronomic destinations and food tourism businesses worldwide, this means investing in online booking technology to reach your target guest with customized, relevant, and timely information *plus* the ability to convert them from 'prospective' to 'booked' guest at that moment.

Whether you own a restaurant that aims to take online reservations, a winery expanding into farm-to-table dinner events, or a local food tour operator looking to capture a new audience, selecting the right system for managing reservations, ticketing & booking online may seem like a daunting task especially if technology is not your primary area of expertise.

The good news is that no matter your business type, size, or location there is a web-based solution to meet your specific booking management needs, which is both cost-effective and integrates relatively seamlessly with your digital ecosystem (viz. your company's website, email marketing system, mobile platform, and social media presence). Which one is right for you?

Getting to Know the Online Booking Space

Before you purchase a solution, you need to know what options are available and learn commonly used terminology. There are three main types of online booking systems geared toward food tourism businesses, and it is important to note that these systems are not the same as those used by airlines or hotels.

1. Online Reservation System – Used primarily by restaurants, these booking systems offer real-time online seating reservations for diners plus reservation and guest management solutions for restaurants. The historical leader in this space has been OpenTable, whose network delivers the convenience of online restaurant reservations to diners and the operational benefits of a computerized reservation book to restaurants. OpenTable has more than 27,000 restaurant customers, and, since its inception in 1998, has seated more than 400 million diners around the world.[10] The landscape is changing with new market entrants seeking to break up OpenTable's virtual monopoly. Urbanspoon, a leading provider of time-critical dining data, saw an opportunity to leverage its broad reach and highly regarded online ratings and review platform with the launch of Rezbook in 2010.

2. Online Ticketing System – Online ticketing systems like Brown Paper Tickets and EventBrite are web-based solutions that allow event organizers around the world to plan, sell and promote events of any size and do so through API integration with the event website, email manager, and social and mobile media tools. Online ticketing system providers typically charge nominal transaction fees to the ticket buyer, rendering the service 'free' to event producers. This category of on-demand ticketing system providers evolved out of a void in the marketplace for streamlined, cost-effective yet feature-rich solutions designed to meet the needs of small businesses and independent culinary event producers. As described by Steve Butcher of Brown Paper Tickets, a "global fair trade ticketing company," mainstream ticketing service providers like TicketMaster cater to large venues and event producers resulting on low service levels, high costs, and no democracy of services to the small or independent business with a need to sell tickets online.

3. Online Booking Management System – For the food tourism business owner who requires a more robust booking management solution but does not have hands-on technical expertise or deep pockets to build custom tools, there are comprehensive booking management solutions like Zerve. Unlike most online reservation and ticketing systems, online booking management systems tend to be more comprehensive in their technologies, providing template-based platforms for food tour and culinary activity businesses to build, publish, and manage dedicated consumer webpages inclusive of calendar widgets, real-time ticketing, embedded customer reviews, and social media sharing features. In addition these solutions offer real-time development, data management, and analytics dashboards plus value-added services such as SEO optimization and marketing support to build awareness, generate demand, and drive conversions for clients.

Robust technology comes at a price. Solution providers like Zerve charge a per transaction processing fee in addition to the transaction fee consumers pay at the time of booking.

Assessing Your Needs

You may have already scoped your technology needs when completing your business plan and budget. If not, this is the time to think about how you want your prospective guests to book with you and how much you want to invest in this system. It may seem like a daunting task, but it is really quite manageable if you allocate a few hours to think through the answers to a number of key questions prior to making a decision.

1. Who are your target guests?

   a. Are they local or regional residents? Global travelers? Both?
   b. Will you need to provide booking information, forms, and confirmation pages in multiple languages?
   c. Do they use mobile devices to manage their travel bookings?

2. What is the online booking experience you aim to provide?

   a. Are guests simply reserving a seat or space for an activity, or will you require full payment at the time of booking?
   b. If you require advance payment, can guests pay in one or multiple currencies?
   c. Will guests be able to purchase gift certificates via your online booking system?
   d. Will you publish discount codes or coupons (digital or printed) that guests can redeem online when booking?
   e. Do you prefer all booking-related transactions take place on your website, or are you fine with redirecting guests to a third party website?
   f. What is your cancelation policy? How will you refund advance payments?

3. How will an online booking solution integrate with your technology and customer service/support infrastructures?

   a. Do you have an existing in-house reservation system that needs to integrate with a web-based booking system?
   b. Do you prefer to manage all transactions solely online including customer support (e.g. live chat, email), or do you want to offer offline support as well (e.g. telephone)?
   c. Will customer support be English-language only, or multiple languages?
   d. Will you need customer support for online bookings to be offered 24/7? Do you have an in-house customer support team, or would you like to outsource this service?
   e. Will you need access to real-time reporting and analytics?

4. How will you integrate a booking system into your marketing, CRM, and PR efforts?

   a. Would you like your booking management system provider to offer enhanced visibility of your business through value-added marketing support?
   b. Do you want your guests to be able to review and rate their experience within your booking system, or on third party review sites with links back to your site?
   c. Do you need social media or email functionality within your online booking system to enable guests to 'share' and/or 'invite others' after they complete a transaction?
   d. Is instant notification of booking, registration, modification and deletion via email or SMS a requirement?

5. What is the maximum you would spend on your booking system?

Making an Informed Decision

Once you have done a thorough audit of all the features and functionality that you require from an online booking system, you can now start to explore what options may be best for our business. You will want to research which solutions are available in your region as not all solutions currently offer global capabilities or support. Plan to interview these potential partners and see demos of their products. As the market for food tourism and event management-based software-as-a-service (SaaS) and web application providers continues to expand then contract, it is important to keep updated with new changes in this area. The payoff for consistent due diligence is the opportunity for partnership with a technology vendor that could offer you significant front-end and back-end enhancements coupled with the potential for increased cost savings. The 'best' online booking system is defined by a) its ease of use for you *and* your guests, b) how innovative the technology is compared to the competition, and c) how well it aligns with the needs of your business today and tomorrow.

"The [food tourism] market is so broad - and the barrier to entry is fairly small - that over the next few years we will see a significant market expansion then a slight collapse, with those businesses who've mastered demand generation + conversion + delivery of great experiences rising to the top," John Dandeneau, Director of Sales, Zerve, Inc.

CONCLUSION

Technology is a moving target. As soon as you have invested in one solution, a better one seems to come along. To prevent remorse over having chosen the wrong solution, do your due diligence in advance. Ask current customers (ones who you find yourself and who are not referred by the company if possible). Search for trustworthy journalist reviews. Search for products in development. Maybe a better solution for your needs is about to launch. Most importantly, stay true to your business strategy or roadmap. Use technology as an enabler. Avoid getting caught up in technical terms and processes or you run the risk of losing focus. Stay focused on the end goals, namely profit and customer satisfaction, and you will do fine.

DISCUSSION QUESTIONS

1. How will technology tools change food tourism development and marketing in the next 10 years? In the next 50 years? Think ahead.
2. After Facebook, what do you think the next "big thing" will be for food or travel marketing, and why?
3. Identify three issues in need of improvement with current online food or travel information resource websites. What would you recommend such websites need to improve?

ENDNOTES

----

[1] "Texting Turns 20", last modified Dec. 3, 2012. www.cnn.com/2012/12/03/tech/mobile/sms-text-message-20
[2] "Gastronomy and the Hunt for Authentic Food Experiences", Last modified Sept. 16, 2012. http://skift.com/2012/09/16/the-future-of-food-tourism/
[3] Global Report on Food Tourism, World Tourism Organization, 2012 Introduction
[4] Ibid, p. 10
[5] "Should you small business advertise on Facebook?", Last modified Jun. 29, 2012. www.businessnewsdaily.com/2771-facebook-ads-effectiveness.html
[6] "How can Foursquare help my Business?", Last modified May 8, 2012. www.getbusymedia.com/how-can-foursquare-help-my-business/
[7] "Making Pinterest Work for Your Travel Brand" Last modified Jun. 6, 2012. www.eyefortravel.com/social-media-and-marketing/making-pinterest-work-your-travel-brand
[8] "How to Use Twitter Hashtags for Business", Last modified Aug. 25, 2009. www.openforum.com/idea-hub/topics/technology/article/how-to-use-twitter-hashtags-for-business-1
[9] Two other popular email marketing services include ConstantContact.com and VerticalResponse.com
[10] OpenTable. www.opentable.com/info/aboutus.aspx

Food & Drink in Meetings & Conventions

Dawn Donahue, Wendy Lange-Faria, & Natalie Lowe

In the case of meetings and conventions, food is typically more of an added value than it is the motivation for travel. With an unsteady global meetings and conventions market, in part due to the ease of communication brought about by technology combined with a distressed global economic climate, food can play a role in increasing loyalty among consumers.[1] Food offers a great point of differentiation for meeting and convention planners to offer their clients as there is a growing interest among individuals for not only locally sourced food, but also for food that is nutritious and which offers a compelling story. While food may not drive attendees to meetings and conventions, it may well support positive word of mouth marketing for the venue and the destination and even create a more positive overall outcome for the meeting/convention organizer. That means repeat business. This chapter discusses current trends in foodservice for meetings and pioneering ideas and best practices which are being used by leaders in large scale food service operations.

INTRODUCTION

When planning a large group event, menu planning can be one of the most rewarding parts of the job, as meals are generally happy, celebratory events. Food is of secondary importance to people who travel for meetings or conventions. They do not travel specifically to sample new foods, but they have traveled and therefore food takes on an important, albeit peripheral role in the success of a meeting/convention. That being said, meetings are absolutely influenced by the food that is served. When the food is of poor quality or is lacking in appeal or quantity, it will be detrimental to the physical comfort of attendees, which cannot bode well for the productivity goals of the meeting. This means food served for large functions must meet a common minimum standard. It must be the right temperature, served in a timely fashion and at the very least, not be offensive in taste. At best, it provides a positive experience for the attendees, delivering feelings of content which will presumably generate positive remarks about the venue and even the meeting/convention itself. That is to say, those who are feeling good about a positive food experience are more likely to feel more positive about the other encounters they have in the same context.

Today's business reality has increased customer expectations. Five years ago, whatever made a meeting venue a leader in its competitive market has now become an expected norm. Excellence in physical comfort and quality food service has become the price of admission in a crowded, increasingly competitive meeting market in which people now have options to work together outside the traditional conference. While it would be hard to prove that a meeting was booked just because the food was good, in recent years we have seen a rise in interest in food from the population in general, whether it be gourmet, ethnic or healthy food. People attending events have started to question traditional banquet food and request more and different options. Proof of this interest is seen by the proliferation of food programs implemented at conference centers and hotels across the world aimed at creating a point of differentiation for the consumer (i.e. organic, local and quality programs in convention centers).

From a historical perspective, dishes would have been chosen for the banquet menu based on the ability to withstand temperature fluctuations without drying out (i.e. if a delay occurs and it needs to be reheated or kept warm), retain heat or cold during the service to the table, and satisfy both the budget and the palate of the client — we will look at the modern banquet offerings and where the trends point to for future years.

In this chapter we will refer to this market as MCIT, which stands for Meetings, Conventions and Incentive Travel, and covers all group business travel but excludes the individual business traveler and traditional road warrior. Generally speaking, "meetings" are smaller in scale and held in hotels while "conventions" are larger and held in convention centers, often where thousands gather. Incentive travel places the highest importance on food and will feature unique venues and be more focused on high end and luxury food experiences. Most of the MCIT market volume is in meetings and conventions, so we will concentrate on these. Incentive travel may give us our greatest future indicators though, as technology and skills grow, convention centers can serve foods that were once the strict purview of small exclusive groups.

The sales process for MCIT is indirect, i.e. the end user or attendee is not typically involved. A third party, such as a meeting planner, meeting manager or conference manager, will deal with the hotel and convention center to make purchases and convey decisions. The skill and training the planner has varies greatly and hotels and convention centers often must understand both the planner and the end user in order to have the best end result.

Attendees range from employees who are directed to attend a company event (to achieve a business objective), to individuals who attend either for their company or for their own personal/professional development.

Assumptions for the MCIT Market

For the purpose of discussion in this chapter, we will make the following assumptions:

1) Creating and consuming local menus is important for both the venue and attendee from an ecological perspective, by reducing the energy footprint of the meeting and an economic perspective as providing good value for the money spent.

2) Some companies have a mandate to support local food initiatives as a way to support locally-based businesses and thus increase economic benefit in the local region.

3) Food well-matched to the experience can provide a richer and better travel experience. While traditionally this was in a cultural sense, mostly with local, traditional food, this interpretation can include what started as spa menus and which has morphed into foods suited for energy, alertness and productivity for business meetings.

4) The first word in business travel is still business. We know travel is an expense approved by companies in order to obtain the benefit it can bring to the business. When we add an expense to the meeting, there needs to be a return on that investment.

Overview of Venues and Suppliers

Due to the indirect nature of the MCIT booking process, where the end user is not making the decision to buy nor using the services for many months, even years after the buying decision, it is not always easy to identify the reasons groups book. Consumer tastes and cultural trends can change in the lag time between booking and the arrival of the group. The logical place to start might be to follow the money. If venues and suppliers have vast sums of resources tied up into acquiring MCIT bookings, then successful businesses will not waste those resources on unneeded or unwanted food programs.

Meetings today can and do feature some great food. Food critics may not start reviewing conference centers any time soon, but high quality, locally sourced menus do exist at convention centers and hotels. This section will primarily focus on what innovation meeting venues, suppliers and planners are involved in to better a meeting's food experience and what we can learn from them.

Working With an Organizing Principle

Necessity is the mother of invention and most great ideas come from one simple idea. With changes in the needs and expectations of consumers, as one might expect, hotel chains are expanding their offerings to meeting clients, such as the nut and spice snacks featured at Ritz Carlton Hotels; the Super Foods program at Westin; or Color Your Plate at Sheraton. Fairmont and other hotel chains have included rooftop or side gardens, apiaries and locally sourced items. A recent initiative, developed in partnership between the Culinary Institute of America and the Harvard School of Public Health, Department of Nutrition, illustrates the growing demand for healthy food by the public and *how* restaurants and convention centers are rising to the challenge.[2] What, if any, are the main reasons such programs are started?

Ecological stewardship seems to push some of the programs. Consider the eco-friendly beehives at 21 Fairmont hotels around the world or their herb and vegetable gardens.[3] Finding their gardens were not pollinated effectively due to the honey bees being affected by Colony Collapse Disorder, the Fairmont Royal York worked within its environmental program and started the first hotel rooftop apiary in the world.[4]

Others programs, such as locally sourced foods through the Sysco "Local Food Program" were started as a way to cut down on expensive transportation of fruits and vegetables negatively affecting the bottom line of many Sysco customers.[5] According to Greg Hall, manager of the Local Food Program at the Ontario (Canada) division of Sysco, customers demanded more local products and lower costs. He was able to source from local farmers who were unable to sell all of their products through traditional channels.[6] Using Sysco's vast network and warehousing, they created a win-win solution.

Still, some initiatives were started as a point of differentiation for their clients. The Super Food and Color Your Plate options offered at the above hotels, for example, address the need for businesses to address the health and welfare of their traveling employees as well as increase productivity at expensive, time consuming meetings.[7] What were once looked upon as strictly "spa menus" have evolved into vegetarian, gluten-free or organic options that are less taxing on the body than the traditional high fat, low fiber meals served for snacks and banquet meals. Some hoteliers feel these food programs do give them an advantage in retaining customer loyalty. According to Christina Ramsay, Director of Sales and Marketing at the Park Hyatt in Toronto, "Hyatt's industry leading effort is our new food philosophy."[8] She is referring to the legacy of Hyatt's Unconventional Cuisine program begun 10 years ago, which sought to give meeting delegates a food experience that was decidedly unlike that found at other conventions.

Perhaps the most powerful, yet risky, principle is to place a high value on quality ingredients. While a focus on high quality may have less of a direct revenue generating or cost saving justification, it does set a tone of quality for the venue. The reality is that local and/or organic supply chains can fluctuate in availability and price, and may not have the infrastructure to support larger volume operations from a single source, so many hotels and convention centers have expanded their culinary operations to include herb and vegetable gardens as well as apiaries for their bees to pollinate and provide honey. The gardens allow chefs access to fresh, pesticide and herbicide free products along with offering a differentiated marketing opportunity. Attaching a company's name with high quality producers, underlines a dedication to a quality product. Presenting a food story with an ecological and health focus conveys an image of cooperation among businesses and addresses customers with a variety of interests and buying triggers.

As a side note, there seems to be little research on hotel gardens, however hotel history suggests this is not so much a new phenomenon as it is the return of an ancient tradition. Hotels, like estates of wealthy families, used to have gardens to supply their kitchens from medieval times. The first known hotel rooftop apiary, however, was started in 2008 by the Fairmont Royal York in Toronto, Canada. So far the Fairmont chain has 19 hotels with rooftop apiaries worldwide.[9]

Make Food Part of the Travel Experience

As you seek ways to enhance the travel experience, you can attract and retain clients that otherwise could stay in their office and use video conference technology rather than explore an area and what it has to offer in terms of food.

This seems to be an idea which the MCIT industry is taking from traditional tourism as they struggle to justify the cost in both time and money for out of office meetings, conferences and events. Taking people out of their everyday environment opens them to new experiences. The richer these experiences are, the greater the change in context and thus, the greater the potential benefit of ideas, creativity and contacts. Food is an easy and flexible way to embrace a new environment and enrich experience in a locale.

Chains are especially interested in embracing the travel experience. For example, Ritz Carlton opened a hotel in Toronto featuring a restaurant named "TOCA" (TOronto, CAnada) that serves local food, wine and beer.[10] This is a marked departure from the concept of a corporate-wide standard menu tailored to that chain's known traveler demographics and tastes. You could be in a chain hotel in New York, London or Shanghai and unless you looked out the window, you would not notice any difference in your surroundings.

In non-temperate climates with harsh winters the ability to buy and serve local foods, as their growing season is short and limits options, forces a business to get more creative. Nevertheless, one can see the passion and creativity of cold climate chefs across the globe. One such example is the use of winter salads in the northern hemisphere. Rather than romaine lettuce or field greens traditionally found on hotel menus, indigenous local fruits, meats and vegetables are used in traditional ways, perhaps with a modern flair. These dishes can provide interest and cost savings as chefs explore the use of local items.

Grow the Network

Most successful local food programs use collaboration with other associations or groups to maximize benefits and minimize risks. Fairmont started their adventures in beekeeping with the Toronto Beekeepers Cooperative and FoodShare which gave them access to beekeeping expertise and a community partner to use their excess honey.[11] This collaboration allows the Fairmont to minimize costly mistakes and enables Fairmont guests to feel good that their purchases are supporting the local community. Fairmont also acquired a great story on the collaboration and two new markets in which to tell their brand story. Beekeepers and community food bank organizers will likely be more receptive to the Fairmont brand due to these partnerships.

If the lesson you need is to help your facility and chef to balance the unique logistics and needs of large groups with quality, locally sourced food, professional pride and a little collegial competition can be a great motivator. The International Association of Conference Centers (IACC)[12] uses an annual Copper Skillet competition to challenge their member chefs to create interesting new menus which are required for the large groups to which their membership caters.[13] Each competition creates an opportunity for interaction and learning amongst the chefs and their teams in order to create better end products for the customer.[14]

Menu Messaging

Several years ago restaurants started using menus to convey more information than just the food offered. The industry norm used to be the menu with a logo on the cover. Now we see the grower or producer who has their product names listed on the menu next to their food item. This type of "naming" usurps past menu branding whereby large commercial operations in food service, beverages or packaged foods would provide sponsorship money in return for a logo on a menu. Your local herb supplier may not have the same budget to provide sponsorship money. Still, their inclusion creates a quality promise that starts with the grower and underlines the venue's commitment to a locally focused food supply chain. This notion of using product names on a menu is just a very small part of what the World Food Travel Association refers to as "menu messaging," where all parts of the menu are used to convey valuable information to diners. Menu messaging is an opportunity for meeting planners to educate convention delegates about locally sourced food and drink that may be entirely unfamiliar to the delegate.

Place High Importance on Customer Satisfaction

It is admirable for companies to embrace social justice and ecological stewardship, but the truth remains that businesses must provide for their customers or risk being replaced by their competitors. Businesses that have embraced the food revolution, specifically the local food revolution, have done so because clients demand it. This section will look at some ways we can bring our customers wants and the needs of businesses into greater alignment.

What is important to your customer must also be important to you. During the two-way education/ dialogue businesses have with customers, you will discover new areas on which you need to concentrate. Hotel chains have developed healthy food options for productive meetings. The IACC requires all members to offer an all-day snack option so meetings do not break around food service, they can break when it is natural for the meeting flow.[15] Meeting Planners International (MPI) recently used the services of experts on productivity to teach its members about movement and nutrition for their meetings. These are objectives which the planner and the venue can work together to accomplish. This can also be more productive for your sales team than simply telling potential clients how wonderful your culinary team is.

Still, tourism organizations can help you market to the meeting planner and the attendees by highlighting the variety and the best choices in your particular destination. In addition, general attendees will get a sense of the destination. By embracing the concept that good food enhances the travel experience, you can include your regional specialty foods as part of your sales experience.

What, if any, effect on sales can a quality food and drink experience have? The Vancouver Convention Centre (VCC) provides one example of how the story of the salmon sold at the Vancouver (Canada) Convention Centre (VCC) can create an emotional bond that will make a sale more likely. The salmon at the VCC is sourced locally, from one supplier, flash frozen for premium quality and delivered to the VCC for their guests. By making the client feel unique and special (that this product was caught and processed only for the VCC and that the person who catches and processes that fish is a member of the local community), helps to create a bridge between the client and the community. If you question the value of drawing the client into the community, listen to the podcast, The Age of Persuasion by Terry O'Reilly, specifically the episode titled "Emotion" to learn about the sales effect when you create an emotional bond with your customer.[16] Generally food forges strong emotional connections because food engages all of the human senses. It stands to reason that a powerful food connection will influence a guest's feelings towards a particular venue.

In addition to creating an emotional bond with your customer, the food quality and service must deliver on the promise made by the sales person. Be careful not to oversell or underdeliver. The consumer in today's marketplace is extremely skeptical of big promises. At a recent food tourism summit, the hotel's General Manager welcomed the group and spoke of the experience and skill of their chef who worked at various high-end restaurants around the world. Twenty minutes later after a rather ordinary meal, the speech meant nothing and there were no raving fans. While the dessert was exceptional, nothing else served left any positive memories. The group felt betrayed.

The General Manager made two errors. First she failed to give the client a reason to care about their expertise and did not show how their expertise would benefit the customer. Secondly, she oversold what was actually a decent meal to the point where it actually became a disappointment. Serving large groups a tasty meal in a timely fashion at the correct temperature is difficult. We know that the sales process is necessary, but concentrate on the value and benefit you bring to your customer with your food program and not how great your program is. You will find your customers happier to be pleasantly surprised than sorely disappointed. The unfortunate risk is that your failure to hit a quality mark will live on for a long time due to the large number of people who experience it. In this day and age of social media, the risk increases.

Getting immediate feedback is also vitally important. To this end, the Vancouver Convention Centre provides tableside comment cards. If there is an issue, managers work to resolve it immediately, which means less likelihood of escalating the issue via social media channels. If the venue has near real-time access to feedback, it can react immediately to any issues or concerns. In larger, ongoing conferences lasting more than a few days, issues can be corrected from day to day and improve the overall rating of your food, rather than repeating something that is not working for another day or two. Real-time feedback on the foodservice needs to be asked by the venue of the end customers rather than only be aggregated into an overall conference evaluation form, the results of which may never find their way back to the convention center staff.

Explore and Experiment

Lastly, let us look at practices that can save a convention center money. The increase in revenue from a new menu might be fleeting because your competition can copy your menu, or consumer tastes may veer in another direction. However, if having an herb garden on the roof reduces your heating and cooling costs and saves your food cost, it will likely last longer than the fancy new main course that is the dish of the moment.

Work with smaller portions. The attendees are less "stuffed" and food cost is reduced. This may also allow you to incorporate small breaks into the day.[17] Research by Cornell University also plays with the idea of customer perceptions, such as serving healthy vegetables on large plates to encourage more consumption and smaller plates to discourage over-eating of heavier type fare. Findings suggest that just by working with consumer perceptions on the serving plate size alon,e we can not only reduce food waste, but also correspondingly reduce costs and at the same time, still satisfy the customer.[18]

Food trends in MCIT will not follow directly in the steps of general food trends. The logistics and planning timelines mean there will always be differences. That does not mean food for larger groups will not evolve. It just means changes will be more conservative. As consumers become

296

more adventuresome and business travelers from further away continue to grow in proportion to overall business and convention travel, we expect to see more and exciting advances in group meals at convention centers and hotels.

CONCLUSION

The food and drink experience is secondary to the meeting and convention purpose. The primary *raison d'être* for a meeting and convention is the actual meeting itself. That said, the discussion throughout the chapter points to ways that meeting/convention venues have managed to separate themselves from the plethora of choices available to the typical meeting planner.

One point of differentiation among meeting planners and meeting venues is to focus on the food. While this action may not necessarily attract meeting attendees by itself, once the attendee has experienced the food and is pleased, there is an increased likelihood that they will share this experience with other colleagues, friends and family, thus generating positive word of mouth for the venue, the meeting/conference, and even the destination.

Another point of differentiation through food is to focus on how the how and where food is sourced. The reality is that social responsibility is very much on the radar of consumers, who tend to be highly interested in where their food comes from and how it is prepared. This action is one of collaboration and can work by partnering with organizations with similar interests, such as the apiary example at Fairmont Hotels. While these type of services may not directly determine one's plan to attend a conference/meeting, it may well indirectly, on a more subconscious level influence which meeting/conference one chooses by affecting consumer choices through their values and perceptions.

While food trends will come and go, some of the more salient ones are here to stay. Focus on health is an ongoing concern, and not one likely to go away. Ensuring our food sources are sustainable long term appears to be a trend that is here to stay. Food is such an essential part of our lives. In spite of fluctuations in the demand for meetings and conventions, food is one component that when creatively managed, can deliver a positive impact on the MCIT market.

DISCUSSION QUESTIONS

1. If you were/are an MCIT planner, what would be your main criteria for choosing a venue? Would you choose a venue based on its food? Why or why not?
2. In this chapter we reviewed what certain venues are doing to increase their offerings, including on-site apiaries and gardens. Aside from the sustainability benefits, do you think meeting planners or other consumers will pay more for this type of experience? If not, what could the hotels and convention centers do to increase the revenue from this type of sustainability commitment?
3. A hypothetical Hotel XYZ wants to host a convention. There are three venues the convention planner is considering at this time, all with comparable rates, space requirements, etc. You are the Director of Sales and Marketing for meetings and conventions at Hotel XYZ. How might you leverage your food product to win the contract (assuming of course, that you have free creativity in what your hotel offers)?

ENDNOTES

[1] As per the Conference Board of Canada's David Redekop interview in December 2012 *Hotelier Magazine,* "Decline in conference attendance is real, and much of this is due to technology."

[2] Culinary Institute of America and Harvard School of Public Health, Department of Nutrition. (2013). Worlds of healthy flavors: Ninth annual invitational leadership retreat for chain restaurants, hotels, supermarkets, and volume foodservice. [Electronic version.] Retrieved June 22, 2013 from www.ciaprochef.com/wohf2013/pdf/WOHF2013_Program.pdf

[3] The District of Columbia. (2009). Case study: The Fairmont. Retrieved June 22, 2013 from http://ddoe.dc.gov/service/case-study-fairmont

[4] Fairmont Hotels & Resorts. (2013). Fairmont abuzz with bees. Retrieved June 22, 2013 from www.fairmont.com/promotions/fairmontbees

[5] Sysco. (2012). Local Sourcing. Retrieved June 22, 2013 from http://bit.ly/16UsfUk

[6] Interview with Greg Hall, Sysco. Spring 2013.

[7] Starwood Hotels & Resorts. Sheraton fitness: Color your Plate. Retrieved June 22, 2013 from www.sheratonfitness.com

[8] Feder, T. (2012). Face time: Canadian hoteliers get creative to attract meetings and conventions. Hotelier Magazine, December 2012 [Electronic version], p. 41. Retrieved June 22, 2013 from www.foodserviceworld.com/MagazinesHotelier/1212-DecemberHotelierMagazine.pdf

[9] Fairmont Hotels & Resorts. (2013). Fairmont abuzz with bees. Retrieved June 22, 2013 from www.fairmont.com/promotions/fairmontbees/

[10] The Ritz-Carlton, Toronto. (2013). TOCA. Retrieved June 22, 2013 from http://bit.ly/NRIRmJ

[11] Toronto Beekeepers Co-operative. (2013). A short history of the Toronto Beekeepers Co-op. Retrieved June 22, 2013 from http://bit.ly/tUc2Ms

[12] www.iacconline.org

[13] IACC. (2013). Copper Skillet Award. Retrieved June 22, 2013 from http://events.iacconline.org/copperskillet

[14] Ibid.

[15] IACC. (2012). Implementing menu change: How to make healthy menus a reality. Retrieved June 22, 2013 from http://bit.ly/14QebdK

[16] CBC Radio. (May 10, 2008). Emotion. Retrieved June 22, 2013 from www.cbc.ca/ageofpersuasion/2008/05/emotion.html

[17] Cornell University Food and Brand Lab. (2006). The perils of large plates: Waist, waste, and wallet. Retrieved June 22, 2013 from http://bit.ly/15tRiK7

[18] Ibid.

Food Tourism in Academia

Tracy Berno, Carol Kline, & Erik Wolf

This chapter discusses which aspects of food and drink tourism are studied at universities and colleges around the world, current research trends, as well as research opportunities.

INTRODUCTION

Food and drink tourism as a field of study hardly existed at the turn of the century. Today, the industry is already 10 years old and it seems as if there are food tourism programs of study on every continent. Because the industry is young, programs of study are still evolving, as is research in the field. Also because the field is young, there is tremendous opportunity to study and research more, to advance our understanding as industry professionals and academicians, and to extend our discoveries to the consumer marketplace. Throughout this chapter, we will look at a variety of case studies that illustrate the state of food and drink tourism in academia.

Emergence of Food Tourism in Education and Research

As tourism has matured as both an activity and an area of study, it has increasingly moved away from the ubiquitous "sun, sea, sand" mass tourism experience to an activity that is now viewed as being much more complex and diverse. The concept of 'niche tourism' has emerged in response to this type of mass tourism. This is reflected in both educational and research trends. In particular, in recent years food and beverage have developed an increasingly more important role in tourism, becoming a significant part of the overall tourism experience rather than just an activity adjunct to the overall tourism experience. As a result, there has been a growing interest in food tourism as an area for research in the academic literature, as well as a concomitant growth of educational opportunities for students to study food tourism as a subject, or indeed a qualification.

Universities and institutes of higher learning are positioned well to contribute to food tourism. Not only do they provide the opportunity for specialist education and training for food tourism, but research can address the growing need to understand more about the phenomenon. In the overall scheme of things, tourism education is a relatively recent newcomer to university study. Over time however, tourism has become part of many universities' offerings, and the focus of what can be studied within tourism has also continued to develop.[1] Food tourism is no exception to this. As it has emerged in importance in tourism, institutions of higher learning have responded.

University Involvement in Food Tourism

From single courses at universities to an entire institution dedicated to gastronomy, food and food tourism studies are increasingly becoming a focus within higher education. The Università degli Studi di Scienze Gastronomiche (The University of Gastonomic Sciences) was founded in 2004 by the international non-profit organization Slow Food in cooperation with the Italian regions of Piedmont and Emilia-Romagna. The university is a private non-profit institution that is recognized by the Italian Ministry of Education. The goal of the university is to create an international research and education center for those working on renewing farming methods, protecting biodiversity, and building an organic relationship between gastronomy and agricultural science.

The university suggests that the result of this higher educational focus on gastronomy is a new professional figure — the gastronome — skilled in production, distribution, promotion, and communication of high-quality foods. Gastronomes are the next generation of educators and innovators, editors and multimedia broadcasters, marketers of fine products, and managers of consortia, businesses, and tourism companies.[2] The Universita Degli Studi di Scienze Gastronomiche offers course work in culinary tourism as part of its curriculum.

With its sole focus on gastronomic sciences, the Universita Degli Studi di Scienze Gastronomiche is somewhat unique. However other institutions also focus on gastronomic studies. For example, Le Cordon Bleu, in partnership with Southern Cross University (Australia) offers three postgraduate qualifications in Gastronomic Tourism comprising a Graduate Certificate, Graduate Diploma and Masters Degree. These programs combine an academic approach to understanding food and drink within historical, cultural and contemporary contexts, integrated with the study of tourism, business and management applications. The aim of the program is to produce graduates with the potential to add value to food and wine-related tourism business operations.

Studying food tourism does not require commitment to a full qualification. Many institutions offer food tourism and related subjects as single course offerings as part of their qualifications. The University of Guelph (Ontario, Canada) for example, offered a course on Culinary Tourism as part of their Current Management Topic offerings in their School of Hospitality and Tourism Management. The course offered students a framework to develop an appreciation for and understanding of the uniqueness of food tourism and its relationship to the tourism and hospitality industries. Similarly, the University of Adelaide (Australia) offers a Wine and Food Tourism and Festivals course as part of its Food Studies program.

Creating a Professional Standard

For the busy professional who wants a useful level of training in a short time period, the World Food Travel Association offers a Certified Culinary Travel Professional (CCTP) program. The program was launched in 2008 in response to requests from food tourism professionals and academics who wanted an industry specific certification. The course is not designed to be a theoretical or research-oriented university-level course, rather it is designed to be detailed, hands-on and interactive for actual practitioners in the industry, as well as recent university graduates. The course is updated annually and taught online in conjunction with telephone meetings with a faculty advisor who is also an industry practitioner. Students can elect to write a final paper or take an online exam. Once the student passes, the CCTP designation is awarded. The Association provides a diploma and customized CCTP logo that the graduate can use in his or her marketing. The Association also promotes the student's CCTP designation in its professional channels.

Another option is the Destination Marketing Association International's Certified Destination Management Executive (CDME) program. These programs are designed to prepare senior executives and managers of destination management organizations for change and competition. The CDME program offers Food Tourism as an elective option on an irregular basis.

Other Industry Certifications

Professional development is not restricted to those in the tourism/destination management areas. Food tourism is something that cookery professionals have an interest in as well. For example, the Northern Ireland Tourist Board has identified food tourism as a key tourism product of the country. In support of this, they published a series of six insight guides on food tourism.[3] As an adjunct to this, and in recognition of the essential nature of food to the tourist experience, they also offered a Master Class for cookery professionals, "Grow Your Food Tourism Product", that explored Northern Ireland's potential to develop an all-round excellent core food offer and to look at the ways in which they could further develop their food tourism offering. Additionally, many Tourism Extension programs at U.S. land grant universities like Michigan State University, Colorado State University, University of Wisconsin, University of Vermont, Clemson University, and California State University, include an emphasis on farm tourism, food tourism, and the development of other niches that mesh with rural livelihoods of food production, processing, and adding value.

Prognosis for Food Tourism Research

Despite the fact that almost every tourist eats as part of their tourist experience, academics have only relatively recently engaged with food tourism as a scholarly pursuit. Since the late 1990s however,[4] there has been an increasing awareness of and interest in food tourism as a subject for research. With the general increase in interest in food as a lifestyle interest, food tourism is now a well-established area in tourism literature. Research on food tourism can be loosely grouped into six thematic areas:[5]

1. The relationship of food and tourism: This thematic area recognizes the close relationship between food and tourism. Research in this area has considered: food as a tourism motivator; food consumption as entertainment or a tourist activity; production and consumption patterns and trends; levels and patterns of tourist engagement with food tourism; impacts on perception and satisfaction; sense of place and place attachment; and globalization of food in tourism and as a result of tourism.

2. Attraction and impediment of cuisine to tourists: With the recognition of food tourism as a niche tourism area, food and food related activities have become viewed as a 'tourism product' and not just an adjunct activity within tourism. This has led to research on: food as an attraction in its own right; food and wine trails and related activities; the role of artisan products in tourism; dimensions of food service across the tourism system; the institutionalization of food tourism; and food as an impediment or detraction in tourism (for example perceptions of safety and hygiene and the effects of food poisoning on the tourist experience).

3. Market segmentation of food tourists: Tourism businesses are not the only industry players who have seen the 'pull factor' of food in tourism. Destination marketers at all levels have also recognized the opportunities that food tourism present. As a result, a literature on market segmentation and marketing of, food tourism has emerged.

4. Food tourism strategies: In recognizing the potential of food tourism as an attraction, many destinations have consciously and purposely developed food tourism strategies, using cuisine as a key means for destination branding. This has provided an important means of differentiating destinations. As such, research on food tourism has considered food tourism planning and strategies, destination branding, assessment of economic benefits (import substitution, economic leakage/retention and multiplier effects), impacts on export markets and tourism-related trade, as a tool for rural development, and a means of environmental protection and preservation of cultural heritage.

5. Promotion and marketing tools: With the recognition of food tourism as a vehicle for destination branding, a concomitant literature on the marketing of food tourism has also emerged.

6. *The application of theories in food tourism development*: As food tourism research continues to mature, there is increasing application of theories from areas such as globalization, economics, sociology, anthropology and cultural studies as a means of understanding food tourism as a phenomenon.

Future Topics and Trends

The involvement of higher education in food tourism studies is only expected to increase. Just as tourism can be viewed through the lens of many disciplines, farming and food systems are equally as multi-faceted. For example, within North Carolina, USA, there has emerged an informal partnership of three major universities within 30 miles (48 km) of each other. Various schools and departments within the universities communicate and collaborate via a "university food studies" listserv. Some of the participating disciplines include public health, nutrition, public administration, political science, history, African-American studies, arts, geography, agriculture, urban planning, adult education, sociology, ecology, and tourism. This kind of interdisciplinary communication is just the beginning, and will likely lead to more comprehensive data on food, stronger educational programs and increased opportunities for students, larger collaborative research projects, and less competition and repetition of efforts.

As the interest in food tourism increases and collaboration across disciplines spreads, one can expect to see holistic and systems approaches to research and education. However, new niches will also emerge as the food tourism scene evolves and gains depth from years of practice. Some future trends of food tourism practice, education and research follow:

1. *Continued multidisciplinary partnerships and networks across campuses, organizations and agencies*: universities will continue to partner with non-governmental organizations, government agencies, and private sector businesses to stay current, pool resources, and find multidisciplinary research-based solutions to complicated problems.

2. *Growth of "systems" approach to food tourism*: Food tourism experiences occur in many forms along a food supply chain that includes agritourism (production and harvest), winery and brewery and bakery tourism (processing), not to mention the retail outlets of gift shops, restaurants, and culinary events.[6][7] Research will begin to encompass a value chain approach to food tourism experiences so as to better the product at all points along the supply chain.[8]

3. *Increased emphasis on sustainability issues and/or the triple-bottom line (economic, socio-cultural, environmental) approach in food tourism*: We will see additional overlap of food tourism and voluntourism as visitors wish to blend a social mission with their business or personal travel; faculty and students will also become involved in many social issues (e.g. farm worker rights, food access, animal welfare) as well as environmental (e.g. food waste and energy use) and economic (e.g. local food campaigns, marketing) by way of classroom projects, research or student club outreach.[9]

4. *Emergence of food tourism certification programs, and the involvement of universities in these programs*: Many tourism certification programs exist, and the food tourism arena will follow suit, perhaps considering energy management, or fair trade,[10] or even locally-based certifications. The World Food Travel Association is the first organization in the world to offer a food tourism industry certification program. The comprehensive program requires about 10 hours of classroom time and one-on-one counsel with a faculty advisor, quite a leap from often-seen 10-minute multiple choice destination "expert" certifications.

5. *Increase of internships and work-study programs in food tourism*: As more and more students are interested in food tourism, they will demand diversified and applied experiences to

learn more about the subject. Additionally, this will lead to the *emergence of student-led clubs and groups that focus on farm tourism and food tourism.*

6. *Increase in niche research programs:* Research in food tourism will continue to hone in on specific topics such as "visitor patronage of food trucks while on vacation" and "comparison of international foodie market travel patterns." New academic food tourism journals will appear. Culinary tourism experiences and the "foodies" themselves will continue to be segmented into more specialized interests.

7. *Transference of sociological, psychological and economic theory to food tourism research:* Tourism research will continue to adapt theoretical frameworks from other disciplines to apply to a food tourism context. An example of this is the Green Building Initiative,[11] which celebrates seven tenets of green building certification. This green building industry's certification is inspiring the World Food Travel Association's emerging food and drink experience accreditation.

8. *Food tourism specialists and ecotourism specialists will find themselves working together:* The overriding societal trends of connecting to local food sources (sometimes called "farm-to-fork"), leading a physically active lifestyle, enjoying the authentic culture and natural resources of a destination, and making travel choices that respect the environment will continue to blur together. Faculty and students in will find themselves working with outdoor recreation professors, urban planners, folk life specialists, and public health faculty to deliver the experience that the future food tourist desires.

A Unique Partnership in Samoa to Promote Food Tourism

Samoa, a small island nation east of Fiji in the South Pacific, has an abundance of fertile land and a tourism-dependent economy. It has been identified that one way of enhancing the benefits of tourism for Samoa is to create a demand for food tourism through the development of a branded Samoan cuisine for the tourism industry, using locally grown and sourced organic products. This in turn will increase the amount of local agricultural products used in the tourism industry.

To help facilitate the development of food tourism in Samoa, a unique partnership between a university academic, a professional chef, a local non-governmental organization (NGO) and the Samoa Tourism Authority was formed. The NGO, Women in Business Development Inc. (WIBDI) works with women and their families to generate cash from the agricultural resources available to them in their village. WIBDI has created a network of women farmers and has worked with them to achieve organic certification. In 2001, five WIBDI farms gained organic certification from the National Association for Sustainable Agriculture, Australia. To date, WIBDI has assisted over 700 farms to become organically certified under NASAA.

The next step for this project is to help the women build the necessary market linkages to supply organic Samoan products to tourism operators. As part of this, it was recognized that a distinctive Samoan food tourism product needed to be developed and promoted as part of the country's tourism attributes. The partners, in collaboration with other stakeholders, including the Samoa Hotel Association, the New Zealand Aid Programme and various government ministries are working to create a branded "Samoan Organic Tourism Cuisine" product inspired by traditional Samoan culinary culture. This is currently being developed as a book on Samoan cuisine, which will be used as a marketing tool to promote food tourism in Samoa.[12]

Research, Teaching and Outreach in Food Tourism Systems

At the Center for Sustainable Tourism (CST) at East Carolina University in the USA, students, staff and affiliate faculty work on a number of programs related to tourism, however one of the key initiatives of the center is Tourism and Food Systems. The center has a unique structure that engages faculty from a variety of departments to address sustainability in all types of tourism. Some of the research programs at CST include:

- the overlap between the food supply chain and the tourism supply chain;
- development of a survey instrument that segments foodies into sub-markets, e.g. the hippie foodie, the upscale foodie, the social media foodie;
- exploring the entrepreneurial ecosystem that private and social sector food and tourism entrepreneurs need to be successful; and
- best practices in agritourism.

Some of the Center's outreach programs include:

- working with livestock farmers to develop and enhance agritourism programs,
- making presentations at farm and food related conferences, and
- the Students for Sustainable Tourism[13] group volunteers at an annual sustainable food festival[14]

Many of these activities are integrated into the classroom as special projects, and research results are discussed as lecture material. Care is taken to introduce students to local organizations that work in sustainable tourism, for example the Appalachian Sustainable Agriculture Project[15] which works with farmers and restaurants within a 60-county region to increase local food tourism, the Asheville Convention and Visitor Bureau which markets the "foodtopia" experiences of Asheville, North Carolina, USA, as well as private companies like Velo Girl Rides which combines fitness, farms and food in their tour offerings.[16]

CONCLUSION

Food tourism is a growing field. All travelers must eat and drink. The industry is still young and will benefit greatly from additional investigation as researchers strive to give the food tourism industry more form and move it along its path of evolution.

DISCUSSION QUESTIONS

1. Name three areas of food tourism in strong need of research within the next five years.
2. What would a food tourism systems model look like? Discuss and create one.
3. The issue of authenticity is raised time after time. How important is authenticity in the food tourism experience? Can food be authentic while the experience itself is inauthentic? Discuss the implications of authenticity in both food itself, as well as the food tourism experience.

ENDNOTES

[1] Janet Chrzan, "Why study culinary tourism?: Answers for a healthy life", Expedition, 48(1) (2005): 40-41.

[2] "History and Mission/Universita Degli Studi di Scienze Gastronomiche", Universita Degli Studi di Scienze Gastronomiche, last accessed 13 March 2013, www.unisg.it/en/storia-e-missione

[3] Northern Ireland Tourist Board, "Revisiting Food Tourism: Business Insight Series 2011/2012", last accessed 13 March 2013, www.nitb.com/ResearchIntelligence/VisitorInterests-SectorInsights.aspx

[4] As one example, Jacinthe Bessière "Local Development and Heritage: Traditional Food and Cuisine as Tourist Attractions in Rural Areas," Sociologia Ruralis 38(1) (1998): 21-34.

[5] Ching-Shu Su & Jeou-Shyan Horng, "Recent Developments in Research and Future Directions of Culinary Tourism: A Review," in *Visions for Global Tourism Industry: Creating and Sustaining Competitive Strategies,* ed. Murat Kasimoglu, last accessed 13 March 2013, http://bit.ly/10b4MOu

[6] Wanching Chang and Jingxue Yuan, "A taste of tourism: Visitors' motivations to attend a food festival," Event Management, 15 (2011): 13 – 23.

[7] C. Michael Hall and Stephan Gossling, Sustainable Culinary Systems: Local Foods, Innovation, Tourism and Hospitality (Routledge: New York, 2012).

[8] Madeleine Pullman and Zhaohui Wu, Food Supply Chain Management: Economic, Social and Environmental Perspectives. (Routledge: New York, 2011).

[9] Yvonne Yen Liu, Y.Y. & Dominique Apollon, The Color of Food. (Applied Research Center: New York, February 2011).

[10] Karla Boluk "In consideration of a new approach to tourism: a critical review of fair trade tourism," The Journal of Tourism and Peace Research 2 (2011): 27-37.

[11] www.thegbi.org

[12] Robert Oliver, Tracy Berno & Shiri Ram, "Mea' Ai Samoa: Recipes and Stories from the Heart of Polynesia (Randon House: Auckland, forthcoming).

[13] www.facebook.com/StudentsForSustainableTourism

[14] http://terravitaevent.com

[15] www.asapconnections.org

[16] http://velogirlrides.com

SECTION FOUR

ISSUES & IDEAS
IN FOOD TOURISM

Sustainability in Food & Drink Tourism

Tracy Berno, Nan Devlin, Ayako Ezaki, David Wilson, & Erik Wolf

Many people, when hearing the word sustainability, immediately think about the environment. In recent years, the concept of sustainability has evolved to be more inclusive. Sustainable tourism is not only about the visitor's experience. There is an increased interest in using local resources to develop tourism along with the concept that host communities should be able to benefit from tourism both socially and economically. This chapter will expand from this perspective on the topic of sustainability in food and drink tourism.

INTRODUCTION

The word "sustainability" conjures a variety of meanings and perceptions, from low carbon footprint, to biodynamic production, organic certification and much more. While these are all important issues in the food industry, a few issues remain neglected, such as food waste. More and more data show how much of our food is actually wasted. The reasons for this run from arcane laws that prevent perfectly fine food from being used, to the expectations of diners as to the amount of food on their plate or how it should look. Yet food waste is just one small issue in sustainability.

Food tourism can leverage the growing interest in sustainability by promoting and using more local products, while at the same time, meeting traveler needs for an authentic, quality experience. The sustainability benefits of food tourism go beyond just what is on the plate and include a range of both direct and indirect positive outcomes. These include a reduction in carbon footprint and other environmental waste; community enrichment; more attractive, vital and viable rural areas; more vibrant and locally distinctive tourism; and greater economic and social well-being for the host community. Through the development and promotion of sustainable food systems, a mutually beneficial relationship between agricultural, tourism and food sectors can be established. By adopting these principles, critical linkages can be forged that will help further promote a holistic approach to sustainable tourism that has positive economic, social and environmental impacts.

The advent of the Boeing 747 in in the late 1960s heralded a new era in international travel. Tourist arrivals rapidly increased in most countries around the planet. Since this profound change to the international travel landscape, tourism and specifically international tourism, have become a critical component of the economies of many nations, generating income, foreign exchange earnings and employment. With the growth of tourism, awareness about sustainability issues has also developed. Over the last decade in particular, various international conventions and declarations have put forward principles and guidelines for "sustainable tourism" with the belief that it is not a discrete or special form of tourism, but rather, that all forms of tourism should strive to be more sustainable.[1]

The concept of sustainable tourism may have started from interpretation of the notion of "sustainable development" as defined by the Brundtland Report, "Sustainable development is development that meets the needs of the present without compromising the ability of future generations to meet their own needs ... and that already had embraced social and economic sustainability, not just environmental."[2] This is reflected in the United Nations World Tourism Organization's (UNWTO) definition of sustainable tourism, "Tourism that takes full account of its current and future economic, social and environmental impacts, addressing the needs of visitors, the industry, the environment and host communities."[3]

The concept of sustainable tourism today has evolved to include increased interest in sustainable ways of using local resources in tourism development, along with the idea that host communities should benefit as much as possible from tourism in terms of social and economic opportunities. Despite this broadening of the understanding and implementation of sustainable tourism, little attention has been paid to sustainability as an essential ingredient of the food tourism experience, namely the relationship between sustainable tourism with food production, consumption and waste.

With increasing public and academic interest in food tourism, it can be beneficial for businesses and even entire communities, to adopt a sustainable approach to food tourism development. Signs of growing interest in sustainability within the food tourism field are reflected in such diverse elements as the new popularity of farms and farmers' markets, green restaurants, food "miles" and sustainability labeling, concerns over food supply and security, Slow Food, Fair Trade, and a desire to buy and 'eat locally.' Food tourism is integral to promoting sustainability practices in all food-related sectors, because food tourism simultaneously acts to globalize and localize food consumption, and create new foodways and commodity chains.[4]

All Tourists Eat, But What Do You Offer Them?

For many countries, particularly those in lesser developed areas, food represents one of the highest areas of economic potential and one of the most underutilized assets. The degree to which tourism in a country relies on imported foods can significantly affect the social, economic and environmental impacts of tourism. For example, islands in the South Pacific import a large amount of food and drink, largely to cater to the expectations and demands of visitors from overseas. This has contributed to an erosion of the importance placed on local food and drink production.[5]

Food importation can bring a number of negative effects, including the reduction of foreign exchange reserves and prevention of opportunities to expand and modernize local food production and processing. This may lead to a loss of local income and employment.[6] Importation also contributes to tourism's carbon footprint, and subsequently, is a key issue for climate change mitigation.[7] Additionally, hotels, restaurants and cruise lines produce significant quantities of food and packaging waste every year, much of which ends up in landfill sites or the ocean.

Triple Bottom Line: Benefits to People, Planet, Profit

The "triple bottom line measurement," a term first coined in 1994 by John Elkington in Great Britain, proposes that sustainability can be defined as endeavors that benefit people (social), planet (environmental) and profit (economic). Rather than measure sustainable efforts by a checklist of tasks, the triple bottom line approach offers realistic goals that can be easily entwined into the business plan of any food and beverage establishment. It also allows more flexibility in how to allocate resources to fulfill the triple promise in ways that are important to the individual business owner. It is beyond the scope of this book to make recommendations about certifications or business practices. That said, the triple bottom line concept should be taken into consideration by food tourism businesses seeking to be more sustainable.

Measuring Sustainability: An Entrepreneurial Approach

Tourism is a unique industry that involves many types of economic activities and it tends to leave a significant environmental footprint. Emissions from aircraft are high and continue to increase.[8] Cruise ships, which bring much needed currency to ports of call, nevertheless can generate as much sewage and wastewater in a single day as a small city.[9] Golf courses in arid areas use enormous amounts of limited water, forcing smooth green surfaces over ground never intended for such coverage. Even entire destinations suffer under the impact of tourism. The governing bodies of both Machu Picchu, Peru and Venice, Italy are considering restricting access so that antiquities can be saved and so that a reduction in visitor numbers can return a better quality of life to local citizens.

Yet tourism is one of the industries that is leading the sustainability movement. Organizations such as The International Ecotourism Society [10] and Sustainable Travel International [11] recognized early on that it was necessary for long-term economic health to protect and preserve the very places travelers want to visit.

GSTC: Internationally Recognized Sustainable Criteria

While each sector of the tourism industry has its own sustainability issues and goals, defining sustainability has always been a moving target, making it more difficult to measure efforts against a standard benchmark. Considering this need, the Global Sustainable Tourism Council (GSTC) was formed in order to start a process for developing guiding principles and minimum requirements in order to protect and sustain natural and cultural resources. To date, GSTC has issued criteria for hotels, destinations and tour operators, and has added revisions as necessary.

The GSTC identifies credible certification programs according to its standards. So far, 15 certification programs around the world have been "recognized as aligned with the Global Sustainable Tourism Criteria for hotels and tour operators" and one has been "approved" as a GSTC-compliant certification program.[12] For food tourism businesses and destinations that are interested in sustainability certification, these programs can be a good place to start.

Social and Cultural Impact of Food & Drink Tourism

The GSTC addresses social benefits of tourism to the host community, including offering minimum standard guidelines for minimizing impact to cultural heritage. The World Food Travel Association considers unique, local, indigenous and historical food and drink as cultural assets worthy of preservation and protection. Such assets help define the destination brand. When travelers think of France or California, they think of wine; India brings thoughts of curry; the Pacific Northwest of the USA conjures an appetite for salmon, coffee and beer. However the mere act of serving local food and drink does not necessarily convey social or cultural benefits especially, when a region's tourism development has not been planned and has occurred spontaneously.

Local Foods as a Destination Experience for Visitors

One of the benefits that tourism brings to a host community is demand for local experiences, including food. Visitors want to know where to go for a good meal or drink, in a restaurant or bar that is unique to the destination, and where there might be an opportunity to meet or learn something about the locals. Sharing food and drink with the locals invites the sharing of stories that may convey a much deeper insight into the culture than just the food.

The availability of local foods, or products made from local ingredients, greatly impacts the sense of place that a tourist experiences. Visitors tend to regard unique local foods as authentic products that symbolize the culture of a destination. They can provide visitors with an insight into the community they are visiting by connecting consumers to the flavors, or terroir, of the region. Recently, food and beverage groups, tourism offices and chefs in many destinations have developed farm-to-table or sea-to-table events, providing the visitor and local resident alike with an opportunity to "meet the maker." These events offer consumers the opportunity not only to experience good, natural foods, often in outdoor surroundings, but also to learn more about the community, nature and society where they are visiting. The farm-to-table concept is quite popular in North America, although one could argue that the farm-to-table concept is business as usual in many other countries, where food is less processed and has to travel less to reach the consumer.

Cultural Preservation as Community Benefit

Sustainable tourism is not only about the visitor's experience. A demand for local experiences translates to opportunities for small business owners and social entrepreneurs including farmers, producers, distillers, brewers, winemakers, restaurant owners and other culinary artisans, who help create a sense of place. Such a sentiment helps to create community appreciation and pride for local foods and beverages. A greater appreciation for local food and drink can lead to greater caretaking of the area's other cultural assets, such as in architecture and traditions.

The City of Portland in Oregon, U.S.A., which until a couple decades ago had a long history of unremarkable food preparation despite the fertile, abundant and nearby agricultural economy, has gained in the past few years, national and international consumer and media recognition for its food and beverage scene, sustained by support of local farmers, fishers and producers, and innovative and unusual preparation of local ingredients by skilled chefs.[13] Examples of noteworthy and visionary Portland chefs include Greg Higgins (Higgins Restaurant), Cory Schreiber (formerly Wildwood Restaurant), and Scott Dolich (Park Kitchen). As in Portland, in many cities and countries, food tours are popular. Such tours introduce visitors to personalized and memorable experiences that everyday tourists would typically miss. Such experiences provide opportunities between culinary artisan and tourist to interact, share stories and ideas.

For example, in Colombia in the "Eje Cafetero" region, tourists can visit coffee plantations, where they can collect, peel and process the coffee beans, like the local workers do. This means that at the end of the tour, tourists can enjoy a cup of coffee made entirely by themselves.[14]

Because sustainable food tourism focuses on local experience and sense of place, it can offer the host community an opportunity to rediscover its roots. For instance, farmers' markets provide exploration and education of local foods and food producers. Culinary-related promotions, such as wine-tasting weekends, "Taste of" events, and even neighborhood fairs, can create a sense of community beyond the scope of tourism.

Bay Area Green Business Program, Napa Valley, California

The (San Francisco) Bay Area Green Business Program was formed in 1996 by the Association of Bay Area Governments (ABAG). Through the program, government agencies help small and consumer oriented businesses become environmental leaders. To be certified as a Green Business, participants must comply with all applicable environmental regulations, as well as implement a variety of additional measures in the categories of solid waste reduction and recycling, energy and water conservation, and pollution prevention. Participants implement measures from industry specific checklists. Some basic measures are required, but others are selected by the business based on what makes sense in light of audits that are conducted as part of the program.

Napa was one of the first regions to participate in the ABAG program but had to withdraw early on due to a lack of funding. In 2006, however, Napa County Supervisor Mark Luce pushed to restart the Green Business program. The relaunch coincided with an effort by the Napa Valley Vintners, a non-profit trade association representing the majority of wineries in Napa, to develop a green winery certification program to complement their successful Napa Green Certified Land program.

The partnership was critical to getting the Green Business Program up and running. County staff were in a good position to conduct third party auditing and certification for the Green Business Program yet lacked resources for consumer marketing. The Vintners group was well suited to do the marketing but needed an objective third party to establish the credible certification program. The County was also able to leverage wine industry resources to launch the Green Business Program for other business types in the county.

About 100 Napa County businesses are currently certified through the program. One of the first steps taken in setting up the program was to update the existing Green Business Winery checklist, the roots of which actually started a little earlier. In 2004, the Napa Green program was founded to protect the Valley's agricultural lands, specifically with regard to soil preservation, water quality, and biodiversity. The program was expanded in 2008 to include sustainable winery management practices in Napa. [15] Napa County's Department of Environmental Management updated the Green Business Winery checklist in cooperation with Sonoma County. Then the program opened for business and the efforts to date have been impressive. For example, Napa wineries have adopted solar power at an unprecedented rate, with more than 60 wineries now having installed systems.[16] While Napa's winemakers have historically been champions of sustainability efforts they have also found that the Green Business measures are a good investment in terms of cost savings and in giving their customers what they want.[17] The Napa Green program has limited metrics based on wineries that have been certified or recertified in the past year. And it is on a path to be able to prove better return on investment in the near future. Napa Green certification began appearing on wine bottle labels with the 2013 vintage. The program is still young, but a leader in the world when it comes to sustainability in wineries and vineyards.

Environmental Considerations and the Five P's

Sustainable food production, consumption and waste management have a range of environmental implications across the entire value chain from "farm-to-fork" and beyond, and involving a broad range of stakeholders. Building on the three-Ps (purchasing, preparation and presentation) of food,[18] it is suggested that extending consideration to five P's (production, purchasing, preparation, presentation and post-consumption), food tourism providers and consumers can contribute to more environmentally sustainable food systems by the choices they make. Table 1 provides an indication of the complexity of addressing environmental sustainability in food tourism. At the same time, it provides an example of how decisions to improve sustainability can be implemented in the food tourism value chain.

Table 1. Environmental sustainability across the food tourism value chain

STAGE	RELATED INITIATIVES
PRODUCTION	• Use of sustainable production techniques • Use of organic production techniques • Implementation of on-site sustainable production
PURCHASING	• Sourcing local and organic ingredients as feasible • Procuring sustainable species (fisheries, etc.), i.e. avoid consuming animals at risk of extinction • Use of seasonal products • Use of Fair Trade products • Reusable and/or returnable containers for products • Planning to avoid waste and spoilage • Use of low impact transportation options
PREPARATION	• Reduction in use of carbon intensive food products • Use more fresh and fewer semi-processed or processed products • Procure rather than produce energy intensive foods in-house • Reduce overall energy consumption and use renewable sources where possible • Shift towards inclusion of more vegetarian items
PRESENTATION	• Use of recyclable and biodegradable service items • Review of portion sizes • Use standardized recipes • Use a la carte rather than buffet-style dining options • Offering at least one plant-based menu option • Educate the consumer and the person selling the product about the impacts of their choices • 'Under-selling' carbon intensive options
POST-CONSUMPTION	• Compost food waste • Separate and recycle food packaging • Donate excess food to local food banks, shelters and hunger relief programs

The Culinary Supply Chain in Koh Samui, Thailand

Under the Tourism Authority of Thailand's (TAT) "Seven Greens Concept" and the Designated Areas for Sustainable Tourism Administration (DASTA) project, Koh Samui has set a goal to be the first low carbon island in the APEC economy. Additionally, the Asia Pacific Energy Research Centre (APERC) selected Koh Samui as its first island to pioneer modeling a low carbon lifestyle to reduce the use of fossil fuel and boost efficient energy use. One way that has been identified for Koh Samui to work towards achieving these 'green goals' is to evaluate the relationship between local agricultural production and food tourism.

Koh Samui is the third biggest island in Thailand and one of the country's most popular island tourism destinations. The island has faced many environmental issues related to tourism development including land use change and conflict, and changes to traditional agriculture production.

Prior to 1990 and the development of tourism, Koh Samui was a small island community that depended on coconut production and fishing for its livelihood. When the market price of coconuts dropped, along with the uncertainty of the crop due to a hispine beetle infestation, tourism's role in economic development grew, with many people leaving agriculture to work in the tourism industry.[19] Because of the significant capital investment required to enter the tourism industry[20] as well as an increase in a demand for land to develop, many locals were forced to sell or rent out their coconut plantations to outside land developers.[21] The following decades have seen Koh Samui develop from primarily a backpacker tourist destination into one of the most increasingly upscale tourist destinations in Thailand.

As a result, currently in Koh Samui there is a scarcity of land to grow coconuts, with much of the available land being used for more lucrative tourism development. Agricultural production however is a socially, culturally and environmentally important activity that nurtures the special relationships between people and the land.[22] Residents of Koh Samui consider coconut plantations to be a part of their natural heritage as coconut products are closely associated with their livelihood, cuisine and history.[23] The use of agricultural products, specifically coconut, is also essential in producing tourism items (e.g. local cuisine, handicrafts, spa products, etc.) so there remains a need for it on the island. As a result of the decline in its production however, coconuts are imported from other areas, such as Indonesia.

Recent research in Koh Samui considered the interrelation between the culinary supply chain and low carbon menus to support sustainable food tourism on the island with particular consideration being given to the uses of coconut (a traditional culinary ingredient) in the supply chain.[24]

The Culinary Supply Chain

This case study considers the three P's (purchasing, preparation and presentation) of climatically sustainable food management across the culinary supply chain in Koh Samui. In each of these categories, foodservice providers were found to have considerable scope to reduce the carbon intensity of the food they provided.

Focusing on farmers and chefs, the process started with a stakeholder meeting to set goals and objectives, and to define the tasks and roles. It was recognized that by applying a 'bottom-up' approach that emphasized the contributions of stakeholders, planned with local people and took local needs into account the outcome of participatory planning was likely to sustain longer since people would identify with the project and see the project as belonging to them. As part of Phase One of the case study, farmers in the Lipa Noi community (in western Koh Samui) participated in in-depth interviews. They were asked to name their primary agricultural products, and explain the relationship between agriculture and tourism. At the same time, local chefs were invited to participate in a focus group about local Koh Samui food, comparing it to the food typically served at hotel restaurants. Additionally, these 12 chefs who participated also organized site visits to their hotel gardens and kitchens.

The interviews discovered that the purchasing of produce was the domain of chefs and purchasing officers in most hotels. In the case of Koh Samui, hotels had been substituting imported products for those that could be sourced locally. In the smaller hotels however, chefs selected the ingredients directly from the nearest local market. There were no standardized energy saving methods applied while preparing and cooking meals in the hotels. All hotels experienced food wastage following meals, but only some hotels had waste separation systems. Others bagged food waste and left it for the local municipality services to pick up once a day.

Taking into account the transition from local networked connectivity to a wider social diversity of the stakeholder groups, internationally well-known chefs representing international hotel chains were also invited to have a better dialogue with local Thai chefs. In working with the expatriate and local hotel chefs together, the case study addressed three issues: (1) can a coconut based menu of three courses be created that would appeal to the international tourist palate?; (2) what are the facilitators and barriers to the procurement of local ingredients and supply to support this?; and (3) what opportunities are there to link local ingredients and local cuisine to tourist food consumption in Koh Samui?

By using a participatory action research process to facilitate deeper dialogue between international expatriate chefs and local Thai chefs, opportunities to create a coconut-based 'glocalised' cuisine were identified. It is anticipated that this cuisine can potentially have a positive effect on the local culinary supply chain. Thus, building a stronger relationship between local agricultural production and the tourism industry through food tourism is one potential way in which Koh Samui can work towards achieving the 'green goals' suggested by the Tourism Authority of Thailand. If sustainable food tourism can be merged with low carbon menus, this will be helpful to Koh Samui's local community and the environment, and potentially, can be applied to other island destinations as well. Koh Samui has a way to go, but it is taking steps in the right direction.

Economic Sustainability in Food and Drink Tourism

While an increasing number of organizations are paying attention to ways to measure tourism's social, economic and environmental impact on destinations, few have tackled the food and drink tourism niche. Tourism economics is vital to all types of destinations around the world, but has a particularly important role in rural communities. Lodging receipts and sales taxes paid by visitors generate revenue that can be used to support schools, housing, roads and hospitals.

At its core, tourism creates jobs and businesses, both through direct employment within the tourism and hospitality industry, and indirectly in sectors such as farming, retail, transportation, manufacturers, suppliers and services. When visitors spend money on local goods and services, and when employees within these sectors spend their wages on goods and services, it leads to what is known as the "multiplier effect," creating even more jobs and small-scale business opportunities. Without tourist spending, a local economy can stagnate. New spending by tourists brings additional profit which can lead to additional investment back in the business, higher wages for employees and additional taxes for the municipality. In some tourism ecosystems, the multiplier effect of spending by tourists can be as high as seven times the impact of cash spent only by local residents.

Counting on the Multiplier Effect

In 2011, the Ontario (Canada) Culinary Tourism Association published a report showing that when a visitor buys local food, there is a 3:1 multiplier effect, and when a visitor buys local wine, the multiplier effect is 12:1. In other words, for every C$1 spent, the impact generates C$3 or C$12 respectively, across the local economy.

Island County in Washington State, USA implemented a culinary tourism plan in 2010, a time when tourism was on a downward trend nationally due to the recession. The county's tourism marketing director, Sherrye Wyatt, worked diligently with local, regional and national media to shine a spotlight on local food, wine and food-related events. She calculated that 60% of media placements between 2010 and 2012 either focused on or mentioned the culinary scene on Island County. During those years, the county saw an average 30% increase in hotel receipts and visitors, bringing much needed tax revenue that benefits local programs. The program is still new and unfortunately there were no prior campaigns for comparison.

Food tourism is an attraction that helps extend the length of stay and increase visitor expenditures. In an example presented by wine economist Karl Storchmann in 2010 in the *Journal of Wine Economics*,[25] Walla Walla, the most prominent wine region in Washington State, USA, found that slightly less than 17% of all restaurant revenue and approximately 40% of all hotel revenue is directly tied to the wine industry.

In 2011, the US State of Ohio determined that visitor spending reached US$26.3 billion, and of that, food and beverage spending captured 26%, or more than US$6.8 billion. The state has been able to estimate that 33% of food and beverage employment is supported by tourism. If suddenly Ohio lost its tourism industry, each household in the state would need to pay an additional tax of US$600 per year to replace the tourism taxes that would be missed by state and local governments.

Locals can also have a big impact on the economic sustainability of food and beverage businesses, and not only when showing out of town guests a good time. According to Michael Shuman, author of *Local Dollars, Local Sense*,[26] when locals buy local products, 45 cents of every dollar spent stays in the community. The Canadian province of British Columbia has been gathering local food purchasing data for several years and has discovered that in that province, there is a 4:1 multiplier effect when locals buy local foods.

Whether the spending on food and drink is by tourists or locals, buying locally produced food and drink provides a positive and measurable economic boost to the local community. According to the World Food Travel Association, visitors spend on average 25% of their travel budgets on food and drink, providing an additional economic boost that would not be present if the visitors never came. And when food and beverages are locally grown, produced or sourced, the impact can bring even greater, lasting, sustainable benefits, regardless of where the purchaser lives.

For those interested in learning more about the economic impact of food and drink tourism, we refer you to the chapter *Economic Impact of Food & Drink Tourism* in this book.

Issues in Food & Drink Tourism Sustainability

Small Local Production

Food and drink establishments are in business to make money. Whether they sell local or imported products, they aim to satisfy the needs and wishes of their customers. However, local wines, beer and spirits are not always available or locally produced. Consider a destination like Singapore, which produces Singha Beer but few other beverages of note. Visitors to the city's luxury or trendy hotels want to order a glass of wine or a mixed drink, so imported products must be used. There is no local wine or spirits industry to speak of, and the beer industry is limited. Food and drink establishments have no choice but to import products, sometimes from great distances.

Consider a different example of 42 Below vodka, which is popular and readily available in New Zealand, where it is made. Its production is limited compared to large international brands such as Absolut or Smirnoff. Two issues are raised here. First, a restaurant or bar may run out of a locally made beverage, such as when a special seasonal beer production runs out. Secondly, the locally made beverage may be difficult or impossible for the consumer to buy when they return home, as is the case with 42 Below Vodka, which is hard to find outside of New Zealand and Australia.[27] This can frustrate consumers who want to buy more of the products. Or it can lend a cachet to the destination, in that the consumer must travel to the destination in order to purchase or taste the product. This then leads to the discussion of reduction of carbon footprint by not importing faraway beverages vs. the consumer creating additional jet exhaust from air travel to the destination in question. Consider Fiji Water. Is it better to fly to Fiji to drink the water, or is it better (i.e. more responsible, more enjoyable, more tasty, or another subjective measurement) to purchase Fiji Water locally where the consumer lives? In a sustainable world, neither solution is truly tenable. Yet, we are in the food and drink tourism business. What is a conscientious consumer or business to do? What is fair for the business?

Fraud

Fraud can happen in a variety of settings, but we will consider a case study at a farmers' market. Farmers' markets are increasingly popular with visitors, especially in North America. While it is true that visitors cannot do much with raw agricultural products like rhubarb or asparagus back in their hotel rooms, a visit to a farmers' market is nevertheless of great interest to foodies. Visitors like to see new and different fruits and vegetables, sample local treats, and maybe even buy lunch. However, who certifies that the produce being sold at the market is local or organic when such claims are made? As a case in point we cite a recent visit to a farmers' market in metropolitan Portland, Oregon, USA.[28] One produce vendor was selling a variety of vegetables and marketing them as locally grown. However, behind the vendor's table was an array of empty produce boxes (the kind you would see at any large grocery store), with origins of Chile, China and Ecuador clearly labeled.[29] We did not confront the vendor, rather we asked the farmers' market management about certifying claims of locally sourced or organic fruits and vegetables. We discovered that no certification process for vendors was in place. In other words, vendors are free to drive to their nearest Walmart, purchase a truckload of fruits and vegetables, drive to the farmers' market, and call them local, organic or anything else they wish. While it seemed that this was the exception and not the rule in this particular farmers' market, *Caveat Emptor.*

Consumer Re-education

It may seem counterintuitive to tell the customer no, but in some cases that is what needs to be done. In a world that celebrates sustainability, restaurants would not serve Atlantic lobster in

318

the Midwest of the USA or Plains of Canada. One highly regarded restaurant in Edmonton, Alberta, Canada served fish from all over the world, including Perth, Australia; Nile River, Egypt; Alaska; California; Chile; and South Africa.[30] While some customers may appreciate the large number of choices, at what cost to the local economy or global environment are these choices made available? By helping consumers to readjust their expectations, business owners can support the march towards sustainable foodservice.

A model business in consumer re-education is the Sooke Harbour House, in Sooke, British Columbia, Canada. Although the inn would not claim that it is proactively reeducating consumers, it does so in a passive way. The inn has made the open commitment to source as much as possible of its food and drink products from Vancouver Island, where it is located. If the chef cannot find an ingredient he needs, he will look elsewhere in the Province of British Columbia. If he cannot find the ingredient locally or regionally, then the chef (and consequently, the diners), do without. The only exceptions to this rule include coffee, sugar, chocolate and orange juice. Still, the inn is a model of best practices in sustainability for this very commitment. Not all lodging properties have the ability to embrace such a program, or access to such local agricultural abundance. Nevertheless, when feasible, it should be considered by food tourism industry businesses.

Moving From Sustainability to Responsibility

Abuzz in our industry is the notion of whether "sustainability" is even the correct word choice, because it can imply to some that preserving and promoting sustainable practices encourages old bad habits to remain (i.e. the ways that things have been done previously are correct and must be preserved.) A better word choice may be "responsible" where an individual takes his or her own responsibility for his food and drink purchase decisions. For example, GoBox is a program in Portland, Oregon, USA that makes it easy for locals primarily to enjoy the popular local food carts while reducing material waste as much as possible.[31] Locals sign up for a Go Box, get a token for a takeaway food box, and redeem it at participating food carts. When they are done with their meal, they can drop used GoBoxes at participating venues nearby. The containers are then thoroughly washed and redelivered to food cart vendors for reuse. While such a solution may not be practical for or known to, food travelers, it is still an interesting program worth further consideration by other foodservice providers.

CONCLUSION

For sustainable food tourism to thrive, it must retain a sense of place and not become a commodity of exploitative exchange or a squandered resource. Sustainable food tourism shelters and nurtures heritage, while investing in the future. Models can be small and built on the strong shoulders of entrepreneurship, or developed with sweeping strategies formed with policy makers and industry leaders. Yet one vital element remains: there is room, and a need, for each person, local or visitor, to participate in and celebrate in the enjoyment of local foods and beverages.

Sustainability as a practice can be applied to both traveler behavior and business practices. It is a system of back and forth, and of mutual understanding and respect, among the visitor, the business, the local resident and the host destination. Sustainability has not yet woven its way fully into the food and drink tourism industry, but its very essence is essential to the success of our industry. Food and drink tourism businesses have the responsibility to be aware of sustainable practices and the importance to achieve balance among the three core aspects of sustainability: economy, environment and local community. Related to this is the need to teach local communities how to be sustainable themselves, and how to benefit from being sustainable.[32] This chapter gave reasons why consumers and businesses can and should strive to be more sustainable, and ideas of how to do so. The food tourism industry value chain must continually evaluate its commitment to sustainability.

DISCUSSION QUESTIONS

1. Promoting food tourism itself may be enough for a destination to undertake, without the additional perceived burden of adding sustainability to the mix. Discuss the pros and cons of factoring sustainability into food and drink tourism.
2. Visitors can be quite demanding and may not take the time to consider the reasons why their favorite distilled spirit from the other side of the planet is suddenly no longer available. Should a business take steps to educate its customers about sustainable food and drink consumption? If so, how can it do so without incurring the wrath of its customers?
3. Sustainability broaches environmental, economic and cultural issues. Which of these is most important to sustainability for your business or destination and why?

ENDNOTES

[1] United Nations Development Programme [UNDP], Making Tourism More Sustainable: A Guide for Policy Makers. (New York: UNDP, 2005).

[2] Prepared by John Drexhage and Deborah Murphy, International Institute for Sustainable Development, for United Nations, September, 2010 www.un.org/wcm/webdav/site/climatechange/shared/gsp/docs/GSP1-6_Background%20on%20Sustainable%20Devt.pdf

[3] Ibid

[4] It helps to globalize food consumption by spreading international awareness of food resources from around the planet. It helps to localize food consumption by underscoring the importance to support local and independent small foodservice businesses.

[5] Author's personal experience from multiple working site visits to various Pacific Islands.

[6] Tracy Berno, "Sustainability on a Plate: Linking Agriculture and Food in the Fiji Islands Tourism Industry". In *Tourism and agriculture: New geographies of consumption, production and rural restructuring,* eds. Rebecca Torres and Janet Momsen (London: Routledge, 2011), 87-103.

[7] Stefan Gössling et al., "Food Management in Tourism: Reducing Tourism's Carbon 'Foot print'". *Tourism Management,* 32, (2011): 534 – 543

[8] www.huffingtonpost.com/jake-schmidt/us-signs-into-law-bill-ca_b_2205079.html. US signs into Law Bill Calling for Global Solution to Aviation`s Carbon Pollution" Hof Post Green, Las modified July 5, 2013, www.huffingtonpost.com/jake-schmidt/us-signs-into-law-bill-ca_b_2205079.html

[9] Van Der Voo, Lee. Green Cruising or Cruise Ship Pollution? The Daily Green. August, 17 2010. www.thedailygreen.com/environmental-news/latest/cruise-ship-pollution-460810

[10] www.ecotourism.org

[11] www.sustainabletravel.org

[12] www.gstcouncil.org/sustainable-tourism-gstc-criteria/gstc-recognized-standards.html "Austrian Ecolabel For tourism" Travel forever, last modified July 5, 2013, www.gstcouncil.org/sustainable-tourism-gstc-criteria/gstc-recognized-standards.html

[13] For those who are interested in learning more about Portland's success, author Karen Brooks provides a wonderful detailed account of how Portland achieved culinary stardom in her book *The Mighty Gastropolis: Portland: A Journey Through the Center of America's New Food Revolution.*

[14] http://hotelfondae.com/turismo-eje-cafetero"Turismo eje cafetero", Hotel Fonda, last modified, July 5, 2013

[15] www.napagreen.org/about

[16] According to the winery's own reporting.

[17] For more information visit www.greenbiz.ca.gov/history.html

[18] Gössling, S., Garrod, B., Aall, C., Hille, J., and Peeters, P. 2011. Food management in tourism. Reducing tourism's carbon 'foodprint'. *Tourism Management* 32(3): 534-543.

[19] Somruthai Soontayatron, "Socio-cultural changes in Thai beach resorts: A case of Koh Samui Island, Thailand" (PhD thesis, Bournemouth University, Bournemouth, UK, 2010). http://eprints.bournemouth.ac.uk/15787/1/Thesis-final_version-_amandements.pdf

[20] Supapong Chaolan, "Lovely coconut bunches return". *Bangkok Post,* 5 March 2011,accessed 4 December 2012, www.bangkokpost.com/print/224905/

[21] Yuthasak Chatkaewnapanon *"Tourism and History: Change and Adaptation of Locals in the Tourism Period. A study of Koh Samui in Southern Thailand"* (Master's thesis, University of Otago, Dunedin, New Zealand, 2011). http://otago.ourarchive.ac.nz/bitstream/handle/10523/1934/ChatkaewnapanonY2011MTour.pdf?sequence=3

[22] Ray Green, "Community Perceptions of Environmental and Social Change and Tourism Development on the Island of Koh Samui, Thailand. *Journal of Environmental Psychology,* 25, (2005): 37-56.

[23] Corazon Catibog-Sinha & Pairin Wechtunyagu, "Natural and Cultural Heritage. Perceived Importance for Tourism: A Case Study in Thailand, *Journal of Tourism and Sustainability,* 1(1), (2011), 29-45.

[24] Thitimar Pruksorranan, Jutamas Wisansing & Tracy Berno, "The Culinary Tourism Supply Chain and the Reduction of Carbon Footprint: A Case Study of Koh Samui, Thailand", paper presented at the Council of Australasian Universities in Tourism and Hospitality Education Conference, Christchurch, February 11-14, 2013 (Christchurch: CAUTHE, 2013), X.

[25] Storchmann, K. (2010). *The economic impact of the wine industry on hotels and restaurants: evidence from Washington State. Journal of Wine Economics* 5(1), 164-183.

[26] Shuman, Michael. *"Local Dollars, Local Sense."* Chelsea Green Publishing. 2012

[27] Recently 42 Below, owned by Bacardi Limited, has been making an effort to enter the US market, which is already oversaturated with premium vodkas. It has not had great success as of this writing. This implies that vodka enthusiasts must travel to New Zealand to try the vodka in its many flavors. Particularly interesting is the manuka honey flavor.

[28] Author's personal visit to a farmers' market in metropolitan Portland, Oregon, USA, 22 June 2013.

[29] It is possible these boxes with other countries of origin were merely used to transport the home-grown produce, although that did not appear to be the case. The overwhelming majority of other farms transported their produce in either boxes correctly labeled with their farm's name, or in plain plastic or wooden crates.

[30] Author's personal visit to said restaurant in Edmonton, Alberta, Canada, February 2007. Restaurant name not cited for reasons of diplomacy.

[31] For more information visit www.goboxpdx.com

[32] For example, in Portland, Oregon, USA, the elected regional government called Oregon Metro which serves approximately 2 million residents in the Portland metropolitan region, decreased its garbage collection fees charged to the public by 1% for the 2013-2014 fiscal year for the sole reason that the program has been so successful largely due to resident participation. Presumably, the program makes sufficient income due to the sale of the recycled materials it collects, that some of the savings can be passed along to the resident. This is the kind of win-win situation that is needed for programs like this to succeed.

Professional Services in Foodservice

Benjamin Brown

This chapter looks at some of the practical issues around professional services such as media relations, legal, and design services in food and drink tourism. What are the benefits of choosing a specialist in food and drink? How do you find such specialists? How do you measure success? This chapter will explore these issues specifically for foodservice businesses, although other food and drink manufacturers and providers may find the information of value as well.

INTRODUCTION

"To succeed in business, to reach the top, an individual must know all it is possible to know about that business." – J. Paul Getty

This chapter is dedicated to the marketing, public relations [PR], design and legal services, which foodservice businesses use to build their reputations, expand loyal customer bases, and develop on the right track. The mentors consulted in this segment hold dozens of years of restaurant management experience in Las Vegas, one of the world's most prominent dining capitals. Many of these concepts can be applied to restaurants in other locations, of different sizes and with both smaller and larger budgets. There is one motif that brings it all together: invest in success, early.

Marketing

Simply put, restaurant marketing is a set of promotional campaigns dedicated to getting more customers through the door. Marketing, unlike public relations [explained later], is often paid, though social media and additional guerilla marketing tactics are often executed at no cost. Those serious about starting a restaurant, however, should be prepared to dedicate part of their budget to marketing.

The Goal of Restaurant Marketing

"The general goal of marketing should be to increase awareness to new and potential customers, while building continual loyalty with current customers," says Marina Nicola, Director of VOX Solid Communications Las Vegas.[1] Nicola spent time with global giant Caesar's Entertainment before going into business on her own, bringing some sizeable clients with her. And whether handling celebrity chefs or local eateries, Nicola agrees that restaurant marketing is a necessity, no matter how good the food is or how popular a restaurant thinks itself to be.

On another note, restaurant marketing allows professionals who specialize in marketing to handle marketing, leaving restaurateurs to do what they do best: handle the restaurant. This may sound like common sense, but restaurateurs often overlook the true time commitment needed to market their product. Again, even great food, service and ambiance will not bring the crowd in unless some medium exists to make your product known to the public. Once people get into the business, they often get so involved with in-house operations that they cannot bring the constant influx of new customers they need, and cannot meet their growth potential as a result. Restaurant marketing agencies use various tactics to spark consumer interest. An array of marketing campaigns, from the formally traditional to the oddly creative, can be tweaked to reach virtually every target audience.

A virtually endless number of tactics exist for restaurants to attract customers. They vary in cost and require significant time and attention. A marketing agency specializes in these procedures. Utilizing an agency will save you substantial time, and eventually money, in the long run.

Quintessential to restaurant marketing is a professional website. Nearly everyone who is interested in a restaurant's marketing materials will google the eatery. Countless potential customers have been steered away from an establishment simply because all they could find was a Yelp page [more on Yelp later]. A Facebook page [also more later] does not work well, nor does a do-it-yourself website that on screen looks like an eight year old's art project. Professional websites create trust, and no marketing campaign can thrive without trust. Invest in a web designer to create your layout, and learn how to update the site yourself from there. Never let a web designer write your copy (the actual words on the site). Come up with that yourself, or better yet, have a marketing or PR agency do it for you to really craft the most effective message possible.

Nearly all marketing initiatives give customers a monetary incentive to dine. Coupons, happy hours, 2-for-1 specials, discounted signature dishes, free house wine with dinner, the list goes on. Publish incentives like these on your website. Print them out if a legitimate outlet exists for distribution, but placing flyers on front doors or car windshields may steer people away rather than bring them in. Some restaurants even publish code words on their websites, giving special discounts for customers in the know.

Participate in community food events whenever possible. Restaurant weeks allow people outside of your traditional target audience to experience your establishment, paving the way for future visits and referrals. Food festivals happen almost everywhere, and any chance for you to get a booth is a great way to promote your business in a new location, extending your outreach in the community. Always stock your booth with menus, business cards and/or any promotional materials you may have.

Advertising space in newspapers, magazines, radio and television generally yields good results, although traditionally it is the most expensive. If you are ready to invest in a traditional media ad, make sure it is professionally designed and vetted by a focus group (which can be comprised of just your peers) before submitting it for publication.

Equally important to marketing to new customers is marketing to current customers. Collect data on your customers in any way possible. Survey cards are a great, affordable way to do this, as well as help improve your business. A small card, handed with the bill, should list 4-5 multiple choice questions about the dining experience, how they heard about you (very important for verifying the benefit of a marketing or PR service) as well as an additional comments section below.

Contact information is useful for sending marketing materials directly. In your survey, offer a coupon for including an email address and/or phone number (customers are usually more willing to give their email). You will inevitably receive false information from time to time, but do not take it personally. Never press a customer for contact information, but giving them the option will allow you to foster more personable relationships though promotional texts or emails. Limit the frequency of these messages, however, to once a month or special occasions.

Point of sale [POS] systems, used for running credit cards, keep track of customer spending habits. This information allows you to see peak hours and which items on the menu are selling, as well as specific customer party sizes, check (bill) sizes, frequency of visits, and ordering preferences.

Use this data to send personalized marketing materials. If you know a customer always skips the appetizers, send him or her an email with a coupon for a free appetizer. This could lead to larger profit per visit.

Social Media

"Like us on Facebook" and "Follow us on Twitter" are actions that have become about as commonplace in restaurant marketing as red wine is with a good steak. Social media is simple, user-friendly, reaches a mass audience, and best of all, can be free. Important to note, however, is that because these glorious features exist, *everyone* uses social media. The market is saturated. When managed strategically, however, major social media outlets still serve as an excellent tool for getting your name out there.

"It's a great, low cost tool for reaching your target audience," says Todd Ford, PR Director for the Stratosphere Hotel, Casino and Tower on the Las Vegas Strip.[2] Ford's day-to-day responsibilities are multifold, involving constant communication with the Stratosphere's marketing team, media, celebrities and major business partners for mutually beneficial projects.

"It has to be done thoughtfully," he cautions. "[It] requires a time commitment to develop interesting content, monitor and then engage with your fans and followers."

Do not waste your time with minor social media sites. This will detract from the attention necessary for a proper Facebook page or Twitter handle. Social media is a 24/7 operation. If you are serious about your social media campaign, be prepared to respond to ugly comments posted at 11 p.m. on a Saturday.

Building Customer Loyalty

Restaurants derive the majority of their income from repeat customers. Marketing campaigns should not only be geared to get customers through the door, but back at a table time after time. Getting a customer to pay full price on repeat visits is the hardest part. Many easy promotional methods can serve restaurants well, but often hurt business instead of help because they do not necessarily build customer loyalty. Make sure your promotional efforts allow you to actually see profit from your patrons over the long term. Keep in mind that marketing to locals can also help turn them into ambassadors for your business or destination. Naturally that is not realistic when marketing to tourists, but tourists gladly share information and experiences with everyone they meet — colleagues who live locally, the hotel where they are staying, and even other travelers. Tourists should not be ignored just because you think they might only buy from you once.

It is easy to bring a person in one time by offering a huge discount. Services like Groupon and LivingSocial are certain ways to get your name out and bring in customers from across the community. However, study after study finds that the massive discount coupon model is not sustainable. Restaurants lose money on customers who pay half the standard price, expecting that these customers will come back to pay full price in the future. Most customers will not return, choosing to move onto the next restaurant that offers a mega-discount. These waves of discount-crazed spenders leave restaurants to recoup from the economic mess they cause, not to mention the cost of running the coupon itself.

Yelp is another service that provides great publicity, but can cost restaurants dearly. Restaurants do not have to pay to appear on Yelp, but Yelp's business subscription service, which costs between US$300-1000/month, has come under serious fire. According to an article on Wired.com, a class action lawsuit against Yelp was filed in Los Angeles, accusing Yelp of extortion.[3] Businesses complained that those who paid Yelp were able to allocate negative reviews to the bottom of the list, and the most positive reviews to the top, hurting the site's reputation for "Real people. Real reviews." Restaurants who offer customers incentive to write positive ratings on Yelp can be called to public scrutiny, losing a great deal of trust in the community as a result.

Remember the goal of restaurant marketing throughout your campaigns as goals change and evolve. Get customers through the door and wanting to come back on their own whim. And while marketing creates the incentive, public relations builds the trust needed to fuel continuing visits.

Public Relations (PR)

Often confused with marketing, PR serves a separate role by building the restaurant's reputation in sync with increasing customer numbers. Advertising through PR is argued by many to be more effective than marketing. Often conducted by different firms, the two professions go hand-in-hand for building a true empire.

The Goal of Restaurant PR

"PR goals for restaurants are multifold: Create recognition and positive awareness. Maintain relevance in the market. Help foster loyalty among customers and generate trust among those who are not yet customers," Ford says.

PR goes beyond the restaurant itself, promoting each individual facet of the establishment in order to better represent the business as a whole. Thinking critically about the restaurant breaks it down into numerous sub-features, from the chef to signature dishes, entertainment and so on. PR brings these features to the public eye.

"We establish a personality for the Chef and/or owner to build customer relationships," says Ford. One of his head chefs, Rick Giffen, was featured on the Food Network's *Chopped*. Additional members of his staff regularly attend community events and industry functions to expand the Stratosphere's brand among potential partners and consumers. Simply said, PR builds trust.

Difference between Marketing and PR

"PR differs from advertising in that it provides information and opportunities to media, which in turn tells the story to the public," says Ford. "Readers assign more credibility to impartial articles and reviews from journalists than they do from paid advertising messages." Marketing and PR hold a complimentary relationship. On one end, marketing creates incentives that attract customer interest, "Let's go here for dinner. I've seen it advertised in my favorite magazine for the past month and have been dying to try it," says your friend. On the other end, PR creates that sense of trust that actually gets people through the door, at a table, writing the check. "Oh, that place! I've seen the same ads. Wasn't too sure about the place but it got a good review in the newspaper. Yeah let's check it out," says your other friend. Oversimplified, but probably you have been involved in a conversation like this at least once, if not many times.

Recognizing a Successful PR Agency

While marketing and PR firms specialize in different skills, the successful businesses in either field hold similar traits. Experts agree that big names do not necessarily guarantee results. "Signs of a successful...agency include the acumen of those who will be working on the account. And I repeat, those who will be working on the account," begins Nicola. "The names on the door don't count unless it truly is a small, boutique agency. Otherwise, you might get a revolving door of 20-somethings working on your account." Don't let age or experience stray you away, however. The key is passion.

"I'd rather than have a person like that who loves my restaurant and has a passion for food versus someone whose client credits are two pages long but without any soul behind the work," says Nicola. She poses the ultimate question for true restaurant PR experts. "Does this team have a passion for food? Those are the people who read Saveur on the weekends and watch the Food Network while they work out – looking for ways to pitch clients."

On a more finite scale, Todd Ford emphasizes the numbers. "Review relevant case studies and measurable results from their other restaurant clientele and information about their process/procedures and cost for services," he says. Ford also discusses the importance peers play in recommending firms that helped lead them to success. "Word of mouth is hard to beat. Ask other restaurateurs for referrals."

Also weighing in on the subject is Michelle Schenk, director at SK+G Public Relations in Las Vegas. Handling multiple high-profile clients across the city has taught Schenk the importance of establishing personable relationships for professional success. "They should be able to provide insights into how they would approach your campaign and illustrate that they understand your brand and competitive set in the market," Schenk says. "Finding someone that meets the above qualifications should complemented by synergistic personalities and good communication skills. Knowing that you will be able to communicate well is just as important as feeling confident in the work they will do on your behalf."

Find people who share your passion. Be sure that they have a successful track record in your industry, or if they are not that established, that they hold the potential to meet your restaurant's goals. Finally, sync your personalities around the common goal and establish open, honest relationships. Establishing firm groundwork will maximize the benefit you will get out of restaurant PR, and will pave the way for campaigns to reach their full potential.

PR Strategies

While restaurant PR serves many roles, handling the media is one of the most important responsibilities.

"The contacts, relationships, outreach, time and writing skills a good publicist has increases visibility in the media and helps create a buzz in the community which in turn leads to increased diners," says Alejandra Gilbert, manager with VirgenGard Inc., who handles restaurants with global prominence. She points out that PR provides an even greater lifeline during holiday rushes or promotional seasons. In one case, VirgenGard handles news coverage and celebrity attendances during Oktoberfest for Hofbräuhaus, famous for German food and beer.

Press releases are a critical asset in PR. Gilbert adds that "writing skills a good publicist has increases visibility in the media," and these skills come out best in press releases that promote restaurant openings, new menus, holiday menus, seasonal specials, promotional events, and related materials. PR firms do a great job of wording content in a way that best glorifies your work, and send the news via an email blast to their list of media contacts.

A good press release will take the form of a pre-written article, and it is commonplace for media to essentially copy/paste this content into their own outlets. Forget for a moment that plagiarism is bad: in this case, the media is publicizing you in exactly the way you want.

For the most part, the more credentialed media coverage that a PR service is able to secure, the better. Working with food critics is an ongoing adventure (explained in detail later), but unbiased reviews are your best bet for generating trust in your business.

Costs and Expectations

"Like with anything else you buy in life, you will get what you pay for," Nicola says. If you're looking to build your empire, the last thing you want is for the wheels to fall off your restaurant's expansion campaign because you skimped out on what could have been a solid outside service. It is like finding the cheapest doctor to perform brain surgery: there are just some cases where you should pay the price, or your will end up paying the price.

Most firms did not specify fees, stating that costs vary according to the restaurant needs. While this is very true, Gilbert says a legitimate PR service will run restaurateurs "between US$2500-5000 per month for a minimum of three months; however, many firms adjust that retainer depending on the restaurant's budget."

As far as a timeline goes, results will vary in terms of when restaurateurs will start to see return on their investment in the form of increased customer draw. Some firms say as little as two to three months, noting that many magazines run a few months out, i.e. a writer may review your restaurant in January, but the article may not show up until the April issue. Some say a year or more. All agree, however, that constant communication is necessary for both parties to meet the common goal.

Best to go into a partnership with the mindset that your investment now will lead to monumental return in the future. Remember that what you spend financially, you will save in time, far and away your most precious resource. By budgeting for outside PR and marketing services, you can fully commit yourself to turning out the best dining experience possible. This way, when those marketing and PR firms do their job and customers start pouring in, they are treated to the quality you sought to deliver. This synergy is what keeps customers coming back.

Food Critics: The Good, The Bad, and The Necessary

Food critics, food journalists, reporters, or whatever other title they may go by, play a vital role in a restaurant's expansion. The job comes with mixed reviews, no pun intended. Some view critics as acclaimed individuals who advance the industry by popularizing the good and doing away with the bad experiences, in a sense evolving the industry with a Darwinian touch. Others find critics to be unnecessary and elitist, out of touch with the true customer, perhaps because they receive some kind of special treatment.

The Role of a Food Critic

When asked if food critics contribute to a restaurant's profit, Todd Ford said, "I'm not at liberty to share data/figures...but [I] can tell you that we hold strong reviews in high regard." Restaurants can report sales increasing anywhere from 5-20% with a good review.

Critics are meant to share the perspective of an average customer. Most food critics, or the legitimate ones at least, do not expect or even want special treatment when they walk through the door. And while you may hear about journalists who wear disguises to protect their anonymity, they are the minority. Most food critics will first contact the restaurant, or more likely, its PR agency, before coming in.

Critics do differ from the average customer in that they sample a wide variety of items from the menu. To judge a restaurant by one appetizer, one main course and one dessert would not do the establishment justice. In addition, it always helps when a manager, general manager and/or chef spends a few minutes with a critic to discuss the restaurant, their personal story, and the inspiration behind the food. These facts add significant personable qualities to the review, building the brand and trust that customers seek.

Different Types of Media Requests

PR directors agree that the standard food review involves the food critic and a guest, where the restaurant will cover the cost of food and drink over several visits, although most reviews are done in one visit. Larger media outlets have the budget to cover meals, but many highly-acclaimed critics will still visit on a comp (i.e. complimentary, or no charge to them). Some restaurateurs gawk at the idea of providing free food, but relatively speaking a free meal falls far below the cost of most advertising spaces, both print and online. Not to mention your publicity comes in the form of a written feature and photo series, far more elaborate than an ad could be, and garners greater trust from readers than an ad could generate. As for allowing a guest: few people like to eat alone, and the company adds critical perspective on atmosphere. In some cases, PR firms will send their representative who handles your account to dine with the critic, but this is more of a rarity.

Be mindful that food critics cannot be bought. Comping (i.e. providing for free) a meal does not guarantee a positive review. "All any restaurant can do is put their best foot forward every time," says Schenk. The critic may bring a camera, but be sure to send them professional high resolution photos to accompany their review (your marketing or PR service should take these when first starting work with you). Even some acclaimed critics will publish photos shot with phones or point-and-shoot cameras, which will not do justice to your food. Some critics lie on the other extreme, bringing in an elaborate lighting setup for their table.

Be sure to go over norms before the review. Critics with large photo setups should come in when the restaurant is less empty. If you are willing to comp food but not drink, say so. Most critics follow good ethics by not ordering pricy wines, but if a problem arises, do not be afraid to speak out. Expect the critic to tip the server. Expect the critic to send you a copy of the review once it is published. This can take anywhere from a few days to a few months, but never hesitate to follow up with them if you have not seen anything.

Media Events

A way to achieve multiple goals with one activity, is by hosting a media night, typically held a few weeks after the restaurant's opening. In this setting, the restaurant dedicates a night to hosting its entire list of media contacts. Traditional media nights are similar to cocktail parties, where the restaurant closes most of its space for a 2-3 hour window. Servers navigate through the crowd with samples of the restaurant's signature food and drink items.

The benefits to media nights are multi-fold. Instead of making separate accommodations for different reviews, you will get them all at once. The mass of press coverage gives your restaurant a strong starting foundation in the community. Media nights, while requiring more effort and a larger expense up front, are far more economic for both time and money over time.

Some reviewers will use media nights to publish teaser articles that make customers aware of the restaurant without going into much depth. They will insist on a follow-up review to cover the full restaurant experience. This is perfectly acceptable and will often earn you double the publicity.

Pros over "Fauxs"

Food critics clearly enjoy some excellent benefits, so naturally everyone wants to be a food critic. It is extremely important to choose your media contacts wisely. Today, there is no shortage of self-proclaimed foodies with blogs, etc." says Ford. "A PR firm can help to separate the pretenders from legitimate, reputable journalists with a sizeable following."

PR firms provide great benefit in laying down the law. While media coverage is of great necessity for long-term success, be sure it comes from a viable source. Ask for work samples and data to verify a writer's following, but do not press too hard. Legitimate journalists will never put up an argument in this matter while the "wannabes" will give you a lengthy excuse for reasons why they are not at liberty to discuss their numbers.

"Our job is to know which ones have merit then react swiftly and communicate the opportunity to the client," says Schenk. "We also know how to politely decline opportunities that are not the right fit." Legitimate critics will never hold a refusal against you.

Maintaining Relationships with Media

Interaction with a food critic should not end when the review publishes. Media contacts are among your best marketing tools, and continued communication allows you to utilize these resources time and time again to promote your establishment. In addition to their readers, critics influence very large peer groups and will always send referrals to the restaurants where they hold the closest relationships. If a journalist contacts you, immediately refer them to your PR representative and/or add them to your contact list. Include them in all news and press releases. Even if you deny them a review, continued communication will open doors to greater opportunity in the future.

Restaurant Design

Great food is only part of the restaurant experience. Customers want atmosphere. They are not just looking for a good meal, they are looking for escape, to transport body and mind away from the world they live in and seek haven under your hospitality. A restaurant's design, done strategically and executed with care, can escalate the dining experience you offer to a whole new level. And while menus are easy to change, you restaurant's layout is intended to last. Dedicate your full time and attention to planning the look and feel of your restaurant and install every possible detail before even thinking about opening your doors.

Selecting Your Space

"Honestly, this was the best location we could afford," said Steve Piamchuntar, who opened his small plates restaurant, Nosh & Swig, in Las Vegas's east side. Piamchuntar comes from years of working on the Las Vegas Strip and well aware that location is everything. But real estate is expensive, and restaurateurs will have to think critically about how they plan to cover overhead costs before writing any checks.

"My wife and I had enough money to buy this place on our own," begins Piamchuntar. His wife, Lorie, manages the front of the house while he serves as Executive Chef. "No investors, no rent. This takes all the pressure off. Now we just get to have fun."

Nosh & Swig may not attract a global audience like restaurants on the Strip do, and may not even be in the most ideal spot for locals, but this location's benefits far outweigh its costs. Location will always be a driving factor in drawing customers, and restaurants should open in an area where the local crowd matches their target audience.

Jeff Kovatch, owner of Greens and Proteins Healthy Kitchen, opened his first location next to one of Las Vegas's most popular gyms. Superfood smoothies and body-conscious sandwiches were an instant winner with the crowd. "We got our regulars after only a few days. Perfect place for a pre- or post-workout meal and a great spot to relax after a tiring session at [the gym]," says Kovatch. "G and P" as he calls it, has opened up a second location across town, also next to a prominent gym.

Selecting Your Designer

Some restaurateurs may want to flex their creative side by designing their own place. Lorie Piamchuntar painted Nosh & Swig's décor herself. Most, however, will save considerable effort and achieve spectacular results with a professional designer. If food is your craft, let that be your focus, and let someone who specializes in design make magic where you cannot.

Look up designers local to your area, as you will want to meet on a regular basis, not just during the restaurant's conception but over time as changes will inevitably take place. Find someone with specific experience in restaurant design: a good residential designer may not be able to apply the same skill set to a dining environment. Ask the designer about his or her connections with suppliers, which will provide significant benefit when it comes to acquiring flooring, tables, chairs and other necessities.

Select a professional who may not agree with you on everything, but whose opinion you value and respect. A professional's reputation, no matter how prestigious, is no match compared to the potential for a lasting relationship.

Fit Your Target Audience

Regardless of who designs your establishment, the most important thing is to center your business around your target audience and not the other way around. Think critically about your restaurant (or B&B or resort, etc.) type: what kind of cuisine are you going to feature; is it low-key, fine dining or somewhere in between; is it fast casual, full service or some other type? These factors, along with location, will likely determine the type of person most likely to dine with you.

Center your restaurant's design around your target audience's interests. See your layout from the customer's point of view. Step into their shoes. What do they do for a living? Families? Kids? How old? What occasion would inspire them to dine with you? What feelings are they hoping to get out of your experience [besides a full stomach]? What other restaurants could they go to, and why does your restaurant set a better scene?

Create a mood that meets these parameters. If you know your restaurant is going to attract a lot of families, aim for amenities that appeal to all ages, allowing parents to enjoy a night out while keeping the kids busy. If you seek a more upscale approach centered around couples and small groups, focus on intimacy. As a restaurant owner you are not only responsible for turning out great taste, you are making memories too.

Design on a Budget

Designing your restaurant should be one of the funnest steps in building your empire. Flex your creativity and tame your stress by approaching your establishment with a resourceful mindset. As much as all restaurateurs would love to hang Swarovski crystal chandeliers from the ceiling, most will be without the budget for the glamor they had hoped for. Those who put their mind to the task, however, will soon find that artistic sense will trumps deep pockets the vast majority of the time.

"We wanted to give our restaurant an organic feel, so why not make it come to life?" says Kovatch about designing Greens and Proteins. Visually enchanting planters and a small waterfall line the walls at this fast-casual health bar, bringing out the food's natural qualities. The design required minimal finances and simple installment for incredibly high yield.

Renew. Reuse. Recycle. The three R's play a vital role in restaurant design. If you are renovating an old restaurant, salvage any décor that may serve aesthetic purpose. Tables, chairs, bars, even glasses and salt and pepper shakers can be made from unusual materials. One of Todd Ford's newest restaurants, McCall's Heartland Grill, melts down wine bottles to use as serving plates, and cuts wine bottles in half to use as water glasses.

Being resourceful may involve turning your head to places you may not think of as 'professional' or 'standard' for the industry. Vintage stores, flea markets and even online listings can become valuable resources for finding materials that can make your restaurant memorable. As long as it meets building and safety codes and fits the desires of your target audience, any material can pave the way for your restaurant's true identity.

Legal Services

As is the case with starting any new business, set legal procedures are in order for establishing your business. And while the restaurateur (or resort owner or food manufacturer, etc.) on a tight budget can manage other facets, there really is no room for flexibility when it comes to legal services. Getting started under the rules and regulations of your trade will take more time from the onset, but will save you substantial heartache, and certainly from potential lawsuits, that could take place later.

Legal Procedures for Opening a Restaurant

The U.S. Small Business Administration, or SBA, offers some basic guidelines (below) for new restaurants.[4] While these principles certainly will vary abroad, they can form a general checklist for restaurateurs anywhere

Zoning laws: Whether you are building a new restaurant or taking over from an existing restaurant, check the area's zoning laws to make sure your concept can operate on that site.

Negotiate your lease: lay out clear guidelines that you agree to follow with the owner of the property. Also check if surrounding restaurants have contracts in the area. For example, if you are opening a breakfast establishment, be sure that the coffee shop around the corner is not the only place allowed to serve food and drink during breakfast hours.

Licenses and permits: restaurants typically require a food service establishment permit, an alcohol beverage license, a general business license and a food safety permit. Permit requirements vary by area or neighborhood, so be sure to search requirements according to your location. Food trucks and other mobile restaurants need to meet permit requirements for all areas where they operate.

Food safety: Health codes vary, but all restaurants must safely handle, store and prepare food. All employees must also maintain proper hygiene. Plan to submit an application for a food safety permit, to your local environmental health department, at least a month before opening.

Insurance: Restaurants have the potential for injuries, which can bring medical expenses and lawsuits. Restaurateurs should invest in property insurance, general liability insurance, worker's compensation insurance and liquor liability insurance. Most establishments that serve alcohol are required to hold liquor liability insurance, or are otherwise responsible for all damages resulting from alcohol consumption, including drunk driving.

Common Potential Lawsuits

Legal issues facing restaurateurs are two-fold, coming from both customers and employees. Best to keep the most common issues in mind when setting up your restaurant and listing procedures, so as to prevent these incidences from ever occurring.

- Slip, trip and fall accidents: Be sure your business layout allows you maximum capacity crowd to navigate the venue safely. Establish policies to immediately clean up any floor spills. Line stairs and walkways with proper non-slip material.

- Food poisoning: Follow all legal guidelines for food preparation, storage and handling, and be sure your suppliers do the same. Always err on the side of caution: better to throw out 100 dollars (or euros or pounds, etc.) worth of meat than spend thousands of dollars (or euros or pounds, etc.) and countless hours in a court case. Post disclaimers on your menu.

- Violent crimes: Post disclaimers and never hesitate to contact authorities.

- Parking lot accidents: Post disclaimers. Address any issues with driving records among your employees.

- Pedestrian accident: Be sure the area surrounding your restaurant is well lit and floors provide proper grip and footing.

- Hot coffee spills: Train employees not to rush when handling hot food and drink.

- Defective stairways, chairs and tables: Routinely inspect all facets of your restaurant. Follow all building codes.

- Alcohol-related cases: Restaurants should not serve intoxicated patrons and are responsible for ensuring these patrons abide by the law on premises and get home safely.

- Lawsuits filed by employees may include all of the above, as well as points below. These cases are common not just in the restaurant industry, but in virtually any working environment.

- Discrimination: In the USA, follow guidelines set by the Civil Rights Act and the Americans with Disabilities Act. Consult with the Equal Employment Opportunity Commission for any issues. Elsewhere, consult anti-discrimination laws in your area (or if none in your area, search online for recommended guidelines).

- Harassment: Harassment cases can come from relationships between any combination of supervisors, coworkers, clients and customers. While sexual harassment is most commonly in the spotlight, which includes comments as well as physical interactions, harassment can include workplace violence or bullying. Maintain open, honest relationships with staff to prevent harassment cases before they start.

- Workplace Injury: Follow building codes and sanitary guidelines to maintain a safe working environment. In addition, become familiar with employee rules and regulations for maximum time worked, break minimums and duty restrictions to ensure you are not violating any labor codes.

- Wrongful Termination: Termination of an employee must be justified with clear evidence. Firing an employee who filed a legitimate complaint is not grounds for termination.

Selecting a Lawyer

No business owner wants to deal with a lawsuit, but every business owner should be prepared for the worst-case scenario. Investing in a lawyer is mandatory. Choosing a lawyer is similar to selecting a marketing or PR service, even if for a different end result. While non-Americans may laugh at the over-litigious American society and believe they have little to worry about, that behavior is rapidly working its way overseas.

Be sure your lawyer has applicable experience in the appropriate industry (foodservice, lodging, manufacturing, etc.). Just because the lawyer has a great reputation for clearing people of traffic tickets does not mean the lawyer can help start a restaurant or defend you in an injury lawsuit. Past clients and cases should reflect restaurant owners and the issues you may have to deal with in the future. Of course it is advisable to have a lawyer with a positive track record who has won more cases than they have lost.

On top of these basic qualifications, however, the most important quality of a lawyer is trust. Find a lawyer who you can truly put your faith in and work with if the times get tough. A strong relationship with your lawyer will allow you to grow your empire at a much quicker pace, keeping everything in order. Lawyers are expensive, costing several hundred dollars (or equivalent in your currency) per hour at least. Investing well early on can save you thousands, if not millions of dollars (or equivalent) in the future.

Invest Now, Profit Exponentially

A common motif exists among marketing, PR, design and legal services for your restaurant: investment. Invest in people who are experts in their trade. They will typically market your restaurant better than you could yourself. They can often design your space in a way you never dreamed possible. They will land your appearances in your community's most prominent media outlets. And unless you have a law degree, they are a necessity for keeping you out of trouble.

The earlier you invest in these experts, the more time and money you will save. Factor in the costs of these services into your budget from the outset. This way, you can approach your investors with one lump request. The last thing you want to do is attempt to do everything on your own, realize you cannot after wasting hundreds of hours and thousands of dollars in the process, and come back to your investors with a request for more money. This will cause nothing but frustration for both parties. A solid investor will appreciate your depth of thought and, provided they have the means, should be very willing to provide the additional funds for these services so long as they are included in your business plan.

Plan your ideal restaurant beforehand. Map out every conceivable detail, and make this plan as clear as possible before approaching any outside service. You are in full control of your dream, and you can only make it happen if a clear picture exists. An exact plan will help others see this picture and bring it to fruition. Even the most accomplished PR executives and designers cannot expand on a product if they do not know enough about the product itself.

The more research and planning you do before opening your doors, the more control you will have once the first customers arrive. You will be incredibly busy handling day to day operations, and the last thing you want to think about then is retracing your steps to the design stages or marketing efforts, or even a legal issue. Granted, you will never be fully ready, but as in most business cases, 80 percent planned and 20 percent learned on the job is a healthy approach to take for your restaurant.

CONCLUSION

Marketing, public relations, design and legal services are quintessential facets for building and expanding your culinary empire. Remember that the most successful asset within a business is its people: recruit professionals who you respect both professionally and personally, for these relationships will allow set an invaluable foundation for a strong and prosperous future. Stay involved with these partners, maintaining constant communication through both the good times and the bad. And never be afraid to speak your mind — it is your business, after all.

DISCUSSION QUESTIONS

1. What are some of the legal and operational issues that are unique to opening a foodservice business in your area?
2. Some professional services such as lawyers require licensing for a particular geographic area. Which professional services require licensing in your area? What are the terms, fees and benefits of these licenses?
3. Outsourced professional services generally imply that a true expert of the service in question will be performing the work needed. Some experts perform better than others. Some small business owners argue that they prefer to do design, legal, or marketing work themselves because they can control every facet of the task. Discuss the benefits and challenges of using outsourced professionals vs. a small business owner doing the work him- or herself.

ENDNOTES

[1] Author interview with Marina Nicola, Director, VOX Solid Communications Las Vegas, Nevada, 14 January 2013.
[2] Author interview with Todd Ford, Public Relations Director, Stratosphere Hotel, Casino and Tower, Las Vegas, Nevada, 16 January 2013.
[3] www.wired.com/threatlevel/2010/02/yelp-sued-for-alleged-extortion
[4] www.sba.gov/community/blogs/community-blogs/business-law-advisor/opening-and-running-restaurant-%E2%80%93-legal-and-regu

Best Practices in Destination Food Tourism Branding

Lena Mossberg, John Mulcahy, Neha M. Shah, & Inger Svensson

What are great examples of food tourism branding by nations, regions and smaller localities? It may not be the destinations you expect. Good marketing helps, but equally important are quality goods and strategic product development. This chapter looks at three case studies and offers models that can be followed by other destinations seeking to develop their food tourism brands.

INTRODUCTION

Often the driver for food tourism development in an area is the destination marketing organization (DMO), which is like the tip of the iceberg with area relationships. The DMO may or may not have a food tourism strategy in place, but at least it should have an idea of the goals it wishes to achieve with a food tourism initiative. This chapter looks at three destinations — Ireland, West Sweden and North Carolina — and what each has done to succeed in its food tourism branding efforts.

Ireland's Journey

The purpose of the section is to share, using case studies, Ireland's journey on the road to branding itself as a food tourism destination, while also maintaining some existing key attributes (e.g. tradition of hospitality, prime agriculture products, 'Irishness') that differentiate Ireland in its primary markets, such as the USA, UK, France and Germany.

The genesis of Ireland's approach to food tourism is best understood through some discussion of the wider environment. Fáilte Ireland,[1] a government organization, is the national tourism development authority in Ireland. Its role is to support the Irish tourism industry and work to sustain Ireland as a high-quality and competitive tourism destination. It provides a range of practical supports to help tourism businesses better manage and market their products and services. The organization also works with other agencies and representative bodies, at local and national levels, to implement and champion positive and practical strategies that will benefit Irish tourism and the Irish economy. With the DiscoverIreland.ie website, it promotes Ireland as a holiday destination through a domestic marketing campaign and manages a network of nationwide tourist information centers that provide help and advice for visitors to Ireland.

In 2010, with food tourism becoming a growing market segment internationally and many destinations, including those in Ireland's competitive set, beginning to develop this sector as a means to gaining competitive advantage, Fáilte Ireland, in consultation with key industry stakeholders, developed the "National Food Tourism Implementation Framework 2011 – 2013".[2]

Historically, Ireland has had a difficult relationship with food driven by its history of colonization, the painful famine and stoic Catholicism.[3] It is only just on the cusp of realizing its own food culture and identity, which is still evolving and emerging. However, Irish food culture has undergone a significant and exciting transformation in the last decade, and in particular in the last five years, with the advent of an emerging, ingredient-driven Irish cuisine. Interestingly, Ireland's current recession has focused the population on the importance of supporting Irish products and producers resulting in changing food purchasing habits and generating a new appreciation of how good Irish food can be. Current research indicates that 83% of consumers believe it is now more important than ever to buy guaranteed Irish goods and services[4] and 69% of diners believe that it is important that restaurants serve local ingredients.[5]

The growing interest in food on the part of the Irish consumer is reflected in many aspects of Irish life and behavior. This is clearly reflected in the increased presence of food features in the media, the expansion in the number of artisanal food producers and farmers' markets, the growth in demonstrations and cooking schools, and the range of restaurants and pubs now proudly and confidently sourcing, serving and shouting about using Irish ingredients.

Despite the recent growth in food related experiences and activities, and the championing of local ingredients and produce by a cohort of chefs and restaurateurs, there is still a disconnect between produce and cuisine, and the relationship between these and the visitor experience. Much has been achieved in a short time, but developing a food tourism culture in Ireland from both a domestic market and an industry practitioner perspective is an on-going process.

On the international stage, Ireland is traditionally seen as a primary source of ingredients, and these do not necessarily appear in local cuisine. High quality foods or ingredients, or the products derived from them, are exported in vast amounts (e.g. milk powder, meat, Kerrygold butter, Bailey's Irish Cream, Jameson whiskey, cheese). This export market shapes Ireland's image internationally, creating high expectations in each visitor of their Irish food experience.

Furthermore, Ireland is one of a small number of countries (besides China, Mexico and Italy, for example) whose cultural background has been commodified, particularly in America, where the media on one hand, and businesses with cultural themes on the other, underline stereotypical imagery resulting in "Hollywoodization" of a culture through consumption.[6] This commodification of Irishness is both a blessing and a curse. On one hand, the use of clichéd, romanticized images and dishes has increased interest in the Irish culture, driving tourism and cultural products. On the other, a visit to Ireland may disappoint if the experience does not live up to expectations, as Ireland now has a modern Irish cuisine which is not consistently reflected in venues outside Ireland. This idea of 'Irishness' in relation to gastronomy is important as its commodification can result in a less authentic tourist experience both gastronomically and more generally in Irish tourism. There is evidence that traditional pubs in Dublin have already changed interior design and gastronomic offerings so that they are more consistent with Irish-themed pubs outside of Ireland.[7] In effect, the local 'authentic' Irish cultural and gastronomic experience upon which the commodification was originally based is evolving, raising obvious authenticity and loss of cultural identity issues and is likely to affect not only the livelihood and lifestyle of the local Dublin population, but Irish tourism generally.

There is a need to be cognizant of how individuals from other cultures and geographies experience Irish gastronomy and for Ireland to take care that it is not being presented in a way which signposts exclusivity and is in conflict with the inclusivity of Irish hospitality.

From a domestic development perspective, consumer understanding of the links between regions and purchase of quality products appears to be good. As Sage (2003) points out, good food is strongly associated with spaces that are sites of transaction, where food transfers from the producer to the person likely to consume it, creating relations of mutual regard.[8] However, there also appears to be a low level of awareness and understanding of Irish regional food labels.[9] Unlike consumers in France and Spain, but in common with those in the UK and Greece, the understanding of "regional" meant country of origin.[10] An obvious implication is that if Irish consumers have difficulty in distinguishing regionality in Ireland, then international visitors will, given the size of Ireland and the visitor's lack of local knowledge, adapt a similar approach. Possible exceptions might include areas that are already components of the international Irish image, such as Connemara, the Ring of Kerry, or the Cliffs of Moher, although visitor and consumer research is required to substantiate this view. Ireland's regional imagery highlights how image is not just that communicated by a tourism promotion, but through a wide variety of other activity such as literature, media, commercial advertising, the sector-specific promotional work of state agencies, and personal experience.[11] Examples of commercial advertising that impact the Irish image internationally are easily found; Guinness, Jameson whiskey, and Kerrygold butter are obvious choices. Specifically in the USA, Lucky Charms breakfast cereal and Irish Spring soap have specifically utilized themes of Irishness to sanitize or romanticize their commodities, and the ads for Irish tourism are perceived to translate the traditional American consumption of Ireland into a touristic concept.[12]

Aside from the fact that Irish images and their meanings may differ between individuals across context, time and geography, the image that is being created for Ireland's food tourism may be a fusion of disparate elements rather than consisting of a holistic entity. The tourist image portrayed by tourism agencies has existed in direct opposition to the modern, technology driven knowledge economy image portrayed by other sectors of economic, political and cultural activity, and continues to do so.[13] [14] Even within the food industry itself, there is evidence of polarization between the agro-food sector and what Sage (2003) calls alternative good food networks. There is also an imbalance between the natural food images intended to attract tourists, and the patterns of consumption of the majority of the Irish population (i.e. strong growth in the convenience and fast food sectors).[15] Ultimately, contradictory messages imply a degree of pretense resulting in a consequent lack of belief and trust in those images in the consumer mind.

From an external perspective, Hall et al[16] see Ireland (along with New Zealand) as being to the forefront of using regional images to market Irish food and tourism products and to reinforce the national brand.[17] They see as significant the use of place in the cross promotion of food and tourism with the development of Brand Ireland, citing the 2002 campaign by Bórd Bia (the Irish government food board) in western USA as an example.[18] It is not clear if Hall et al assumed a collaborative state agency approach, but the example does highlight the idea of a national brand, which is of advantage to all. There are reciprocal effects between a country's food and drink industry and its tourism industry. When the products do well overseas, it has a [positive] effect on tourism, and when visitors enjoy products on their home ground, this creates a market for those products elsewhere.[19]

Against this background, the emergence, and subsequent success, of food tourism in Ireland has been a result of a combination of both public policy and private enterprise. Utilizing four case studies, the leadership and coordinating role and 'ground up' approach of national agencies will emerge as a common theme. The case studies will demonstrate the use of social media, animation, and product development through various types of collaboration locally and nationally.

Place on a Plate: Using Local Food to Promote Your Business

Place on a Plate is an industry focused initiative to encourage all food and hospitality providers to offer fresh, locally sourced, seasonal food on their menu and just as importantly, make sure they are telling their customers about it. Research has shown that in recent years experiencing local foods and beverages, which express the identity of a destination through food culture and heritage, has become a highly sought travel experience for both domestic and international visitors. Indeed, in Ireland 35% of total visitor spending is on food and drink.

Place on a Plate is an ethos that can be embraced by any business serving food. It challenges them to think differently about their food offering. Fáilte Ireland has developed a wide range of business supports and workshops tailored to help industry to implement Place on a Plate.

Workshops covered topics such as menu engineering, using a menu as a selling tool, profitable kitchen management, skill training and refresher courses for chefs and front of house staff training. These supports focus on operational efficiency and productivity from a business perspective and the consumer focus ensures the visitor receives a high quality, authentic, Irish food experience.

The overarching message is that food is important. For consumers, it provides a true sense of the locality they are visiting by experiencing quality local food sourced from local producers who are passionate about ensuring the quality of their products. For businesses it will help to sustain their business, drive profitability and create a platform for producers and providers to work together. This will raise the profile of the locality and bring increased business to the area which ultimately benefits the local economy.

A Bottom-Up Approach

A successful food tourism model should be grounded in a bottom up approach as most innovation comes from local community driven networks and collaboration. For Ireland to truly triumph in the food tourism market it was agreed that a community-led approach was needed, so in September 2012, Fáilte Ireland embarked on a journey of discovery by launching a campaign, utilizing primarily social media, to seek nominations for emerging food champions with a resounding passion and belief in Irish food, together with the commitment and drive to actively influence and shape the future of Irish cuisine and food tourism in their region.

With no predecessor to the initiative there was nothing to benchmark against which gave raise to many uncertainties for example; how many people would respond, what type of individuals would be nominated, would they be able to work together, would they want to work with Fáilte Ireland and where would the journey lead to? This was a seismic shift for Fáilte Ireland from a traditionally very action orientated role to that of a more enabling and facilitative role in their capacity of supporting the industry. The initial campaign to recruit the champions was highly successful resulting in over 160 peer nominations in less than a week confirming the energy and commitment within the industry to create a sustainable food tourism proposition for Ireland.

The selection criteria and process were very clear and fully transparent with all details available on Fáilte Ireland's corporate website. Fourteen nominees were selected, representing a mixed group of owner-managers of food service businesses and members of the wider food tourism community, who had demonstrable commitment in playing a role in developing Ireland's food tourism proposition and reputation.

Once established, the group traveled on a food tourism benchmarking program to Prince Edward Island (PEI), Canada where they met with met with 15 business owners. PEI faces similar challenges to Ireland and has an established range of successfully integrated food tourism products and activities.

The trip reinforced the thesis that ultimately food tourism is driven by experiences, community pride and passion through proactive local networks and collaborations. It also provided the newly appointed champions with tangible ideas to help further develop Ireland's food experiences. Not everything they experienced was 'perfect' but this lead to the realization that nothing is perfect and that you should be prepared to make lots of mistakes along the way. They returned as a cohesive group primed and ready to take their learning's back to their local communities and networks to start working on how they could transfer this information into practical initiatives and develop engaging food experiences to encourage visitors to stop, spend and stay longer.

Most of the group had never met so there was an informal meeting the evening before departure which acted as an icebreaker and assisted in setting the scene and establishing the expectations of all parties. Throughout the educational visit the group held a couple of informal discussion sessions and reconvened for a formal meeting a month after their return. They reflected upon the experience in Canada and established their role and agreed activities. Fáilte Ireland's role was defined as one of facilitation and support, but ultimately the group was in charge of its own agenda in their capacity as a conduit to build and develop food tourism.

Food Strategy Group: Stakeholder Driven Development

During the development of Fáilte Ireland's Food Tourism Framework 2011 – 2013, it was clear that the development of a food tourism destination could not be achieved with a 'top-down' only approach. There were many parties directly and indirectly involved in food tourism including producers, suppliers, providers and food-related attractions/events and other experiences. There are also important state agencies such as Bord Bia (Food Board) and Tourism Ireland (International Tourism Group), in addition to private representative bodies and marketing groups, which all have a vital role to play in developing and promoting the sector.

Fáilte Ireland was clear in its assertion that they were not seeking to replicate, or indeed replace the existing efforts of these stakeholders but rather to serve as a facilitator for greater cohesion and direction between all concerned. In order to harness direct stakeholder involvement in the development and delivery of the Food Tourism Framework and to integrate the strategic objectives of the related government agencies, Fáilte Ireland established an *Industry Working Group* in 2010. The Group comprised of representatives drawn from relevant government agencies, industry representative groups, marketing associations, the foodservice sector, sector entrepreneurs and food focused events/activities. This Group was chaired by an independent, experienced food expert who had no affiliation to the groups involved and so was in a position to be objective in his approach.

The primary role of the Industry Group was to guide the development and implementation of the national food tourism framework. As a result of this stakeholder-driven approach, Fáilte Ireland was in a better position to not only achieve its own stated goals regarding food tourism, but also to deliver real benefits for all stakeholders, including: enhanced marketing and promotion, increased visitor awareness and satisfaction, better business opportunities for producers, and ultimately the potential for greater profitability and sustainability for all those involved in food tourism.

The Food Tourism Framework has a three year timeframe and while the principles remain true, during implementation the focus has somewhat shifted due to changes in the macro environment, emerging priorities and the natural evolution of the project as it evolves into areas and ideas not previously considered. Ireland also remains in a difficult financial position and as a result, resources for implementation are more limited resulting in a shift whereby the focus of Fáilte Ireland's engagement with the trade is to 'enable' rather than 'do'.

After two and a half years it was decided that the activities of the Industry Working Group, in its original form, had reached a natural conclusion. The group has achieved many objectives; probably none more important than the introductions that were made and the working relationships that developed, inspiring various initiatives that have helped strengthen Ireland's food tourism product. It is hoped that these working relationships will continue. The focus on implementation will now be supported by the 'Food Champions' selected in 2012.

This approach is a partnership between the private and public sector which facilitates the identification and mentoring of young Irish chefs who are helping to create the dishes that are part of an emerging Irish cuisine. Fáilte Ireland is committed to strengthening Ireland's food tourism reputation. However, research to date has shown that Ireland does not feature as a consideration for travel in the minds of consumers, domestically or internationally, when asked about food destinations. Yet, Ireland is very well-known and recognized for the quality of ingredients and produce. Consequently, the dishes produced have unmistakably positive connotations for visitors as being pure, natural, and good. It is essential, if Ireland is to build its reputation for food, that Irish cuisine is as recognized, known and valued as Irish food produce.

Euro-Toques is a pan-European organization representing over 3,500 chefs and cooks, with national branches in many European countries. Euro-Toques Ireland is comprised of about 180 chefs with a core philosophy of promoting local sourcing and protecting culinary heritage, therefore delivering foods of flavor, authenticity and provenance; all of the desired elements for an emerging Irish cuisine. Fáilte Ireland partnered with Euro-Toques Ireland on this venture to strategically capitalize on the wealth of existing and potential culinary talent within the country. They have a well-established and highly regarded Young Chef of the Year competition which has development potential and could be more effectively used to develop the pool of young culinary talent within the context of an emerging Irish cuisine. They also have links with European-wide sister groups, some of which have strong presence in our key markets and could be utilized for promotional purposes.

Ultimately the key objectives of the project are to drive the identification of young chef talent in Ireland and develop them as food ambassadors, in to order to propel the establishment of a recognizable and well known Irish cuisine. It will also act as a continuing professional development initiative for young chefs within the industry.

Some of the key steps in the collaboration process included:

- Engagement with proposed partner around project objectives to secure agreement on working together. Euro-Toques Ireland still owned and managed the competition.
- The priorities of Fáilte Ireland included a much greater use of social media, the incorporation of key concepts such as food heritage, taking focus off the existing fine dining approach, and a change in the final event to something that is more consumer versus industry focused.
- Agree on a sponsorship structure e.g. in this case it was agreed that the support model would be for three years with a decreasing amount of support each year as part of Fáilte Ireland's exit strategy. It was also recognized that it would take a few years for new approach to gain traction in the market place.
- Application process for Young Chef Competition was reviewed to help increase in number of applications.
- The 'Meet the Press' event for the five finalists was to include a consumer element.
- A time commitment to their role as 'Food Ambassadors' was agreed and will be reviewed as necessary. All five finalists would be involved in promoting Irish cuisine and media plan and training to be arranged as necessary.
- Agree on key performance indicators (KPIs) and establish a tracking system to monitor activity and media pick up e.g. equivalent advertising value; social media activity – Twitter, blogs etc. and international pick up.

The five finalists each year become Irish cuisine ambassadors who will inspire other young professionals in the industry and raise the profile of Irish cuisine in the marketplace. The ambassadors may be utilized both domestically and internationally and ultimately, Ireland's food tourism reputation is strengthened.

For food tourism to be authentic and sustainable, it must be developed through community driven networks and collaboration. This has led to a change in Fáilte Ireland's approach from action- to partnership-orientated, with an enabling and facilitative function which helps to create the right environment for those networks to learn and develop within their regions.

If food tourism is to truly reflect local and regional food, the collaboration between the agricultural and tourism sectors has proven to be important, particularly in the gastronomy and economics of rural tourism where scale and volume are factors of success. Notwithstanding that, the authenticity and sustainability of food tourism depends on sectors that may not perceive tourism as important, as well as the indigenous population itself. Within the wider tourism industry, food tourism may not be a product in itself, but is something that is integral across all sectors, markets and populations.

From a public policy perspective, the conclusion is that food tourism is a people business, in terms of both those who provide and consume the experience. Consequently, the span of food tourism provision needs to be very broad, and although the infrastructure elements are in place, this has implications for the industry. Food tourism is a cost effective, profitable option for all stakeholders, and adds value, which attracts a premium. So there is a substantial economic, social and developmental rationale for a place in public policy for food tourism.

West Sweden: Food as a Reason to Visit

The West Sweden Tourist Board has worked with food for just over 10 years. It serves as an excellent case study as to how different types of food can be used strategically for different ends in destination development.

Few would argue that it is not just products that compete for customers; even countries, cities and regions are competing to be attractive in the eyes of different target groups. Tourist organizations highlight the range of tourist services, Chambers of Commerce promote local goods and services, while municipalities point to culture, childcare, healthcare and other public services that contribute to making that a good place to live. It is therefore about building a brand for a place. Many places also have great opportunities for creating a unique position by taking advantage of their history, culture, landscape and of course, their culinary traditions.

In many ways, marketing a place is similar to the efforts required to create a durable brand for a physical product. You need to have an overall view, know what makes the place attractive and be conscious of its identity. It is difficult to market a destination if you do not know how different groups perceive the place or region. Therefore, during discussions about a destination's brand, the destination's image is a central concept; i.e. the individual's mental perception of the place. What do the residents of the region think of the place, how is it perceived by tourists, and do people in other countries know that the place exists?

When choosing a holiday destination, many alternatives are frequently compared with each other. The destination's image is one of the most important factors when tourists choose to visit a specific place, because this symbolizes the advantages that different tourists associate with that place. There are many destinations that have made great efforts to market themselves, but they have chosen to communicate an image that is too uninteresting. The reason could be that it is difficult to agree on the destination's core values. Destinations chose, perhaps, to use and communicate core values such as the friendliness of the local people or the beauty of the natural surroundings, but what travel destinations do not have friendly people and beautiful countryside? Quite simply, they have not demonstrated what is original and unique. Thus, the destination does not promote any distinctive characteristics.

Creating and maintaining an image, therefore, is fundamental when working with a brand. This field of place branding has developed considerably over the last ten years. There are many research groups worldwide that specialize in this field, many books and scientific articles have been written and a scientific journal, *Place Branding & Public Diplomacy,* is published several times a year. Many studies have also pointed to the importance of cuisine to a destination's image. It is not especially remarkable that we see links between countries/regions and culinary products. When it comes to wines and spirits, for example, we can point to champagne, Scotch whisky, Irish whiskey, German beer and Russian vodka, and for food to Greek salad, French cheese and Spanish paella. If we look at fish and seafood, Norwegian salmon, Maine lobster, Maryland crabs and Bouillabaisse from Marseille stand out.

Knowledge of a product's place of origin is often important when evaluating the product's quality. The studies performed show that, if the country/place has a positive image in the market, it could be appropriate to emphasize the product's country/place of origin. Increasingly, consumers are consciously concerned about the country or the place of origin. The origin not only creates a feeling about the product but also a character and identity. It can provide reinforcement for the product, the place and other products that are also from the region. In the literature, terms such as *'manufactured in', 'produced in', 'made in'* and *'designed in'* are used when focusing on countries of origin and brand creation.

Most regions would say they have good food. It is difficult for a destination to claim it has the best fish, the best vegetables, the best fruit or the best meat. For the local consumer, the product does not need to be the best; instead it needs to maintain acceptable standards. On the other hand, the situation is different for a tourism office that wants to claim that these products are worth taking a detour for, and that they themselves are a reason for visiting. If the aim is to be a culinary meeting place, with the emphasis on a specific product, or a destination where the range on offer has a good variation to meet the needs of different visitors, then collaboration is required between many different actors. These include everyone from restaurants, growers, fishermen, processors, and tourist organizations, to politicians. In several successful cases, it can be seen that interested parties from private trade and industry came together with representatives from the public sector, and also with University researchers.

The question then is which products could be suitable for emphasis? Certain products are so commercially attractive that they can be sold without branding. They can be sold in sacks or boxes, such as mushrooms and shellfish. Naturally, the more unique and in demand a product is, the easier it is to market. This uniqueness is often due to taste and availability. Many unique products are not readily available, because they do not grow anywhere other than just one or a couple specific locations. Examples are saffron and truffles.

The argument for shellfish was made in one project in West Sweden as follows. Each kind of shellfish (lobster, crayfish, oysters, etc.) is imbued with its own myths, but they can also complement each other well in a shared brand. For goods and services with mythical associations, their consumption becomes symbolic. Many people associate lobsters and oysters with luxury and they are often accompanied by champagne. They also have a symbolic significance in a social context, to show who we are or who we want to be. To return home and tell others that "I have eaten lobster" conveys "bragging rights" that matter to some people. Crayfish do not have the same luxurious image as lobsters and oysters, but they are certainly linked to pleasure and good appetite. In Sweden, crayfish largely represent symbolic consumption with many associated rituals; crayfish hats, lanterns and special napkins as well as drinking-songs and more. Prawns and mussels are also among the delicacies from the sea's larder. Even if both of these can be part of our daily diet, they are surely considered by many to be at home in feasts and banquets.

Shellfish are also unique, because they are only available in limited quantities and are available fresh for a very short season. Shellfish are "culinary fast food" and do not need a lot of preparation time. They are healthy, wholesome and contain low levels of fat. Shellfish are ecologically beneficial products. For example, there is now evidence that mussels help to clean the sea. The more mussels we eat, the better the marine environment we will have — that is to say, a win-win solution. Shellfish are at their best when it is low season for tourism. Therefore, tourist products based on shellfish can act to lengthen the season. There is great interest, tradition and knowledge connected with shellfish. They also have a long culinary history, which is a major advantage in a brand context.

A project was started to build a brand around shellfish and tourism, with the aim of strengthening the attractiveness of Norra Bohuslän, a region on the Swedish west coast. A concept was developed based on the idea of a Seafood Safari. The first test was made in the autumn of 2009. The theme was "All of Bohuslän on one plate." Bohuslän as a brand is symbolized here by its foremost primary products.[20] The interest from all actors involved has grown over the years and it is now considered a success story.

When many tourists think of West Sweden, their thoughts go at once to the sea and the coast. Coastal tourism is one of the oldest forms of tourism, at least in this region. Some of the coastal resorts in Bohuslän have been tourist destinations since the early 19th century. For a long time, Bohuslän has lived on sun and sea-bathing, but it is now subject to increasing competition and has a major need to develop and quality assure the coast's other assets, as well as to create new year-round products. Seafood is a central part of the product development.

With its access to shellfish, West Sweden's coastal destinations are blessed with good conditions to enable them to offer a wide and competitive range of meals and to create reasons for visiting, particularly now that Sweden is to be one of the world's new culinary nations, according to Eskil Erlandsson, the Swedish Minister for Agriculture. However, in the Västra Götaland region of West Sweden there are also lakes and canals as well as the sea. Across the region, the number of farm shops is on the increase. Apart from the specialties they produce themselves, many of them also offer accommodation and various forms of activity. Restaurants that consciously pursue the culinary arts are growing steadily. There are also many entrepreneurs who are daring to invest in specific products, such as beestings pudding, beaver safaris, or cheese maturation.

An action plan for a Culinary Sweden was presented a couple of years ago. A framework budget has been established and most things appear to be going as intended by the Minister for Agriculture. At the same time, the local population in West Sweden is showing an increasing interest in preserving their identity, environment, nature, history and culture, and as a consequence, are making clear the importance of local primary products and traditions in their cultural offering. While traveling, meal stops, like place markers on Google maps, have to be year-round goals for short or long culinary trips by boat, car, bicycle or on foot. On the culinary journey, the visitor will choose the number of taste experiences and where they are to be eaten, complement them with overnight stays, events and travels — with food as the reason for the journey — through the region's different culinary places.

The West Sweden Tourist Board has regularly managed projects focusing on food. Its work started with the Taste of West Sweden project, which was first discussed in 2000 and launched in 2001. The activities primarily include restaurant meals, meals with a media relations purpose, marketing the destination's food by activities and product sampling at trade fairs and events as well as developing tour packages with food as a major reason for visiting. Taste of West Sweden, a shared brand, is the link between these activities and guides all of the efforts. The key words have been quality and locally produced products. During recent years, collaboration began with 'Lokalproducerat i Väst' (Locally Produced in the West) with the trademark 'Smaka på Västsverige' (Taste the West of Sweden) with the aim of giving both the local population and visitors the chance to taste and consume locally produced food from the whole region. This is a question of creating a dialogue between restaurants, producers and shops, as well as cooperating with producers and distributors, about developing environmentally friendly and effective systems for logistics, having quality assured farm shops and helping them reach the market via the Internet.

In the beginning, there was resistance. Marie Linde, Project Leader for Taste of West Sweden (2000–2004) said, "It will never work. Chefs are individualists; they compete and they will never consider joining a joint project." Then she changed her tone. "They spurred me on," says Marie. "The West Sweden Tourist Board, in this case Gunilla Mitchell and I, [were] totally convinced that we must invest in a project to stimulate West Swedish restaurants. We saw the culinary experience as a possible reason for visiting, in exactly the same way as it works for the major culinary nations, such as France and Italy. And, gratifyingly, it turned out that the critical and doubtful were in the wrong."

The project was not without its challenges. Marie continues, "Initially, it was difficult for the Tourist Board to unite the different provinces into a whole. The arguments at that time were more about what divided than what united. Taste of West Sweden, which was intended to promote the development of food and local primary produce, met the need for a 'common denominator', something that united without anyone losing their distinctive character. It was important for us that the collaboration did not become a type of 'club', which could be joined by paying a fee. This was about uniting restaurants with a shared view on quality, who see their role as the trustees and developers of local traditions, and who were prepared to base their menus on local fresh produce as far as possible considering the season."

The invitation to participate in West Sweden's first quality project for restaurant meals was sent out, and a large number of applications were received. The tourist board recognized the need to establish criteria. "Not to be chosen was a great surprise to many. There was some grumbling," remembers Marie. "Nevertheless, I never had any problems dealing with the arguments. We had planned the project so thoroughly that, once we were launched, there was no difficulty at all in explaining the purpose and goals."

The process of spreading information was very important for its acceptance. Marie traveled around the region, meeting with key players. During this period, it became increasingly clear to Marie that the restaurants spread across West Sweden led a rather isolated life, with limited opportunities for improving their skills and meeting others in the industry. She saw that there was a pent-up need to meet, exchange opinions and learn new things. "What characterized all the restaurants participating in the project was a desire to get to the heart of what they did. There was a wish to develop together, and the project and its high level of ambition was genuinely inspirational."

During the second part of the project, the restaurants and producers met for the first time in a workshop followed by a food fair, where contacts were made. In the spring, the first group qualified. Brass signs with "Taste of West Sweden" were handed out, as of course, was a diploma for visible placement in the restaurant. "I'll never forget the feeling I had during the celebrations of the diploma presentations, when all the participants expressed their appreciation and enthusiasm. They were really proud to have been chosen and they also saw that this was the start of a long-term venture."

During the quality development process, food as a reason for visiting was the tourist board's focus. The next step was to clarify the complete experience: the food and the environment as well as what else the destination could offer. It was time to market food as part of destination development. "A Culinary Guide to West Sweden," a travel guide and cookbook, published by "Natur & Kultur," was a great success. The group worked with one of Sweden's best food photographers, and the book was penned by well-known and professional writers. The pictures of nature were attractive and the layout combined aesthetics with pedagogy, explains Marie. "The fact is that the book, which sold out long ago, still beats today's competition."

Then the group sought to broaden and deepen the interest of agricultural and other associations. Their shared values meant that they could help and support each other's work with small-scale producers. "Naturally, the collaboration worked a bit differently; partly depending on location and partly depending on the season, but the ice was broken and the understanding of the restaurateurs' needs increased among the producers, and vice versa."

During the final phase of Marie Linde's time as a project leader, the West Sweden Tourist Board's focus was mainly on foreign markets. The country managers in the West Sweden Tourist Board showed great skill in selling the idea of food as a reason for visiting, which gave a result that — not least in column inches of newsprint — was rather overwhelming. "Naturally, this was gratifying, but personally I consider our home market to be at least as interesting, with all the opportunities for culinary events and the other public attractions that this offers," concludes Marie. And the rest is history.

Increased Collaboration and Meals on the Web

An organization is needed to coordinate the efforts. There are innumerable interested parties in a region who work with food and meals, and each one has different goals and wishes. The argument must be strong and the message clear to convince the actors to take part in a long-term venture. Otherwise, doubts arise, for example from restaurants, about whether it is profitable to cooperate with the competition. Visitors have to find out what the destination has to offer as well as what local culinary traditions, primary produce, food and drink combinations et cetera are characteristic. One way is to present information virtually about what is on offer.

Ever since the launch of its Virtual Tourist Agency, Taste of West Sweden has had its own website.[21] The Taste of West Sweden name focuses on food as a reason to visit and the reader can obtain more information about a restaurant's location and specialization, the owner's philosophy, and more, from a 'product sheet'. Also all food related activities such as food festivals, trade fairs and food journals are presented with information, films, links etc. In 2012 the website had four million unique visits, proving the marketing and sales potential.

Nevertheless, the West Sweden Tourist Board also wants to provide all tourism companies in West Sweden, via the Internet, with the chance to develop their quality, their hospitality, and to do more business through partnerships, for example with activity companies, event organizers, carriers, tour operators etc. This need has resulted in the development of Basetool 2.0, a complete intranet tool that tourism companies need to develop their products, create business concepts, communicate and raise their profitability by attracting new customers and taking market share. Today, around 13,400 visiting sites, hotels and restaurants are entered in Basetool. It fulfills one of the most important functions for cooperation and collaboration and contributes to augmenting important knowledge and competence, which are all important parts of both company and regional development.

West Sweden Tourist Board Contributes to New Opportunities

Food tourism is an important economic growth area and contributes by strengthening the region's identity and external profile, thereby helping to marketing the region nationally and internationally. The challenge for the tourist industry in West Sweden, according to the business plan, is to turn the region into Scandinavia's most visited, appreciated and profitable tourist region in the long-term. The West Sweden Tourist Board has the regional mandate and responsibility to communicate and spread the vision's challenge and create commitment to it with commercial and state interested parties. It is a clear challenge, which assumes a viable trade and industry that is focused on development, and with food tourism as an important element. Meals that are considered pleasurable experiences, where the region's tastes and traditions are highlighted. This is not just economic sustenance but also sustenance for body and soul — for the good life.

Down Home Goodness in North Carolina

Chatham County, North Carolina, USA is a rural county surrounded by several urban counties. The local DMO is a one-person organization housed under county government and fully funded by an occupancy (lodging) tax. Unique foods that are hard to find elsewhere serve as a draw to the county and a base for itinerary creation. The county celebrates its rural landscapes, comfort foods, fine dining, and current favorites in a format that is uniquely local but with a twist. While unique and trendy cuisines are part of the food landscape, the classic and comfort food eateries are becoming increasingly popular as they are revisited and updated. Barbecue, burgers, and buttermilk biscuits are now what travelers seek, along with recipes to take home.

Country ham, chicken and dumplings, crackling cornbread, and other country favorites are part of the itinerary as much as those searching for the New American dishes. The enthusiasm for "mom's cooking" is as significant as the deconstructed dishes honoring traditional fare. Travelers seek to explore dining while sightseeing; the itinerary is a part of the foodie's landscape of fine dining, food trucks, beer gardens, and more. The stories and the background of the paw paw ingredient in craft beer or the chow chow bottled for inn guests enhances the visit, whether for locals for the day or for long-haul travelers overnight.

Southern Supreme[22]

This region is home to the largest nutty fruitcake producer in North Carolina. What began as a gift to clients at a hair salon became a business for Berta Lou Scott who was encouraged to open a business and she did just that — in her garage. Almost 30 years later, she still runs a family-owned and operated business in Bear Creek that now offers tours and tastings (not just nutty fruitcake); an annual holiday open house; and a cookbook compiled by family, staff, and guests. Visitors can take the tour and see the story in pictures; ask questions of the tour guide and witness the cake, chocolate, and jam operations; taste a sampling of their many products; and roam the showroom for edible souvenirs. Lucky visitors might get a glimpse of Berta.

Small B&B and Cafe[23]

Bed & breakfast café and inn owners, Dave Clark and Lisa Piper, moved to Pittsboro, North Carolina[24] from Minnesota. Their casual and inviting style, which emanates beyond their personalities into the inn and café operations made this spot a welcome addition to the mix of eateries in town. Their B&B is not 'your mama's B&B'. Rooms are offbeat, funky, and architecturally cool. Originally, the site had four tiny rooms and the owners could see the restaurant with windows open to the east for morning exposure, a chance to reuse the walls and floors, windows higher on the wall to provide light but not distract, music outside and porch seating in warm temperatures, and a glimpse into the kitchen. Always on the menu, lemon ricotta hotcakes, with that just right hint of lemon, tastes light and is a tasty breakfast or brunch dish sought after by every visitor. Small B&B and Café is a member of Piedmont Grown,[25] a certification program that wants to make sure that farm products grown, raised, and made in the Piedmont Region of North Carolina are clearly identified and promoted everywhere where food and farm fresh products are for sale. Small B&B and Café's Southern Benedict made with biscuits and local country ham, a big favorite among local residents. Seasonal eating is important, as is showcasing local farms so along with the regular good eats that are always on the menu, Facebook fans await to hear the day's specials, which include grilled strawberry and brie sandwiches with balsamic and fresh basil or quiche made with a cornmeal crust, both at the top of the favorites list.

Angelina's Kitchen

One of the earliest local eateries, with almost 90% local ingredients in many dishes, Angelina Koulizakis, is a friend to all farmers. Entering her restaurant is genuinely like entering her kitchen. Standing in line, one sees a fun but busy kitchen. Visitors can sample the latest local eats, and learn something about how the day's special was made. Super local with a Greek twist, Angelina makes everything from Frito pie (her way), spicy enchiladas, a cheesy bake, Avgolemono, Shepard's pie, falafel, gyro, and much more. Even the kid's meals include a locally handcrafted toy. Angelina's Kitchen is a Piedmont Grown member and she is a Best Dish North Carolina finalist. She works alongside several local eateries, championing their food and making it a food community that gives travelers a reason to plan their dining smartly. Angelina considers healthy and all dietary options. Visitors will find gluten-free pitas available and a chef who finds time for chats with guests throughout her small café.

Heartfriends B&B

A lovely southern B&B that is owned and operated by Yvonne Stegenga, Heartfriends Inn is a bed and breakfast that offers breakfast feasts. No menus are repeated for second-time guests, unless requested. Three dishes that are most complimented and requested and that are supposedly naware of being served elsewhere in the vicinity include the "souffled" pumpkin pancake, breakfast quinoa, and French toast stuffed with blueberries and cream cheese and topped with blueberries. All of Yvonne's dishes are customized and these have become her signature dishes.

Paw Paw in Craft Beer[26]

Grower Wynn Dinnsen has a 250 tree paw paw orchard in Chatham County near Pittsboro. Paw paw is used in Fullsteam Brewery's Belgian-style Golden Ale, by Chatham County resident and Fullsteam Brewery owner Sean Lilly Wilson who dubs Dinnsen the modern Johnn Pawpawseed, for harvesting this tropical plant.[27] Paw Paw is a seasonal beer for late summer. It is challenging to brew, according to Wilson, and is a small batch beer because of the rarity of the ingredients and the high risk inherent to brewing it. One year, Fullsteam Brewery successfully brewed the beer, yielding 40 kegs. They plan for a single batch, approximately 20 kegs, another year based on current conditions, and will always try to have it available, at least for the foreseeable future. Why this tropical plant and what to pair with it? Says Sean Lilly Wilson, "Paw paws are beautiful and odd, with that fatal flaw of quick spoilage relegating it to semi-obscurity. I don't know where I learned about paw paws, but Wynn Dinnsen was the first person to get me a taste. Paw Paw is a higher alcohol beer, around 9%. It's delicious on its own, with some light cheeses, or perhaps with some toasted pound cake."

Starrlight Mead[28]

A family of Starrs formed Starrlight Mead, our first honey winery (making honey wine). Owners Becky Starr (Sales/Tasting Room Manager) and Ben Starr (Meadmaker) have made this a family affair. Son Chris is the beekeeper. All of the honey is from North Carolina. Their award-winning mead surpassed more than 200 entries in the International Mead Association's 2006 competition, winning Best in Show in the Home Mead-Maker category for their Starrlight Mulled Apple Cyser. Starrlight Mead's Herb Infused Meads are their second line of meads, a nice complement to their regular honey and fruit based meads. These meads are based on their Off-Dry Traditional Mead and made with organic herbs, which are infused into the mead, creating new unique flavors that are very different from traditional grape wines. They offer seven in the line: Lemon Balm, Chamomile, Lavender, Apple Mint, Sage, Ginger, and a blend of Caraway, Fennel, and Anise Seed that they call Nordic Blend (a riff off of Aquavit, a Scandinavian liqueur). They launched them in early March in small 10 case batches to gauge market reaction. So far, the best sellers have been Chamomile, Ginger and the Nordic Blend. They have decided to continue to carry those three, adding others randomly as inspired; sage was suggested for the fall.) They are currently available only at the meadery. Becky's inspiration with the herb meads came from years of making herbal teas and tinctures (large amount of herb in a small amount of alcohol, usually vodka, where it steeps for a month). Ben and Becky are always talking about new flavors, so upon discussing with employee Jenn Hansen, they jointly decided to test 12 of their favorite herbs in very small test batches (in quintessentially Southern quart mason jars of course). They let the mixtures soak for approximately two weeks, tasted them and put the herb meads in green bottles with a new label. Becky Starr, "Flavors that failed: Rosemary — bummer, one of my very favorite herbs, but tasted too piney/sappy/woody. Cardamom — tasted like honey-eucalyptus cough drops! Lemon Thyme — another of my favorite cooking herbs — the notes on the tasting say "Ick! Medicinal, tasted like wooden sticks, bitter!" Because it is an alcohol extraction, it can extract some of the resin-y or bitter flavors of some herbs."

Chatham Marketplace is a grocery store/cafe with a huge emphasis on local foods. The Chatham Mills historic complex also includes a pollinator garden, with guided tours offered seasonally/monthly. One of the newest restaurants, Oakleaf, also has a focus on local and seasonal dining. Starrlight Mead is located here too. Chatham Marketplace offers a variety of local cheese, wines, and more, including the award-winning Kerala Curry products. Kerala Curry's Tomato Chutney won the Outstanding Condiment at the 2008 SOFI™ Awards presented by the National Association for the Specialty Food Trade at the Fancy Food Show in New York City. While tomato chutney is not unique, Kerala Curry's items certainly began that way...Indian food in a predominantly rural and vast county. They quickly became a big hit.

While Chatham County may not be on every foodie's travel itinerary, it nevertheless boasts a respectable array of quality and unique food and drink experiences that contribute to the region's own culinary sense of place. The area has achieved a critical mass of producers, with products that seem to play well off of each other. The Piedmont Grown certification further supports the draw of the region. A combination of unique products made with unique ingredients, served up with classic Southern hospitality, combine to make this a popular foodie destination. Destination marketers seeking to brand their own areas should try to take elements of the unique products, unique ingredients and hospitality equation and combine them into their own success story.

CONCLUSION

Destinations face different challenges when it comes to food tourism marketing. Some DMOs may have no budget, while others have large budgets. Some areas may have sparse agricultural production, while others are awash in fresh fruits and vegetables. Still other areas may have difficulty with public opinion or local politics, while in other places, the residents and leaders understand the value of food tourism. There is no one-size-fits-all prescription when it comes to branding a food tourism destination. Still, these destinations offer some solid sustainable advice on ways to develop food tourism in other destinations.

DISCUSSION QUESTIONS

1. How could an area with few or no agricultural resource brand itself as a culinary destination?
2. Consider some destination food tourism branding failures. Which destinations come to mind and why do you think they failed?
3. As a tourism marketer, how would you respond to complaints from visitors that they are unable to find "authenticity" in your destination?

ENDNOTES

[1] www.failteireland.ie

[2] http://bit.ly/R0U4mJ

[3] A History of Irish Food, Frank Armstrong, 2012

[4] Amárach Consulting. (2011). Attitudes to Irish brands and the Guaranteed Irish logo. Accessed 4 April 2013: www.slideshare.net/amarach/guaranteed-irish-research-report august-2011 and www.amarach.com

[5] Bord Bia, 2013

[6] Wood, Natalie T., and Caroline Lego Munoz. 2007. "'No rules, just right' or is it? The role of themed restaurants as cultural ambassadors." Tourism & Hospitality Research no. 7:242 - 255.

[7] Wood and Munoz 2007, 252. See also Cohen, E., and N. Avieli. 2004. "Food in tourism - Attraction and impediment." Annals of Tourism Research no. 31 (4):755 - 778. doi: 10.1016/j.annals.2004.02.003.
Connolly, Claire. 2003. Theorizing Ireland, Readers in cultural criticism. Basingstoke: Palgrave Macmillan.

[8] Sage, Colin. 2003. "Social embeddedness and relations of regard: alternative 'good food' networks in south-west Ireland." Journal of Rural Studies no. 19 (1): 51.

[9] Henchion, Maeve, and Bridín McIntyre. 2000. "Regional Imagery and Quality Products: the Irish Experience." British Food Journal no. 102 (8):642

[10] Parrott, Nicholas, Natasha Wilson, and Jonathan Murdoch. 2002. "Spatializing Quality: Regional Protection and the Alternative Geography of Food." European Urban and Regional Studies no. 9 (3):253. doi: 10.1177/096977640200900304

[11] Henchion, Maeve, and Bridín McIntyre. 2000. "Regional Imagery and Quality Products: the Irish Experience." British Food Journal no. 102 (8):631 - 633

[12] Negra, Diane. 2001. "Consuming Ireland: Lucky Charms Cereal, Irish Spring Soap and 1-800-Shamrock." Cultural Studies no. 15:76 - 97.

[13] Quinn, Bernadette. 1994. "Images of Ireland in Europe: A Tourism Perspective." In Culture, Tourism and Development: The Case of Ireland, edited by Ullrich Kockel. Liverpool: Liverpool University Press, page 68.

[14] Graham, Colin. 2001. ""Blame it on Maureen O' Hara": Ireland and The Trope of Authenticity." Cultural Studies no. 15:69

[15] Sage, Colin. 2003. "Social embeddedness and relations of regard: alternative 'good food' networks in south-west Ireland." Journal of Rural Studies no. 19 (1): 54

[16] Hall, C. Michael, Richard Mitchell, and Liz Sharples. 2003. "Consuming places: the role of food, wine and tourism in regional development." In Food Tourism around the World: Development, management, and markets, edited by C. Michael Hall, Liz Sharples, Richard Mitchell, Niki Macionis and Brock Cambourne, 25 - 59. Oxford; Boston: Butterworth-Heinemann.

[17] Hall, Mitchell, and Sharples 2003, 53

[18] Interestingly, the participating companies were all quite industrial, with the exception of the Farmhouse Cheese Group. The others were Nestlé Ireland Ltd., McCann's Irish Oatmeal, Irish Biscuits Ltd., Jacob's Biscuits, Barry's Tea and the Irish Dairy Board. Obviously, the cost of such a promotion is prohibitive to small producers.

[19] Canavan, Orla, Maeve Henchion, and Seamus O'Reilly. 2007. "The use of the internet as a marketing channel for Irish specialty food." International Journal of Retail & Distribution Management no. 35: 188, 192 -193

[20] www.skaldjursresan.se

[21] www.vastsverige.com

[22] www.southernsupreme.com/

[23] http://discoverpittsborosilercity.wordpress.com/2012/02/05/small-bb-cafe-big-flavors/

[24] http://visitpittsboro.com/about-us and see also http://visitpittsboro.com/eat

[25] www.piedmontgrown.org

[26] www.fullsteam.ag/blog/2011/09/forager-3-paw-paw-belgian-style-golden-ale/

[27] http://growingsmallfarms.ces.ncsu.edu/growingsmallfarms-paw-paw-harvest/

[28] http://starrlightmead.com

Towards A Cookie Cutter Future

Vicki Mavrakis

While chains are growing at an unprecedented rate, they bring consumers many benefits that are hard to dispute. In this respect, chains help independent businesses understand the need for greater consistency in food, experience and predictability. That said, with the globalization of businesses, are we in fact, stampeding towards a look-alike world, or is cuisine the sole remaining differentiator among destinations? What lessons can we learn from chains? How are chains helping or hurting smaller, local and independent businesses? Can global and local businesses work together? How can we account for global cuisine choices at the local level? How should we view local and regional chains? This chapter will explore these issues. Benefits and drawbacks of chains to consumers will also be presented.

INTRODUCTION

Chain businesses are the bane of many small, local and independent businesses, yet many consumers love them and many are fiercely devoted to their favorites. Why is this? It might be the consistency of product, a fun experience, convenience, a rewards program or any number of other reasons. According to the Restaurant Report, in the USA, "in the 1970s the independent restaurant held a commanding 85% of the market share. During the 1980s, chains perfected their strategies through their own survival, and mastered their ability to identify with consumer demand. Today, chains now hold 88% of the market share, leaving independents scrambling to find their voice in the industry."[1] In many cities around the planet, chains are pervasive. While independent hotels and restaurants often struggle with fierce competition from chains, those chains must be doing something right.

Defining a "Chain"

According to Wikipedia, "chain stores are ... outlets that share a brand and central management, and usually have standardized business methods and practices. Before considered a chain, stores must meet a litmus test, it must have more than 10 units under the same brand and have a central headquarters. [...] These characteristics also apply to chain restaurants and some service-oriented chain businesses. In retail, dining and many service categories, chain businesses have come to dominate the market in many parts of the world. A franchise retail establishment is one form of chain store. ... A restaurant chain is a set of related restaurants with the same name in many different locations that are either under shared corporate ownership or operated under franchising agreements. Typically, the restaurants within a chain are built to a standard architectural format and offer a standard menu. Fast food restaurants are the most common, but sit-down restaurant chains (e.g. in the USA, Outback Steakhouse, T.G.I. Friday's, Ruby Tuesday, and Olive Garden) also exist. Restaurant chains are often found near highways, shopping malls and tourist areas."[2] Chains comprise a wide variety of business types. Chains can be international (such as Starbucks or McDonald's), national (such as Hell Pizza in New Zealand or Max Burgers in Sweden), regional (such as Burgerville in the Pacific Northwest of the USA), or local (such as Gray's Papaya hot dogs in New York City or Masala Zone in London).

The chain business model leverages the success of scaling. The bigger the chain, the greater the efficiency and ideally, the better the financial result. In many areas, the opening of an anchor store, or well-known fast food chain increases real estate values. Chains leverage a turn-key business process, using pre-fabricated buildings, well-trained corporate launch teams, and astute real estate investors. For smaller independent food tourism business owners, such are goals worthy of consideration.

Chain businesses offer consumers three key benefits, namely a consistency of product and experience; predictability of price; and standardized customer service. Due to pre-negotiated product purchase contracts that reflect advance purchase bulk buying discounts, chain businesses receive preferential pricing from suppliers and are able to offer their customers prices that meet or often beat prices offered by locally-owned businesses. In other words, independently owned businesses cannot buy in the same volume and therefore typically do not qualify for high volume purchasing discounts.

Benefit #1: Consistent Experience

Customers can expect consistent food and drink at most chain locations. In many ways, consistency is a byproduct of the chain business model. It allows scale to work. Some chains such as McDonald's partially localize menus to suit the taste of the local markets (e.g. by serving beer in Germany or the McArabia sandwich in the Middle East). A Starbucks venti latte should taste the same at any Starbucks in the world. Some customers are comforted knowing that they can expect a similar food or drink experience at any chain outlet in the world. Chain customers can also expect an overall consistent *experience*. For example, Subway sandwich stores look pretty much the same everywhere in the world. There is no guesswork about the ordering process when ordering a sandwich in a Subway location on the other side of the world. The Nando's restaurant design is the same everywhere in the world. Hyatt Hotels feel almost the same in every city in the world, often with the signature atrium lobby. A customer unhappy with his or her Starbucks coffee in Hong Kong knows that (s)he can have it remade or refunded without fuss — a corporate policy that gives a consistent customer experience everywhere. Chains can also offer loyalty cards or programs that reward the customer no matter which outlet they visit (although the ability to earn and redeem loyalty points does not always cross national borders easily).

Benefit #2: Convenience

Chains carefully scope out locations before agreeing to build an outlet. The reason is that they want to build in a location that will be convenient for customers, but also where the real estate stands to increase in value. This is why chains are usually found in shopping malls, highway on/off ramps, service stations (in the UK), airports and hotel lobbies. People walk or drive by them constantly. The potential for a large volume of sales is high. Customers do not have to think too hard about choosing where to eat or stay.

Benefit #3: Predictability of Price

Chains offer customers predictable prices. They are able to do so with high volume contract discounts with foodservice and material suppliers. While prices will not always be the same due to a variety of factors like different costs of living, a customer knows that a McDonald's Big Mac, for example, is going to be one of the more affordable burger options in the area, irrespective if the city happens to be extremely expensive. In other words, chain pricing is relative to the area. More recently, chains have been dabbling in more premium (i.e. higher priced) offerings in an effort to compete with other premium options in theor competitive area.

Benefit #4: Service

Chains tend to organize customer service and employee training programs at the corporate level. Starwood Hotels uses this practice. Their trainers travel from property to property to train the company's staff on computer systems, service and other issues. Regardless of which of the Starwood brands is being discussed, the training will be consistent at all locations. That is the expectation at least. Many chains of all types experience a high turnover rate, which can actually result in a consistently inconsistent experience.

Larger corporations are driven by generating revenue and earning profits for shareholders. When the primary driver is profit, the business needs to streamline the management of its operations to reduce expenses. In doing so, a number of characteristics that are important to foodies can often get lost, such as quality and sense of place.

Larger corporations that generate higher earnings than local and independent businesses have an additional advantage that they can have more cash and more employees that can engage in community programs, charitable donations, and so on. There are as many corporations as stars in the sky and it is nearly impossible to categorize the wide variety of corporate goals. Large corporations have an opportunity to establish a leadership position with regard to their business practices and corporate social responsibility. Specifically with regards to things like commitments to sustainability, fair treatment of employees, worker rights, and so on. Large corporations also have the power to be able to foster consumer opinion and drive change by their sheer size and buying power.

The US chain Chipotle is just one such example of a large corporation that is helping to change consumer awareness about the benefits of healthy eating, by educating its customers about why its menu choices are healthy. That said, Chipotle's clever marketing causes people to have a high regard for the Chipotle brand. However, a fine print disclaimer states on product wrapping that if there is not enough all natural chicken available, they reserve the right to substituting with another suitable product. Therefore, an unwitting consumer cannot be guaranteed that he or she is getting the product they thought they were buying.

In the documentary film *WAL-MART: The High Cost of Low Price*, the filmmakers show how chain businesses are often welcomed with open arms into communities because of the promise of jobs, but the movie presents the case that this is often a case of selling out to the devil. Ninety-nine percent of the workers hired are trapped in hourly positions. While some food products might be purchased locally or regionally, the overwhelming majority of profits generated by the franchise are shipped back to the corporate headquarters to pay dividends to stockholders. Meanwhile, according to Tommy Klauber, a serial entrepreneur and owner of Pattigeorge's Restaurant, Polo Grill & Bar and other independent foodservice businesses in Florida, USA, "the big corporate marketing budgets drown out the quieter voices of the less cash-flush independent food and drink businesses, which are closing in rising numbers." He continues, "We're losing our culinary cultures around the world — even in food-centric countries like France and Italy. The independents don't have the same deep pockets as the chains. It's harder for us to survive."

While food in independent restaurants and hotels may cost more than in chains, it is important to support independents for the major reason that they help keep money in the community. When money is spent in a chain, some money stays in the community in terms of wages, local taxes paid and possibly some supplies purchased. Some of a chain's earnings are sent back to headquarters, at a minimum 5% of its gross earnings as a franchise fee and an additional 3-5% for its corporate marketing fund. As much as 100% of an independent's earnings can stay in the local community.

According to Chicago, USA-based restaurant industry analysis company The NPD Group, in 2008, 87% percent of the loss in restaurant visits came from independents, even though only a little over a quarter of all restaurant visits going into the [2008] recession took place at independents. As such, since 2009, chains' share of the industry grew from 60 percent to 61 percent. At the same time, the percentage of restaurant visits that took place at independents dipped from 28 to 27 percent. And the number of independent restaurants in the USA declined by 7158, while the number of chain restaurants increased by 4511. NPD analysts said that, among independents, higher-end restaurants in large urban areas fared relatively well during the recession. It was smaller, mom-and-pop establishments that were hit hardest.

Independent Businesses

With such a favorable light cast on chain businesses, it may sound as if chains are the best deal for consumers. However, independently owned businesses are able to offer their customers different benefits which can often be easily overlooked. Independents can adapt more quickly to local tastes and demands. So if customers decide to stop eating beef for a while due to a possible threat from mad cow disease, the independent restaurant owner can quickly reprint menus without any beef on the menu, and also will not have to worry about months' worth of beef in the supply chain for dozens or hundreds of outlets. Independents can also vary the menu more frequently, giving their customers a greater choice more often. If a fisherman brings in a fresh catch of mussels, the restaurant can put them on the menu that night. The chain restaurant cannot usually react as quickly, and if it does, the price of that particular commodity rises on the open market due to demand.

Secondly, independent businesses often reflect local character, which is important to some customers. Why would a foodie travel across the globe for a predictable chain coffee or burger? They most likely would not. But they would try a locally-owned burger restaurant or a locally-owned café because they know that their experience in such establishments could be unique and memorable, which is an underlying tenet of food tourism. One could have a memorable experience at a chain business, but one would have that same great experience in each of the chain's outlets. In an independent outlet, the experience is unique.

Independents are free to focus on higher quality ingredients than many of the chain businesses. It does not matter whether such ingredients are locally sourced or imported. The overall quality of the ingredients can typically be higher than in chains.

Perhaps we should place our support behind "local operators" who are doing something truly worthwhile. A community needs to support its local chefs and food scene by developing and patronizing it. Chains like Seasons 52, which are operated by local owners, are incorporating seasonality, sustainability, health and wellness and culinary passion. [3]

Independents also tend to be more personal. For example, there is a high likelihood that locals know the business's founding family or its relatives. It would not be unrealistic to meet one of the owners inside the business. This would rarely if ever happen at a chain. When customers meet the owners, stories are told and customers invest more emotions in the overall experience, creating longer lasting memories. Stories can revolve around the current or former owner, the building or area's history or a dish that the restaurant is known for. Chains might have one big story to tell, but it will likely be the same story told across all locations and not unique to one location or area as would be the case for independents. In local and close-in regional chains, the experience may still be unique enough to warrant a visit from a bona fide foodie.

Staff who work for an independent may have more input into the menu development, whereas staff at a chain will usually have little to no say in menu development. This allows an independent's kitchen staff to develop and hone creative skills in menu planning, and incorporate customer requests, rather than simply reheating frozen, pre-portioned food. Independents can also take the risk to try new things (approaches, menu items, ingredients) than a chain may not try. A chain will conduct research to see what will sell and focus on that.

> If independents could organize together, such as around a common food and drink experience assessment system, they could help ease the decision making process for new potential customers and compete more effectively against chains.

Chains do not typically give foodies a reason to explore. According to the WFTA, foodies tend to be explorers and have a propensity to want to actively search for unique and memorable food and drink experiences. It is hard to search for a unique and memorable food experience at a busy intersection with well-known chain business on each of its four corners. The act of making the food or drink convenient takes away the excitement foodies get from discovering new food or drink experiences.

According to the WFTA, in the USA, the largest number of members in state restaurant associations are independent businesses, but the majority of the funding for state restaurant association memberships comes from chains. This inherent conflict of interest represents an opportunity in that the needs of independents are not fully met. While there are actually greater numbers of independent restaurants overall, this wide variety of independent restaurants gives consumers more choice than is available from the few chains in a given geographic area. For example, exiting a highway in the United States, chain restaurants and hotels will be congregated near the highway on and off ramps. However, less than 1-2 miles (0.6-1.3 km) from the highways, a much larger choice of independent restaurants and hotels is often found. The challenge for independents is getting potential customers (at least those traveling by car), to drive a bit further afield and to take the risk to try their business.

Challenges

Independent restaurants especially face some serious challenges from chain restaurants. First, chains can serve as a positive memory recall. For example, Tim Horton's, a Canadian donut chain, does brisk business at its outlets in overseas military bases, perhaps helping soldiers to overcome homesickness.

Many chain businesses are in touch with the "buy local" mantra. Rosenberger is a chain of freeway truck stops throughout Austria.[4] It is known for its emphasis on a high quality, locally sourced Austrian menu which bonds the restaurant chain to its area. Rosenberger features a rotating menu of seasonal Austrian specialties. Despite its many locations, the company remains a family-owned and operated business. It is quality combined with convenience.

There are still examples of chains that could be said to help preserve culinary cultures in a way. Both Moti Mahal and Haldiram, chains in India, have taken street recipes and codified them, creating mass-produced copies of authentic regional foods that are safe, convenient and affordable for anyone to enjoy.

Travelers do not need help locating chains but travelers do need help finding suitable choices of local and independent hotels and restaurants. This is where popular consumer review websites like Yelp or UrbanSpoon come in.[5] Chain consistency and predictability take the risk and doubt out of decision-making around food and drink. If independents could organize together, such as around a common food and drink experience assessment system, they could form a net of consistency across the world and compete more effectively against chains. This has been tried unsuccessfully by a number of organizations like Dine Originals in the USA and even Slow Food.

Reality dictates that travelers will not eat every meal at a locally owned restaurant. Factors such as lack of time, inexperience with a foreign language, lack of familiarity with new neighborhoods, and influence of friends and colleagues can all affect restaurant choice.

In some areas, chains face fierce competition from local providers. For example in Portland Oregon, USA, it is notoriously difficult for large chains to maintain a presence in the downtown business district, and only a handful can be found. Similarly throughout even the close-in neighborhoods of Portland, it is difficult for large chains to gain traction. Yet further out in the suburbs, chains abound. Portland's city residents are fierce advocates of buying local whenever feasible. They prefer local grocery stores, local restaurants, local wines and beers, and local food products. This behavior is endemic throughout the region of Cascadia, although not all area residents subscribe to this ethos. Portland is admittedly an anomaly among U.S. cities but it is an excellent model of community-supported approach to commerce and economic development. Some chains provide quality food and an above average experience, but most float in the "sea of sameness." Such chains are for the uneducated or indifferent sustenance seeker, not someone who knows about or cares about food.

Towards a Cookie Cutter Future?

While chain businesses come with both positives and negatives, an important question remains. If smaller local businesses continue to be bought by large multinational corporations, or if they continue to close, is our food and drink experience destined to become "rubber stamped"? Will our hamburger, pizza or donut experience be prescribed to exactly the same specifications in every country?

Large or small cities, provincial towns or remote locations all offer varying forms of food and drink hospitality. Even more so, local and regional cuisines have been used as a draw for tourism.[6] Food experiences complement the traveling experiences for the tourist and make them more memorable. World Food Travel Association research shows that travelers commonly spend 25% of their budget on food and drink while traveling, although travelers tend to spend a higher percentage (up to 40%) in more expensive destinations.[7] Travelers may look for types of foods they are familiar with or they may be passionate or curious to try foods of other cultures or different foods to those they are used to.[8] With so many offerings, one is inclined to believe that variation is the norm. Yet in a shrinking world, similar offerings can be found on every continent, in almost every sector.

Are All Cookie Cutters Created Equal?

The cookie cutter is a metaphor for standardization. This can mean standardizing the product (food, drink or accommodation), the offering (service delivery, atmosphere or physical location) or both. Standardization of product or experience brings to mind large food and drink chains, such as those often found in large cities across the globe, which are often the first port of call for travelers. Here, illuminated billboards and signs promote access to fast food in a very visible way. One can find McDonalds in over 100 countries selling a standardized and largely predictable menu.

Ultimately, success breeds success. Chains have a very sophisticated vetting process for decision making. The trend now is the "Un-chain" chain, i.e. one that does not celebrate its carbon copy outlets, and wants to be identified as a genuine socially responsible member of the community. Chipotle, a U.S. chain featuring Mexican food, is one such example.

Standardized vs. Unique Products and Offerings

The many facets of the tourism industry all produce different experiences. People travel for a variety of reasons including to visit friends and relatives, business meetings, conventions, exploration, genealogy, cultural and sports performances, and health/medical reasons. Food itself is a motivator for travelers to visit new places and seek out unique food experiences. Yet all travelers must (and do) eat even if they do not travel seeking culinary experiences.

In developed countries, standardized products, such as fast-food restaurants and limited service hotels can represent good value. They are easily replicated and lend themselves well to multi-site expansion.[9] These types of global food chains also provide a level of security to certain travelers because they are familiar.

Chains do well in terms of managing expectations of their product. A Big Mac is pretty much the same anywhere. Those exposed to this type of food, know what to expect when they enter the fast food restaurant. However, for those that travel widely, differences are often felt and tasted in the offering and the product respectively. The style of service at the Coffee Club in Brisbane, Queensland, Australia is different to the service of the Coffee Club in Bangkok, Thailand. The coffee tastes different because the milk is quite often reconstituted in Thailand whereas it is fresh in Brisbane. While this variation may seem insignificant, it can reinforce how the supporting products may let the product down or how the customer interaction with the service delivery system falls short of the tourist's benchmark.

Independent restaurants, more variable in their offering and their product than their chain counterparts, are often used as a draw to an area, providing a non-standardized experience. As long as any variation in quality is used to enhance the product or augment the experience as may be the case with seasonal produce, or summer/winter tourist destinations, such variation is acceptable or even welcomed. Building such variations into the offering lessens the likelihood of the tourist having a bad experience. Variation is an element that goes beyond the mold, providing unique culinary experiences where a chain cannot compete and is a competitive advantage of the non-standardized, non-chain offering.

Large fast-food chains attract visitors with a combination of their "comfort of home" combined with culture-specific and nation-specific products. For example, according to Foreign Policy Magazine,[10] one of the top 10 selling McDonald's products world-wide is the McArabia, a grilled chicken or kofta pita sandwich sold in the Arab World. Whether this product is purchased by locals or visitors, the attraction remains: a consistent product served in a familiar environment at a predictable price.

Destinations – More Than Just Food

Within the familiar, easily replicated offering, providing good value to target markets, and variations in product allow the chains to appear culturally relevant. But for those tourists seeking a more authentic culinary experience, chains represent a loss of authenticity in the product. Authentic and interesting food can attract visitors to a destination and through its uniqueness, may serve as a competitive advantage.

While a range of offerings from global to national to regional caters for most travelers, competitive advantage comes from differentiation. This could be in terms of a highly customized product such as the Caesar Ritz hotels or Maxim's Restaurant which cannot be reproduced easily. As unique products they are able to draw customers throughout the designing and managing of the tourism and hospitality products.

In many cases, the rich tapestry of the national and the local that many people come to see when traveling, may be buffered with the global offering of the mass produced chain. So is cuisine then, becoming the only differentiator among destinations? What about language, culture and location? All these things must work together in synergy to provide the memorable or even unforgettable tourist experience. How many times have you, in your travels come across a culinary moment so special, that you seek to buy the wine, or the oil or whatever it was, that you could take back home with you to replicate the experience? And on trying to recreate the experience back home, you failed miserably? The wine tastes too cheap, the oil not quite right, etc. Heston Blumenthal summed it up nicely when he said that your particular experience was only what it was — that experience — because of the combination of all the senses taking part, in a unique location at that moment in time. If it were just about cuisine, taking food elements home with you should have been enough. But they were not. So while on paper and rather objectively, one may argue that an experience may appear to fall short, the power of the senses in the location and the role of food in the real world should not be under-estimated as a means to cement that particular experience as a memorable one.

New World vs. Old World "Cuisine"

If everything is headed toward a cookie cutter future, perhaps the size and shape of the cookie cutters are the differentiating factors that can be manipulated. Such sentiment is possibly the result of globalization. Finding Italian food in Bangkok, a country which has its own very strong authentic cuisine and uses food tourism as a draw, is in itself a version of standardization. Yet is eating Italian in Bangkok the same as eating it in Rome?

New world countries like Canada and Australia are multicultural and their very identity comes from this multiculturalism. A great and diverse food offering offers a competitive advantage for food and drink tourism in that many different types of good quality food can be found in these places. It is relatively easy to seek out Chinese, Spanish or Greek restaurants in a place like Australia. Ironically, when one travels through China, Spain or Greece, one does not usually seek a kind of cuisine different from that of the host country. Most of the food served through local restaurants and bars is Chinese, Spanish or Greek, respectively. In this sense, new world countries may be seen to have lost some of their authenticity — the items making it onto menus are usually those considered delicacies of those cultures, and with the passing of time, these delicacies become the markers of the cultural cuisine in the new world landscape. In that way, food presented at these restaurants is not necessarily authentic; it is more special occasion food that took off from its humble roots to cater for the country's immigrants.

Countries like Australia and Canada have grasped this cultural assimilation and added a level of integrity to the diverse offering, creating their own competitive advantage. People come to Australia for the outdoors and the landscape. The way people eat in Australia is different to the USA or Canada. While Australians do not have a distinct culinary tradition, how Australians eat is a differentiator; what they do with food and how they use produce is in effect an expression of themselves. So perhaps eating Italian in Australia may be as authentic as eating it in Italy or Bangkok yet culturally different at the same time. The location adds a further dimension to the experience.

While regional cuisine is being touted as a differentiator, especially in the state of South Australia, there are too many similar elements in the products and offerings to allow for enough of a competitive advantage to make the approach worthwhile. Destination marketers need to align their strategies with the interests of independent food and drink businesses so both parties can find a return on their investment. The opportunity for complementing the tourist experience offering to a high quality food and drink one has greater potential in regional areas. But the key lies in being able to offer a non-standard offering, where every second food experience is not the same as the previous one. Creativity is a major element to keep it interesting for the tourist, where they want to see and spend more.

In new world countries like Australia, with no historical national cuisine to call their own, the industry relies more heavily on various cultural nuances to help shape its food and drink offering. The failure of "bush tucker"[11] to be a major draw for Australia perhaps further indicates that food is not the sole differentiator among destinations. To succeed, uniqueness must have a market. Australian Native Food made attempts in the mid-1990s to commercialize products that were native to Australia but did not succeed. The irony of being able to find more "bush tucker" alternatives outside Australia than within is not lost on food industry professionals. But Australian food and drink tourism professionals have a long way to go before they can use native Australian fare as a draw or even as part of a tourist experience. One of the possible reasons for this lack of success was that this type of cuisine did not fit into a known offering; no core group of people ate it all the time. There was no grassroots promotion and no real demand for this cuisine, unlike what occurred with Asian or European cuisine which had core groups of people following that food.

Perhaps a reinvention of Australian Native cuisine presents an opportunity to utilize elements of standardized offerings (in terms of service delivery) to provide unique products in a unique setting which transcends the acculturation of cuisine to place. Tourists in Australia are likely to seek out places where they can eat crocodile, emu and kangaroo. Just recently there has been a push, especially in South Australia, to promote kangaroo as it is a meat that is more environmentally friendly to produce, and it is tasty and lean. This is something that will need to be developed further but the healthy eating push certainly helps boost the popularity of this typical dish.

CONCLUSION

Standardized options come in varying shapes and sizes. While the obvious food, drink and accommodation chain offerings can present both good value to their target markets through their familiar, safe and easily replicated offerings and products, a competitive advantage can be found with the culturally relevant and unique product offering. Local restaurants are part of the charm and culinary experience for the tourist. But for many, food is not the sole reason for travel. While cuisine does have an impact on a traveler's decision when choosing their vacation destination, provincial variation through culture, language and landscape provides the edge and makes for a more differentiated food, drink and accommodation offering as, the Barossa, Napa, Franschhoek and the South of France all demonstrate. New world countries like Australia display a level of integrity in their multicultural offerings and products which may be an example of how we move beyond synergy. Taking the familiar, such as Italian cuisine, and moving outside of a standardized offering will allow the creativity of the other dimensions of the tourist experience (perhaps why one traveled in the first place) to be realized and make for a more memorable one. And for those in the business, if all players display a level of integrity, then perhaps the chains, the locals and the independents can coexist. Will chains put the independents out of business? People will always seek out good food, and there will always be gifted cooks. Independent businesses should take note that chains are raising the stakes.

The standard cry is always global versus local, and this is a faulty premise. Globalization of food in some form is here to stay, at the very least because some cuisines are so ingrained into our global culture they will likely not fade any time soon. Increasing environmental pressure means food with a high energy cost, like strawberries in January in the northern hemisphere will have to give way to locally sourced alternatives. Nevertheless, we as food tourism professionals have a duty to educate our customers as to the reasons why locally owned, smaller food businesses must be supported. And consumers have a duty to support our local economies by buying as many food and drinks locally as possible.

DISCUSSION QUESTIONS

1. What can multicultural new world countries do to further differentiate their cuisine than what is already presented herein?
2. What can food tourism professionals do to educate their customers about the need to buy locally and support locally owned businesses?
3. If a national chain purchases and serves high quality local food and drink ingredients, should it be supported by foodies?

ENDNOTES

[1] www.restaurantreport.com/Departments/biz_guerilla_mkt.html

[2] http://en.wikipedia.org/wiki/Chain_store, Accessed 23 March 2013.

[3] www.seasons52.com

[4] www.rosenberger.cc

[5] See the chapter *The Power of the People* in this book for a more in-depth discussion of consumer influence.

[6] Lucy Long, *Culinary tourism* (Lexington, KY: The University Press of Kentucky, 2004).

[7] International Culinary Tourism Association, Report on U.S. Culinary Travelers, 2007.

[8] S. Karim and C. Chi, *Journal of Hospitality Marketing & Management,* 19 (2010) 531-555

[9] P. Kotler, J. Bowen, & J. Makens. *Marketing for Hospitality and Tourism: International Edition* (Pearson Higher Ed USA, 2009)

[10] foreignpolicy.com/articles/2012/10/08/10_best_mcdonalds_meals_you_wont_find_in_the_us?page=0,2

[11] "Bush" is Australian jargon for "countryside" and "tucker" is Australian jargon for "food".

Food Tourism in the Far East: Cracking the Code

Tim Alper

Asian dishes are some of the most revered in the world. Ask any group of people their favorites and there will be no shortage of replies, from Vietnamese *pho* to Thai *khao man gai* to Chinese hot and sour soup, just to name a few. Yet two countries, notably South Korea and Japan, have attempted to make their mark in the world of food tourism, with mixed results. Issues of language, culture and politics are partly the reason, but so is the world's lack of familiarity with these cuisines apart from commonplace sushi or kimchi. We will look at what Japan and South Korea are doing to brand their food and tourism experiences and offer a prescription of what national foodservice industries and tourism offices can do to market better the finer nuances of rich cuisines such as these.

INTRODUCTION

Asia's Far East is undoubtedly the continent's economic powerhouse. At its most easterly edge lie Japan and South Korea. Both are wealthy nations, and not only in terms of GDP, but also when it comes to diversity of food. [1] As many visitors to these countries will attest, Westernization may have radically altered much of the heritage and social landscape of Japan and Korea, but the native food culture is alive and well. [2]

Yet when most non-Asians think of Asian food, they probably think of sushi, Chinese dishes, Thai food and possibly even Indian curry. Outside Asia, and in areas with large Korean or Japanese populations, such as major US or Canadian cities, London, or certain parts of Brazil, Korean and Japanese dishes are still considered exotic and unknown — almost undiscovered.

Certain Japanese and Korean dishes have made a breakthrough on the international food scene. Japanese sushi is now easy to come by in many countries since it exploded into the American mainstream in the last quarter of the 20th Century. [3] The inhabitants of the (mainly urban, North American) areas with large Korean populations have also had their heads turned by certain Korean dishes, such as kimchi[4] and so-called "Korean barbecue," with mainstream media and heavy-hitting chefs starting to talk about Korean food. [5] [6]

However, these caveats aside, the vast canon of Japanese and Korean cuisine does seem largely uncovered, even by the more intrepid of food explorers. Finding outlets that claim to sell Japanese food in London is not difficult. If you Google "Japanese restaurant London", you will find no shortage of hits. However, upon closer examination, it would seem that Japanese restaurants are almost synonymous with a single dish: sushi. In fact finding a Japanese restaurant in the UK that is not all about sushi, is hard. Almost one third of all the Japanese restaurants in London even feel the need to feature the word "sushi" in their names. [7] The fastest-growing and most successful chain of Japanese restaurants in the UK, *YO! Sushi* has never even been owned by anyone of Japanese extraction. [8]

Indeed, despite the huge interest sushi garnered in Western markets beginning in the 1980s, it would be still be hard to make the argument that Japanese food has successfully invaded the US or EU markets. However, since the turn of the millennium, both countries have been talking big about increasing food tourism through the sales of food products, and turning Korea and Japan into destinations where food is a major draw.

When former South Korean President Lee Myung-bak announced in 2008 that he wanted to put Korean food "amongst the top five cuisines in the world by the year 2011," Korean food entrepreneurs must have liked what they heard. The Hansik Jaedan (Korean food federation) was created, and the President's own wife, Kim Yoon-ok, was appointed to lead the group's work. The initiative has gone by the unofficial moniker of "The First Lady's Project." The flagship mission of the Hansik Jaedan, announced in 2010, was to be the establishment of a Korean government-run restaurant in New York's Manhattan.

Japan has also been exceptionally active, embracing the cultural phenomenon of "Cool Japan." "Cool Japan," a term first coined in 2002 by international observers,[9] suggests Japan's international image is attractive to non-Japanese. The Japanese government believes it can harness the power of "Cool Japan"[10] and use it to boost sales of Japanese food and drink products.

And according to Japan's Agency for Cultural Affairs, South Korea spent 117 billion yen on "cultural activities" in 2008, while Japan spent just under 101.8 billion yen in the same period — figures that include spending on projects aimed at increasing tourism and food-related events. In the wake of the tragic tsunami and the Fukishima disaster of 2011, Japanese food trade has been hit in terms of production and demand from home and abroad.[11][12] Nonetheless, Japan still aims push ahead with the international promotion of its food. A government cabinet action paper published in August 2012 says Japan aims to be bringing in 1 trillion yen (over US$11 billion) in food and beverage exports by 2020.[13] This is an ambitious goal indeed, seeing as pre-Fukishima export revenues in 2010 amounted to about half that amount – US$4.7 billion.[14]

The central governments and related groups from both countries have been exceptionally active in the realm of food tourism promotion. The past few years have seen advertisements for Korean food placed in *The New York Times*,[15] as well as a Korean food advertisement in New York's Times Square.[16]

Japanese tourism promotion advertisement videos, featuring food, were screened on US television channel CNN in 2009,[17] and 2011 advertisements featuring the pop band Arahi appeared in 133 countries in 2011. They, too, have also been aired in Times Square.[18]

Yet even within both countries, it seems there is some level of public dissatisfaction with the way that the government is going about its efforts. Japanese and Korean food tourism promotions, it seems, are not without their, often quite vocal, critics. In many cases, plans to push local food to international consumers have hit major snags.

In an article in *Japan Today*, Umezawa Takaaki, Partner and Managing Director of A.T. Kearney Japan, was quoted as saying, "Japan is generally strong in the area of creativity, but weak in several critical areas: [the] ability to appraise overseas markets, [and] businesspersons with [the] ability to lead the development of overseas markets."[19]

In South Korea, a large setback was endured in 2005 when three of Seoul's largest and most prestigious hotels, The Westin Chosun, The Grand International and The Shilla, each announced the closure of many of their government-subsidized Korean restaurants.[20]

All hotels sited lack of trade at restaurants that were just too unprofitable to continue. At the time of writing, only four of Seoul's 20 "exclusive-level" hotels have Korean restaurants, in spite of a government point scheme that rewards hotels that offer Korean food.[21]

More recently, serious questions have been raised by Koreans as to the efficacy of the Hansik Jaedan. One of its projects was to establish a "flagship Korean restaurant," paid for by public funds, in New York City. A budget of around about US$500,000 was set aside for the restaurant and promotional activities tied to the project but the restaurant failed to open, amidst some serious public criticism.[22]

In early 2013, the Hansik Jaedan ran into yet more difficulty when the Korean parliament voted unilaterally in favor of launching a public inquiry into the federation and the restaurant that still has not materialized, three years after plans to launch it were announced. The Hansik Jaedan foundation claimed that it had spent the budget on developing its website and preparing materials that would allow for the correct Anglicization of Korean food names, but parliament alleges that there are reasons to believe the funds were misappropriated.[23][24]

Whatever difficulties Japan and South Korea are experiencing need to be kept in context. It is worth remembering that up until less than 150 years ago, Japan actively shunned any sort of contact or trade with the outside world. It was not until 1868 that Japanese citizens were even allowed to leave the country. The idea of tourism and trade with the outside world is still in its nascent stages in Japan, despite the breathtaking speed at which it has become one of the largest global trading nations on the planet.

Korea, too, was still being referred to as a "hermit kingdom" at the turn of the 20th Century. It was not until end of the Korean War and the "Miracle on the Han"[25] in the late 1960s that South Korea started to emerge as an active participant in the world trade economy. Food promoters in both nations might well cast an envious eye at their Chinese neighbors. Despite never really having an active food tourism promotion campaign, Chinese cuisine has become an international hit. Try finding a town anywhere without a Chinese restaurant. It may be harder than you think. Tthere are an estimated 41,000 Chinese restaurants in the US alone.[26]

It is often thought that countries like Korea and Japan compete with the Chinese. China dwarfs both in terms of size and population, and "Chinese food" is a lazy term given to food that comes from a huge variety of ethnic groups within China. If you talk about Chinese cuisine, you could be talking about anything from raw Mongolian horsemeat preparations to Tibetan yak butter tea. The international network of Chinese expatriates is also astounding. Some 50 million Chinese live outside their own country,[27] and many are involved in the catering industry.

It is only since the end of World War Two, or even later, that South Korea and Japan decided to step out onto the global food scene. As much effort and economic investment they commit to the food tourism cause, we cannot expect to see success overnight. It is clear that, despite the lofty goals of both the South Korean and Japanese governments, the task of popularizing Far Eastern food to the wider world will not be easy. Both nations are certainly aware, now more than ever, as dire financial forecasts predict tough economic times ahead for the entire Asian economic bloc, that simply throwing money at the problem will not solve it.

Evidence from both countries, and abroad, suggests the time may be right for Korean and Japanese food promoters, though the path to mainstream acceptance will be littered with obstacles unique to both Japanese and South Korean cuisine.

A Question of Semantics?

Semantics plays an enormous, and potentially divisive, role in spreading knowledge about any foodstuff; but the cases of Japan and Korea are particularly troublesome, precisely because the cooking techniques they use are so advanced. The few Japanese food-related words that many non-Japanese are familiar with — sushi, sashimi, and sake — are simply untranslatable because few other countries have any words in their lexicon to describe them.

The English expression "raw fish", for most foodies, describes as-yet uncooked fish, rather than fish that is never intended to be cooked. The connotations of "raw fish" sound unappetizing to a Westerner; it sounds like something that will give the diner stomach problems. If you are a Japanese chef writing "raw fish" on a menu, you are already fighting an uphill battle to keep your potential customers interested. Fortunately, much of the world is aware of what sushi is. The real problem for Far East Asian food tourism promoters is creating a desire for food that most average non-Korean/non-Japanese have never tried before. When the vocabulary to even describe such food does not exist, this becomes a mammoth task.

However, the further you explore the world of sushi, the more confusing the language difficulties become. The word "sushi" does not actually mean raw fish; it means "sour taste." Non-Japanese culinary adventurers may be dismayed to hear that preparing sushi does not just involve hacking up freshly-caught fish. It involves complex knives, difficult-to-learn knife skills, and sophisticated preservation techniques that use vinegar and cold water. And if you are trying to make sushi commercially in the EU or the US, you will need to follow an array of uncompromising health guidelines that will almost certainly impair the taste of the food. Ignore these and you could risk having your restaurant shut down.[28] [29] [30]

Cities with large Korean populations, like Toronto, New York, London and Los Angeles, are seeing the popularity rise of restaurants known to non-Koreans as "Korean barbecue," with American media outlets starting to feature restaurant articles that focus on Korean barbecue eateries or chefs using Korean barbecue as a fusion ingredient.[31] [32] Yet, although "Korean barbecue" is a convenient moniker, it is actually a misnomer. There is no way of even saying "barbecue" in Korean, and the average Korean would be confused if you asked him or her to direct you to a such a restaurant. What the rest of the world refers to as "Korean barbecue" could be a whole variety of *gogigui*, or grilled meat. The correct Korean word for what most North Americans term "Korean barbecue" is most likely *samgyupsal*, marbled pork belly meat with three layers of fat between each layer of flesh. But also popular is *ogyupsal*, five layers of fat to five layers of flesh. *Galbigui*, rib meat, is another local favorite. But many restaurants offer beef variations rather than pork, and to confuse matters more, many restaurants offer *ddakgalbi* — chicken cooked at a similar-looking table-top grill, but in a thick and spicy pepper paste marinade. Just asking for *gogigui*, Korean barbecue's most appropriate name, will not be enough to get exactly what you want in Korea. The frightening variety and complexity of Korean food is often its own worst enemy when it comes to feeding foreigners.

Even more of a challenge, though, is that Korean food that is less well-known among non-Koreans, is the same food that Koreans might like to promote to potential food tourists.

There are a whole host of Korean gadgets that have quite remarkable cooking qualities quite unusual to other cultures. The dolsot[33] is a quite remarkable device that plays a vital role in Korean cooking. It is a carefully-crafted stone bowl that can retain heat for an extraordinarily long time, meaning that a broth served at the table stays piping hot throughout the meal. It can also be used for cooking at the table, in the case of dolsot bibimbap (a rice dish served with various vegetables, meat and egg and mixed with sesame oil and pepper paste).

However, the most common form of bibimbap is Jonju bibimbap (Jonju is a Korean city), which is served in a metal bowl. Ordering the dolsot style means you are eating a piping hot dish, while the Jonju style means you are getting something more akin to room temperature. Yet the literal English translation of dolsot bibimbap is "stone pot bibimbap,"[34] while Jonju bibimbap just translates to "Bibimbap, Jonju-style". Perhaps the more aesthetically-inclined foodies will care whether their dinner is served on a bronze platter or a plastic plate, but most will judge food on its taste. And there is a huge difference between eating food that is served piping hot versus lukewarm.

For Koreans, or even non-Koreans who know about Korean food, seeing the word "dolsot" makes them understand that the food will be served hot, but the uninitiated just see "stone pot" and "Jonju" and think, "what is the difference?" Considering how different languages work when describing food may become the biggest challenge for anyone in the Far East who hopes to promote as-yet-unfamiliar food.

Fermented food: A Food Journey into the Unknown?

The heavy presence of fermentation in Japanese and Korean food is also a potential stumbling block for East Asian food tourism promoters. Although fermented foods have been proven to have extraordinary health benefits, and perhaps even help in the fight against colon cancer,[35] their global popularity is somewhat limited, especially in the West.

What little fermented food Westerners do consume, such as pickled cucumbers, sauerkraut and so on, is often fermented in vinegar, which tastes totally different to the salt-fermented vegetables so prominent in Japanese and Korean food. Large-scale, Western-style vinegar-based fermentation, does not provide anything close to the health benefits of salt-based fermentation.[36]

For this reason, much of Japan and Korea's fermented foodstuffs, such as natto, miso and dwenjang (all salt-preserved soybean products), have no point of reference in non-Oriental societies. Non-Far Eastern languages, once again, lack the vocabulary to describe fermented soy products, the backbone of most Korean and Japanese meals.[37] The unfamiliarity of these staple foods of Far Eastern cuisine provides a large obstacle for food tourism promoters, but not an insurmountable one. The health properties are immense of the most humble of all possible Korean meals: rice, dwenjang, tofu and nameul (various green shoots, often prepared with garlic); or the simple Japanese breakfast of miso soup, rice, nori (seaweed) and fermented tsukemono pickles.

High in protein, vitamins and iron,[38] low in saturated fat, and full of macrobiotic goodness, both foods far surpass coffee and a pastry when it comes to nutritional value. A literal "breakfast of champions" is available to the average Korean or Japanese every day. As the rest of the world panics about the unhealthiness of its breakfasts,[39] [40] Korea and Japan have the potential to claim their place in the food tourism industry if they can exploit the image of being purveyors of a healthier way of life.

James Howe, professor of culinary arts at Korea's Woosong University, is a gastronomic veteran of Korea, and lived 12 years in the country. Howe agrees that health benefits need to be accentuated in marketing efforts. He says, "Look at what the average Korean family eats for dinner: Most likely they will have a meal consisting of fish, dwenjangjigae [fermented bean stew], steamed vegetables and rice. You have Omega 3 and 6 fatty acids in the fish, antioxidants in the dwenjangjigae, and calcium in all the green leafy vegetables. Korean food should be marketed and promoted as healthy."

There can be little arguing that a Korean food product has managed to make it onto the North American A-list of trending health food ingredients in last few years. A plethora of US food articles mentioning black garlic, an ingredient made in Korea using many of the traditional Korean fermentation techniques, have started to appear in major Western media outlets since 2009.[41] [42]

Yet the biggest name in international black garlic sales is not the Korean government, or a large Korean food manufacturer like Nongshim or Ottogi. It is a US venture, Black Garlic Inc., owned by Korean-American Scott Kim, who claims to even own three black garlic-related patents.[43] However, the black garlic story does serve to show that Far Eastern food has the potential to garner some serious interest from global food enthusiasts, if it can only tap into the ever-expanding health zeitgeist at key moments. As cancer fatalities continue to rise, we are living in the era of the antioxidant. As both Japanese and Korean food abound in nutrients to help in the fight against cancer, the world food stage would seem to be set for both countries to make an entrance.[44]

Cultural Sensibilities

Although most culinary adventurers might like to harbor the romantic notion that they would only ever eat the authentic food enjoyed by locals, the reality is often very different. Many food exporters or restaurants catering to largely non-native customers do make slight alterations in their food in order to pique the interest of potential food tourists.

The taste of the food served in Chinese restaurants, for example, in Paris, in New York, in Seoul and in Beijing varies a lot, as the expat Chinese chefs quickly learn which flavors sell well to the crowds in their adopted homes.

Some believe, too, that the key to success for Japanese and Korean food could be the application of a gentle tweak to some traditional specialties. Haruhara Yoko, journalist for the *Japan Times* and an instructor at the Japan campus of Philadelphia's Temple University, certainly thinks so. Haruhara believes that wagashi, traditional Japanese sweets often served during tea ceremonies, could appeal to foreign consumers on an aesthetic level, but need adjustment if they are to become a major draw for foreign consumers.

She says, "Wagashi are typically made with bean paste, which has very delicate flavor. It is less appreciated abroad, though, because foreigners are not used to coming across beans in confectionery. One way to increase wagashi's appeal would be to substitute beans with ingredients that are more acceptable to a Western palate."

Dina Yeon is the Head of Sales at US food company Ingredion's Korea operations. Yeon argues that there could even be very slight cultural differences that could ruin a non-Korean's experience of Korean food. She says that marketing efforts aimed at bringing in foreign consumers need to be planned with care.

"We truly need to understand what makes food appetizing for specific groups of consumers. For example, Koreans tend to eat several different kinds of food at the same time. Multiple flavors all mix in your mouth at once. Sometimes this might mask or even ruin the (otherwise distinctive) taste of a specific dish. If first-time eaters of Korean food do likewise, the first impression that they go away with might be less favorable," says Yeon.

Kim Young-chool, chef-owner of Uhchun, a hoe (Korean sashimi-like raw fish) restaurant in Songsu-dong, Seoul, and a 40+ year veteran of the catering trade, agrees with the idea that foreign visitors ought not to mix up flavors in the local style.

Kim says, "You might see a lot of locals in *hoe* restaurants daubing their fish in red pepper paste, wrapping it in sesame leaves or eating it in the same mouthful as garlic or green peppers. I'd actually suggest not doing that if it is your first time trying hoe, as you won't really be able to pick up on the delicate taste of the carefully-prepared hoe that way." The evidence would suggest that, quite possibly, Far Eastern food promoters have to consider not just *what food* they want us food tourists to eat, but *how* they want us to eat it.

368

The Future of Far Eastern Food Tourism?

With new heads of state coming into power only recently in both countries, we can certainly expect changes in the form of food tourism promotion from both countries, as central government has unquestionably been the driving force in all major food promotion efforts made by both Japan and Korea. What the food tourism future holds under current and future leadership is unclear.

In these transitory times, the opportunity exists for both governments to tinker, adjust or even totally rethink their investment and strategy on food tourism promotion. Some voices from within the food trade suggest that there is the opportunity for these sleeping Far Eastern food giants to learn from each other. Jung Hye-sook is the Editor-in-Chief of *Essen*, one of South Korea's biggest-selling food monthlies. Jung suggests that certain food tourism promotion efforts made in Japan could be adapted to showcase the rich and regionally-variable culture of Korean food. She explains, "A lot of Japanese railways stations sell take-out bento boxes, filled with regional specialties, displaying a lot of the local flavor. I feel that booths in Korean railway stations could do the same kind of thing, but in our case, the take-out would be ddeok (rice cakes), which is very much a take-out friendly item. Ddeok varies enormously in terms of shape, color and taste from one part of Korea to the next."

As both countries are still relatively new to food tourism promotion, this is certainly a time when promotion efforts will have to adopt a trial-and-error strategy. But, it could be argued, there might be no harm in carefully examining the successes and failures of each other's food promotion policies.

In these days of big data and customized advertising, skeptical and world-weary consumers need a lot of convincing in order to part with their money. Indeed, some believe that methods resembling targeted marketing, rather than generalized, broader-sweeping marketing strategies represent the way forward for both Japan and Korea.

Sake sommelier Tsujino Nobuko says that in the case of Japanese traditional alcohol, this would certainly be beneficial. Tsujino explains, "Unlike, say, French wine, Japanese sake is not internationally well-known. I think it is necessary to advertise its taste and qualities outside of Japan. I think targeted marketing is very important if we want to improve sake's international reputation. Various sake tasting events should be held, we could invite people who consider themselves 'sake lovers'. Their thoughts on the events — shared online — could be powerful PR."

CONCLUSION

Japan and South Korea rank fifth and seventh, respectively, as the world's biggest export economies.[45] They both certainly know a lot about selling products to the outside world. The food culture of both countries is unique, distinct, technologically-advanced, and most of all, varied.

There can be little question that eventually, bento will be as globally ubiquitous as the McDonald's Big Mac, and kimchi will be as freely-available as ketchup, but we cannot expect this overnight. Expansion into foreign markets requires not just financial investment, but a true understanding of global culinary preferences if more rapid progress is required.

The unexplored world no longer exists as a concept, certainly not for 21st century foodies, who think nothing of keeping a bottle of pilipili oil next to a jar of garam masala in their cupboards. As general tourism to both Korea and Japan grows, and as efforts to globalize Korean and

Japanese food remain relentless, time must surely be running out before the lid is blown off the Far East's treasure trove of culinary secrets.

DISCUSSION QUESTIONS

1. What other cuisines might face positioning issues similar to those experienced with Japanese and Korean cuisines, and why?
2. What role could multinational corporations, such as airlines, grocery stores and restaurant chains, play in solving these kinds of positioning issues?
3. What could small providers like independent restaurants do to prevent their menus from turning into one homogenized offering with the same 10 main course choices, no matter where in the world the food is served?

ENDNOTES

[1] For more information of Japanese food diversity see www.insidejapantours.com/japanese-culture/food/

[2] Eager readers might seek commentary on food and drink tourism issues and ideas from other Asian countries. To include such commentary in this book would be an enormous and unfair task, as such information could fill its own volume. Therefore we have chosen to focus solely on Japan and South Korea in this chapter.

[3] How Sushi Ate the World http://observer.guardian.co.uk/foodmonthly/story/0,,1715295,00.html The Observer, 26 February 2006

[4] "L´épicerie – Le Kinchi un plat coréen", Youtube, posted July 22, 2010, last accessed July 22, 2013, www.youtube.com/watch?v=BKmhvwKmWY4 (Radio Canada TV feature, 22 July 2010)

[5] Sang, Choe, "Starship Kimchi: A bold taste goes where it has never gone before" The New Yor Times, Last modified 24 February 2008, last accessed July 22 2013, www.nytimes.com/2008/02/24/world/asia/24kimchi.html?_r=1&,

[6] Gold, Jonathan, "Counter Intelligence: The basics of life at Kang Ho-dong Baekjeong", LA Times, last modified November 10 ,2012, last accessed July 22, 2013, http://articles.latimes.com/2012/nov/10/food/la-fo-gold-20121110

[7] Data gathered from: www.london-eating.co.uk January 2013

[8] Harrington, Ben "Yo! Sushi sold for £51m" The Telegraph, last modified March 11, 2008, last accessed July 22, 2013,
 www.telegraph.co.uk/finance/newsbysector/retailandconsumer/2785864/Yo-Sushi-sold-for-51m.html

[9] Mc Gray, Douglas, "Japan´s Gross National Cool" Foreign Policy, last modified may 1 2002, last accessed July 22, 2013, www.foreignpolicy.com/articles/2002/05/01/japans_gross_national_cool Foreign Policy,

[10] Ministry of Economy, Trade and Industry, last modified June 2010, last accessed July 22 2013, www.meti.go.jp/english/press/data/20100608_01

[11] Fackler, Martin" Japanese take food safety into their own hands", The New York Times, Last modified January 21, 2012, last accessed July 22, 2013, www.nytimes.com/2012/01/22/world/asia/wary-japanese-take-food-safety-into-their-own-hands.html?pagewanted=all&_r=1&

[12] "Radioactive cesium found in Japan´s fish, seawater", Russia Today, last modified August 5 2012, last accessed July 22, 2013, http://rt.com/news/radioactive-cesium-japan-fish-seawater-895/

[13] "Rebirth of Japan: A Comprehensive Strategy", Japan's National Policy Unit, Published 8 August 2012, last accessed July 22, 2013, www.cas.go.jp/jp/seisaku/npu/pdf/20120821/20120821_en.pdf

[14]Johnson Renée, "Earthquake and Tsunami: Food and Agriculture Implications", Congressional Research Service, last modified April 13 2011, last accessed July 22, 2013, http://fpc.state.gov/documents/organization/161583.pdf

[15] "Bibimbap Commercial at Times Square", Maangchi, last modified July 22, 2013, www.maangchi.com/talk/topic/bibimbap-commercial-at-times-square

[16] "How about bibimbamp for lunch today", Maangchi, last accessed July 22, 2013, www.maangchi.com/talk/?bb_attachments=2051&bbat=107

[17] "Food of Japan Policy", 2009, Japan's Ministry of Agriculture, Forestry and Fisheries, last modified July 22, 2013, www.maff.go.jp/e/export/campaign/cm09.html

[18] "New Japan Tourism Promotion Campaign", Japan Probe, last accessed July 22, 2013, www.japanprobe.com/2011/07/13/new-japan-tourism-promotion-campaign/

[19] Hori, Yoshito,"Creating a vision of Japan; Promoting Cool Japan", Japan Today, last modified January 12, 2012, last accessed July 22, 2013, www.japantoday.com/category/opinions/view/creating-a-vision-of-japan-promoting-cool-japan

[20] "Re-install the operating ... Shilla Korean Restaurant", Biz Focus economic, last accessed July 22, 2013, http://news.sportsseoul.com/read/economy/1106995.htm

[21] "Dress Code on the difficult, changing horses in the bitter Shilla" The Korea Herald , last accessed July 22, 2013, http://m.heraldbiz.com/detail.jsp?newsId=20110414000480&menu=life&categoryId=010503&page=1, 14 April 2011

[22] "Korean Foundation inverted spoon", Naverblogs, last modified July 22 2013, http://m.blog.naver.com/foodi2/30122334275

[23] "Parliament, Mrs Food Globalization business audit requirements up down", JoonganglIbo, last modified 5 January 2013, last accessed July 22 2013, http://article.joinsmsn.com/news/article/article.asp?total_id=10344994&ctg=1000,

[24] www.seoul.co.kr/news/newsView.php?id=20130105008014&spage=1 Seoul Shinmun, 5 January 2013

[25] Kane, Daniel, "Seoul´s Green Revolution", Time magazine, last modified October 7, 2002, last accessed July 22, 2013, www.time.com/time/magazine/article/0,9171,501021014-361781,00.html

[26] Bonsal, Stephen, "The obliteration of the Kingdom of Korea, last modified July 28, 1907, last accessed July 22, 2013, http://travel.cnn.com/explorations/eat/usa/50-best-chinese-restaurants-usa-145368

[27] Xinhua, "Reforms urged to attract overseas Chinese", China.org, last modified March 11, 2012, last accessed July 22, 2013, www.china.org.cn/china/NPC_CPPCC_2012/2012-03/11/content_24865428.htm

[28] "Guidelines for the preparation of sushi products" Albertha Health Services, last accessed July 22, 2013, www.albertahealthservices.ca/EnvironmentalHealth/wf-eh-guidelines-for-sushi-prep.pdf

[29] Wallop, Harry "Sushi chefs fume over EU freezing law", The Telegraph, last modified July 28, 2007, last accessed July 22, 2013, www.telegraph.co.uk/news/uknews/1558738/Sushi-chefs-fume-over-EU-freezing-law.html

[30] Hollingworth, William, "Suchi chefs in Europe slam fish – freezing regulation", The Japan Times, last modified August 31 2007, last accessed July 22 2013 www.japantimes.co.jp/text/nn20070831f1.htmlTheJapan Times 31 August 2007

[31] "Korean barbecue Dos and Don'ts", The Food Section, last accessed July 22, 2013, www.thefoodsection.com/foodsection/2005/04/korean_barbecue.html

[32] Olmsted, Larry, "10 most memorable restaurant meals of 2012", Forbes, last accessed July 22, 2013 www.forbes.com/sites/larryolmsted/2012/12/27/10-most-memorable-restaurant-meals-of-2012/

[33] "Dolsot Stone Bowl", Sous Chef, last accessed July 22, 2013, www.souschef.co.uk/dolsot-stone-bowl.html

[34] "Dolsot Bibimbap", Terms. Naver, last accessed July 22, 2013 http://terms.naver.com/entry.nhn?cid=200000000&docId=1286424&mobile&categoryId=200000400

[35] L. Brady, D. Gallaher and F. Busta "The Role of Probiotic Cultures in the Prevention of Colon Cancer", last accessed July 22, 2013, http://m.jn.nutrition.org/content/130/2/410.full.pdf (2000)

[36] Sisson, Mark, "The definitive guide to fermented foods", Mark´s Daily apple, last modified, December 10, 2009, last accessed July 22, 2013, www.marksdailyapple.com/fermented-foods-health/#ixzz1jrwWeNoe

[37] "Japanese fermented food", Trends in Japan, last accessed July 22, 2013, http://web-japan.org/trends/11_lifestyle/lif120223.html

[38] "Standard Tables of food composition in Japan Fifth Edition", Ministry of Education, Culture, Sports, Science and Technology, Japan, last modified 2005, last accessed July 22, 2013, www.mext.go.jp/b_menu/shingi/gijyutu/gijyutu3/toushin/05031802.htm

[39] Jampolis, Melina, "What can I eat for a really healthy breakfast", CNN, last modified December 18 2009, last accessed July 22, 2013, http://edition.cnn.com/2009/HEALTH/expert.q.a/12/18/nutritious.breakfast.jampolis/index.html. Jampolis, Physician Nutrition Specialist on CNN, 18 December 2009

[40] Penquin, Lawrence 2008 "*Eat Your Heart Out: Why the food business is bad for the planet and your health* by F. Lawrence (Penguin, 2008)

[41] Benwick Bonnie,"Black Garlic, the next it ingredient" The Washington post, last modified February 25, 2009, last accessed July 22, 2013, www.washingtonpost.com/wp-dyn/content/article/2009/02/24/AR2009022400755.html

[42] Adriani, Lynn, "Super food list 2012" Eating well, last modified February 14, 2012, last accessed July 22, 2013, www.oprah.com/food/Superfoods-List-2012-Sunchokes-Adzuki-Beans-Chia-Seed/2

[43] Latimer Joanne "Digging up the dirt on black garlic", last modified February 9, 2012, last accessed July 22, 2013, www2.macleans.ca/2012/02/09/digging-up-the-dirt-on-black-garlic/

[44] To see cancer statistics comparisons between US population and Korean`s and Japan´s population consult this web page: onlinelibrary.wiley.com/doi/10.3322/canjclin.49.1.33/full

[45] "CIA World Factbook", last modified July 22 2013, www.cia.gov/library/publications/the-world-factbook/rankorder/2078rank.html

The Need to Get Creative

Anne Klein, Kostantinos Nikolopoulos, & Erik Wolf

What motivates a foodie to choose one destination over another? This chapter addresses primary and secondary food tourism destinations, and why food tourists might be more prone to choose a primary over a secondary destination. Ideas are presented for how a secondary destination can be more proactive in raising its image as a food tourism destination. The chapter concludes with a short case study of how one smaller destination managed to successfully increase its popularity as a food tourism destination.

INTRODUCTION

Both tourists and tourism marketers recognize that some destinations are more popular than others, and for different reasons. This is not to say that one destination is better than another, rather, it is simply more popular with a specific target market. While the popularity may be based on historic importance, cultural icons, or special landmarks, specific definitions of food tourism destinations are lacking. Our industry needs to understand better how we measure the differences between primary and secondary destinations and what secondary destinations can do to raise their profiles.

Primary-Secondary-Rural

The following popularity categories are helpful for food tourism destinations to understand their positioning.

Primary destination. A primary food or drink destination is one where visitors come primarily for the food or drink experience. The destination is *already very well-known* and well-regarded for its food and drink offerings. Examples of primary food destinations include Paris, France; Tuscany, Italy; New Orleans and San Francisco.

Secondary destination. A secondary food or drink destination is one that has great food and drink but the destination is *less known* as a food or drink destination. Visitors may come for another reason first, and may have heard something about the food before their arrival. They then experience great food and drink while there. Examples of secondary food destinations include Scotland; British Columbia, Canada; Seoul, South Korea and Ecuador.

Tertiary destination. A tertiary food or drink destination is one that has great food and drink but the destination is *almost entirely unknown and unexpected* as a food or drink destination. Visitors would usually come for another reason first, and then be pleasantly surprised as they discover great food and drink while there. A tertiary destination may also be completely rural or remote, lacking extensive transportation options and infrastructure. This type of destination may be more theme-based, and as such, the food experiences may need to match a theme. For example, a Spanish fiesta in the remote part of Spain would entail a festival experience complete with traditional Spanish fare and particular methods of preparation. Another example would be the areas of Pallini and Peania, East Attica (suburbs of Athens, Greece), which are rural and not so famous; but the tourists are able to experience the wine culture of Mesogia area and all the wine festivals that take place there each summer together with religious celebrations (e.g. Birth of Virgin Mary on August 15). Additional examples of tertiary food and drink destinations include Vancouver Island, Canada; Daegu, South Korea; Nova Scotia, Canada and Vermont, USA.

The Given: What Foodies Seek In Most Destinations

Generally speaking, foodies visiting certain destinations have in mind expectations about certain food and drink or experiences. For example, a first time visitor to New Orleans wants to try Cajun food or beignets at Café du Monde. A first time visitor to Indonesia wants to try beef rendang, and a first time visitor to South Africa may want to try grilled kudu.

Preferences vary widely, but generally foodies consider criteria such as the following when it comes to destination selection:

- Food quality, including freshness, sanitation, taste, smell, and of course, service (an example of which may include restaurants that follow the farm-to-table movement)
- Destination authenticity, evidenced by local specialties, local methods of food preparation, etc. (such as a hot sausage with mustard served by a street vendor in Germany)
- Uniqueness of the food experience. Visitors seek and remember food and drink experiences that cannot be replicated easily elsewhere (such as hawker centers in Singapore)

Primary Destinations

From the perspective of many primary destination marketers, nothing is wrong with their destination. The destination is well-known, has a great food scene, lots of other attractions and is popular already with visitors. These facts may be true, but primary destination marketers should be aware of a trap, which is the danger of resting on their laurels.[1] Foodies are inherently explorers. Many food travelers have already been to many of the famous primary destinations, and are seeking new and different places. Despite a popular reputation, even primary destinations must still market their food and drink as attractions, and show potential visitors that they continue to innovate. Otherwise the chance is high that visitors will be lured by sexier, newer, and different food destinations all around the planet.

Many well-known service providers face a similar issue of reputation by charging a lot for their products or services, even if the actual cost of product inputs does not warrant the high end cost. Many foodies, as well as other travelers, resent being seen as open wallets. Word-of-mouth promotion is pervasive in the foodie world. If your business has a reputation as being a rip off, the word will spread. If your product or service is expensive for good reason, be transparent and explain to visitors the reasons why. If you justify it in a sensible manner, they will understand and even defend your position when talking about their experience with your business in the future.

The Unique: Why Foodies Might Choose Secondary & Tertiary Destinations

How might a secondary or tertiary destination gain competitive advantage over a primary destination? Primary destinations tend to have larger budgets for marketing and branding than do smaller destinations. However, primary destinations usually need to be all things to all people. For example, visitors and residents alike in Paris, France expect to be able to dine on Chinese, Thai, Mexican, Indian and other cuisines, whenever they wish. In smaller destinations, this wide variety of choice might not be available or even expected. Secondary and tertiary destinations can focus on differentiated products as mentioned above.

Piraeus, Greece (outside Athens) has been very lucky to be known as the "right place" for fresh fish sourced directly from the Aegean Sea. Visitors expect the fish to be cooked using traditional recipes, especially those of the Aegean islands, served with the appropriate Greek or non-Greek

374

wine and with all the traditional dips, such as melitzanosalata (creamed eggplant) or skordalia (mashed potato and garlic cream). Piraeus benefits from the most effective and least expensive kind of promotion: word-of-mouth.

Ways to Help Smaller Destinations Succeed

To attain success as a food destination, a secondary or tertiary destination needs to gain the support of the local government and stakeholders in the area. Doing so is not always easy. In such instances, showing policy stakeholders the money — the economic benefit of food and inbound tourism purchases may help. Working in partnership, they can promote the area by creating a common food "brand" experience. Creating a unique food experience in the destination is the first benefit of working together. The second benefit is creating a long term strategy and plan that may be funded by regional, national, or in some cases, international means.

Building a brand for the destination's food tourism is essential to drive traffic to the area, regardless of whether it is a primary or smaller destination. For example, East Sussex, United Kingdom is called 'The Sunshine Coast'. It is connected to sunny and sandy beaches, the Eastbourne Pier, the notorious Beachy Head, numerous classic hotels and the traditional fish 'n' chips, which may be found in restaurants all over town.

The ultimate goal in branding a food tourism experience should not be one-dimensional. In other words, a single product by itself (e.g. fish and chips) is not always sufficient to brand a destination. The entire experience becomes of utmost importance. For example, olive oil produced in a specific region may be of the finest quality. In a secondary destination, the oil is critical to branding but to attract visitors, the entire experience must be created. Not only the "oil" but the people who serve the food, the local produce of the area, the type of customer service, the way meals are presented — all of these elements need to be finely tuned. The visitor is coming not just for the product, but for an entire experience.

China Date Ranch

It may start as the "best kept secret" or a small destination geographically located within a larger primary destination. On a recent visit to Las Vegas, Nevada, USA, one of the authors of this chapter discovered the China Date Ranch 45 miles (72 km) west of "Sin City" (Las Vegas). The ranch is a hidden gem nestled in gorgeous terrain with 20+ varieties of high quality dates grown on the oasis-like farm. It was the highlight of the trip and only stumbled upon following a tip from a local chef.

A secondary or tertiary destination may also be a location that is more remote or one that has not organized its culinary offerings, so it is more fragmented than a location that has a packaged product with marketing efforts to support it. In either of these scenarios, a secondary or tertiary destination has benefits and can maximize its culinary offerings to create a desirable and profitable product. Secondary destinations often have an element of discovery, under-promising and over-delivering and may also offer a more "organic" and less commercial experience.

Durango Colorado: City of "Brewerly" Love

By its geographic location, Durango, Colorado, USA is a tertiary culinary destination. People often come to the historic southwestern American town to experience the Durango & Silverton Narrow Gauge Railroad or to ski Purgatory at Durango Mountain Resort. Upon their arrival, tourists discover that the outdoor mecca is also an incredible food and agricultural destination. The town of 16,000 residents at 6512 feet (1985 meters) above sea level has five craft breweries, over 100 restaurants, working ranches, honey bees, elk ranches, wine education classes, cooking schools, farm-to-table dinners, wineries and food-centric festivals. While culinary travel may not have been their primary purpose to visit, tourists leave Durango with an appreciation and passion for the local food scene.

A secondary or tertiary destination, whether a working ranch or a city, should start its food tourism program with a passion to understand and create a marketable product. Durango began with a SWOT (Strengths-Weakness-Opportunity-Threats) analysis to better understand what its region had to offer and to be able to define its "product." Once the culinary asset inventory was complete, the local farmers lobbied the tourism office, city government, restaurants and brewers to create a map of all the locations that people could experience "local" cuisine, products and tours.

To support the message, a public relations campaign organized by the local tourism office offered maps, product information, sampling and ideas of culinary events through their website, e-newsletters, FaceBook page and other social media sites, news releases, videos and the local tourism office. The tourism office made sure that the locals knew about the local food scene so that they could serve as "salespeople." The city adopted names and claims to fame like: "Napa Valley of Beer," "City of Brewerly Love," and even challenged the culinary reputation of San Francisco as to which city had more restaurants per capita, which resulted in the discovery and subsequent positioning of Durango having "more restaurants per capita than San Francisco." The tourism office leveraged the strength in public relations to apply for culinary destination awards and build awareness of the area.

As a secondary or tertiary destination, the challenge is to market the product and deliver on the brand promise. Help lead potential tourists to discover your destination's "hidden gem" or a "local's favorite" — something off the beaten path or unknown to the everyday tourist. People will leave not as a tourist but a traveler, one who has had a personal experience with the location.

Just because a destination becomes known for food does not mean it should aspire to become a primary food destination. In the case of a small farm, for example, there would be insufficient infrastructure or product supply for it to become inundated with tourists. It is rewarding when a secondary destination evolves into a more organized food destination like the case of Durango. Destination marketers should be certain to include metrics as part of their development strategy so that they can prove their results to stakeholders.

Lessons Learned

It is impossible to prescribe a roadmap for success for the world's secondary and tertiary destinations. Still, some basic steps can be followed to help these destinations on the path to success. While the discussion of a full marketing plan is beyond the scope of this chapter for space reasons, destination marketers nevertheless be sure to should perform a SWOT analysis and a competitive analysis. What are your destination's strengths, weaknesses, opportunities and threats compared to the competition from other possible tertiary, secondary and even primary destinations? And consider competition beyond food and drink. Perhaps your smaller destination has great food and drink but if a popular outdoor adventure destination, for example, is nearby, it may be hard to compete effectively. Also consider segmenting your unique selling propositions to meet the interests of smaller markets, for example, people who buy only organic, only vegetarian, or only local foods. In other words, perhaps "all foodies" is too big a market to taken on for your smaller destination. You may also want to look at a cost-benefit analysis. If your smaller or less-known destination only has one or two culinary resources of note, what would it cost you to promote them? Could you package your one or two culinary resources with other activities and attractions to lure more visitors? Would the return on investment be worthwhile? Naturally a complete marketing plan or lean business model canvas referenced earlier in this book would help to answer these questions. However, in the absence of limited time and resources, addressing these very fundamental questions will help.

CONCLUSION

Almost everywhere in the world, politics and personalities can prevent a destination from succeeding, not just in food tourism, but as a tourism destination in general. For example, in one region of Greece, plans have been drawn up to develop and promote olive oil production as a visitor attraction, but officials cannot agree on who will manage the project so it has gone nowhere, creating no new jobs, and doing nothing to ameliorate the region's current 56% unemployment. Unfortunate destinations such as these would benefit from a paradigm shift in how they view and manage tourism. The rest of the world is their competition, and such destinations have fallen so far behind, they will never be able to compete with more popular destinations unless circumstances and views change, and quickly.

Smaller destinations should be proud of what they are and not strive to be New York City or Tuscany. Destinations should lead with their strengths, even if their strengths are modest, and build on those strengths sustainably, over time. Product development and marketing can help support food tourism initiatives in smaller destinations, but such work should be rooted firmly in a destination food tourism strategy. Lastly, partnerships between secondary and primary destinations, while not always possible, can hold synergistic benefits and may be worth exploring.

DISCUSSION QUESTIONS

1. What advice would you give destinations that are primarily known for only one product such as wine, cheese or chocolate, if they are looking to diversify?
2. How can a secondary or tertiary destination that is in close proximity to a primary destination, compete effectively for attention from food travelers?
3. The brand promise to travelers is sometimes different from the brand reality. What advice would you give to DMOs creating a new brand promise, to avoid misleading potential food travelers?

ENDNOTES

---

[1] Colloquial English phrase meaning "to be overly confident and/or proud of past accomplishments."

New Marketing Tactics in Food Tourism

Carmina Fandos-Herrera and Neha M. Shah

This chapter explores the various conventional and digital marketing trends and tools available to food and drink tourism destinations and related businesses. It will also provide practical marketing tips and techniques to leverage these tools to acquire new customers, and enhance the customer experience to drive increased loyalty and repeat business. Lastly, ways to develop marketing strategies will be presented, both for large or small businesses.

INTRODUCTION

Over the past 10 years, new media and marketing channels have evolved at lightning speed, offering exciting and sometimes unchartered ways for food tourism destinations and businesses to reach and engage with customers. The resulting arsenal of marketing tools now available to owners of food and drink establishments, tourism businesses, and destination marketers has expanded well beyond traditional mass advertising, print collateral, and direct mail. Digital tools such as social media, mobile apps, podcasts, and quick response (QR) codes offer immediate and lower cost ways to reach target customers with the food, drink, and travel planning information they want, when they want it, and where they want it...be it on their smartphone, tablet, or laptop...at home, in the office, or on the road.

Gone are the days of brands investing most of their marketing budgets in one-size-fits-all mass advertising and marketing campaigns. Today's web-savvy customers are in greater control over which marketing messages and promotional offers they wish to receive...which brands they 'like' and evangelize through blog posts, tweets, and online reviews...making the art of food tourism brand building and customer relationship marketing (CRM) that much more complex. In a hyper-connected culture, it is the customer who should at the center of a successful marketing strategy, with all communications channels and touch points being personalized and tailored to impact the customer journey of the food tourist in a positive way.

In this chapter we will define the modern-day marketing toolbox and explore tips and techniques for: 1) building awareness; 2) driving trial and purchase; 3) incenting repeat purchase; and 4) creating and growing customer loyalty. We will provide examples of effective customer marketing campaigns and loyalty programs by food tourism business type (gourmet & specialty food shops, eateries, food truck vendors, bakers, chefs, farmers and farmers markets, and wineries).

The Evolution of Marketing in Food Tourism

For decades, tourism-related business owners, destination marketers and their creative partners have viewed 'tourism' like any other commodity, resulting in marketing strategies and promotional campaigns that concentrate solely on the purchasing transaction and increased visitation to an establishment and/or locale. Until recent years, they relied primarily on glossy printed brochures, and discount-laden direct mail to 'sell' to a prospective customer. The rise of food and drink travel as a high-growth, specialty category in the tourism industry has demonstrated a need for marketers and small business owners to think about the customer journey from a more sensory-perspective and to focus their marketing efforts on the customer experience ... both on premise and virtual. Tastings, tours, behind-the-scenes looks, private dinner with the wine maker, foodie events, tweet-ups, and other events have opened the doors for food and drink entrepreneurs to share their products and services with visitors in a unique, intimate way.

Culinary entrepreneurs are now sharing their secrets and their customers are returning the appreciation of the food and drink by blogging, posting photos and tips, providing feedback and input. Customers show their loyalty to the brand by serving as brand evangelists. While promoting the food and drink businesses, customers are also marketing the business, its local and the quality of its product or service...summing up the experience beyond the business and encompassing the destination as one for self-described foodies, food travelers and adventures.

The Customer Service Journey[1]

This is a marketing model whereby the customer is aware of a purchase need, searches for suitable options, plans to make a purchase, browses actual purchase candidates, finds the right product to buy, tries the product, buys the product, experiences and reflects upon the product, and shares their experience with friends, family and colleagues. Keep this in mind as you plan your new marketing strategy.

Social Networking Changes the Marketing Landscape

Social media has created unprecedented marketing opportunities for the food tourism industry, offering new ways to engage directly and one-on-one with prospects and customers as outlined below.

The Art of the Check-in as Marketing Tool

Foursquare, a location-based social media tool that allows users to 'check in' to a locale or establishment, can be a powerful tool for business owners to view frequent visitors and track other information about the visitors' profile. Consumer rewards include check-in specials. Monetarily, customers only receive payment in pride. Badges, ousting someone else from mayor, and adding 'tips' (useful information) are virtual rewards but what is the value exactly? The value for the consumer to participate in the branding of the food tourism business is not necessarily quantifiable.

Sharing Food Experiences and Images Goes Mobile

Foodspotting allows users the opportunity to share images of their food and drink. It is a web-based mobile app that allows users to upload their images later, if they choose. Comments, images, mapping, tagging, and social media integration with Facebook, Twitter, and Foursquare. Users earn badges at different levels but no financial rewards are currently available; however, Foodspotting may be working with businesses soon to offer gift certificates or other rewards and incentives. OpenTable acquired Foodspotting in January 2013, so integration of social media and mobile and web marketing in this partnership forges additional opportunities for menu sharing, authentic images in real time, point — earning perks for diners, reviews, and more.

Online Reservation Systems Offer 360° Marketing Solution

OpenTable, the de facto global leader in online dining reservations, allows users to book reservations for a table at participating restaurants. Reminder emails are sent to the user, with an opportunity to modify or cancel their reservation if needed. After the reservation date, OpenTable sends an electronic invitation for the customer to post a review of their dining experience. OpenTable captures significant diner preference data, allowing restaurants to earn accolades based on user votes, such as Most Romantic Restaurant, Best Place for Power Lunches, Best View, etc. Visitors earn points for making reservations and checking in and extra points for special promotions and points accumulate to convert into dining certificates.

Consumer Review Websites

Review sites are the boon and the bane of a visitor-related business, especially for lodging and dining. Many business owners are leery of the review sites and find it frustrating trying to find the time to stay informed of the volumes of posts. Furthermore they have difficulty finding time to respond to negative reviews. While monitoring and addressing issues can be time-consuming, reviews are critical for the marketing of a destination and its food businesses.

Originally, review sites like TripAdvisor were lodging-centric, but have since expanded to encourage consumer reviews and ratings of their experiences at restaurants, wineries, breweries, cooking classes, food tours and festivals. Genuine customer impressions, particularly those with credibility (e.g. from frequent posts) can help the marketing message. Thoughtful responses from the business owner are significant in identifying issues (if valid) and allow readers to distinguish between quality of the business and the authenticity of the reviewer's judgments.

Many travelers check at least one or more review sites for images and impressions of a food and drink business when planning a trip. Most often, if a visitor can sift through the "noise" and see images and reviews that are pertinent and responses by business owners (when necessary), then posts with less than favorable comments may keep a traveler from visiting, depending on what the consensus of the reviews was, and how the business owner replied to any issues.

QR Codes

QR codes are useful modules to store information on a dot matrix or two-dimensional bar code, widely used in direct marketing as geolocation systems. These codes are still a benchmark in terms of communication through smartphones or tablets, so that trade is being promoted via

mobile and customer loyalty through its capture in magazines, billboards, cards visit, marquees, wine bottles, etc. The QR code of the World Food Travel Association is pictured left. Try it out by scanning a QR reader on your smartphone.

Some examples of QR code use in tourism would be when you are enjoying a meal in a restaurant and choose a trout, you can scan or capture with mobile code on the page menu and you can see a video your mobile phone in which you see the process from how trout is caught, to how it is processed. Or similarly, you could watch a video in which the winemaker of the wine you are drinking walks you around the winery and vineyards. Another example refers to the ability to purchase any product, for example the grocery chain TESCO South Korea, which enables consumers to shop for groceries using their smartphones at virtual supermarkets in subway stations in Seoul.[2] In Valencia, Spain, you can buy up to five different bottles of wine directly from the winery via QR code and it will be delivered to your door.

It is also increasingly common use by tourists who can read the code of a business card for a restaurant, and automatically view its phone number, address, website, etc. Tourists no longer need paper brochures since information is scanned with your mobile device. Recently, a reputed Spanish company producing milk, Central Lechera Asturiana (pictured below), began using QR codes more creatively. Its codes can accomplish different tasks, like offer grass to feed the cows, show actual cows or milk bottles, or provide the user with an instant coupon.

Daily Deal Websites

In November 2008 the local marketing landscape changed forever with the launch of a new start-up called Groupon. It was the first crowd buying coupon website (aka daily deal site) designed to bring highly discounted products and services to local audiences around the globe. Following closely on the heels of Groupon's meteoric success, the market exploded with the launch of LivingSocial (2009), kgbdeals (2010), Google Offers (2011), and Amazon Local (2011), to name a few.

The idea of pairing hyper-local marketing for businesses of all sizes with local, national and global budget-conscious consumers led to the explosive growth of the daily deal as both a business model and marketing tool. However, business and marketing industry experts who have been closely monitoring and analyzing this space for the past five years, suggest the decision to offer a daily deal is not right for every business, and perhaps the benefits of a daily deal promotion favor more established, well-known brands and not small, independent businesses. An increase in customers does not always lead to increased revenue.

One example of a daily deal promotion gone wrong is Posies Cafe, an independent coffee shop in Portland, Oregon.[3] In 2010, Posies signed up with Groupon, which promised the small business it would deliver a certain minimum number of customers if the owner agreed to sell them US$13 worth of product for US$6, a typical discount of 50% or more on the Groupon site. What Posies was not prepared for was the overwhelming response. Nearly 1,000 people bought the Groupon in the single day it was advertised, according to Posies, swamping the small coffee shop for three months. In a blog post, the owner said that the volume of sales coupled with the steep discount threatened her business, forcing her to spend US$8,000 of her personal savings to pay her employees and the rent. "It has been the single worst decision I have ever made as a business owner thus far," she wrote on the Posies blog that same month. While Posies Café is not the norm, it is a widely held belief that daily deal promotions attract one-time bargain hunting customers who are often put off by the full retail price. These are customers who often do not return until they encounter another daily deal of the same or greater value that suits them.

Before adding a daily deal promotion to your marketing mix, it is imperative to do a proper cost and operational assessment of the net impact this type of offer may have on your bottom line, on your product inventory, and on your staff who will be servicing a potential influx of customers.

Apps

The use of apps in food tourism is becoming increasingly visible. However, just as some businesses felt a few years ago that they had to participate with Groupon and hurry to offer a Groupon deal, the same phenomenon is happening with apps. Many businesses feel like they need one, but for no strategic reason. It certainly makes sense for a restaurant chain to have an app so customers can check nutrition information or place an order or find locations in advance. It does not necessarily make sense for a local restaurant to have an app.

Apps are perhaps more useful to food tourists in destination marketing scenarios. Taste of Nova Scotia is a food and drink industry trade association in the Canadian province of the same name. The group has published Adventures in Taste: Nova Scotia,[4] which has been tremendously popular with visitors and locals alike. Among other ideas, the app cleverly plays on a visitor's yearning for typical regional food with its promotion of the Chowder Trail. Users can also search by the taste experience they seek. The app focuses squarely on the province's food and drink experiences, and does not pretend to be all things to all people. Such an app helps pre-arrival visitors do research in advance. It helps current visitors navigate an itinerary of taste and it also helps locals to discover new food and drink experiences they may not know about.

Frequent Shopper Loyalty & Rewards Programs

For many years the preferred customer loyalty program of lodging, casual dining, and some retail and grocery establishments was the frequent shopper or buyer rewards program, whereby new customers were handed a wallet-size paper card to be 'punched' or marked with each subsequent in-store purchase. The inherent problems of this type of physical card, mainly personally identifiable customer data was not tied to the card, and the customer needed to have the card with them at the point-of-sale (POS) otherwise their transaction would not be counted, has led to use of POS swipeable plastic cards the size of a credit card with a unique card number and tied to a customer's email address or phone number for use in the event the customer did not have the card with them. Wallet-size loyalty cards soon gave way to keyfobs, easily clipped to a customer's key chain and scanned via a card reader at the POS to track purchases and points earned more easily that their credit card-sized companions.

Fast-forward to today's loyalty rewards programs and the cards that once filled a customer's wallet or keychain have gone digital. Many businesses that play a role in the food tourism industry — airlines, hotels, retailers, restaurants, museums — have developed mobile loyalty applications (apps) available for download right to their customers' smartphones and tied to their personal loyalty card number. With these apps customers not only have the ability to scan their phone at POS via a bar code, but they can also opt in to receive e-coupons, special offers, and promos delivered right to their smartphone, often leading to increased and immediate savings, leading to ongoing loyalty and brand preference. Examples of businesses successfully managing digital customer loyalty programs include the Tesco Clubcard (UK, Ireland, Hungary, Poland) and Starbucks (worldwide). In addition, companies like Apple have launched loyalty program apps for users to store all their disparate loyalty cards in once place on their smartphone. Apple's Passbook, which was launched in the US in September 2012, allows users to store digital versions of all their loyalty cards (plus airline boarding passes and electronic movie tickets) in one place on their iPhone or iPod Touch. Apple's Passbook has paved the way in new loyalty-based app development, with Samsung coming out with its Samsung Wallet app in early 2013 that included partnerships with Walgreens, Belly, Major League Baseball Advanced Media, Expedia, Booking.com, Hotels.com, and Lufthansa for the app's launch.

In order for business and marketers to optimize their loyalty programs and create long-term opportunities with their customers, social media integration is a critical component of success. Culinary businesses can track valuable information from the statistics provided from these electronic reward programs. It would also be interesting to examine the varying levels of loyalty. It would be worthwhile to explore travelers' habits including the distance of their trip from home, whether they only visit to use promotional mobile coupons, the amount of their purchases (do they make frequent small purchases or sparingly make a few large ones), if they purchase just the minimum for the rewards or are buying the service or product regardless of what is required for the reward.

Business-Specific New Marketing Tactics Drive Customer Loyalty

Small Production or Boutique Wineries

Small production and boutique wine producers and wineries have a different relationship with their customers than large, 'big brand' wineries known globally. Both types of wineries certainly have their share of customer loyalty, but the dynamics of the relationships are different.

Small wineries attract a clientele that views the relationship in various ways. Some consider the winery a great find initially, and then work as ambassadors to share their 'best-kept secret' with their neighborhood, friends, family, etc. They frequent the winery for gifts, they often have closer access to the winemaker and/or winery owners, and they are thrilled to be privy to special events. Private tastings and events, reserve wines, barrel room dinners, and other promotions are most often publicized through the winery's mailing list, most often in the form of electronic newsletters.

Large wineries also appeal to customers who will consistently purchase their wines. The customers will show their loyalty by buying the wine, but also subscribing to newsletters and visiting the website. Recognition of the brand, often at food and wine shows, is one way that customers follow their favorite wineries, as well as through learning more about food pairings.

Some partnerships such as groups of wineries, wineries with gourmet food products, and wineries with acclaimed chefs, etc. are some of the marketing tools that strengthen customer loyalty and build networks as well. Wineries have evolved in the customers' minds, due both to marketers working on expanding the appreciation for a winery, but also as travelers have sought multi-functional itineraries. Enjoying a tasting of a selection of wines, taking pictures and touring the vineyards, visiting with the winemaker, and buying wines to take home are part of a 'standard' trip to a winery. Today, wineries offer picnic tables for guests to linger, gourmet nibbles to purchase while opening a bottle on-site (and then buying more to take home), barrel room dinners, and even a site for weddings or corporate functions. Guests have become loyal as the winery's products and services have expanded beyond simply wine provider. The allure of hosting an event in a location that will draw appeal have brought repeat visitors, particularly guests who bring their friends and family to revel in what they have been experiencing. Many winemakers offer wine clubs or barrel sponsor opportunities, furthering the relationship with their customers who in turn, feel (and share) pride and perhaps even higher status or bragging rights.

Breweries

Breweries around the world have increasingly grown a cult-like following for their products. Distilleries, microbreweries, and nano-breweries are an integral item on the itinerary of many foodie adventures. Various business models have served the purpose of drawing customers to breweries, from free tastings and tours with the brewmaster, great meals with pairings, menu items inclusive of the beer as an ingredient, or events like Oktoberfest.

Travelers attend events, bring back pint glasses and shirts, accumulate points ('brew crew' as an example of one brewery's loyalty program), and are often rewarded with private events or exclusive opportunities from the brewery, much like winery guests. Newsletters, banners at other events, social media, seasonal menu pairings, and other marketing promotions. Again, unique or common sense collaborations are mutually beneficial and continue to expand the strategic marketing opportunities for visitor-related businesses while reaffirming the branding of a destination.

Farms and Farmers' Markets

Marketing by farms and farmers' markets has evolved tremendously in recent years. Once primarily a word-of-mouth campaign, farmers have focused their efforts on websites, occasional email notices to their circle, joining agritourism organizations, partnering with and promoting eateries that use their ingredients, hosting informational tours, and even conducting workshops at agriculture and agritourism conferences. Farmers' market websites promote the farms and events (customer appreciation, market opening and closing for the season festivities) and while farmers' markets and farms traditionally marketed to local residents, their circle of audience has expanded to include travelers seeking local food for picnics, hikes, and/or to meet the farmer serving food at the restaurant they will visit. Farms that welcome visitors are also now marketing through agritourism, with limited tours offered seasonally or as part of an annual farm tour for a self-guided tour of multiple farms, or farm-to-fork dinners that appeal to travelers.

Food Trucks

Food trucks play a unique and increasingly popular role in the global food tourism industry. In some cities like Portland, Oregon, USA, there are so many food trucks (called "carts" in Portland), that they become tourist attractions themselves. Their marketing efforts are largely comprised of social media, but have also included work with the tourism office, brochures/flyers, websites, area bloggers, "following" customers on social media, etc. New television shows like "Eat Street"[5] allow people to experience food carts vicariously through the show's host. While such carts or trucks are all the rage in the USA and Canada, the notion of street food has been around much longer in Asia, Europe and Latin America.

Bed & Breakfasts and Inns

Inns are heralded by visitors for their gourmet menus and innovative culinary creations, often as much as dining destinations unto themselves. Marketing through the tourism offices, themed promotions, newsletters, and package specials that focus on food are a few strategies to reach culinary travelers. Distinctive touches, from printed menus autographed by the chef to remembering guests' preferences to extra amenities not listed on the website such as beautifully wrapped handmade chocolates are also marketing mementos that make or keep visitors loyal.

Gourmet and Specialty Food Shops

Gourmet and specialty food shops use a combination of experiential and interactive marketing tools to build customer loyalty, including tastings/samplings, specials, electronic newsletters, catalogs, website promotion, and coupons. Frequent shopper programs are also a popular marketing tool for specialty culinary businesses. The visiting friends/family market is a big sector for these businesses and their loyal customers often bring out-of-town guests for tastings and tours.

Gastronomic Societies and Supper Clubs

Membership-based gastronomic societies or gourmet clubs are an increasingly common attraction. These societies use new technologies as the primary source of communication, such as videos showing how to cook a particular food, food fairs, upcoming news, links to the ranking of the best restaurants in the world, societies or directory links to area tourism attractions and so on. Gourmet clubs can typically help you find information about recipes, culinary events, local products, restaurants, shops, wineries, wine, books, etc.

Food Events

Food events like "Good Food Month" in Sydney, Australia provide the opportunity for a large audience to learn about smaller food and drink businesses. This event brings together restaurants, bars and leading food business and in effect, creates a national food event where entertainment and food celebration are fundamental.[6] Another example of a successful food event is "Alimentarte" in Bogotá, Colombia where a variety of Bogotá's restaurants come together for two weekends of gastronomic celebration.[7] Small businesses are usually part of this event, giving the public the opportunity to learn about them.

CONCLUSION

Marketing practices have evolved in the past decade to include tools beyond the traditional or conventional ones. Websites, newsletters (print and electronic), brochures, and business cards are among the obvious and initial marketing materials used by food and drink businesses. Today, consumers engage in marketing alongside food and drink business professionals. They serve as brand ambassadors, they define the landscape of the destination, and they share information that lends authenticity to the marketing message.

Apps, review sites, and social media each offer powerful promotional opportunities and when intermingled, they profoundly impact a marketing campaign. Today's marketers also realize the value of retaining the traditional tools and embracing new ones, especially weaving them into each other as appropriate.

Food tourism marketing goes beyond websites and social media. Alternatives that engage customers and build loyalty are essential. Private, exclusive, behind-the-scenes and highly customized events present opportunities for businesses to both connect with and reward their loyal customers. Food and drink tastings, food truck rodeo events, culinary classes and demos, tours and tastings are additional ways to leverage marketing opportunities and increase loyalty.

DISCUSSION QUESTIONS

1. Why is it important to put the customer at the center of your marketing communications plan?
2. How can your food tourism destination or business take advantage of social media to increase customer loyalty?
3. What types of interactive or digital marketing tools can you leverage to more effectively showcase your establishment and/or destination?

ENDNOTES

[1] Interested parties should refer to *The Food & Drink Tourism Service Journey* chapter earlier in this book.

[2] "Tesco Homeplus virtual subway store in South Korea", Youtube video, posted by Recklessnutter, June 24 2011, www.youtube.com/watch?v=fGaVFRzTTP4

[3] Ylan Q. Mui (September 17, 2010). "Some businesses are victims of social-couponing (Groupon, Living Social) success" Washington Post, last accessed July 31, 2013, www.washingtonpost.com/wp-dyn/content/article/2010/09/17/AR2010091707048.html

[4] "The adventures in taste app", Adventures in Taste Nova Scotia, last accessed July 31 2013, http://adventuresintaste.ca/mobile-app/

[5] "Eat Street", Fox Life TV, last accessed July 31 2013, www.foxlife.tv/co/shows/eat-street

[6] "Introducing good food month", Good Food Month, last Access July 31 2013, www.goodfoodmonth.com

[7] "This Saturday begins Alimentarte, the recognized gastronomic festival" El Tiempo, last accessed July 31 2013, www.eltiempo.com/colombia/bogota/ARTICULO-WEB-NEW_NOTA_INTERIOR-12091429.html

Let's Tell a Story

Kevin Fields, with Ginger King and Lynn Ogryzlo

Every human on Earth tells stories as part of how we experience life. Food tourism also involves the making and sharing of stories. Whether we met a famous chef at the London Borough Market, or a cheeky dog at a winery in Australia's Barossa Valley, we take home those experiences as memories. Food artisans tell stories, too. This chapter will look at how storytelling can be an effective promotional tactic.

INTRODUCTION

"If more of us valued food and cheer and song above hoarded gold, it would be a merrier world." J.R.R. Tolkien, author of Lord of the Rings (1892-1973)

The art of storytelling is as old as the human race, whether we tell our stories in the art on walls of caves, in the written word, or by the foods we eat. We tell stories to put children to sleep, or to recount our adventures from faraway lands. Storytelling was how we entertained and conveyed information long before broadcast media existed. Storytelling has stayed with us into modern times and now, telling stories, i.e. sharing content, is considered an effective promotional strategy.

Storytelling as a Common Denominator

Whether we are promoting a pair of running shoes or a meal, effective marketers know they need to tell a story about the product or the experience. When we share stories about a meal or other food experience, our fellow humans can put themselves in our place and almost taste and smell the experience. In food tourism, storytelling is one of our most powerful promotional tools.

Regardless of our differences in the world; language, culture, beliefs, race, age, or gender, the one need and interest that all humans share is food, we all need to eat and most people enjoy doing so. Food is a common denominator that bonds us together in emotional ways. Yet, when tourists eat in restaurants, it is usually an unremarkable act. Visitors go into a restaurant (single person, couple or family), eat and usually leave having gained no relationship with the food, the people, or the restaurant. In food tourism, a meal is considered an opportunity to tell a story, engage the customers and create an emotional relationship. Dining out is not just a meal, it should be a memory. Telling a story takes an ordinary act and turns it into a personal experience: the tourist now has a relationship with the cuisine.

Dining out is not just a meal, it should be a memory.

It makes sense then to share stories with visitors. Using food as a medium enhances the personal experiences tourists have when traveling and creates fond memories, goodwill, trust, potential repeat customers, and ultimately grows the business.

Food and tourism are inextricably linked because tourists need to eat. However, food as a visitor attraction can play a much broader role than merely providing nourishment to visitors. It is a form of cultural capital through which a tourist's experiences of a destination can be explored. Through food we can learn about local history, local culture, local people, logical climate, and geographical factors. Food is about enjoying the sensory experiences and personal relationships that good food can deliver. Food brings added value to tourism and enriches the tourist's experience. Telling stories has the ability to shape our culinary present and record historical food trends.

New vs. Old Ways We Experience Stories

Food tourism connects us to our surroundings and each other. However, what drives food tourism in each part of the world paints a different picture. For example, in the new world (North and Latin America, Oceania) food tourism is led more by consumer interest, where consumers have come to demand local food. As the industry in the New World continues to develop, small businesses often find themselves in new and unfamiliar territory. Those businesses that engage in food tourism through storytelling often find themselves at the leading edge of culinary hospitality. In the New World consumers will travel across a continent to visit a restaurant just for the experience.

The character of food tourism in the Old World (Europe, Asia and Middle East) is more about the connection between food, history and tradition. Centuries of evolution through food, food trade, and food development can be understood through the many stories told of where things grew, what was traded and by who, and the evolution of food preparation to result in the culinary experiences available today. Regions in the old world market their cuisine in the way of traditional foods, culinary customs and dishes that represent a history and culture. In the Old World, consumers will travel to a country to immerse themselves in a food culture.

Collaboration

Telling stories through culinary collaborations almost always involves local food. It is about knowing your own food history, dishes, people, region, and agriculture. When local food is involved, storytelling becomes a collaboration among as many as four partners: agriculture, hospitality, viticulture, and tourism. When these four industries work together they can produce authentic, distinct culinary stories and traditions that are unique to the food region in which they are created.

Authenticity, distinctiveness, and engagement are important elements to telling food tourism stories about local food and what is grown, raised or produced within the region. Sharing this information works towards creating consumer trust. Therefore, these are not foods brought into a region, but foods grown in a region.

Distinctiveness addresses the unique aspects of a region that supports growing, raising, or producing foods of a region. Key elements here include geography, geology, and climate. More importantly is how these three elements are reflected through food in terms of flavor and overall style of the dish. This connects consumers to a place and is often referred to as "terroir." The wine industry in general does a great job of telling the story of their terroir and how it affects the flavor of the wine.

Authenticity and distinctiveness can be two key factors of a food/region and their delivery requires engagement. This means giving the consumer opportunities to meet the trusted faces behind local food dishes. This could be a farmer, a chef, restaurant owner, culinary entrepreneur, etc. Engagement, or sharing unique and special stories, turns eating at a restaurant into a personal culinary experience with connections to people, food and place. Examples include:

- Religious orders transported vines to the 'New World' to ensure a supply of wine for their rituals.

- Romans introduced their foods throughout the empire they created to feed their soldiers. The empire eventually faded and the Romans went home, but their food stayed and became part of the staple diet of the indigenous population.
- Portuguese explorers brought foodstuffs back from the New World and introduced them into European cuisines — potatoes, tomatoes, peppers, etc.

Each of these stories begat hundreds if not thousands of stories about the local food and drink.

A Food Culture

Telling the story of a food culture is a bit different. Tourists increasingly seek local, authentic, and novel experiences linked intrinsically to the places they visit. Both at a regional and national level, foods can become unique elements of the brand image of places and help to create distinctiveness.[1]

Switzerland is a good example. How does a country that does not produce cacao beans earn a worldwide reputation for chocolate? This food culture was dependent on culinary entrepreneurs with a passion for food (chocolate in this case). Switzerland's success has created a food culture not authentic to a region, but authentic to a people and place. Through the distribution of consistently high quality chocolate at a price commensurate with its quality, chocolate has become part of Switzerland's culinary brand. Part of Switzerland's chocolate culture is the exchange of gifts, often for Christmas and Easter. When such gifts are high quality (and that usually means expensive) Swiss chocolate and if they are received on a regular basis, a story begins to be attached to the Swiss chocolate. Holidays and gift giving are part of Switzerland's chocolate story.

Another example is Italy, which does not cultivate coffee, yet it is regarded by many to have some of the world's best coffee. Again, this food culture was created by culinary entrepreneurs with a passion for food and drink (coffee in this case). Part of Italy's coffee culture is the small local cafés or bars where customers stand up to drink their morning coffee, with loud mopeds and honking car horns directly outside. The experience of the noise, the dirt from the street, and the loud shouts in Italian are part of Italy's coffee story.

While these are obvious examples of a country's accepted culinary flavors, many countries and regions have passionate culinary entrepreneurs who create products from global foods that are celebrated. It could be someone who crafts a line of gourmet sauces with ingredients sourced locally and globally. Blending ingredients into products such as a chocolate raspberry sauce cannot be promoted as locally sourced, rather it can be promoted as locally made by a unique local business. With these examples, success is built on sharing the food story. Italy's gelato, New York Bagels, and Irish whiskey are all examples of foods or drinks that do not necessarily use local ingredients, but which have their own food culture and interesting stories to tell.

Telling a Story

Most places have a rich food history and captivating stories to tell of food past, present, and extreme. Many stories are anecdotal and definitive versions of the same story. It matters not, as long as there is a nucleus of truth at the center. For example, there are multiple versions of how dishes such as Tarte Tatin, Cornish pasties, and Caesar salad were initially created. The stories are no less interesting for their variance; indeed they introduce an element of mystique which actually enhances the stories.

Storytelling can be as simple as a strawberry dessert featured during strawberry season while wait staff tout the beauty of strawberry fields throughout the region. It could be the story of a chef with a passion for charcuterie who personally serves the platter of cured meats and cheeses. These stories create excitement, especially when told by the butcher, baker, or winemaker, and add anticipation on the dining experience. Many food stories can be told from the perspective of the producer, a chef or restaurateur, an artisan creating food products through the use of local produce, or merely a local sharing knowledge of their indigenous cuisine.

Food tourism is not just about fine dining. Food tourism is about the assets, large and small, that make a culinary region. Food tourism does not have to mean gourmet food. It is increasingly about unique and memorable experiences.[2] The speed at which the food cart scene in Portland, Oregon, USA, has grown is testimony. While some of the cart food approaches gourmet, much of it does not. Yet a visit to the food carts is on the top of the to-do list for most tourists there.

Ways to Tell the Story

When consumers travel for food, they make decisions of the heart. When they taste the flavors and meet the people of a place, their culinary experience becomes an endearing experience. Many times they do not want the experience to end. Other times, they use social media to keep in touch. They share their stories, good or otherwise on social networks, and often with photos and videos which help tell their stories. They have the ability to reach out to many more people than destinations, restaurants, hotels and other tourism businesses can do on their own. By engaging tourists through stories, as well as enhancing the touristic experience we are ultimately reaching a wider audience who we may then convert into visitors and consumers.

Websites are potentially one of the greatest tools to tell a story because they offer unlimited space. Stories can include the history of a tourism property, culinary philosophy, and culinary collaborations. A static website such as simple lists of farmers with whom a restaurant works or pictures of a region's agricultural prowess will not quite carry the same weight as will an interview with the farmer or chef, and even better, a video interview.

Cooking shows aimed at discovering the small, undiscovered, local restaurants have gained in popularity and created an entire population of foodies who travel specifically to eat at the little known place with an incredibly enticing story. Since visitors seek culinary experiences and cannot generally eat nonstop all day, they may look to fill the rest of their non-meal time at museums and theaters, or by shopping, listening or watching performing arts and festivals and undertaking outdoor recreation, thereby driving economic benefits for other sectors in the community. Some visitors who go on full-day tasting tours would argue that they can, in fact, eat all day long. In such instances we would applaud them for experiencing the area's culture through its cuisine, and politely suggest they try also the art museums or theater.

Menus, blackboards, and features are all opportunities to tell a story, and create trust without personal contact. This is good for food tourism statements such as "we buy from local farmers" or "it's asparagus season, ask your server for the chefs new creation from the daily harvest." Displays of fresh potted herbs, a bowl of apples or baskets of bread go a long way to tell a story. Italian restaurants do this very well by setting the mood by displaying olive oil bottles, decorative bottles of dried pasta, wine carafes, and photos from Italy on the wall. Servers are a great way to engage visitors in storytelling, however it can also be the most difficult. The success of this method relies on your servers and their personal beliefs in, and excitement about, the story. If a server or owner is not inherently socially outgoing, then the great stories may never be told to your customers.

Self-guided food tourism products like "trails" and "routes" tell a story of regional specialties. In Ontario, Canada, there is a Butter Tart Trail, an Apple Route, a Wine Route, an Apple Pie Trail, a Cheese Trail, a Chocolate Trail, the Bacon and Ale Trail, and a Taste Trail. Food tours with set days, times, and a guide allows a region to present its culinary prowess. For example, Washington DC, USA, offers DC Metro Food Tours where a guide walks consumers through neighborhoods that offer a wide range of exciting cuisine with personal introductions to people and places.

Stories Worth Telling

Cornish Pasties (Cornwall, England)
Photo Source: Wikimedia Commons

The pasty is a pastry filled with meat and vegetables and sealed with a crimped edge. Pasties originated in Cornwall, England, but surrounding areas have had similar versions. Since 2012, the Cornish pasty has been covered by Protected Geographical Indication (PGI) status under European law. Cornish pasties can now only be called such if made in Cornwall.

The pasty's history itself is interesting. It is alleged that they were initially designed for workers in coal mines who worked far underground and would need to take their lunch down with them. As there were no facilities for the cleaning of hands before eating lunch, pasties were finished with a crimped pastry edge that could be held in dirty hands while they main part was eaten - the crimped edge then being discarded. There is anecdotal evidence that one half of the pasty would have the meat and vegetable filling, and the other half a sweet filling, so main course and dessert were available in the one product. There appears to be no conclusive evidence that this was ever the case, but it does add interest to the story.

Alheira Sausages (Portugal)

The Portuguese Inquisition started in 1536, with a primary purpose of forcing Portuguese Jews to convert to Catholicism. While many pretended to do so to avoid persecution, torture and death, many still continued to practice Judaism in secret. These Jews had a variety of ways of deceiving the Inquisitors, one of which involved food. Portuguese families would preserve pork by making it into sausages and hanging them in a smoke house, or even in living areas which had an open fire. As Jews did not eat pork, households without links of sausages hanging up would be very suspect. Jewish families contrived to make sausage from chicken, rabbit, or game, with bread added. These would then be suspended in the same way as pork sausages and those households would not come under automatic suspicion. When visitors eat Alheira sausages in Portugal, they will hear this story. Whether the story is true is uncertain, but it has become folklore and adds interest for tourists.

Tarte Tatin (France)

The story goes that Tarte Tatin was first created by accident in the 1880s at the Hotel Tatin in Lamotte-Beuvron, France, about 100 miles (162 km) south of Paris. One of the two sisters that ran the hotel overcooked apples in butter and sugar when preparing an apple pie. The sugar had caramelized so the sister put a pastry top on the pan then baked it in the oven, turning out the result onto a plate. It met with such positive comments in the dining room that the dish was then served on a regular basis. This is another story that has several variations, but it does seem clear that the dish was created by accident, but has proved so successful that it is still cooked throughout the world today, and still with its original name.

Saddleworth Cheese

Sean Wilson was an actor who played a part in one of the United Kingdom's most popular soap operas, Coronation Street. After 21 years in the role, he resigned in order to pursue his dream as an artisan cheese producer, forming the Saddleworth Cheese Co.[3] He now produces four cheeses and has won a variety of awards for them. Each is named to show its Lancashire roots:

- Muldoons Picnic: a Lancashire term given to a room full of screaming kids!, "What dya think this is, Muldoons Picnic?"
- Hows yer father: a common term using Lancashire dialect, when enquiring after the health of somebody's father.
- Mouth Almighty: what those from Lancashire would call somebody who is very outspoken. The cheese is so named as it has a very intense and strong flavor that will fill the mouth and excite the taste buds.
- Smelly Apeth: more Lancashire dialect. 'Apeth' is a diminutive of halfpenny, a small coin that no longer exists. It would be commonly applied to a small child covered in muck after a full day's play is a Smelly Apeth. The name was chosen to reflect that fact that this is a strong smelling blue-veined cheese.

Lymestone Brewery

This microbrewery situated in the town of Stone, Staffordshire, UK, was started in 2008 by the husband and wife team of Brad and Viv, and ably assisted by their spaniel, Lollie, who is listed on the workforce. Lollie is always ready to welcome visitors to the brewery and often goes out on the truck delivering beer to local outlets. Besides the story of how the brewery began, each of the beers has an interesting name incorporating 'Stone', apart from their German-style lager which is known as Ein Stein (which actually means "a stone" in German). Some of the names of the beers come from brewery staff, but customers can enter a competition to create names for their seasonal beers. Thus we have Lymestone Cowboy, Gaul Stone, Stone the Crows, Cobble Stone, Heart of Stone, and many others.[4] Consequently, the history of the brewery is an interesting story, but the names of the beers themselves are also talking points.

Titanic Brewery

While this company does not have a specific story of its own, by choosing such a unique name there is a connection to another story. The company started as a microbrewery, but as it now produces over 2.3 million pints a year perhaps that description no longer fits. The company name was chosen as Captain Edward John Smith, the captain of the Titanic, was born just down the road from the brewery in the town of Etruria, Staffordshire. All of their beers are named with some sort of connection to the Titanic, or the White Star Line, to whom the Titanic belonged. Examples of their standard brews include: Titanic Mild; Titanic Steerage; Titanic

Lifeboat; Titanic Anchor; Titanic Iceberg; Titanic Stout; Titanic White Star; and Titanic Capt. Smith's.[5] They also produce seasonal brews, giving them the opportunity to create additional names based upon the same Titanic or maritime themes. While the company has no direct link to the Titanic or the White Star line, they have created a related identity to what is the most famous ocean-going liner of all, and one of the highest grossing films of all time. This link to the Titanic, while not a story in its own right, creates a focus and talking point for customers and generates interest over and above their actual products.

Ben & Jerry's Ice Cream

This has become a very well-known story. The business was started in a dilapidated gas (petrol) station in Burlington, Vermont, USA. The total knowledge of owners Ben and Jerry was gained via a US$5 correspondence course in ice cream making. The store did not last long and they closed it down while they figured out if they were actually making money, which they were not. What they had learned resulted in their selling pints of ice cream from Ben's Volkswagen camper van. They slowly built the business and their forte became creating unusual flavors and names for their ice creams. The business is now global and there are very few countries where you will not find Ben and Jerry's products in supermarket freezers. This story is particularly interesting as it focuses upon two people with creative ideas but no apparent professional training, just a passion.

Ontario Butter Tarts

While Quebec is known for its dominating French culture, in Northern Ontario just north of Sudbury there is a large French population. It is here where the Ontario butter tart is believed to have been invented. While no one knows for sure what the origins of the Ontario butter tart is, it is a common understanding that in the early 1900s butter tarts began as a version of the French sugar pie, but in miniature form. The Ontario butter tart has become so popular and iconic that today you can find them in most bakeries throughout the province and almost all on-farm markets with an in-house bakery. Butter tarts have evolved and there are great debates over whether the filling should be runny and gooey or firm like a sugar pie. Others debate the addition of raisins or pecans while purists claim neither. It is not uncommon when travelling to other bordering provinces or USA states to find signs on deli counters that say, "Ontario butter tarts coming today."

Canadian Bacon

Canadians call it peameal bacon or back bacon, which is not really bacon but a roast taken from the back of the pig and cured in a brine solution. It has no fat marbling other than a top layer of fat and a covering of cornmeal is applied (in old times, crushed yellow peas were used). Peameal bacon is not smoked although back bacon is. Both are an iconic Canadian food with some fame coming from a movie starring John Candy called *Canadian Bacon*. It is indeed a food story worth sharing.

CONCLUSION

Telling food tourism stories is about creating relationships between people and places. Few foods lack interesting stories and they need to be told through a collection of various means. They may be based upon why certain produce thrives in a particular locality, an interesting production method, the culture of a location, the success of culinary entrepreneurs, or how it reached that locality in the first place. History is littered with stories about how food has moved around the world, through migration, trading, and even warfare. Telling these stories is a new form of personal tourism. Stories have an impact on others, the environment, and our food culture. And ultimately, stories can make a social and political statement.

DISCUSSION QUESTIONS

1. What food stories can you share from your area? What is the origin of each?
2. Can food stories exist without people behind them? In other words, can a product have a story by itself, without its creator?
3. Do you see new food stories emerging in your area? If so, what are they?

ENDNOTES

---

[1] Richards, G. (2012) In OECD (2012) Food and the Tourism Experience: The OECD - Korea Workshop, OECD Studies in Tourism, OECD Publishing, p.9

[2] Gazzoli, C. (2012) in World Tourism Organisation (2012) Global Report on Food Tourism, UNWTO, Madrid, p. 23.

[3] www.saddleworthcheese.co.uk Saddleworth is a village in the county of Lancashire, England. Not only is there a story behind the cheese company, there is a story behind each of the cheeses names.

[4] www.lymestonebrewery.co.uk

[5] www.titanicbrewery.co.uk

Don't Forget the Locals

Lisa Chase and Travis Antonio Sinckler

Food tourism is not exclusively for out-of-town visitors.[1] The success and longevity of any food or drink business that supports local tourism hinges in great part on engaging and involving the local community throughout every step of business planning, launch, and day-to-day operation. This chapter discusses ways to work successfully with locals, including residents, government officials, and business leaders. It offers key lessons and opportunities presented in a dynamic case study of the evolution of Barbados into a tourism destination that is both community-centric and culinary-centric.

INTRODUCTION

Local residents and businesses are your best customers and advocates. They can also be your biggest threat. The role they play for your business depends on how you treat locals and work with or without them. For food and drink tourism businesses, local support and involvement is critical in many ways. Beginning with business planning and start-up, to the development of a regional outreach campaign, to identifying and building long-term relationships with local brand advocates, local residents and business partners are often the key to success. This chapter describes how local residents can help or thwart food tourism endeavors.

What about Locals?

Food tourism sometimes has the image of an elitist activity: dining at fine restaurants with white linen tablecloths and a china place setting, main courses costing US$50+ per plate, sipping French champagne costing US$300 or more per bottle, or sampling artisanal cheeses that costs US$30+ per pound or kilogram. Food tourism might be considered exclusive and expensive, inaccessible for everyday folk, but nothing could be further from the truth.

That is not to say expensive dinners and fine wines do not have their place in food tourism. They do, but they are just a small part of it. In fact, the World Food Travel Association recently changed its name from the International Culinary Tourism Association, in part to broaden the concept and our industry's understanding. The Association's research proved that the phrase "culinary tourism" was potentially misleading to native English speakers and sounded elitist and narrow, in a way that food travel does not.

Food travel is defined by the Association as "the pursuit and enjoyment of unique and memorable food and drink experiences, both far and near." The specific mention of "far and near" emphasizes the importance of locals as participants in food travel, because it involves close experiences in local traditions, religion, history and culture. Locals can enjoy a good food experience, such as at Fisherman´s Wharf (San Francisco, California) a place where you can learn and get to know all the history and tradition involved in fish trade that is still very popular nowadays among locals and visitors alike.[2] If you seek out special food or drink experiences, you are a food traveler, regardless of whether these experiences are in your hometown, across the continent or on the other side of the planet.

Types of Local Involvement in Food Tourism

There are three primary ways for locals to be involved in food travel. They can be as customers, employees or as owners/partners.

The three roles are not mutually exclusive. More often than not, especially for small enterprises, locals are involved in at least two of the above roles, sometimes all three. While each type occupies its own unique space, there is often overlap. When the three types of local involvement come together in a collaborative way, then new food tourism opportunities can result.

Locals as Customers

Many food tourism businesses, restaurants in particular, rely on locals as a significant part of their core customer base. Special offers may be developed to attract locals, especially during slow times such as mid-week and shoulder seasons. These offers can be very effective for penetrating new markets and generating public interest and support. For example, in Honolulu, Hawaii, USA at the Sansei Seafood Restaurant and Sushi Bar, upon presentation of valid State of Hawaii issued identification, locals can get up to a 50% discount on any menu item.[3]

Another example of this is the Napa (California, USA) Neighbor program, where Napa Valley Vintners members offer product discounts (often 10% off wine purchases), and complimentary tours and wine tastings to anyone living in the Napa Valley.[4] This encourages locals to experience wines and tours with several positive results:

- Increased customers and sales mid-week, as many of the special deals are offered on Tuesdays or other slow times.
- Creation of a strong base of local support for Napa Valley Vintners. This can be helpful when zoning, taxes and other issues need to be decided locally.
- Mobilization of the most powerful marketing tool: word of mouth. When locals or out-of-town visitors ask where to go, friends and those working in the tourism industry will suggest the places they know and like.

Of course, the more locals try their area's culinary delights (whether a food cart or five star extravaganza), the better they will be able to recommend to visitors where they should dine, or culinary attractions that they should experience. According to the World Food Travel Association, one of the top three visitor questions is, "Where should we eat?".[5] Locals can serve as brand advocates and ambassadors when it comes to marketing and spreading the word about services via word of mouth. Locals have the "insider's only" knowledge and influence that can guide the tourist where to spend their money.

Locals as Employees

Across the counter from the customers, figuratively and often literally, are employees. From managers to servers to maintenance to delivery, employees are the backbone of many businesses as well as the face of the business to the public. Often locals are the only source of available labor, and attracting and retaining competent employees is critical. As with any workforce, fair pay, fair treatment, and opportunities for advancement and professional development are important ingredients for a successful food tourism business.

Restaurants are notoriously demanding on their staff, with long hours and difficult work conditions. But the successful ones carefully pick their staff to thrive in these conditions. A unique example is the Willows Inn on a small island off the coast of the US State of Washington. There, Chef Blaine Wetzel and his staff use only ingredients sourced from the nine-square-mile (23.3 sq km) rocky island. While they buy fish and other ingredients from locals on the island, the staff forages and farms much of the food themselves. The other chefs at Willows Inn were certainly not trained to forage and farm as part of their culinary schooling, but Chef Blaine carefully selected them during the hiring process to ensure that they would embrace this part of the job, along with the usual food preparation.[6] While many of the staff at Willows Inn were not 'locals' in the sense of having spent their whole lives there (the island has a population of less than 1000), the staff have become 'locals' in a sense and have become an integral part of the community, along with the Willows Inn.

Another example is the case of two burrito shops, one in Sacramento (Oscars Very Mexican Food) and the other in San Francisco (Ocean Taqueria), both in California, USA. Both shops employ local workers which helps to generate local economic impact. In fact, Oscar's Very Mexican Food recently opened a new location just so it could continue to employ its workers while it remodeled its main location. This dedication to its staff not only helped the business generate interest in local media but helped it maintain its image as the leading burrito shop in the Sacramento area.[7] Customers anxiously await the opening of the remodeled location and continue to visit the new location even though it is located farther away.[8]

Locals as Owners

Many food and drink businesses are locally owned. Whether it is a high-end restaurant like the Willows Inn or a street cart selling falafel, the chefs and cooks are often also the owners. The same applies to specialty grocery stores, farms, and many other food travel attractions. Partnerships between these businesses can strengthen regional efforts to promote food travel. By combining resources, small businesses can make their lean marketing budgets go further and create a unique brand for their region. A prime example of this is Ceja Vineyards in Carneros, California, USA, a family-owned business and the USA's first Hispanic-owned winery, which started 20 years ago producing just a few bottles of wine.[9] Well known for their touching and inspiring story, the owners' active presence and ability to 'tell their story' has helped them grow to where they are now.[10]

Another example is Floating Bridge Food & Farms Cooperative which is a group of working farms, food producers, lodging properties and dining establishments located in central Vermont, USA.[11] Individual member businesses offer locally produced farm products, farm tours, cooking classes, on-farm workshops, events, farm vacation packages, and farm stays. Made up of a group of farm, food, and lodging businesses owned by families, the co-op is dedicated to locally grown food and sustainable agriculture and is working to build a strong community of like-minded businesses within central Vermont. The Floating Bridge Food & Farms Cooperative's mission is threefold:

1. Develop a collective of agricultural businesses as a model of local sustainability.
2. Provide visitors with an authentic experience that deepens their appreciation and understanding of a working agricultural community.
3. Provide farm and food-based educational opportunities.

Co-op members provide their communities and area visitors with farm and food experiences, including locally raised meats, vegetables and prepared foods — available at their farms, restaurants, and bed & breakfasts, as well as at local farmers' markets and food co-ops. In this example, locals are owners, producers and ambassadors.

To share new developments about products, food tourism businesses often hold open houses for other producers and businesses as a chance to talk and get to know about each other's businesses. These can help locals experience food and drink, and they have the additional benefit of giving owners and employees of businesses a chance to develop relationships.

The members of the Floating Bridge Food & Farms cooperative are owners, employees, and customers collaborating to promote food travel in their region, and they are reshaping their community at the same time, resulting in an impact larger than the simple sum of the parts. They are engaging in community-based food travel.

Community-Based Food Travel

When local food and drink businesses collaborate, they can create a powerful alliance of locals and visitors who support the businesses and the community as a whole. Indeed, they can change the economy, the environment, the culture, and the image of a community by banding together around food, as has happened in several places around the world, not just in Vermont.[12]

Countless efforts are underway on every continent to develop community-based food travel and tourism opportunities. By focusing on local food, landscapes, and traditions, food travel can create transformational change in all types of ecosystems, from the mountains of Vermont to the tropics of Barbados, as described in the case study below.

Creating Community-Based Food Tourism in Barbados[13]

Despite being a mature tourism destination, the evolution of tourism activities in Barbados has not necessarily always had a direct link to local communities. An innovative pilot project which commenced in 1999 under the caption *De Heart uh Barbados®* sought to change this by integrating a local food tourism element within the broader community and nature tourism initiative.[14] This is an ongoing initiative that seeks to combine various aspects of Barbados heritage including local small farm and kitchen-garden production systems; community interaction; and the tradition and experiences of local food artisans. Based on accomplishments to date, the *De Heart uh Barbados®* food tourism model has demonstrated significant progress in adding an authentic, local community and culinary-centric dimension to the existing Barbados tourism product.

Impetus for Integrating Local Residents into Barbados Tourism

In 1999, as part of the Government of Barbados Feasibility Study for Harrison's Cave and its Associated Sites, the Natural Heritage Department (previously known as the Environment Special Projects Unit) worked with the communities of upland Barbados in piloting an integrated community and nature tourism festival. The festival, officially called *De Heart uh Barbados®*, celebrations, which highlighted the area's natural, cultural, and rural features including:[15]

- Natural attractions including the Flower Forest, Harrison's Cave, Jack-In-the-Box Gully, Welchman Hall Gully
- Scenic vistas of the west coast and east coast of Barbados
- Rural communities including residents, heritage sites, and local businesses
- Agricultural use including sugar cane production
- Attractive karst landscape
- Historic and adventure tours

Before establishing the festival, the baseline assessments in 1998 highlighted a number of issues between residents and area tourism operations, including:[16]

- The absence of significant interaction between visitors and tourists;
- A high-level of indifference among residents to local tourism-based activities; and
- Respondents expressing an interest in possible small business ventures.

The *De Heart uh Barbados*® celebrations were therefore viewed as a major intervention designed to develop the relationship between "community and tourism."[17] The celebration was first held in 1999 and continued until 2008, missing only one year (2007). 'Heritage Passports' were sold at a fixed nominal cost and allowed entry to many of the nearby nature-based attractions, which would normally cost (in total) almost four times as much as the passport. To connect with local residents and encourage the participation, households in the Welchman Hall/Sturges district were exempt from having to pay for their Heritage Passports. Local food establishments, farmers and craft persons were also engaged in the establishment of a Farm and Craft Market, and a small business sub-committee was established to manage and support the market. The Celebration was transformational in creating a mutually beneficial, two-way dialogue between local residents and key tourism operators. Specific to the Farm and Craft Market, it was noted that the event brought together diverse members of the communities and created linkages that could be carried forward with similar activities in the future.

Leveraging Local Gastronomy to Diversify the *De Heart Uh Barbados*® Program

The move to embrace and develop the local farm and food component of the celebration was rooted in the review of the 1999 pilot. Festival participants identified among several growth opportunities, including:[18]

- Guided tours along nature trails/gardens
- Local craft, foods and music
- Educational programs

In 2006, in an effort to explore practical avenues for culinary tour offerings within the celebration, Natural Heritage Department volunteers administered a sample survey on local gastronomy to attendees of the Farm and Craft Market.[19] The survey sought feedback on:[20]

- Favorite food offerings and key drivers for food purchase(s)
- Awareness of grapefruit's origin and potential for a branding and marketing program
- Willingness to support local farmers
- Preference for culinary products using local produce
- Experience in participating in local food-based tours
- Willingness to participate in local food tours and ideas for area food tour offerings
- Ideas for marketing the area's food and culture

The survey findings indicated:[21]

1. The majority of the respondents were not aware of grapefruit's origin, but were generally knowledgeable of the varied uses of grapefruit.
2. Over 90% of respondents preferred to buy locally grown produce on the basis of supporting the local economy.
3. Only 17% of the respondents had experienced a food tour, while on the other hand 84% indicated their willingness to participate in a *De heart uh Barbados*® food tour.
4. Recommended components for a *De heart uh Barbados*® food tour included ready-to-eat traditional meals, food preparation demonstrations and sampling, historical interpretation, landscape and ecology, and local fruits and vegetables.

Leveraging key insights from the survey, the Natural Heritage Department (NHD) representatives and community members commenced a consultative process to design a local food tourism component to *De Heart uh Barbados*®. In 2007 a group of residents in the Welchman Hall/Sturges community with the support of the NHD and volunteers involved in

401

execution of the festival agreed to develop an institution in order to promote the gastronomic heritage of the *De Heart uh Barbados*® region. The community organization was called the "Grapefruit & Molasses Foodies Inc.®" (GMF) and their mission statement is, "To share our common community heritage in food using our local ecology and agriculture to produce exportable products and gastronomic-based tours."[22] As part of their focus, the group would prove to be the strategic community partner for developing two distinct yet related features of the Welchman Hall/Sturges food tourism landscape, namely:

- The Sturges Farmers' Market
- The Farm and Food Lovers' Trail

Other targeted activities were identified by Grapefruit and Molasses Foodies Inc.®:[23]

- Developing products based on grapefruit and molasses
- Strengthening community linkages
- Establishing an institutional mechanism to drive the organization's vision
- Documenting local recipes

Implicit in the group's focus was the desire to integrate the surrounding community into their activities, while at the same time continuing to pursue economic development opportunities through tourism.

Milestones in Building Community Linkages and the Local Food Tourism Product

In pursuit of additional trail and market development, the organization undertook several successful activities. The Natural Heritage Department was again instrumental in supporting the Grapefruit and Molasses Foodies Inc.®'s food tourism development efforts, as below:

Community Food and Farm Development

1. Undertaking a food asset inventory by community members
2. Surveying the local food production practices[24]
3. Conducting a literature search on nutritional profiles of produce grown in the area[25]
4. Documenting community food heritage through interviews and undertaking an oral history program, the latter was done under the auspices of the Natural Heritage Department.
5. Instituting collaborations between members of the Grapefruit and Molasses Foodies Inc.® and the local primary school, Holy Innocents Primary, in developing the 4-H Club as well as various culinary products utilizing local produce.

Farm-to-Market Development

1. Collaborating with Slow Food International in December 2009 in piloting a Community Farmers Market as part of the annual Terra Madre Day celebrations, and subsequently instituting the monthly community Sturges Farmers Market under the auspices of the Natural Heritage Department and the Grapefruit and Molasses Foodies Inc.®.
2. Initiating a community grapefruit distribution and planting program as a means of rebuilding the grapefruit stock following devastation caused by a storm in 2010.
3. Engaging community graphic designers in the production of a visual brand identity for the Grapefruit and Molasses Foodies Inc.® and related products.

1. Securing inputs from residents, farmers, shop owners and food artisans in a community planning and mapping exercise towards the design of the Farm and Food Lovers Trail (see photo below).
2. Engaging staff and guests of environmentally focused hotels in piloting the Food and Farm Lovers Trail at *De Heart uh Barbados* in 2008.
3. Undertaking a preliminary risk assessment and management strategy for the Trail.[26]
4. Facilitating regional dialogue of community groups involved in food tourism towards the development of a Caribbean community food tourism network.[27]
5. Establishing relationships with international food experts and social media experts.[28]

Key Accomplishments & Future Opportunities

So far Grapefruit and Molasses Foodies (GMF) Inc.®, with the continued support of the Natural Heritage Department, has been able to maintain the monthly Sturges Market. Market visitors are primarily Barbadians living outside of the Welchman/Hall Sturges area. Community-based attendance to the market is generally viewed as low despite various innovations introduced to stimulate local patronage including:

1. The experimental development of market-branded dishes such as the Sturges Market Breakfast Platter and Sturges Farmers' Market Relish.
2. The introduction of social media into the local marketing strategy.
3. Investment in signage including banners and posters.
4. Strengthening collaborations with other community organizations such as churches and local transport operators in the market promotion.
5. Co-hosting special community events on select market days.

Community members mapping the trail. *Photo Credit: Travis Sinckler*

With respect to the Farm and Food Lovers Trail, following its 2008 pilot, tours were offered on a periodic basis as an adjunct to the Sturges Farmer's Market when requested by local institutions or required by special events. Overall the pilot trail was deemed a success and several factors were highlighted following an analysis of a questionnaire survey executed at that time. According to Clarke (2008c), the pilot Farm and Food Lovers Trail was indeed a success, as it:

- Involved the community
- Used and therefore promoted the existing local landscape and historic features
- Served food made from local products
- Created an additional market for farmers and food vendors in the community.
- Adhered to the carrying capacity limit calculated in the risk management study[29]

As such, the process to develop and execute this tour should be regarded as a best practice approach for sustainable rural community-based tourism.

Overall, both activities contributed to a deepened sense of awareness of local food and farm among community members given the central role played by the GMF as a community-based organization. Economic benefits, though relatively small, continue to be realized particularly through the farmer's market.

In moving ahead, the institutional evolution of the GMF will prove critical to the long-term sustainability of the community food tourism enterprise. The partnership with the Natural Heritage Department has proven invaluable in building the credibility of the initiatives as well as providing financial and technical support on an ongoing basis. There is also the recognition that the surrounding community as the visitor base for the Sturges Market is insufficient. A target market approach to neighboring districts in central and eastern segments of the country will have to be explored, as well as new institutional collaborations with government and community based institutions.

Specific to the Farm and Food Lovers Trail, and based on results from a confidential SWOT analysis, a mixture of infrastructural, institutional, financial and marketing developments needs to be considered.[30] Local engagement was essential to the development of the latter and financial sustainability will depend on the GMF building strategic alliances with big tourism.

Lessons from Barbados

A number of key learnings garnered from the Barbados experience can serve as a blueprint for the development of similar initiatives designed to engage and involve your local communities, specifically:

1. Using a lifecycle approach to localize food tourism development whereby residents can be involved in strategic phases of business planning, operational development & management, and ongoing evaluation.
2. Community-based tourism involves geographic, environmental and cultural aspects of the local community and should be built on local agriculture and its gastronomic products– critical components for new brand development and marketing.[31]
3. Systematic study of impacted communities should be undertaken to understand consumption and production patterns, and related demographics through research partnerships with local government, community-based institutions, and universities.
4. Building trust among stakeholders is time consuming but essential in order to create long lasting food tourism partnerships.
5. Institutional and financial sustainability of local institutions should be considered in the development of community-based food tourism programs.
6. Government support is often required for catalyzing community economic development. Agencies involved in agriculture, tourism, community development, culture and environment can each provide entry points for building food tourism partnerships with community organizations and tourism operations.
7. Sound analysis of potential business risks and roadblocks is essential for sustainable development models.

CONCLUSION

Food tourism businesses and destinations should keep in mind the following ideas and principles about engaging with locals to help make your business a success:

1. Locals can be an important part of your target market mix. For example, in Ontario, Canada, 80% of the province's visitors are from within the province.[32]
2. Use public relations to tell your stories to locals, who can continue to share those stories outside their local area.
3. Adopt a motto that "tourism is everyone's business," a concept that is well-known and used in the tourism industry in Scotland.
4. Offer special programs and pricing for locals, as with the Heritage Passports program in Barbados.
5. Hold open houses for other producers and businesses and proactively seek to learn more about each other's businesses.

It is imperative to look at local residents as potential customers, employees, and partners of your business. When they become all three and work together collaboratively as a region, community-based food travel is the result and it has the potential to transform a region's economy, landscape, and culture in positive ways.

DISCUSSION QUESTIONS

1. What food tourism products or services can best involve the local community?
2. Does government have a role in facilitating the involvement of local stakeholders in food tourism? Explain your position.
3. What is required to sustain and grow community food tourism initiatives?

ENDNOTES

[1] "What is food tourism", World Food Travel Association, accessed July 6, 2013, www.worldfoodtravel.org/what-is-food-tourism

[2] "Attractions at Fisherman's Wharf, Fisherman's Wharf, accessed July 6, 2013, www.visitfishermanswharf.com/mosets-directory/dining/seafood-stands

[3] "Menu for Sansei Seafood Restaurant", Sansei, accessed July 6, 2013, www.restauranteur.com/sansei/menu.htm

[4] Napa Valley Vintners. Napa Neighbor Discounts www.napavintners.com/programs/pe_2_discounts.asp

[5] PsychoCulinary Profile Research Report, World Food Travel Association, 2011.

[6] Jacobsen, Rowen. "Eating the Island". *Outside Magazine*. March 2013.

[7] "Oscar's Very Mexican food closes for construction adds west Sacramento location". Sacramento Business Journal, last accessed July 7, 2013, www.bizjournals.com/sacramento/blog/mark-anderson/2012/11/oscars-very-mexcian-food-closes-for.html

[8] "Oscar's Very Mexican Food", Yelp, last accessed July 7, 2013, www.yelp.com/biz/oscars-very-mexican-food-sacramento

[9] Ceja Vineyards: Marketing to the Hispanic wine consumer, Ceja Vineyards, last accessed July 7, 2013, http://hbr.org/product/ceja-vineyards-marketing-to-the-hispanic-wine-cons/an/NA0108-PDF-ENG

[10] "Ceja Vineyards motto marries the past and present", Ceja Vineyards, accessed July 6, 2013, www.cejavineyards.com/Press/Solano-Magazine-Vinum-Cantus-Amor

[11] "Floating Bridge food and farms Trail", Dig in Vermont, accessed July 6, 2013, www.diginvt.com/trails/detail/floating-bridge-food-and-farms-trail

[12] Hewitt, Ben. 2010. *The Town that Food Saved: How One Community Found Vitality in Local Food*. Rodale Books.

[13] The authors gratefully acknowledge the input from the following persons in the preparation of the Barbados Case Study: Ms. Shawn Sharon Carter, Ms. Judi Clarke, Mr. Steve A. Devonish, Dr. Mark D. Griffith and Ms. Stacia Thorne.

[14] Devonish, S. Personal Communication with Mr. Steve A Devonish as Director of the Natural Heritage Department and founder of De Heart uh Barbados®.

[15] http://heritage.gov.bb/Dhub_what_is_it.html "What is it", The Natural Heritage Department, last modified July 6, 2013, http://heritage.gov.bb/Dhub_what_is_it.html

[16] Axys Environmental Consulting (B'dos) Inc., Environmental Planning Group Ltd, Gillespie and Steel Associates, and Bellairs Research Institute, 2000a. Harrison's Cave and Associated Sites Baseline Report. Feasibility Studies of Harrison's Cave and Associated Sites, Carlisle Bay, and Folkestone Park and Marine Reserve. March 2000.

[17] Devonish, S. personal communication.

[18] Axys Environmental Consulting (B'dos) Inc., Environmental Planning Group Ltd, Gillespie and Steel Associates, and Bellairs Research Institute, 2000b.Harrison's Cave and Associated Sites Baseline Report. Feasibility Studies of Harrison's Cave and Associated Sites, Carlisle Bay, and Folkestone Park and Marine Reserve. March 2000.

[19] Carter, S. Personal Communication with Miss Shawn Carter in her role as a former De Heart uh Barbados ® Coordinator and current member of the Grapefruit and Molasses Foodies Inc.®.

[20] Clarke, J. 2008a.Preliminary Assessment of Local consumption and Production Patterns in rural Communities of Barbados: Identification of Opportunities for Sustainable Local Economic Development in the Welchman Hall Area: Final report. Prepared for the Environment Division of the Ministry of Family, youth, Sports and Environment. Government of Barbados. P17-25.

[21] Clarke, J. 2008a.

[22] Shorey-Bryan, N.2008.Outcomes from the Grapefruit & Molasses Foodies Strategic Planning Meeting- August 1, 2008.

[23] Shorey-Bryan, 2008.

[24] Clarke, J. 2008a.

[25] Clarke, J. 2008b. Nutritional Profile of Fruit, Vegetables and Herbs Grown in De Heart uh Barbados®. Final Draft. Prepared for the Ministry of Family, youth, Sports and Environment. Government of Barbados. 56 p.

[26] Sinckler, T. 2008. Application of the risk Management Decision process- "The development of a Village-Based Farm and Food Lover's Trail". Risk and Loss Control Management. February 25th – 29th, 2008. Dalhousie University College of Continuing Education.

[27] Caribbean Policy Development Centre, 2009. Establishing Sustainable Development Partnerships, Rethinking Environmental Sustainability, Local Gastronomy and Rural Development: Workshop Report. Prepared for the Environment Division of the Ministry of Environment, Water Resources and Drainage. Government of Barbados.

[28] Heather Johnston, "Video: Barbados Food Tour", *So good.TV* video,4:28, July, 2009, www.sogood.tv/heather_johnston/2009/07/video-barbados-food-tour.html

[29] Clarke J.2008c. Consultant's report; Analyses of the Gastronomy Survey and the Farm & Food Lover's Trail, June 21, 2008.Ministry of Family, Youth, Sports and Environment. Government of Barbados. 60 p.

[30] Clarke J.2008c.

[31] "What is geo- tourism" Food reference, accessed July 6, 2013, www.foodreference.com/html/a313-geotourism.html

[32] Leheup, Rebecca, Executive Director, Ontario (Canada) Culinary Tourism Alliance. Presentation entitled "Foccus congreso turismo enogastronomico" in Bilbao, Spain, 7 November 2012.

It's Who You Know:
Sustainable Industry Partnerships & Memberships

Neha M. Shah and Erik Wolf

The food tourism industry is enormous and spans the world. Hospitality professionals are more often than not a social bunch who appreciate the opportunity to share a glass of wine or cup of coffee and exchange industry stories. It is difficult for small business owners to learn about and take advantage of the enormous realm of networking opportunities. Similarly destination marketing organizations also need to know about different partnership opportunities available to them and their members or constituents. Organizations like chef associations and other niche travel industry groups can be of enormous benefit to our industry. What are the best ways to network at industry events? What advantages and disadvantages does each type of group offer? Which groups are worth your time? What are opportunities for these groups to expand? This chapter endeavors to answer these questions.

INTRODUCTION

There are so many organizations in the world that the number of potential partnerships you might pursue is truly overwhelming. Whether you join an organization depends on time, cost and relevance. Some of us might become members of an organization with the best intentions, only to realize that we may not have time to get the most out of what the organization has to offer. Or perhaps the organization did not offer any real benefits so we choose not to renew our membership. Still, the right partnerships used correctly can drive progress in your own business by enabling faster product development, facilitating sales or distribution, and more.

Memberships & Strategic Partnerships

Partners or Members?

When we refer to a partnership, we usually mean a strategic partnership. This is typically between two organizations whose goals, programs and activities may be complementary, but could also have divergent goals (discussed below). Unfortunately too often in business, a strategic partnership is announced, but it is nothing more than the organizations exchanging links and logos on their respective websites. In other words, it is often a passive partnership, which is of little strategic value to either organization. A more valuable strategic partnership would include actions like developing and packaging products; joint education or research; undertaking cooperative marketing and media relations campaigns; attending and/or speaking at each other's conferences, and so on. By membership, we mean an organization that you would join as a member. Some membership organizations charge dues while others are free.

Memberships Types

In the food and drink tourism industry, logical partnerships naturally focus on food, drink, travel or hospitality organizations. The most obvious type of organization food tourism professionals will encounter is a trade association, such as those for restaurants, lodging, and food or drink producers. Not every food tourism industry sector has a trade association in every geographic area, so identifying suitable partners can take some time. It is beyond the scope of this chapter to detail all of the possible organizations in the world, or to make recommendations as to which are worthwhile, so you will need to do some research on organizations that meet your own specific needs.

What do you need in a membership organization? Are you looking for general education about the industry? If so, does the organization in question offer suitable education resources? Maybe you just need research for your business plan or a new business venture. Does the organization offer research that would be useful for your goals? Maybe you need help with sales or marketing? In that case, does the organization offer various resources that will help you to sell or market your products or services? Your time is valuable and therefore you need to make sure that the type of organization you join is one that will meet your immediate needs.

Know Your Focus

The first step to exploring suitable industry partnerships and memberships is to consider the geographic focus as well as the sector focus of your business, group or destination.

Geographic Focus

It may not make immediate sense for a small area producers association to pursue relationships with national or international organizations. Such small producer organizations should understandably pursue partnerships with each other first. In the English language, we say that it is advisable to "take baby steps." An example would be a group of farmers' markets throughout one city that could come together under a common vision to align their opening days, market policies, products offered, vendors included and so on. Once these kinds of partnerships are created and stable, then additional partnerships can be explored. It may never make sense for one individual business owner to pursue strategic partnerships with larger regional or national organizations, but it may make sense for the small producers group of which the business owner is a member, to pursue such far-reaching strategic partnerships. To do so, a producers association with, for example, 50 members, only needs to make one phone call to the regional or national association rather than each of its members making their own calls to the same association.

The small producer may find more benefit in being a member of the producers association in his or her area. The same concept applies for a different kind of small business with a similar small business association in the area. Recalling the question of what you want to get out of such an organization, find out if such organizations in your area support your business goals.

Aggregating communications, purchasing power, marketing campaigns and development plans together is best carried out at a strategic level between the two organizations, for maximum efficiency and effect. That said, there may be one or two larger producers in the smaller area that would benefit from partnerships at the regional or national level. In such a case, those producers could contact the regional or national organizations directly.

Open and transparent communication among all parties at all levels is preferred whenever feasible. Obviously issues of privacy, confidentiality, or competitiveness should not be publicly revealed. In the previous example where the single large producer in a smaller area that contacts the national Association by itself is something that would be of interest to potentially benefit the other smaller producers in the same local area. Email is obviously an easy tool to share news and developments, and may be sufficient for small artisan producers, farmers, brewers, winemakers and so on, for occasional communication. Ongoing communications and groups with more structure are best realized using an online team collaboration system.[1]

Sector Focus

Similar to the geographic focus, businesses should seek to partner within their own sector first before exploring cross-sectoral promotions. For example, at a minimum, a winemaker should know about his or her area winery association, if one exists. Whether he or she finds value in being involved in such an association is another matter. Perhaps that same winemaker might find more value working with a larger winery association, or something like a Chamber of Commerce or tourism office. This broaches the idea of cross-sectoral partnerships, where businesses in different sectors within the food tourism industry matrix find value in working together. [2] Examples of suitable cross-sectoral partnerships can include foodservice and lodging; foodservice and tour operations; tour operators and lodging; media and academics; destinations and most business types; and so on. There are nearly an unlimited kind of partnerships that can be forged. We encourage you to think differently and explore untraditional relationships.

Types of Organizations

Next, evaluate which kind(s) of organizations make sense for your business objectives.

Artisanal Food and Drink Producers Associations

One type of organization that works to serve the needs of small food and drink (artisanal) producers are groups like Good Food Ireland and Taste of Nova Scotia. [3] These groups undertake sales, marketing, awareness, education and research activities that may be of great interest and help in your business.

Chamber of Commerce

A Chamber of Commerce is a local organization whose purpose is to support the area's local businesses through visibility, networking and promotional opportunities. Chambers usually charge a fee to become a member. Chambers have meetings regularly, often on a monthly basis. At chamber meetings, attendees have the opportunity to stand up and introduce themselves and their business. If there is no chamber of commerce in your area, look for a "business association," "business guild" or "small business group" which serve similar functions.

Destination Marketing Organizations (DMOs)

DMOs are one type of organization that is often overlooked by food and drink providers, who unfortunately sometimes take the view that they are food or drink producers and nothing more. Actually, food and drink producers are part of the area's branding ecosystem. For example, when in Perugia, Italy, a visitor expects to eat chocolate. In San Francisco, California, a visitor expects to eat sourdough bread. In Singapore, a visitor expects to eat laksa. Producers of chocolate, sourdough bread and laksa in their respective destinations help comprise the destination character — and brand — whether or not they do so intentionally.

A DMO is like the tip of an iceberg in that it is the one entity that can potentially oversee all other travel and hospitality businesses in the region. In essence, the DMO is the "glue" that holds the destination together. Some destinations do not have a DMO, or may have one with severe operating restrictions, in which case aligning with a DMO may not be possible or even advantageous. If you are unsure if your area has a DMO, search online for nearby tourism offices or convention and visitor bureaus. Be aware that some media publishers position their media outlets (i.e. websites and visitor guides) to look like websites for official tourism offices, yet they are not even affiliated with the official tourism office for the area. Look for words like "Official" that may indicate a true DMO. You can also ask colleagues what they know.

DMOs can be structured to be membership-based (i.e. you pay to join) or constituent-based (no fee to join and oversees an area in general). Some DMOs may exist by mandate of local, regional or national economic development or other government agencies and may be prohibited from having members.

Networking 101[4]

Some of us are more social than others. And some of us may be social enough, but simply too busy to do a good job of getting visibility for our name or that of our company or product. Here are a few tips that can help you get the most out of networking in the food tourism industry:

Business Cards

It may seem obvious, but many of us still do not have business cards, or we forget to carry them with us. There is no easier way to stay in touch with someone new than to hand them your business card (although that is changing slowly, as NFC[5] technology now allows people to touch smartphones and send their contact details to another person wirelessly). While you go to the trouble to print business cards, make them two-sided. Be sure not to print glossy on both sides (glossy on one side is fine) in case the recipient wants to write notes on your card (this happens often at trade shows). Also leave some space for notes on the back side of your card. Avoid cute or overly artistic designs (unless you are a graphic designer or artist), use a large enough font size to be easily readable, and do not forget to include your email and website addresses. Use the standard international telephone format (+xx) x-xxx-xxxx[6] if you expect to get business from outside your country or if you travel internationally. Lastly, avoid free or Internet service provider email addresses (i.e. those using gmail.com, aol.com, wanadoo.fr, telecom.co.nz, etc.). If you have your own business website or own a domain name, you can easily get your own business email address at no extra cost. If you do not know how to do this, ask a colleague or university student for help. Take your business cards with you everywhere you go, and especially to trade shows, meetings and conventions, and even on holiday.

Trade Shows

There are plenty of trade shows in both the food and drink, and travel and hospitality, industries. Examples include both ANUGA[7] and the Fancy Food Show[8] for food and drink, or World Travel Market[9] for travel and hospitality. At such shows, you could potentially meet dozens if not hundreds of new contacts. Such shows allow you to hone in on exactly who you want to meet, or to find new people to meet that you might not have thought of before. Suitable trade shows take place all around the planet. Ask yourself which shows might be most relevant to your needs. If you are unsure, ask your colleagues or your local tourism office for their recommendations. Be aware that a trade association of which you are a member might already have plans to attend a trade show. Joining them might add value to their presence, or your presence might be unnecessary if they can adequately represent you. Do a cost-benefit analysis to determine if the return on investment for your time and money would be worth it. Attending and/or exhibiting at such trade shows is usually quite expensive, so producers are beginning to look towards online tools to help facilitate sales and marketing relationships in a more affordable and time-sensitive way.

Industry Meetings & Conventions

Similar to trade shows, industry meetings and conventions are another excellent place to meet new people. Of course there will be people looking to sell to you, but there will also be people looking to buy, or who can help distribute or promote your product. Journalists often attend industry meetings and conventions and are always looking for new newsworthy content. If you are unsure which meetings and conventions would be worth your time, ask your colleagues or your local tourism office for recommendations.

Volunteer Committees

Working with local events or campaigns is another great way to meet people who could be in a position to promote your product or service. You might find an amazing new sales person, or meet someone who can help design labels for your new line of gourmet honey, for example. If nothing more, volunteering for a committee is a great way to break up your everyday work schedule and it forces you to experience new people and situations.

Online Communities

Many businesses have Facebook pages and many food and hospitality professionals are already members of LinkedIn. Each of these community platforms has inherent pros and cons. We cannot tell you whether it is worth your effort personally to network via these platforms. One common complaint we hear is that current online business communities are too general. A food or hospitality professional is not typically looking to network with realtors (estate agents), lawyers (barristers), chemical engineers or Linux programmers. Our industry would benefit tremendously from a global online community focused on food, drink, travel and hospitality. For now, pick and choose your online communities carefully. Your time and money are limited.

Ideas to Actions

It does take time to research and sort through suitable industry partnerships, especially if you run a small business. Rather than taking valuable time to do the work yourself, make it easy with the following suggestions:

- Visit the chamber of commerce, if your area has one. Attend a meeting and learn about the organization, its resources and its members. The savvy business owner will know quickly if it is worth his or her time to pursue.
- Talk to your peers in other businesses. What organizations are they members of? Which do they consider to be of value or not?
- Meet with the closest tourism office to your area. Is it effective in tourism promotions? Does it actively develop new tourism products? Is food and drink tourism part of its strategic plan (or will it be soon)?
- Invite a university student to conduct the research for you. Many students seek internships to gain practical work experience. Some internships are paid and others are not. The choice is yours whether you pay the student. Ask a student to research organizations in your industry and make recommendations as to those which can benefit your business.

CONCLUSION

Whether we are born with the "social gene" does not really matter, as there is still an inherent benefit in networking with others in our industry. You can network with others directly at trade shows and meetings, or you can do so in a more structured way such as at a convention or on a committee. If you have not done so already, you will realize that there are too many

411

opportunities for networking, so you must pick and choose where to focus your time, money and effort. If you are new to this approach, ask your colleagues or your area tourism office for guidance.

DISCUSSION QUESTIONS

1. What kind of professional business or networking groups in food, drink, travel and hospitality are available in your area?
2. What local, regional, national or international membership organizations would be of use to your business and why?
3. What would be the purpose of a food or drink professional attending a travel or hospitality trade show, and vice versa?

ENDNOTES

[1] The World Food Travel Association successfully uses TeamWorkPM.net for communications and collaborations with distributed teams, which have embraced it as a robust, easy, and intuitive collaboration system. For tracking personal task lists, currently todoist.com is the Association's preferred product.

[2] Refer to food tourism industry sectors matrix in the *Introduction to the Food Tourism Industry* chapter in this book.

[3] Refer to the *Tourism Offices & Trade Groups* chapter in this book for more detailed information about this type of producers association.

[4] Appending "101" after a word implies a reference to the US university system, whereby a course name followed by "101" indicates that it is a first year, or introductory overview course for the subject.

[5] Near field communication (NFC) is a wireless technology for the transmission of information between two capable devices.

[6] In the formula (+xx) x-xxx-xxxx, (+xx) is the international direct dial country code. Next is "x" which is the regional area code and is often preceded by a "0". If a zero is used in your country as a prefix for domestic phone calls, then use the format (+xx) (0)x-xxx-xxx to indicate that the "0" might not be required by international direct dialers. Then xxx-xxxx is the local number (often 6, 7 or 8 digits).

[7] www.anuga.com

[8] www.specialtyfood.com/fancy-food-show

[9] www.wtmlondon.com

Evolution of Guidebooks, Ratings, & Reviews in Food & Drink Tourism

Jenn Bussell and Erik Wolf

This chapter addresses the broad spectrum of food and drink rating systems, review forums, and guidebooks from industry cornerstones like the Michelin star system and MICHELIN Guide, to consumer review websites like TripAdvisor and Yelp, to the rise of the food bloggers and amateur critics. Each of these opinion-based options offers benefits to both the food tourism industry and consumers alike, yet they also have inherent drawbacks. This chapter will explore the evolution of these different choices, discuss the impact they can have on a food or drink business, and identify opportunities for future development of new systems that are more inclusive to the broad range of businesses that comprise the food tourism industry.

INTRODUCTION

Ask 50 people what they think of a new restaurant and you will most likely hear 50 unique opinions. Some of these opinions will be based on a single dining experience, while others may be the aggregated view of multiple visits over a period of time. A similar spectrum of divergent opinions exists in the food tourism industry as well. Since 1900 when the first MICHELIN Guide appeared in France, consumers have had access to an increasingly broad, and at times confusing, array of industry-tolerated food and drink rating systems and guides designed to aid consumer decision making. While many of these sources of professional opinion have set the standards of excellence for eating and drinking establishments around the world, their criteria for success are often vague and conflicting. Rating systems and guides evaluate either front-of-house (FOH) and/or back-of-house (BOH) operations, including décor and kitchen efficiency; others focus heavily on value for money. A restaurant reviewed in one guide may be missing in a second, competitive guide for the same city. And a restaurant that may appeal to one type of person, or a particular demographic or psychographic profile, may or may not appeal to someone with different characteristics, making it nearly impossible for a foodie to really know the mindset of the person who wrote the review.

Hotels have their own measures of quality, rating systems, and consumer guides such as The Leading Hotels of the World and the American Automobile Association (AAA) and its British counterpart, the Automobile Association (AA). To complicate matters further, in Europe there exists an umbrella association called HOTREC that serves and supports hotels, restaurants and cafés as a single hospitality category, or sector. One of the core missions of HOTREC is to bring the myriad of hotel classification systems in various European countries closer to one another, creating a unified set of criteria of one through six stars.[1] Many European and non-European consumers alike are unfamiliar with the HOTREC system.

The growing focus on sustainability coupled with the increase in agritourism interest over the past 10 years has resulted in yet another category of rating systems and certification programs for restaurants, food retail, and food service operations. 'Conscious consumers,' as described by Fair Trade USA, make educated food, drink, and travel purchases based on certifications of sustainable business practices. The entities whose certifications they abide by is not always consistent or even necessarily known to, or discoverable by, other travelers.

As you develop and implement your business plan, it is important to understand the cluttered landscape of food and drink rating systems, review forums, and guides in order to make sound business decisions on whether to invest time, effort, and budget to secure industry certifications and top rankings that could result in global PR and marketing opportunities, increased brand awareness, and new customers.

The MICHELIN Guide for Restaurants and Hotels

In 1900, tire manufacturers and brothers André and Edouard Michelin printed and distributed free guidebooks to help motorists find quality lodging options around France. *Le Guide Michelin* began listing restaurants by category in 1920. Between 1926 and 1936, the Michelin brothers introduced their eponymous one-, two-, and three-star restaurant rating system as follows:

- One star: "A very good restaurant in its category" ("Une très bonne table dans sa catégorie")
- Two stars: "Excellent cooking, worth a detour" ("Table excellente, mérite un détour")
- Three stars: "Exceptional cuisine, worth a special journey" ("Une des meilleures tables, vaut le voyage")

What grew out of an innovative and strategic marketing ploy to drive increased consumer demand for cars and tires (and specifically Michelin tires), evolved into the gold standard for rating fine dining establishments around the world, with the Michelin three-star system still alive and well today.

The longstanding success of the MICHELIN Guide has been predicated on the use of anonymous reviewers called 'inspectors' who are recruited and reimbursed by the Michelin Corporation to visit and evaluate restaurants. Inspectors write reports on their dining experiences that are then distilled into rankings of three, two, one and in some cases, no stars, during annual "stars meetings."[2] In addition to honoring the vision, product, and exemplary service of chefs and restaurateurs around the globe, the MICHELIN Guide also awards Rising Stars, an indication that a restaurant has the potential to qualify for a star, or an additional star if already rated.

Yet the personal and professional pressure of attaining the respect and global recognition that comes with a Michelin star has changed the shape of dining for many. Chefs became hyper-focused on creating menu items for the potential visit of an anonymous inspector rather than catering to the palates of their guests. So guests themselves started to evolve, spawning a unique subset of diners flush with cash and the means to travel seeking to dine only in Michelin-starred restaurants. For this group of self-proclaimed gourmands, it was less about the communal sharing of food and more about checking off another entry on their Michelin Red Guide list, earning bragging rights among their peers for having scored a near-impossible reservation.

Despite its efforts to keep pace with technology and reach new audiences by offering mobile apps and digital tools to demystify their rating system including *The MICHELIN Guide Dictionary* and *How to Use This Guide*, there has been increasing backlash against the MICHELIN Guide and what it represents. Castigated as a dinosaur by a number of outspoken journalists, critics, and chefs alike, they view the MICHELIN Guide as out of touch with modern travel and dining experiences, and forcing unattainable and outdated standards on an industry that seeks to achieve increased transparency and approachability. This backlash has spawned alternative publications such as *Le Fooding*. Founded in 2000 by Alexandre Cammas, a French journalist and food critic, Le Fooding is a Paris-based restaurant and culinary event guide that aims to abandon the classic seriousness and stuffiness associated with French cuisine. While Le Fooding's editorial team is quite serious about the world of food — reviewing, ranking, and reporting on some of France's best chefs and tables — its style is more irreverent than the MICHELIN Guide and other restaurant guidebooks.

Some leading chefs, however, including Eric Ripert of Le Bernadin in New York City still see the value of the MICHELIN Guide and its star rating system. They believe it can coexist in a new world order of restaurant guidebooks, restaurant critics, restaurant and beverage industry bloggers, amateur food bloggers, and consumer review sites. "In defense of the Michelin ... this is like pop music versus classical music," commented Chef Ripert.[3]

Zagat

First published in 1979, the *Zagat Survey*® began as a personal hobby for husband and wife Tim and Nina Zagat in New York City. While at a dinner party with friends that year, one of the dinner guests complained about the restaurant reviews of a major newspaper, and everyone agreed that the paper's reviews were unreliable. It was then that Tim Zagat suggested taking a survey of their friends as a better gauge for assessing a restaurant's worth. This novel idea led to 200 amateur critics rating and reviewing 100 top restaurants in and around New York City for food, décor, service and cost based on a 30-point scale. The survey results, printed on legal-sized paper, were an instant success with copies being hoarded all over town.

Unlike the MICHELIN Guide, Zagat aims to give consumers a vehicle to express their opinions on various leisure dining categories (food, service, décor, price) through their proprietary surveying methods. Zagat editors then distill consumer feedback into numeric scores and concise reviews that incorporate short, often witty, quotes from consumer survey responses. In addition to print versions, Zagat launched its website in 1999 offering free content to users. In 2002, Zagat moved to a paid subscription model whereby members gained full access to all review content for a monthly fee.

After selling one-third of the company to a private equity firm in 2000, Zagat was acquired by Google in 2011. In 2012, Zagat was officially integrated into Google's services, with Zagat consumer reviews integrated into Google Maps, Google+ Local pages, and users' Google+ profiles. Zagat content is once again free to access provided users have registered on zagat.com with their Google+ account.

Much like the MICHELIN Guide, Zagat also has its supporters and detractors. While some industry experts view the Zagat 30-point system as a means to democratize dining reviews, others view it and the accompanying anecdotal consumer commentary to be pedantic and non-authoritative.

White Guide

The *White Guide* is Sweden's leading restaurant guide, ranking the country's top 250 restaurants and reviewing more than 500 restaurants of all types and sizes annually. The White Guide employs a rating system of 'International master class', 'Swedish master class', 'Very good class', 'Good class', 'A nice place' and 'A suggestion' and includes descriptive reviews designed to educate readers about regional dishes, local specialties, and prices. In addition to this proprietary rating system, the White Guide proudly markets Sweden's Michelin-starred restaurants. The White Guide does a great job of marketing Sweden's worthwhile food experiences. Unfortunately, travelers outside of Scandinavia have rarely heard of the White Guide, perhaps largely because the White Guide currently publishes very little information in languages other than Swedish.

Australian Good Food and Travel Guide

Founded in 1977, the *Australian Good Food and Travel Guide* (AGFG) was inspired by the MICHELIN Guide and Gault Millau, and has long been considered Australia's most comprehensive restaurant, accommodation, and travel rating authority throughout the continent.

As described on the AGFG website which launched in 1999, "ratings are based on the facilities and services of each establishment. In the interest of uniformity, a standardized point criteria assists [sic] inspectors in their critique. Each establishment must meet the minimum requirements and receive a rating score equal to or above that of the corresponding rating, standardizing the ratings throughout Australia and further ensuring that irrespective of where or who is rating an establishment, the rating will be consistent with international standards."

Like its American and European contemporaries, AGFG has leveraged technology to expand its product suite, which currently includes the AGFG website and mobile site; mobile apps; and GPS-based, in-car navigation tools.

A Brief Look at Lodging

As with dining, there is an equally wide variety of rating schemes used in the global hospitality and lodging space. Most classifications are star-based, with a greater number of stars indicating greater luxury for guests. The *Forbes Travel Guide* (formerly the Mobil Travel Guide) launched its star rating system in 1958, whereas the American Automobile Association (AAA) and its Canadian cousin the CAA use a system of diamonds to rate hotel and other lodging establishments in the US and Canada. AAA also publishes printed *AAA TourBooks®* and downloadable *eTourBook® Guides* which provide members access to travel information for major cities, national parks and other destinations across North America and the Caribbean.

Like the MICHELIN Guide, the majority of hotel guides that have been published since the mid-20th century were created in response to the boom in automobile ownership. More cars meant more drivers in need of road trip-related information such as where to stay and where to eat.

Options Breed Consumer Confusion

With so many systems for rating food, drink, and lodging establishments — stars, points, diamonds, forks, spoons, wine glasses, currency signs and more — as well as their varying sources for raw data — professional inspectors, consumer surveys, public reviews — it is no wonder that consumers are confused about which source offers the most impartial yet reliable information.

For the local, regional, and international food tourist looking to research and plan their next adventure, this vast selection of ratings, reviews, and guides offer little in the way of information about alternative dining and drinking options such as culinary tours, food trucks, wineries, breweries, farms, and epicurean markets.

This void in the food and drink ratings and review marketplace — coupled with the desire for authentic, peer-based point of views — has opened the door for consumers and personal bloggers to fill the gap with their own highly subjective and real-time opinions via review websites, blogs and a variety of social media platforms like Instagram and Pinterest.

Travel, Restaurant & Food Review Websites

As detailed in the *Power of the People: Word of Mouth Marketing in Food Tourism* chapter in this book, consumer review websites and other online community-based forums have permanently changed how consumers make their food travel choices.

416

Prior to the mid to late 1990s and early 2000s, when the dot com boom facilitated the explosive growth of travelogues, travel websites, and online travel agencies, consumers were limited to three main sources for dining and travel-related information: 1) printed travel and restaurant guides, 2) restaurant, bar, hotel, and destination reviews written by professional critics, and 3) friends and family (also called 'word of mouth,' as defined in the above-mentioned chapter).

But then new yet pivotal players like TripAdvisor, Expedia, Orbitz, Travelocity, and Hotels.com launched and changed the ratings and review game forever. In addition to providing consumers with web-based travel content and booking engines, this new category of industry players created online forums whereby everyday travelers could recount their travel and dining experiences and share their recommendations with the world. They also enabled site visitors to rank the very businesses they were reviewing by using a star-based system similar to those used by their guidebook predecessors. Proprietary algorithms aggregated this consumer input to assign a score on a scale of one to five stars. Algorithms were also designed to capture key words in consumer-generated review content and build tags to enable more customized online searches for specific destinations and establishments.

The popularity and success of these new business models plus the digital expansion of the MICHELIN Guide and Zagat Survey in turn opened the doors to another new category of ratings and review sites: the localized, pure-play digital restaurant review sites and food discussion forums. Yelp, Urbanspoon, CHOW, OpenTable, Gayot, Fodor's, RestaurantRow, and MenuPages are all examples of virtual community websites where like-minded consumers can post and read reviews, chat, and direct message one another about their eating, drinking, and travel experiences.

Rise of the Blogger

In its *2013 Digital Influence Report*, Technorati, a full-service media company that provides services to blogs and social media sites and connects them with advertisers and consumers, found that personal blogs outrank social networks such as Facebook and Twitter in influencing consumer purchasing decisions. Their research discovered that, in general, consumers view personal bloggers (e.g. not working for or representing a company or brand) as honest and sincere in their reviews of products and services. By presenting both the positive and negative aspects of a product, service, or destination they have personally experienced, many bloggers have garnered a reputation as a trusted source of information. As bloggers increase their reach and following, their clout increases, as does their appeal to advertisers. The food, drink, and travel blogosphere encompasses thousands of bloggers, writers and content creators worldwide, with more than 1,300 attending the 2013 TBEX (Travel Blog Exchange) Conference held in Toronto, Canada. This growing community shares a common love of all things food, drink, and travel, and are a driving force behind the evolution of ratings and reviews platforms. Their collective voice will continue to influence consumers in search of detailed and often intimate accounts of the very dining, drinking and travel experiences they are considering.

The Fate of the Professional Critic

Professional food, drink, and restaurant critics have often been perceived as an elite and privileged few, representing their well-honed palates and points of view to the masses. For decades, this select group of industry experts was a leading voice of influence in helping consumers choose where and what to eat. Much like the professional inspectors employed by the MICHELIN Guide, critics have remained a fairly anonymous group when in the field, often booking a table under a pseudonym, and going to great lengths to conceal their true identities when sampling new restaurants. The objective was to ensure the FOH and BOH teams treated him or her as an average guest, thereby ensuring a more accurate assessment of what everyone could expect in food, drink, and service. Critics approach their reviews with a discerning, evaluative, and sometimes scholarly perspective that often incorporates a rating system that they, their editors, or their publishers have developed.

In December 2010, a Los Angeles-based restaurant made headlines when it publically outed Los Angeles Times restaurant critic S. Irene Virbila. Her photo was snapped and immediately posted online by Red Medicine managing partner Noah Ellis, who justified his actions stating "Irene is not the person any of us wanted reviewing our restaurant. ... This was not a rash decision."[4]

Virbila's anonymity, which she had successfully maintained for 16 years in her role as the Times' restaurant critic, was obliterated. This sparked debate among restaurant owners, chefs, critics, and diners over the fate of professional critics and their anonymity, questioning whether it is still possible or even advisable in industry that is striving for increased transparency. The debate continues today.

The Future of Food & Drink Rating Systems

It is no wonder that consumers and the food and drink tourism industry alike are confused about which people and systems to trust. An extensive survey performed by the World Food Travel Association in 2011 revealed that there is no globally accepted system to rate food and drink experiences comprehensively and objectively. As such our industry has an opportunity to develop a globally recognized, industry-wide rating and review platform that breaks down geographic, cultural, and language barriers.

Such a system should be based on a set of criteria with inherent flexibility and scalability to accommodate all business categories that comprise the food and drink tourism industry, as well as meet the global consumer need for accuracy, immediacy, and impartiality of ratings and review information.

The New Criteria

The World Food Travel Association has been working on identifying a new set of criteria that could be used in a universal food and drink experience rating system. How your customers experience your business can involve many different criteria, from the quality of the products you use, to the service capabilities of your staff and their knowledge of local area and ingredients, to the perceived value of the experience, to minute, yet important, details such as the cleanliness of the restrooms or WCs. Even the healthfulness of food preparation or whether or not your coffee is fair trade can affect the customer experience. As a starting point, the World Food Travel Association has so far identified eight possible criteria, or success pillars, than could serve as the foundation of a new, universal rating system.

1. Memorability

One of the underlying tenets of the food tourism industry is that food and drink experiences should be memorable. Memorability does not necessarily mean white tablecloths and choreographed table service. What aspects of your business are unique and memorable for the visitor? The answer may not be the food. It could be service, venue, view, history, architecture a number of other things, or a combination of these. Or is your offering indistinguishable from other businesses or areas? For example, if you represent a destination, do you promote "outdoor recreation" as do 500 other communities within a day's drive? If you represent a restaurant or hotel, is it itself a "destination"? What is unique about your business? Are your customers or visitors affected emotionally after their food tourism experience?

2. Popularity

A second pillar of the new system could be popularity. We cannot dispute popular opinion, but do we make choices based on informed opinions, or are we the victims of large marketing budgets or groupthink? People either like a place or they do not, but do they like a place because the food or drink is actually good? Not necessarily. In coffee-loving Portland, Oregon, this author saw a line of customers literally queued up out the door of a large national coffee chain, while a locally owned café with superior locally-roasted coffee (by accounts of fellow foodies) literally right next door to this national chain, was only half as busy, with no line to place an order. How do we account for this difference? Generous marketing budgets of multinational corporations may be part of the reason influencing what we, as consumers, call desirable. That said, both cafes are popular, but for different reasons.

3. Business Readiness

How ready is your business or destination to deliver an outstanding food or drink experience? Have you done research to understand thoroughly your target market? Have you written a business plan, and if so, do you update it regularly? Do you hold annual planning meetings with your staff and/or investors? The amount of preparation that a business owner or destination marketer puts into their product is directly related to the end experience of the customer.

4. Consistency

A fourth pillar could be consistency. It is one thing to achieve high scores in customer experience at one point in time, but circumstances change all the time. Owners sell businesses, chefs move on, inns get sold, and destinations fall out of favor. What steps do you practice to ensure that your customer experience is consistent over time? Regular service training is just one way to help achieve this. You may also require employees to pass a test on the history of your business or area. If you represent a destination, you may have a destination-wide training program that a majority of your area's front-line staff have completed. Even better is that such training should be transferable to another business when the employee moves on. Measuring consistency can be hard. You could compare survey scores over time, as long as the same survey is used each time. If you do not measure consistency, you are missing out on a serious factor of the overall food and drink experience.

5. Sustainability (or Responsibility)

Another pillar could be sustainability. We recognize many ways to measure sustainability, such as economically, environmentally and socially — often called "the triple bottom line." Economic sustainability may include buying local ingredients or supplies and/or spending as much as possible of your income in your local area. Environmental sustainability means that you take quantifiable steps to reduce energy and water consumption, and to reduce solid waste. You can show exactly what your business does every year to reduce your environmental impact. Social sustainability relates to how you support your local community. For example, are you active in charity programs? One example is Jamie Oliver's program to train homeless youth to work in the kitchen and even to become chefs. What do *you* do? Not all businesses are surrounded by great local agriculture that is in season 12 months out of the year and that is OK. Customers are more demanding and judgmental than ever. How do you prove that you are a steward of sustainability in various areas of importance to today's consumer? If nothing else, your business should adopt the "reduce, reuse recycle" approach to bring it closer to triple bottom line performance goals.

6. Training

Service is a critical component of reviews and ratings. So many times, the food can be great but an irate server sours the experience, even causing irreparable damage with customers. Does your business have a formal training system in place? Do you train your staff on your business philosophy, customer service philosophy, and logistics of your daily business operations? A well-informed server (or tasting room host, or inn receptionist etc.) can make an enormous difference in the overall food or drink tourism experience.

7. Hygiene

This particular metric is of particular importance in warmer climates or in areas with less stringent food safety laws. Think about the health of your customers. Could the mayonnaise be slightly old now and should it be thrown out? Do you reuse bread from another table to save money, forgetting that someone may have coughed on that bread? Do you use water or ice in drinks that may adversely affect your customers' or visitors' gastrointestinal tract because they are not used to your local water? Such issues may seem obvious but need to be factored in.

8. Community Integration

The last suggested metric is how well integrated a business is with the local tourism office and trade associations, and vice versa. Do you operate your business like an independent unit, avoiding "distraction" from outside parties? Or perhaps you already understand the benefit of networking, and spreading the word about what you do to everyone you know in the community as well as to local businesses like the tourism office. To help foodies to find your business, or your destination, you may need to be a little more social and a little more involved in your community.

New Criteria Require New Measurement Tools

So how would new criteria be measured? The answer is most likely, in a way that has never been measured before. Popular opinion is important. Even with the problems that plague online review websites, if 3000 people like a place and only 500 do not like it, the overwhelming majority approves. That counts for something. However who performs the quality control, and how do we even define "quality"? There is something to be said for the assessor model provided that assessors could be trained in a consistent manner. However, to leave subjectivity out of the equation as much as possible, the assessors would need to rate on a pass-fail or low-medium-high basis. Trying to decide if something is really worth 3 instead of 3.5 stars is not only highly subjective, it is nearly impossible to do and could drive one crazy. More importantly, would that rating be consistent every time? However, discovering if a business owner buys a minimum percentage of produce locally, the answer is a simple yes or no. Pass or fail. That can be assessed with ease.

CONCLUSION

There is a style of ratings and reviews to appeal to every type of diner, imbiber, and food traveler. While each platform has inherent pros and cons in their metrics, savvy business owners and consumers will recognize this and gravitate to the sources and systems that work best for them.

Initial steps have been taken to further democratize the ratings and reviews that drive the food tourism industry, with the World Food Travel Association taking the lead in a move towards a universal food and drink experience rating system that can benefit both businesses and consumers. If the past 100 years have taught us anything, it is that the market is far from static, and that change is always in the works.

DISCUSSION QUESTIONS

1. Will the role of the professional restaurant, food, and hotel critic need to change over the next five years? If yes, how? If no, why not?
2. How do mystery diners or shoppers (also called "secret shoppers") fit into a food and drink rating system? Is there opportunity for their roles to expand? If so, how?
3. Consider the new rating criteria proposed by the World Food Travel Association, what are the pros and cons of each one? Which new criteria would you introduce, taking care not to overcomplicate the system?

ENDNOTES

[1] www.hotrec.eu/hotel-stars-in-europe.aspx

[2] "Lunch with M.: Undercover with a Michelin inspector" by John Colapinto, *The New Yorker*, November 23, 2009
www.newyorker.com/reporting/2009/11/23/091123fa_fact_colapinto#ixzz29X2lhNlo

[3] Anthony Bourdain: No Reservations, Paris Episode. Aired first September 6, 2010

[4] "Food critic outed and ousted from restaurant" by Christopher Reynolds and Rene Lynch, December 23, 2010, Los Angeles Times http://articles.latimes.com/2010/dec/23/local/la-me-critic-20101223

Power of the People:
Word of Mouth Marketing in Food Tourism

Jenn Bussell and Kim Roberts

Word of mouth has always been a powerful and low-to-no cost marketing tool for every category of business. Yet in the age of digital connectivity, instantaneous media, and amateur journalism, the balance of power is shifting and the collective consumer voice is now stronger than ever. As a result, word of mouth can truly make or break a food tourism business or destination in its critical first year, a seemingly daunting task for any new organization to manage strategically, tactically, and operationally.

Knowing about your brand's reputation is actually easier now than when word of mouth was comprised primarily of "water cooler conversations" among colleagues planning their next holiday, and friends and family sharing personal accounts of their latest leisure excursion over the dinner table. Today's word of mouth conversations are both offline and online, and are traceable and measurable to some extent. This chapter will discuss the new world of word of mouth marketing and provide ideas on how to leverage it for your business.

INTRODUCTION

Most marketers agree that word of mouth is one of the best marketing tools available. It is low-to-no cost yet high value. It is also one of the key drivers in how and why travelers and locals alike choose a destination to visit as well as where they will stay, eat, and drink while there.

People tend to solicit the recommendations of friends and family when it comes to decisions about where to go, what to see, where to eat and drink. Conversely, we tend to feel tremendous satisfaction and a heightened sense of value when asked our opinions. In pre-Internet days these conversations happened offline and out of earshot of a business owner.

With the explosive growth of technology and global reach of social media, digitally connected consumers simply log into their Twitter, Facebook, Foodspotting, Vine, or Yelp accounts and share their experiences in real-time — the good, the bad, and the mediocre — before their bill has even been presented. The net result is a significant increase in the 'power of the people,' and their collective social influence over food travel-related planning and purchasing decisions.

Word of Mouth Marketing

In its most simple definition, word of mouth (WOM) marketing is a nonpaid and unsolicited form of marketing in which satisfied and unsatisfied customers tell other people how they like (or dislike) a business, brand, product, service, or event.[1] According to Entrepreneur Media, word of mouth is one of the most credible forms of marketing because people who do not stand to gain personally by promoting something put their reputations on the line every time they make a recommendation or write a review. Also referred to as 'buzz' marketing, the merging of word of mouth techniques with social media networks has created a dynamic, and at times fraudulent, new communications channel for businesses launching new products and services, and for consumers to share their unfiltered opinions with the world at the press of a button. The combination of online and offline word of mouth is what marketing experts refer to as "social voice."

Despite historically being a nonpaid marketing channel, word of mouth marketing spending by marketers is expected to hit US$3 billion in 2013, according to a report based on extensive word of mouth research from PQ Media.[2] "The most influential marketer in a consumer's life is someone they know and trust, such as a family member, friend or colleague," said Patrick Quinn, President and CEO of PQ Media, in an exclusive PQ Media press release in July 2009. "This report shows that brands value and invest in word-in-mouth. Our research indicates that brands are allocating more of their budgets to long-term word-of-mouth campaigns, executing effective online and offline activities that resonate with consumers and their core groups."

The Evolution of Word of Mouth

Word of Mouth 1.0

Word of mouth revolved around the idea that one satisfied customer tells friends and family about the good service they received, or their positive experience with a product they purchased.

Word of Mouth 2.0

Brands started to capitalize on the potential of word of mouth marketing by developing strategies to actively gain brand advocates and set up affiliate models of selling, rather than simply using paid marketing and advertising tactics. The rise of online shopping, comparison and review sites, social media, and experiential marketing all helped the spread of word of mouth.

Word of Mouth 3.0

In 2012 brands started to put their businesses in the hands of the consumer. Affiliate selling moved from advertising agencies pushing links to drive sales, to consumers becoming the curators of their own websites. Consumers now recommend and share products on a variety of platforms, whether that is through virtual stores, apps or online storefronts, and earn rewards, points and cash.

Source: World Food Travel Association

Word of mouth as paid marketing allows consumers to take control of the brand message, while providing opportunities for them to earn incentives for referrals and actual sales. Tesco, Debenhams, Pizza Hut and Iceland (the actual name of a retail grocery outlet) are among a growing number of UK high street retail brands encouraging people to share products and experiences, in return for some kind of reward. In July 2012, Tesco launched its 'Share & Earn' campaign where Tesco's Facebook fans earn Clubcard points for sharing products with their friends online, as depicted in the image below.

Source: WaveMetrix, www.wavemetrix.com

In the week after the campaign launched, 54% of comments on the Tesco Facebook page recommended an item to others, compared to just 26% before the launch of Share & Earn. This shows that small incentives can have a major impact on consumer engagement and brand advocacy levels. In addition, overall consumer sentiment with Tesco became more positive with the introduction of Share & Earn, showing that it has generated an uplift in positive buzz about the Tesco brand in general.[3] Consumers may not realize that this is a paid type of word of mouth (Tesco's customers are incented to spread the word). Therefore while credibility and reliability of the word of mouth promotion is suspect, few consumers seeing the shares or likes will take the time to dissect the marketing message and realize that Tesco's supporters actually received a type of compensation for their support.

To better understand how word of mouth can be incorporated into your marketing plan, brand messaging platform, and promotional campaigns, consider the three forms of word of mouth marketing as defined by McKinsey, detailed below.[4]

Experiential

Experiential word of mouth is the most common and powerful form, typically accounting for 50 to 80 percent of word of mouth activity in any given product category. It results from a consumer's direct experience with a product or service, largely when what they experience deviates from what they expect. Keep in mind that consumers rarely complain about or praise a company when they receive what they expect. Complaints when airlines lose luggage are a classic example of experiential word of mouth, which adversely affects brand sentiment and,

425

ultimately, brand equity, reducing both receptiveness to traditional marketing and the effect of positive word of mouth from other sources. Positive word of mouth, on the other hand, can generate a tailwind for a product or service. It is important to set right expectations for consumers and consistently deliver to them high quality products and services that they expect.

Consequential

Marketing activities also can trigger word of mouth. The most common is what we call *consequential* word of mouth, which occurs when consumers directly exposed to traditional marketing campaigns pass on messages about them or the brands they publicize. The impact of those messages on consumers is often stronger than the direct effect of advertisements, because marketing campaigns that trigger positive word of mouth have comparatively higher campaign reach and influence. Marketers need to consider both the direct and the pass-on effects of word of mouth when determining the message and media mix that maximizes the return on their investments.

Intentional

A less common form of word of mouth is *intentional,* for example, when marketers use celebrity endorsements to trigger positive buzz for product launches. Few companies invest in generating intentional word of mouth, partly because its effects are difficult to measure and because many marketers are unsure if they can successfully execute intentional word-of-mouth campaigns. And hiring a celebrity is not cheap.

What marketers need for all three forms of word of mouth, is a way to understand and measure its impact and financial ramifications, both good and bad.

Why Word Of Mouth Matters

A white paper published in 2012 by MarketShare and the Keller Fay Group provided new and compelling evidence that online and offline word of mouth, or social voice, drives sales to a considerable degree, providing both direct and indirect impact on sales, amplifying the impact of marketing campaigns as people talk about the campaigns or share it via social media.[5] Their study found that social voice increased marketing effectiveness up to 54%, and that a 10% increase in social voice resulted in a sales life of up to 1.5%. They found also that offline word of mouth had a more significant impact on buying outcomes than social media.[6][7]

While it may seem challenging at first, including word of mouth in your marketing mix offers a number of real benefits for your business, including:

1. Allowing you to establish a unique identity and brand voice, online and offline.
2. Better understanding of your customers' needs and expectations.
3. Identifying potential opportunities for product or service improvements.
4. Demonstrating brand goodwill by actively engaging with customers and responding quickly and sincerely to issues or complaints voiced by first-time or long-term customers.
5. Nurturing relationships with brand loyalists and key influencers among diverse customer audiences.

Harnessing the Power of the People

A 2011 study conducted by KellerFay Group and commissioned by Procter & Gamble's in-house word of mouth marketing agency identified the following key insights about word of mouth marketing:[8]

426

1. The majority (59%) of word of mouth conversations occur at home, whether offline or online.
2. Offline conversations occur most among females, those with a higher education, older consumers and married respondents, or those living with a partner.
3. Online conversations are more likely among males and younger consumers.
4. Online word of mouth advice is more likely to come from younger consumers while those over 40 years of age provide such advice offline.
5. Most offline advice is likely to come from spouses, family or co-workers.

Despite who your target customer is, remember that a loyal customer is not born; they are a product of their environment, their expectations, and their experiences. The evolution of a brand advocate (also called a brand loyalist, evangelist, or fan) starts when someone is first made aware of your product or service. Upon trying/buying your product or service, they become a customer. Trying/buying your product or service again makes them a repeat customer. But it is not until they share their experience with your product or service that word of mouth marketing occurs. A single positive mention of your product or service starts this customer on the path to advocacy. Multiple, consistently positive experiences with your product or service — and the team behind it — is when the brand advocate emerges. This is when you can start to harness the power of the people to deliver your brand message and drive business growth. But how and where exactly do you find these amazing customers offering to evangelize your business to the masses? Step one is to answer the following questions:

1. Where do prospective customers get information about my industry in general, and my business in particular?

   a. Personal contacts (friends, family, colleagues)?
   b. Mass advertising (TV, print, radio, out-of-home)?
   c. Targeted online advertising?
   d. Direct mail?
   e. Branded collateral (brochures, sell sheets)?
   f. Industry publications and websites?
   g. Search engines?
   h. Corporate blogs?
   i. Personal blogs?
   j. Consumer review websites?
   k. Other?

2. How do prospective customers interact in my industry?

   a. Do they connect through brick and mortar and/or virtual social communities or professional networks?
   b. Are they active or passive participants?

3. What factors influence prospective customers in my industry?

   a. Price?
   b. Location?
   c. Availability?
   d. Accessibility?
   e. Prestige?
   f. Professional opinions?
   g. Personal opinions?
   h. Other?

These answers will both help to define your broader marketing ecosystem, and highlight your online and offline word of mouth marketing touch points. It is with this information that you can begin developing and implementing a plan to identify, monitor, and if you choose, engage with prospects, customers, and advocates that influence your brand through their real-world conversations, online chats, comments, likes, shares, posts, tweets and retweets.

360° Word of Mouth Marketing in Washington State Wine Country

Word of mouth occurs all the time in food and drink tourism. Doubters just look at how you yourself recommend (or not) a restaurant, wine, or beer to your friends. However, additional dialogue about the application of word of mouth can be beneficial to the food tourism industry. A business that has successfully harnessed the power of word-of-mouth marketing is Westport Winery & Vineyards By-the-Sea in the U.S. State of Washington. The hallmark of Westport Winery's success has been the ongoing ability of the owners and their staff to create and maintain honest and open lines of communication with their customers.

Founders Kim and Blain Roberts purchased the land now known as Vineyards By-the-Sea in early 2007 and opened Westport Winery a year later. Their son Dana is the winemaker and daughter Carrie serves as the general manager. Prior to entering the wine business, the Roberts previously owned the largest charter scuba diving business in Hawaii. During that time a consultant with whom they partnered shared these profound and impactful words: "Find out what your customer wants and give it to them."

The Roberts took that statement to heart when laying the ground for the then western-most vineyard in Washington State, and have faithfully practiced this principle ever since...instilling it in their employees as well.

If winery guests asked for a certain style of wine they did not produce, the Roberts and their staff would learn how to make it. In a relatively short period of time, Westport Winery went from producing 14 to 33 award-winning wines, driven in large part by their collective willingness to both listen and respond to what their customers were saying on social media, via email, and on premise at the winery. When word started trickling in that locals were experiencing a lack of social and community-centric activities in their area, the Westport Winery team responded by developing culinary classes, lectures, festivals, and tours.

When Westport Winery hears about or directly receives negative feedback from a guest, they know nothing is more valuable than a genuine and immediate apology, and that a lack of communication in any form is unacceptable. The winery recently adopted a policy of asking their guests what form of resolution or tangible remedy they preferred in the event a problem arises. It took some time, but they discovered it is not effective to simply assume what type of resolution an unsatisfied guest prefers most. The goal is to have the guest leave feeling "wowed," in spite of any service hiccups, and feeling more inclined to share a positive review of their winery experience than talking about what they disliked. However, the winery's management is even happy to have the guest tell their friends they had a problem as long as the conversation includes how the winery team listened to and, ultimately, solved the issue in the best possible way.

So far this story showcases word of mouth marketing in one direction: Guests telling their friends, family, followers, and even the winery staff about personal experiences at Westport Winery. In an effort to take a more proactive and innovative approach to managing their social (aka word of mouth) reputation, the Roberts and their staff started a two-way dialogue, telling guests what they would like from them in exchange for delivering great experiences. These requests included: "Tell your friends about the food, we'd love to have them visit, and "be sure to vote for us, we want to be named the Best Winery Destination in the Northwest."

The goal of Westport Winery & Vineyard By-the-Sea is that of a great wine: Be approachable and top-quality, be memorable and offer a strong sense of place at a great value. The owners and team take a strategic and hands-on approach to managing word of mouth marketing.

Tracking and Measuring Word of Mouth

As your brand's social voice is somewhat of a moving target, measuring the net impact of word of mouth on your business poses inherent challenges. The good news is that as quickly as this space evolves, measuring the return on investment (ROI) of word of mouth marketing is less challenging than in the past and new analytics tools are coming to market to keep pace with the market need.

Determining which tools are right for you requires a clear definition of your measurement objectives. Traditional survey methods remain the most effective tools for measuring offline brand buzz, brand health, and customer loyalty. For measuring online word of mouth, the current suite of tools is expansive and still growing. Some solutions are free, and others are fee-based depending on the level of customization and depth of data capture you seek. Some solutions offer real-time, highly customized dashboards that enable you to manage multiple accounts, use shared workspaces, and respond on multiple social networks with one click. Others are simple, effective, and lightweight, and provide the right amount of functionality. Key players in this space change from year to year, but a good source for lists of the top solution providers is Social Media Today LLC,[9] a leading curator and publisher of social media and marketing content by industry thought leaders and academics in the areas of business, marketing, and public policy.

The Dark Side of Word of Mouth Marketing

The power of word of mouth marketing lies in the honest, candid conversations and reviews by actual customers who feel compelled to share their experience with your product or service. However, with great power comes great responsibility and with the advent of consumer-generated content and review websites, unscrupulous business practices have come into play.

While it is far from the norm, there has been a significant rise in the number of fake reviews permeating dining and travel review forums that can have a potentially devastating effect on your business. These 'fakes' come in many forms, from the local restaurant owner posting a glowing five-star review of his/her own menu to the hotel employee posing as a recent guest and writing how they found bed bugs at a competitor's property. Another common form of trickery is the business that directly or indirectly solicits reviews by people who have never been to either their establishment or a competitor's. Other businesses have resorted to hiring intermediaries to offer consumers money and other incentives in exchange for a positive review. Readers are fooled into thinking these paid reviews are genuine and unbiased. This questionable activity has found a comfortable home on Freelancer.com and on Craig's List, a global online community of classified advertisements where on any given day, postings in the 'jobs' and 'gigs' categories offer users a chance to make extra cash and get free food for reviewing restaurants, bars, spas, and other businesses that play a role in the local food tourism industry. Rarely does this user have any contact with the original poster of the ad other than by email, nor do they know whether the original poster is an intermediary or the owner of the business they are asked to review. It is this anonymity and lack of accountability that makes this bad business behavior feasible and hard to eradicate.

In an attempt to crack down on this type of abuse and intent to mislead consumers, the U.S. Federal Trade Commission has implemented penalties and fines for merchants who post fake reviews about themselves, or harsh reviews about their competitors. In addition, a number of leading travel websites such as TripAdvisor police their own web properties in an effort to maintain review integrity. According to Steve Kaufer, CEO of TripAdvisor, the site takes steps to validate reviews by surveying users on their experiences. Other sites like OpenTable and Zerve only allow reviews to be submitted by people who have actually booked with them, sending an invitation for feedback via email to users shortly after their booked dinner reservation or food tour date. That said, there remains potential for fraud on many of today's consumer review websites.

As the keeper of your brand, responsibility falls to you and your team for managing and maintaining the authenticity of any content about your business, whether that content is developed by you, by your creative agency, or by consumers. Keeping a watchful eye on reviews of your business across different websites and platforms, while simultaneously becoming acquainted with your guests on a personal level during their visit with you is a great way to spot reviews that read disingenuous or fabricated. Look for concrete and specific details in reviews, details like an employee's name, a room number, or a current menu item. It is these nuances that lend credibility to a consumer review, be it in reference to a positive or negative experience. Abstract descriptions that lack specificity tend to be written by someone with more nefarious intentions.

CONCLUSION

No matter where you are in your business lifecycle, word of mouth marketing can be a powerful way to grow your business and develop impenetrable bonds between your brand and your customers. The secret to word of mouth marketing success is fairly simple and straightforward:

1. Deliver a great product or service experience, and you will garner great recommendations and reviews from your customers, both online and offline.
2. Be consistent in your delivery, and you will consistently garner positive recommendations and reviews from your customers.
3. Encourage (but do not incent) your customers to share their experiences online.
4. Invest in social media monitoring tools and hire a social media or online community manager to actively listen to online conversations about your brand where you know your customers interact.
5. Empower your team to participate in conversations when it makes sense; provide guidelines and training for how they should respond to both positive and negative commentary.

DISCUSSION QUESTIONS

1. What form of word of mouth marketing might spark conversations about a new seasonal promotion?
2. How does word of mouth integrate with and support other marketing channels, in order to impact reservations or sales?
3. How much should a business owner spend to measure word of mouth effectiveness?

ENDNOTES

[1] www.businessdictionary.com/definition/word-of-mouth-marketing.html

[2] www.pqmedia.com/about-press-20090729-wommf.html

[3] "Tesco's 'Share and Earn' scheme generates advocacy on its Facebook page" by Leonie Bulman, July 12, 2012 http://wave.wavemetrix.com/content/tesco-s-share-and-earn-scheme-generates-advocacy-its-facebook-page-00954

[4] Bughin, Jacques., Doogan, Jonathan, and Vetvik, Ole Jørgen. "A new way to measure word-of-mouth marketing: Assessing its impact as well as its volume will help companies take better advantage of buzz". McKinsey Quarterly, April 2010.

[5] "Executive Summary: Quantifying the Role of Social Voice in Marketing Effectiveness," prepared by MarketShare & KellerFay Group, October 25, 2012.

[6] Ibid.

[7] The reader should take note of this fact, although limited space in this chapter precludes a more detailed discussion of offline word of mouth promotion.

[8] Belicove, Mikal E. "Measuring Offline vs. Online Word-of-Mouth Marketing", November 23, 2011 Entrepreneur.com

[9] http://socialmediatoday.com

SECTION FIVE

WRAPPING IT UP

Bringing in the Dough: Creative Funding Models

Erik Wolf

This chapter presents and evaluates a variety of innovative ways to fund food tourism development and promotion.

INTRODUCTION

The ability to fund a business or project is the ability to give life to a business or project. In the food tourism industry we see projects that are noble and worthwhile but which are largely volunteer efforts. We also see projects without strong funding but somehow continue to carry on. And we also see projects that are in fact well-funded. Funding can come from a wide variety of sources, which we will look at and let you determine which might give your project the best chance for success.

The first question to ask is, are you funding a business, product, or a strategic destination plan? The right solutions depend on how you answer this question. This chapter looks at a variety of funding models, some of which may be more appropriate for a tourism office, while others may be better suited to an individual business. Choose what works for you and your situation.

Creating a Budget

Before an organization embarks upon its food tourism development or marketing it should create a budget along with an additional 10% contingency buffer that it can realistically implement over the course of the fiscal year. The organization should project its budget five years into the future so it will have an idea of its cash flow over the short and medium-term. If the organization does not have a strategy or project plan, it could run the risk of wasting money without a clear goal or result.[1]

One-Off Projects & Events

If your focus is a project such as a food event, it should strive to be self-funding after no more than three years. The first year is to understand the business model and make mistakes. The second year is devoted to refining the business model and correcting the mistakes from the first year. The third year is to prove the business model and demonstrate that the business can be self-funding. If a project cannot be self-funding after period of three years, then it might be considered a labor of love or a volunteer project. There is nothing wrong with projects that do not earn money, but few of us are in a position to work for free. Ideally a project should sustain itself financially.

The Small Business Funding Process

Getting funded sounds as easy as writing a business plan, applying for funding, and taking the check to the bank. While this would be nice, it usually does not work so easily or quickly. There can sometimes be a significant delay (months or even years) between when you finish your business plan and when you get funding, if you ever do get funding. Keeping that in mind, remember two important points:

1. Keep your day job. Many entrepreneurs quit their jobs to write their business plans, spend a long time to write the business plans, and are never able to qualify for loans,

grants or other revenue resources. Keep your full-time job until you have funding in place.

2. Plan on no salary for a while. Even if you get funding, you may not be in a position to take a salary for some time. Make sure you have sufficient savings to live on until you know you will have either funding or customers.

Government Grants

Grants are often available from a wide variety of government bodies, including ministries of agriculture; ministries of tourism; ministries of economic development and the regional and local equivalents of these bodies. The European Union has been known to offer grants for food tourism projects under the auspices of economic development initiatives. Some government grants for which you are unsuccessful can be applied for again in subsequent years. In such situations when follow-on funding is available, it is not uncommon for the amount of the next grant to be less than that of the first. In such scenarios it should be the goal of the funding entity to wean the recipient organization off of the funding entity after a period of time, often approximately three years.

Foundation Grants

There exist both private and public foundations whose business is to provide grants to nonprofit organizations for a variety of reasons. Some may include capacity building such as hiring staff and expanding office space, while other grants may be project related, with a clear expected project outcome and measurable results. Foundation grants are usually restricted by geography so it is best to check which grants might be available in your particular area. A library or a conversation with an economic development officer are good ways to begin your search.

Cooperative Funding

For one or more individual businesses, one option may be to fund the business or a cooperative project together with one or more businesses. For example, a group of restaurants on one street could come together and fund a cooperative marketing project, such as a walking map and guide to dining and activities on the street. While one might view such a project as competitive, our view is that the bigger the (financial) pie, the larger is everyone's slice.

Self-Funding and Realistic Needs

For an individual business, funding a project or business yourself might be feasible. Bank loans tend to be very difficult to qualify for, interest rates are high and such loans also require collateral, which is an uncomfortable risk for the business owner. First, consider what you wish to buy. Do you need all new equipment for a café kitchen? Do you need the most prestigious (and expensive) advertising agency? Do you need to print menus on the highest quality paper? Maybe you can buy used furniture. Compare prices online to find better prices. Ask your local supplier to match the price of something you found online. Lower your expectations a bit to see how you can afford more for less. Then see how you can build a budget for your project. Do you have savings? Is getting a cash advance on credit cards an option? The goal is cash in, not cash out (i.e. be stingy with spending money). Your available cash will go a lot further.

Friends & Family

Maybe you do not have quite enough money to fund your project or business, but you may not need to go as far as considering a formal bank loan. Could friends or family provide a short-term, low interest loan? It cannot hurt to ask. Negotiate a written agreement with repayment terms. Use an online tool like www.Prosper.com to track the repayments and make it official.

Seed Funding

In some cities, business incubators exist to provide small seed capital funding and guidance to start-up companies. One example is GrowLab in Vancouver, BC, Canada.[2] Another is the Portland Incubator Experiment (PIE) in Portland, Oregon, USA.[3] A third is StartUp Chile.[4] Incubators like these exist around the world. Typically, the incubator invests a small amount of capital (e.g. the local equivalent of US$15,000-40,000). In exchange, the business gives up a small percentage ownership in the company (e.g. often 5-12%, depending on the terms you negotiate). One benefit of incubators and their seed funding is that typically advisors are available to help guide your startup towards success. For some, this type of arrangement may be exactly what you are looking for. Check in your area to see if you have access to a similar business incubator program.

Bank Financing

If you have a "bullet-proof" business plan and collateral to secure a loan, bank financing may also be an option. The major advantage of such financing is that you know the loan terms up front. Painful negotiations behind closed doors with Silicon Alley venture capitalists are not required. When your bank loan is paid off, you still have 100% of your equity. For start-up food, drink, travel and hospitality businesses, however, securing a bank loan can be hard. It banking circles, the food tourism industry is not well understood. We do not import supplies from overseas to make widgets in a factory, which will then be shipped out to a network of distributors. Our industry's businesses do not fit the classic mold to whom banks like to lend. That prejudice is slowly beginning to change, especially in agricultural communities where the value of entrepreneurship is appreciated, as is the investment in the agricultural system. A rare but great example is the Bank of North Dakota[5] in the US State of North Dakota. It is a state-funded bank that guarantees loans to agricultural producers and food manufacturers.

Customer Revenue

Often overlooked, revenue from your current and future customer base is an additional way to fund a business endeavor. If you use this approach, you might be able to ask customers to pre-pay for future orders. You might also be able to contract with a larger distributor to carry your product once it is produced. If a distributor (customer) believes in your product, they might give you a small advance on the payment.

Third Parties

Sometimes a business or even a project needs a larger investment that is beyond the reach of individuals and small companies. An example might be the development of a culinary history museum or renovation of a historic chef's house as a culinary attraction. Consider pursuing investment from third party angel investors or venture capital (VC) firms. Going after a VC is actually easier in today's business climate than it has ever been. This is because VCs were getting a lot of competition from angel investors and learned they needed to be more competitive. Therefore many VCs now fund smaller projects with better terms for the business. Still, securing VC or angel funding takes a lot of hard work and connections.

Crowdfunding

Crowdfunding solutions like Kickstarter and Indiegogo have received tremendous press over the years. Overnight successes like Nomiku, a product designed to bring sous vide cooking to the home chef, raised a phenomenal US$586,061 in less than 30 days. Some crowdfunding solutions are international (Indiegogo), and others like Kickstarter are country-specific (currently US and UK only). Wikipedia has an excellent list of crowdfunding platforms and the countries they serve.[6] Crowdfunding is not a panacea. Most projects eligible for funding on these platforms need to be for a short-term project with a specific end goal. You must actively market your fundraising campaign and you need a large network of engaged supporters to help spread the word. Succeeding without any of these circumstances will be difficult.

Special Purpose Taxation Assessment

For public-funded organizations and some tourism offices, a special tax assessment might offer a short-term solution to fill a budgetary need. About ten years ago, the US State of Oregon recognized the need to raise money for tourism promotion. The state's tourism office was ranked in the bottom five of the 50 US states in terms of its budget funding. With a lot of lobbying and negotiating, the state's tourism industry was able to pass a 1% tax increase on lodging in the state. Almost overnight, the state's tourism budget nearly quintupled. Today, Travel Oregon (the state's DMO) now has the budget to hire sufficient staff and engage in creative and forward thinking tourism development and marketing. This never would have been possible had the bill to increase lodging tax by 1% not passed. One caveat: if the funding need is short-term, build in an automatic expiration date for the tax. Failing to do so could incur the wrath of visitors and residents alike. If the funding need is long-term, then plan accordingly. A second caveat: visitors resent being singled out for taxation. In the example of the State of Oregon, there was already a lodging tax, so adding another 1% was not perceived as a new tax and it was a minimum burden to bear. It was also a tax paid by visitors, not residents. Adding a brand new tax to a restaurant bill will anger residents and visitors alike. The Canadian province of British Columbia is still feeling the effects of a major misunderstanding of the proposed benefits of consolidation both provincial and federal taxes. The mistake severely hurt the province's foodservice sector. The program backfired and the taxes have been separated again. Use a special purpose taxation assessment lightly, if at all.

Offering Equity

Another funding option is the issuance of shares of stock, but that takes considerable planning, with many legal considerations that vary considerably by country. The issuance of stock requires a valuation, which is often hard to estimate with a new company. To avoid having to set a valuation at a very early stage, many start-ups choose to issue convertible notes instead of equity. If you use convertible notes, you avoid having to set a valuation.

A quite new alternative to convertible notes is "convertible equity," which is essentially convertible debt without the repayment feature at maturity and without interest. Y Combinator has very recently come out with something similar to convertible equity, called "simple agreement for future equity" or "safe."[7]

No matter how you intend to structure a proposed financing, there is a law in the United States that US businesses may only solicit to "accredited investors," i.e., high net-worth individuals within the meaning of the U.S. securities laws, with whom the business owner has a preexisting relationship and not through any kind of general solicitation or general advertising. If you engage in general solicitation or general advertising, there are additional and often undesirable measures to take before any investment can be accepted. While these regulations apply to the solicitation of investment to US residents and companies, other countries may have similar strict solicitation rules.

Also, if you have not already formed an entity and issued founders' shares, you should engage legal counsel to do that as soon as possible. At least by US law, if you issue founders' shares for a nominal price too close to when you conduct fundraising, adverse tax consequences can flow to the founders.

The equity landscape is changing quickly and varies considerably by country. While this section presents US-centric advice, it is still food for thought. Be sure to consult with your legal counsel to achieve optimal results for your investment scenario.

CONCLUSION

There is no "one size fits all" solution when it comes to funding resources. Different national laws and banking systems, differing cultural norms and different business or project needs can all affect which path you pursue. Weigh each choice carefully. Ask within your professional network to see if anyone you know has used any of these tools and see what their experience was. Will they share with you lessons learned? Good luck in your business or project.

DISCUSSION QUESTIONS

1. Which funding models might work for your business or your area?
2. How might a tourism office creatively fund its annual operating budget?
3. Consider a scenario where you ask your current or future customers to pre-pay for a product you will produce in the future. What kind of reassurance could you provide to your customers that you will actually deliver the product?

ENDNOTES

---

[1] Please refer to the *Business Model Generation* chapter for more information.

[2] http://growlab.ca

[3] www.piepdx.com

[4] http://startupchile.org

[5] www.banknd.com

[6] http://en.wikipedia.org/wiki/Comparison_of_crowd_funding_services

[7] http://blog.ycombinator.com/announcing-the-safe-a-replacement-for-convertible-notes

Sharing the Recipe: Metrics in Food & Drink Tourism

Wendy Lange-Faria and Erik Wolf

Gone are the days of undocumented spending. Any campaign or project today needs clear metrics. Today's business owners, especially of small and locally owned operations, are keener than ever to justify cash outlays. In this chapter we will look at the importance of measuring the ROI (return on investment) in food tourism. How do we measure success in our industry? Which food tourism sectors or businesses have been most successful and why? What are the top success indicators? By the end of this chapter, you should have an idea of a measurement tools that you can apply to your own food tourism campaigns and projects.

INTRODUCTION

Defining success in food tourism can be elusive at times. How does one ascertain whether or not a visitor is happy with their food experience? How does one measure whether or not food tourism initiatives or projects are successful? Indeed, what exactly should we measure? Do we measure profit alone? Visitor satisfaction? Environmental costs? Any and all of these are relevant concerns when measuring success in food tourism.

The Triple Bottom Line: People. Planet. Profit.

Success or lack thereof may be determined by any number of means, including change in number of arrivals, change in duration of stay, change in visitor spending, change in in word-of-mouth messaging, change in quality service ratings, and change in impact on environmental factors. In some instances, at first glance, success may appear hard to measure, in which case we suggest breaking down the proposed metric further to the point where ROI measurement is easier. These questions encompass measurements of people, planet and profit, all of which are important to creating a sustainable business. This concept is particularly relevant to food tourism. True success in all three areas can lead to a memorable visitor experience, an increase in visitor spending, and arguably add value to the community.

People

Since visitors are at the heart of food tourism, finding ways to communicate the food tourism product through marketing is critical to business growth. Prominent actions that can drive a positive return on investment are as follows:

- Launching new models of public and private cooperation for promoting a strong and coherent image internationally.
- Collaborating with chefs and local producers for the preservation of gastronomic knowledge and the promotion of the destination.
- Taking a proactive approach to image-building across all major channels of media, tourist guides, food blogs and social networks.
- Developing food and beverage exports and a network of good quality restaurants abroad.
- Being honest and accurate with marketing, to set realistic expectations. The level of a tourist's satisfaction with a destination depends largely on the product's performance compared to the tourist's expectations.[1]

Staying current by networking with people not only within your own area, but globally as well, is key to staying competitive in the food tourism arena.

A good example of collaboration and the proactive approach suggested by the above bullets is Savour the Flavours of Dumfries & Galloway in Scotland. Dumfries & Galloway is the second largest region in Scotland and geographically diverse, not to mention an area that is sparsely populated. It was faced with the challenge of bringing people together to communicate, work together, and share the array of food in this area of Scotland.

Noteworthy from the Savour the Flavours initiative is the annual September food festival celebration called Flavour Fortnight.[2] Spanning the entire region of Dumfries & Galloway, this festival is now in its fourth year. In 2012, it drew over 100 different events and activities to promote the offerings of this part of Scotland. More than 10,000 locals and visitors participated in the events which included a plethora of activities, such as producer days, tastings and samplings, special menus, collaborative food festivals, wild food foraging, talks, and workshops. Today, Flavour Fortnight is a key driver for tourism in Dumfries & Galloway.[3]

An industry driven initiative, this organization illustrates the pride and passion that bring together everyone from the artisan food producer to the independent retailer to the small hotel and café sourcing the best of the region to drive the project forward.[4] The food tourism strategy is broken down into four component parts that center around the following people:

- Producers: Dumfries & Galloway identifies new producers, explore ways to help get produce to market, and assist with funding and packaging issues for small producers.
- End user: i.e. restaurants, hotels. People have to be able to see, taste and experience local produce if they are going to use it so the producers and restaurateurs are very much interrelated.
- Consumer: the consumer needs to be educated to understand about the quality producers in the region and gradually build up a mark of people who recognize where the produce comes from (i.e. be able to trace the journey of where food comes from).
- Children: getting into schools. Be sure that kids understand fresh produce and especially local produce.[5]

Savour the Flavours was very much a grassroots movement and now is driven by the needs of the industry. Some of the specific outcomes of this initiative are outlined as follows:

- Drawing the region's farmers' markets together to explore a joined up approach, which has led to the establishment of the Dumfries & Galloway Farmers' and Communities Markets Association
- A group of leading chefs from across Dumfries & Galloway have joined forces to support Savour the Flavours to launch the D&G Chefs Association. The organization aims to raise professional standards across the region with training, mentoring and support; encouraging the use of fresh, local ingredients by chefs, cooks and caterers throughout Dumfries & Galloway and it will continue to work closely in helping raise the profile of Dumfries & Galloway as a food destination.
- Development of a private chef to chef forum on the Savour the Flavours website for knowledge sharing and exchange.
- Supporting members who are looking for advice and support in terms of growing their businesses, updating marketing and promotional literature.
- Highlighting opportunities to members to encourage business growth.[6]

Liz Ramsay, project manager for Savour the Flavours says about the organization, "By working together with our committee members and the business community we have created a forward momentum that is very much driven by the grassroots approach of Savour the Flavours. The

442

micro business, the artisan producer, the independent retailer, the small hotel and cafes that go out of their way to source the very best that our region has to offer and that invest their products and services with such pride and passion. These are our local food heroes, these are the people who are helping to drive this project forward and these are the people who, together, are co-creating a strong, vibrant and sustainable food and drink industry in Dumfries and Galloway."[7]

While the approach above outlines some of what Dumfries & Galloway has achieved, the table below provides a snapshot of their success metrics.

What's measured	• The impact of the projects to businesses in the region (quantitative/qualitative). • The effectiveness of the program in meeting the objectives related to funders.
How it's measured	• Stakeholder interviews (DMOs, funders) • Review of activities/milestones (project management level) • Sub-project interviews (actual chefs association, farms, community association and school programs departments) • Business/member surveys (online) • Visitor survey during the events at the festival
Funding mechanism	• Dumfries & Galloway LEADER program (government program for communities revitalization projects) at 50% • Dumfries & Galloway Council at 50% • Fixed nature of project by project funding poses a constant challenge
ROI metric	• In the case of the festival, financial impact year over year is measured • Measure whether there is a yearly increase in interest and profits for individual businesses participating in the initiatives

The measure of success or defining moment is the point when the region becomes a food destination in its own right. The impetus is to bring people to the region because of strength of the local producers who have the wonderful produce. This strength of local producers will be how success is measured and what the organization is working towards.

Planet

While it may appear out of place to some, we can no longer ignore the cost to our planet and our environment. With an increase in global population and corresponding increase in the number of people traveling, for both leisure and business, the need for sustainability is here to stay. That is to say that today's food tourism strategies now need to calculate the costs and benefits of adhering to sustainability practices and protocols. The United Nations World Tourism Organization summarizes practices that food tourism businesses in today's world should consider:

- Decrease the food environmental footprint through encouraging more local and seasonal product use.
- Commit to social responsibility by supporting local food businesses, farmers and entrepreneurs.

- Invest in agritourism opportunities that enable the visitor to partake in local farm activities and gain an appreciation for what all is involved in food production and the food experience in its entirety, from field or hoof to plate. And furthermore, "[b]uilding agritourism initiatives through collaboration between tourism ministries, agriculture ministries, NGOs and local businesses helps inject investment back into local communities, sustainable tourism and agriculture practices."[8]

An excellent example of a region taking the culinary offerings to this level of sustainability is that of the wine region of the Napa Valley (USA). The following except outlines how sustainability lends to their success, and how it can contribute to the success of any food tourism organization.

"Along with our hospitality programs, the infrastructure of our wine-growing region has experienced a renaissance in sustainability practices that define the Napa Valley as second-to-none in land use, transportation, water usage and education of the local community. It is well-recognized that "the sustainability of Napa as a visitor destination involves the relationship between the basic agricultural character of the county, the existing public infrastructure and the range of options offered to visitors." [9] However, it is critical that wine tourism businesses realize the importance of their organizations to the overall guest experience. In many cases, wineries in emerging regions may view wine tourism as a secondary activity to their primary operation of growing and producing wine. This is a perspective that is diminishing, but still lingers in many organizations. A wine tourism company needs to determine the priority of being guest-focused, or product-focused. Most will choose and attempt to achieve both objectives, which is exactly what they need to do to be successful."[10]

It should be noted at this point that Napa Valley has been widely recognized as being first in class when it comes to sustainability. The Napa Valley Vintners have really been a driver and industry lead in the Napa Green Winery and Napa Green Farming – devising leading edge ideas and technologies that have been recognized in the sustainability world.[11]

Some of the actual success metrics shared by Visit Napa Valley are outlined in the following table.[12]

What's measured	<ul><li>Lodging guests</li><li>Visiting friends and relatives staying in peoples' homes (VFR)</li><li>Day trip guests</li><li>Nights stayed are the metric, food tourism being a subset of the evaluation (the longer people stay, the more they will be engaging in food and drink related activities)</li></ul>
How it's measured	<ul><li>Visitor intercept study questionnaire which interviews a random sample of guests around Napa Valley</li><li>Lodging guest survey</li><li>Telephone survey of Napa county homes</li><li>Economic impact study (most recently in 2012 and previously in 2006)</li><li>Smith Travel Research data to evaluate room revenues</li></ul>
Funding mechanism	<ul><li>Private, not for profit agency (Visit Napa Valley) funded by the Special Assessment on Lodging (the Tourism Improvement</li></ul>

	District Assessment; a lodging assessment that goes directly to private industry such as Visit Napa Valley)
	• For specific events, private sponsors and donors are solicited
ROI metric	• Measured by amount of room revenue generated and growth. Food tourism success is measured anecdotally and considered to be secondary (a subset of rooms).

The measure of success is dependent on a number of factors for Napa Valley, but one of the defining measures that differentiate them is the commitment to sustainability.

Profit

The Ontario Culinary Tourism Alliance (OCTA) is a not-for-profit organization dedicated to bringing together viticulture, agriculture, and aquaculture to promote food tourism in the Canadian province of Ontario. Its mandate is to foster strong relationships between the various stakeholders in the food tourism industry.

How organizations like this are funded is always an interesting discussion. Since OCTA is the organization chosen to implement the Government of Ontario's 10-year strategy and action plan for food tourism, its funding model and evaluation plan provide a useful example of how one destination is approaching financial metrics.

In a time of fiscal restraint, a number of organizations that were previously dependent on government grants are now forced to find alternate sources for funding. Founded in 2005 and originally fully funded by the Government of Ontario, by 2008, the organization was receiving 80% of its funding through two provincial ministries, namely agriculture and tourism. The other 20% came from industry stakeholders via membership dues and project funds. In 2012 a major funding shift took place, with only 20% of funding arising from government and the remainder from industry participants and project funds. The current model as of 2013 is 20% of the funding from government grants, 15% from membership fees, and 65% from consulting fees and project funds.[13] Rebecca LeHeup, Executive Director for OCTA surmises that this new funding model will continue to lead the organization into the future.

The OCTA Four-Year Culinary Tourism Strategy expands on and updates the original Provincial Strategy and Action Plan 2005-2015 that was created in 2006 and was intended to drive the Ontario food tourism sector. The strategic plan outlines 10 goals and objectives and, as one would expect, the corresponding outcomes and strategies by which to accomplish those outcomes. A vision is critical to any strategy and the one projected by Ontario is as follows.

"By 2015, culinary tourism in Ontario is valued as a leading contributor to a vibrant and sustainable tourism economy in the province."[14] The leading values of the strategy are commitment, collaboration and communications — values that permeate every one of the 10 goals and objectives. One of the goals set forth by OCTA, specifically on the funding side of the strategy is "a funding structure and mechanism to access funds for food tourism projects that is both long-term and sufficient to address the priorities of stakeholders."[15] Specifically, the funding mechanism formulated for the OCTA is as follows:

- Develop a financial funding model. OCTA has worked with the provincial government and other funders to augment the membership model designed to support annual operational costs.
- Invest in communities and regions. OCTA continues to work with 26 destinations and communities to support the development of food tourism.

- Create seed funding for regions creating food tourism product strategies. OCTA has been able to invest in some regional initiatives that support food tourism.
- Invest in research. OCTA has been able to support several research initiatives that help OCTA achieve its goals and objectives.
- Invest in recognition program for food tourism – OCTA awards.
- Create workbooks and resource materials – toolkits and website.
- Invest in partnerships.[16]

The actual goals, and ultimately, criteria for success, as outlined by the Ten Year Ontario Culinary Tourism Strategy and Action Plan, are outlined as follows:

1. [Competent] Leadership
2. Market-ready or near-market-ready culinary products and resources
3. Integrated strategy
4. Partnership and community-based collaboration
5. Financial support and performance measures
6. Destinations with good access from key origin markets
7. Sufficient market intelligence
8. Culinary tourism resources distinctive to the region
9. Destination with multiple culinary tourism experiences
10. An effective destination marketing organization (DMO)[17]

The goals give rise to expected outcomes. Measurement is based on what has been accomplished on each project (project outcomes measured against the goals and objectives). As with any project, the goal is to deliver results on time, on budget and within the scope of the goal/objective.

In terms of measuring success, so far OCTA has identified three measures of success: client satisfaction, membership satisfaction and project goal achievement. That being said, one of the project outcomes is to design and implement a balanced scorecard (see below). The scorecard is a Harvard University model attributed to Dr. Robert Kaplan and Dr. David Norton, and lauded for its usefulness in measuring both the financial and non-financial measures of business success.[18] The OCTA is in the process of developing a balanced scorecard to measure its success.

A Balanced Scorecard

How this model might work in the food tourism context is outlined in the table below. The individual performance measures are derived from the business or organization's strategic planning mission statement and goals. Each organization will have different standards of what success will look like and correspondingly how to measure that level of success. A balanced scorecard approach is outlined in Table 1 below.

Any tourism business or organization undertaking this form of evaluation of course would begin with its own mission statement and from there, create a list of strategic objectives. These objectives, remembering that they should arise out of the mission statement, would form the backbone of all the activities in which the organization engages. In other words, you need to devise a strategy that starts with the mission statement. Once these items are in place, you would develop the food tourism scorecard. This balanced scorecard approach, which is labeled here the "food tourism scorecard," is a solid, well-researched means by which to measure the financial and non-financial metrics of success for any food tourism related business.

Table 1: Hypothetical model of a food tourism scorecard. Each sector shows one category that determines success. In each category, the organization creates specific goals and tangible ways to measure those goals. Categories and sample measurement techniques are provided.

PROFIT

Food tourism financials (shareholder value)

How do we add value to the food visitor while keeping our costs under control, and in the case of a business, generate revenue?

In this quadrant list your objectives, your measures (examples in bullets below), the revenue targets, and the activities that would be implemented.

- Cash flow
- Sales growth

PEOPLE

Food tourism visitors (customer perceptions)

Who are our visitors and how do we create value for them?

In this quadrant list your objectives, your measures (examples below), your target, and the actual initiatives you are planning.

- Number of repeat visitors
- % of new sales that are derived from a new food product/experience (customer acceptance)
- Market share
- Number of requests for information on specific food products in an area
- Feedback surveys from visitors
- Word of mouth metrics derived from social media initiatives

PEOPLE

Food tourism internal business operations (business excellence)

Which business processes do we need to really be good at to excel?

In this quadrant list your objectives, the measures, the target (your aim), and the initiatives (some examples are below).

- Tourism business awards
- Quality assurance
- Movement to being a self-supporting organization versus a government grant supported organization
- Service quality standards development in the food industry

PEOPLE & PLANET

Food tourism innovation/learning

What do we need to do as an organization to grow, to keep with the trends, to stay modern, to stay "ahead" with the times and current with the needs of our food visitors?

In this quadrant list your objectives, your measures (some examples are below), your target, and the list of activities you will engage in to reach this target.

- Time taken to develop new tourism experience
- Reducing the environmental footprint
- % of local foods being used in restaurants

Cluster Analysis

Lastly, cluster analysis can be used in situations where it is helpful to gain an aggregate view of data. For example, when the Association performs a Food Tourism Asset Inventory Analysis, the reporting can include cluster analysis, which is a statistical tool that uncovers associations, patterns and relationships among large amounts of data. This can especially be used in factoring a return on investment. A cluster analysis is performed during the first asset inventory analysis. Then a period of time passes, such as an annual fiscal cycle. Later, another asset inventory analysis is performed and cluster analysis on the second set is performed. We are able to draw conclusions about the overall performance of the development efforts by analyzing the differences (either growth or shrinkage) between the first and last analyses.

CONCLUSION

At the beginning of this chapter we determined that any food tourism business first needs to create its own definition of success. Success also must be examined through the lens of the visitor, the perspective of profit for a business or a region, and finally, encompass sustainability, arguably the three pillars of food tourism success. Food tourism ROI can be somewhat difficult to measure for an organization.

While funding models may differ, many regions depend on some form of government and/or industry partnership to fund programs or projects. The project faces serious limitations if the only measure of return on investment is financial. To measure success as a whole, take into account non-financial measures, incorporate the three measures of success proposed in this chapter (people, planet, profit) and implement a balanced scorecard approach for food tourism businesses and organizations.

DISCUSSION QUESTIONS

1. What is your definition of success in food tourism?
2. In these times of government cutbacks and global business, propose a type of funding model that you could use in your business. What are some of the drawbacks and advantages of each type of funding model?
3. Create a food tourism scorecard for your business. Decide what you will measure under each category and then how you will practically measure each one of your defined goals.

ENDNOTES

[1] UNWTO. (2012). Flavours of the Silk Road International Conference on Food, Culture, & Tourism: Global report on food tourism. Baku-Azerbaijan, 6-7 September 2012. Retrieved June 1, 2013 from http://bit.ly/ZC8K26
[2] www.flavourfortnight.co.uk
[3] Ramsay, Liz. (October 12, 2012). Personal Communications.
[4] Ibid.
[5] Savour the flavours. Retrieved June 1, 2013 from http://bit.ly/1aPgsWr. [YouTube.]
[6] Ramsay, Liz. (October 12, 2012). Personal Communications.
[7] Ibid.
[8] UNWTO. (2012). Flavours of the Silk Road International Conference on Food, Culture, & Tourism: Global report on food tourism. Baku-Azerbaijan, 6-7 September 2012. Retrieved June 1, 2013 from http://bit.ly/ZC8K26
[9] Napa County League of Governments Task Force, Page 41, May 2005
[10] MacNeil, I. (n.d.). Lessons for emerging wine regions: Napa Valley transportation & eco-tourism. Napa Valley College Hospitality & Tourism Management. [Electronic version.]
[11] Napa Valley Vintners. (2013). Retrieved June 13, 2013 from http://bit.ly/13l39oa
[12] Visit Napa Valley. (2013). Retrieved June 13, 2013 from http://bit.ly/11chqLH
[13] Rebecca LeHeup. (2012). Personal Correspondence.
[14] OCTA. (2011). Ontario's Four-Year Culinary Tourism Strategy and Action Plan 2011-2015. Accessed electronically June 7, 2013 from http://bit.ly/12wZlp0
[15] OCTA . (n.d.) Ontario's four-year food tourism strategy and action plan 2011-2015. Retrieved June 1, 2013 from http://bit.ly/yCHEDX
[16] Ibid.
[17] Ibid.
[18] Balanced Scorecard Institute. 2013. Balanced Scorecard Basics. Retrieved June 8, 2013 from http://bit.ly/bn09GQ

Consumer Changes in Food & Drink Tourism

Erik Wolf

Since the Association's founding in 2003, the food tourism industry has evolved, and consumers have matured. In essence, a "new" kind of food consumer has emerged, one that is better educated, and also more demanding with regard to food and drink. This chapter looks at recent consumer changes and predicts how consumers will continue to evolve as active participants in the food and drink tourism industries.

INTRODUCTION

The year 2013 marked the tenth anniversary of the founding of the World Food Travel Association and of the formal food tourism industry.[1] In the industry's early years, the notion of "cuisine" was not as widely appreciated as it is today. The media has created a legion of educated consumers, and technology has armed them with powerful new tools like smartphones, apps and fast mobile broadband access. Food travelers of today are not what they were 10 years ago, nor are they the same consumers we will see 10 years into the future.

Consumers & Media

In the past decade, we have witnessed a deluge of food and travel television programming. We have also seen the cross-over of food shows on travel channels and vice versa. Shows like Anthony Bourdain's *No Reservations* or Rachel Ray's *$40 a Day* are purely standalone food travel shows. This plethora of programming has created a very well educated group of consumers. It is not unusual for foodies now to know more about the food than the wait staff at the business in question. The advent of chef reality shows like *Master Chef*, *Iron Chef* and Gordon Ramsay's *Kitchen Nightmares* continue to feed the appetites of hungry consumers. Celebrity chefs like Wolfgang Puck and Jamie Oliver are now household names around the world. It is not an exaggeration to say that the public is obsessed with food and chefs. Shows like *Man v. Food* only underscore this point. The phenomenon is not limited to the United States. Food television is on the rise in many countries around the world.

Consumers & Technology

The past 10 years have brought the advent of smartphones, along with pervasive broadband internet access and smartphone applications that give us a tremendous amount of information at our fingertips. Today we can go to a restaurant and get an approximate calorie count and other nutritional information about our meal. Apps like Fooducate or FoodMeter help us shop for groceries and present healthier alternatives to limit sugar intake, avoid wheat gluten, and other specific criteria. Or the Tesco QR app which helps Korean consumers do their grocery shopping while they are waiting for the subway in downtown Seoul.[2] Consumer review websites like FoodSpotting and Yelp help guide us towards suitable food purchase decisions, although their reliability is arguably hit and miss. Imagine being able to make these kinds of well-informed and fast decisions 10 or 20 years ago? It was not possible then, but it is now.

Technology will continue to improve and make it easier for us to participate successfully in food tourism. When Google Goggles become commonplace, we will be able to walk down a street and see real-time reviews of every restaurant we pass. Imagine being able to link a smartphone app with your car's GPS so you can navigate to only those wineries in the area that produce a claret or sangiovese that has achieved a minimum score of your choosing. Or wave a wristband over your food to assess its nutritional value and ingredients.[3] Consumers will continue to be better educated because websites, mobile apps and new hardware devices will deliver more relevant content than ever, with better search results, and in a timelier manner.

Power of the People

The popularity of websites like TripAdvisor, Yelp and UrbanSpoon, despite their criticisms, mean that the voice of consumers is more powerful than it ever was. Like it or not, consumers have the power to make or break a new restaurant, brewpub or really any kind of food or drink tourism business. These websites are not without their limitations and flaws, however. For example, there is nothing to stop a disgruntled former employee from writing a scathing review about the restaurant where he used to work. In time, the accuracy, reliability and trustworthiness of reviews like these will improve. Refer to the *Power of the People: Word of Mouth Marketing in Food Tourism* chapter for more information about the power of the people.

Consumers & Lifestyle

There is a trend in the developing and developed world alike towards a more comfortable lifestyle. The very mention of "wellness tourism" and "vegan spa cuisine" no longer gets strange looks from people. Consumers are learning new, healthy eating behaviors and taking their behaviors on the road with them. Combine a love of good food and drink with family travel, pet travel, or gay and lesbian travel and the astute marketer will see a nearly unlimited array of product development and marketing opportunities. Special interest travel has become mainstream.

The End of Demographics?

For many years, marketers sought to build elaborate profiles of their consumers. Data points that were collected included age, gender, level of education completed, postal code and block of residence and other quantifiable data. Then something happened. People did not behave as predicted. Marketers realized that not all women eat salads, and not all men eat steak. The era of psychographics was born, where we began to understand more about the behavior that people exhibit when making purchase decisions. Marketers now realize that not all Baby Boomers or Generation X people behave the same. For example, not all Baby Boomers are rich and appreciate gourmet experiences. Now our understanding of marketing is evolving yet again. Enter today's era of nanodemography,[4] which introduces the notion of individuality and time into the equation. In other words, we can and do change our preferences and behavior many times per day, depending on where we are, who we are with, and what we have just heard or seen. With the advent of smartphones and broadband mobile internet, consumers are able to source enough information fast enough to make more informed — and more accurate — decisions, and to change our opinions, likes and preferences at a moment's notice. We might want a steak one night, but then hear about floods in Bangladesh and the next night seek a Bengali restaurant to show our support for the plight of the owner's relatives in that country. Readers interested in learning more about motivations for food and drink purchase decisions should read the chapter *How Foodies Make Decisions* in this book.

Shifting Brand Loyalties

There is no arguing that consumers fiercely support their mega-burger and mega-coffee preferences. That said, we see changes in those loyalties occurring every day. Reasons for a shift in brand loyalty can include product price, company reputation (and transparency or lack thereof), celebrity endorsement and new product entries. While some consumers value the €200 bottle of Dom Perignon, or SEK 1250 for a multi-course menu at Sweden's Fäviken, rated in the 2013 list of the top 50 of the world's restaurants, many consumers are finding new joys in less expensive food and drink experiences. For example, authentic chicken vindaloo from a hawker stand in Singapore, or a Whiffie pie from a food cart in Portland, Oregon, USA. The price aside, each is a worthwhile food and drink *experience*. New research like that of PsychoCulinary profiling will help small business and destination marketers to better match consumer preferences with the product offered.

Dichotomy among Lesser & More Developed

The 2007-2008 Global Financial Crisis taught us that the presumably "developed" world is indeed financially vulnerable. The severity of the crisis has forever changed how developed world residents consume. Conversely, the formerly "lesser developed" world is quickly accessing the same opportunities as were previously available in the more developed world. While more opportunities are available to more consumers everywhere, not all consumers behave in the same manner. Emerging market consumers buy things that express their personality much more (62%) than their counterparts in other countries (20%) and similarly, emerging market consumers consider the environmental impact of what they buy more (64%) than developed market consumers (32%).[5] In much of the world, the mobile broadband network has surpassed terrestrial broadband network in both number of subscribers and speed.[6] The implication for food tourism professionals is that, depending on your target market and your type of business, you might be better served by a mobile website or app than a regular website.

Renunciation of Waste

As the world becomes a more expensive place, and prices soar for everything including beef, bottled water and liquor, consumers are thinking twice about two kinds of waste: 1) waste of money; and 2) waste of food. While there is some truth to the joke often made by international travelers to the USA, that one meal portion can serve their family of four, portion sizes in the USA are on the decrease. Restaurateurs are paying more attention to what gets thrown away or sent back to the kitchen. The march towards healthy eating continues, with obesity, diabetes, high cholesterol and gluten-free issues on the top of consumer minds. Consumers are taking this new behavior with them out to eat or when they travel as well. That means the free bread and tap water are increasingly being replaced with better quality bread or bottled water that must be paid for. And as for waste of money, consumers are thinking twice if a £20 bowl of pasta is really worth £20. We are also seeing consumers order starters as main courses, which saves both calories and money. To be fair, the renunciation of waste is a relatively new approach in consumer behavior, which does not seem rooted in any one particular geographic area. It is being embraced by a new kind of consumer who survived the Global Financial Crisis and rethought everything from how they spend money to how they eat. This approach is by no means pervasive, but it is increasing.

Advent of Agility

Ours is a fast-moving world. It is no longer enough to create a product, put it "on the shelf" and hope people will buy it. Savvy business owners have learned that they need to continually innovate. They must use agile methodologies in product development and marketing. Improvement in analytics technologies is now making this possible. Companies like Tellagence[7] furnish business owners with clever, real-time dashboards that let owners make decisions that can instantly affect their earnings, as well as customer satisfaction. Is consumer opinion about this year's Chardonnay less than flattering? Analytical tools like these can give you enough information fast enough to help you adjust price, distribution and customer experience, as needed.

CONCLUSION

Food and drink tourism development and promotion includes a lot of moving parts. We find ourselves preoccupied with business strategy, consumer marketing, creating trade partnerships and increasingly, having to prove a return on investment. In this equation, the notion of consumer marketing is not a constant. It is a variable. The chapter *How Foodies Make Decisions* explains new ways to look at foodie consumers today. Yet consumers continue to evolve. Preferences change, new products emerge and new competition comes to market. It can make a marketer's head spin to try and follow all the changes. Hopefully the seed has been planted to put you at the front of the line in anticipating and meeting the coming consumer changes in food and drink tourism.

DISCUSSION QUESTIONS

1. How will consumers experience restaurants differently in 25 years?
2. How will emerging technologies make it easier, safer and faster for consumers to make food and drink purchase decisions, whether they are in a grocery store, restaurant, winery or anywhere else?
3. What would be the imlications if countries started outsourcing their food and drink needs to other countries where food and drink are cheaper to produce?

ENDNOTES

[1] The Association was founded in 2003 as the International Culinary Tourism Association. It rebranded as the World Food Travel Association in 2012. The mission, goals and programs remain the same.

[2] See for yourself at www.youtube.com/watch?v=nJVoYsBym88

[3] www.livescience.com/40756-can-new-wristband-sense-what-you-re-eating.html

[4] Term first coined by the World Food Travel Association.

[5] www.accenture.com/SiteCollectionDocuments/us-en/landing-pages/energizing-global-growth/Energizing-Global-Growth-Final.pdf   Accessed 18 June 2013.

[6] www3.weforum.org/docs/GITR/2012/GITR_Chapter1.5_2012.pdf

[7] www.tellagence.com

Food & Drink as Communication

Diana Laskaris, Sue Reddel, & Erik Wolf

Food is a basic human need, common to all people regardless of their culture, history, belief system, geography or other demographic or psychographic profile. Food connects people and turns strangers into friends. Food is a tool for expressing culture, history, appreciation and affection through the lens of travel. Food in a host community communicates cultural values, nationality, geography, ethnicity, tradition, a moment in time and the personality and character of a locale. Beyond nutrition and the gustatory, food and drink carry meaning and symbolism. They may express our commonalities and our differences, both of which are of interest to the traveler. For this subtle knowledge transfer to take place, intermediaries in the host communities or destinations and those working in the travel and communication industries play a vital role in packaging or extracting the story of a local foodway for an exciting and meaningful exchange which promotes crosscultural understanding through the universal language of food and drink.

Food is a tool for breaking down barriers, offering opportunities for learning truths and dispelling misconceptions. The opportunity to use food as a springboard to broader learning about a society, its people, and culture cannot be undervalued in creating meaningful connections in an increasingly globalized world. Food can communicate for us in ways that language sometimes fails to do, opening ways to remove boundaries and create relevance in us for one another. Food consumption during travel opens the door to non-threatening opportunities to learn about others in an intimate way that is typically unavailable through other modes of communication. The meaning of a particular food may change between cultures and may be embedded with a myriad of learnings for the traveler, ranging from geography and agriculture to social context. In its highest service, food may be a tool that we can use to promote a more peaceful coexistence in this world. Because, there is likely one thing we can all agree upon: nothing quite makes us enjoy ourselves like sharing a good meal.

INTRODUCTION

Food is meaning not just nourishment, ritual not just consumption, ceremony not just act, familial and social relationship not just individual ingestion. But profound and increasingly global changes in the way people eat have eclipsed these truths.[1]

"The way to a man's heart is through his stomach," proclaims an old English proverb. While this adage may have been pithy advice for ladies hoping to woo a mate, it also embodies a universal truth. Good food has long been and continues to be a form of communication that overcomes barriers of language, culture, history and tradition, enriching those who share it on a deep and basic human level. Food can be an exalted expression of artistry, individuality and passion. It can also be a form of comfort, stability and connection. Understanding what we eat can help us know who we are. Sharing and experiencing what others eat can help us know who they are.

Striving Towards a Common Understanding

"Over two decades ago, van den Berghe argued that food sharing serves as a bridge for crossing ethnic divides and can provide a basis of multicultural harmony. Food, he writes, is a "paradigm for ethnicity" and "internal tourism" enables inter-ethnic contact. Through such safe crosscultural experiences, individuals vicariously experience another culture and foster crosscultural understanding. Undoubtedly there are many motivations for "food tourism" and various consumers attach myriad meanings to their crosscultural food experiences, some of which are more meaningful than others."[2]

We can learn how to seek out and discover meaningful connections with others through culinary experiences. By breaking bread together we can break through boundaries that keep us from understanding one another. Encouraging food tourism so that people travel to different places of the world and learn more about each other through the intimate experience sharing meals can provide one way of doing that.

As the world becomes more interdependent and interwoven both economically and politically, it is important that the social and cultural aspects of globalism are not extracted or ignored. In this chapter, we will discuss how food is a basic human need, creating a common ground for all people. We will explore how meals can provide an expression of who we are, culturally and in relation to one another. We will look at examples of how we can use food as a tool for understanding, communication and ultimately more peaceful relationships among cultures.

Through this discussion, we hope to show that the value of food travel extends beyond the excitement of individual discovery and deserves its place among the meaningful tools of ambassadorship, cultural exchange and diplomacy.

"Food is our common ground, a universal experience." – James Beard

Despite advances in technology that have helped us map our DNA, cure once-deadly diseases, send people and animals into outer space and place global communication devices in the palms of our hands, no one has yet found a way for human beings to live without food. Food is a basic human need and hunger is still one of the unsolved problems in much of the world. It seems quite natural that such a basic human necessity should be a good place to find common ground among people of all sorts, despite any other differences they may have.

How many times have you sat at a table, beginning to eat a meal when someone starts discussing a previous meal, or one that he or she is anticipating in the future? Does the conversation immediately begin to transform into a sharing of stories and explanations surrounding those food memories or expectations? This sort of discussion is a common occurrence among many cultures because food is such a deeply embedded part of our social structure. The common pleasures we find in talking about food make the differences between us melt away as we each find ways of expressing how pleasurable our food experiences were or what we hope that they will be.

Beyond the food experiences that we discuss with those who share our language, there are times when the food experience itself transcends language altogether. We see this when someone takes a bite of food and the look on his or her face tells it all — this is delicious or this is awful — without having to say a single word. Humans share a common reaction to food delight or distaste. When seeing someone bite into a delicious dessert, for example, we know what he or she is enjoying without the need for language. A gigantic smile, a rolling of the eyes or maybe even a satisfied moan tells us that the pleasure of that bite is something wonderful. This delighted response is usually also something to which we can relate. Even if we do not have experience with the particular food being tasted, we know from our own personal experience what wonderful tasty desserts are like and so we can empathize with the taster.

Even when a food type is not part of our common experience, the need for food to sustain us and permeates our humanity on universal level. Expressions of hunger are easily understood, whether through gestures, like fingers pointing at a hungry mouth, or longing looks directed at food that remains just out of reach. There is a deep connectedness we feel toward others not because of who they are or where they are from, but because we all need to sustain ourselves. We are dependent on food for the very basic premise of survival. This aspect of food surpasses the need for common tradition, history or language and binds us all to that most basic commonality — the need to eat to keep ourselves alive.

"Tell me what you eat, and I will tell you what you are." – *Jean Anthelme Brillat-Savarin*

While food itself is a necessity of life, we often get emotional sustenance in addition to physical sustenance by sharing food with others. Meals have been eaten throughout history, from small family everyday gatherings to expansive feasts celebrating national holidays. Meals have been used to bring people together not only when they have much in common but also when they do not, and when they seek better relations and understanding.

We enjoy meals and share them with friends and family. Meals are an expression of culture, tradition and history. They are often an expression of appreciation and caring, and can help form a bond among participants. For meals shared among family members, even those members who may live far away and are infrequently seen, the act of inclusion in the shared dining experience takes on a significance that binds the family together. Food-sharing at holidays is often symbolic of unity and inclusion. How foods are prepared also communicate meaning, in China chicken is served whole to symbolize family unity and togetherness.[3] Recipes from common ancestors may be shared and family traditions maintained.

Even though time and distance may keep family members apart much of the time, these special meals are a way to reconnect and rekindle or even strengthen the familial ties. Celebrations of religious feast days, historical holidays as well as the more personal birthdays and anniversaries frequently involve the sharing of family recipes as well as dishes customarily enjoyed at such events, again engaging the sense of relationship and bonding that many people seek, even as the structures of "family" undergo tremendous transition in society.

When others outside the family are brought into such events and celebrations, whether friends or acquaintances, business associates or even vacationing visitors, they often experience a sense of connectedness and belonging that is facilitated by the easily comprehensible and universal act of sharing food, regardless of conversations, histories or customs that may elude their understanding. People of all cultures have an opportunity to express themselves through their preparation of good food. A symbolic greeting or acceptance, guests invited into the sharing of that experience, even if there is minimal relationship to the family unit, usually feel a great appreciation and a sense of attachment to those who have invited them.

We celebrate many meals as part of a cultural heritage involving particular traditional dishes that carry with them a sense of cultural pride. A Thanksgiving turkey in America, *Yebeg Wot* stew for Christmas in Ethiopia, Devil's Curry on Boxing Day in Singapore, Empanadas at *Fiestas Patrias* in Chile, lentils for an Italian New Year, pickled herring for *Midsommar* in Sweden, *Magiritsa* soup at Easter in Greece — these are just a few customary dishes that carry with them a wealth of history, tradition, and cultural identity. Sharing these with family and friends can provide a powerful combination of past and present by melding modern experience and traditional customs, most often highlighted by food tastes and food memories.

If you are traveling out of your own country, you may be on the receiving end of hospitality in a culture that believes in sharing meals as a way of deepening relationships. In this way, you have the opportunity to get to know people in a different context and to be drawn into a new social structure through customs of different cultures.

For example, Sunday dinner is a ritual in many cultures. It is an opportunity for busy family members to slow down, and connect with one another, their children and other families. The invitation to join in a Sunday dinner is an invitation to be included in a group of family and friends gathering to enjoy one another's company on arguably the most precious day of the week.

For coworkers, having Sunday dinner with an associate's family and friends may not provide a concrete transition from workmate to friend, but it does make a subtle, perceived one. The mere act of sharing favorite foods with the family and friends of a colleague apart from the business environment encourages greater depth in a relationship and precipitates the understanding that such a relationship can endure even after the business relationship ends.

Sharing meals together also provides us with an opportunity to understand who we are culturally and in relation to one another. When we extend an invitation to someone we do not know well to "grab a bite" or "get a drink," we are opening the door to a different level of communication and an extending the offer to a more meaningful relationship. We choose to spend time in pleasurable pursuits with people we like. When we ask someone to share a meal with us, particularly if we also involve our family or friends along with us, we are, in effect, telling the invitee that we enjoy their company enough to want to spend some time getting to know them better — and for them get to know us better as well. There are few ways of initiating an invitation to friendship that are as positively met as an invitation to dine together.

"Sharing food with another human being is an intimate act that should not be indulged in lightly." M.F.K. Fisher

Once the invitation is extended and accepted, the focus turns to what we will eat. Whether going out to a restaurant or inviting someone into your home, we know that whatever food is shared will carry a great amount of significance, even if only on a subconscious level. Many societies consider that the greatest expression of affection and appreciation comes from preparing a meal for someone else. Exposing someone to the important tastes and traditions of our own food culture is just as important as having them share theirs with us.

Some of the most meaningful meals we want to share with others are those that have been shared with us, whether by a beloved family member, a dear friend or as part of a history or memory that has importance to us. When we look to connect more deeply with others, we tend to seek ways to shorten the path to understanding by using positive associations. We silently express our desires by putting the same attention and affection into the preparation and serving of food. We want the positive feelings that we associate with the meal to be experienced by our guest and to pave the way for an easy transition from one level of acquaintance to another.

An invitation to a meal can be seen as an invitation to friendship. Since communication is the key to understanding, we should encourage exploration of food culture as a way of understanding others and creating or deepening bonds of friendship. Thus, it becomes important for people who seek opportunities to create such bonds, not to shy away from foods that are unfamiliar or even potentially unappealing to them. The more adventurous we become in seeking to communicate with and be communicated to through food, the more friendships and better understanding we open ourselves up to experiencing.

Currently there exist two excellent examples of fostering friendship through food. The first is EatWith,[4] a new global community that invites people to dine in homes around the world.[5] Guests can connect with hosts they think they will like, share stories and unforgettable experiences, and enjoy delicious homemade cuisine. Both the visitors and the host can potentially enjoy a satisfying experience and gain a greater understanding of other peoples and cultures with an EatWith meal. While EatWith is enjoyed by tourists, locals are also finding it to be a fun social experience. The World Food Travel Association says that food tourism takes place not just while you are traveling, but can happen in your own area as well, especially when you visit a new neighborhood or section of your city. EatWith is headquartered in Israel, a country that loves its wide variety of foods, and which understands the need for understanding other cultures.

Another example is *hemmahos*, a Swedish concept that means "at home." Popular in the Jämtland region of Sweden, the concept is similar to EatWith. Visitors to the region find out about *hemmahos* through the local tourism office. If the visitor is interested, the tourism offices matches the visitor(s) with an area family. The tourists enjoy (usually) Swedish cuisine and get to know their hosts on a much deeper level than they would in an area restaurant. While still new, the concept has been very popular with visitors.

The cultural component of shared meals is also often seen as an opportunity for the hosting party to show off some part of their culture, which, it is hoped, can be appreciated by the guests. The desired result is to build a bridge toward understanding of other matters that may require more profound conversation or deeper thought. If we are willing to extend ourselves, whether through preparing dishes that are special to us or accepting those dishes prepared by our hosts as being special to them, then whether or not the dishes are "to our taste" is less important than the message that is being communicated by our desire to share them with one another.

Allowing a free flow of communication in the form of meal-sharing is one of the best ways we can encourage understanding, appreciation and connection among those with different cultural backgrounds, traditions and histories. Promoting food travel is a way to expose travelers to a variety of cultures while allowing them also to absorb them in a way that is individually meaningful, even on a subconscious level, through their own associations with the common value of sharing food with others.

"If you reject the food, ignore the customs, fear the religion and avoid the people, you might better stay at home." - James A. Michener

When crossing borders, we can learn about other cultural traditions, customs and history through food. We can approach understanding, acceptance and appreciation of those cultures through the experience of sharing food. Many cultures have deeply rooted traditions and customs that are expressed through food, and on a certain level, to reject an experience of food is to reject a culture. It becomes important then to be culturally sensitive not only to what foods are commonly used in the cuisine of a locale, but also cultural, historical or traditional associations that go along with them.

For example, while many people who have never traveled to Turkey may be familiar with "Turkish Coffee," the fact is that drinking tea is much more of a Turkish pastime. In practically every corner of Istanbul where there are shops, bazaars, cafes and people, you will find tea purveyors and tea drinkers. Tea is often used as a tool for bargaining merchants to find an opportunity to turn their prospective customers into friends, at least for the duration of a negotiation. Tea is offered frequently and freely to prospects as a testament to the merchant's good character and trustworthiness. The hospitality is hoped to translate into a purchase.

An interesting aspect of the omnipresent tea that populates the area is that it is served in a unique manner unused outside of Turkey. The tea is served in tulip-shaped cups made from thick glass. If one is unfamiliar with this service, they will grab the glass by the middle and find it uncomfortably hot. With exposure and understanding, one learns that the glass is to be grasped by the top and tilted toward the mouth. Because the tea is prepared by adding boiling hot water to a concentrated tea, which has been steeping all day, a visitor may be unaware of the potential hazards. Worse, if unaware of the cultural significance of this tea service, one might ask for tea to be served in a regular teacup, which may not even be available. Aside from being perceived as uncouth, one might unintentionally be insulting.

The cultural significance of the Turkish manner of serving tea is one of which the Turks are proud. Tea drinking was encouraged as an alternative to coffee after World War I, when the fall of the Ottoman Empire turned coffee into an expensive import. Founder of the republic, Ataturk, encouraged tea consumption instead because domestic resources could easily sustain it. The unique shape of the tulip cup and the fact that it is made from glass resulted from the low cost and ready availability of glass for manufacturing and the ease of producing the vessels without a handle. The Turks continue to drink tea in this same manner as a custom with which they are proud, even though the initial historical reasons for doing so have long since faded away.

For many travelers, the discovery of unique culinary items, customs and traditions is part of the thrill for which they travel. Exploring the intricacies of culinary culture can even be the deciding factor for food travelers to choose one destination over another. The more we can learn about the culinary practices and dishes of a place, the more likely we are to want to get to know its people. For destinations seeking a greater tourism advantage, one way to gain attention and favor is to promote the unique and appealing elements of its food culture. For those travelers hungry for travel that integrates cultural and culinary experiences, the clear explanation of what one will find when exploring a destination's culinary highlights will certainly strike a chord.

This sort of exercise has value too for the destination seeking to achieve a higher profile among experienced global travelers. While historic, cultural and artistic attractions alone may be enough to attract the novice traveler, when combined with culinary exploration, the appeal of a destination becomes greater for those experienced travelers who may be looking for something more out of a destination. Identity, distinctiveness, and diversity in the culinary arena may provide destinations with a closer look from travelers who desire to gain a greater understanding of its people, places and plates. Food can be a tool for communicating the inherent uniqueness of a culture through the authentic appeal of its food.

"How can you govern a country which has 246 varieties of cheese?" - Charles de Gaulle

Communication through food and drink can dispel misconceptions and misunderstandings and help replace fear and bias with common ground. For many people, it is easier to identify a group through the action of a few than to differentiate the limitless variety of human experience among those within such groups. We sometimes use culture or religion or politics as boxes in which to classify people. In so doing, we can perpetuate fallacies and create barriers that get in our way of truly understanding our fellow humans. Food, because it is a basic need for all of humanity, might be used as a way to dispel such misconceptions and open a path of communication that may otherwise remain closed. Traumatic events, celebrations, weddings, graduations, deaths, births and birthdays all have a way of bringing people together, which usually involves eating.

Ongoing education should be nurtured when dealing with divergent cultures, especially where there may be a tendency to oversimplify cultural complexities and varieties of experience. Communicating through food and drink can provide a doorway to understanding such variation and complexity.

"If more of us valued food and cheer and song above hoarded gold, it would be a merrier world." – J.R.R. Tolkien

460

Even in places where political differences can stifle communication among people living in the same region, food can serve as a common ground for interaction. One such location is the city of Jerusalem, a land that is rich in delicious foods and flavors that may be overlooked while the world focuses on political tensions instead.

When chefs, friends and business partners Sami Tamimi and Yotam Ottolenghi first met in London more than a decade ago, they discovered that they both came from Jerusalem, from two sides of one complex city, in which they experienced two different cuisines.

Tamimi comes from the Arab east side of the city, Ottolenghi from the Jewish west side. Although they did not meet until almost 30 years later, they discovered that they shared many of the same food experiences during their childhood and enjoyed many of the same tastes. "We like the same things and share the same palates," says Tamimi. Those common culinary bonds formed the basis for a business relationship that spawned multiple restaurants and most recently a jointly authored *Jerusalem: A Cookbook* (Ten Speed Press, 2012), which is dedicated to sharing favorite flavors from their homeland.

"You can't ignore the political situation there, but it's a beautiful place. All the recipes in the book are things we love to eat," says Tamimi. "Also, Middle Eastern food is not getting that much attention. It's full of flare, but it's not exposed enough," he states.

Sharing a meal can help people communicate on an unconscious level, regardless of our political beliefs. "People forget that food is to enjoy, it's a pleasurable thing. Food is a basic thing, a comforting thing," says Tamimi. Food can bring people together and communicate the similarities between us. "Jerusalem started with trying to go back and understand how we are. We did the book because we always like to share and feed people," says Tamimi.

This desire to share ourselves, our heritage, the flavors of our youth, to expose others to food experiences that have meaning to us is a way of communicating that goes beyond words. We use food to communicate where we are from and who we are. In that way, we can transcend boundaries, even political ones, by nourishing others through sharing our food.

"What I say is that, if a man really likes potatoes, he must be a pretty decent sort of fellow." – A.A. Milne

When cultures have some significant differences, sharing food may be one way to bridge the divide. We find that opening ourselves to the hospitality of others creates a new common vocabulary, even if each of us brings a different world of meaning to the table from our own cultures and lives.

Middle Eastern hospitality is an important cultural element, and a source of pride. The United Arab Emirates, particularly Dubai with its gleaming tall buildings and outward displays of wealth, can seem like a place that is all business and spending, not hearth and home. But this is not the case.

When United States business travelers attend dinner with the family of a Dubai colleague, they may discover that their associate is delighted to provide a full experience of food and engage in an exchange of cultural information.

Dubai is a place that honors refreshment. Being a country with a large Muslim population, alcohol is not served apart from hotel bars and hotel-affiliated establishments. Thus, an extraordinary array of fresh juices can be found nearly everywhere. A host family can offer a tremendous variety of freshly made foods, including ample vegetables and juices, and express a generosity of spirit in everything that is served.

Over courses of delicious food and fresh juices there is an opportunity to share many cultural exchanges and dispel myths. Misconceptions can be corrected and discussed through a concurrent exploration of realities and sharing of flavors that are fresh and close to nature. Each participant in the experience may realize that the differences between them are actually quite small, while what they have in common is much more than first imagined.

Food makes a wonderful platform from which dialogues and exchanges of culture can take place. When one opens up the palate, the world becomes a wonderful place to explore. If we are able to use food as a starting point for dispelling misconceptions, we may be able to replace fear and intolerance with understanding and compassion. There are times when a good meal speaks volumes and words mean very little. It is our hope that we can all better learn to use food as a tool for cross-cultural understanding and to promote peace.

CONCLUSION

"There is no sincerer love than the love of food." – George Bernard Shaw

Food is a basic human need, common to all people regardless of their culture, history, belief system, gender, age, level of education or geography. Food can create connectedness and belonging, turning strangers into friends. Food is a tool for expressing culture, history, appreciation and affection. And food is a tool for breaking down barriers, offering opportunities for learning truths and dispelling misconceptions. Food can communicate for us in ways that language sometimes fails to do, opening ways to remove boundaries and create relevance in us for one another. In its highest service, food may be a tool that we can use to promote a more peaceful coexistence in this world. Because, there is likely one thing we can all agree upon, namely that there is no thing that few of us enjoy more than sharing a good meal.

DISCUSSION QUESTIONS

1. How are food and drink good tools for communication?
2. How can food and drink be used to break down barriers across borders?
3. What are some ways the food and drink tourism industry can use the concept of food and drink as communication to promote its value to participants?

ENDNOTES

[1] www.hangoverguide.com/factbook/food.html

[2] www.warscapes.com/retrospectives/food/consuming-other#sthash.5xgzSydi.dpuf

[3] www.bbc.co.uk/news/magazine-16631679

[4] www.eatwith.com

[5] Guy Michlin, one of EatWith's co-founders, explains the company's philosophy at the TechCrunch Disrupt Battlefield presentation on April 30, 2013 in New York City. Watch his presentation here: www.youtube.com/watch?v=gO3zmUrTjLs

Ongoing Development for Food Tourism Professionals

Kathryn McAree

As we progress in our careers, we can easily forget that change affects our relevance to the work we do. Events like the 2008 Global Financial Crisis force us to change both personally and professionally. We learn something new every day. This chapter addresses tools available to food tourism professionals to help them stay current in our industry and in their own professional development.

INTRODUCTION

To be successful, both personally and professionally, it is important to understand why professional development is important to your overall goals in life, and options available to achieve professional development. When thinking of professional development, what first comes to mind? Going back to school to learn new skills or sharpen existing ones? Enrolling in a course at a local college? Learning a second language? Or do you think about ways to grow in your own personal development? Sometimes looking at the career paths of others can provide a guide of sorts to follow.

Your Path to Learning

The corporate world understood long ago that it was well worth their while to invest in developing their human resources. By encouraging staff to enroll in personal development, companies benefit from the employee knowing more about themselves and, by extension, more about others. Both of these lead to a more productive work environment for the company. For the individual, it is a chance gain insights into their personality, behavior and strengths.

A personality assessment tool called Myers-Briggs[1] was once commonly used throughout many companies and corporations. Through completing detailed exercises, individuals learned about their personality type, such as whether they preferred to be guided by intuition, feeling, and/or thinking. The process was an entire learning experience about yourself as an individual and, intrinsically, about others who you work with.

"Understanding self and others can have the single greatest impact on creating a career that's both fulfilling and rewarding," agrees Anna Harvey, a Vancouver Island (Canada)-based life coach and Lumina Learning facilitator. "We all have natural preferences when it comes to our behavior — introverted, extroverted, people focused, detail driven, visionary, etc. Knowing this about *oneself* creates a set of 'winning conditions' that allows us to play to our strengths and be mindful of our blind spots. Understanding *others'* preferences, strengths and communication style allows us to bring out the best in our relationships with team members and managers."

One needs to look no further than the field of food tourism for a case in point for being emotionally connected to one's work. For many, your work is incredibly meaningful and fulfilling, not unlike other creatively based careers. The next hurdle is how to leverage that passion into career success. Professional development is the key. No worries — you will love the learning. That is the benefit of working in a field that emotionally inspires you.

Building Your Professional Development Plan

Professional development can also be referred to as continuing education, skills training or career development. Depending on your career path, the right area of professional development for you might be narrowly focused on foodservice, tour operations, destination marketing, farming, writing and so on. By connecting with professional organizations in your particular area of concentration, you can explore courses, seminars, and the availability of coaches and mentors.

You can take advantage of many informal learning opportunities by becoming a member of your local chamber of commerce, local tourism association, and by attending professional networking events. You never know who you will meet or when. When you take an interest in others, you will always find opportunities to learn. An excellent way to meet new people and learn something new is to attend a Meetup. Meetup.com is a global network of interest groups. You register and search for groups near you that may be of interest to you. Sometimes there is a fee to attend a meeting, and other times not. Meetups are a new way to network and find business contacts, or to learn something new.

For food tourism specialists, the World Food Travel Association offers accreditation as a Certified Culinary Travel Professional.[2] This certification was the first of its kind in the food tourism industry and is still the most comprehensive non-university food tourism training available. It remains the Association's most popular product.

A wealth of information is also available by researching trade publications and food tourism industry articles in areas of hospitality management, wine production, farming, restaurant management, destination marketing, and more.

Attending food, travel and tourism conferences in the geographic area of your work will not only give you an excellent opportunity to learn about the industry, it will also give you the chance to meet like-minded people who may have an interesting overlap with your own business venture.

It is important to know the time commitment you are able to make and also your optimum learning environment. For example, explore both in-person and online courses, weekly classes and intensive one-day or weekend seminars. One of these should fit your best learning style.

Also keep in mind that a career path you choose to follow may require specific licenses or training in your region or country. Do you have the time, money and interest to pursue such training and licenses, if required?

Professional Development: A Personal Story

It was in 2000 when Laura Gustafson made the decision to become a culinary tour operator. There was not yet a World Food Travel Association and there was very little information available so Laura created her own opportunities.[3]

As a young adult, Laura had the opportunity to attend the Dale Carnegie course. "I thought I was just going to learn how to be an effective public speaker," she said. "Well I did – and so much more!" The Dale Carnegie books, originally written in the 1950s, play to our human nature and are as applicable today as when they were written. During the early days of her career, Laura attended the Phoenix Seminar on the Psychology of Achievement, where she learned about drive, success, and how to know what you want. Suddenly she knew what she wanted, but needed to do the work to get there.

464

Laura spoke to as many industry professionals as she could find in the tourism, food and restaurant sectors and to people in her city's destination marketing organization. Soon she was volunteering at a local farm that taught cooking classes. Lucky for her, the operator had limited computer and organizational skills. Laura was able to offer her experience and proficiency in those areas, and was able to serve the cooking school while gain hands-on experience. Today, Laura brings her clients to this farm.

Next, Laura connected with a chef who led culinary tours in Italy. Before long, she was in Tuscany serving as his assistant. Her role was wonderfully diverse: greeting international guests, driving the winding roads, searching for a lost traveler in an ancient city, assisting in the kitchen, buying food and wine, staying up late talking with travelers, eating fabulous food and getting very little sleep. She learned a great deal in Italy and, more importantly, learned first-hand what tour participants liked the best about their culinary tour and what they could do without. There is nothing more valuable than hands-on learning.

When Laura returned home, she knew she needed to do more to develop her business and herself professionally. Having worked in the restaurant industry for only a short time when she was younger, Laura learned early on in her new food tourism career that she needed to know more about food, local food in particular, and food handling. She took the British Columbia accredited Food Safe course to learn about the safe preparation, handling, and storage of food.

During this time, Laura also read many books and watched food documentaries. Michael Pollan's books are a great tool for learning and *Food Inc.* is her favorite food documentary. Learning about food issues has helped expand her horizons and understand the concerns of many of her artisan suppliers. More volunteering brought Laura into connection with a local chef association at a food event they were hosting. It was here where she realized the benefit of having her *Serving It Right* certification, a program that communicates the legalities and complexities of serving liquor in the province.

Today, Laura continues to create learning opportunities for herself. For example, there is a charcuterie that she regularly visits with her culinary walking tour groups. Being a city-girl, she was a little uncomfortable with the whole beast coming through the front door. So Laura asked the owner if she could watch him break down and butcher a pig. He kindly agreed and Laura went into the shop very early one morning and got a crash course in butchering a whole animal. It was not at all what she expected and she even enjoyed it.

During harvest, Laura often helps a small winery to hand-pick grapes. If the winery is short of people, she recruits chefs, servers, and industry friends to help. This brings a whole new meaning to hands-on learning.

Laura receives Google Alerts for topics that affect her business and which are worthwhile for her to stay well-informed about. The web is an endless teacher and she finds Google Alerts are a great way to keep her up to date. She also subscribes to various RSS news feeds, which bring relevant industry news directly to her computer. A quick scan of the daily industry news is how Laura starts every day.

After over a decade of business, she continues to participate in courses and seminars, attend conferences, and volunteer with like-minded professionals.

CONCLUSION

There is no prescription for learning. Professional and personal development is never out of style. As we grow as individuals, we grow as professionals. The more you learn about yourself, your industry, and your colleagues, the more excitement and inspiration you will find. Explore some of the tools mentioned in this chapter, and rise to the next level in your career. If you seek a career in food tourism, start by looking for opportunities in your region. You might find that opportunities exist to allow you to create your own path.

DISCUSSION QUESTIONS

1. Where are the gaps in current food tourism professional development offerings?
2. Which is better: online learning (including distance learning) or learning in person? Discuss the pros and cons of each.
3. Does professional development need to be focused on one's career path (e.g. foodservice or journalism) or does development work in other areas still benefit professionals in these areas?

ENDNOTES

---

[1] A popular and free online version of the Meyers-Briggs test is available here: www.humanmetrics.com/cgi-win/jtypes2.asp
[2] More information is available at www.worldfoodtravel.org/cctp
[3] Author interview with Laura Gustafson, 11 June 2013. Ms. Gustafson has asked not to mention details of her company for privacy reasons.

Future of Food Tourism

Jenn Bussell, Annette Tomei, & Erik Wolf

This chapter looks at some of the issues our industry can expect to face in the next few years.

INTRODUCTION

Predicting where our industry is headed is almost impossible. Nevertheless, there are some emerging trends that should be of interest to food tourism practitioners. Hopefully our look into the crystal ball will provide some insight to help you be well prepared to adjust to changes expected in our industry over the next several years.

The Hard BRICs

Over the past decade much has been written about growth in outbound tourism from BRIC countries (Brazil, Russia, India and China). A cursory analysis of outbound travel from those countries indicates that a higher percentage of residents of those countries are traveling than are residents of the more developed world. As these visitors travel, they bring their own cultures and expectations with them. Sometimes their expectations are in sync with the local (destination) food culture, other times they are not. Destinations and food tourism businesses hosting travelers from these (and other) countries may need to consider the pros and cons of adapting to changing consumer expectations. For example, the wine industry may need to make accommodations for people who do not drink alcohol, but who still want to know about wine. Restaurants may need to begin serving more vegetarian meals, or learn how to cater to guests with religious dietary preferences, as airlines currently do. Some businesses and destinations will not adjust, and others will. Neither approach is right or wrong. Simply put, times are changing.

Many destination marketers regard Chinese travelers as a panacea. 'Build it and they will come' and 'their sheer numbers will support our hotel occupancy for years to come' are common perceptions among destination marketers throughout North America and Europe. While the number of outbound Chinese is increasing, their per capita spending tells another story. Interestingly, in recent years China has become actually one of the world's top markets for premium wines.[1] While sales are significant, research shows that the Chinese in general have a preference for sweet or fruity wines. That said, the palates of Chinese middle- and upper-class consumers are evolving to match those of their Western counterparts. According to the Boston Consulting Group, "The Chinese will have the second largest number of citizens travelling overseas next year, having overtaken the Japanese, and a total of 8% of the outbound global tourist market. Much of that outbound tourism will be to Europe and the United States, and with it, an introduction to Western food and wines."[2] While the Chinese are trying other styles of wine, such styles may not actually be their preference. And whether Chinese travelers in the USA or Europe can import the wines they try back home is another matter. With Western experiences and values (some call it cultural imperialism, others call it progress), came the *aspiration* by Chinese consumers towards Western tastes. Did they drink the dry red wine because they really liked it or did they drink it because they thought they would like it or were expected to like it?

Technology: The Moving Target

The speed at which technology evolves makes it challenging at best to leverage it in the food tourism industry, whether it is digital content development and distribution, reservations and booking systems, sales and marketing or really any kind of technology solution. As a bellwether, look at the fast evolution of mobile phones, from Motorola Razr to Blackberry Pearl to the iPhone and now the Samsung Galaxy. What can we expect next? Solutions last for a year or two and then something better comes along. It is the nature of the business.

With technology, content authorship and ownership has changed hands as well. Consumers now have the ability to share their food and drink experiences with the power of the "send" button, and in great detail with photos and video as supporting evidence. The power of the people cannot be ignored. What is next in food tourism content? Better quality and faster mobile devices like tablets and smartphones will mean more electronic brochures, high resolution videos and even 3-D videos will come to life. Virtual reality visits of a winery or cooking school might also be possible in the not too distant future.

Regarding reservations and booking systems, software as a service (SaaS) continues to be the approach of choice for savvy business owners with a variety of needs ranging from accounting to reservations and more. SaaS reservations tools like Kayak.com or Priceline.com are becoming easier than ever for consumers to use. OpenTable.com is solving a lot of operational issues for restaurants. There are plenty of technology development companies that will gladly accept your money to build bespoke booking systems. Not only do such systems start at several hundred thousand U.S. dollars (or equivalent in your currency) and quickly reach into the millions of dollars, the technology is often outdated before the product comes to market because these platforms take so long to build. The advantages of a SaaS solution are many. First, they are orders of magnitude cheaper, typically charging a reasonable monthly or per transaction fee. Secondly, no huge overhead investment in software or staff is required. Thirdly, the software developer does what it does best so updates are made much more frequently. Leave the software development to the developers. Of course larger companies may have sophisticated needs that are not met by SaaS and may elect to still build their own bespoke systems.

Another major improvement our industry can expect is from database-driven solutions such as restaurant or visitor information websites, which will become more useful as their results become more relevant. Instead of searching for a type of cuisine and getting thousands of results, you will be able to specify a few more parameters and get a highly targeted, manageable and more relevant list of only a few dozen nearly perfect choices. This will help both consumers and trade immensely as both groups stand to reap considerable benefits from better targeting technologies. Another tool that will make these improvements even more useful is a better, globally recognized food experience rating system, such as the one being designed by the World Food Travel Association.[3] Such a system is being designed to minimize the fear of risk and loss that often plagues foodie travelers when presented with opportunities to try new food and drink experiences.

Related to improvements in targeting technology are improvements in contextual search results. We already see this today, such as when the Google app on your smartphone tells you about restaurant recommendations nearby, even without your asking. There has been much talk of Google glasses, which are designed to display information in the lens of the glasses about everything currently being observed through the glasses. In many ways, this bypasses the current process of scanning a QR barcode for information. The idea is that you can point the camera of your smartphone at a restaurant or famous landmark and you will receive relevant information about the history, pricing, bookings/reservations and more.

Old-School Marketing on Its Way Out

Not even 20 years ago, we regarded print media as a viable vehicle for food and travel marketing. Place an ad and hope for results. Today, print media is not often favored (with a few notable exceptions of course). In favor today are all forms of interactive or online marketing, with social media at the top of the list. There is still a place for printed brochures, but print runs are down. Visitors need information before they leave home. Once in a new destination, it is usually too late to promote a seasonal event for example, because the visitor's itinerary is largely decided before they leave home.

Increasing Role of Consumer Influence

As we explored in the *Evolution of Guidebooks, Ratings and Reviews in Food & Drink Tourism* and *Power of the People: Word of Mouth Marketing in Food Tourism* chapters in this book, a combination of increased consumer skepticism in traditional ratings and review systems plus advances in digital and mobile hardware and software, has resulted in an influx of consumer-generated content in the food and drink tourism industry. Leveraging a real-time, global platform of review sites, video sites, podcasts, blogs, tweets and social networking sites, consumers are exercising their right to share like never before. As our connected culture grows, the collective social influence of consumers will continue to have tremendous impact on the purchase process of food travelers.

While the concept of consumers influencing other consumers is not new, *how* consumers exert their influence has evolved. Prior to social platforms and review websites, consumers exerted what marketing industry experts refer to as 'passive influence,' whereby they responded when asked for advice or recommendations. Today, they are 'active influencers,' using digital tools to proactively give advice and offer recommendations without being asked.

In order for business owners and marketers to effectively harness this power of the people, they must first identify the most trusted voices among consumer influencers in their respective markets. Then they must develop strategic and creative ways to seed messages with those who have both the ability and willingness to amplify brand messages across their individual social circles comprised of friends, family, colleagues, and perhaps even other like-minded consumers. This requires finesse and tact, as most consumers are aware when brands are trying to control or direct social conversations and public opinion. While consumers are keen to participate and share, they want to do it on their terms.

The Need for Local Cooperation

It will become increasingly difficult for smaller, local and independent businesses to compete, which is a clarion call to these businesses that it is finally time to work together. Small businesses can no longer ignore the reality that united they stand and divided they fall. Working together benefits all cooperating businesses. Small business owners need to put aside their differences and stop seeing each other as competition. And to be fair, many of them already have this perspective, but many do not. Instead, they should try to view each other as "coopetition" (cooperative competition). The real competition is the multinational corporations with a marketing army with coffers flush with cash. A simple solution would be the creation of local consortia or national trade associations that lobby strongly on behalf of small foodservice and hospitality business owners. Another solution is to "fight fire with fire," namely to influence the very trendsetters in the market, namely teenagers, college students, and celebrities.

The general public falls into line quickly when a new fad is introduced, and then the fad becomes ingrained in the culture. Look at the success of the Tickle Me Elmo children's toy years ago, as well as Blackberry and now iPhone smartphones, and the availability of endless customizations at Starbucks. Many small business owners do participate in programs to support local initiatives, especially when they work with local tourism offices. However, finding success in such initiatives is hard because they do not serve to sway public opinion, which is what is needed. One of the few organizations in the world that has the potential to drive significant change among consumer opinion is Slow Food, based in Bra, Italy. However, Slow Food has its own focused initiatives and so far has not made such a broad global campaign a high priority. Therefore the trade must take the lead ourselves to continue to spread the message to our customers about the need to preserve and promote the local culinary culture. Similarly, customers need to listen to the trade about why it is important for them to support local and independent businesses. We need to make it worth their while to listen.

Global Issues = Local Impact

Unfortunately, sickness and disease are parts of both tourism and foodservice. Travelers still suffer from 'Montezuma's Revenge,' pollen and environmental allergies and motion sickness. Serious threats are afoot from mad cow disease, contaminated water, and food-borne illnesses and poisoning. For example, Listeria Monocytogenes is a pathogen found in contaminated water. Salmonella Typhimurium is found in undercooked beef, and still with us are bird flu, swine flu and similar diseases from farming animals kept in unsanitary and cramped conditions with little to no access to fresh air or water.

With an ever-increasing population, resources such as water are becoming increasingly scarce. And the cost to ship and prepare food is increasing because of decreased availability of oil and other energy sources. These factors will drive changes in consumer behavior. For example, the practice in US restaurants of serving tap water for free without guests asking for it might wane. The cost of bottled water will also increase, largely due to the increased transportation costs and scarcity of fresh water. As consumers become increasingly aware of the cost of food and drink, their purchase decisions may shift as well. According to Vegsource.com, it takes up to 200 times more water to produce a pound of beef than a pound of potatoes.[4] With the availability of fresh, clean water decreasing, beef will become increasingly expensive, not to mention the fact that red meat increases the number of free radicals and carcinogens in the body. Consumers are already slowly starting to change their eating habits, and they are taking their new eating habits with them on the road.

Food allergies are on the rise as well. Wheat gluten, dairy, food coloring, mustard, peanuts, soy and MSG are just a few of the most common allergens. Rampant allergies (or more precisely, a significant increase in awareness among consumers about their food allergies), are revolutionizing restaurant menus. There is no longer a stigma associated with offering a significant number of vegetarian main courses, for example, and gluten-free choices are seen more and more. Countries like Jordan, where the cuisine has significant vegetarian options and largely free of additives and preservatives, stand to benefit more from consumers conscious about what goes into the food they eat.

Food waste is unfortunately on a dramatic rise, and for no good reason. Food waste is detrimental for many reasons, the most obvious of which is the cost, both in actual product wasted, but also in the cost of its transportation. A hidden cost is the amount of methane released into the air by decaying food, which is a contributor to global warming. In many restaurants and foodservice outlets, perfectly good fruits and vegetables are thrown out because they do not "look good" although nothing is wrong with the flavor. The perception is that consumers will not buy the product if it does not look good. This is a thorny issue that varies in almost every jurisdiction in the world. Some businesses such as New Seasons Market[5] in Portland, Oregon, USA have found a way to achieve "Zero Waste," whereby there is no net negative impact on the local environment or food system from the store actually being in business. More foodservice businesses should look at the New Seasons zero waste business model and consider the benefits of emulating it. At the very least, owners of foodservice businesses stand to reduce the cost of their ingredients substantially. Buy less product to start with, in order to waste less product. If a restaurant runs out of chicken that night, so be it. The restaurant has not wasted any chicken, the owner has reduced resource consumption and decreased food waste, and perhaps the consumer is educated in the process.

Business Diversification as the Key to Longevity

Diversification is a potential means to sustained business growth and longevity, and can help small, local, and independent businesses survive in the tough economic climates. Business diversification comes in many forms ... new products or services, new markets, and new revenue streams. In her June 13, 2012 article on the *Guardian* small business network, contributor Alison Coleman defined the key to successful small business diversification as "spotting and exploiting new market opportunities for their products, using their core skills to offer complementary businesses services or simply taking their brands into uncharted territory."[6]

For example, a 40-seat Basque restaurant in New York City could continually receive requests from their guests for their chef's authentic pintxo dishes. They decide to create a series of pintxo making classes on Monday evenings when the restaurant is normally closed. These classes, priced at US$65 per person, offer an education on regional Basque cuisine and cooking demos on how to prepare pintxos, cocktail pairings, plus creative ideas for home entertaining. To start, the classes are limited to 10 people to ensure the experience is both intimate and interactive. As word of mouth spreads and the popularity of these classes grows, the restaurant begins offering the class on Sunday mornings as well, before the restaurant opens for dinner service. The restaurant has successfully generated new sources of revenue, while building brand loyalty and customer goodwill.

Similar examples include the boutique winery that partners with a nearby farmer to launch a farm-to-table dinner series; and the independent kitchen gadgets shop that does on-premise coffee tastings to showcase the different types of coffee makers they sell, while providing tips and techniques for customers to achieve the perfect cup of coffee at home.

CONCLUSION

There are more consumers than ever, faced with more choices than ever. We also have more tools than ever, which allow us to take advantage of literally anything at anytime and anywhere on the planet. As new economic powerhouses like China and Brazil mature, the world's tourism industry will begin to witness an even greater increase in consumer expectations and preferences originating from these cultures. Should the receptive culture change its offerings to match the preferences of its visitors? Perhaps not, but sometimes a little "taste of home" is a nice comfort when a visitor is thrust into a completely different food culture. Destinations and businesses alike should take steps to ensure they preserve their food culture and not kowtow to perceived visitor demands unless those demands are, in fact, real.

DISCUSSION QUESTIONS

1. How will changing consumer tastes change the food and drink industry in the short-term?
2. How will growth in travel from emerging countries and contraction in travel from more developed countries change the food and drink industry?
3. Should cultures change their food offerings en masse to the culinary norm of their main source of visitors? Discuss the pros and cons of doing so.

ENDNOTES

[1] www.china-briefing.com/news/2012/05/21/chinas-exploding-wine-consumption.html

[2] www.china-briefing.com/news/2011/11/21/chinas-wine-market-shows-great-potential.html

[3] Those interested in learning more should read the *Evolution of Guidebooks, Ratings and Reviews in Food & Drink Tourism* chapter in this book.

[4] www.vegsource.com/articles/pimental_water.htm

[5] www.newseasonsmarket.com

[6] www.guardian.co.uk/small-business-network/2013/jun/14/diversify-die-explore-new-markets-business-grow

Conclusion

Erik Wolf

Just like a great Hollywood movie, this book conveys love, fear and passion, but instead of playing out on the big screen, this is real life and in a situation that we call our livelihoods.

The pages you hold now represent the collective work of more than 70 authors and writers, two dozen or so proofreaders and five editors from nearly 24 countries. In other words, this is our industry's braintrust. We have attempted to leave no stone unturned. Naturally space precludes too much discussion of some of the issues herein. We welcome comments and feedback on this book or recommendations from savvy professionals about the next book. Please visit: www.worldfoodtravel.org/have-fork-will-travel to share your thoughts or email us at fork@worldfoodtravel.org.

We are all human and these loves and concerns are the same for all of us, no matter whether our work is for a government, a trade organization, a nongovernmental or nonprofit organization, a tourism office, or a small to medium sized business. We also work in a very special industry, in which we can easily find kindred spirits — someone to lend a hand or make a suggestion, or just to give us the support we need to succeed. In many ways, our family of food, drink, travel and hospitality professionals is quite unique. No matter our cultural background or the language we speak, the hospitality gene is programmed into who we are and how we behave. And we suspect that is why you found your way to this book. Welcome to our food and drink tourism family. We hope that you have gleaned a few tasty morsels from this book to help you and your business or destination to grow and succeed with food and drink tourism.

Thank you for reading. Good luck with your food and drink tourism work!

Be sure to connect with us socially at: www.worldfoodtravel.org/social

Food & Drink Tourism Industry Glossary

Erik Wolf, with Kristina Lupp

INTRODUCTION

The food tourism industry is like other industries in that we use our fair share of jargon and acronyms. The terms our industry uses however are sourced from a wider set, namely the entire food, drink, travel and hospitality industries. Professionals used to terminology in only one of these industries may be perplexed by terms used in a different part of our industry. Only the initiated will be able to decipher instructions such as "Ask the DOS to book 50 pax into a double double to be guaranteed by the DMC. Call the DMO if you need more information." For those new to the industry, or food professionals working with the travel industry for the first time, the glossary below will be a tremendous help in deciphering the meaning of food-tourism-speak.

À la Carte: French phrase meaning "from the menu." Each item is individually priced.

Acceptance: Agreement to purchase products or services under specified terms.

Accommodation: Any seat, room or service provided and/or sold to a guest or passenger.

Accompanying person: Guest or spouse of an attendee.

Accreditation: To provide with credentials. Also an approval given by various trade associations to a travel agency or similar business type which gives the accredited organization a competitive advantage in sales.

Act of God: A weather-related, seismic or similar natural event over which a travel provider has no control and, hence, no legal responsibility. Usually an exclusion included in the fine print.

Actual cash value: Replacement cost of lost or damaged property less depreciation.

Ad hoc tour: A tour designed around a specific theme. Most such tours provide an expert tour leader and visit places and/or events of special interest to the participants.

Add-on: Any component of a package tour that is not included in the package price.

Adventure tour: a tour designed around an adventurous activity such as rafting of hiking.

Advisory board: A group that offers advice or counsel to management on planning of specific projects or strategies.

Affinity group: a group sharing a common interest, usually from the same organization. See also pre-formed group.

After-departure charge: expenses such as telephone charges that do not appear on a guest s account at check out.

Agent: one who acts or has the power to act as the representative of another. Most frequently in travel anyone other than a principal, such as a retail travel agent, receiving agent, ticket agent, local operator or wholesaler.

Agritainment: a contraction of "ag" from "agriculture" and "entertainment". The term is typically used in the context of farm visits by school children who have an entertaining experience while at the farm. An example is a "pizza farm" where children learn the origin of the different ingredients used on a pizza.

Agritourism: a contraction of "ag" from "agriculture" and "tourism". The term is broad and can encompass everything from families visiting a farmers' market to kids experiencing agritainment as part of a school outing, to professional visits by farmers and biologists. Not the same as food tourism or culinary tourism.

Air Sea: a cruise/travel program which includes both air/sea arrangements. Often combined with local hotel arrangements for pre/post stays

Air Transport Association (ATA): The former name of the trade association now known as Airlines for America (A4A). Comprised of American and Canadian scheduled airlines, including international, major, national, intra-Hawaiian, intra-Alaskan, helicopters and cargo carriers. www.airlines.org

Air wall: An operable wall panel system used to subdivide exhibit, meeting or ballroom space.

Airline classes of service: variety of terms used to express a particular type of aircraft cabin service. Classes vary with types of compartments, seating comfort, and amenities, with variation between domestic and international flights, and denoted by a fare code on the ticket.

Airline fares: Price charged for an airline ticket.

Airline Reporting Corporation (ARC): A corporation consisting of airlines, both domestic and international, whose main purpose is to authorize and govern travel agencies. www.arccorp.com

All-expense tour: a tour offering all or most components, usually with meals, for a pre-established price. The terms all-expense or all-inclusive are often misused. The terms and conditions of a tour contract should always specify exactly what is covered.

All-suite hotel: A hotel whose entire inventory of sleeping rooms have separate bedroom, bathroom, living room or parlor areas, and possibly a kitchenette or other special features.

American Automobile Association (AAA): A nationwide organization that provides members with services, such as travel agencies, and travel and automobile insurance. www.aaa.com

American Bus Association (ABA): A trade organization consisting of member motorcoach lines throughout the country. www.buses.org

American Hotel & Lodging Association (AH&LA): A federation of lodging industry trade associations covering the United States, Canada, Mexico, and Central and South America. www.ahma.com

American Society of Association Executives (ASAE): Considered the advocate for the nonprofit sector, it has 25,000 members who manage leading associations, and represents vendors that offer products and services to the association community.www.asaenet.org

American Society of Travel Agents (ASTA): The oldest and largest organization in the world for travel agents. Other companies providing travel industry products and services can be associate members. www.asta.org

Americans with Disabilities Act (ADA): U.S. civil rights statute passed in 1990 to meet the needs of disabled people, requiring public buildings to meet minimum standards to make their facilities accessible to individuals with physical disabilities. Applies to hotels, motorcoaches, restaurants and other hospitality and foodservice businesses in the USA.

Analog: Conveying data electronically in relation to a television, radio or telephone signal by varying frequency or amplitude.

Association executive: A full-time professional administrator who is employed by an association and is responsible for planning and promoting annual conventions and association meetings.

Association of British Travel Agents (ABTA): The principal trade association of United Kingdom travel agents and tour operators. www.abta.com

Association: An organized group of individuals and/or companies who band together to accomplish a common purpose, usually to provide for the needs of its members, and is usually organized under a nonprofit legal status. Also called a trade association.

Attendance: Number of people at a meeting, event, show or exhibit.

Attendees: A combination of delegates, exhibitors, media, speakers and guests/companions who attend an event.

Attraction: A location or activity that offers items of specific interest. Examples of attractions include a natural or scenic wonder, a man-made theme park, a cultural or historic exhibition, or a wildlife/ecological park. Culinary attractions are museums, homes of famous chefs, or places where recipes were first invented or made popular.

Attrition: Shortfall of sleeping room block pick-up or food-and-beverage projections from numbers agreed to in a contract. Penalties for attrition may be outlined in a contract's attrition clause.

Audio/visual (A/V or AV): Equipment used in audio/visual presentations, such as television monitors and video equipment.

AVA: American Viticultural Area, a term used to describe a wine appellation with a prescribed geographic boundary. Often mistakenly used to describe wine appellations outside the United States, this term applies only to those regions in the USA.

Average room rate: The total guest room revenue for a given period's occupied rooms divided by the number of rooms occupied for the same period.

Back of the house: A term used in hotels to refer to areas for staff only.

Back-to-back: Travel program operating on a continuous uninterrupted basis so that one group arrives as another departs.

Banner advertising: An advertisement on a website that allows users to "click through" to the advertiser's website.

Banquet event order (BEO): A form used to provide details to personnel concerned with a specific food or beverage function or meeting room setups.

Bed and breakfast (B&B): A facility, often a home, which offers an overnight room accommodation with breakfast.

Bed tax: Tax placed on hotel/motel room rentals. Generally all or part of the revenues generated are used in financing convention facilities or tourism offices. Also called room tax, hotel tax and transient occupancy tax.

Bias: preferential display on a reservations computer of a host carrier flight schedule.

Block: Number of sleeping rooms reserved for one specific group. Also called a "room block".

Blocked space: Sleeping rooms, exhibit, meeting or other space reserved for use by an organization intending to hold a meeting.

BOH: back of house, usually with regard to restaurants

Bonding: the guarantee of protection for a supplier or consumer. In the travel industry, certain bonding programs are mandatory. The ARC insists that travel agents be bonded to protect the airlines against defaults. Professional operators and agents buy bonds voluntarily to protect their clients.

Booking form: a document which tour purchasers must complete which gives the operator full particulars about who is buying the tour. It states exactly what is being purchased, (including options) and must be signed as acknowledgment that the liability clause has been read and understood.

Booth: One or more standard units of exhibit space. In the United States, a standard unit is a 10 feet x 10 feet (3 m x 3 m) space. However, if an exhibitor purchases multiple units side-by-side or back-to-back, the combined space also is referred to as a booth.

Break-out sessions: Smaller group sessions, panels, workshops or any presentations that are offered concurrently within the meeting and are formed to focus on specific subjects.

British Guild of Travel Writers (BGTW): An association of media professionals who focus on travel. Members include journalists, authors, editors, photographers and broadcasters.

Business attire: Business suits or jackets with shirts and ties for men, and day dresses or suits for women; usually means office wear.

Business casual: A style of dress that is less formal than the standard office attire of suit and tie or dress.

Cafeteria: a food-service operation of a limited menu, in which customers carry their own trays to seating.

Canadian Automobile Association (CAA): A Canadian organization that provides members with services, such as travel agencies, and travel and automobile insurance, as well as roadside assistance. www.caa.ca

Carrier: transportation company such as an airline, motor coach, cruise line, or railroad which carries passengers and/or cargo

Carrying capacity: the number of visitor arrivals that a destination can handle without creating new or unnecessary strain on its infrastructure

Cash flow: monies available to meet a company's daily operating expenses, as opposed to equity, accounts receivable, or other credits not immediately accessible

Ceiling height: The maximum height of the ceiling of an exhibition hall or meeting room. Dimensions quoted by halls and hotels often do not take into account any light fixtures hanging from the ceiling.

Certified Association Executive (CAE): Certification program offered by ASAE designed to elevate professional standards, enhance performance and designate those who demonstrate knowledge essential to the practice of association management.

Certified Culinary Travel Professional (CCTP): A designation conferred by the World Food Travel Association upon professionals who have completed the certified culinary travel professional program and who demonstrate knowledge essential to working in the food tourism industry.

Certified Meeting Professional (CMP): Program offered by the Convention Industry Council to certify competency in meeting management.

Certified Speaking Professional (CSP): Accredited designation offered by the National Speakers Association. This is earned from extensive, documented speaking experience and client satisfaction.

Certified Tour Professional (CTP): A designation administered by the National Tour Foundation and conferred upon tour professionals who complete prescribed evaluation requirements.

Certified Travel Counselor (CTC): A designation conferred upon travel professionals who have completed a travel management program offered by the Institute of Certified Travel Agents.

Charter operations: (1) term referring the transportation of pre-formed groups which have the exclusive use of the vehicle. (2) An operator authorized to arrange transportation, however, is not limited to dealing with pre-formed groups, but can itself form the tour group.

Charter: to hire the exclusive use of any aircraft, motor coach, or other vehicle for the purpose of conveyance

Chef's table: A special table in a restaurant, usually near the kitchen, where the patrons (often VIPs) receive special attention from the chef. Can also refer to the opportunity for a meeting professional to sample a menu in advance of the event, usually in the company of the chef.

Circle trip: a journey with stopovers that returns to the point of departure

City guide: a person who specializes in tours of the local city area only

Closeout: finalization of a tour, cruise, or similar group travel project after which time no further clients are accepted. Any unsold air or hotel space is released, and final payments are sent to all suppliers.

Coach: The largest cabin in an aircraft; car on a train; the type of standard price paid for a ticket with no upgrades or discounts. Also short for "motorcoach".

Commercial rate: A special rate given by a hotel or rental car company to an organization based on either the volume of business done or the type of accommodation or rental car. Also referred to as a corporate rate.

Commercial recreation system: recreational products, services, and facilities created and operated by privately owned businesses or corporations as opposed to public facilities

Commission: a percentage of a selling price paid to a retailer by a supplier. In the travel industry, travel agents receive commissions for selling tour packages or other services.

Commissioned tours: A tour available for sale through retail and wholesale travel agencies, which provides for a payment of an agreed upon sales commission either to the retail or wholesale seller.

Common carrier: a privately owned carrier that offers transportation for a fee

Complete meeting package: An all-inclusive plan offered by conference centers; includes lodging, all meals and support services.

Complimentary (comp): Service, space or item given at no charge.

Complimentary ratio: The number of rooms provided at no cost based on the number of occupied rooms. The industry standard is one complimentary room per 20 to 50 rooms occupied per day.

Complimentary registration: Waiver of registration fees.

Concessionaire: a firm that, under contract rights, operates for another party (in many cases, a government agency) food and beverage services, lodging facilities, and other services on-site at an attraction.

Concierge: a hotel employee who handles restaurant and tour reservations, travel arrangements, and other details for hotel guests.

Concurrent sessions: Multiple sessions scheduled at the same time; programs on different themes or subjects offered simultaneously.

Conditions: the section or clause of a transportation/tour contract which specifies what is not included and which may spell out the circumstances under which the contract many be invalidated

Conference: An event used by any organization to meet and exchange views, convey a message, or open a debate. No tradition, continuity or periodicity is required to convene a conference. Conferences are usually of short duration with specific objectives.

Confidential tariff: a schedule of wholesale rates distributed in confidence to travel wholesalers and agents. Better known as a net rate.

Configuration: the interior arrangement of a vehicle, particularly an airplane. The same airplane, for example, may be configured for 190 coach-class passengers, or it may hold 12

first-class passengers and 170 coach passengers, Configuration is also used in conjunction with how the plane is arranged such as three seats on each side or in larger planes two seats on each side with four middle seats (which would be referred to as 2-4-2, designating the number of seats each on the left, middle and right portions of the plane).

Confirmed reservation: an oral or written agreement by a supplier that he has received and will honor a reservation. Oral confirmations have no legal weight. Even written or telegraphed confirmations have specified or implied limitations. e.g.: a hotel not honoring a reservation after 6 pm., unless late arrival has been guaranteed in some manner.

Consolidation: cancellation by a charter tour operator of one or more tours/flights associated with a specific charter departure or departure period, with the transfer of passengers to another charter tour/flight to depart on or near the same day.

Consolidator: A person or company with the resources to contract bulk airline seats and resell to the public or through travel agencies.

Consortium: A trade association formed by travel agencies, tour operators and hotels to increase the buying power of its collective members. These associations help an independent company compete with a major chain in areas such as override commissions and availability of discounts.

Contract: a legally enforceable agreement between two or more parties

Contractor: an operator who provides services to wholesalers, tour operators and travel agents

Convention & Visitors Bureau (CVB): A nonprofit organization supported by bed taxes, government budget allocations, private memberships or a combination of these. A CVB promotes tourism, encourages groups to hold meetings and trade shows in its city, and assists groups before and during meetings. Its scope of operations may be more extensive depending on the organization's charter.

Convention Industry Council (CIC): A federation of national and international organizations representing individuals, firms or properties involved in the meetings, conventions, expositions and travel and tourism industries. www.conventionindustry.org

Convention Service Manager (CSM): Facility manager or CVB staff member responsible for the logistics of an event.

Convention: An event where the primary activity of attendees is to attend educational sessions, participate in meetings and socialize. There is a secondary exhibit component.

Co-op tour: a tour that is sold through a number of wholesalers, cooperatives, or other outlets in order to increase sales and reduce the possibility of tour cancellations.

Corporate meeting: Gathering of employees of a commercial organization. Usually, attendance is required, and travel, room and most meal expenses are paid for by the organization.

Corporate planner: Meeting planner who works for a corporation.

Costing: the process of itemizing and calculating all costs the tour operator will pay on a given tour. Costing is usually the function of the operations manager.

Courier: European terminology to mean tour manager/guide

Cover charge: a fee, usually a flat amount per person, charged to patrons to cover the cost of music and entertainment. Also called simply "cover". The number of "covers" a restaurant handles means how many people it served for a specific meal.

Customized tour: a tour designed to fit the specific needs of a particular target market.

Customs: the common term for a government agency charged with monitoring and/or collecting duty on items imported into that country. The agency can also restrict the entry of persons and forbidden items.

Cut-off date: Designated date when the facility will release a block of sleeping rooms to the general public. The date is typically three to four weeks before a convention. Also called reservation review date. Can also mean the designated day when the buyer must release or add commitments to their event or tour.

Day rate: a reduced rate granted for the use of a guest room during the daytime, not overnight occupancy. Often used when someone needs a display room, office, or is in-transit due to odd airline schedules.

Definite booking: Space reservations confirmed in writing.

Deluxe tour: in travel usage, presumably of the highest standard.

Departure date: Date when majority of meeting participants check out of a facility.

Departure tax: fee collected from the traveler by the host country at the time of departure

Deposit policy: a specified amount or a percentage of the total bill due on a specified date prior to arrival

Deposit: an advance payment required to obtain confirmed space

Deregulation: the act of removing regulations from the U.S. transportation industry. The Airline Deregulation Act of 1978, which amended the U.S. Federal Aviation Act of 1958, provided for the end of the Civil Aeronautics Board's regulating authority over domestic airlines on January 1, 1985. It also provided for removing travel agent exclusivity, thus paving the way for carriers to appoint and pay commissions to non-travel agents, and for the removal of antitrust immunity for travel agents. The motorcoach industry was deregulated in 1982.

Destination management company (DMC): company or professional individual engaged in organizing tours, meetings of all types and their related activities. Also referred to as a ground operator.

Destination Marketing Association International (DMAI): the professional association of DMOs, largely in the United States, but also includes other countries. Formerly known as the International Association of Convention & Visitors Bureaus (IACVB). More information at www.destinationmarketing.org

Destination marketing organization (DMO): an organization for a city, state, province, country, region or other area whose primary purpose is the promotion of tourism to the destination. Can be structured in many different ways including a non-profit organization, a

482

membership organization, a chamber of commerce, a government office, an office of economic development, or a public-private partnership. Usually funded by membership dues, grants, hotel taxes or program fees.

Destination: A city, area or country that can be marketed to groups or individuals as a place to visit or hold a meeting. Also refers to the place where a traveler is going. In the travel industry, "destination" generally means any city, area, or country which can be marketed as a single entity for tourists.

Dine around: Use of a number of restaurants in a destination with reservations and billing arrangements to one particular client.

Direct flight: A flight that does not require a passenger to change planes, although the flight may have intermediate stops. Not the same as a non-stop flight.

Direct spending: money that goes directly from a tourist into the economy of the destination

DOC: denominazione di origine controllata ("Controlled designation of origin") is a quality assurance label for Italian food products, especially wines and various cheeses. Modeled on the French AOC, the Italian DOC began in 1963 and was updated in 1992 to comply with new EU laws on Protected Designation of Origin, which also came into effect that year.

DOM: director of marketing (usually in hotel industry)

Domestic escorted tour: a packaged, pre-planned itinerary, including the services of a tour manager (escort) within a traveler s own country

Domestic independent tour (DIT): A custom-made tour of a part of the USA planned exclusively for a client by a travel agent.

DOS: director of sales (usually in hotel industry)

Double-occupancy rate: The price per person for a room shared with another. Rate most frequently quoted in tour brochures.

Double double: a hotel room with two double-size beds in the same room.

Double-room rate: The full price of a room for two people.

Downgrade: to move to a lesser level of accommodations or a lower class of service

Duty-free imports: item amounts and categories specified by a government that are free of tax or duty charges when brought into the country

Eco-tour: A tour to environmentally sensitive areas, or designed to focus on preserving the environment.

Educational tour: tour designed around an educational activity, such as studying art

Emerging market: A group of customers who do not provide as much business as the primary target markets, but show a new interest in the destination or product.

Errors and omissions (E&O) insurance: insurance coverage equivalent to malpractice insurance, protecting an agent s or operator s staff if an act of negligence, an error, or an omission occurs which causes a client great hardship or expense.

Escort: (1) a person, usually employed or subcontracted by the tour operator who accompanies a tour from departure to return, acting as a troubleshooter. This term is often incorrectly interchanged with courier, conductor, host, manager, director, or leader, since each term designates different duties although they do perform the escort function.

Escorted tour: (1) a pre-arranged travel program, usually for a group, escorted by a tour manager or leader. In a fully conducted tour, the escort will also provide guide service throughout.

Escrow account: funds placed in the custody of licensed financial institutions for safekeeping in a specific account with restricted access. Many contracts in travel require that agents and tour operators maintain customers' deposits and prepayments in escrow accounts until the time of service.

Ethnic tour: tour designed for people usually of the same heritage traveling to their native origin, or to a destination with ethnic relevance

European Incentive & Business Travel & Meeting Exhibition (EIBTM): A trade show for European incentive operators. www.eibtm.com

Excursion: journey where the traveler returns to the original point of departure

Executive coach: A luxury motorcoach with seating of 25 or less that can include such amenities as television, galley (kitchen), wet bar, card tables, etc.

Exhibit booth: An individual display set up to show products or convey a message.

Exhibit: The display materials and product housed in a booth.

Extensions: an arranged sub-tour offered optionally before or after a tour or cruise at an extra charge

Familiarization tour (FAM or famil): A program designed to acquaint participants with specific destinations or services. Offered in groups and on an individual basis.

Fare, Advanced Purchase Excursion (APEX): Heavily discounted excursion fares for international travel, usually with cancellation penalties attached.

Fare, base: The price of an airline ticket without the taxes.

Fare, bulk: A discounted, net price offered only to tour operators who directly purchase a specified block of seats from a carrier. The operator must then sell the seats at a marked-up price.

Fare, economy: in U.S. domestic airline operations, passenger carriage at a level below coach service; in international operations, carriage at a level below first class

Fare, excursion: A discounted airline ticket that has the following restrictions: must be round trip, comply with minimum and maximum stay, and be purchased in advance.

Fare, group: Usually round-trip travel in a specified period of time with a minimum number of participants required.

Fare, open jaw: Fare established where the passenger departs the originating city to a destination, but returns to the originating city from another destination.

Fare, promotional: Usually round-trip, restricted tickets that have been discounted for a limited amount of time to stimulate sales or introduce a new travel product or service.

Fare, regular: Unrestricted fare.

Federal Aviation Administration (FAA): The U.S. Department of Transportation agency that is primarily concerned with the promotion and regulation of civil aviation. www.faa.gov

Feeder service: Air service that provides convenient connections to other air services. Typically refers to air service from very small destinations to larger airports with more connections.

Fixed expense: an expense related to a tour as a whole, which does not vary with the number of passengers such as a meal or a per person entrance to an attraction

Flag carrier: a transportation carrier designated by a country to serve international routes

Folio: an itemized record of hotel guest charges and credits, maintained in the front office until departure. Also referred to as guest bill or guest statement.

Foodie: a colloquial English language word used to describe a food enthusiast. Sometimes mistakenly ascribed by non-foodies to mean someone who prefers premium and expensive experiences, the term actually means any kind of food enthusiast, regardless of the amount of money spent.

Food cover: a unit of food service provided to a customer (also see "cover"). The term is not synonymous with meal because a food cover may comprise only a cup of coffee or bowl of soup

Force Majeure clause: Contract clause that limits liability should an event be prevented due to acts of God, acts of war, civil disturbances, labor strikes or other disruptive circumstances beyond a facility's control. Usually inclement weather does not apply.

Foreign flag: any carrier not registered in the USA (applies to air and sea transportation)

Franchise: the right to market a product or service, often exclusively for a specified area by a manufacturer, developer, or distributor in return for a fee

Frequent independent travel (FIT): A trip planned for an individual client's specifications, and is normally prepaid and usually unescorted. Also referred to as "foreign independent travel". The terms are frequently interchanged and confused.

Front office: office situated in the lobby of a hotel, the main functions of which are (1) control/sale of guest rooms, (2) providing keys, mail, and information, (3) keeping guest accounts, rendering bills/payments, and (4) providing information to other departments

Front of the house (FOH): the front-facing, or guest-facing side of hotel and restaurant operations.

Full house: a hotel with all guest rooms occupied

Full-service restaurant: a food-service establishment with several menu selections and table service

Function room: room used for functions, can often also be a banquet room

Function: a pre-arranged, catered group activity, usually held in private room/area

Gateway: city, airport, or area from which a flight or tour departs; a city with an international airport

General session: one meeting within a larger convention that all delegates attend simultaneously

GM: general manager (usually in hotel industry)

Ground operator: a company or individual providing such services as hotel, sightseeing, transfers, and all other related services for groups. Also see receptive operator.

Group booking: reservation for a block of rooms for a single group.

Group leader: an individual, acting as liaison to a tour operator, acts as escort

Group tour: A prearranged, prepaid travel program for a group usually including transportation, accommodations, attraction admissions and meals. Also referred to as a package tour.

Guarantee: The minimum number of servings to be paid for by the client, whether they are actually consumed or not. Always required to be provided in advance, but cut-off dates vary widely for guarantee numbers.

Guaranteed tour: a tour guaranteed to operate

Guest account: an itemized record of a guest s charges and credits

Guide: (1) a person qualified to conduct tours of specific localities or attractions (many reliable guides are licensed), (2) an airline, bus, railroad, or ship manual of schedules and fares, usually printed seasonally

Guided tour: a local sightseeing trip conducted by a guide

Head tax: fee charged for arriving and departing passengers in some countries

Headquarters hotel: facility, as the center of operations, where registration, general sessions, and conference staff office are located.

Heads in beds: term that refers to sleeping room reservations at a hotel, usually quoted by DMO staff whose goal is often to get more sleeping room bookings at its member hotels

High season: the period of the year when occupancy/usage of a hotel or attraction is normally the highest. High usage invariably means higher prices for rooms or admission. Also referred to as in-season or peak season.

Hospitality Sales & Marketing Association International (HSMAI): The leading international organization of sales and marketing professionals representing all areas of the hospitality industry. www.hsmai.org

Host: (1) a representative of the group (organizer) that may arrange optional excursions and answer questions but does not have escort authority (2) liaison to the tour operator or tour manager, or (3) a representative who provides only information or greeting services or who assists at the destination with ground arrangements without actually accompanying the tour.

Hotel classifications: Classification of a hotel by its amenities, facilities, service and cost. Qualifications and terms may vary by country.

Hotel, deluxe: A top-grade hotel or resort offering the highest service and the maximum variety of amenities. All rooms have a private bath, and all the usual expected services are provided.

Hotel, first class and luxury: this type of hotel offers a number of special services to the business/leisure traveler. They may offer first-rate restaurants, banquet and conference rooms, valet service, room service, cable television with international channels and a complimentary morning newspaper.

Hotel, limited service or economy, budget or service: A hotel or motel reasonably priced, generally providing a bed, telephone, television, shower and sometimes parking. They often do not have room service or a restaurant.

Hotel, moderate: a medium-priced hotel with services and amenities such as a restaurant and possibly small conference rooms.

Hotel, upper moderate: hotel or motel that offers special services such as a first-rate restaurant, banquet and conference rooms, valet service, room service, cable TV, and a host of other amenities.

Hub and spoke tours: tours which utilize a central destination with side trips of varying length to nearby destinations

Immigration: the process by which a government official verifies a person's passport, visa or origin of citizenship with the intent of admission to the country

Inbound tour operator: company specializing in domestic tours for (usually foreign) visitors in the strictest sense. Can also be used interchangeably with receptive operator.

Inbound tour: group of travelers whose trip originated in another city or country

Incentive event: Celebratory event intended to showcase persons who meet or exceed sales or production goals.

Incentive meeting: Reward meeting, usually of high quality, in payment for achieving goals.

Incentive tour: (1) a trip offered as a prize, particularly to stimulate the productivity of employees or sales agents, or (2) the business of operating such travel programs

Incentive Travel & Meeting Executives (ITME): Also known as the Motivation Show. Each year, more than 20,000 top business executives attend this show to learn the latest in effective motivation program planning. In addition, more than 2,000 suppliers of merchandise and travel services exhibit their products. www.motivationshow.com

Incentive travel company: Company that designs and handles some or all elements of incentive travel programs.

Incentive travel: A travel reward given by companies to employees to stimulate productivity. Also known as an incentive trip.

Incentive: Reward offered to stimulate greater effort.

Incidentals: Expenses other than room and tax billed to a guest's account. Examples include phone charges, wireless Internet, minibar and room service.

Inclusive tour: A specific package in which all components of the package are part of the price. Generally, an inclusive package includes transportation, lodging, meals, gratuities and taxes, and some form of sightseeing or rental car. The terms and conditions of a tour contract should specify exactly what is covered. Also referred to as an all-expense tour and an all-inclusive tour.

Independent contractor: a person contractually retained to perform specific tasks. The other person has no control over the independent contractor other than what is written in the contract. In the context of group travel, the tour operator often retains a tour manager, or tour brochure designer/writer might be hired in this capacity.

Independent tour: an unescorted tour sold through agents to individuals. For one price, the client guaranteed air travel, hotel room, attraction admissions and (typically) a car rental.

Indirect air carrier: generally synonymous with charter tour operator. A tour operator, travel agent, or other promoter who (under federal regulations) contracts for charter space from a carrier for resale to the public. In theory, indirect air carriers act as independent, risk-taking entrepreneurs, promoting their own product

Indirect spending: not money spent by a tourist, rather the extended impact of the visitor's total spending after the visitor has left

Intermediate carrier: a carrier that transports a passenger or piece of baggage as part of an inter-line movement, but on which neither the point of origin or destination is located

Intermodal tour: tour using several forms of transportation such as airplanes, motorcoaches, cruise ships, and trains to create a diversified and efficient tour package

Internationale Tourismusbörse (ITB): An annual trade show held in Berlin, Germany with 50,000+ tourism professionals from around the world, including travel agents, tour operators and media. More info at www.itb-berlin.de.

IT Number: a registration number that is assigned to a tour package

Itinerary: the travel schedule provided by a travel agent or tour operator for the client. A proposed or preliminary itinerary may be rather vague or very specific. A final itinerary spells out all details, including flight numbers, departure times, and similar data, as well as describing planned activities.

Land operator: a company that provides local services. See also ground/receptive operator

Lead time: Time between when arrangements are made and when an event occurs.

Leads: Requests for proposals generated by direct sales, participation in trade shows, etc. Leads also are provided to DMO members whose services and/or products meet the needs of a DMO client company.

Leg: portion on a journey between two scheduled stops

Letter of agreement: a letter from the buyer to the supplier accepting the terms of the proposal. This may also be the supplier s initial proposal that has been initialed by the buyer

Load factor: average number of seats occupied, e.g. motorcoach or air

Lost business: A group that was bid on, or was holding tentative dates, which was subsequently booked in another city or facility.

Low season: that time of the year at any given destination when tourist traffic, and often rates, are at their lowest. Also referred to as off-peak or off-season.

Manifest: final official listing of all passengers and/or cargo aboard a transportation vehicle or vessel

Market segments: Categorization of people, organizations or businesses by professional discipline or primary areas of interest for the purposes of sales analysis or assignment.

Market share: the sales made by an enterprise divided by the total sales of a service or product.

Marketing: a process of identifying customer wants and needs, and developing a plan to meet those wants and needs for a profit.

Markup: (1) difference between the cost and the selling price of a given product; (2) difference between the net rate charged by a tour operator, hotel, or other supplier and the retail selling price of the service.

Master account: All items charged to a group. May include room, tax, incidentals, food and beverage, audio/visual equipment, decor, etc. Also known as a master bill.

Master bill: all items contracted by the operator and supplier that will be paid by the operator

Meals, American plan (AP): Includes three full meals and a room.

Meals, Bermuda plan: Includes an American-style breakfast and a room.

Meals, continental breakfast: breakfast includes juice, toast, roll or sweet roll, and coffee or tea.

Meals, continental plan (CP): includes continental breakfast and room.

Meals, demi-pension: includes breakfast, and lunch or dinner, and a room.

Meals, European plan (EP): rate includes only a room; no meals.

Meals, modified American plan (MAP): rate includes breakfast, dinner and a room.

Meet and greet: pre-purchased service for meeting and greeting a client upon arrival in a city, usually at the airport, and assisting the client with entrance formalities, baggage and transportation.

Meeting management company: Handles site selection, negotiations and turnkey support. Also handles the day-to-day management of the organization. Also see DMC.

Meeting planner: person whose job it is to oversee and arrange every aspect of a meeting.

Meeting Professionals International (MPI): MPI is the largest trade association for the meetings industry and provides its members with the latest research and trends, professional development and networking opportunities. www.mpiweb.org

Meeting profile: a written report outlining statistics of previous meetings, anticipated use of services, profile of attendees, etc.

Meeting specifications: Information about a meeting (e.g. function space, food and beverage requirements) that is sent directly to a venue or circulated by a CVB.

Meeting: an event where the primary activity of the attendees is to attend educational sessions, participate in meetings, socialize or attend organized events. There is no exhibit component to this event.

Minimum land package: the minimum tour expressed in terms of cost and ingredients that must be purchased to qualify for an airline inclusive tour, or contract bulk inclusive tour fare. Such packages usually include a certain number of nights lodging, other specified ingredients such as sightseeing tours and/or entertainment and/or car rental. The minimum rate for the combined air fares and ground package is often expressed as a percentage (often 100% or 110%) of the lowest regular fare for the air travel scheduled.

Minimum: smallest number of covers and/or beverages served at a catered event. A surcharge may be added to the client's bill if the minimum is not reached.

MOD: manager on duty (in hotel industry)

Motor coach tour operator: a company that creates tours in which group members are transported via motor coach to their destination, itinerary activities and back.

Motor coach (or motorcoach): a large, comfortable, well-powered bus that can transport groups and their luggage over long distances. Motor coaches are normally able to accommodate 46 to 54 passengers.

Move-in/move-out dates: dates set for installation/dismantling of an exposition.

Mystery tour: a tour to an unpublished destination -- passengers get a surprise!

National Tour Association (NTA): a trade association of North American motor coach tour operators. www.ntaonline.com

Net wholesale rate: a rate usually slightly lower than the wholesale rate, applicable to groups when components are specifically mentioned in a tour brochure. The rate is marked up by wholesale sellers to cover tour costs.

NGO: non-governmental organization, any non-profit or voluntary group which is organized on a local, national or international level.

Non-stop flight: a flight from one city to another with no stops in between. Not the same as a direct flight (see direct flight).

No-show: reservation made, but participant did not attend or cancel according to cancellation guidelines.

Occupancy rate: the total number of rooms occupied during a given time period divided by the total number of rooms available for occupancy during that same period.

Off-peak: a period in which a hotel or attraction is not in its busiest season

Off-site event: activity scheduled away from headquarters facility.

On-demand public transportation: transportation services, such as taxicabs that do not have regular schedules

Open jaw: an arrangement, route, or fare, authorized in a tariff, granting the traveling public the privilege of purchasing round-trip transportation from the point of origin to one destination, at which another form of transportation is used to reach a second destination, where a passenger resumes the initial form of transportation to return to the point of origin. Used mainly for airline travel.

Operations: performing the practical work of operating a tour or travel program. Operations usually involve the in-house control and handling of all phases of the tour, with both suppliers and clients.

Operator: A loose term that may mean contractor, tour operator, wholesaler, or a combination of any or all of those functions.

Option date: the date agreed upon when a tentative agreement is to become a definite commitment by the buyer

Option: tour feature extension or side trip offered at extra cost

Outbound operator (or outbound tour): a company or tour that takes groups from a given city or country to another city or country.

Outbound tour: any tour that takes groups outside a given city or country, opposite of inbound

Outfitter: a business that provides services or equipment at a recreational facility

Overbooked: Accepting reservations for more hotel guest rooms than are available. Also refers to oversold airline flights.

Overflow: attendees booked into other facilities after headquarters' facilities are full.

Override: A commission over and above the normal base commission percentage, often paid in conjunction with volume business. Also referred to as an incentive or incentive commission.

Pacing: the scheduling of activities within an itinerary to make for a realistic operation and give a certain balance of travel time, sightseeing, events and free time

Package tour: a combination of several travel components provided by different suppliers, which are sold to the consumer as a single product at a single price

Package: travel arrangements with two or more components offered for one price, inclusive of all taxes. Also refers to a single-fee booth package offered by show management.

Packager: an individual or organization that coordinates and promotes the development of a package tour and establishes operating procedures and guidelines for that tour.

Passport: government identification document permitting a citizen to enter and depart a country

Pax: industry abbreviation for "passengers", usually used with a number, e.g., 46 pax (= 46 passengers)

Peak fare, rate, or season: highest level of charges assessed during a year

Peak night: referring to the night during a meeting when those in attendance occupy most rooms.

Per diem: a limited amount of money a meeting attendee can spend per day on food and other expenses.

Permission marketing: an e-mail marketing campaign that only sends messages to users who have requested (or opted-in) to receive specific types of information.

Pick-up: number of guest rooms actually used from a room block.

Pipe and drape: light-weight aluminum tubing and drapery used to separate exhibit booths, staging areas, and other similar locations.

Port of entry: point at which persons enter a country where customs and immigration services exist

Pow Wow International: a computerized scheduled appointment show for international tour operators always held in the United States and sponsored by the U.S. Travel Association. Also called simply "Pow Wow". www.ipw.com

Pre- and post-trip tours: optional extension or side trip package offered before or after a meeting, gathering or convention.

Pre-con meeting: a meeting at the convention center or hotel just before the show begins to set up. Attended by staff, contractors and building people to review the details of the event.

Pre-formed group: a tour group in existence prior to the tour, the members of which share a common bond, interest, or organization affiliation. Also referred to as an affinity group.

Pre-function space: area adjacent to the main event location. Often used for receptions prior to a meal or coffee breaks during a meeting.

Press release: a prepared statement released to the news media about a company, product, service, individual or show.

Pricing strategy: method by which cost of a room or service is derived, based on whether or not near term income is critical, and rapid market penetration for eventual market control is desired.

Pricing: decision-making process of ascertaining what price to charge for a given tour, once total costs are known. Pricing involves determining the markup, studying the competition, and evaluating the tour value for the price to be charged; function performed by the operations manager.

Proof of citizenship: a document, necessary for obtaining a passport, which establishes one's nationality

Protected: guarantee by a supplier or wholesaler to pay commissions, plus all refunds to clients, on pre-paid, confirmed bookings regardless of subsequent cancellation of a tour or cruise.

Professional Convention Management Association (PCMA): a nonprofit international association of professionals in the meetings industry whose mission is to deliver education and promote the value of professional convention management. www.pcma.org

Public space: space in a facility that is available for general use by guests; may also be available for rental for a fee.

Publicity: a media campaign, normally consisting of a series of public notices and advertising activities, aimed at ensuring maximum attendance by focusing attention on an event.

Receptive operator: a tour operator who provides local services, transfers, sightseeing, guides, etc. Many large receptive operators develop packages and sell them through wholesale tour operators in foreign countries. Also referred to as a ground operator, an inbound tour operator, a land operator and a receiving agent.

Release: (1) signed form giving the tour operator permission to use a person s name, picture or statement in an advertisement; (2) to give up space, as in returning unsold hotel room reservations

Religious Conference Management Association (RCMA): RCMA, the society for religious meeting professionals, provides resources to enhance the professionalism of its members and improve the experience of religious meeting attendees worldwide. www.rcmaweb.org

Rental charges: cost of renting equipment or exhibit space for a period of time. It may or may not include ancillary services.

Request for proposal (RFP): a document that stipulates what services the organization wants from an outside contractor and requests a bid to perform such services.

Resort casual: Attire for warm weather destinations, including mid- to knee-length shorts;

collarless or golf shirts; khakis and sandals. Women can wear linen, casual skirts or sundresses.

Resort: a hotel, motel or condominium complex located in an area associated with recreation and leisure, such as the mountains or the seashore. Normally offer facilities for sports and recreational activities. Often positioned in an upscale way.

Resort fee: an add-on fee charged by hotels and resorts, ostensibly for their guest's use of common hotel facilities like the swimming pool, gym, business center, etc. Many travelers hate this kind of add-on as they are of the opinion that these hotel services should already be added into the room rate. To them, the resort fee is a "profit surcharge".

Responsibility clause: the section of a brochure that spells out the conditions under which a tour is sold. The clause should name the party responsible for the tour financially.

Retailer: (1) travel agents or (2) one who sells directly to the consumer

Return on investment (ROI): net profit divided by net worth. A financial ratio indicating the degree of profitability.

Revenue per available room (RevPAR): A measure used by hotels that divides revenue for a given time period by the number of available rooms for the same time period.

Right of first refusal: a courtesy extended to a previously booked party to approve/disapprove a concurrent booking or to save uncontracted space for program growth.

Right-to-work state: in the USA, a state where joining a trade/workers' union is not a condition of employment.

Risk monies: funds that an agency would not recoup should a tour not take place, such as nonrefundable deposits, promotional expenses, and printing costs

Room capacity: number of people that can function safely and comfortably in a room.

Room nights: number of rooms blocked or occupied multiplied by number of nights each room is reserved or occupied.

Room pick-up: the number of sleeping rooms actually used by show attendees and exhibitors.

Room rate, convention rate: a discounted rate for a particular group.

Room rate, corporate rate: special rates assigned to corporations, usually priced to reflect the corporation's bulk buying requirements.

Room rate, day rate (or use rate): usually the regular rate of a room for use by a guest during a given day up to 5:00 p.m.

Room rate, flat rate (or group rate): specific room rate for a group agreed upon by the hotel and group in advance.

Room rate, group rate: room rate negotiated for booking multiple guests. It usually reflects a percentage reduction from the rack rate.

Room rate, inclusive: the amount charged for a room, usually including breakfast (or other meals), taxes and service charge.

Room rate, net group rate: a wholesale rate for groups (usually a minimum of 10-15 people) to which an operator may add a mark-up.

Room rate, net wholesale rate: a rate usually lower than the group rate, applicable to groups or individuals when a hotel is specifically mentioned in a tour folder

Room rate, rack rate: the regular published rate of a hotel or other tourism service. Not a discounted rate.

Room rate, run-of-the-house rate: flat rate for which a hotel or motel agrees to offer any of its available rooms to a group. Final assignment of the rooms is the discretion of the hotel.

Room rate: the amount charged for the occupancy of a room.

Room service: food or beverages served in a guest's sleeping room or suite

Room setup, banquet round: round table used for meal service; depending on the diameter, can comfortably seat up to 12 persons.

Room setup, classroom: tables lined up in rows, one behind the other with chairs facing forward.

Room setup, conference: tables set in rectangle or oval shape with chairs on both sides and ends. Same as boardroom setup.

Room setup, crescent rounds: uses rounds with seating on two thirds to three quarters of the table and no seating with its back to the speaker. Used for banquet-to-meeting or meeting-to-banquet quick set. Also called buzz style setup or half-moon seating.

Room setup, herringbone: rows of chairs or tables set in a V shape facing a head table, stage or speaker. Also referred to as chevron seating.

Room setup, hollow square: tables set in a square or rectangle with chairs around the outside of the table. The center of the tables is hollow.

Room setup, reception: the room is typically empty with no chairs or tables. If tables are used, they tend to be tall, have a small diameter, and be used without chairs.

Room setup, theater: chairs are set up in rows with no tables. Also referred to as auditorium seating.

Room setup, U-shape: series of tables set up in the shape of a U with chairs set all around on one or both sides.

Room type, double: a room for two people, normally with a double bed.

Room type, double-double: A hotel room for two with two double beds or two queen beds.

Room type, hospitality suite: A hotel suite, parlor or studio engaged for the entertaining of those attending a convention, meeting or event.

Room type, single: Accommodations for one person only.

Room type, suite: A room providing a separate bedroom and living room.

Room type, twin: A room for two guests with two single beds.

Rooming list: List of guests and room data supplied to facility prior to arrival.

Royal Automobile Association (RAA): An Australia organization that provides members with services, such as travel and automobile assistance. www.raa.com.au

Sales mission: intense selling effort in a particular locality; cold calling to qualify leads. Usually performed by a group of people from one organization who may or may not all be in a sales capacity.

Seasons, off-season: the time of year when tourist traffic, and often rates, are at their lowest because of decreased demand. Also referred to as low season, off-peak or value season.

Seasons, peak season: the time of year when demand and price is at a premium. Also known as high season.

Seasons, shoulder season: the season between peak season and off-season when demand is average and the travel product will not produce the highest price but does not need a deep discount to generate traffic.

Series operator: a travel agent, wholesaler, tour operator or broker who blocks space in advance for a series of movements (tours) over a given period of time, not necessarily on a back-to-back basis.

Service charge: a specified percentage of a hotel's daily rate (often 10-15%) charged to the guest so a guest is relieved of the responsibility for tipping. Also a fee charged by a travel agent.

Service: non-physical, intangible attributes that management controls, including friendliness, efficiency, attitude, professionalism, and responsiveness.

Shore excursion: a land tour, usually available at ports of call and sold by cruise lines or tour operators to cruise passengers

Single supplement: an extra charge assessed to a tour purchased for single accommodations

Site destination selection company: company that investigates and suggests potential meeting sites to suit corporate or association needs

Site inspection (also called site selection): personal, careful survey of property, facility or area, usually with the idea of holding a meeting or convention there.

Site: area, location, property or specific facility used for a meeting.

SMERF: meeting industry acronym for a category of meeting market segments including social, military, educational, religious and fraternal groups. These organizations often are looking for value when selecting a meeting destination.

Society of American Travel Writers (SATW): a professional association whose purpose is to promote responsible journalism and provide professional development. Members are writers, photographers, editors, electronic media, and public relations representatives. www.satw.org

Society of Government Meeting Professionals (SGMP): a nonprofit professional organization of persons involved in planning government meetings and those individuals who supply services to government planners. www.sgmp.org

Society of Incentive & Travel Executives (SITE): a worldwide organization of business professionals dedicated to the recognition and development of motivational and performance improvement strategies of which travel is a key component. www.site-intl.org

Special event tour: a tour designed around a particular event, e.g.: Mardi Gras

Special interest tour: a tour designed to appeal to clients with a curiosity or concern about a specific subject. Most special interest tours provide an expert tour leader and usually visit places and/or events only relevant to that interest.

Spouse programs: educational and/or social events planned for spouses and guests of meeting participants.

Step-on guide: an independent guide who comes aboard a motorcoach to give an informed overview of the city or attraction to be toured

Stopover: an allowance made for leaving a flight for an indefinite period of 24 hours or more. Some flights offer stopovers en route, sometimes free and sometimes for a nominal fee.

Subcontractor: a local operator who provides services for a wholesaler

Supplier: the provider of a travel product or service such as a hotel or restaurant, not the travel agent or tour operator selling the product.

Surety bond: insurance to guarantee that an insure will carry out the specific work he or she was hired to do

Sustainability: an approach that ensures the business processes and resources can maintain their performance over time; implies respect for reduce, reuse, recycle and environmental considerations.

Target market: the group of customers who will be the focus of a company's marketing efforts.

Tariff: (1) fare or rate from a supplier; (2) class or type of a fare or rate; (3) published list of fares or rates from a supplier; (4) official publication compiling rates or fares and conditions of service

Teleconference: meeting that brings together three or more people through telecommunications. Also known as a conference call.

Territory: a salesperson's exclusive region or area of prospects and clients.

Terroir: flavor characteristics imparted to a product by the environment where it is produced. Originally used to describe wine, the term is now being used to apply to coffee, chocolate and other value-added agricultural products. Its usage today implies that terroir embodies not just the soil of the area, but the air, water, weather and geography of the region and even the love bestowed upon the product by its producer

Themed tour: a tour designed around a specific theme such as fall foliage, also a special interest tour

Third party: person or organization who is not considered the end user of a product.

Through fare: the price of an airline ticket from origin to a destination; one price even though traveling may involve two or more airlines to reach the destination.

Tour basing fare: a reduced-rate excursion fare available only to those who buy pre-paid tours or packages. Tour basing fares include inclusive tours, group inclusive tours, incentive tours, contract bulk inclusive tours, and group round-trip inclusive tours.

Tour broker: an individual licensed and bonded by the (U.S.) Interstate Commerce Commission to operate motorcoach tours in the United States and, in some cases, Canada. Also known as a motorcoach broker or tour operator.

Tour catalog: a publication produced by tour wholesalers listing all of their tour offerings. Catalogs are distributed to retail agents who make them available to their customers. Also referred to as a tour brochure or tour tariff.

Tour consultant: individual within a travel agency selling and advising clients regarding a tour.

Tour coupon: a voucher that can be exchanged for a travel product

Tour departure: the date of the start by any individual or group of a tour program, also used in referral to the entire operation of that single tour

Tour escort: the tour company staff member or independent contractor who conducts the tour. Often called the tour manager or tour director. It is technically a person that only escorts the group and does not have charge of the commentary portion.

Tour guide: a person who takes people on local sightseeing excursions of limited duration

Tour leader: usually a group leader, also see escort

Tour manager: a person employed as the escort for a group of tourists, usually for the duration of the entire trip, perhaps supplemented by local guides. The terms tour director, leader, escort, conductor, and (in Europe) courier have roughly the same meaning and are used interchangeably. A person with this title is usually at a professional well trained level.

Tour manual: (1) a summary of facts about a company's rules, regulations, and official procedures; (2) a compendium of facts about a destination, including its attractions, accommodations, geography, and special events, used by destination marketing organizations to attract tour operators and visitors and their area

Tour menu: a menu that limits a group's clients to just two or three choices at a special price

Tour operator: a person or company that negotiates discount rates, packages travel products, prints brochures, and markets these travel products through travel agents or to the general public

Tour option: any component of a package tour that is not included in the package price, but may be purchased as an added feature to extend the length of the package or enhance the trip.

Tour order: a coupon given to the purchaser of a tour package, identifying the tour, the seller, and the fact that the tour is pre-paid. It is used as a form of proof of payment and receives vouchers for meals, porterage, transfers, entrance fees, and other expenses. Also see tour vouchers.

Tour organizer: person who locates and creates groups for preformed tours. The tour organizer is often compensated only with a free trip

Tour vouchers: documents issued by tour operators to be exchanged for accommodations, meals, sightseeing, admission tickets and other services. Also referred to as coupons and tour orders.

Tour: any pre-arranged journey to one or more destinations

Tourist card: a kind of visa issued to tourists prior to entering a country (required in addition to a passport or other proof of citizenship

Tracking: a cause of action or method of monitoring, such as tracking the number of tours that come into a specific destination

Trade association: an organization that coalesces a group of individuals in a common trade, for a common purpose. Mission can range from advocacy, to cost reduction, to education or other strategic initiatives

Trade mission: a group tour with a business purpose, rather than for vacationing. The mission is usually planned for business or government representatives traveling overseas to secure new business in international markets.

Trade publication: a magazine that targets a specific industry.

Trade show: exhibit of products and services that is targeted to a specific clientele and not open to the public.

Transfer: local transportation and porterage from one carrier terminal to another, from terminal to hotel, or from hotel to activity.

Transit visa: an official document allowing the holder to stop over in a country for a brief visit in order to make a travel connection.

Transit: passenger changing planes without going through security and/or customs.

Travel agent (or travel agency): person or firm qualified to advise and arrange for travel needs such as hotel rooms, meals, transportation, tours and other travel elements. Represents all travel suppliers worldwide. Also referred to as a retailer.

Trip director: an escort for an incentive company. Larger companies reserve this title for the person who directs all personnel and activities for a trip.

Triple bottom line: a new approach to adding environmental and social responsibility to financial responsibility with regard to company performance

United States Tour Operators Association (USTOA): a nationwide organization of tour operators offering protection for travelers purchasing member travel products by way of a multi-million dollar bond. www.ustoa.com

Universal Credit Card Charge Form (UCCCF): the form travel agents use to apply travel charges to a traveler's credit card.

Upgrade: provide a higher level of product or service than was ordered/expected.

Value season: a time of year when prices are lower than peak, also called low or off-season

Value-added tax: a tax that is added to a product at each step of the manufacturing and marketing process reflecting value that has been added to the product by processing.

Variable cost: a cost that changes according to how many people take a tour, such as motorcoach expenses

VAT/TVA/MWS/GST: acronyms for value-added tax, a tax system which adds a fixed percentage of taxation on products and services at each step of production or service delivery. Common in Europe, Canada and Oceania.

Vendor: One who sells services or supplies.

Venue: Location, site or destination of meeting, event or show.

Video conference: A meeting between two or more people or groups across a distance utilizing telecommunications or communications satellites for transmission of the signal.

VIP: very important person. A person or group of people to whom a higher level of service is either expected or which should be rendered.

Virtual conferencing: any meeting where people at two or more distant locations are linked using video, audio and data for two-way communication via satellite communications or the internet. Each party sees and hears the other through a TV screen or computer monitor and audio speakers.

Visa waiver: a program initiated by the US government to eliminate the visa requirement for selected countries

Visa: stamp of approval recorded in a passport to enter a country for a specific purpose

Visit USA Committee: A volunteer committee formed by parties who have a common interest in promoting, increasing and generating Visit USA travel and tourism. www.visitusa.org

Visit USA fares: air tariffs offering visitors to the USA reduced fared on domestic travel, also called VUSA fares

Waitlist: list of clients awaiting transportation or accommodations at times when they are not available, confirmed as a result of subsequent cancellations

Walk-through: review of meeting details, or inspection of function room or trade show floor prior to event.

Web conferencing: web-based videoconferencing.

Welcome reception: opening event where drinks and food are served.

Wholesaler: a company that creates and markets inclusive tours and FITs for sale through travel agents. Often used interchangeably with "tour operator," but several distinctions should be drawn: a wholesaler presumably sells nothing at retail, a tour operator does both; a wholesaler does not always create his or her own products, a tour operator virtually always does; and a wholesaler is less inclined than a tour operator to perform local services.

World Tourism Organization (WTO): an organizational branch of the United Nations that was created to promote and develop tourism in the interest of the economic, social and cultural progress of all nations. *www.*unwto.org

World Travel Market (WTM): a trade show taking place in London, UK that is a dedicated business-to-business forum with more than 40,000 industry professionals from 150 countries in attendance. More information at www.wtmlondon.com

Yield management: computer program that uses variable pricing to maximize the return on a fixed (perishable) inventory, such as hotel rooms; based on supply-and-demand theory.

Editors & Contributing Authors

The World Food Travel Association would like to acknowledge and thank the following writers and editors without whose work this book would not have been possible. Names are listed alphabetically by surname. The names of chapters to which authors contributed are italicized and follow their names. Please also consult the Acknowledgements chapter for a list of other people who contributed in other ways to the book.

TIM ALPER
Cracking the Far East Food Tourism Code

Journalist, Seoul, South Korea
(+82) 10-8647-1121   tda7@hotmail.com

Tim Alper is a journalist based in Seoul, South Korea. He has written about both Korean and Western cuisine and food culture for a variety of publications, including 행복히가득한집 and Joongang Daily. He is a regular contributor to Essen magazine, where he currently writes a column entitled "Tim Alper's 30-minute cooking", and Aju Good Day, where he writes a column called "Tim Alper's Korean food". He has also been featured on Korean food TV channel, Olive TV, and was co-host of Arirang TV's food documentary, "Taste of Wisdom". He has also written about a variety of other subjects for magazines and newspapers both in South Korea and his native Britain, including The Guardian, The Jewish Chronicle, MorningCalm (Korean Air's in-flight magazine), Weekly Chosun, Kyunghyang Shinmun, M25 and The Korea Times.

GEORGIA BAILLIEU
Culinary Retail & Grocery

Freelance Journalist, Perth, Western Australia
giorgiabaillieu@gmail.com   www.unapanciapiena.wordpress.com

Georgia graduated with a Journalism degree in 2008. After working in radio for a year she moved to Italy to pursue her passion for food, writing and traveling. Three years later she is still there, finishing her Masters in Tourism at the L'Universitá degli Studi di Bergamo and doing freelance food writing about her European culinary adventures.

LYNNE MARIE BENNETT
Culinary Attractions
Farms & Farmers' Markets
Cooking Schools & Classes
Culinary Lodging

Owner, California Culinary Adventures, Sonoma, California, USA
(+1) 707-484-2151   lynne.bennett@att.net   www.CaliforniaCulinaryAdventures.com

Lynne is a certified Natural Chef, Nutrition Educator, Wellness Consultant and certified Culinary Travel Professional (CCTP) through World Food Travel Association. Lynne established a culinary and wellness tourism business in the San Francisco Bay Area and Northern California to combine food, wine, travel, wellness, adventure, and fun. This includes sustainable tourism, farm-to-table activities, spa and wellness experiences, and hands-on cooking classes.

Lynne is well traveled and has visited numerous countries around the world. She takes extra delight in tasting the savory flavors of each region, while learning about food customs, farming, and agricultural practices. Lynne brings all of her world travel and nutritional knowledge home to the Sonoma and Napa Valleys of California, a region she has lived in for over 20 years. These Valleys are known for their award-winning wineries, famous health spas, agritourism practices, renowned culinary schools, restaurants, organic and biodynamic farms, and local gourmet artisan food.

TRACY BERNO

Special Role of Agriculture
Food Tourism in Academia
Sustainability in Food & Drink Tourism

Associate Professor, Lincoln University, Christchurch, New Zealand
(+64) (3) 423-0481   tracy.berno@lincoln.ac.nz

Tracy Berno is an Associate Professor in Tourism and Development at Lincoln University, New Zealand and Deputy Director of the University's Centre for International Rural Development. Tracy has over 20 years' experience as a tourism development academic and consultant. With a catering and cooking background, Tracy has always had a strong interest in sustainable cuisine. This grew into a research program focusing on how the produce and cuisines of the South Pacific could be highlighted as part of tourism, and how these agriculture-tourism linkages could support rural development and sustainable livelihoods. Tracy has researched and published in this area, as well as contributed to cookery books in New Zealand and the Pacific. She is co-author of Me'a Kai: The Food and Flavours of the South Pacific, Winner: Best Cookbook in the World 2010, Gourmand World Cookbook Awards.

NICOLE BISCARDI

Culinary Tours, Guides, Packages & Agents

Director of Marketing and New Business Development, Your Private Italy
Annapolis, Maryland, USA; Salerno, SA, Italy
nicole@yourprivateitaly.com   www.yourprivateitaly.com

Nicole directs all of the marketing and new business development activities for Your Private Italy, a boutique luxury destination management specialist to Italy, providing a full range of exclusive services including direct access to an extensive portfolio of luxury properties, private tours and excursions, logistics and transportation, private guides and concierge services, as well as wedding and event planning. Nicole has a BBA in Hospitality and Tourism Management as well as an MBA in Finance, both from Pace University in New York City. In addition, she has recently completed a Master's in Marketing, Communications and New Media at the University of Bologna's Alma Graduate School in Italy. Nicole currently resides in Rome with her fiancé, a well-known Italian Chef, and would be more than happy to assist you in discovering "Your Private Italy."

BENJAMIN BROWN, M.ED.
Professional Services in Foodservice

Food Critic, Las Vegas Food & Beverage Professional Magazine, Las Vegas, Nevada, USA
Ben@lvfnb.com   www.examiner.com/ethnic-restaurants-1-in-las-vegas/benjamin-brown
www.lvfnb.com

Benjamin Brown is a food and travel journalist in Las Vegas and Southern California. A contributor for Las Vegas Food & Beverage Professional Magazine, CBS and Examiner.com, Ben's love for dining and adventure has taken him to explore tastes and thrills in more than two-dozen countries across six continents. His coverage of the Las Vegas restaurant industry includes profiling more than 200 establishments, partnering with some of the nation's most prominent names in hospitality and interviewing culinary celebrities such as Gordon Ramsay, Todd English, Adam Richman and Guy Fieri. Ben is currently developing an online media business that will "create euphoria in food journalism." An amateur Track & Field athlete as well, Ben's love for exercise qualifies an appetite that 'devours entire restaurant menus.' You can find Ben on Twitter @BenBrownLV or reach him directly at Ben@lvfnb.com.

DR. KAROLINA BUCZKOWSKA, PhD
Food & Drink Events: Great Ideas or False Panaceas?

University School of Physical Education (AWF), Department of Tourism and Recreation, Poznan, Poland
turystykakulturowa@interia.pl   www.awf.poznan.pl

Dr. Karolina Buczkowska, is a cultural tourism lecturer at the University School of Physical Education (AWF) in Poznan, Poland. There she is also the tutor of Cultural Tourism and Tourism Journalism courses and the Departmental Coordinator of the LLP/Erasmus Program. She is the Deputy Editor-in-Chief of Cultural Tourism, a Polish scientific journal (Turystyka kulturowa), and a member of the Association for Tourism and Leisure Education (ATLAS) Cultural Tourism Research Group. She has already published three books: two in Polish and one in English (Cultural Tourism – Heritage, Arts and Creativity) and over 25 articles concerning cultural tourism. She is also an international tour leader and a tour guide in Poznan city. Her research interests are: cultural tourism (especially tourists' motivations, behaviors, typologies), creative tourism, cultural heritage, and food travel.

JENN BUSSELL, Editor
Restaurants, Catering & Other Foodservice in Tourism
Technology in Food & Drink Tourism
The Evolution of Guidebooks, Ratings, and Reviews in Food & Drink Tourism
Power of the People: Word of Mouth Marketing in Food Tourism
Future of Food Tourism

Brand Strategy Consultant & Marketing Coach
Washington, DC, USA
(+1) 202-658-8037   jenn@jennbussell.com
www.jennbussell.com   www.linkedin.com/in/jennbussell

Jenn Bussell is a highly regarded brand strategy consultant and marketing coach who has been solving complex business, marketing, and communications challenges for clients in the US, UK, Europe, Russia, and Latin America since 1991. With a practical focus on optimizing the customer experience in a connected culture, Jenn has led the research, planning, design, and implementation of award-winning digital and integrated brand marketing solutions for global leaders in the CPG, beverage, hospitality, restaurant, retail, and financial services industries. Jenn is the published author of food, drink, travel, fashion, personal branding, and digital marketing content. In 2010 and 2012 she was a featured speaker on the role of social media and mobile apps in driving increased outreach, engagement, and revenue for nonprofits. Jenn grew up in Boston and graduated from Wheaton College in Massachusetts with a degree in International Relations.

CARALYN CAMPBELL, Editor

Former Travel Editor, The Vancouver Sun / The Province
Vancouver, British Columbia, Canada
(+1) 604-605-1066   caralync@gmail.com

Caralyn Campbell recently retired as Travel Editor for The Vancouver Sun and The Province newspapers after 30 years with the company. Her lifelong love of food and cooking led to a passion for cookbook collecting and she has an extensive and treasured personal library. In 1994 Caralyn published Urban Foraging: A Cook's Guide to Vancouver and beyond. She has travelled extensively throughout the world taking cooking classes and visiting markets, farms and vineyards wherever possible. She divides her time between Yaletown, Vancouver, BC and Mayne Island, off the southernmost tip of British Columbia's West Coast. You can contact her at caralync@gmail.com or through www.urbanforaging.ca

CARLOTTA CASCIOLA

Culinary Tours, Guides, Packages & Agents
Developing a Food Tourism Destination

Director/Founder, Alacarta Luxury Wine & Gourmet Tours, Salamanca, Spain
(+34) (0)62-657-9603   info@alacarta.es   www.alacarta.es   www.alacartawinetours.com

Carlotta Casciola, founded Alacarta luxury wine & gourmet tours in 2003, a tour operator that designs and organizes customized wine and gourmet experiences in the most prestigious regions of Spain, Italy, France and Portugal. She is also a Food & Wine Tourism consultant and active in social media, writing articles related to Food & Wine, Tourism and Marketing. She grew up surrounded by the aromas and flavors of her father's village gourmet shop in Italy, and developed her professional marketing career in tourism in Italy, France and Spain. Her educational background combines her degree in Economic Sciences at the University of Perugia with a master course in Marketing at the IAE in Lille, France. After receiving instruction as a sommelier and working as a wine consultant for several wineries in her adopted home country of Spain, and considering her insatiable culinary curiosity, she decided to convert her life's passion into her own business.

LISA CHASE

Food Tourism Industry Stakeholders
Don't Forget the Locals
Benefits of Food Tourism
Economic Impact of Food & Drink Tourism

University of Vermont Extension, Vermont Tourism Data Center, Brattleboro, Vermont, USA

(+1) 802-257-7967 ext 311   lisa.chase@uvm.edu   www.uvm.edu/extension
www.uvm.edu/tourismresearch

Lisa Chase is the Director of the Vermont Tourism Data Center and Natural Resources Specialist with University of Vermont Extension. As a member of the Vermont Council on Agricultural and Culinary Tourism, Lisa works closely with many types of culinary ventures including fine dining restaurants, sugarhouses, and apple orchards. Spanning the spectrum of possibilities from farm to plate, Lisa's work links Vermont's culinary arts and agricultural bounty, promoting the authentic taste of Vermont. Her research and outreach focus on the intersection of sustainable tourism development, working landscapes, and community vitality. Prior to working in Vermont, Lisa conducted research and outreach in New York, Colorado, Costa Rica and Ecuador, among other places. She received her B.A. in Economics from the University of Michigan, her M.S. in Resources Economics from Cornell University, and her Ph.D. in Natural Resource Management and Policy from Cornell University.

SARIKA CHAWLA
How Foodies Make Decisions
Culinary Media

Editorial Director, Peter Greenberg Worldwide, Los Angeles, California, USA
(+1) 323-449-5084   schawla1@hotmail.com   www.petergreenberg.com
www.sarikachawla.com

Sarika Chawla is a Los Angeles-based writer and editor who covers food, travel and lifestyle for print, television, web, and radio. She is the editorial director for Peter Greenberg Worldwide, where she runs the editorial division to produce content for travel guru and CBS News Travel Editor Peter Greenberg.

LIVIO COLAPINTO
Food & Drink Manufacturing

Founder/MD, FoodPeckers /Zest of Italy Tours/Consulting, Trani, Apulia, Italy
(+39) 338-141-6526   liviocolapinto@yahoo.it   www.zestofitaly.com   www.foodpeckers.com

Livio was born in Turin, northern Italy with Apulian roots and a great passion for his mother's and grandmothers' kitchens. At 8 he was cooking his first meal for the family and since then has never stopped searching, smelling and hunting for the best foods. After his engineering studies and ten years of work in finance between London, Zurich and Tokyo he returned to his origins, studying food communication at the Slow Food University in Italy, working with its International president, Carlo Petrini. Eating and traveling are the most social activities one can do which explains how he made his way into the hospitality industry. Today he is a marketing and tourism consultant, private culinary tour organizer and passionate chef. When he plans tours with his wife Kathrin he brings together fellow travelers and his favorite food artisans for experiences that exceed all hopes and expectations.

NAN DEVLIN
Sustainability in Food & Drink Tourism

Principal, Devlin Endean Marketing Group and Avid Traveler Consultants
Portland, Oregon, USA
(+1) 971 235-9785   nan@devlinendean.com   www.devlinendean.com   www.avidtraveler.com

Nan Devlin is an award-winning freelance writer, rural tourism consultant, and marketing professional with a Master's in Tourism Administration from the George Washington University. As the principal of Avid Traveler Consultants and Devlin Endean Marketing Group, she specializes in agritourism, cultural and culinary tourism in the Pacific Northwest, helping destinations develop tourism strategies, build their brands, tell their stories, engage in social media, and improve visitor relations. She is an adjunct professor in the graduate school of Hospitality Management Resources at the University of Alabama. Nan is a native of, and lives in, Portland, Oregon.

DAWN DONAHUE
Food & Drink in Meetings & Conventions

President and CEO, Go Golf Events Management Inc., Vancouver, British Columbia, Canada
(+1) 604-628-9547   dawn@gogolfevents.com   www.gogolfevents.com
www.festivalofchocolate.ca

Raised on a 2,000 acre working farm in central Ontario, Canada, Dawn Donahue was born into the agritourism world. Her father was one of the first culinary retail – butcher, poultry, market gardeners selling local, fresh products daily, including home delivery, farmer's markets, roadside kiosks, and U-Pick. Fresh and local food was the center of the family model as well as the business model. Dawn studied languages and psychology at the University of Guelph, and Kinesiology at Simon Fraser University, however work always revolved around the hospitality industry. As progress in education and occupation paralleled, the love of the hospitality, service and culinary industry won. Career development included restaurant, neighborhood pub, and club ownership; food played a key role in business success. Conference, meeting and event planning came next, a key factor in the success of events revolves around the food and beverages incorporated into every event.

JESSE THOMAS EISENHUTH
Restaurants, Catering & Other Foodservice in Tourism

Director Food Service & Catering, The Henry Ford, Dearborn, Michigan, USA
(+1) 248-719-5021   jesse_eisenhuth@hotmail.com   www.thehenryford.org/food

Jesse Eisenhuth is a graduate of Michigan State University in Hospitality Business. He began his career traveling throughout the US with Levy Restaurants' Sports and Entertainment Division, but eventually went back to Michigan where he joined Starwood Hotels and Resorts, traveling all over North America as a member of their Corporate Food and Beverage team. He now works at The Henry Ford as Director of Food Service and Catering, where he is responsible for creating, coordinating and leading both short- and long-range strategic goals aligning with the institutional mission of ensuring high quality culinary experiences for all food service and catering. Throughout the 200 acre campus The Henry Ford strives to provide exciting food service options for visitors and continues to expand the organization's network of local and regional use of Michigan products, vendors and farmers, constantly bringing fresh ideas to The Henry Ford's banquet and catering operations.

STATIA ELLIOT, PhD
How Foodies Make Decisions

Associate Professor, School of Hospitality and Tourism Management, University of Guelph, Ontario, Canada
statia@uoguelph.ca   https://www.uoguelph.ca/htm/node/319

Dr. Statia Elliot joined the University of Guelph's School of Hospitality and Tourism Management in 2007 with a combination of academic study in business, and over 10 years work experience in tourism. From Consultant with Tourism Ontario, to Director of Marketing for Travel Manitoba, Statia's career spans the fields of marketing, research, policy, and management. A graduate of Carleton University in Ottawa, she has published in top journals, such as Cornell Hospitality Quarterly, and the Journal of Business Research. Statia is the 2014 President of the Travel and Tourism Research Association Canada Chapter, and actively participates in hospitality and tourism conferences and committees in North America and abroad. She researches destination image, food and wine tourism, and e-marketing. Statia has traveled extensively, lived and studied in South Korea, and now calls Guelph her home.

AYAKO EZAKI
Food Tourism in Emerging Destinations: The Case of Ecuador
Sustainability in Food & Drink Tourism

Managing Partner & Co-Founder, TrainingAid, Hamburg, Germany
ayako@trainingaid.org   www.trainingaid.org

Ayako is Managing Partner and Co-Founder of TrainingAid, a company that focuses on providing tools and solutions for practical online professional training programs in the international development field. Prior to starting this new company, Ayako worked for The International Ecotourism Society (TIES) as Director of Communications, focusing on areas including member communications, social media marketing, content development, training and education program management, and leading TIES blog and newsletter editorial team. She is originally from Japan, and has traveled extensively especially in Asia and Europe. As a long-time vegetarian and ethical and sustainable food advocate, she enjoys discovering local markets, street food, and authentic flavors when she travels

MÅNS FALCK
Culinary Retail & Grocery

CEO, Cajsa Warg, Stockholm, Sweden
mans.falck@cajsawarg.se   www.cajsawarg.se

Måns Falck completed a Master of Science at Stockholm School of Economics in 2000. Parallel to his studies and as a food enthusiast, Måns worked at the revolutionary grocery store Cajsa Warg, opened in 1996. After graduation from SSE in 2000, Måns joined Coop, the second largest food chain in Sweden as a management trainee. At Coop Måns primarily worked in the area of controlling business development projects. During his years at Coop he also worked 6 months as store manager for Cajsa Warg, by then acquired by Coop as a development concept store. In 2003 Måns purchased back Cajsa Warg together with the original founders from Coop. Since then Cajsa Warg has developed into an institution in the Swedish food market and with the opening of the second store in 2010, the company is now one step closer to its target of becoming a chain of food stores.

CARMINA FANDOS-HERRERA
New Marketing Tactics in Food Tourism

Senior Lecturer, Department of Marketing Management and Market Research
Universidad de Zaragoza, Zaragoza, Spain
cfandos@unizar.es   http://marketing.unizar.es/fichas/c_fandos/index.html

Carmino Fandos-Herrera's research interests include agro-food marketing, food tourism and complaint behavior. Her work has been published in journals such as the Journal of Food Products Marketing, Journal of International Food & Agribusiness Marketing, British Food Journal, International Journal of Wine Business Research, Managing Service Quality, Journal of Product and Brand Management, the book "Turismo Gastronómico. Estrategias de Marketing y Experiencias de Éxito" and participated in the most recent UNWTO report, "Global Report on Food Tourism".

KATHRIN FEHERVARY
Food & Drink Manufacturing

Food/Wine Tour Operator, Zest of Italy/Foodpeckers, Stainz, Styria, Austria
(+43) 660 1227248   kfeherv@hotmail.com   www.zestofitaly.com   www.foodpeckers.com

Kathrin grew up in a 200 year-old farmhouse in Styria, southeastern Austria. Her parents own a small-scale biodynamic farm and have cultivated a variety of fruits and vegetables for the last 30 years for family use. After her A-levels, Kathrin specialized in Tourism and Management in school, followed by 2 years of work experience on cruise ships. During her undergraduate studies in Business Management in London, she rediscovered in a local cheese shop her love for the world of food and wine. After a few years of learning how to age cheeses, she decided to do a second degree at the Slow Food University of Gastronomic Sciences. This is where she met her husband Livio and opened the tour operator, Foodpeckers, in 2009. Over the last 15 years she has been realizing her passion for natural winemaking.

KEVIN FIELDS
Let's Tell a Story

Senior Lecturer, University of Gloucestershire, Gloucester, UK
(+44) 07968193527   kfields@glos.ac.uk   www.glos.ac.uk

Kevin Fields is a senior lecturer at The University of Gloucestershire in the UK. His teaching areas encompass Hospitality, Tourism & Event Management, but he has a particularly keen interest in Gastronomy. He has been at Gloucestershire for just over 6 years, having previously held positions at universities in Birmingham and London. Prior to that, he held a range of positions in the hospitality industry. Kevin is currently the coordinator of the Gastronomy and Tourism special interest group of ATLAS, a global association for tourism academics. He is a regular keynote speaker at gastronomy-related conferences throughout Europe.

COLM FOLAN

Food & Drink Events: Great Ideas or False Panaceas?

Manager, Casadh
colm.folan@gmail.com

Colm Folan is a graduate of the Dublin Institute of Technology in Culinary Arts and Tourism (MSc. Tourism Management) and the Dublin Business School in Tourism Marketing Management. He has a keen interest in Gastronomy, food history and travel and is a fully qualified Chef, having worked for CERT, the National Tourism Training Authority as a Chef Instructor. Colm now works in the field of addiction rehabilitation helping persons in recovery access treatment aftercare, further education and work.

JEREMY FREEMANTLE

Cooking Schools & Classes

Co-owner and Managing Director, African Relish Culinary Tourism (pty) Limited, Prince Albert, Great Karoo, Western Cape, South Africa
(+27) 23 5411381   jeremy@africanrelish.com   www.africanrelish.com
www.sustain360.co.za

Jeremy spent 32 years in advertising, conceptual marketing, brand building and brand management and, most recently, advising CEOs on investor communication strategies, corporate governance, the triple bottom line and integrated reporting. He has always had a deep passion for the culinary world and spent most of his free time from the corporate treadmill exploring the cultures of the world through their diverse and colorful cuisines. In 2008 he launched into the culinary tourism industry by starting African Relish, a recreational cooking school in the remote rural village of Prince Albert in the Great Karoo. African Relish shares the diversity of South Africa's multicultural culinary heritage with visitors from around the world through offering interactive cooking experiences. SUSTAIN 360, a non-profit company was established adjacent to African Relish to train and mentor underprivileged rural youth in the hospitality and tourism industry through entrepreneurship and life skills programs.

MARCO FUSO

Developing a Food & Drink Tourism Framework

Founder & CEO, VacationAndCuisine.com, Italy
Marco@VacationAndCuisine.com   www.vacationandcuisine.com
Blog: http://vacationandcuisine.wordpress.com/

Marco graduated from Westminster University in London with a BA (Hons.) in Tourism and Planning. After graduation he worked in product marketing roles for US and UK B2B companies, before starting up Vacation & Cuisine, a booking company dedicated to the promotion of cooking holidays and food and wine tours around the world with the purpose of giving visitors a website where they can find great holiday destinations and experience local food. Vacation & Cuisine gathers tour operators or cooking experience providers who would otherwise not be able to offer their tours to a worldwide audience on the web so that visitors can find and book the vacation of a lifetime. Tours are hand-picked by Marco to ensure the highest standards for food and local experience.

CARLOS GALLARDO

Food Tourism in Emerging Destinations: The Case of Ecuador

President of the Chefs Association of Ecuador, Quito, Pichincha, Ecuador
cgallardo@udla.gob.ec

Carlos Gallardo de la Puente has dedicated a decade to the research and study of the inherited and traditional culinary techniques and tendencies, the historical value, the sociological impact and the anthropological roots, as well as the modern avant-garde applications of Ecuador's most significant and valuable culinary products, which are known worldwide for their delicacies, richness and importance. He is the fiercest advocate of Ecuadorian cuisine and his most invaluable mission is and always will be, to contribute and place Ecuador's gastronomy as one of the finest and richest cuisines in the world. Carlos is Director of the Gastronomy Faculty at Universidad de Las Americas, he is the Executive Director of The Rescue of The Traditional Flavors of Ecuador, President of Ecuador's Chefs Association, he has and still writes articles and publications related to Ecuadorian gastronomy in all forms of media such as television, radio and digital.

DONALD GETZ

Demographic History of Food Travelers

Professor, School of Tourism, The University of Queensland
(+1) 403-241-9773   don.getz@haskayne.ucalgary.ca

Dr. Getz retired in July 2009 from his full-time academic position at the University of Calgary, Canada, where he remains Professor Emeritus. He is currently a 50% Professor on the School of Tourism, The University of Queensland, and he is a Visiting Professor at several other universities. Professor Getz is a leading international proponent of event studies, drawing from his extensive research, volunteering, teaching and consulting experience in many countries. His book, Event Studies, defines the field of study, establishes the theoretical and policy framework, and provides a detailed reference work on related research. He is also active in researching a variety of special-interest market segments, including food and wine tourism, culture and sports. His latest book, Event Tourism, was published in early 2013.

Dr. Getz received a BES from the University of Waterloo, an MA from Carleton University, and PhD from the University of Edinburgh.

MARTIN HRABEC

Culinary Tours, Guides, Packages & Agents

Chairman, Hospitality Training Institute, Mikulov, Czech Republic
(+420) 721 427 854   info@hospitalitytraining.cz   www.hospitalitytraining.eu

Martin Hrabec is founder and Chairman of the Hospitality Training Institute, an association of experts in Hospitality, Tourism and the Food Industry. He has been working 25 years in hospitality, the last ten years as trainer, lecturer, consultant and researcher in hospitality and sustainable tourism. As a member of Slow Food, World Food Travel Association and Global Sustainable Tourism Council, he is intensively engaged in issues of sustainable tourism & regional development, small-scale farming, artisan food production and networking of farmers/producers and hospitality enterprises.

He also cooperates intensively with a number of like-minded organizations and individuals, universities and professional bodies across the European Union. He participates in research & development of strategic studies, organizing of didactic journeys and thematic excursions and providing consultancy activities & training in mentioned areas of interest.

MARGARET JEFFARES
Tourism Offices & Trade Groups

Founder and Managing Director, Good Food Ireland, Ireland
(+353) 539158693   info@goodfoodireland.ie   www.GoodFoodIreland.ie

Margaret Jeffares has worked in the tourism and travel industry in Ireland for almost 25 years. She grew up on a farm in the West of Ireland and now lives with her husband Des on a farm in County Wexford, as such she is very much aware of the premium quality of Irish produce. Margaret pioneered the first all-island food travel experience brand for Ireland, Good Food Ireland, by linking Ireland's agri-food and hospitality sectors. She has truly been an innovative force in Ireland's culinary tourism initiatives through her appointments on a number of government boards and influence on destination brand messaging around food. Margaret's passionate commitment and inspiring entrepreneurship has led her to speak at numerous conferences in Ireland and overseas.

LEE JOLLIFFE
Culinary Lodging

Professor, University of New Brunswick, Canada
ljolliff@unb.ca

Professor Lee Jolliffe is a tourism academic with an interest in culinary tourism. She is the editor of three culinary related volumes - Tea and Tourism: Tourists, Traditions and Transformations (2007); Coffee Culture, Destinations and Attractions (2010); Sugar Heritage and Tourism in Transition (2013) - all published by Channel View Publications in the U.K.

GINGER K KING
Let's Tell a Story

Author, Carolina Wine Country Cooking / Owner Carolina Wine Cooks
Lumberton, North Carolina USA
(+1) 910-734-7933 ginger@carolinawinecooks.com www.carolinawinecooks.com
www.gingerkking.com

Ginger King is the author of Carolina Wine Country Cooking, all about cooking with wine from the Carolina vines, featuring recipes using the famous North Carolina Muscadine as well as European varietals produced in the western part of the state. She is also a contributor to the just-released Second Helpings, a compilation of holiday short stories and author's recipes. She is also working on a second volume in the Carolina Wine Country Cooking series.

RASTO KIRN

Farms & Farmers' Markets

Architect, Slovenia
rastokirn@me.com

Rasto Kirn is an architect by profession, dealing with sustainability planning with an emphasis on early stage tourism. His work involves GIS studies, planning and traveling. He lives with his Russian wife and two sons in Slovenia but has worked in Vienna and Austria and his friends are from Italy and Croatia, so internationalism is his life. His profession often leads him out of the office which is where he gets in touch with his great loves - people and food. He loves to eat, and thankfully the food is quite good in Slovenia where people still know the recipes of their grandmothers, be it for soups, vegetables, meat, or sweets. Oh, and Slovenia has some great wines too! You're cordially invited!

ANNE KLEIN

The Need to Get Creative

Public Relations, Durango Area Tourism Office, Durango, Colorado, USA
(+1) 970-749-0991   anne@durango.org   www.durango.org

Anne Klein began her career as a food stylist for major food companies, holding a BA degree in foods and nutrition and a culinary certificate from LaVarenne in Paris. She received a Masters in Marketing Communication and pursued a career in public relations. Anne enjoys the fast pace of public relations and has a flair for special events and media relations. She taught Introduction to Marketing at California State University and has been a media spokesperson for food, fitness and equestrian products. She started Giraffe Marketing to provide innovative and cost-effective marketing and public relations consulting. Current clients of Giraffe Marketing include: Durango Area Tourism Office, Royal Robbins, 5.11 Tactical, Western United Dairymen and Artemis Strategy. She lives in Durango, Colorado, is a mother of 3 teens and enjoys horseback riding, travel, fund raising and cooking.

CAROL KLINE, PhD

Food Tourism in Academia

Assistant Professor, Center for Sustainable Tourism (CST)/ Recreation and Leisure Studies (RCLS)
East Carolina University, Greenville, North Carolina, USA
(+1) 919-306-1705   RCLS: www.ecu.edu/rcls   CST: http://sustainabletourism.org

Carol Kline currently works at East Carolina University where she holds a joint appointment with the Center for Sustainable Tourism and the Department of Recreation and Leisure Studies. She received her Ph.D. in Parks, Recreation and Tourism Management from North Carolina State University, where she instructed classes and provided outreach on tourism issues to North Carolina communities. Carol has worked in a variety of geographical and cultural settings including New England, Colorado, Germany, the Republik of Moldova, Grenada, Peru and the South Eastern U.S. Her research interests focus on rural tourism development including how to create a supportive environment for tourism entrepreneurs, the role of sustainable food systems in tourism, the impacts of tourism on various community 'capitals', and early tourist markets in burgeoning and rural destinations.

SANTOSH KUMAR MISHRA
Food Tourism Industry Stakeholders

Technical Assistant, Population Education Resource Centre (PERC), Department of Continuing and Adult Education and Extension Work, S. N. D. T. Women's University, Mumbai, Maharashtra, India
(+91) 022-22066892   drskmishrain@yahoo.com   http://sndt.ac.in

Santosh Kumar Mishra is a researcher and demographer with PERC, Department of Continuing & Adult Education & Ext. Work, S. N. D. T. Women's University, Mumbai, India. He is associated with 14 international journals as an editorial board member and reviewer. He has contributed papers at international conferences held at Karachi, Manila, Hong Kong, Dar es Salaam, Stockholm & Chicago. Dr. Mishra has over 30 books, book chapters and research papers published to his credit.

WENDY LANGE-FARIA, Editor
Food Tourism Where Little Agriculture Exists
The Role of Drinks: Promoting Tourism through Beverage Trails
Sharing the Recipe: Metrics in Food & Drink Tourism
Food & Drink in Meetings & Conventions

Food and Tourism Consultant, Ottawa, Ontario Canada
Skype: wendy.lange.faria   wlangefaria@gmail.com   www.wendy.faria.ca

Wendy holds a Masters of Education from University of Ottawa and a Masters of Business Administration in tourism and hospitality management from University of Guelph in Ontario, Canada. Passionate about food tourism, she has participated in everything from planning the first Klondike Harvest Fair in Canada's far north to helping develop a local, agricultural taste trail in eastern Ontario. Wendy is always on the lookout for new and authentic culinary experiences seeing food as a means by which to connect people – the act of eating as the bridge that can connect people beyond the confines of language, culture, worldviews and belief systems. From cooking for a youth camp in a converted mansion in the Dundee region of Scotland to enjoying a homemade feast in Košice, Slovakia, Wendy sees food and travel as being closely connected. A published author on social media in the academic journal Tourismos, Wendy has also worked in the areas of research, branding and marketing, product development, training and writing/editing.

DIANA LASKARIS
Food & Drink as Communication

Chief Food Officer, Food Travel Network, Inc., Chicago, Illinois, USA
(+1) 312-334-9777   diana@foodtravelist.com   www.foodtravelist.com   www.poshports.com

Diana Laskaris is Co-Founder and Chief Food Officer of Food Travel Network, Inc., a Chicago-based leisure and entertainment company focused on the food and travel markets. She leads the culinary team for the Food TravelistTM brand, the first media and social network dedicated entirely to the culinary travel sector. She is a Certified Culinary Travel Professional with a lifelong appetite for food culture. A veteran entertainment industry professional, Diana was Vice President of National Lampoon where she produced licensing ventures, motion pictures, television specials, live events and merchandise lines for the iconic comedy brand. She is also a licensed business attorney. Diana's many philanthropic activities have recently focused on integrating initiatives into Food Travelist's brand identity to create a social enterprise in which "Doing Good and Giving Back" is a foundational part of its business profile. She loves to cook and enjoys entertaining guests with creative food and drink menus.

URBAN LAURIN, Ph.D.
Special Role of Agriculture
Developing a Food Tourism Destination

Progrezzum, Austria
(+43) 6641946391   urban.laurin@telia.com   www.urban-laurin.com

Since 2001 Urban Laurin has owned his own company and worked both as a consultant and an author, with areas of expertise concentrated in food, tourism, rural development, storytelling, entrepreneurship and integration. Urban has his Ph.D. in political Science, from Skytteanum Uppsala University in Sweden, with research on tax behavior and mass media power. However, since letting his interest in wine take over, he has become a wine writer with his own magazine and several books to his credit.   Urban believes development is best achieved through transparency, open systems, collaboration and participation, with a culture of sharing and openness. He regularly works with open innovation, crowdsourcing, open systems and integrative or holistic management, which are transparent and reward learning, even from mistakes. He finds it especially important to stimulate dialogues with those who think otherwise, dare to listen to their intuition and then blend theoretical knowledge with practical experience.

NATALIE LOWE, CMM
Food & Drink in Meetings & Conventions

President, Celebrate Niagara DMC, Niagara, Ontario, Canada
(+1) 905-984-5725   natalie@celebrateniagara.ca   www.celebrateniagara.ca

Natalie is a food, wine and travel enthusiast – who, coming from Northern Alberta, has a keen appreciation for the bounty provided in Niagara. The luxury of eating food grown in your own postal code is a thrill that just never gets old. Natalie went to school at Ryerson University in Toronto and took her Certification in Meeting Management from Meeting Professionals International in 2005. She now specializes in group travel into the Niagara and before starting her own company Natalie worked in the hotel and gaming industry in Toronto, Niagara and Alberta. She is known for her passion and high energy, for being obsessive about the details, her voracious reading habits and her curiosity about the world.

KRISTINA LUPP
Food & Drink Tourism Industry Glossary

Gastronomical Editor and Translator, Tallinn, Estonia
(+372) 5399 1873   kriss.lupp@me.com   www.kristinalupp.com

Kristina Lupp is a Toronto native based in Tallinn Estonia. She works as a freelance editor and translator, specializing in gastronomical texts. She holds a Master's degree in Gastronomy from the University of Adelaide in Australia and a Diplôme Universitaire du Goût, de la Gastronomie et des Arts de la Table from the University of Reims Champagne-Ardenne in France.

GEORGIOS MALTEZAKIS, PhD
Special Role of Agriculture

Heraklion, Crete, Greece
gmaltezakis@gmail.com   www.cretanpaths.com

Dr. Maltezakis is founder of Tasting Crete a small, regional excursion agency focusing on culinary tourism. In 2013 he joined Cretan Paths, another regional excursion and travel agency that aims to promote the beauty of Crete through culinary tours. He holds his first degree in Anthropology from University of Aberdeen, his MA in Psychology and Counseling from City College in Thessaloniki and his PhD in Anthropology from Ljubljana Graduate School of The Humanities in Slovenia with a thesis on food and consumption. He joined WFTA as a coach for Greece and conceptualized the idea of a culinary excursion agency in Crete; in 2012 he gained his CCTP accreditation. He works to promote and develop culinary tourism in Crete because he deeply believes in the potential the island has as a culinary and cultural haven. He has also published works in collaboration with the renowned Professors Ken Albala and David Hassenzal.

VICKI MAVRAKIS, PhD Candidate
Towards a Cookie Cutter Future

Senior Policy Officer, Agribusiness and Regions, Faculty of Health Sciences, Flinders University, PIRSA
Bedford Park, South Australia, Australia; Adelaide, South Australia, Australia
(+61) 413-530-011   vicki@mavrakis.net.au

Vicki is a PhD candidate within the Discipline of Public Health at Flinders University. Vicki holds a Bachelor of Science, Bachelor of Arts and a Masters in Environmental Studies from the University of Adelaide. She has worked with food in both the private and public sectors in distribution, processing, sales, policy and food industry development. Vicki's research is on understanding how the everyday attitudes and behaviors of people's food consumption results in the generation of food waste in household settings. Vicki is an avid traveler and passionate cook. She is interested in food value chains, food tourism, food equity and access and the translation of research into policy as well as practice. She is currently writing her thesis.

KATHRYN MCAREE, Editor
Ongoing Development for Food Tourism Professionals

Owner, Travel With Taste Tours Ltd & Taste: Victoria's Festival of Food and Wine, Victoria, British Columbia, Canada
info@VictoriaTaste.com   www.VictoriaTaste.com   www.TravelWithTaste.com

Kathryn McAree has blended the perfect ingredients to form a successful career of pure indulgence. Passion for exploration, food expertise and a splash or two of wine have mixed well to create Travel With Taste, Vancouver Island's premier culinary tour company. On a trip to Italy many years ago, Kathy realized how precious her own backyard is, so she now brings the world to feast at the plenteous tables of Vancouver Island. She provides an opportunity to get to know the amazing organic farmers, winemakers, chefs, cheesemakers, etc. which make the area so special. She also hosts a four-day extravaganza each July, Taste: Victoria's Festival of Food and Wine. An enthusiastic culinary world traveler and a board member of Les Dames

517

d'Escoffier, her knowledge, skill and passion is evident as she awakens your senses on her culinary tours, and through her writing and speaking, including her weekly hour-long radio show on CFAX 1070.

F. XAVIER MEDINA, PhD
The Role of Drinks: Promoting Tourism through Beverage Trails

Director, Department of Food Systems, Culture and Society
Universitat Oberta de Catalunya, Barcelona, Spain
(+34) 646326373   fxmedina@gmail.com   www.uoc.edu

Dr. Medina has his PhD in Social Anthropology from the University of Barcelona. Since 2009 he has been the Academic and Programmes Director in the Department of Food Systems, Culture and Society at the Universitat Oberta de Catalunya (UOC). Between 1991 and 2009 he was the senior researcher and head of projects at the European Institute of the Mediterranean (IEMed). His main subjects of research include food culture and heritage, food and wine tourism, and regional and local development. He is author of more than a dozen books and more than seventy articles in published journals, mainly on food issues. He was also member of the Mediterranean Diet team to be considered as a World Heritage Site, adopted by UNESCO in November 2011. He is also currently Chair for Europe of the International Commission of the Anthropology of Food and Nutrition (ICAF).

CRYSTAL L. MILLER
Farms & Farmers' Markets

Graduate Student, Department of Community, Agriculture, Recreation and Resource Studies, Michigan State University, Michigan, USA
(+1) 517-803-7663   millerl.crystal@gmail.com

Crystal Miller is a graduate student in the Department of Community, Agriculture, Recreation and Resource Studies at Michigan State University. She studies community sustainability and collaboration within local and regional food systems and is passionate about community-engaged scholarship. Applied research projects include partnering with Oakland County Parks and Recreation in Waterford, Michigan to enhance recreation and leisure at the Oakland County Farmers Market and the Waterford Oaks Greenhouse Complex. She is the recipient of the 2011 Mildred B. Erickson Fellowship and the 2013 C.S. Mott Predoctoral Fellowship in Sustainable Agriculture. Crystal lives in Lansing, Michigan and after many years in Southern Georgia, she thoroughly enjoys the Great Lakes and beautiful seasons of Michigan.

CATHERINE MORELLON representing TOURISME MONTRÉAL
Culinary Attractions

Manager, Media and Leisure Market, Montréal, Québec, Canada
(+1) 514-844-3840   morellon.catherine@tourisme-montreal.org   @mocali232

Catherine Morellon is a Manager in the Media and Leisure Market Department at Tourisme Montreal. She oversees the development of the culinary niche for the organization and promotes Montreal's gastronomy scene by highlighting its restaurants, chefs, terroir products, markets, food tours and food events. Culinary tourism is one of Tourisme Montreal's priority markets, and in 2011 the Organization launched an integrated marketing strategy to attract
518

food lovers to the city. Tourisme Montréal is also responsible for the city's new restaurant week, TASTE MTL (held annually in early November). Tourisme Montreal is responsible for providing leadership in the concerted efforts of hospitality and promotion in order to position "Montréal" as a culinary destination on leisure and business travel markets. Prior to joining Tourisme Montréal, Catherine Morellon contributed in the launching of the Martinique Gourmande event in Montreal for the Martinique Promotion Bureau, in 2007.

LENA MOSSBERG
Best Practices in Destination Food Tourism Branding

Professor, University of Gothenburg, Gothenburg, Sweden
(+46) 31786 1539   lena.mossberg@handels.gu.se

Lena Mossberg is professor in marketing in the School of Business, Economics and Law at the University of Gothenburg and also Professor II at the University of Nordland. She was also professor in experience economy at BI Norwegian School of Management in Oslo for two years and guest professor at Örebro University, in the department of culinary arts for three years. She holds a Ph.D. in Business Administration and has interests in tourist behavior, consumer experiences, service encounters, and destination image. She has published several articles and books related to consumer experience and has been involved in several international tourism and marketing programs, not least in her capacity as tourism management expert for the UN and the EU.

JOHN D. MULCAHY
Best Practices in Destination Food Tourism Branding

Head of Food Tourism, Hospitality Education, & Standards, Fáilte Ireland, the National Tourism Development Authority, Dublin, Ireland
(+353) 18847751   john.mulcahy@failteireland.ie   www.failteireland.ie
http://ie.linkedin.com/in/gastronomy

Highly qualified in food, wine and gastronomy, John has a special interest in Irish food and its tourism potential, informed by over 30 years' experience in tourism and hospitality. John formalized his excitement for food in tourism by graduating from University of Adelaide in 2010 with the Cordon Bleu Master of Arts in Gastronomy, adding to other academic awards from Cornell (USA), Oxford Brooks (UK), the Institute of Wine & Spirits (UK), and Dublin Institute of Technology. His dedication to food in tourism is thanks to both a personal ardor for gastronomy and also his experience at various times as a pub, restaurant or food service operator on three continents, as an educator in hospitality management and wine, and most recently as a public servant with the National Tourism Development Authority in Ireland. John leads a dedicated Food Tourism team who have all contributed to the work in this book.

KONSTANTINOS NIKOLOPOULOS
The Need to Get Creative

Business Developer/Olive oil of "MEGA SPILEO" Monastery,
Holy Diocese of Kalavryta and Aigialeia, Aigion, Achaia, Greece
(+30) 2691023008   kwn_nikolopoulos@yahoo.gr   www.im-ka.gr

Konstantinos has served as Sales Advisor for Chevrolet Greece, Chevellas, and Electronet; as a translator for AMC 2000 Ltd, Belgium; as a lecturer of Greek language for foreigners at the Nicolaus Copernicus University in Torun, Poland; and currently as business developer on behalf of the Holy Diocese of Kalavryta and Aigialeia in Greece. This position deals with the packaging, branding and distribution of extra virgin olive oil from Mega Spileo Monastery. Konstantinos speaks English, French, Italian and Polish, and holds a BSc in Business Administration from Deree College and an MA in Tourism Management from the University of Brighton, he is also an undergraduate at the Theological School of the University of Athens. His hobby and main love is tourism, especially Religious Tourism, which is a very important niche in Greece, and it can also include culinary aspects.

LYNN OGRYZLO
Let's Tell a Story
Economic Impact of Food & Drink Tourism

Writer/Promote/ Local Food Ambassador, Queenston, Ontario, Canada
(+1) 905-262-4941   ogryzlo@sympatico.ca   www.ontariotable.com

Lynn is an international award-winning author, writes on food and wine for various magazines and was culinary host for CHCH-TV's Niagara Express. A culinary activist, Lynn has been a champion of local foods for over 22 years, Slow Food President (1998/9, Toronto/Niagara chapter) and founder of the local food $10 Challenge©. She is the founder of The Niagara Culinary Trail, an agricultural organization that introduces consumers to the best farmers in the region. For Lynn, food, wine and travel are a delicious way to communicate that personal 'sense of place' that exists in each destination. Follow her on Twitter @OntarioTable.

HAROLD D. PARTAIN, CTC, CCTP, DS
Culinary Tours, Guides, Packages & Agents

Owner, Epicopia Culinary Journeys
Founder & Executive Director, Epicopia Culinary Journeys
Partner & Executive Director, McCabe Travel Group LLC
(+1) 972-771-3510
hpartain@epicopia.com   www.epicopia.com   facebook.com/Epicopia

Harold was born and raised on a farm in Northwest Arkansas, but admits he "grew up" the year he lived in New York City. His passion for travel and exotic foods was instilled in him from his mother who always dreamed of traveling. She introduced him to foraging at a very young age when she would take him into the woods and fields on the hunt for local wild berries, herbs and other edible greens. After completing his university degree from University of Arkansas at Little Rock, Harold moved to Dallas and began his 40+ years travel career managing travel agencies and eventually owning several. Never one to stop learning, Harold earned the CTC – Certified Traveler Counselor and later was the first to be awarded the CCTP – Certified Culinary Travel Professional. He continues today mentoring and counseling others to earn their CCTP. He is recognized as a Destination Specialist and Travel Lifestyle Advisor. Harold, a seasoned tour director, has focused on food and wine travel experiences the past 15 years and is the Founder and Executive Director of Epicopia Culinary Journeys, specializing in small group experiences. He is also Senior Partner and Managing Director of McCabe Travel Group, LLC based in Rockwall, Texas. Harold returned to the farm and currently lives in a restored 100 years old Texas Farmhouse just outside Dallas. Harold has served on the Board of Directors of the World Food Travel Association since 2004 and as Chairman since 2011.

CAROLINA PÉREZ
Food Tourism in Emerging Destinations: The Case of Ecuador

Culinary Tourism Coordinator, Ministry of Tourism of Ecuador, Quito, Pichincha, Ecuador
(+593) 9 9806-1153   cpperez@turismo.gob.ec

Carolina Pérez has a master's degree in Food Culture and Communications from UNISG - University of Gastronomic Sciences in Bra, Italy, founded by the international non-profit Slow Food Movement. She trained in the food and communications area in Switzerland in "Walker AG Cheese" in Bitsch, the Hotel Mont Cervin Palace and the store "Cheese and Wine" in Zermatt. She returned to Ecuador to work in the Ministry of Tourism where she coordinates Culinary Tourism, developing strategies to strengthen and promote Ecuadorian gastronomic potential. She also has a bachelor's degree in Organizational Psychology and has experience in cultural and human development projects.

SUE REDDEL
Food & Drink as Communication

Chief Travel Officer, Food Travel Network, Inc., Chicago, Illinois, USA
(+1) 312-334-9777   sue@foodtravelist. www.foodtravelist.com www.poshports.com

Sue Reddel is Co-Founder and Chief Travel Officer of Food Travel Network, Inc., a Chicago-based leisure and entertainment company focused on food and travel. A Certified Culinary Travel Professional, Sue's passion for travel has taken her to exciting and memorable destinations around the world. She has logged as much as 150,000 miles in a 6-month period. Sue leads the travel team for the Food Travelist™ brand, the first media and social network dedicated entirely to the culinary travel sector. Sue's extensive management experience includes serving as Vice President and Media Director for Starcom Worldwide where she managed major food and beverage accounts for Fortune 500 clients. A natural teacher, Sue is an adjunct professor for Roosevelt University's Integrated Marketing Communications program and an executive trainer in integrated marketing, media planning and social media for global corporations. An accomplished eater, Sue enjoys music and the arts, and perfecting her golf swing.

PRAJAKTA REMULKAR
Culinary Media

Culinary Writer & Cook, Spice Up Your Soul, Dallas, Texas, USA
(+1) 214-676-6588   praj.r2006@gmail.com   www.spiceupyoursoul.com

Prajakta Remulkar writes her own cooking blog, called Spice up Your Soul where she creates new recipes that blend different cultures. She has contributed recipes to CNN Go Asia. A believer of cooking for the soul, she loves to write about comfort foods from around the world.

KATRIN RIPPEL

The Food and Drink Tourism Service Journey

Menu International, Inc., Tenino, Washington, USA
(+1) 360-451-0039   krippel@menuintl.com   www.menuintl.com

Katrin Rippel has a passion for cultures, languages and technology. She developed a deep appreciation for multilingual communication during 16 years of front-line customer service in the food and hospitality industry in her native Germany, in France, and in North America. She then completed rigorous training in language translation and international software and website applications. With MENU International, a translation and web services company, she provides services to the food, hospitality and tourism industries.

CORRINE ROBER

Restaurants, Catering & Other Foodservice in Tourism

Owner, Margarita Grill Restaurant, Glen, New Hampshire, USA
Bearrockadventures@gmail.com

Corrine has been in the hospitality industry for over thirty years and is an active contributor to the states' movement in Farm-to-Table and sustainable practices. In 2013 she was awarded The Sustainable Business of the Year from the New Hampshire Travel & Tourism Governor's Council and Entrepreneur of The Year from the Chamber of Commerce in the Mount Washington Valley. Margarita Grill is the only restaurant in the state to be awarded both the Environmental Champion Status from the NHSLRP and the NH Certified Local certification. Corrine is a member of The Valley Originals and is the driving force behind the area's independently-owned restaurants working collaboratively to strengthen the connection between the restaurants and local agriculture. She is also the creator of S.O.H.L., an integrity-based set of principles that assists businesses in connecting to their passion and the greater good of the local communities. Corrine is committed to creating organic solidarity in the areas she loves. She works closely with her husband in land investment and management. Currently they are creating an outdoor adventure company that will help strengthen the economic standing for the Great North Woods of New Hampshire.

KIM ROBERTS

Power of the People: Word of Mouth Marketing in Food Tourism

Co-owner, Westport Winery, Aberdeen, Washington, USA
(+1) 360-648-2224   kim@westportwinery.com   www.WestportWinery.com

Kim Roberts has written for The Daily Planet, Western-Farmer Stockman, Ocean Observer, Spokane Coeur d'Alene Living, Discover Diving, Log Home Living, RV Life, American Fitness and the Leavenworth Echo where she won the Washington State Newspaper Publishers Association Best General Column award. Roberts and her husband, Blain, formerly owned Lahaina Divers on Maui. Together they founded Westport Winery on the Washington coast where they live within their Vineyards By-the-Sea. Westport Winery was named "Washington Winery to Watch" in 2011 by Wine Press Northwest and has been voted Best Northwest Destination Winery and Wine Tour by King 5 Evening Magazine 2010, 2012 and 2013. The Roberts family was selected as one of the top three small family businesses in Washington in 2012 by Seattle Business Magazine.

RICHARD N.S. ROBINSON, PhD
Demographic History of Food Travelers

Senior Lecturer, Hospitality Management, University of Queensland
St Lucia, Queensland, Australia
(+61) 7 3346-7091   richard.robinson@uq.edu.au   www.tourism.uq.edu.au/richard-robinson

Richard joined the University of Queensland's School of Tourism in 2005, after an extended career as a chef, predominantly managing foodservice operations in the private club and heritage facility sectors. He has since taught a suite of hospitality and tourism management classes and currently supervises several higher degree research students. He has coordinated and worked on research teams for funded national and international projects relating to tourism workforce issues and food tourism. Richard's work in these areas has been shared in leading academic journals, edited books, international conferences and industry periodicals and he has received university, national and international awards for his teaching and research.

GLORIA RODRIGUEZ
Developing a Food & Drink Tourism Framework
Creating a Food or Drink Tourism Product Inventory

Researcher/Consultant on Culinary Culture & Tourism, Madrid, Spain
gloria@worldfoodtravel.org   http://lnkd.in/wQstwf

Gloria Rodríguez is an independent researcher and consultant specialized in culinary heritage and culinary tourism. She is a regular research contributor at the Ferran Adrià Chair on Culinary Culture, hosted by the Universidad Camilo José Cela in Madrid, Spain, and a regional project manager for the World Food Travel Association's activities in Spain. Gloria holds a M.A. in Culture Management and Cultural Tourism, which she focused on culinary heritage and culinary tourism. Her research work is centered in the sustainable development of culinary tourism as a tool for local development and as a vehicle for intercultural communication. Gloria is also an Electronic Communications Engineer and a certified Project Manager with over ten years' experience in large international environments; an expertise that she strives to contribute to the fields of culinary culture management and culinary tourism by promoting effective project management practices in these areas.

KATERINE-LUNE ROLLET
Culinary Attractions

Freelance Gastronomic Tourism Journalist, Montréal, Québec, Canada
klr.presse@gmail.com   www.katerinerollet.com

After working for 16 years in front of CBC's cameras (national public television), Katerine-Lune Rollet has veered into the web as food blogger for Tourisme Montréal. She currently teaches social media at INIS (Institut National de l'Image et du Son) and has a journalism career in culinary tourism (canoe.ca + radio). Traveling around the world, she attends food congresses, meets chefs, and inspires Canadians to discover food specialties and restaurants from abroad. Addicted to her iPhone, she spends time searching, reading, and sharing information on the culinary and gastronomic trends on her blog katerinerollet.com and on social media (@katerinerollet).

PAULINA SALACH
Technology in Food & Drink Tourism

Owner, Spoon Food Tours, San Juan, Puerto Rico
(+1) 787-249-4488 info@spoonfoodtours.com   www.PRrestaurantweek.com
www.spoonfoodtours.com

Paulina is a culinary and travel entrepreneur, a native of Poland, a New Yorker at heart and current resident of Puerto Rico. In New York, Paulina worked as a public relations account executive at a boutique firm and managed catered events throughout the city. In 2008, she relocated to San Juan and continued her PR work at an affiliate of Ogilvy & Mather. In her spare time, she began perfecting local recipes and traveling throughout the Island, finding the best culinary spots. Paulina left her job at the agency and decided to be an entrepreneur in the culinary industry.   In 2010, she co-founded Puerto Rico Restaurant Week™, bringing the worldwide dining celebration to San Juan. In 2012, Paulina founded Spoon Food Tours, a food and culture tour company. Her goal is to continue positioning Puerto Rico as the top culinary destination in the Caribbean. Paulina also manages social media for several restaurants in Puerto Rico, sells Hungarian wines, organizes private events and is a culinary consultant in San Juan.

MICHAEL SCHAFER, ESQ.
The Food & Drink Tourism Service Journey

Sommelier, CSW (Certified Specialist of Wine), The Wine Counselor®
(+1) 248-219-7301   winecounselor@gmail.com   www.WineCounselor.net

Michael Schafer Esq., The Wine Counselor®, is the charismatic speaker, educator, trainer, Sommelier, C.S.W., writer and consultant who entertains while educating. His humorous and fun approach is reflected in his trademark phrase "I taste bad wine so you don't have to"®. Michael teaches at The International Culinary Schools @ the Art Institute of Michigan and at Dorsey Schools. He is an international keynote speaker at food and wine expos/festivals/conferences around the globe. Michael has authored numerous articles in various publications, including Hour Detroit's Menu Guide, the cover stories for Michigan Wine Country magazine and Edible Grand Traverse, Midwest Wine Press, 944 Magazine, and NW Michigan's Second Wave. He writes monthly columns for the Michigan Chefs de Cuisine, and the Windy City Chefs. Whether training restaurant teams, conducting private tastings, or customizing a wine event, Michael demystifies wine and leaves his clients laughing and learning! Michael also enjoys judging international wine competitions.

NEHA M SHAH
New Marketing Tactics in Food Tourism
Best Practices in Destination Food Tourism Branding
It's Who You Know: Sustainable Industry Partnerships & Memberships

Writer, Cary, North Carolina, USA
(+1) 919-824-0290   Nehatraveler@gmail.com   http://TravelWordsmith.com
www.foodspotting.com/nehamshah

Neha M Shah was born in India and raised in south Florida. She has a Master of Science in Tourism and Bachelor of Science in Business Administration (Marketing and Management),
524

both from the University of Florida. She has presented a paper in Italy on Social Media in Tourism as well as co-presented in Canada, most recently. Ms. Shah has worked for the Pittsboro-Siler City Convention & Visitors Bureau in Chatham County, North Carolina since December 1999; it is a one-person destination marketing organization. She has traveled to more than 14 countries and is a foodie and traveler who loves to explore.

TRAVIS ANTONIO SINCKLER
Don't Forget the Locals

Senior Environment Officer, Environment Division, Government of Barbados
St. Thomas, Barbados
espumarine@caribsurf.com

Travis' interest in food was founded in his family's farming heritage, nurtured in his mother's kitchen, and refined through his work in sustainability. He views community food tourism as a challenging, yet promising approach to localizing sustainability action. Travis says "it's about creating a common space for dialogue among farmer, fisher, restaurateur, chef, food traveler (local and international), and regulator around an issue common to all - food. That dialogue will yield solutions." His efforts to explore links among community, island gastronomy and nature-based tourism started in 1998 during development of the sustainable tourism initiative, "de Heart uh Barbados ®". Today, he continues to promote those linkages through programs such as the UN 10-Year Framework of Programmes on Sustainable Consumption and Production. Travis is trained in business administration and environmental management; he has been member of Slow Food International since 2006 and enjoys creating farm-inspired fusion-cuisine for family and friends.

INGER SVENSSON
Best Practices in Destination Food Tourism Branding

Copywriter, Svenssons Ord ab, Gothenburg Sweden
(+46) (0) 705131224   inger.svensson@vastsverige.com   www.svenssonsord.com

Inger loves to communicate, he is known for telling stories that inspire others. Fortunately for him, his professional background is head of Public Relations and Communication for a large bank. He loves people, travel, wine and opera, though not necessarily in that order. He loves life.

STORMY SWEITZER
Business Model Generation

Owner, Maoomba, LLC., Utah, USA
(+1) 801-671-8785   stormy@maoomba.com   /www.maoomba.com

Stormy Sweitzer, MPH, MBA, is a Utah-based writer, entrepreneur, teacher, and consultant with a love of amazing flavors, exotic ingredients, lifelong learning, global travel, and exploring new ideas and places. She focuses on these topics on her blog, Maoomba.com, and weaves them throughout her educational programs and the work she does in helping people and organizations make their ideas real in the world. In other words, she loves a great business model as much as a great curry! Stormy is author of Paleo Power Lunch, leads intrepid eaters through Travel the World in a Day Experiences of ethnic food markets and ingredient use in her home city, and is working on her next projects – a food adventure novel and an online course that helps the "culinarily" curious bring adventure into their everyday eating and cooking.

NADIA THEUMA, BA BA (HONS) MPhil PhD (Strath), Editor

Director, Institute for Tourism, Travel and Culture, University of Malta
(+356) 7924 9889   nadia.theuma@um.edu.mt

Nadia holds degrees in Anthropology and Tourism Studies. She is a Senior Lecturer at the University of Malta where she teaches tourism, research, heritage and food. Nadia has held advisory posts with the Ministries of Tourism and Education, Malta Tourism Authority, Heritage Malta, Malta Crafts Council and Ministry for Resources and Competitiveness and Communications. She was a Board Director of Malta Tourism Authority where she was influential in the Ministry for developing a cultural tourism policy and participated in the developing of the brand identity for Malta. She is also a freelance consultant to Maltese entities and private companies on identity, image and product development. Nadia has initiated the group Fuklar whose main objective is to promote the Maltese and Mediterranean food culture. She has conducted research and written papers on Maltese food and food identities, in particular the roles of food markets and food and religious celebrations.

ANNETTE M. TOMEI
Future of Food Tourism

Chef/Food & Beverage Educator/Consultant, VinEducation, Brooklyn NY USA
Annette@vineducation.com   www.wandereatandtell.com

After nearly two decades as a chef and educator in Napa Valley and New York City, Annette Tomei has launched VinEducation where she applies her signature blend of academic rigor with her ability to make even the most complex concepts fun through education programs, tastings, and events in the US and abroad. Annette became passionate about wine while living in Napa Valley, where she pursued professional wine studies at Napa Valley College, the CIA at Greystone, and through the Court of Master Sommeliers. In 2008, she was awarded a Masters of Arts in Gastronomy from the University of Adelaide in South Australia. Annette is an adjunct instructor at The International Culinary Center, co-author of Chile Aphrodisia and a contributor to two books and also a contributing editor for Life of Reiley Publications and writes a weekly column, "Wine of the Week".

SANJA VUJICIC, PhD
Demographic History of Food Travelers

Consultant, Experience Consulting Company, Gothenburg, West Sweden, Sweden
(+46) 706-62 02 21   sanja@experiencec.com   www.experiencec.com

Sanja Vujicic has more than ten years of academic research and advisory experience within the field of market communication, tourism experience design and destination marketing. Experience Consulting is an experience consultancy founded by Sanja Vujicic in 2010. Before founding Experience Consulting she held an academic and an Assisting Director position at the Centre for Tourism, School of Business, Economics and Law, University of Gothenburg, where she also received her PhD in Business Administration in 2008. Sanja has, among other things, worked as a freelance photographer on a national and an international basis, and was responsible for planning and producing photographs for destinations.

BRIAN WANSINK, PhD
How Foodies Make Decisions

Professor of Marketing & Director of Food & Brand Lab, Cornell University
Ithaca, New York, USA
(+1) 607-254-6302   foodandbrandlab@cornell.edu   http://foodpsychology.cornell.edu
http://smarterlunchrooms.org

Brian Wansink is the John Dyson Professor of Marketing and the Director of the Cornell Food and Brand Lab and Co-Director of the Center for Behavioral Economics in Child Nutrition Programs at the Dyson School of Applied Economics & Management at Cornell University in Ithaca New York. He earned his Ph.D. in marketing at Stanford (1990) and was marketing professor at the Amos Tuck School at Dartmouth College (1990–1994), the Vrije Universiteit in Amsterdam (1994–1995), and the Wharton School at the University of Pennsylvania (1995–1997) and the Julian Simon Faculty Scholar and Professor of Marketing, Nutritional Sciences and Agricultural and Consumer Economics at the University of Illinois at Urbana–Champaign (1997–2005). He is also the author of over 150 peer-reviewed papers and of the best-selling book Mindless Eating: Why We Eat More Than We Think (2006).

JANET WELCH
Culinary Media

www.RoadTripFlavors.com, Mission Viejo, California, USA
Janet@RoadTripFlavors.com

Janet Welch is a 25-year corporate marketing communications veteran gone A.W.O.L. for the food and drink tourism industry. She is a published food tourism writer, blogger and cookbook author. She and her partner, K.O. Lett co-write RoadTripFlavors.com, a travel, dining and recipe blog. They also self-published their first cookbook in 2013: "Mediterranean Flavors, Easy Recipes and Menus in the RoadTripFlavors Style". The RoadTripFlavors brand began with a passion for cooking together for family and friends. Collaborative efforts for preparing regionally authentic meals boosted their appetite for more intriguing culinary experiences. They are the quintessential food tourists, seeking out places that promise great dining, local and fresh ingredients, inspired chefs and cuisine true to a regional heritage. Back in their kitchen, they craft new recipes that are both inspired by the flavors tasted on the road and influenced by their California roots.

DAVID WILSON
Food & Drink Manufacturing
Sustainability in Food & Drink Tourism

Chicago, Illinois
d.wilson180@my.chicago.chefs.edu

David is the author of a book on visual arts, and he is also an artist. He recently added an associate's degree in applied sciences from Le Cordon Bleu College of Culinary Arts in Chicago to his life-list of career activities. After an internship with NASA's, Johnson Space

Center in Houston, Texas, in their Space Food Systems Laboratory, and culinary graduation, David returned to Le Cordon Bleu to gain his baking and pastry certificate. David now volunteers regularly at a local Chicago soup kitchen. His interests include food as it relates to culture, social dynamics and history.

ERIK WOLF, CCTP, Publisher

Executive Director, World Food Travel Association, Portland, Oregon, USA
www.worldfoodtravel.org   erik@worldfoodtravel.org   (+1) 503-213-3700

Erik Wolf is the visionary founder of the world's food tourism industry. His career has included time with leading travel industry brands such as Travelocity, Royal Caribbean, Marriott and American Express. He is a popular speaker in the USA and abroad, and is considered as the go-to food tourism resource for media world-wide, including CNN, the BBC, the Wall Street Journal, Newsweek, Forbes, PeterGreenberg.com, Ariang Korea, and many more. Erik also advises to UNESCO's Creative Cities Network gastronomy program. Erik holds a B.A. in languages from the University of Virginia and an M.A. in Travel Marketing and International Communication from The American University in Washington, D.C. For Erik, food and drink are the best ways to communicate and connect with local people. A command of several languages has helped him navigate through dozens of countries. He has lived in Australia, Denmark, New Zealand, Singapore and South Africa. The more Erik traveled, the more he realized that many destinations have wonderful but untold stories in the form of truly unique food and beverage experiences. Erik enjoys recommending unusual and remarkable food and beverages experiences from obscure lands. Don't ever let him loose in a grocery store in another country — you won't see him for hours.

References & Bibliography

In addition to endnotes specific to each chapter, the authors have made the following list of additional references and bibliography available.

Andersen, A. *Science and Agriculture: Advanced Methods for Sustainable Farming. 2nd Ed.* USA: USA, 2000.

Arnott, Margaret L. *Gastronomy: the anthropology of food and food habits.* The Hague: Mouton, 1975.

Boniface, Priscilla. *Tasting Tourism: Traveling for Food and Drink.* London: Ashgate Publishing, 2003.

Boyne, S. and Hall, D. (2003) "Managing food and tourism developments: issues for planning and opportunities to add value" in Hall, C.M., Sharples, L., Mitchell, R. et al (eds) (2003) Food Tourism Around the World: Development, Management and Markets. Oxford: Butterworth-Heinemann, p.285-295.

Cai, Liping A., William C. Gartner, and Anna M. Munar. *Tourism branding communities in action.* Bingley, UK: Emerald Group Pub., 2009.

Carol M. Devine, M. M. Connors, Jeffrey Sobal, and Carol Bisogni, "Sandwiching It In: Spillover of Work onto Food Choices and Family Roles in Low- and Moderate-Income Urban Households," Social Science & Medicine (February 2003), vol. 56, no. 3, pp. 617-63

Černič, Irena. Rating and Presenting Statistics of Tourism in Slovenia for the Satellite Accounts for Tourism (Thesis, May 2005, www.cek.ef.uni-lj.si/u_diplome/cernic1898.pdf)

Croce, Erica, and Giovanni Perri. *Food and wine tourism: integrating food, travel and territory.* Wallingford, Oxfordshire, UK: CABI, 2010.

Espeitx, E. (2007). "Los espacios turísticos del patrimonio alimentario" in: Tresserras, F. y Medina, X. (eds) Patrimonio gastronómico y turismo cultural en el mediterráneo. Barcelona: Ibertur, p. 153-176.

Failte Ireland (2010). National Food Tourism Implementation Framework. [Online document]. Available at: www.failteireland.ie/FailteIreland/media/WebsiteStructure/Documents/3_Research_Insights/1_Sectoral_SurveysReports/Food_Tourism_Implementation_Framework-1-19-07-2012.pdf?ext=.pdf [1 June 2013].

Goeldner, C. R. & Brent Ritchie, J.R. (2009) Tourism: Principles, Practices, Philosophies. Eleventh Edition. Hoboken, NJ: John Wiley & Sons.

Gunter, Barrie and Adrian Furnham (1992), Consumer Profiles: An Introduction to Psychographics, London: Routledge.

Hall, C.M (2012) Boosting food and tourism-related regional economic development. In: OECD. Food and the Tourism Experience: The OECD-Korea Workshop, OECD Studies on Tourism. OECD Publishing, p. 49-61.

Hall, C.M. & Sharples, L. (2003) "The consumption of experiences or the experience of consumption? An introduction to the tourism of taste" in Hall, C.M., Sharples, L., Mitchell, R. et al (eds) *Food Tourism Around the World: Development, Management and Markets.* Oxford: Butterworth-Heinemann. 14057/27312

Hall, C.M. & Sharples, L. (2003) The consumption of experiences or the experience of consumption? An introduction to the tourism of taste. In Hall, C.M., Sharples, L., Mitchell, R. et al (eds) Food Tourism Around the World: Development, Management and Markets. Oxford: Butterworth-Heinemann, p.314-335.

Hall, C.M. (2008) Tourism Planning Policies, Processes and Relationships. Essex, UK: Pearson Education.

Hall, C.M., Mitchell, R. & Sharples, L. (2003) Consuming places: the role of food, wine and tourism in regional development. In Hall, C.M., Sharples, L., Mitchell, R. et al (eds) Food Tourism Around the World: Development, Management and Markets. Oxford: Butterworth-Heinemann, p. 25-59.

Hall, Colin Michael. *Wine, food, and tourism marketing.* Binghamton, NY: Haworth Hospitality Press, 2003.

Kamakura, Wagner A. and Thomas P. Novak. Journal of Targeting, Measurement and Analysis for Marketing, 3:1, 18-30 (1992), "Value-System Segmentation: Exploring the Meaning of LOV," Journal of Consumer Research, June 119-132.

Marlene B. Schwartz, H. O. Chambliss, Kelly D. Brownell, Steven N. Blair, and Charles Billington, "Weight Bias Among Health Professionals Specializing in Obesity," Obesity Research (September 2003), vol. 11, no. 9, pp. 1033-1039.

Medina, X. & Tresserras, F. (2007). "Patrimonio gastronómico en el mediterráneo dese una perspectiva turística" in: Tresserras, F. y Medina, X. (eds) *Patrimonio gastronómico y turismo cultural en el mediterráneo.* Barcelona: Ibertur, p. 11-14.

Medina, X. & Tresserras, F. (2007). Patrimonio gastronómico en el mediterráneo dese una perspectiva turística. In: Tresserras, F. y Medina, X. (eds) Patrimonio gastronómico y turismo cultural en el mediterráneo. Barcelona: Ibertur, p. 11-14.

Mojca Rozman (MKO), Registry of Farms (PowerPoint presentation, January 2009)

Oliver, R, Berno, T. & Ram, S. *Mea'Ai Samoa: Recipes and Stories form the Heart of Polynesia.* Auckland: Random House, (forthcoming).

PMI (2008). A Guide to the Project Management Body of Knowledge. Newtown Square, Pennsylvania: Project Management Institute.

Pristovšek, Ksenija. An Empirical Analysis of Slovenian Tourism (Thesis, September 2009, www.cek.ef.uni-lj.si/UPES/pristovsek363.pdf)

Rasto, Kirn, Central European Bibliography: Literature & Sources. Applying the Eurostat methodological guidelines in basic tourism and travel statistics, A Practical Manual, March 1996.

Reynolds, T.J. & Gutman, J. (1988). Laddering theory, method, analysis, and interpretation. Journal of Advertising Research, February/March, 1988, pgs.11-31.

Richards, G. (2012) "Food and the tourism experience: major findings and policy orientations" in Dodd, D. (ed.) *Food and the tourism experience*. Paris: OECD, p.13-46.

Richards, G. (2012) An overview of food and tourism trends and policies. In: OECD. Food and the Tourism Experience: The OECD-Korea Workshop, OECD Studies on Tourism. OECD Publishing, p. 13-43.

Richards, G. (ed) (1996) *Cultural Tourism in Europe. Global and Local Perspectives.* Wallingford, UK: CABI Publishing. (tb. en PC) 15634/29164
Richards, Greg. *Cultural tourism: global and local perspectives.* New York: Haworth Hospitality Press, 2007.

Rogina, Marjeta. Layer Pie of the Prekmurje Region ("Prekmurska gibanica") and Wine (thesis, 2009, www.digitalna-knjiznica.bf.uni-lj.si/dn_rogina_marjeta.pdf)
Ruiz de Lera, E. (2012) Gastronomy as a key factor in branding Spain. In: OECD. Food and the Tourism Experience: The OECD-Korea Workshop, OECD Studies on Tourism. OECD Publishing.

Schulte, S. (2003) Guía conceptual y metodológica para el desarrollo y la planificación del sector turismo. Santiago de Chile: United Nations. Available at www.eclac.org/publicaciones/xml/2/13092/manual25.pdf [20 June 2013].

SECTUR (2001). "Cómo crear clubes de producto" in SECTUR, Serie de Documentos Técnicos Competitividad, fascículo 7. Available at: www.sectur.gob.mx/work/models/sectur/Resource/14774/fasciculo7.pdf [4 June 2013]

Slovenian Agriculture, Forestry and Food Processing Industry – Basic Characteristics and Numbers, Ministry of the RS of Agriculture, Forestry and Food, May 2007

Sonoma County Economic Development Board and Sonoma County Tourism Bureau (2012). 2012 Annual Tourism Report.

Torres, Rebecca Maria, and Janet Henshall Momsen. *Tourism and agriculture: new geographies of consumption, production and rural restructuring.* London: Routledge, 2011.

Tresserras, J.; Medina, F. X. & Matamala, J.C. (2007) El patrimonio gastronómico como recurso en las políticas culturales y turísticas en España: el caso de Cataluña. In: Tresserras, J. y Medina, X. (eds) Patrimonio gastronómico y turismo cultural en el mediterráneo. Barcelona: Ibertur, p. 217-242.

Tribe, J. (2005) "Strategy for Tourism" in: Pencer, L. and Sharpley, R. (eds) The Management of Tourism. London: SAGE Publications, p. 119-134.

Tribe, J. (2010) Strategy for Tourism. Oxford, UK: Goodfellow Publishers. ISBN: 978-1-906884-07-9. 17204/31435

United States Department of Agriculture. (2013). "Know Your Farmer, Know Your Food", Retrieved from www.usda.gov/wps/portal/usda/knowyourfarmer?navid=KNOWYOURFARMER

UNWTO (1998). *Introducción al turismo. Madrid:* Organización Mundial del Turismo.

UNWTO (2005). *Indicadores de desarrollo sostenible para los destinos turísticos: Guía práctica*. Madrid: Organización Mundial del Turismo. 14838/28277

UNWTO (2007) A Practical Guide to Tourism Destination Management. Madrid: World Tourism Organization.

Van der Stoep, G.A. (2000) "Community Tourism Development" in Trends in Outdoor Recreation, Leisure and Tourism. Oxon, UK : CABI Publishing, p.309-321.

Virginia Tourism Corporation (2011). FY2011 Profile of Leisure Travel in Virginia. TNS Travels America.

Wansink, B. (2000).New techniques to generate key marketing insights. Marketing Research, (Summer), 28-36.

Wansink, B. (2003). Using laddering to understand and leverage a brand's equity. Qualitative Market Research: An International Journal, 6:2, 111-118.

Wansink, B. (2005). Marketing Nutrition: Soy, Functional Foods, Biotechnology, and Obesity. Champaign, IL: University of Illinois Press.

Wansink, B. and JaeHak Cheong, "Taste Profiles That Correlate with Soy Consumption in Developing Countries," Pakistan Journal of Nutrition (December 2002), vol. 1, no. 6, pp. 276-278.

Wansink, B.and Keong-mi Lee, "Cooking Habits Provide a Key to 5 a Day Success," Journal of the American Dietetic Association (November 2004), vol. 104, no. 11, pp. 1648-1650.

Wansink, B.and Randall Westgren, "Profiling Taste-Motivated Segments," Appetite (December (2003), vol. 41, no. 3, pp. 323-327.

Wansink, B.Ganaël Bascoul, and Gary T. Chen, "The Sweet Tooth Hypothesis: How Fruit Consumption Relates to Snack Consumption, Appetite (2013), forthcoming.

Wansink, Brian (1994), "Developing and Validating Useful Consumer Prototypes,"

Wansink, Brian and SeaBum Park (2000), "Accounting for Taste: Prototypes that Predict Preference," Journal of Database Marketing, 7:4, 308-320.

Weinstein, Art (1994), Market Segmentation, Chicago, IL: Probus Publishing.
Wells, William D. (1975), "Psychographics: A Critical Review," Journal of Marketing Research, May 196-213.

Wolf, Erik (2006). Culinary Tourism: The Hidden Harvest. US: Kendall/Hunt Publishing.

The World Food Travel Association (WFTA) is a non-governmental organization (NGO) and the world's leading authority on food tourism, shepherding a community of over 18,000 professionals in 135 countries. The WFTA is at the forefront of food and drink tourism development with cutting-edge products and services that meet the needs of today's food, drink, travel, hospitality and media professionals. The Association promotes food, drink & culinary cultures through travel. We serve as the central hub connecting key industry segments and partners with business to business (B2B) and business to consumer (B2C) relationships. We accomplish our work through destination marketing organizations, industry trade associations, the media, universities and consumer food communities.

www.WorldFoodTravel.org

Made in the USA
Las Vegas, NV
21 January 2022